《云南统计年鉴—2021》

Yunnan Statistical Yearbook—2021

编 者 说 明

一、《云南统计年鉴—2021》是一部全面反映云南省国民经济和社会发展情况的统计资料工具书，汇集了全省及各州市、县（市、区）2020年和主要年份经济和社会发展主要统计数据。

二、本年鉴对上年度年鉴章节内容进行了部分调整，调整后全书共18章，即：1.省情概况；2.国民经济核算；3.固定资产投资；4.城乡市场消费；5.公共财政；6.对外经济贸易；7.农业和农村；8.工业和能源；9.建筑业和房地产业；10.交通运输、通信和服务业；11.金融和保险业；12.旅游业；13.教育、科技和文化业；14.卫生、体育和社会管理；15.人口与就业；16.资源与环境；17.民族自治地方经济概况；18.县域经济概况。

三、本年鉴每个章节后附有主要统计指标解释，对主要统计指标的含义、统计范围和统计方法作了简要说明。本年鉴的资料来源，大部分来自年度统计报表。由于统计口径范围和调查方法的差别，部分指标各州市、县（市、区）数字相加可能不等于全省总计，对于一些统计指标的统计口径范围发生变化的，本年鉴对有关数据作了相应的调整，并在有关统计表中作了解释，在使用中请注意。

四、度量衡单位均采用国家颁布的国际统一标准计量单位。本年鉴中对计量单位进一步统一调整，符号使用说明："空格"表示无该项统计指标数据，或不足本表最小单位数，或资料不详；"#"表示指标的其中主要项。

五、对各级党委、政府和有关部门给予《云南统计年鉴—2021》编辑工作的关心和大力支持，以及参与此项工作的同志付出的辛勤努力表示衷心感谢！为不断改进和提高本年鉴质量，更好地满足社会各界的需要，希望广大读者提出宝贵的意见。本年鉴如有差错之处，欢迎读者批评指正。

EDITOR' S NOTES

I.*Yunnan Statistical Yearbook 2021* is an annual statistics reference book which fully reflects the national economy and social development in Yunnan province. The present yearbook covers comprehensive data in each city, county and prefecture in 2020as well as some key data in significant years of the whole province.

II. After revision, this book contains the following eighteen parts: 1.Provincial survey; 2.Economies; 3.Investment in Fixed Assets; 4.Urban and Rural Consumption; 5.Public Finance; 6.Foreign Trade; 7.Agriculture and Country; 8.Industry and Energy; 9.Construction and Real Estate; 10.Transport and Communications Industry; 11.Banking and Insurance; 12.Tourism; 13.Education, Science and Technology and Culture; 14.Public Health, Sports and Social Services; 15.Population and Employment; 16.Resources and Environment; 17.Survey of National Autonomous Area; 18.Survey of Intra–county Economies.

Ⅲ. Explanatory Notes on Principal Statistical Indicators are provided at the end of each part to describe the content, scope and method of provincial statistical indicators briefly. The major data in this publication are obtained from annual statistical reports. It is advisable to note in the reference that the sum of data of each city, county and prefecture may not correspondingly equal the total of the whole province in some statistical indicators due to different statistical ranges and investigation methods. As for changes of statistical ranges, the relevant data are adjusted and explained accordingly in the present yearbook.

Ⅳ. The units of measurement used in this book are international standard measurement units issued by the state. Notations used in this yearbook, "(Blank)" indicates that the data are not available; or refers to numbers of minimum units or refers to numbers which are not in detail. "#" indicates that the major items of the total.

Ⅴ.Thanks for the great support and attention given by party members and governments at each level, and colleagues who participate in this editing work. In order to perfect the yearbook and meet the requirements of the society better, comments from various readers are highly appreciated. At the same time, readers are welcome to correct our mistakes made in this book.

目　　录

CONTENTS

一、省情概况

Chapter 1 Provincial Survey

二、国民经济核算

Chapter 2 National Accounts

三、固定资产投资

Chapter 3 Investment in Fixed Assets

四、城乡市场消费

Chapter 4 Urban and Rural Consumption

五、公共财政

Chapter 5 Public Finance

六、对外经济贸易

Chapter 6 Foreign Trade

七、农业和农村

Chapter 7 Agriculture and Country

八、工业和能源

Chapter 8 Industry and Energy

九、建筑业和房地产业

Chapter 9 Construction and Real Estate

十、交通运输、通信和服务业

Chapter 10 Transport, Communication And Service Industry

十一、金融和保险业

Chapter 11 Banking and Insurance

十二、旅 游 业

Chapter 12 Tourism

十三、教育、科技和文化

Chapter 13 Education , Science , Technology and Culture

十四、卫生、体育和社会管理

Chapter 14 Public Health , Sports and Social Management

十五、人口与就业

Chapter 15 Population and Employment

十六、资源与环境

Chapter 16 Resources and Environment

十七、民族自治地方经济概况

Chapter 17 Survey of National Autonomous Area

十八、县域经济概况

Chapter 18 Survey of Intra - county Economies

Chapter 1

一、省情概况
Provincial Survey

1−1 人口和资源（2020年）
Population and Resources (2020)

指 标	Item	2020
全省年末人口总数（万人）	Total Population (year-end) (10 000 persons)	4 722.0
人口密度（人/平方千米）	Population Density (person/sq.km)	119.8
全省土地面积（万平方千米）	Total Land Area (10 000 sq.km)	39.41
民族自治地方土地面积（万平方千米）	Autonomous Area of Nationalities (10 000 sq.km)	27.67
全省年末耕地总资源（万公顷）	Total Cultivated Land Resources at Year-end (10 000 hectares)	620.91
牧草地面积（万公顷）	Area of Grassland (10 000 hectares)	14.69
全省森林面积（万公顷）	Forest Area (10 000 hectares)	2 493.58
全省森林覆盖率(%)	Forest Coverage Rate (%)	65.0
全省森林蓄积量（亿立方米）	Standing Stock Volume (100 million cu.m)	20.67
全省水域及水利设施用地面积（万公顷）	Water Area and Water Conservancy Facilities Area (10 000 hectares)	70.25
全省水能资源理论蕴藏量（亿千瓦）	Hydropower Resources by Theoretic (100 million kW)	1.04
全省水资源总量（亿立方米）	Total of Water Resources (100 million cu.m)	1 799.19
全省铁矿保有资源储量（亿吨）	Ensured Reserves of Iron Ore (100 million tons)	43.48
全省煤矿保有资源储量（亿吨）	Ensured Reserves of Coal Ores (100 million tons)	363.85
全省磷矿石保有资源储量（亿吨）	Ensured Reserves of Phosphate Ores (100 million tons)	52.01

注：由于全国第三次国土调查数据尚未公布，本表中土地利用数据沿用2018年数据。
Note: Because the data of the Third National Land Survey has not been released , data of land use in this table are used in 2018.

1-2 全省行政区划及代码(2020年)
Administrative Divisions and Their Codes in Yunnan (2020)

单位：个 (unit)

州市 Autonomous Prefectures and Municipalities	县级单位名称 County Units	县级单位数 Number Of County Units		
		市辖区 Districts under Municipal Jurisdiction	县级市 Cities at County Level	县 Counties
昆 明 市 Kunming	五华区 盘龙区 官渡区 西山区 东川区 呈贡区 晋宁区 富民县 宜良县 石林县 嵩明县 禄劝县 寻甸县 安宁市 Wuhua District, Panlong District, Guandu District,Xishan District, Dongchuan District,Chenggong District, Jinning District, Fumin, Yiliang, Shilin,Songming, Luquan, Xundian, Anning City	7	1	6
曲 靖 市 Qujing	麒麟区 沾益区 马龙区 陆良县 师宗县 罗平县 富源县 会泽县 宣威市 Qilin District,Zhanyi District,Malong District, Luliang, Shizong, Luoping, Fuyuan, Huize, Xuanwei City	3	1	5
玉 溪 市 Yuxi	红塔区 江川区 通海县 华宁县 易门县 峨山县 新平县 元江县 澄江市 Hongta District, Jiangchuan District,Tonghai, Huaning,Chengjiang City Yimen, Eshan, Xinping,Yuanjiang	2	1	6
保 山 市 Baoshan	隆阳区 施甸县 龙陵县 昌宁县 腾冲市 Longyang District, Shidian, Longling, Changning, Tengchong City	1	1	3
昭 通 市 Zhaotong	昭阳区 鲁甸县 巧家县 盐津县 大关县 永善县 绥江县 镇雄县 彝良县 威信县 水富市 Zhaoyang District, Ludian, Qiaojia, Yanjin, Daguan, Yongshan, Suijiang, Zhenxiong, Yiliang, Weixin, Shuifu City	1	1	9
丽 江 市 Lijiang	古城区 玉龙县 永胜县 华坪县 宁蒗县 Gucheng District,Yulong, Yongsheng, Huaping, Ninglang	1		4
普 洱 市 Pu'er	思茅区 宁洱县 墨江县 景东县 景谷县 镇沅县 江城县 孟连县 澜沧县 西盟县 Simao District, Ning'er, Mojiang, Jingdong, Jinggu, Zhenyuan, Jiangcheng, Menglian, Lancang, Ximeng	1		9
临 沧 市 Lincang	临翔区 凤庆县 云县 永德县 镇康县 双江县 耿马县 沧源县 Linxiang District, Fengqing, Yunxian, Yongde, Zhenkang, Shuangjiang, Gengma, Cangyuan	1		7
楚 雄 州 Chuxiong	楚雄市 双柏县 牟定县 南华县 姚安县 大姚县 永仁县 元谋县 武定县 禄丰县 Chuxiong City, Shuangbai, Mouding, Nanhua, Yao'an, Dayao, Yongren, Yuanmou, Wuding, Lufeng		1	9
红 河 州 Honghe	个旧市 开远市 蒙自市 弥勒市 屏边县 建水县 石屏县 泸西县 元阳县 红河县 金平县 绿春县 河口县 Gejiu City, Kaiyuan City, Mengzi City, Mile City, Pingbian, Jianshui, Shiping, Luxi, Yuanyang,Honghe, Jinping, Luchun, Hekou		4	9
文 山 州 Wenshan	文山市 砚山县 西畴县 麻栗坡县 马关县 丘北县 广南县 富宁县 Wenshan City, Yanshan, Xichou, Malipo, Maguan, Qiubei, Guangnan, Funing		1	7
西双版纳州 Xishuangbanna	景洪市 勐海县 勐腊县 Jinghong City, Menghai, Mengla		1	2
大 理 州 Dali	大理市 漾濞县 祥云县 宾川县 弥渡县 南涧县 巍山县 永平县 云龙县 洱源县 剑川县 鹤庆县 Dali City, Yangbi, Xiangyun, Binchuan, Midu, Nanjian, Weishan, Yongping, Yunlong, Eryuan, Jianchuan, Heqing		1	11
德 宏 州 Dehong	瑞丽市 芒市 梁河县 盈江县 陇川县 Ruili City, Mangshi City, Lianghe, Yingjiang, Longchuan		2	3
怒 江 州 Nujiang	泸水市 福贡县 贡山县 兰坪县 Lushui City, Fugong, Gongshan, Lanping		1	3
迪 庆 州 Diqing	香格里拉市 德钦县 维西县 Shangri-La City, Deqin, Weixi		1	2
全 省 **Yunnan**	**8个省辖市、8个民族自治州；17个市辖区、17个县级市、29个民族自治县、66个县** **8 Provincial Jurisdiction Cities,8 Ethinic Minority Autonomous Prefectures, 17 Municipal Jurisdiction Districts，17Cities at County Level,29 ethinic minority autonomous counties，66 counties**			

1-2 续表1

单位：个

州 市	Region	县级单位数 Total	#县级市 Cities at County Level	#市辖区 Municipal Districts	#民族自治县 Ethnic Minority Autonomous Counties	#边境县 Counties of Border
全 省	**Yunnan**	**129**	**17**	**17**	**29**	**25**
昆 明	Kunming	14	1	7	3	
曲 靖	Qujing	9	1	3		
玉 溪	Yuxi	9	1	2	3	
保 山	Baoshan	5	1	1		2
昭 通	Zhaotong	11	1	1		
丽 江	Lijiang	5		1	2	
普 洱	Pu'er	10		1	9	4
临 沧	Lincang	8		1	3	3
楚 雄	Chuxiong	10	1			
红 河	Honghe	13	4		3	3
文 山	Wenshan	8	1			3
西双版纳	Xishuangbanna	3	1			3
大 理	Dali	12	1		3	
德 宏	Dehong	5	2			4
怒 江	Nujiang	4	1		2	3
迪 庆	Diqing	3	1		1	

continued

(unit)

乡镇单位数 Total	街道办事处 Community Offices	镇 Towns	乡 Townships	民族乡 Townships of Ethnic Minority	社区村单位数 Total	居委会 Community Residents' Committees	村委会 Villagers Committees
1 413	**191**	**680**	**542**	**140**	**14 589**	**2 755**	**11 834**
139	80	43	16	4	1 681	760	921
137	46	51	40	8	1 674	414	1 260
75	24	25	26	10	713	284	429
75	6	35	34	10	951	110	841
146	7	99	40	17	1 379	301	1 078
65	7	26	32	15	467	67	400
103	1	65	37	10	1 052	59	993
77	2	32	43	13	940	51	889
103		65	38	4	1 103	137	966
135	9	64	62	5	1 352	243	1 109
104	3	42	59	16	977	95	882
33	2	19	12	7	257	34	223
112	3	69	40	11	1 153	81	1 072
51	1	23	27	5	401	65	336
29		13	16	2	294	39	255
29		9	20	3	195	15	180

1-2 续表2 continued

单位：个 (unit)

州市县	Region	行政区划代码 Administrative Division Codes	乡镇单位数 Total	街道办事处 Community Offices	镇 Town	乡 Township	民族乡 Townships of Ethnic Minority	社区村单位数 Total	居委会 Community Residents' Committees	村委会 Villagers Committees
全 省	**Yunnan**	**530000**	**1 413**	**191**	**680**	**542**	**140**	**14 589**	**2 755**	**11 834**
昆明市	**Kunming**	**530100**	**139**	**80**	**43**	**16**	**4**	**1 681**	**760**	**921**
五华区	Wuhua	530102	10	10				91	91	
盘龙区	Panlong	530103	12	12				103	71	32
官渡区	Guandu	530111	10	10				129	129	
西山区	Xishan	530112	10	10				117	117	
东川区	Dongchuan	530113	9	2	6	1		169	39	130
呈贡区	Chenggong	530114	10	10				82	82	
晋宁区	Jinning	530115	8	2	4	2	2	137	12	125
富民县	Fumin	530124	7	2	5			75	6	69
宜良县	Yiliang	530125	9	3	4	2	2	138	88	50
石林县	Shilin	530126	7	3	3	1		93	6	87
嵩明县	Songming	530127	5	2	3			75	36	39
禄劝县	Luquan	530128	17	2	9	6		197	17	180
寻甸县	Xundian	530129	16	3	9	4		175	29	146
安宁市	Anning	530181	9	9				100	37	63
曲靖市	**Qujing**	**530300**	**137**	**46**	**51**	**40**	**8**	**1 674**	**414**	**1 260**
麒麟区	Qilin	530302	16	13	3			143	89	54
沾益区	Zhanyi	530303	11	4	2	5		134	45	89
马龙区	Malong	530304	10	5	2	3		75	47	28
陆良县	Luliang	530322	11	2	7	2		148	36	112
师宗县	Shizong	530323	10	3	4	3	3	110	21	89
罗平县	Luoping	530324	13	3	4	6	3	154	45	109
富源县	Fuyuan	530325	12	2	9	1	1	161	36	125
会泽县	Huize	530326	25	5	7	13	1	389	45	344
宣威市	Xuanwei	530381	29	9	13	7		360	50	310
玉溪市	**Yuxi**	**530400**	**75**	**24**	**25**	**26**	**10**	**713**	**284**	**429**
红塔区	Hongta	530402	11	9		2	2	105	95	10
江川区	Jiangchuan	530403	7	1	4	2	1	76	23	53
通海县	Tonghai	530423	9	2	4	3	3	76	27	49
华宁县	Huaning	530424	5	1	3	1	1	77	23	54
易门县	Yimen	530425	7	2	1	4	3	58	19	39
峨山县	Eshan	530426	8	2	3	3		76	21	55
新平县	Xinping	530427	12	2	4	6		124	27	97
元江县	Yuanjiang	530428	10	3	2	5		81	24	57
澄江市	Chengjiang	530481	6	2	4			40	25	15

1-2 续表3 continued

单位：个 (unit)

州市县	Region	行政区划代码 Administrative Division Codes	乡镇单位数 Total	街道办事处 Community Offices	镇 Town	乡 Township	民族乡 Townships of Ethnic Minority	社区村单位数 Total	居委会 Community Residents' Committees	村委会 Villagers Committees
保山市	**Baoshan**	**530500**	**75**	**6**	**35**	**34**	**10**	**951**	**110**	**841**
隆阳区	Longyang	530502	21	6	5	10	4	348	80	268
施甸县	Shidian	530521	13		5	8	2	138	5	133
龙陵县	Longling	530523	10		5	5	1	121	5	116
昌宁县	Changning	530524	13		9	4	3	124	6	118
腾冲市	Tengchong	530581	18		11	7		220	14	206
昭通市	**Zhaotong**	**530600**	**146**	**7**	**99**	**40**	**17**	**1 379**	**301**	**1 078**
昭阳区	Zhaoyang	530602	20	3	10	7	4	198	88	110
鲁甸县	Ludian	530621	12		10	2	2	103	33	70
巧家县	Qiaojia	530622	16		12	4		184	37	147
盐津县	Yanjin	530623	10		6	4		97	20	77
大关县	Daguan	530624	9		8	1	1	84	8	76
永善县	Yongshan	530625	15		8	7	2	144	32	112
绥江县	Suijiang	530626	5		5			43	12	31
镇雄县	Zhenxiong	530627	30	3	20	7	2	263	29	234
彝良县	Yiliang	530628	15		10	5	5	147	15	132
威信县	Weixin	530629	10		7	3	1	87	18	69
水富市	Shuifu	530681	4	1	3			29	9	20
丽江市	**Lijiang**	**530700**	**65**	**7**	**26**	**32**	**15**	**467**	**67**	**400**
古城区	Gucheng	530702	11	7	2	2	1	60	34	26
玉龙县	Yulong	530721	16		7	9	3	104	7	97
永胜县	Yongsheng	530722	15		9	6	6	151	9	142
华坪县	Huaping	530723	8		4	4	4	61	10	51
宁蒗县	Ninglang	530724	15		4	11	1	91	7	84
普洱市	**Pu'er**	**530800**	**103**	**1**	**65**	**37**	**10**	**1 052**	**59**	**993**
思茅区	Simao	530802	7	1	4	2	2	73	17	56
宁洱县	Ning'er	530821	9		6	3		89	4	85
墨江县	Mojiang	530822	15		12	3	1	168	8	160
景东县	Jingdong	530823	13		10	3		170	4	166
景谷县	Jinggu	530824	10		6	4		142	5	137
镇沅县	Zhenyuan	530825	9		8	1		111	2	109
江城县	Jiangcheng	530826	7		5	2		52	4	48
孟连县	Menglian	530827	6		4	2		43	4	39
澜沧县	Lancang	530828	20		5	15	6	165	8	157
西盟县	Ximeng	530829	7		5	2	1	39	3	36
临沧市	**Lincang**	**530900**	**77**	**2**	**32**	**43**	**13**	**940**	**51**	**889**
临翔区	Linxiang	530902	10	2	1	7	2	104	15	89
凤庆县	Fengqing	530921	13		8	5	3	187	4	183
云　县	Yunxian	530922	12		7	5	3	194	4	190
永德县	Yongde	530923	10		3	7	2	121	5	116
镇康县	Zhenkang	530924	7		3	4	1	75	4	71
双江县	Shuangjiang	530925	6		2	4		77	7	70
耿马县	Gengma	530926	9		4	5	1	87	7	80
沧源县	Cangyuan	530927	10		4	6	1	95	5	90

1-2 续表4 continued

单位：个 (unit)

州市县	Region	行政区划代码 Administrative Division Codes	乡镇单位数 Total	街道办事处 Community Offices	镇 Town	乡 Township	民族乡 Townships of Ethnic Minority	社区村单位数 Total	居委会 Community Residents' Committees	村委会 Villagers Committees
楚雄州	**Chuxiong**	**532300**	**103**		**65**	**38**	**4**	**1 103**	**137**	**966**
楚雄市	Chuxiong	532301	15		12	3		154	31	123
双柏县	Shuangbai	532322	8		5	3		85	8	77
牟定县	Mouding	532323	7		4	3		89	5	84
南华县	Nanhua	532324	10		6	4	1	128	12	116
姚安县	Yao'an	532325	9		6	3		77	13	64
大姚县	Dayao	532326	12		8	4	1	129	17	112
永仁县	Yongren	532327	7		3	4	1	63	3	60
元谋县	Yuanmou	532328	10		3	7		78	10	68
武定县	Wuding	532329	11		7	4	1	135	9	126
禄丰县	Lufeng	532331	14		11	3		165	29	136
红河州	**Honghe**	**532500**	**135**	**9**	**64**	**62**	**5**	**1 352**	**243**	**1 109**
个旧市	Gejiu	532501	10	3	5	2		119	59	60
开远市	Kaiyuan	532502	7	2	2	3	1	78	24	54
蒙自市	Mengzi	532503	13	4	5	4	2	107	24	83
弥勒市	Mile	532504	12		10	2		144	42	102
屏边县	Pingbian	532523	7		4	3		80	4	76
建水县	Jianshui	532524	14		8	6		153	16	137
石屏县	Shiping	532525	9		7	2		115	3	112
泸西县	Luxi	532527	8		5	3		87	15	72
元阳县	Yuanyang	532528	14		3	11		138	4	134
红河县	Honghe	532529	13		5	8		91	3	88
金平县	Jinping	532530	13		4	9	1	100	7	93
绿春县	Luchun	532531	9		4	5		92	21	71
河口县	Hekou	532532	6		2	4	1	48	21	27
文山州	**Wenshan**	**532600**	**104**	**3**	**42**	**59**	**16**	**977**	**95**	**882**
文山市	Wenshan	532601	17	3	7	7	5	141	28	113
砚山县	Yanshan	532622	11		4	7	4	108	22	86
西畴县	Xichou	532623	9		2	7		73	4	69
麻栗坡县	Malipo	532624	11		4	7	1	105	12	93
马关县	Maguan	532625	13		9	4		127	9	118
丘北县	Qiubei	532626	12		3	9	5	101	6	95
广南县	Guangnan	532627	18		7	11		177	10	167
富宁县	Funing	532628	13		6	7	1	145	4	141
西双版纳州	**Xishuangbanna**	**532800**	**33**	**2**	**19**	**12**	**7**	**257**	**34**	**223**
景洪市	Jinghong	532801	12	2	5	5	2	107	21	86
勐海县	Menghai	532822	11		6	5	3	91	6	85
勐腊县	Mengla	532823	10		8	2	2	59	7	52

1-2 续表5 continued

单位：个 (unit)

州市县	Region	行政区划代码 Administrative Division Codes	乡镇单位数 Total	街道办事处 Community Offices	镇 Town	乡 Township	民族乡 Townships of Ethnic Minority	社区村单位数 Total	居委会 Community Residents' Committees	村委会 Villagers Committees
大 理 州	**Dali**	**532900**	**112**	**3**	**69**	**40**	**11**	**1 153**	**81**	**1 072**
大理市	Dali	532901	13	3	9	1	1	142	31	111
漾濞县	Yangbi	532922	9		4	5		66	1	65
祥云县	Xiangyun	532923	10		8	2	1	139	7	132
宾川县	Binchuan	532924	10		8	2	2	90	11	79
弥渡县	Midu	532925	8		6	2	1	89	7	82
南涧县	Nanjian	532926	8		5	3		81	4	77
巍山县	Weishan	532927	10		4	6		83	4	79
永平县	Yongping	532928	7		3	4	3	75	3	72
云龙县	Yunlong	532929	11		4	7	2	88	3	85
洱源县	Eryuan	532930	9		6	3		90	2	88
剑川县	Jianchuan	532931	8		5	3		93	5	88
鹤庆县	Heqing	532932	9		7	2	1	117	3	114
德 宏 州	**Dehong**	**533100**	**51**	**1**	**23**	**27**	**5**	**401**	**65**	**336**
瑞丽市	Ruili	533102	6		3	3		47	18	29
芒 市	Mangshi	533103	12	1	5	6	1	103	23	80
梁河县	Lianghe	533122	9		3	6	2	66	4	62
盈江县	Yingjiang	533123	15		8	7	1	108	11	97
陇川县	Longchuan	533124	9		4	5	1	77	9	68
怒 江 州	**Nujiang**	**533300**	**29**		**13**	**16**	**2**	**294**	**39**	**255**
泸水市	Lushui	533301	9		6	3	1	86	15	71
福贡县	Fugong	533323	7		1	6	1	64	7	57
贡山县	Gongshan	533324	5		2	3		29	3	26
兰坪县	Lanping	533325	8		4	4		115	14	101
迪 庆 州	**Diqing**	**533400**	**29**		**9**	**20**	**3**	**195**	**15**	**180**
香格里拉市	Shangri-La	533401	11		4	7	1	64	5	59
德钦县	Deqing	533422	8		2	6	2	48	6	42
维西县	Weixi	533423	10		3	7		83	4	79

1-3 云南国民经济主要指标数据（2013-2020年）

指　　标	Item
云南生产总值(当年价)(亿元)	**Gross Domestic Product of Yunnan Province (at current prices) (100 Million yuan)**
#非公经济增加值	Added Value of Individual and Private Economy
年末总人口数（万人）	**Total Population at Year-end (10 000 persons)**
年末城镇人口比重	Proportion of Urban Population at Year-end
年末就业人员数 （万人）	**Total Number of Employed Persons at Year-end (10 000 persons)**
#城镇单位在岗职工人数	Number of employees on duty of urban entities
全省居民人均可支配收入 （元）	**Per Capita Disposable Income of Households (yuan)**
城镇居民人均可支配收入	Annual Per Capita Disposable Income of Urban Households
农村居民人均可支配收入	Annual Per Capita Disposable Income of Rural Households
工农业总产值 （亿元）	**Gross Output Value of Industry and Agriculture (100 million yuan)**
农业总产值	Gross Output Value of Farming, Forestry, Animal Husbandry and Fishery
工业总产值(当年价)	Gross Output Value of Industry (at current prices)
轻工业产值	Total Output Value of Light Industry
重工业产值	Total Output Value of Heavy Industry
主要农产品产量(万吨)	**Output of Major Agricultural Products (10 000 tons)**
粮　食	Grain
油　料	Oil-bearing Crops
甘　蔗	Sugarcane
烤　烟	Flue-cured Tobacco
水　果	Fruits
茶　叶	Tea
猪、牛、羊肉	Pork,Beef and Mutton
水产品	Aquatic Product
主要工业产品产量	**Output of Major Industrial Products**
原　煤（万吨）	Raw Coal (10 000 tons)
粗　钢（万吨）	Steel (10 000 tons)
钢　材（万吨）	Steel Products (10 000 tons)
发电量（亿千瓦小时）	Electricity (100 million kWh)
成品糖（万吨）	Sugar of Finished Product (10 000 tons)
卷　烟（亿支）	Cigarettes(100 million pieces)
水　泥（万吨）	Cement (10 000 tons)
布（万米）	Cloth (10 000 m)
机制纸及纸板（万吨）	Machine-made Paper and Paperboards (10 000 tons)

Principal Indicators on National Economy of Yunnan (2013-2020)

2013	2014	2015	2016	2017	2018	2019	2020
12 825.46	**14 041.65**	**14 960.00**	**16 369.00**	**18 486.00**	**20 880.63**	**23 223.75**	**24 521.90**
–	–	–	–	–	9 864.32	10 954.75	11 411.25
4641.0	**4653.0**	**4663.0**	**4677.0**	**4693.0**	**4703.0**	**4714.0**	**4722.0**
39.99	41.21	42.93	44.64	46.29	47.44	48.67	50.05
2 835.00	**2 859.00**	**2 823.00**	**2 855.00**	**2 831.00**	**2 822.00**	**2 812.00**	**2 806.00**
352.27	347.06	343.25	345.80	357.38	359.20	310.48	305.34
12 578	**13 772**	**15 223**	**16 720**	**18 348**	**20 084**	**22 082**	**23 295**
22 460	24 299	26 373	28 611	30 996	33 488	36 238	37 500
6 724	7 456	8 242	9 020	9 862	10 768	11 902	12 842
15 813.02	**16 101.94**	**15 552.76**	**16 527.90**	**16 985.88**	**18 716.19**	**21 720.25**	**22 895.72**
3 056.04	3 261.30	3 383.09	3 704.69	3 872.93	4 108.88	4 935.73	5 920.52
12 756.98	12 840.64	12 169.67	12 823.21	13 112.95	14 607.31	16 784.52	16 975.20
3 911.54	4 017.84	4 257.51	4 650.60	4 563.72	4 671.10	5 117.95	5 056.80
8 845.44	8 822.80	7 912.16	8 172.61	8 549.23	9 936.21	11 666.57	11 918.40
1 897.61	1 940.82	1 969.79	1 815.10	1 843.40	1 860.54	1 870.03	1 895.86
60.68	64.68	65.92	56.34	56.26	60.98	62.51	63.09
2 146.25	2 110.40	1 930.05	1 523.77	1 516.15	1 640.08	1 569.69	1 597.17
103.85	94.50	90.34	87.89	83.85	82.29	81.00	81.60
634.52	669.02	726.54	797.77	783.90	813.35	860.32	961.58
30.17	33.55	36.58	37.30	39.30	42.33	43.72	46.32
597.48	627.46	627.03	369.60	374.10	378.47	346.58	353.28
78.16	87.01	93.74	60.15	63.12	63.75	63.65	64.40
8 185.53	4 013.66	4 590.14	4 251.82	4 392.91	4 534.90	4 779.61	5 265.63
1 884.80	1 689.07	1 418.08	1 417.33	1 517.50	1 925.04	2 154.68	2 233.02
2 053.92	1 935.05	1 695.37	1 654.65	1 607.38	1 940.74	2 323.31	2 640.72
1 954.62	2 347.21	2 352.40	2 469.50	2 730.09	3 007.72	3 251.88	3 451.17
236.52	249.68	249.58	220.77	227.13	244.98	238.70	261.22
3 787.75	3 848.06	3 903.63	3 736.89	3 589.36	3 501.52	3 496.45	3 515.88
9 009.16	9 492.64	9 305.31	10 963.53	11 292.89	11 798.42	12 844.85	12 984.71
298.00	156.00	118.00	104.00	93.00	23.00	–	–
41.43	46.58	58.89	78.46	89.55	88.51	85.26	74.29

1-3 续表

指　　标	Item
全社会固定资产投资总额增速(%)	**Growth Rate of Total Investment in Fixed Assets (%)**
社会消费品零售总额（亿元)	**Total Retail Sales of Consumer Goods (100 million yuan)**
进出口总额(亿美元)	**Total Value of Exports and Imports (USD 100 million)**
出口额	Exports Value
进口额	Imports Value
实际利用外商直接投资总额(亿美元)	**Actually Utilized Foreign Investment Value (USD 100 million)**
财　政（亿元)	**Government Finance (100 million yuan)**
财政总收入	Government Revenue
#地方一般公共预算收入	Government Expenditure
地方一般公共预算支出	Government Expenditure
交通运输邮电	**Transport, Posts and Telecommunication Services**
货运周转量（亿吨公里)	Freight Traffic(100 million ton-km)
铁　路	Railways
公　路	Highways
水　路	Waterways
民用航空	Civil Aviation
旅客周转量（亿人公里)	Passenger Traffic(100 million passenger-km)
铁　路	Railways
公　路	Highways
水　路	Waterways
民用航空	Civil Aviation
邮电业务总量（亿元)	**Total Post and Telecommunication Services(10 000 yuan)**
旅游总收入(亿元)	**Total Tourism Revenue(100 million yuan)**
#国际旅游收入(亿美元)	Foreign Exchange Earning from International Tourism(USD 100 million)
职工工资	**Wages of Staff and Workers**
职工工资总额（亿元)	Total Wages of Staff and Workers (100 million yuan)
#国有单位职工工资总额（亿元)	Total Wages of Staff and Workers of State-owned Entities (100 million yuan)
职工平均工资（万元)	Annual Average Wages of Staff and Workers (10 000 yuan)
#国有单位职工平均工资（万元)	Annual Average Wages of Staff and Workers of State-owned Units (10 000 yuan)
居民消费价格指数（%)(上年=100)	**Consumer Price Index (%)(preceding year = 100)**
教育文化	**Education and Culture**
高等学校数（所)	Number of Regular Institutions of Higher Education (unit)
高等学校在校学生数（万人)	Student Enrollment of Regular Institutions of Higher Education (10 000 person)
中等专业学校在校学生数（万人)	Student Enrollment of Specialized Secondary Schools (10 000 person)
普通中学在校学生数（万人)	Student Enrollment of Regular Secondary Schools (10 000 persons)
小学在校学生数（万人)	Student Enrollment of Primary Schools (10 000 persons)
艺术表演团体（个)	Number of Art Performance Groups (unit)
报纸出版数量（亿份)	Number of Newspapers Issued (100 million pieces)
各类杂志出版数量（亿册)	Number of Magazines Issued (100 million pieces)
图书出版数量（亿册)	Number of Books Published (100 million copies)
卫　生	**Health Care**
卫生机构数（个)	Number of Health Institutions (unit)
床位数（万张)	Number of Sickbeds of Health Institutions (10 000 units)
#医院病床数（万张)	Number of Sickbeds of Hospital (10 000 units)
专业卫生技术人员（万人)	Number of Medical Technical Personnel (10 000 persons)
#执业（助理）医师(万人)	Doctors (10 000 persons)

注：1.进出口总额包括边境贸易。
2.财政总收入包括上划中央的"两税"收入。
3.2012年以前卫生机构数包括主要卫生机构、诊所、卫生保健所、医务室等，从2013年开始还包括村卫生室。

continued

2013	2014	2015	2016	2017	2018	2019	2020
27.3	**15.4**	**17.4**	**19.4**	**17.5**	**11.3**	**8.3**	**7.2**
5 053.71	**5 744.42**	**6 390.83**	**7 222.73**	**8 194.79**	**9 197.26**	**10 158.23**	**9 792.87**
258.29	**296.22**	**245.27**	**199.99**	**233.94**	**298.95**	**336.92**	**389.46**
159.59	188.02	166.26	115.82	114.30	128.12	150.22	221.40
98.70	108.20	79.01	84.17	119.64	170.83	186.70	168.06
25.15	**27.06**	**29.92**	**8.67**	**9.63**	**10.56**	**7.23**	**7.59**
2 976.79	3 156.73	3 250.02	3 204.95	3 392.08	3 719.77	4 003.56	3 995.36
1 611.30	1 698.06	1 808.15	1 812.29	1 886.17	1 994.35	2 073.56	2 116.69
4 096.51	4 437.98	4 712.83	5 018.86	5 712.97	6 075.03	6 770.09	6 974.02
1 325.30	1 407.63	1 465.30	1 569.20	1 798.67	1 943.85	1 524.03	1 551.07
390.24	390.59	371.83	379.44	420.62	436.08	489.86	441.38
921.98	1 002.35	1 077.89	1 173.06	1 360.37	1 489.23	1 015.20	1 101.54
11.65	13.09	14.08	15.20	16.21	17.33	17.44	7.18
1.43	1.60	1.51	1.50	1.46	1.21	1.54	0.97
720.33	573.63	599.49	585.55	596.70	595.88	632.51	375.63
99.34	103.22	111.38	110.92	131.90	150.99	181.95	117.39
323.10	321.06	330.21	319.99	308.27	269.63	251.27	138.47
2.23	2.37	2.50	2.70	2.88	3.02	2.30	0.74
125.40	146.98	155.40	151.93	153.66	172.23	196.99	119.03
402.61	**567.23**	**791.55**	**1 285.81**	**1 210.26**	**2 567.46**	**4 304.34**	**5 805.92**
2 111.24	**2 665.74**	**3 281.79**	**4 726.25**	**6 922.23**	**8 991.44**	**11 035.20**	**6 477.03**
24.19	24.21	28.76	30.75	35.50	44.18	51.47	4.03
1 630.67	1 727.71	1 958.70	2 284.05	2 636.42	2 922.04	2 905.61	3 050.83
797.61	916.93	1 065.57	1 323.26	1 565.96	1 659.47	1 648.62	1 808.24
4.40	4.78	5.50	6.36	7.35	8.05	9.18	9.83
4.90	5.44	6.45	7.89	9.57	10.41	10.65	11.36
103.1	**102.4**	**101.9**	**101.5**	**100.9**	**101.6**	**102.5**	**103.6**
67	67	69	72	77	79	81	82
54.86	57.70	61.46	65.66	70.59	76.47	86.40	96.42
30.13	30.84	30.97	31.25	32.12	31.97	30.81	29.53
261.07	266.55	267.60	267.78	270.69	272.64	275.45	279.53
392.08	382.69	377.78	376.61	375.21	379.51	385.10	389.22
259	284	276	221	316	268	304	99
6.51	6.14	4.61	4.00	3.56	3.33	3.26	3.13
0.42	0.40	0.38	0.34	0.28	0.31	0.22	0.19
1.72	1.53	1.90	1.52	1.64	1.05	1.08	1.70
24 267	24 285	24 186	24 241	24 688	24 958	25 590	26 626
21.01	22.49	23.76	25.36	27.48	29.12	31.19	32.52
15.61	16.97	18.13	19.47	21.08	22.33	24.13	25.25
19.33	20.89	22.80	25.02	28.39	30.20	33.97	36.65
7.49	7.54	7.96	8.59	9.39	9.97	11.40	12.26

Note: a.The total value of imports and exports includes frontier trade value.
b.The government revenue is the total government revenue,including two taxes turned over to the central government.
c.Health institutions include main medical institutions, clinics， health care centers,infirmaries and so on in 2012 and before,and since 2013, village clinics are also included.

1-4 主要年份云南国民经济主要指标总量和增长速度

指　标	Item	总量指标 1978	1990
年末总人口(万人)	**Total Population at Year-end (10 000 persons)**	**3 091.50**	**3 730.60**
城镇人口	Urban Population	375.70	1 510.10
乡村人口	Rural Population	2 715.80	2 220.50
就业人员数(万人)	**Employment (10 000 persons)**	**1 313.40**	**1 922.70**
第一产业	Primary Industry	1 130.90	1 537.80
第二产业	Secondary Industry	100.70	184.80
第三产业	Tertiary Industry	81.80	200.10
生产总值(GDP)(亿元)	**Gross Regional Product of Yunnan Province (100 million yuan)**	**69.05**	**451.67**
第一产业	Primary Industry	29.46	168.13
第二产业	Secondary Industry	27.58	157.80
第三产业	Tertiary Industry	12.01	125.74
人均生产总值（元）	Per Capita GDP	226	1 224
全省城乡居民人均可支配收入(元)	**Per Capita Disposable Income of Households (yuan)**		
城镇常住居民人均可支配收入	Annual Per Capita Disposable Income of Urban Households	328	1 515
农村常住居民人均可支配收入	Annual Per Capita Disposable Income of Rural Households	131	541
全社会固定资产投资总额(亿元)	**Total Investment in Fixed Assets (100 million yuan)**	**15.04**	**75.74**
#房地产开发	Real Estate Development	-	2.06
社会消费品零售总额(亿元)	**Total Retail Sales of Consumer Goods (100 million yuan)**	**28.38**	**145.59**
旅游业	**Tourism**		
入境过夜游客（万人次）	Overseas Tourists (10 000 person-times)	-	-
#外国人（万人次）	Foreigners (10 000 person-times)	-	-
国内旅客（亿人次）	Number of Tourists (Domestic Visitors) (100 million person-times)	-	-
国际旅游收入（亿美元）	Foreign Exchange Earnings from International Tourism (100 million USD)	-	-
国内旅游收入（亿元）	Earnings from Domestic Tourism (100 million yuan)	-	-
进出口总额(亿美元)	**Total Value of Exports and Imports (USD 100 million)**	**1.04**	**5.48**
出口额	Export Value	0.69	4.34
进口额	Import Value	0.35	1.14
财　政（亿元）	**Government Finance (100 million yuan)**		
财政总收入	Government Revenue	11.76	77.43
#地方一般公共预算收入	General Public Budget Revenue		
地方一般公共预算支出	General Public Budget Expenditure	18.28	90.76
农　业	**Agriculture**		
农林牧渔业总产值（亿元）	Gross Output Value of Agriculture, Forestry, Animal Husbandry and Fishery	40.02	211.72
主要农产品产量(万吨)	**Output of Major Agriculture Products(10 000 tons)**		
粮　食	Grain	864.05	1 061.21
油　料	Oil-bearing Crops	5.51	13.31
甘　蔗	Sugarcane	160.01	661.88
烤　烟	Flue-cured Tobacco	12.26	43.60
水　果	Fruits	11.62	31.97
茶　叶	Tea	1.78	4.48
猪、牛、羊肉	Pork,Beef and Mutton	29.23	74.74
水产品	Aquatic Products	1.12	4.60

Growth Rate and Total Amounts of Principal Indicators on National Economy in Significant Years of Yunnan

Aggregate Data			各年比上年增长(±%) Growth Rate over Last Year				年平均增长速度(%) Average Annual Growth Rate(%)			
2000	2010	2020	1990	2000	2010	2020	1979-2020	1991-2020	2001-2020	2011-2020
4240.8	**4601.6**	**4722.0**	**2.3**	**1.2**	**0.7**	**0.2**	**1.0**	**0.8**	**0.5**	**0.3**
990.6	1601.8	2363.4	-0.9	-50.3	3.1	3.0	4.5	1.5	4.4	4.0
3250.2	2999.8	2358.6	4.6	47.7	-0.6	-2.5	-0.3	0.2	-1.6	-2.4
2 295.40	**2 794.00**	**2 806.00**	**2.2**	**2.3**	**4.1**	**-0.2**	**1.8**	**1.3**	**1.0**	**0.0**
1 695.90	1 687.58	1 226.00	2.3	-1.4	0.9	-2.7	0.2	-0.8	-1.6	-3.1
210.40	352.04	497.00	0.5	6.5	9.6	5.8	3.9	3.4	4.4	3.5
389.20	754.38	1 083.00	3.4	19.3	9.2	0.1	6.3	5.8	5.3	3.7
2 030.08	**7 735.33**	**24 521.90**	**8.7**	**7.5**	**12.3**	**4.0**	**9.7**	**9.7**	**9.8**	**9.4**
442.29	1 090.31	3 598.91	8.5	5.6	4.2	5.7	5.2	4.9	5.5	6.1
836.15	3 267.69	8 287.54	9.8	5.8	15.6	3.6	10.8	11.2	11.1	10.6
751.64	3 377.33	12 635.45	7.1	10.4	11.6	3.8	11.9	11.1	10.2	9.2
4 814	16 866	51 975	6.7	6.2	11.6	3.7	8.6	8.8	9.2	9.1
6 277	15 528	37 500	16.1	2.1	11.1	3.5	11.9	11.3	9.3	9.2
1 508	4 327	12 842	13.2	3.5	18.2	7.9	11.5	11.1	11.3	11.5
697.94	**5 528.71**	**-**	**11.7**	**-2.7**	**22.1**	**7.2**	**19.4**	**21.9**	**20.0**	**15.3**
83.23	900.44	4 505.19	-	-9.6	22.1	8.5	-	31.6	24.2	20.2
630.53	**3 057.12**	**9 792.87**	**2.4**	**9.3**	**25.6**	**-3.6**	**14.9**	**15.1**	**14.7**	**12.3**
100.11	329.15	57.65	—	-3.7	15.7	-92.2	—	—	-2.7	-16.0
66.59	231.23	51.36	—	-8.1	20.6	-91.2	—	—	-1.3	-14.0
0.38	1.38	5.29	—	4.6	15.1	-33.9	—	—	14.1	14.4
3.39	13.24	4.03	—	-3.2	12.9	-92.2	—	—	0.9	-11.2
183.19	916.82	6 449.21	—	4.6	25.5	-39.6	—	—	19.5	21.5
18.13	**133.68**	**389.46**	**0.1**	**9.2**	**66.7**	**15.6**	**15.2**	**15.3**	**16.6**	**11.3**
11.75	76.03	221.40	16.0	13.6	68.4	47.4	14.7	14.0	15.8	11.3
6.38	57.62	168.06	-34.1	2.1	64.4	-10.0	15.8	18.1	17.8	11.3
432.95	1 809.30	3 995.36	22.4	1.8	21.4	-0.2	14.9	14.0	11.8	8.2
180.75	871.19	2 116.69		4.7	24.8	2.1	-	-	13.1	9.3
414.11	2 285.72	6 974.02	10.8	9.5	17.1	3.0	15.2	15.6	15.2	11.8
680.86	1 810.53	5 920.52	6.6	6.5	4.7	5.8	5.8	5.9	6.2	6.2
1 467.80	1 650.00	1 895.86	6.3	4.9	4.6	1.4	1.9	2.0	1.3	1.4
26.98	34.23	63.09	29.0	30.8	-31.8	0.9	6.0	5.3	4.3	6.3
1 420.29	1 750.92	1 597.17	20.1	-7.0	-0.6	1.8	5.6	3.0	0.6	-0.9
64.61	95.40	81.60	-4.5	6.0	8.4	0.7	4.6	2.1	1.2	-1.6
76.95	397.91	961.58	-6.8	4.2	16.1	11.8	11.1	12.0	13.5	9.2
7.94	20.73	46.32	5.0	5.7	13.3	5.9	8.1	8.1	9.2	8.4
191.51	474.82	353.28	9.4	6.2	75.3	1.9	6.1	5.3	3.1	-2.9
16.62	48.17	64.40	4.3	7.0	11.9	1.2	10.1	9.2	7.0	2.9

1-4 续表

指　标	Item	总量指标 Aggregate Data 1978	1990
主要工业产品产量（万吨）	**Output of Major Industrial Products (10 000 tons)**		
原　煤	Raw Coal	1 483	2 227
粗　钢	Steel	35.12	80.15
成品钢材	Steel Products	25.59	68.97
发电量（亿千瓦小时）	Electricity (100 million kWh)	52.51	125.78
水　泥	Cement	131	471.00
卷　烟（亿支）	Cigarettes (100 million pieces)	315.0	2240
机制纸及纸板	Machine-made Paper and Paperboards	5.12	15.43
成品糖	Sugar of Finished Product	14.00	51.00
建筑业	**Construction**		
建筑业总产值（亿元）	Gross Output Value of Construction (100 million yuan)	5.46	36.68
交通运输	**Transportation**		
货运周转量（亿吨公里）	Freight Traffic (100 million ton-km)	62.34	260.67
旅客周转量（亿人公里）	Passenger Traffic (100 million passenger-km)	24.25	87.67
邮电业务总量（亿元）	**Total Post and Telecommunication Services (10 000 yuan)**	**0.30**	**1.27**
国有单位职工平均工资(元)	**Average Wages of Staff and Workers of State-owned Entities (yuan)**	**623**	**2 200**
科学技术	**Science and Technology**		
研究与试验发展经费支出（亿元）	Expenditure on R&D (100 million yuan)	–	–
发明专利申请批准数（万件）	Number of Patent Applications Granted (10 000 pieces)	–	24.00
技术合同成交额（亿元）	Transaction Value in Technical Contract (100 million yuan)	–	–
教　育	Education		
专任教师数（万人）	Full-time Teachers (10 000 persons)		
#普通高等学校	Regular Institutions of Higher Education	0.37	0.78
普通高中	Regular Senior Secondary Schools	1.16	1.23
普通初中	Junior Secondary Schools	4.74	5.69
普通小学	Regular Primary Schools	16.41	17.42
在校学生数（万人）	Total Enrollment (10 000 persons)		
#普通本、专科	Regular Undergraduates and College Students	1.59	4.35
普通高中	Regular Senior Secondary Schools	23.78	18.06
普通初中	Junior Secondary Schools	104.76	105.89
普通小学	Regular Primary Schools	436.03	446.86
教育经费支出（亿元）	Government Expenditures on Education (100 million yuan)	1.86	15.93
卫　生	**Health Care**		
医院病床数(万张)	Number of Hospital Sickbeds (10 000)	5.41	7.61
专业卫生技术人员(万人)	Number of Medical Technical Personnel (10 000 persons)	6.55	10.16
#执业（助理）医师(万人)	Number of Doctors	3.11	5.39
城镇职工参加社会保险人数（万人）	**Social Insurance (10 000 persons)**		
参加城镇职工基本养老保险人数	Contributors in Basic Pension Insurance	–	–
参加城镇职工基本医疗保险人数	Contributors in Basic Medical Care Insurance	–	–
参加失业保险人数	Number of Employees Joining Unemployment Insurance	–	–

continued

总 量 指 标 Aggregate Data			各年比上年增长(±%) Growth Rate over Last Year(±%)				年平均增长速度(%) Average Annual Growth Rate(%)			
2000	2010	2020	1990	2000	2010	2020	1979-2020	1991-2020	2001-2020	2011-2020
2 215.61	9 763.38	5 265.63	2.1	-16.8	9.4	10.2	3.1	2.9	4.4	-6.0
189.41	1 293.77	2 233.02	11.0	6.0	23.3	3.2	10.4	11.7	13.1	5.6
183.71	1 214.99	2 640.72	11.5	0.9	24.8	11.8	11.7	12.9	14.3	8.1
317.46	1 364.85	3 451.17	10.2	6.5	16.3	6.1	10.5	11.7	12.7	9.7
1 642.80	5 786.16	12 984.71	4.1	1.2	14.7	0.8	11.6	11.7	10.9	8.4
3 063.85	3 573.78	3 515.88	10.0	1.5	3.4	0.6	5.9	1.5	0.7	-0.2
22.32	44.87	74.29	1.4	-6.6	-2.5	-12.5	6.6	5.4	6.2	5.2
152.25	179.78	261.22	9.9	-6.3	-19.7	8.8	7.2	5.6	2.7	3.8
311.34	1 511.85	6 724.82	8.5	-0.7	26.3	9.8	18.5	19.0	16.6	16.1
479.52	915.04	1 551.07	15.7	8.2	8.5	1.8	8.0	6.1	6.0	5.4
237.94	523.64	375.63	-6.7		16.8	-40.5	6.7	5.0	2.3	-3.3
99.07	**268.94**	**5 805.92**	**15.5**	**61.7**	**14.8**	**34.9**	**–**	**–**	**23.5**	**36.0**
9 422	**34 330**	**113 623**	**13.6**	**11.5**	**13.2**	**6.7**	**13.2**	**14.1**	**13.3**	**12.7**
–	44.20	246	–	–	18.6	11.8	–	–	–	18.7
139.00	652.00	2 458	71.4	90.4	37.0	13.1	–	16.7	15.4	14.2
–	11.21	50.10	–	–	14.4	-39.5	–	–	–	16.2
0.92	2.65	5.81	-2.5	10.8	2.8	40.0	6.8	6.9	9.7	8.2
1.46	4.12	11.20	1.7	8.1	3.8	79.2	5.5	7.6	10.7	10.5
9.10	11.98	13.00	6.0	6.6	3.7	-2.8	2.4	2.8	1.8	0.8
21.05	23.75	23.57	0.1	4.7	1.6	2.1	0.9	1.0	0.6	-0.1
9.04	43.69	96.42	-3.5	22.3	12.2	11.6	10.3	10.9	12.6	8.2
22.21	63.28	97.16	2.1	14.4	3.5	6.9	3.4	5.8	7.7	4.4
163.76	207.35	182.37	4.0	10.6	1.7	-1.2	1.3	1.8	0.5	-1.3
472.06	435.21	389.22	-2.3	-1.8	-2.0	1.1	-0.3	-0.5	-1.0	-1.1
95.58	540.93	1 162.02	19.0	11.0	23.5	8.6	16.6	15.4	13.3	7.9
6.61	11.25	25.25	1.5	2.3	12.8	4.6	3.7	4.1	6.9	8.4
12.41	14.17	36.65	2.5	2.6	5.9	7.9	4.2	4.4	5.6	10.0
6.26	6.21	12.26	3.9	3.1	4.5	7.5	3.3	2.8	3.4	7.0
252.28	317.42	701.34	–	12.9	3.5	7.9	–	–	5.2	8.3
69.48	414.77	548.42	–	54.4	4.4	3.9	–	–	10.9	2.8
196.03	209.61	307.39	–	8.3	5.5	6.3	–	–	2.3	3.9

1—5 按经济类型划分的云南国民经济主要指标数据（2020年）

Principal National Economical Indicators by Types of Economy of Yunnan (2020)

指　　标	Item	全　省 Yunnan	比重 (%) As Percentage to Total (%) (total=100)
规模以上工业增加值(亿元)	**Added Value of Industry above Designated Size (100 million yuan)**	–	**100.00**
国有企业	State-owned Enterprises	–	3.46
集体企业	Collective-owned Enterprises	–	0.25
股份合作制企业	Joint Stock Cooperative Enterprises	–	0.01
股份制企业	Joint Stock Enterprises	–	92.70
外商及港澳台资企业	Foreign-funded and Enterprises funded by Hong Kong,Macao and Taiwan	–	2.79
其他工业	Other Enterprises	–	0.79
全社会固定资产投资总额(亿元)	**Total Investment in Fixed Assets (100 million yuan)**	–	**100.00**
国有经济	State-owned Economy	–	38.50
集体经济	Collective-owned Economy	–	0.10
个体私营经济	Individual and Private Economy	–	0.30
其他各种经济	Other Types of Ownership Economy	–	58.50
农村农户投资	Investment of rural households	–	2.60
社会消费品零售总额(亿元)	**Total Retail Sales of Consumer Goods (100 million yuan)**	**9 792.87**	**100.00**
公有经济	Public Ownership Economy	1 847.65	18.87
#国有经济	Of which:State-owned Economy	1 484.83	15.16
非公有经济	Individual and Private Enterprises	7 945.22	81.13
#私有经济	Of which: Private Economy	7 050.96	72.00
就业人员总数(万人)	**Total Number of Employed Persons (10 000 persons)**	**2 806.00**	**100.00**
城镇就业人员	Employed Persons in Urban Entities	1 292.00	46.04
乡村就业人员	Rural Employed Persons	1 514.00	53.96

1-6 云南省国民经济主要数据占全国的比重（2020年）
Proportion of Principal Indicators of National Economy of Yunnan Province to the Whole Country (2020)

单位：% (%)

指　标	Item	全　国 China	云　南 Yunnan	云南占全国的比重(%) Proportion of Yunnan to National Total(%)
生产总值(GDP)(亿元)	**Gross Regional Product (100 million yuan)**	**1015 986.20**	**24 521.90**	**2.4**
第一产业	Primary Industry	77 754.10	3 598.91	4.6
第二产业	Secondary Industry	384 255.30	8 287.54	2.2
第三产业	Tertiary Industry	553 976.79	12 635.45	2.3
人均生产总值(元/人)	**Per Capita Gross Regional Product(yuan/person)**	**72 000**	**51 975**	**72.2**
年末总人口(万人)	**Total Population at the Year-end (10 000 persons)**	**141 178**	**4 722.0**	**3.3**
城镇化率(%)	**Urbanization Rate(%)**	**63.89**	**50.05**	**78.3**
全部职工平均工资(元)	**Average Wages of All Staff and Workers (yuan)**	**100 512**	**98 287**	**97.8**
城镇常住居民人均可支配收入(元)	**Annual Average Disposable Income of Urban Households (yuan)**	**43 834**	**37 500**	**85.6**
农村常住居民人均可支配收入(元)	**Rural Per Capita Net Income (yuan)**	**17 131**	**12 842**	**75.0**
社会消费品零售总额(亿元)	**Total Retail Sales of Consumer Goods (100 million yuan)**	**391 980.60**	**9 792.87**	**2.5**
对外贸易进出口总额（亿美元）	**Total Value of Export and Import in Foreign Trade(USD 100 million)**	**46 462.57**	**389.46**	**0.8**
#出口总额	Total Export Value	25 906.46	221.40	0.9
实际利用外商直接投资(亿美元)	**Actually Utilized Direct Foreign Investment (USD 100 million)**	**1 443.70**	**7.59**	**0.5**
工农业主要产品产量(万吨)	**Output of Major Industrial and Farm Products (10 000 tons)**			
粮　食	Grain	66 949.0	1 895.86	2.8
油　料	Oil-bearing Crops	3 586.4	63.09	1.8
烤　烟	Flue-cured Tobacco	202.2	81.60	40.4
猪、牛、羊肉	Pork , Beef and Mutton	5 278.09	353.28	6.7
原　煤(亿吨)	Coal (100 Million tons)	39.02	0.53	1.4
粗　钢	Steel	106 476.7	2 233.02	2.1
钢　材	Steel Products	132 489.2	2 640.72	2.0
发电量(亿千瓦小时)	Electricity (100 million kWh)	77 790.6	3 451.17	4.4
水　泥(亿吨)	Cement (100 Million tons)	23.95	1.30	5.4
农用化肥(折100%)	Chemical Fertilizer (Converted into 100%)	5 496.0	213.77	3.9
成品糖（万吨）	Sugar of Finished Product (10 000 tons)	1 431.3	261.22	18.3
卷　烟（亿支）	Cigarettes (10 billions cigarettes)	23 863.7	3 515.88	14.7
普通高等学校在校学生数(万人)	**Student Enrollment of Regular Institutions of Higher Education(10 000 persons)**	**3 285.29**	**96.42**	**2.9**
卫生机构病床数(万张)	**Number of Hospital Sickbeds (10 000 beds)**	**911.3**	**32.52**	**3.6**
卫生技术人员(万人)	**Medical Technical Personnel (10 000 persons)**	**1 067.1**	**36.65**	**3.4**
#执业（助理）医师	Doctors	408.2	12.26	3.0

注：本表全国数据主要来自《中国统计摘要(2021)》。全国钢材产量数据中含企业之间重复加工钢材约30566万吨。
Note: The national data in this table is from China statistical summary (2021). The national steel production data contains about 306 million tons of terra processed steel among enterprises.

1-7 全省按国民经济行业门类分的法人单位数（2016—2020年）
Number of Legal Entities by National Economy Indicators (2016-2020)

单位：个 (unit)

国民经济行业	National Economy Indicators	2016	2017	2018	2019	2020
全　省	**Yunnan**	**451 891**	**579 001**	**532 830**	**619 318**	**741 669**
农、林、牧、渔业	Agriculture, Forestry, Animal Husbandry and Fishery	78 056	109 423	84 771	94 033	104 282
采矿业	Mining	7 080	7 568	5 434	5 876	6 271
制造业	Manufacturing	26 905	32 978	34 606	38 381	43 405
电力、燃气及水生产和供应业	Production and Supply of Electricity, Gas and Water	3 206	3 521	2 975	3 116	3 367
建筑业	Construction	18 936	26 555	28 058	37 604	52 690
批发和零售业	Wholesale and Retail Trades	127 986	166 569	141 696	166 541	203 469
交通运输、仓储和邮政业	Transport, Storage and Post	8 685	11 046	10 675	13 113	16 717
住宿和餐饮业	Hotels and Catering Services	11 186	14 873	14 348	15 795	18 052
信息传输、软件业和信息技术服务业	Information Transmission, Computer Software and Information Technology Services	11 683	17 568	15 285	20 258	26 952
金融业	Financial Intermediation	4 080	4 385	2 948	3 016	3 434
房地产业	Real Estate	12 215	14 489	14 998	19 533	24 672
租赁和商务服务业	Leasing and Business Services	39 115	54 745	48 736	61 548	79 834
科学研究和技术服务业	Scientific Research, Technical Services	14 057	18 964	21 870	26 572	32 954
水利、环境和公共设施管理业	Management of Water Conservancy, Environment and Public Facilities	3 220	4 194	4 061	5 279	6 803
居民服务、修理和其他服务业	Services to Households and Other Services	12 280	14 686	13 888	15 853	18 573
教　育	Education	11 604	12 641	15 492	17 045	19 353
卫生和社会工作	Health, Social Security and Social Welfare	5 713	5 956	5 887	6 216	6 964
文化、体育和娱乐业	Culture, Sports and Entertainment	9 216	12 425	14 315	15 930	18 086
公共管理、社会保障和社会组织	Public Management and Social Organizations	46 668	46 415	52 787	53 609	55 791
国际组织	International Organization					

1-8 各州市法人单位数（2013-2020年）
Number of Legal Entities by Region (2013-2020)

单位：个 (unit)

州 市	Region	2013	2014	2015	2016	2017	2018	2019	2020
全 省	**Yunnan**	**191 663**	**279 006**	**372 755**	**451 891**	**579 001**	**532 830**	**619 318**	**741 669**
昆 明	Kunming	63 683	93 825	125 560	151 657	196 315	167 380	204 895	253 850
曲 靖	Qujing	16 960	25 755	37 439	46 183	57 596	45 681	55 140	65 051
玉 溪	Yuxi	13 871	17 546	23 511	27 784	32 310	29 566	32 824	37 568
保 山	Baoshan	6 888	10 233	13 267	17 003	21 621	20 697	23 216	28 330
昭 通	Zhaotong	9 521	13 541	18 572	23 378	29 076	29 124	32 947	40 797
丽 江	Lijiang	5 203	9 231	12 231	15 086	18 229	18 512	20 205	24 169
普 洱	Pu'er	9 123	13 873	17 624	20 678	24 841	23 751	26 582	30 863
临 沧	Lincang	6 046	9 846	12 701	15 452	20 996	21 976	22 930	26 490
楚 雄	Chuxiong	10 226	16 337	22 513	26 940	34 438	33 025	35 879	41 081
红 河	Honghe	14 894	18 879	23 483	24 327	38 199	39 281	42 926	50 699
文 山	Wenshan	7 780	10 847	13 596	19 125	23 637	21 581	24 415	30 565
西双版纳	Xishuangbanna	4 787	6 533	8 934	11 429	16 294	15 376	21 125	24 079
大 理	Dali	12 899	18 610	25 292	31 958	38 096	40 099	44 341	50 001
德 宏	Dehong	5 743	7 756	9 798	11 554	14 082	13 538	16 642	20 871
怒 江	Nujiang	2 124	3 619	4 451	5 430	6 361	6 430	7 558	8 701
迪 庆	Diqing	1 913	2 575	3 783	3 907	6 910	6 813	7 693	8 554

1-9 各州市按三次产业分的法人单位数（2020年）
Number of Legal Entities by Three Strata of Industry and Region (2020)

单位：个 (unit)

州 市	Region	法人单位数 Number of Impersonal Entities	第一产业 Single-industry Corporation	第二产业 Multi-industry Corporation	第三产业 Activity of Multi-industry Corporation
全 省	**Yunnan**	**741 669**	**97 737**	**105 141**	**538 791**
昆 明	Kunming	253 850	10 631	38 051	205 168
曲 靖	Qujing	65 051	11 683	8 677	44 691
玉 溪	Yuxi	37 568	3 470	5 977	28 121
保 山	Baoshan	28 330	4 729	4 507	19 094
昭 通	Zhaotong	40 797	8 261	5 010	27 526
丽 江	Lijiang	24 169	6 392	2 266	15 511
普 洱	Pu'er	30 863	6 578	4 973	19 312
临 沧	Lincang	26 490	5 025	4 769	16 696
楚 雄	Chuxiong	41 081	9 595	5 834	25 652
红 河	Honghe	50 699	4 520	6 772	39 407
文 山	Wenshan	30 565	4 986	3 994	21 585
西双版纳	Xishuangbanna	24 079	2 967	3 081	18 031
大 理	Dali	50 001	9 711	6 615	33 675
德 宏	Dehong	20 871	2 569	2 754	15 548
怒 江	Nujiang	8 701	3 081	901	4 719
迪 庆	Diqing	8 554	3 539	960	4 055

1-10 各州市按机构类型分的法人单位数（2020年）

Number of Legal Entities By Type of Institutions and Region (2020)

单位：个 (unit)

州 市	Region	法人单位数 Number of Impersonal Entities	企业法人 Single-industry Corporation	机关法人 Government Entity	事业法人 Institution Entity	社团团体 Multi-industry Corporation	其他 Activity of Multi-industry Corporation
全 省	**Yunnan**	**741 669**	**599 648**	**29 454**	**10 828**	**14 279**	**87 460**
昆 明	Kunming	253 850	236 753	3 840	1 394	1 938	9 925
曲 靖	Qujing	65 051	50 893	3 229	827	989	9 113
玉 溪	Yuxi	37 568	29 586	2 518	780	1 612	3 072
保 山	Baoshan	28 330	22 262	914	438	392	4 324
昭 通	Zhaotong	40 797	27 697	3 000	902	1 014	8 184
丽 江	Lijiang	24 169	18 197	864	464	617	4 027
普 洱	Pu'er	30 863	20 649	2 197	733	720	6 564
临 沧	Lincang	26 490	18 386	1 799	657	754	4 894
楚 雄	Chuxiong	41 081	32 087	1 440	706	937	5 911
红 河	Honghe	50 699	39 919	2 940	1 037	1 238	5 565
文 山	Wenshan	30 565	22 162	1 666	627	523	5 587
西双版纳	Xishuangbanna	24 079	18 954	999	370	433	3 323
大 理	Dali	50 001	35 551	2 737	962	1 957	8 794
德 宏	Dehong	20 871	16 679	744	395	547	2 506
怒 江	Nujiang	8 701	4 941	301	292	303	2 864
迪 庆	Diqing	8 554	4 932	266	244	305	2 807

1-11 各州市按控股情况分的企业法人单位数（2020年）

Numbers of Corporate Enterprises by Region and the Status of Holdings (2020)

单位：个 (unit)

州 市	Region	法人单位数 Number of Impersonal Entities	国有控股 Single-industry Corporation	集体控股 Collective-holding	私人控股 Private-holding	港澳台商控股 Hong Kong, Macao and Taiwan-holding	外资控股 Multi-industry Corporation	其他 Activity of Multi-industry Corporation
全 省	**Yunnan**	**599 648**	**8 610**	**5 150**	**570 451**	**676**	**894**	**13 867**
昆 明	Kunming	236 753	2 784	1 023	227 516	406	465	4 559
曲 靖	Qujing	50 893	717	552	47 651	22	32	1 919
玉 溪	Yuxi	29 586	477	278	27 966	20	20	825
保 山	Baoshan	22 262	457	198	21 203	11	21	372
昭 通	Zhaotong	27 697	394	542	26 117	14	7	623
丽 江	Lijiang	18 197	274	101	17 442	11	30	339
普 洱	Pu'er	20 649	385	444	19 283	14	17	506
临 沧	Lincang	18 386	323	373	17 037	14	9	630
楚 雄	Chuxiong	32 087	409	319	30 740	26	24	569
红 河	Honghe	39 919	730	562	37 881	33	23	690
文 山	Wenshan	22 162	421	115	20 841	11	12	762
西双版纳	Xishuangbanna	18 954	264	123	18 073	17	98	379
大 理	Dali	35 551	490	335	33 692	35	48	951
德 宏	Dehong	16 679	267	67	15 914	28	68	335
怒 江	Nujiang	4 941	105	48	4 576	6	3	203
迪 庆	Diqing	4 932	113	70	4 519	8	17	205

1-12 各州市基本单位数（2020年）

Number of Basic Entities by Region (2020)

单位：个 (unit)

州市	Region	法人单位数 Number of Impersonal Entities	单产业法人 Single-industry Corporation	多产业法人 Multi-industry Corporation	产业活动单位数 Number of Industrial Activity Entities	多产业法人单位所属产业活动 Activity of Multi-industry Corporation
全　省	**Yunnan**	**741 669**	**717 502**	**24 167**	**853 539**	**136 037**
昆　明	Kunming	253 850	245 422	8 428	277 905	32 483
曲　靖	Qujing	65 051	63 311	1 740	75 813	12 502
玉　溪	Yuxi	37 568	36 236	1 332	44 008	7 772
保　山	Baoshan	28 330	27 263	1 067	35 421	8 158
昭　通	Zhaotong	40 797	39 858	939	46 570	6 712
丽　江	Lijiang	24 169	23 301	868	28 306	5 005
普　洱	Pu'er	30 863	30 065	798	34 551	4 486
临　沧	Lincang	26 490	25 719	771	30 963	5 244
楚　雄	Chuxiong	41 081	39 755	1 326	48 963	9 208
红　河	Honghe	50 699	48 802	1 897	60 961	12 159
文　山	Wenshan	30 565	29 344	1 221	37 559	8 215
西双版纳	Xishuangbanna	24 079	23 439	640	27 570	4 131
大　理	Dali	50 001	48 222	1 779	59 804	11 582
德　宏	Dehong	20 871	20 069	802	25 131	5 062
怒　江	Nujiang	8 701	8 433	268	10 075	1 642
迪　庆	Diqing	8 554	8 263	291	9 939	1 676

注：本表产业活动单位的汇总范围，包括外省(地、州)法人单位在本地的产业活动单位，但不包括本省(地、州)法人单位在外地的产业活动单位。

Note: The number of industrial activity entities by region does not include the number outside the province.

1-13 各州市一套表调查单位数（2020年）

Numbers of Survey Units in a set of Table by Region (2020)

单位：个 (unit)

州 市	Region	法人单位数 Number of Corporation Units	房地产业 Real Estate	规模以上工业 Industry above Designated Size	规模以上服务业 Service Enterprises above Designated Size	限额以上批发和零售贸易业 Enterprises above Designated Size of Wholesale and Retail Trades	限额以上住宿和餐饮业 Enterprises above Designated Size of Hotel Industry and Catering Services	有资质建筑业 Qualified Construction Industry	其他有5000万以上在建项目 Projects under Construction are over 50 million yuan
全 省	**Yunnan**	**23 116**	**2 962**	**4 363**	**1 977**	**3 893**	**1 539**	**3 648**	**4 734**
昆 明	Kunming	5 825	763	982	944	742	360	1 373	661
曲 靖	Qujing	2 789	234	646	115	383	112	292	1 007
玉 溪	Yuxi	1 602	158	428	98	293	75	261	289
保 山	Baoshan	1 087	149	269	74	212	56	159	168
昭 通	Zhaotong	945	113	145	64	134	65	114	310
丽 江	Lijiang	591	92	49	78	80	71	95	126
普 洱	Pu'er	892	132	165	62	159	36	177	161
临 沧	Lincang	758	101	177	28	163	37	96	156
楚 雄	Chuxiong	2 008	215	345	89	406	278	209	466
红 河	Honghe	2 110	280	441	108	329	71	237	644
文 山	Wenshan	968	141	175	61	196	47	130	218
西双版纳	Xishuangbanna	615	169	112	60	94	32	63	85
大 理	Dali	1 542	211	244	106	364	186	260	171
德 宏	Dehong	951	158	145	44	286	68	118	132
怒 江	Nujiang	187	13	19	13	22	15	31	74
迪 庆	Diqing	246	33	21	33	30	30	33	66

1-14 云南省一套表调查单位数（2011-2020年）

Numbers of Survey Units in a set of Table of Yunnan Province（2011-2020）

单位：个 (unit)

年份 Year	法人单位数 Number of Corporation Units	房地产业 Real Estate	规模以上工业 Industry above Designated Size	规模以上服务业 Service Enterprises above Designated Size	限额以上批发和零售贸易业 Enterprises above Designated Size of Wholesale and Retail Trades	限额以上住宿和餐饮业 Enterprises above Designated Size of Hotel Industry and Catering Services	有资质建筑业 Qualified Construction Industry	其他有5000万以上在建项目 Projects under Construction are over 50 million yuan
2011	10 477	2 675	2 777		2 098	700	2 227	
2012	13 128	2 707	3 211	1 423	2 616	809	2 362	
2013	14 121	2 736	3 537	1 463	2 990	926	2 469	
2014	14 748	2 783	3 783	1 587	3 161	914	2 520	
2015	14 719	2 649	3 862	1 552	3 088	917	2 651	
2016	15 653	2 618	4 180	1 720	3 289	1 086	2 760	
2017	19 226	2 605	4 172	2 000	3 356	1 150	2 865	3 078
2018	20 716	2 768	4 393	1 986	3 581	1 270	3 126	3 592
2019	21 635	2 860	4 351	1 953	3 709	1 350	3 456	3 956
2020	23 116	2 962	4 363	1 977	3 893	1 539	3 648	4 734

Chapter 2

二、国民经济核算
National Accounts

2-1 云南生产总值（一）（1952−1977年）

Gross Domestic Product (Ⅰ)（1952-1977）

单位：亿元 (100 million yuan)

年 份 Year	生产总值 Gross Domestic Product	第一产业 Primary Industry	第二产业 Secondary Industry	第三产业 Tertiary Industry	人均生产总值（元/人） Per Capita GDP (yuan/person)
1952	11.78	7.27	1.82	2.69	70
1953	14.86	8.87	2.88	3.11	87
1954	17.03	9.92	3.57	3.54	97
1955	18.34	10.44	4.13	3.77	103
1956	21.33	11.60	5.11	4.62	117
1957	22.53	12.47	5.43	4.63	121
1958	23.21	9.57	7.99	5.65	122
1959	25.35	9.00	10.01	6.34	133
1960	25.43	8.83	10.50	6.10	134
1961	22.90	11.16	7.28	4.46	121
1962	24.50	13.64	6.55	4.31	127
1963	25.63	14.01	7.11	4.51	129
1964	29.25	16.18	8.19	4.88	142
1965	33.62	17.31	11.01	5.30	158
1966	36.39	18.37	12.18	5.84	166
1967	34.18	18.49	10.17	5.52	151
1968	26.51	17.36	4.74	4.41	114
1969	34.34	18.63	10.01	5.70	144
1970	38.52	18.87	13.38	6.27	156
1971	43.47	21.99	14.57	6.91	171
1972	49.50	24.84	16.89	7.77	188
1973	54.57	27.23	18.85	8.49	202
1974	51.78	24.29	18.98	8.51	186
1975	54.29	26.34	19.12	8.83	190
1976	49.27	25.70	14.96	8.61	169
1977	55.84	24.36	21.45	10.03	187

注：生产总值按当年价格计算。

Note: Data of gross product are calculated at current prices.

2-2 云南生产总值（二）（1978-2020年）

单位：亿元

年 份 Year	生产总值 Gross Domestic Product	第一产业 Primary Industry	第二产业 Secondary Industry	第三产业 Tertiary Industry	农林牧渔业 Agriculture,Forestry, Animal Husbandry,and Fishery Industries	工 业 Industry	建筑业 Construction
1978	69.05	29.46	27.58	12.01	29.46	20.91	6.67
1979	76.83	32.38	30.50	13.95	32.38	23.56	6.94
1980	84.27	35.89	33.98	14.40	35.89	25.86	8.12
1981	94.13	41.23	35.80	17.10	41.23	28.62	7.18
1982	110.12	47.04	42.39	20.69	47.04	34.21	8.18
1983	120.07	49.33	47.28	23.46	49.33	39.08	8.20
1984	139.58	57.33	54.38	27.87	57.33	44.14	10.24
1985	164.96	66.07	65.41	33.48	66.07	52.51	12.90
1986	182.28	71.32	70.83	40.13	71.32	61.09	9.74
1987	229.03	84.06	84.30	60.67	84.06	73.30	11.00
1988	301.09	103.47	112.40	85.22	103.47	99.19	13.21
1989	363.05	119.01	138.06	105.98	119.01	124.73	13.33
1990	451.67	168.13	157.80	125.74	168.13	142.77	15.03
1991	517.41	169.48	179.56	168.37	169.48	162.32	17.24
1992	618.69	186.80	219.03	212.86	186.80	193.90	25.13
1993	783.27	191.45	325.57	266.25	191.45	284.65	40.92
1994	983.78	236.25	428.68	318.85	236.25	383.91	44.77
1995	1 222.15	302.69	534.78	384.68	302.69	480.95	53.83
1996	1 517.69	360.48	669.06	488.15	360.48	599.82	69.24
1997	1 676.17	387.02	743.82	545.33	387.02	657.05	86.77
1998	1 831.33	403.43	818.26	609.64	403.43	705.55	112.71
1999	1 899.82	406.87	811.90	681.05	406.87	686.09	125.81
2000	2 030.08	442.29	836.15	751.64	442.29	707.00	129.15
2001	2 159.00	444.42	871.39	843.19	444.42	734.52	136.87
2002	2 358.73	463.44	942.09	953.20	463.44	796.47	145.62
2003	2 633.39	494.60	1 059.78	1 079.01	494.60	895.59	164.19
2004	3 136.38	607.75	1 267.79	1 260.84	607.75	1 060.41	207.38
2005	3 497.69	646.30	1 387.30	1 464.09	661.69	1 144.61	242.69
2006	4 090.66	704.50	1 674.19	1 711.97	724.40	1 387.79	286.40
2007	5 077.35	849.60	2 057.40	2 170.35	870.52	1 728.25	329.15
2008	6 016.59	1 001.92	2 476.07	2 538.60	1 024.29	2 092.58	383.49
2009	6 574.36	1 049.71	2 605.38	2 919.27	1 072.39	2 135.02	470.36
2010	7 735.33	1 090.31	3 267.69	3 377.33	1 114.57	2 674.99	594.94
2011	9 523.13	1 396.60	3 811.40	4 315.13	1 423.95	3 076.48	737.41
2012	11 097.39	1 640.43	4 458.40	4 998.56	1 670.96	3 557.36	903.66
2013	12 825.46	1 878.46	5 000.52	5 946.48	1 912.82	3 903.40	1 100.00
2014	14 041.65	2 007.43	5 376.49	6 657.73	2 045.43	4 085.03	1 294.64
2015	14 960.00	2 079.31	5 491.69	7 389.00	2 121.79	4 044.54	1 450.49
2016	16 369.00	2 225.49	5 747.37	8 396.14	2 272.60	4 087.54	1 663.38
2017	18 486.00	2 338.37	6 317.82	9 829.81	2 388.55	4 347.84	1 973.69
2018	20 880.63	2 498.67	7 267.50	11 114.46	2 552.58	4 911.71	2 360.03
2019	23 223.75	3 037.69	8 060.35	12 125.71	3 096.16	5 400.45	2 664.64
2020	24 521.90	3 598.91	8 287.54	12 635.45	3 663.21	5 457.96	2 834.06

注：1.生产总值按当年价格计算。
2.1992年以前,批发和零售业包含住宿餐饮业。
3.2020年度为快报数。

Gross Domestic Product (Ⅱ) (1978-2020)

(100 million yuan)

批发和零售业 Wholesale and Retail Trades	交通运输、仓储和邮政业 Transport,Storage and Post	住宿和餐饮业 Hotels and Catering Services	金融业 Financial Intermediation	房地产业 Real Estate	其他 Others	人均生产总值(元/人) Per Capita GDP
4.49	2.34		1.54	0.33	3.31	226
5.21	2.72		1.79	0.38	3.85	247
5.16	2.80		1.85	0.39	4.20	267
6.09	3.33		2.20	0.47	5.01	294
7.41	4.01		2.65	0.57	6.05	339
8.37	4.56		3.01	0.65	6.87	363
9.94	5.42		3.57	0.77	8.17	416
11.94	6.51		4.29	0.92	9.82	486
14.20	7.84		5.16	1.11	11.82	528
21.66	11.80		7.77	1.67	17.77	653
33.01	14.57		9.98	3.11	24.55	845
39.48	18.47		13.03	4.55	30.45	1 003
40.44	19.82		18.45	6.28	40.75	1 224
52.76	23.70		26.45	8.42	57.04	1 377
58.32	25.19	15.32	34.52	10.64	68.87	1 625
75.90	30.52	19.94	52.66	10.96	76.27	2 030
90.84	39.01	23.86	63.34	12.41	89.39	2 515
106.84	49.93	28.07	74.89	15.01	109.94	3 083
127.72	67.97	33.55	83.59	25.82	149.50	3 779
134.11	77.37	35.23	99.98	26.90	171.74	4 121
145.04	90.76	38.10	102.50	30.42	202.82	4 446
153.97	110.48	40.45	79.73	60.51	235.91	4 558
173.70	92.89	45.63	79.35	83.40	276.67	4 814
180.16	115.63	43.48	86.59	94.49	322.84	5 063
197.58	132.60	46.88	103.19	108.86	364.09	5 472
203.92	159.48	48.96	106.73	125.97	433.95	6 048
245.65	180.83	58.00	117.21	147.01	512.14	7 136
297.62	164.20	92.75	127.11	196.07	570.95	7 890
310.85	230.28	87.99	140.71	233.83	688.41	9 158
371.09	278.57	118.42	169.94	298.29	913.12	11 287
512.32	247.55	142.40	280.10	320.19	1 013.67	13 286
631.97	283.43	154.10	355.43	357.61	1 114.05	14 427
766.96	321.06	179.88	379.38	394.25	1 309.30	16 866
1 050.24	378.78	260.77	458.79	437.26	1 699.45	20 653
1 187.13	454.23	308.30	547.38	508.59	1 959.78	23 992
1 345.75	528.82	346.98	737.08	586.69	2 363.92	27 665
1 469.82	591.56	384.79	881.26	659.74	2 629.38	30 217
1 583.34	650.47	398.12	1 000.98	709.70	3 000.57	32 117
1 732.48	740.15	435.37	1 121.26	819.40	3 496.82	35 051
1 941.14	888.07	486.42	1 245.66	1 006.11	4 208.52	39 458
2 187.26	1 041.18	539.18	1 312.61	1 278.18	4 697.90	44 446
2 386.22	1 101.14	589.45	1 393.11	1 417.42	5 175.16	49 323
2 456.70	1 109.77	534.89	1 500.41	1 503.67	5 461.24	51 975

Note: a.Data of gross product are calculated at current prices.
b.Before 1992,wholesale and retail included the hotel industry and catering services.
c.Data of 2020 in the table are express numbers.

2-3 云南生产总值构成（1978-2020年）

单位：%

年份 Year	生产总值 Gross Domestic Product	第一产业 Primary Industry	第二产业 Secondary Industry	第三产业 Tertiary Industry	农林牧渔业 Agriculture,Forestry, Animal Husbandry,and Fishery Industries	工业 Industry
1978	100.0	42.7	39.9	17.4	42.7	30.3
1979	100.0	42.1	39.7	18.2	42.1	30.7
1980	100.0	42.6	40.3	17.1	42.6	30.7
1981	100.0	43.8	38.0	18.2	43.8	30.4
1982	100.0	42.7	38.5	18.8	42.7	31.1
1983	100.0	41.1	39.4	19.5	41.1	32.5
1984	100.0	41.1	39.0	20.0	41.1	31.6
1985	100.0	40.1	39.7	20.3	40.1	31.8
1986	100.0	39.1	38.9	22.0	39.1	33.5
1987	100.0	36.7	36.8	26.5	36.7	32.0
1988	100.0	34.4	37.3	28.3	34.4	32.9
1989	100.0	32.8	38.0	29.2	32.8	34.4
1990	100.0	37.2	34.9	27.8	37.2	31.6
1991	100.0	32.8	34.7	32.5	32.8	31.4
1992	100.0	30.2	35.4	34.4	30.2	31.3
1993	100.0	24.4	41.6	34.0	24.4	36.3
1994	100.0	24.0	43.6	32.4	24.0	39.0
1995	100.0	24.8	43.8	31.5	24.8	39.4
1996	100.0	23.8	44.1	32.2	23.8	39.5
1997	100.0	23.1	44.4	32.5	23.1	39.2
1998	100.0	22.0	44.7	33.3	22.0	38.5
1999	100.0	21.4	42.7	35.8	21.4	36.1
2000	100.0	21.8	41.2	37.0	21.8	34.8
2001	100.0	20.6	40.4	39.1	20.6	34.0
2002	100.0	19.6	39.9	40.4	19.6	33.8
2003	100.0	18.8	40.2	41.0	18.8	34.0
2004	100.0	19.4	40.4	40.2	19.4	33.8
2005	100.0	18.5	39.7	41.9	18.9	32.7
2006	100.0	17.2	40.9	41.9	17.7	33.9
2007	100.0	16.7	40.5	42.7	17.1	34.0
2008	100.0	16.7	41.2	42.2	17.0	34.8
2009	100.0	16.0	39.6	44.4	16.3	32.5
2010	100.0	14.1	42.2	43.7	14.4	34.6
2011	100.0	14.7	40.0	45.3	15.0	32.3
2012	100.0	14.8	40.2	45.0	15.1	32.1
2013	100.0	14.6	39.0	46.4	14.9	30.4
2014	100.0	14.3	38.3	47.4	14.6	29.1
2015	100.0	13.9	36.7	49.4	14.2	27.0
2016	100.0	13.6	35.1	51.3	13.9	25.0
2017	100.0	12.6	34.2	53.2	12.9	23.5
2018	100.0	12.0	34.8	53.2	12.2	23.5
2019	100.0	13.1	34.7	52.2	13.3	23.3
2020	100.0	14.7	33.8	51.5	14.9	22.3

注：1.生产总值按当年价格计算。
2.1992年以前,批发和零售业包含住宿餐饮业。
3.2020年度为快报数。

Composition of Gross Domestic Product（1978-2020）

(%)

建筑业 Construction	批发和零售业 Wholesale and Retail Trades	交通运输、仓储和邮政业 Transport,Storage and Post	住宿和餐饮业 Hotels and Catering Services	金融业 Financial Intermediation	房地产业 Real Estate	其他 Others
9.7	6.5	3.4		2.2	0.5	4.8
9.0	6.8	3.5		2.3	0.5	5.0
9.6	6.1	3.3		2.2	0.5	5.0
7.6	6.5	3.5		2.3	0.5	5.3
7.4	6.7	3.6		2.4	0.5	5.5
6.8	7.0	3.8		2.5	0.5	5.7
7.3	7.1	3.9		2.6	0.6	5.9
7.8	7.2	3.9		2.6	0.6	6.0
5.3	7.8	4.3		2.8	0.6	6.5
4.8	9.5	5.2		3.4	0.7	7.8
4.4	11.0	4.8		3.3	1.0	8.2
3.7	10.9	5.1		3.6	1.3	8.4
3.3	9.0	4.4		4.1	1.4	9.0
3.3	10.2	4.6		5.1	1.6	11.0
4.1	9.4	4.1	2.5	5.6	1.7	11.1
5.2	9.7	3.9	2.5	6.7	1.4	9.7
4.6	9.2	4.0	2.4	6.4	1.3	9.1
4.4	8.7	4.1	2.3	6.1	1.2	9.0
4.6	8.4	4.5	2.2	5.5	1.7	9.9
5.2	8.0	4.6	2.1	6.0	1.6	10.2
6.2	7.9	5.0	2.1	5.6	1.7	11.1
6.6	8.1	5.8	2.1	4.2	3.2	12.4
6.4	8.6	4.6	2.2	3.9	4.1	13.6
6.3	8.3	5.4	2.0	4.0	4.4	15.0
6.2	8.4	5.6	2.0	4.4	4.6	15.4
6.2	7.7	6.1	1.9	4.1	4.8	16.5
6.6	7.8	5.8	1.8	3.7	4.7	16.3
6.9	8.5	4.7	2.7	3.6	5.6	16.3
7.0	7.6	5.6	2.2	3.4	5.7	16.8
6.5	7.3	5.5	2.3	3.3	5.9	18.0
6.4	8.5	4.1	2.4	4.7	5.3	16.8
7.2	9.6	4.3	2.3	5.4	5.4	16.9
7.7	9.9	4.2	2.3	4.9	5.1	16.9
7.7	11.0	4.0	2.7	4.8	4.6	17.8
8.1	10.7	4.1	2.8	4.9	4.6	17.7
8.6	10.5	4.1	2.7	5.7	4.6	18.4
9.2	10.5	4.2	2.7	6.3	4.7	18.7
9.7	10.6	4.3	2.7	6.7	4.7	20.1
10.2	10.6	4.5	2.7	6.8	5.0	21.4
10.7	10.5	4.8	2.6	6.7	5.4	22.8
11.3	10.5	5.0	2.6	6.3	6.1	22.5
11.5	10.3	4.7	2.5	6.0	6.1	22.3
11.6	10.0	4.5	2.2	6.1	6.1	22.3

Note: a.Data of gross product are calculated at current prices.
b.Before 1992,wholesale and retail included the hotel industry and catering services.
c.Data of 2020 in this table are express numbers.

2-4 云南生产总值指数（一）（1953-1977年）

Indices Gross Domestic Product (Ⅰ)（1953-1977）

本表按不变价计算
(上年=100)

Data in this table is calculated at constant price
(preceding year=100)

年 份 Year	生产总值 Gross Domestic Product	第一产业 Primary Industry	第二产业 Secondary Industry	第三产业 Tertiary Industry	人均生产总值 Per Capita GDP
1953	120.8	114.7	157.1	112.6	118.3
1954	115.1	113.2	122.0	113.9	112.7
1955	108.8	107.8	114.9	105.2	106.5
1956	117.6	110.6	133.4	119.8	115.2
1957	99.6	97.5	104.5	98.9	97.2
1958	106.8	85.1	145.3	112.5	104.8
1959	109.2	91.2	129.6	110.0	108.8
1960	96.7	93.7	97.8	99.3	97.2
1961	85.2	115.0	70.6	68.8	85.5
1962	98.4	109.5	86.4	94.4	96.7
1963	104.4	101.7	108.1	105.4	101.3
1964	114.5	116.1	116.0	107.4	111.1
1965	116.5	106.9	133.8	110.7	112.7
1966	109.7	106.1	113.6	111.0	106.1
1967	92.1	100.6	82.1	93.2	89.5
1968	75.9	94.0	49.7	79.2	73.8
1969	132.2	107.2	197.9	131.1	128.5
1970	114.6	99.7	137.4	110.8	111.3
1971	107.8	105.7	108.7	111.2	104.3
1972	112.7	110.6	115.3	111.5	109.3
1973	110.2	109.4	110.1	112.4	107.1
1974	96.3	91.7	100.2	97.4	93.6
1975	105.2	109.3	102.0	104.3	102.6
1976	90.6	97.6	80.9	99.0	88.6
1977	113.6	94.4	134.7	114.4	110.9

注：生产总值按当年价格计算。
Note: Data of gross product are calculated at current prices.

2-5 云南生产总值指数（二）（1978−2020年）

Indices Gross Domestic Product (Ⅱ)（1978-2020）

本表按不变价计算
(上年=100)

Data in this table is calculated at constant price
(preceding year=100)

年份 Year	生产总值 Gross Domestic Product	第一产业 Primary Industry	第二产业 Secondary Industry	第三产业 Tertiary Industry	农林牧渔业 Agriculture,Forestry, Animal Husbandry,and Fishery Industries	工业 Industry	建筑业 Construction
1978	121.7	113.8	129.0	119.1	113.8	128.3	132.7
1979	103.1	92.9	105.8	114.8	92.9	106.3	103.3
1980	108.5	109.8	110.1	102.5	109.8	109.4	114.0
1981	107.8	109.3	103.3	117.3	109.3	105.7	91.5
1982	115.5	112.8	115.1	120.4	112.8	115.7	111.6
1983	108.4	104.2	108.9	113.3	104.2	110.3	100.3
1984	114.5	113.8	112.9	118.9	113.8	111.8	120.0
1985	113.0	106.8	113.6	119.6	106.8	112.6	119.3
1986	104.3	97.7	106.6	107.1	97.7	106.6	106.7
1987	112.3	107.7	110.4	120.6	107.7	110.3	111.0
1988	116.0	107.8	118.5	119.0	107.8	118.1	120.8
1989	105.8	103.2	103.9	111.3	103.2	104.5	100.4
1990	108.7	108.5	109.8	107.1	108.5	110.1	107.8
1991	106.6	101.1	108.9	111.0	101.1	109.3	105.5
1992	110.9	103.0	116.8	113.4	103.0	115.2	133.5
1993	111.1	102.5	113.7	117.0	102.5	113.2	117.8
1994	112.2	103.0	117.3	114.7	103.0	117.7	114.0
1995	111.7	105.0	113.4	115.2	105.0	114.2	107.1
1996	111.1	105.2	111.5	115.1	105.2	112.0	106.6
1997	109.7	104.6	110.6	112.3	104.6	109.6	120.4
1998	108.1	103.0	109.2	110.3	103.0	107.2	126.6
1999	107.3	104.5	107.0	109.3	104.5	106.5	110.8
2000	107.5	105.6	105.8	110.4	105.6	107.0	97.2
2001	106.8	103.9	104.0	111.5	103.9	104.0	103.9
2002	109.0	103.9	109.4	111.4	103.9	110.0	105.8
2003	108.8	105.5	110.0	109.2	105.5	110.2	109.0
2004	110.3	105.4	111.3	111.6	105.4	110.5	116.0
2005	108.9	104.8	108.5	111.2	104.8	107.6	113.4
2006	111.8	105.3	117.5	109.2	105.5	117.4	118.0
2007	112.2	104.1	115.5	112.4	104.2	117.3	107.0
2008	110.6	106.2	112.0	110.9	106.3	113.4	105.2
2009	112.1	105.3	113.6	113.2	105.2	111.3	126.0
2010	112.3	104.2	115.6	111.6	104.2	114.5	120.9
2011	113.7	105.9	117.9	112.1	106.0	117.2	121.1
2012	112.0	106.6	115.3	110.3	106.7	115.2	116.1
2013	112.2	106.8	112.6	113.2	106.8	110.8	120.7
2014	108.1	106.2	108.8	107.9	106.2	107.2	115.2
2015	108.7	105.9	108.5	109.7	106.0	106.7	114.3
2016	108.7	105.6	109.1	109.4	105.7	107.1	114.7
2017	109.5	106.1	110.8	109.5	106.1	110.5	111.6
2018	108.9	106.3	111.6	107.6	106.3	112.0	110.7
2019	108.1	105.5	108.5	108.4	105.5	107.7	110.4
2020	104.0	105.7	103.6	103.8	105.7	102.4	106.5

注：1.生产总值按当年价格计算。
2.1992年以前,批发和零售业包含住宿餐饮业。
3.2020年度为快报数。

Note: a.Data of gross product are calculated at current prices.
b.Before 1992,wholesale and retail included the hotel industry and catering services.
c.Data of 2020 in this table are express numbers.

2-5 续表 continued

本表按不变价计算
(上年=100)

Data in this table is calculated at constant price
(preceding year=100)

年 份 Year	批发和零售业 Wholesale and Retail Trades	交通运输、仓储和邮政业 Transport,Storage and Post	住宿和餐饮业 Hotels and Catering Services	金融业 Financial Intermediation	房地产业 Real Estate	其他 Others	人均生产总值(元/人) Per Capita GDP (yuan/person)
1978	121.1	94.1		112.5	116.7	147.6	119.0
1979	117.2	115.7		112.3	112.2	111.7	101.3
1980	98.3	103.2		107.8	94.5	107.9	107.1
1981	111.9	119.1		115.1	111.7	127.4	106.3
1982	129.2	120.5		109.1	106.0	115.5	113.6
1983	115.2	113.8		114.7	104.2	110.2	106.6
1984	120.6	119.2		117.4	102.7	118.5	113.0
1985	116.7	124.9		110.6	106.6	127.4	111.5
1986	100.4	114.6		107.2	104.9	113.3	102.7
1987	112.0	120.5		117.3	105.9	136.0	110.4
1988	115.5	115.8		131.5	112.2	120.7	114.2
1989	104.5	120.5		119.4	85.1	111.9	104.1
1990	104.5	104.7		102.9	229.1	107.9	106.7
1991	102.9	110.0		122.5	126.0	114.3	104.7
1992	119.4	111.6		114.5	120.7	105.9	109.5
1993	112.3	118.1	112.3	131.6	131.8	112.5	109.6
1994	114.3	121.1	114.3	108.0	135.9	114.2	110.7
1995	109.3	116.8	109.3	124.0	111.3	117.3	110.3
1996	111.3	121.5	111.3	119.8	109.1	114.6	109.7
1997	104.7	119.1	104.6	116.9	107.7	115.7	108.3
1998	109.4	108.8	109.4	102.1	108.8	117.9	106.7
1999	107.9	116.6	107.9	75.8	202.2	116.3	106.0
2000	114.8	107.5	114.8	102.5	130.1	106.5	106.2
2001	103.2	114.7	109.4	106.5	110.5	117.8	105.6
2002	110.1	110.1	103.4	119.1	106.2	113.3	107.8
2003	102.4	108.7	108.8	101.8	108.0	115.5	107.7
2004	119.7	109.5	102.8	108.0	104.8	112.1	109.2
2005	116.3	104.8	117.9	108.3	114.4	109.6	108.0
2006	110.6	103.8	104.7	116.4	105.4	110.3	110.9
2007	110.7	115.1	108.1	116.7	106.4	114.3	111.4
2008	111.6	103.4	105.7	116.7	106.7	113.3	109.9
2009	121.4	108.8	107.9	125.4	108.9	109.4	111.4
2010	112.9	109.8	116.6	105.7	107.3	113.8	111.6
2011	114.0	108.9	110.1	106.4	106.2	115.6	113.1
2012	107.0	110.9	111.3	126.5	106.2	108.8	111.7
2013	106.0	110.8	104.4	134.6	106.1	114.5	111.9
2014	106.8	107.9	105.1	113.4	105.5	107.3	107.8
2015	107.6	108.8	106.5	113.5	106.2	111.3	108.5
2016	107.2	106.4	107.2	110.6	107.8	111.5	108.5
2017	107.5	110.0	107.9	106.5	108.7	111.9	109.2
2018	106.9	106.8	107.5	103.3	107.7	109.6	108.6
2019	107.6	108.4	106.6	106.4	105.9	110.1	107.8
2020	103.4	100.9	88.2	103.9	103.4	106.4	103.7

注：1.生产总值按当年价格计算。
2.1992年以前,批发和零售业包含住宿餐饮业。
3.2020年度为快报数。

Note: a.Data of gross product are calculated at current prices.
b.Before 1992,wholesale and retail included the hotel industry and catering services.
c.Data of 2020 in this table are express numbers.

2-6 各州市生产总值（2020年）

Gross Regional Product by Region（2020）

单位：亿元 (100 million yuan)

州市	Region	生产总值 Gross Domestic Product	第一产业 Primary Industry	第二产业 Secondary Industry	第三产业 Tertiary Industry	工业 Industry	建筑业 Construction	三次产业构成 Composition (%) 第一产业 Primary Industry	第二产业 Secondary Industry	第三产业 Tertiary Industry	人均GDP（元/人） Per Capita GDP (yuan/person)
全省	**Yunnan**	**24 521.90**	**3 598.91**	**8 287.54**	**12 635.45**	**5 457.96**	**2 834.06**	**14.7**	**33.8**	**51.5**	**51 975**
昆明	Kunming	6 733.79	312.35	2 102.93	4 318.51	1 324.98	778.53	4.6	31.2	64.2	80 586
曲靖	Qujing	2 959.35	553.53	1 094.92	1 310.90	822.81	273.04	18.7	37.0	44.3	51 244
玉溪	Yuxi	2 058.14	207.26	864.29	986.59	736.91	127.91	10.1	42.0	47.9	91 290
保山	Baoshan	1 052.58	243.30	392.61	416.67	216.91	175.87	23.1	37.3	39.6	43 200
昭通	Zhaotong	1 288.74	226.12	482.78	579.84	304.80	178.12	17.5	37.5	45.0	25 255
丽江	Lijiang	512.75	77.53	165.50	269.72	90.70	74.99	15.1	32.3	52.6	40 841
普洱	Pu'er	945.42	235.13	228.62	481.67	137.46	91.27	24.9	24.2	50.9	39 172
临沧	Lincang	821.32	242.34	203.84	375.14	120.21	83.74	29.5	24.8	45.7	36 213
楚雄	Chuxiong	1 372.16	261.93	545.89	564.34	336.07	210.07	19.1	39.8	41.1	56 433
红河	Honghe	2 417.48	344.78	940.44	1 132.26	603.09	337.96	14.3	38.9	46.8	53 925
文山	Wenshan	1 185.12	241.28	396.78	547.06	229.44	167.66	20.4	33.5	46.1	33 798
西双版纳	Xishuangbanna	604.18	138.26	151.56	314.36	71.87	79.76	22.9	25.1	52.0	46 619
大理	Dali	1 484.04	338.96	405.94	739.14	274.28	131.84	22.8	27.4	49.8	44 346
德宏	Dehong	575.54	120.41	121.52	333.61	67.68	53.94	20.9	21.1	58.0	43 817
怒江	Nujiang	210.73	30.63	74.01	106.09	38.23	35.78	14.5	35.1	50.4	38 141
迪庆	Diqing	266.94	18.47	102.67	145.80	69.18	33.53	6.9	38.5	54.6	68 711

注：本表数据为快报数。

Note: Data in this table are express numbers.

2-7 非公有制经济增加值（2018-2020年）
Added Value of Non-Public Ownership Economy (2018-2020)

单位：亿元 (100 million yuan)

州 市	Region	非公经济增加值 Added Value of Non-Public Ownership Economy	第一产业 Primary Industry	第二产业 Secondary Industry	第三产业 Tertiary Industry
2018		9 864.32	823.22	3 619.05	5 422.05
2019		10 954.75	1 002.87	3 992.63	5 959.25
2020		11 411.25	1 177.63	4 131.86	6 101.76
昆 明	Kunming	2 656.07	126.51	830.45	1 699.10
曲 靖	Qujing	1 495.29	225.77	618.16	651.36
玉 溪	Yuxi	957.93	57.73	334.93	565.26
保 山	Baoshan	576.25	61.94	293.22	221.09
昭 通	Zhaotong	531.86	79.14	181.93	270.78
丽 江	Lijiang	278.04	26.81	101.95	149.27
普 洱	Pu'er	439.64	83.78	139.98	215.88
临 沧	Lincang	381.71	71.66	150.34	159.71
楚 雄	Chuxiong	664.64	76.54	299.85	288.25
红 河	Honghe	1 293.91	94.26	477.35	722.30
文 山	Wenshan	619.45	71.60	217.39	330.45
西双版纳	Xishuangbanna	325.55	44.77	97.20	183.58
大 理	Dali	710.15	107.73	241.31	361.12
德 宏	Dehong	311.90	39.17	77.54	195.20
怒 江	Nujiang	73.07	7.71	29.54	35.82
迪 庆	Diqing	115.87	5.29	43.99	66.58

注：1.生产总值按当年价格计算。
2.2020年数据为快报数。

Note: a.Data of gross product are calculated at current prices.
b.Data of 2020 in this table are express numbers.

主要统计指标解释

国内（地区）生产总值 指按市场价格计算的一个国家（或地区）所有常住单位在一定时期内生产活动的最终成果。国内（地区）生产总值有三种计算方法，即生产法、收入法和支出法。三种方法分别从不同的方面反映国内生产总值及其构成。

生产法 是从生产的角度衡量常住单位在核算期内新创造价值的一种计算方法。即从生产的全部货物和服务总产品的价值中，扣除生产过程中投入的中间产品的价值，得到增加值。全社会所有常住单位增加值的总和就是生产总值。计算公式为：

增加值 = 总产出 – 中间投入

国（地区）外净要素收入 是指本国（或本地区）居民对国（或本地区）外从事投资和提供劳务所得的要素收入，与外国（或本地区）居民对本国（或本地区）从事投资和提供劳务所得的要素收入的差额。

三次产业 三次产业的划分是世界上较为常用的产业结构分类，但各国的划分不尽一致。中国的三次产业划分是：

第一产业：是指农（种植）、林、牧、渔业（不含农、林、牧、渔服务业）。

第二产业：是指采矿业（不含开采辅助活动），制造业（不含金属制品、机械和设备修理业），电力、热力、燃气及水生产和供应业，建筑业。

第三产业即服务业，是指除第一产业、第二产业以外的其他行业。第三产业包括：批发和零售业，交通运输、仓储和邮政业，住宿和餐饮业，信息传输、软件和信息技术服务业，金融业，房地产业，租赁和商务服务业，科学研究和技术服务业，水利、环境和公共设施管理业，居民服务、修理和其他服务业，教育，卫生和社会工作，文化、体育和娱乐业，公共管理、社会保障和社会组织，国际组织，以及农、林、牧、渔业中的农、林、牧、渔服务业，采矿业中的开采辅助活动，制造业中的金属制品、机械和设备修理业。

支出法国内（地区）生产总值 是从最终使用的角度反映一个国家或地区一定时期内生产活动最终成果的一种方法，包括最终消费支出、资本形成总额及货物和服务净出口三部分。计算公式为：

支出法地区生产总值 = 最终消费支出 + 资本形成总额 + 货物和服务净出口

最终消费支出 指常住单位为满足物质、文化和精神生活的需要，从本国经济领土和国外购买的货物和服务的支出。它不包括非常住单位在本国经济领土内的消费支出。最终消费支出分为居民消费支出和政府消费支出。

居民消费支出 指常住住户在一定时期内对于货物和服务的全部最终消费支出。居民消费支出除了直接以货币形式购买的货物和服务的消费支出外，还包括以其他方式获得的货物和服务的消费支出，即所谓的虚拟消费支出。居民虚拟消费支出包括如下几种类型：单位以实物报酬及实物转移的形式提供给劳动者的货物和服务；住户生产并由本住户消费了的货物和服务，其中的服务仅指住户的自有住房服务和付酬的家庭雇员提供的家庭和个人服务；金融机构提供的金融媒介服务。

政府消费支出 指政府部门为全社会提供的公共服务的消费支出和免费或以较低的价格向居民住户提供的货物和服务的净支出，前者等于政府服务的产出价值减去政府单位所获得的经营收入的价值，后者等于政府部门免费或以较低价格向居民住户提供的货物和服务的市场价值减去向住户收取的价值。

资本形成总额 指常住单位在一定时期内获得减去处置的固定资产和存货的净额，包括固定资本形成总额和存货增加两部分。

固定资本形成总额 指常住单位在一定时期内获得的固定资产减处置的固定资产的价值总额。固定资产是通过生产活动生产出来的，且其使用年限在一年以上、单位价值在规定标准以上的资产，不包括自然资产，耐用消费品、小型工器具。固定资本形成总额按购买者价格计算，并在所有权发生变化时记录。核算内容主要包括住宅，非住宅建筑物，机器和设备（包括武器系统），知识产权产品中的研发支出、计算机软件、矿藏勘探费、文学艺术品原件，新增役、种、奶、毛及娱乐用牲畜和新增经济林木价值等培育资产，住宅产权和非生产资产所有权转移费用等。

存货变动 指常住单位在一定时期内存货实物量变动的市场价值，即期末价值减期初价值的差额，再扣除当期由于价格变动而产生的持有收益。存货增加可以是正值，也可以是负值，正值表示存货上升，负值表示存货下降。存货包括生产单位购进的原材料、燃料和储备物资等存货，以及生产单位生产的产成品、在制品和半成品等存货。

货物和服务净出口 指货物和服务出口减货物和服务进口的差额。出口包括常住单位向非常住单位出售或无偿转让的各种货物和服务的价值；进口包括常住单位从非常住单位购买或无偿得到的各种货物和服务的价值。由于服务活动的提供与使用同时发生，一般把常住单位从非常住单位得到的服务作为进口，非常住单位从常住单位得到的服务作为出口。货物的出口和进口都按离岸价格计算。

Explanatory Notes on Main Statistical Indicators

Gross Domestic (Regional) Product refers to the final products at market prices produced by all resident units in a country (or a region) during a certain period of time. There are three methods reflect Gross Domestic Product and its composition from different aspects.

Production Approach refers to the calculation method for measuring the newly increased value of resident units in the accounting period from the perspective of production, i.e. the value of total goods and services produced minus that of intermediate products input in the process of production is added value. The sum of added value created by all resident units makes GDP. The formula is as follows: Added Value = Total Output – Intermediate Input.

Net Factor Income from Abroad refers to the difference between factor income earned by residents of a country (or territory) from their investment and labor services in foreign countries (or territories) and that earned by residents of foreign countries (or territories) from their investment and labor services in that country (or territory).

Three Industries Classification of economic activities into three industries is a common practice in the world,although the grouping varies to some extent form country to country. In China, economic activities are categorized as follows: Primary industry refers to farming, forestry, animal husbandry and fishery.Secondary industry refers to mining and quarrying, manufacturing, production and supply of electricity, water,fuel gas and construction.Tertiary industry refers to all other economic activities not included in primary or secondary industry,including services of farming, forestry, animal husbandry and fishery, communications and transportation, storage and postal services, information transmission, computer and software services wholesale and retail trade, hotel and food services, banking, real estate, lease and commercial services, scientific research and technical service,geological prospecting, management services of water conservancy, environment and public facilities, resident and other services, education, health care, social security and welfare, culture, sports and entertainment, public management and social organizations.

Gross Domestic (Regional) Product Calculated by Expenditure Approach refers to the method of measuring the final results of production activities of a country or region during a given period from the perspective of final uses. It includes final consumption expenditure, gross capital formation and net export of goods and services. The formula for computation is.:

Gross Regional Product by expenditure approach = final consumption expenditure + gross capital formation +net export of goods and services

Final Consumption Expenditure refers to the total expenditure of resident units for purchases of goods and services from both the domestic economic territory and abroad to meet the needs of material, cultural and spiritual life. It does not include the expenditure of non-resident units on consumption in the economic territory of the country. The final consumption expenditure is broken down into household consumption expenditure and government consumption expenditure.

Household Consumption Expenditure refers to the total expenditure of resident households on the final consumption of goods and services. In addition to the consumption of goods and services bought by the households directly with money, the household consumption expenditure also includes expenditure on goods and services obtained by the households in other ways, i.e. the so-called imputed consumption expenditure, which includes the following: a) the goods and services provided to households by employers in the form of payment in kind and transfer in kind; b) goods and services produced and consumed by the households themselves, in which the services refer to the owner-occupied housing and services offered by payed family employees; c) financial intermediate services provided by financial institution.

Government Consumption Expenditure refers to the consumption expenditure spent for the provision of public services provided by the government to the whole country and the net expenditure on the goods and services provided by the government to households free of charge or at reduced prices. The former equals to the output value of the government services minus the value of operating income obtained by the government departments.The latter equals to the market value of the goods and services provided by the government free of charge or at reduced prices to the households minus the value received by the government from the households.

Gross Capital Formation refers to the fixed assets acquired less disposals and the net value of inventory, thus including gross fixed capital formation and changes in inventories.

Gross Fixed Capital Formation refers to the value of acquisitions less those disposals of fixed assets during a given period. Fixed assets are the assets produced through production activities with unit value above a specified amount and which could be used for over one year. Natural assets,consumer durables and small tools are not included.The gross fixed capital formation is calculated at the buyer's price and is recorded when ownership changes. Accounting content mainly includes residential and non-residential buildings, machinery and equipment (including weapons systems), spending on research and development of intellectual property products, computer software, mineral exploration, original works of art, literature, the value of draught animals, breeding stock and animals for milk, for wool and for recreational purposes and the newly increased forest with economic value, residential property and unproductive assets ownership transfer fees, etc.

Changes in Inventories refers to the market value of the change in the physical volume of inventory of resident units during a given period, i.e. the difference between the values at the beginning and at the end of the period minus the gains due to the change in prices. The changes in inventories can have a positive or a negative value. A positive value indicates an increase in inventory while a negative value indicates a decrease in inventory.The inventory includes raw materials, fuels and reserve materials purchased by the production units as well as the inventory of finished products, semi-finished products and work-in-progress.

Net Export of Goods and Services refers to the exports of goods and services subtracting the imports of goods and services. Exports include the value of various goods and services sold or gratuitously transferred by resident units to non-resident units. Imports include the value of various goods and services purchased or gratuitously acquired resident units from non-resident units. Because the provision of services and the use of them happen simultaneously, the acquisition of services by resident units from abroad is usually treated as import while the acquisition of services by non-resident units in this country is usually treated as export. The exports and imports of goods are calculated at FOB.

Chapter 3

三、固定资产投资
Investment in Fixed Assets

3－1　全社会固定资产投资增长速度（1979－2020年）

Growth Rate of Total Investment in Fixed Assets in the Whole Province (1979-2020)

单位：%　　(%)

年 份 Year	固定资产投 资 Investment in Fixed Assets	国有经济 State-owned Entities	集体经济 Collective-owned Entities	其他经济 Others	个体经济 Self-employed Entities	农 村 Rural
1979	11.5	7.6	9.6		132.6	132.6
1980	24.6	10.4	15.1		227.1	227.1
1981	-10.6	-12.3	1.4		-8.0	-8.6
1982	31.4	44.7	19.0		-20.8	-21.9
1983	-0.2	-0.1	-36.6		23.5	24.4
1984	34.7	19.3	253.2		56.8	55.3
1985	40.3	32.6	89.5		38.7	36.2
1986	7.9	6.0	14.1		9.9	8.7
1987	8.9	6.4	18.2		9.8	8.0
1988	24.6	26.4	7.8		37.2	31.7
1989	0.0	-8.5	29.6		6.4	2.3
1990	11.7	22.8	-10.2		-1.0	6.3
1991	29.8	39.0	13.0		8.0	9.5
1992	43.1	46.0	43.0		27.2	22.9
1993	78.7	74.5	83.4		39.7	33.3
1994	28.0	21.9	3.8	172.8	53.2	59.2
1995	18.3	18.9	-0.4	48.2	12.4	13.9
1996	17.7	13.6	23.4	39.5	17.5	16.8
1997	20.6	22.9	7.9	24.5	14.6	12.9
1998	24.4	31.8	-0.2	13.0	11.9	8.6
1999	6.7	3.0	2.4	-15.1	68.5	-11.4
2000	-2.7	-6.5	-9.5	12.3	9.6	9.0
2001	5.3	5.2	-10.5	-0.6	16.5	12.3
2002	12.8	6.5	25.7	58.7	6.0	0.4
2003	23.2	4.2	2.9	91.2	45.7	17.1
2004	30.3	13.4	5.7	68.1	40.8	10.4
2005	31.9	32.1	36.9	64.7	-13.7	-12.7
2006	26.5	30.9	72.2	3.1	56.7	125.8
2007	26.1	13.5	41.8	26.2	55.5	63.8
2008	26.0	17.8	18.0	38.6	28.3	11.8
2009	28.4	50.3	-51.3	65.6	-44.2	47.7
2010	22.1	22.3	-3.7	37.7	-94.2	-41.9
2011	11.9	-6.1	-7.5	30.6	44.2	15.1
2012	26.6	22.1	85.2	28.6	130.8	7.5
2013	27.3	31.3	24.2	25.0	13.9	24.8
2014	15.4	20.6	34.0	11.1	-37.3	22.6
2015	17.4	32.1	56.8	4.5	35.9	1.5
2016	19.4	37.4	-5.9	4.4	-4.8	6.0
2017	17.5	24.8	-29.2	12.0	34.2	0.9
2018	11.3	6.5	-72.7	19.5	8.4	1.9
2019	8.3	-5.0	-10.5	22.9	58.7	2.2
2020	7.2	-5.8	-60.5	19.0	47.0	-9.1

注：1.2006年国家对全社会固定资产投资口径和计算方法做了调整。
2.2010年国家对全社会固定资产投资口径范围、统计起点和计算方法做了调整，投资项目统计起点由50万元提高到500万以上。

Note: a.In 2006,the National Bureau of Statistics adjusted the coverage and calculation method for calculating total investment in fixed assets.
b.In 2010,the National Bureau of Statistics adjusted the coverage ,statistical starting point and calculation method for calculating total investment in fixed assets.Statistical starting point of investment project raised to 5 million yuan from 0.5 million yuan.

3-2 按经济类型分固定资产投资构成（1978-2020年）

Composition of Fixed Assets Investment by Economic Types (1978-2020)

单位：%　　(%)

年 份 Year	固定资产投资构成 Investment in Fixed Assets	国有经济 State-owned Entities	集体经济 Collective-owned Entities	其他经济 Others	个体经济 Self-employed Entities	农 村 Rural
1978	100.0	89.3	7.6		3.1	3.1
1979	100.0	86.2	7.5		6.3	6.4
1980	100.0	76.3	6.9		16.8	16.7
1981	100.0	74.9	7.9		17.2	17.1
1982	100.0	82.5	7.1		10.4	10.2
1983	100.0	82.6	4.5		12.9	12.7
1984	100.0	73.1	11.9		15.0	14.6
1985	100.0	69.1	16.1		14.8	14.2
1986	100.0	67.9	17.0		15.1	14.3
1987	100.0	66.4	18.4		15.2	14.2
1988	100.0	67.3	15.9		16.8	15.0
1989	100.0	61.5	20.6		17.9	15.3
1990	100.0	67.6	16.6		15.8	14.6
1991	100.0	72.4	14.5		13.1	12.3
1992	100.0	73.9	14.4		11.7	10.6
1993	100.0	72.1	14.8	3.9	9.2	7.9
1994	100.0	68.7	12.1	8.3	10.9	9.8
1995	100.0	69.1	10.1	10.4	10.4	9.4
1996	100.0	66.7	10.5	12.4	10.4	9.4
1997	100.0	67.9	9.5	12.7	9.9	8.8
1998	100.0	72.0	7.5	11.6	8.9	7.7
1999	100.0	69.5	7.3	9.2	14.0	6.4
2000	100.0	66.8	6.8	10.6	15.8	7.1
2001	100.0	66.7	5.8	10.0	17.5	7.6
2002	100.0	63.0	6.4	14.1	16.5	6.8
2003	100.0	53.3	5.4	21.9	19.4	6.4
2004	100.0	46.4	4.4	28.3	20.9	5.4
2005	100.0	46.4	4.5	35.3	13.8	3.6
2006	100.0	48.1	6.2	28.8	16.9	6.4
2007	100.0	43.3	6.9	28.8	21.0	8.4
2008	100.0	40.5	6.5	31.7	21.3	7.4
2009	100.0	47.4	2.5	40.9	9.3	8.5
2010	100.0	47.5	1.9	46.1	0.4	4.1
2011	100.0	39.8	1.6	53.8	0.6	4.2
2012	100.0	38.4	2.4	54.7	1.0	3.5
2013	100.0	39.6	2.3	53.7	0.9	3.5
2014	100.0	41.4	2.7	51.7	0.5	3.7
2015	100.0	46.6	3.6	46.0	0.6	3.2
2016	100.0	53.7	2.8	40.2	0.5	2.8
2017	100.0	57.0	1.7	38.4	0.5	2.4
2018	100.0	49.8	0.2	46.6	0.2	3.2
2019	100.0	43.8	0.2	52.7	0.3	3.0
2020	100.0	38.5	0.1	58.5	0.3	2.6

3-3 固定资产投资（不含农户）增长速度（一）（2020年）

Growth Rate of Total Investment in Fixed Assets (Excluding Rural Households)(Ⅰ)(2020)

单位：% (%)

国民经济行业	National Economic Sector	固定资产投资 Total Investment in Fixed Asset
固定资产投资增速	**Growth Rate of Total Investment in Fixed Assets**	**7.7**
按登记注册类型分	**Grouped by Registration Status**	
内　资	Domestic Fund	7.6
国　有	State-owned	-21.6
集　体	Collective-owned	-65.3
联　营	Joint Ownership	- 71.1
股份制	Share Holding	-8.4
其　他	Others	22.7
港澳台商投资	Fund from Hong Kong,Macao and Taiwan	2.9
# 合资经营	Joint Venture	80.3
合作经营	Collaborative Operation	1478.6
独　资	Solely Foreign-owned	14.9
外商投资	Fund from Overseas	11.0
# 合资经营	Joint Venture	-19.5
合作经营	Collaborative Operation	304.7
独　资	Solely Foreign-owned	181.5
按隶属关系分	**Grouped by Jurisdiction of Management**	
中　央	Central Investment	16.4
按建设性质分	**Grouped by Type of Construction**	
# 新　建	New Construction	11.6
扩　建	Expansion	-20.3
改建和技术改造	Reconstruction and Technical Transformation	6.6
单纯建造生活设施	Housing	19.2
迁　建	Removal and Reconstruction	6.4
恢　复	Resumption	52.9
单纯购置	Purchase only	-50.8

3-4 固定资产投资（不含农户）增长速度（二）（2020年）

Growth Rate of Total Investment in Fixed Assets (Excluding Rural Households) (Ⅱ) (2020)

单位：% (%)

类 别	Category	全 省 Yunnan	地 方 Local
固定资产投资额	**Total Investment in Fixed Assets**	**7.7**	**7.0**
#住宅投资	Residential Buildings	4.8	9.6
#经济适用房	Economically Affordable Houses		
按构成分	**Investment by Structure**		
建筑安装工程	Construction and Installation	7.4	6.1
设备工器具购置	Purchase of Equipment and Instruments	16.5	27.4
#购置旧设备	Purchase of Second-hand Equipments	217.8	218.1
其他费用	Others	7.4	8.5
#旧建筑物购置费	Purchase of Used Buildings	43.4	43.5
#土地购置费	Purchase of Field	8.5	8.0
本年新增固定资产	**Newly Increased Real Estate**	**3.1**	**4.1**
本年施工房屋面积	Project under Construction		
#住 宅	Residential Building		
#经济适用房	Economically Affordable Houses		
本年竣工房屋面积	Project Completed and Put into Use		
#住 宅	Residential Building		
#经济适用房	Economically Affordable Houses		
本年竣工房屋价值	Project Completed and Put into Use		
#住 宅	Residential Building		
施工项目个数	Number of Projects under Construction	14.0	13.2
#本年新开工	Started This Year	34.9	33.8
本年投产项目个数	Number of Projects Put into Use This Year	3.6	3.0
规划用地面积	Land Space Planned		
本年实际征用和购置土地面积	Land Space Purchased and Used This Year		
本年实际征用和购置土地成交价款	Value of Land Purchased and Used This Year		
本年资金来源合计	**Total Fund of Different Sources**		
上年末结余资金	Fund Left Last Year	32.8	35.9
本年资金来源小计	Total Fund of This Year	5.3	2.3
国家预算内资金	State Budgetary Appropriations	114.8	99.1
国内贷款	Domestic Loans	-10.7	-18.7
债 券	Stock	-99.4	-100.0
利用外资	Overseas Funds	2.8	2.8
#外商直接投资	Direct Foreign Investment		
自筹资金	Self-raising Fund	-5.0	-5.9
#企事业单位自有资金	Fund of Enterprises		
其他资金来源	Other Sources of Funds	13.8	12.2
本年各项应付款合计	**Total of Account Payable**	**16.1**	**15.5**
#工程款	for Projects	17.7	16.3

3-5 按国民经济行业分的固定资产投资增长速度及占比（2020年）

Growth Rate and Percentage of Investment in Fixed Assets by National Economic Sector (2020)

单位：%　　　　(%)

国民经济行业	National Economic Sector	全　省 Yunnan	占比 Percentage
固定资产投资	**Total Investment in Fixed Assets**	**7.7**	**100.0**
农、林、牧、渔业	**Farming, Forestry, Animal Husbandry and Fishery**	**42.0**	**7.4**
农　业	Farming	8.4	3.0
林　业	Forestry	60.1	0.4
畜牧业	Animal Husbandry	87.2	2.8
渔　业	Fishery	104.0	0.1
农、林、牧、渔服务业	Services for Farming, Forestry, Animal Husbandry and Fishery	73.9	1.1
采矿业	**Mining**	**-1.7**	**1.4**
煤炭开采和洗选业	Mining and Washing of Coal	-19.1	0.6
石油和天然气开采业	Extraction of Petroleum and Natural Gas	7.1	
黑色金属矿采选业	Mining and Dressing of Ferrour Metal Ores	2.7	0.1
有色金属矿采选业	Mining and Dressing of Nonferrour Metals Ores	17.6	0.5
非金属矿采选业	Mining and Dressing of Nonmetal Ores	14.5	0.3
开采辅助活动	Mining Auxiliary Activities		
其他采矿业	Mining and Dressing of Other Ores		
制造业	**Manufacture**	**5.9**	**9.6**
农副食品加工业	Processing of Farm and Sideline Food	6.2	1.3
食品制业	Manufacture of Food	9.1	0.3
酒、饮料和精制茶制造业	Manufacture of Wine, Beverage and Refined Tea	9.8	0.3
烟草制品业	Tobacco Products	-59.5	0.1
纺织业	Textile Industry	177.4	
纺织服装和服饰业	Manufacture of Textile Garments, Apparel	82.9	0.1
皮革、毛皮、羽毛(绒)及其制品业	Feather, Furs, Down and Related Products	-8.9	
木材加工及木、竹、藤、棕、草制品业	Timber Processing, Bamboo, Cane, Palm Fiber & Straw Products	-27.9	0.1
家具制业	Manufacture of Furniture	-28.2	0.1
造纸及纸制品业	Papermaking and Paper Products	209.9	0.1
印刷业和记录媒介的复制	Printing and Record Medium Reproduction	76.1	0.1
文教体育用品制业	Manufacture of Cultural, Educational and Sports Goods	75.1	
石油加工、炼焦及核燃料加工业	Petroleum Refining, Coking and Nuclear Fuel Processing	30.3	0.2
化学原料及化学制品制业	Manufacture of Raw Chemical Materials and Chemica Products	11.7	0.5
医药制业	Manufacture of Medicines	11.7	0.5
化学纤维制业	Chemical Fiber Manufacturing		
橡胶和塑料制品业	Rubber and Plastic Products	46.6	0.2
非金属矿物制品业	Nonmetal Mineral Products	14.4	1.6
黑色金属冶炼及压延加工业	Smelting and Pressing of Ferrour Metals	37.8	0.4
有色金属冶炼及压延加工业	Smelting and Pressing of Nonferrour Metals	20.8	1.1
金属制品业	Metal Products	26.1	0.3
通用设备制业	Manufacture of General Purpose Equipment	60.3	0.1
专用设备制业	Manufacture of Special Purpose Equipment	-7.2	0.1
汽车制业	Automotive Industry	-58.9	0.1
铁路、船舶、航空航天等制业	Manufacture of Transport Equipment for Railway,Boats and Aerospace and Other Transport Equipments	82.2	
电气机械及器材制业	Electric Equipment and Machinery	-28.7	0.2
计算机、通信和其他电子设备制业	Communication Equipment, Computers and Other Electronic Equipment Production	-28.2	0.3
仪器仪表制业	Instrument Industry	8.2	
其他制业	Other Goods Production	-9.2	1.2
废弃资源综合利用业	Comprehensive Utilization of Discarded Resources and Waste	17.7	0.3
金属制品、机械和设备修理业	Manufacture of Metal Products, Machine and Equipment Maintenance		
电力、热力、燃气及水生产和供应业	**Production and Supply of Electric, Heat，Gas and Water**	**6.7**	**4.4**
电力、热力生产和供应业	Production and Supply of Electric Power and Heat Power	-1.3	3.3
燃气生产和供应业	Production and Supply of Gas	-34.5	0.2
水的生产和供应业	Production and Supply of Tap Water	71.0	1.0
建筑业	**Construction**	**29.0**	
房屋建筑业	House Building	7.2	
土木工程建筑业	Construction Industry of Civil Engineering		
建筑安装业	Construction Installation	-86.2	
建筑装饰和其他建筑业	Building Decoration and Other Construction Industry	46.6	

3-5 续表 continued

单位：% (%)

国民经济行业	National Economic Sector	全省 Yunnan	占比 Percentage
交通运输、仓储和邮政业	**Transport, Storage and Postal Services**	**4.1**	**24.2**
铁路运输业	Railway Transport	17.7	2.0
道路运输业	Road Transport	3.2	21.0
水上运输业	Waterway Transport	336.0	0.1
航空运输业	Air Transport	-63.1	0.2
管道运输业	Pipeline Transport	42.1	
多式联运和运输代理业	Multimodal Transport and Forwarding Agencies.	23.4	
装卸搬运和运输代理业	Lording, Unlording, Carrying and Storage	40.5	0.9
邮政业	Postal Services	-58.9	
信息传输、软件和信息技术服务业	**Information Transmission Computer Service and Software Service**	**32.7**	**0.7**
电信、广播电视和卫星传输服务业	Telecommunication and Other Information Transmission Service	35.2	0.6
互联网和相关服务业	Computer Service	24.7	0.1
软件和信息技术服务业	Software Service	25.8	0.1
批发和零售业	**Wholesale and Retail Trades**	**-0.4**	**1.5**
批发业	Wholesale Trade	11.7	0.6
零售业	Retail Trade	-7.4	0.9
住宿和餐饮业	**Hotels and Catering Services**	**-19.2**	**0.8**
住宿业	Hotels	-14.8	0.6
餐饮业	Catering Services	-33.3	0.2
金融业	**Finance and Insurance**	**-20.4**	
货币金融业	Banking	-43.0	
资本市场业	Securities Industry		
保险业	Insurance	1154.6	
其他金融业	Other Financial Trade		
房地产业	**Real Estate Trade**	**-0.8**	**30.1**
租赁和商务服务业	**Leasing and Business Services**	**94.1**	**0.6**
租赁业	Leasing Services	41.4	0.0
商务服务业	Business Services	95.2	0.6
科学研究和技术服务业	**Scientific Research,Technology Service**	**75.9**	**0.2**
研究与试验发展	Research and Experimental Development	330.6	
专业技术服务业	Special Technical Services	4.4	0.1
科技交流和推广服务业	Scientific & Technological Exchange and Promotion Services	333.6	0.1
水利、环境和公共设施管理业	**Management of Water Conservancy,Environment and Public Facilities**	**15.7**	**11.9**
水利管理业	Management of Water Conservancy	18.6	3.4
生态保护和环境治理业	Protection of Ecological Environment and Admistration of Environment	12.8	1.3
公共设施管理业	Management of Public Facilities	14.9	7.2
居民服务和其他服务业	**Services to Households and Other Services**	**71.6**	**0.4**
居民服务业	Services to Households	74.1	0.3
机动车、电子产品和日用产品修理业	Repair Industry of Automotive Vehicles、Electronic Products and Daily Products	96.2	0.1
其他服务业	Other Services	-85.9	
教　育	**Education**	**27.8**	**2.8**
卫生和社会工作	**Health Care, Social Work**	**48.6**	**1.7**
卫　生	Health Care	59.1	1.5
社会工作	Social Work	-3.5	0.2
文化、体育和娱乐业	**Culture, Sports and Recreation**	**15.3**	**1.3**
新闻出版业	Publication	23.9	
广播、电视、电影和音像业	Radio, Television, Film and Video	47.8	
文化艺术业	Culture and Arts	-2.1	0.2
体　育	Sports	61.8	0.3
娱乐业	Recreation	9.8	0.8
公共管理和社会组织	**Public Administration and Social Organizations**	**3.7**	**0.9**
中国共产党机关	Organs of Communist Party of China	-63.5	
国家机构	Government Agencies	9.2	0.3
人民政协和民主党派	CPPCC and Democratic Parties		
社会保障	Social Security	-74.7	
群众团体、社会团体和其他成员组织	Mass Groups, Social Groups and Religion Organization	-53.4	
基层群众自治组织	Self-governing Mass Organizations at the Grass-roots Level	8.2	0.6
国际组织	**International Organizations**		

3-6 新增生产能力（2020年）

Newly Increased Production Capacity (2020)

单位：万吨/年 (10 000 tons/year)

生产能力(或)效益名称	Item	建设规模 Total Construction Size	本年施工规模 Under Construction This Year	本年新开工 Started This Year	累计生产能力 Accumulative Production Capacity	本年新增 Newly Increased This Year
原煤开采	Coal Mining	380.50	260.00	62.00	153.00	138.00
洗　煤	Coal Washing					
焦　炭	Coke					
天然气开采(亿立方米/年)	Natural Gas Extraction (100 million cu.m/year)	3.40	2.80	2.00	0.80	0.80
铁矿开采(原矿)	Iron Ore Mining	614.60	592.60	92.60	82.60	82.60
生　铁	Pig Iron					
铁合金	Ferroalloy					
钢　材	Rolled Steel					
铜冶炼	Copper Smelting					
锌冶炼	Zinc Smelting	2.50	2.50	2.50	2.50	2.50
#电解锌	Electrolytic Zinc					
氧化铝	Aluminum Oxide					
原铝(电解铝)	Aluminum (Electrolytic Aluminum)	413.00	261.50	194.50	205.50	97.00
铝加工材	Aluminum Machining	8.00	8.00	8.00	8.00	8.00
铜加工材	Copper Machining					
发电机组容量(万千瓦)	Installation Capacity of Power Generation(10 000 kW)					
水力发电	Hydro Power Generation	2 410.90	1 490.40	7.50	1 253.50	349.80
火力发电	Thermal Power Generation					
其他发电	Others	73.30	60.70	30.00	51.60	38.30
输电线路长度(11万伏及以上)(公里)	Length of Transmission Line (over 110kv) (km)	8425.40	4798.50	2719.00	6136.40	2805.50
水　泥	Cement	1257.20	1156.50	690.30	883.20	782.50
氮　肥	Nitrogen Fertilizers					
磷　肥	Phosphate Fertilizers					
塑料树脂及共聚物	Plastics,Colophony and Copolymer					
合成橡胶	Synthetic Rubber					
载货汽车制造(辆/年)	Truck Manufacturing (unit/year)					
其他汽车制造(辆/年)	Other Automobile manufacturing (unit/year)	500	500	500		
酒	Liquor					
啤　酒	Beer					
白　酒	Wine					
其他酒	Others					
机制纸浆	Machine-made Pulp					
新建铁路里程(公里)	Newly Railways (km)	1651.40	1301.30	1.20	548.80	202.00
复线里程(公里)	Double Track (km)	801.80	484.10		317.70	
电气化铁路里程(公里)	Electrified Railway (km)					
新建公路(公里)	Length of Newly-built Highway (km)	6 660	5 698	790	2 471	1 610
#高速公路	Expressway	5 809	4 963	651	2 316	1 543
一级公路	Class-A Highway	86	58	16	37	18
二级公路	Class-B Highway	590	587	34	3	
改建公路(公里)	Length of Reconstructed Highway (km)	1 123	536	140	523	150
一级公路	Class-A Highway	3	3		3	3
二级公路	Class-B Highway	960	376	3	411	42
新建独立公路桥梁(延长米)	Length of Newly-built Bridges (m)	4 579	2 347	1 278	1 827	900
新建独立公路桥梁(座)	Number of Newly-built Bridges (set)	8	7	5	5	4
新(扩)建客、货运站(个)	Cargo or Passenger Terminals (unit)	5	5	3	3	3
新(扩)建客货运站(万平方米)	Cargo or Passenger Terminals (10 000 sq.m)	2.52	1.57	0.77	1.94	0.99
民航机场跑道(条)	Airport Runway(unit)	1	1		1	1
民航机场跑道(米)	Airport Runway(m)	1 500	1 500		1 500	1 500
飞机购置(架)	Aircraft Purchase(unit)					
候机楼(座)	Terminals (unit)	3	2		1	1
候机楼(平方米)	Terminals (sq.m)	52 743.00	5 421.00		2 131.00	2 131.00
城市自来水供水能力(万吨/日)	Urban Volume of Water Supply (10 000 tons/day)	65.40	58.50	28.30	32.30	26.80
城市污水处理能力(万吨/日)	Urban Capacity of Sewage Treatment(10 000 tons/day)	54.70	41.40	24.10	33.00	28.40

主要统计指标解释

固定资产投资 是以货币形式表现的在一定时期内建造和购置固定资产的工作量以及与此有关的费用的总称。该指标是反映固定资产投资规模、结构和发展速度的综合性指标，又是观察工程进度和考核投资效果的重要依据。固定资产投资按登记注册类型可分为国有、集体、个体、联营、股份制、外商、港澳台商、其他等。固定资产投资统计口径为各种登记注册类型的法人单位及个体经营进行的计划总投资500万元及以上的建设项目投资。

房地产开发投资 指各种登记注册类型的房地产开发法人单位统一开发的住宅、厂房、仓库、饭店、宾馆、度假村、写字楼、办公楼等房屋建筑物和配套的服务设施，土地开发工程（如道路、给水、排水、供电、供热、通讯、平整场地等基础设施工程）和土地购置的投资；不包括单纯的土地开发和交易活动。

固定资产投资按国民经济行业分 根据建设项目建成投产后的主要产品或主要用途及社会经济活动性质来确定国民经济所属行业。一般情况下，一个建设项目或一个企业、事业单位只能属于一种国民经济行业。

固定资产投资按隶属关系分 是按调查单位的主管上级机关确定的。

（1）中央：是指中共中央、人大常委会和国务院各部、委、局、总公司以及直属机构直接领导的建设项目和企业、事业、行政单位。这些单位的固定资产投资计划由国务院各部门直接编制和下达，建设中所需物资、主要设备以及建设中的问题都由中央有关部门安排和解决。

（2）地方：是由省（自治区、直辖市）、地区（州、盟、省辖市）、县（旗、县级市）三级政府及业务主管部门直接领导和管理的建设项目、企业、事业、行政单位。地方项目还包括不隶属以上各级政府及主管部门的建设项目和企业、事业单位，如外商投资企业和无主管部门的企业等。

固定资产投资按建设性质分 根据整个建设项目情况来确定。建设项目的性质一般分为新建、扩建、改建和技术改造、迁建、恢复等。

（1）新建：一般指从无到有开始建设的项目。现有企业、事业、行政单位一般不属于新建。但如有的单位原有基础很小，经过建设后新增的固定资产价值超过该企、事业、行政单位原有固定资产价值（原值）三倍以上的也应作为新建。

（2）扩建：为扩大原有产品的生产能力（或效益）或增加新的产品生产能力，而增建主要的生产车间（或主要工程）、分厂、独立的生产线。行政、事业单位在原单位增建业务用房（如学校增建教学用房、医院增建门诊部、病房等）也作为扩建。

现有调查单位为扩大原有主要产品生产能力或增加新的产品生产能力，增建一个或几个主要生产车间（或主要工程）、分厂，同时进行一些更新改造工程的，也应作为扩建。

（3）改建和技术改造：指对原有设施进行技术改造或更新（包括相应配套的辅助性生产、生活福利设施）的建设项目。调查单位为适应市场变化的需要，而改变企业的主要产品种类（如军工企业转产民用品等）的建设项目，应作为改建。原有产品生产作业线由于各工序（车间）之间能力不平衡，为填平补齐充分发挥原有生产能力而增建不增加本企业主要产品设计能力的车间，也应作为改建。技术改造是指调查单位在现有基础上，用先进的技术代替落后的技术，用先进的工艺和装备代替落后的工艺和装备，以改变企业落后的技术经济面貌，实现以内涵为主的扩大再生产，达到提高产品质量、促进产品更新换代、节约能源、降低消耗、扩大生产规模、全面提高社会经济效益的目的。技术改造具体包括以下内容：机器设备和工具的更新改造；生产工艺改革、节约能源和原材料的改造；厂房建筑和公共设施的改造；保护环境进行的“三废”治理改造；劳动条件和生产环境的改造等。

固定资产投资按构成分 固定资产投资活动按其工作内容及其实现方式分为建筑工程，安装工程，设备、工具、器具购置，其他费用四个部分。

（1）建筑工程：指各种房屋、建筑物的建造工程，又称建筑工作量。包括各种房屋建造工程；各种用途设备基础和各种工业窑炉的砌筑工程及金属结构工程；为施工而进行的各种准备工作和临时工程以及完工后的清理工作等；铁路、道路的铺设，矿井的开凿及石油管道的架设等；水利工程；防空地下建筑等特殊工程；列入房屋工程预算内的暖气、卫生、通风、照明、煤气等设备的价值及装设油饰工程；列入建筑工程预算内的各种管道（蒸汽、压缩空气、石油、给排水等管道）、电力、电讯电缆导线等的敷设工程；房地产开发单位进行的商品房屋开发建设工程、土地开发工程。

（2）安装工程：指各种设备、装置的安装工程，又称安装工作量。包括各种需要安装设备的装配和安装，与设备相连的装设工程及附属于被安装设备的其他工程；为测定安装工程质量，对设备进行的试运工作。但不包括被安装设备本身的价值。

（3）设备、工具、器具购置：指报告期内购置或自制的，达到固定资产标准的设备、工具、器具的价值。新建单位及扩建单位的新建车间，按照设计或计划要求购置或自制的全部设备、工具、器具，不论是否达到固定资产标准均计入“设备、工具、器具购置”中。

（4）其他费用：指在固定资产建造和购置过程中发生的，除上述几项内容以外的各种应分摊计入固定资产的费用。

新增固定资产 指在报告期已经完成建造和购置过程，并已交付生产或使用单位的固定资产的价值。包括已经建成投入生产或交付使用的工程投资和达到固定资产标准的设备、工具、器具的投资及有关应摊入的费用。属于增加固定资产价值的其他建设费用，应随同交付使用的工程一并计入新增固定资产。

施工房屋面积 指报告期内施工的全部房屋建筑面积。包括本期新开工的面积和上期开工跨入本期继续施工的房屋面积，以及上期已停缓建在本期复工的房屋面积。本期竣工和本期施工后又停缓建的房屋，其建筑面积仍计入本期施工房屋面积中。

房屋新开工面积 指报告期内新开工的全部房屋建筑面积，以单位工程为核算对象。房屋新开工面积指整栋房屋的全部建筑面积，不能分割计算。

竣工房屋面积 指在报告期内房屋建筑按照设计要求已全部完工，达到住人和使用条件，经验收鉴定合格（或达到竣工验收标准），可正式移交使用的各栋房屋建筑面积的总和。

竣工房屋价值 指在报告期内竣工房屋本身的建造价值。竣工房屋价值按房屋设计和预算规定的内容计算。

施工项目 指报告期内进行过建筑或安装施工活动的项目。凡是报告期内施过工的建设项目，不论施工时间长短，均作为施工项目统计。施工项目个数可以反映一定时期固定资产投资的实际规模，与同期全部建成投产项目个数相比，可以从建设速度的角度反映固定资产投资的效果。

全部建成投产项目 报告期内按设计文件规定建成主体工程和相应配套的辅助设施，形成生产能力或工程效益，经验收合格，并且已正式投入生产或交付使用的建设项目。

新增生产能力 指通过固定资产投资活动而增加的设计能力或工程效益，它是用实物形态表示的固定资产投资的成果。新增生产能力的计算，是以能独立发挥生产能力或效益的工程为对象。当工程建成，经有关部门鉴定合格，正式移交投入生产，即可计算新增生产能力。

固定资产投资的资金来源 根据固定资产投资的资金来源不同，分为上年末结余资金和本年资金来源。其中本年资金来源又分为六种：

（1）国家预算资金包括中央预算资金和地方预算资金。

（2）国内贷款指报告期固定资产投资项目单位向银行及非银行金融机构借入的用于固定资产投资的各种国内借款。包括银行利用自有资金及吸收的存款发放的贷款、上级主管部门拨入的国内贷款、国家专项贷款（包括煤代油贷款、劳改煤矿专项贷款等），地方财政专项资金安排的贷款、国内储备贷款、周转贷款等。银行贷款、非银行金融机构贷款等。

（3）债券指企业或金融机构为筹集用于固定资产投资的资金向投资者出具的承诺按一定发行条件还本付息的债务凭证，包括金融债券和企业债券。

（4）利用外资指报告期收到的用于固定资产建造和购置投资的境外资金（包括设备、材料、技术在内）。计算利用外资时，需要折算成人民币，折算中所使用的外汇汇率按现汇计算，即按使用外汇时的汇率计算。

（5）自筹资金指在报告期内筹集的用于项目建设和购置的资金。包括自有资金、股东投入资金和借入资金，但不包括各类财政性资金、从各类金融机构借入资金和国外资金。

（6）其他资金来源指在报告期收到的除以上各种资金之外其他用于固定资产投资的资金。包括社会集资、个人资金、无偿捐赠的资金及其他单位拨入的资金等。

Explanatory Notes on Main Statistical Indicators

Total Investment in Fixed Assets refers to the volume of activities in construction and purchases of fixed assets and related fees, expressed in monetary terms during the reference period. It is a comprehensive indicator which shows the size, structure and growth of the investment in fixed assets, providing a basis for observing the progress of construction projects and evaluating results of investment. Total investment in fixed assets includes, by type of ownership, the investment by State-owned units, collective-owned units, individuals, joint ownership units, share-holding units, as well as investments by entrepreneurs from foreign countries and from Hong Kong, Macao and Taiwan, and by other units. Its statistical range is construction projects involving a total planned (or required) investment over 5 million yuan by enterprises of various types of ownership, institutions, administrative units and individuals in urban areas.

Investment in Real Estate Development refers to investment by real estate development companies, commercialized buildings construction companies and other real estate development units of various types of ownership in the construction of buildings, such as residential buildings, factory buildings, warehouses, hotels, guesthouses, holiday villages, office buildings, and the complementary service facilities and land development projects, such as roads, water supply, water drainage, power supply, heating supply, telecommunications, land leveling and other infrastructural projects. It does not include activities in pure land transactions.

Investment in Fixed Assets by Sector The classification of construction projects by sector is determined by the major products or the purpose of the projects when they are put into production or use, and by the nature of their social economic activities. In general, one project or one enterprise or institution can only be classified into one sector.

Investment in Fixed Assets by Jurisdiction of Management refers to the classification of investment by the competent authorities under which investment is made by construction units, enterprises, institutions or administrative units.

(1)Central investment refers to the investment in projects or by enterprises, institutions or administrative units which are under the direct leadership and management of the State Council and of the national commissions, ministries, agencies and State-owned large corporations. Various ministries and departments of the State Council prepare and implement plans for investment in fixed assets by those departments, and arrange and ensure the supply of materials and key equipment required for the projects.

(2)Local investment refers to the investment in projects or by enterprises, institutions or administrative units which are under the direct leadership and management of departments under the provincial, prefecture and county governments. Also included are projects by foreign-invested enterprises and enterprises without competent managing authorities.

Investment in Fixed Assets by Type of Construction Construction projects in general can be classified, by the type of construction, into new construction, expansion, reconstruction and technical transformation, moving and restoration.

(1)New construction in General refers to construction projects, which start from scratch, of enterprises, institutions, administrative agencies. Construction in existing enterprises, institutions or agencies is generally not considered as new construction. In case the size of the existing unit is quite small, and the value of newly added fixed assets is more than three times of the original value, the expansion will be considered as new construction.

(2)Expansion refers to construction of new major production workshop, branch factory or independent production line within a factory or in other locations, for the purpose of increasing the production capacity (or improving efficiency) or adding new production capacity. Newly constructed accommodation for the operation of institutions and administrative organizations (such as newly constructed buildings for teaching in schools, buildings for clinics or wards in hospitals, etc.)are also classified as expansion.

Also included in expansion are investments by existing enterprises or institutions in building major production lines or branch factories along with some work on innovation, for the purpose of expanding the production capacity of original products or producing new products.

(3)Reconstruction and technical transformation refers to construction projects by existing enterprises or institutions in innovation or technical transformation of the old facilities (including auxiliary production equipment and welfare facilities). Also considered as reconstruction is the construction of new workshops by the existing enterprises or institutions to change the variety of products to meet the market demand (such as the production of civil products by defense industries), or to bring the designed production capacity into full play through a more balanced production process on production lines. Technical transformation refers to replacement of old technology or equipment by new technology or equipment, in order to expand the reproduction through improvement of technology contents in production, to improve product quality, to promote new products, to save energy, to reduce consumption, to expand the production scale and to improve overall social-economic efficiency. Contents of technical transformation include: updating of machinery, equipment and tools; reforming production process by using energy or materials saving technology; construction of factory workshops and transformation of public facilities; improvement of working conditions and environment, etc.

Investment in Fixed Assets by Structure By their contents and the mode of implementation, investment activities are classified into 3 categories, i.e. construction and installation, purchase of equipment and instrument, and other expenses.

(1)Construction (work volume of construction) refers to the construction of houses and buildings, They include construction of houses; equipment foundations, industrial kilns and stoves, and metal structure work; preparation works and temporary works for project construction, and clearing up works post project construction; pavement of railways and roads, drilling of mines and putting up of oil pipes; construction of water conservancy; construction of underground air-raid shelters and construction of other special projects; value of equipment for heating, sanitation, ventilation, lighting, gas, painting, etc. that are covered by the budget of housing projects; laying out of various pipelines (for steam, compressed air, petroleum, tap water and sewage) and wiring and cabling for electric power and for communications; installation of various machinery and equipment; testing operation for pre-testing the quality of installation projects, and land and other development work conducted by real estate developers for commercialized housing.

(2)Installation (work volume of installation) refers to the installation of various kinds of equipment and instruments, the installation projects connected with the equipment and other projects attach to the installation equipment; preparing work of the equipment to test the quality of the installation projects. The value of equipment installed is itself not included in the value of installation projects.

(3)Purchase of equipment and instrument refers to the total value of equipment, tools, and instruments purchased or self-produced which come up to the cut-off point for fixed assets by the construction units or investing enterprises or institutions. Equipment, tools and instruments purchased or self-produced for new workshops by newly established or expanded units are categorized as "purchase of equipment and instruments" no matter whether they come up to the cut-off point for fixed assets.

(4)Other Expenses refer to expenses arising during the construction or purchase of fixed assets other than those mentioned above.

Newly Increased Fixed Assets refer to the newly increased value of fixed assets, constructed or purchased, that have been transferred to the investors. This is an indicator that demonstrates the results of investment in fixed assets in monetary terms, and an important indicator to reflect the speed of construction and to calculate the efficiency of investment.

Floor Space under Construction refers to total floor space of all buildings under construction during the reference period, including floor space of newly started buildings during the reference period, floor space of construction extended from the previous period to the current period, and floor space of construction suspended during the previous period and resumed in the current period. Floor space of construction completed in the current period, and floor space of construction started and then suspended in the current period are also included in the floor space under construction of the current year.

Floor Space of Newly Started refers to the total floor space of buildings of newly started in the reference period and its accounting coverage is the unit construction. It is the total floor space of the whole building and it should be calculated as a whole.

Floor Space Completed refers to the floor space of all buildings completed in the reference period, which has been appraised and accepted (or come up to the designed standards) and has been transferred to owner units.

Value of Floor Space Completed refers to the value of floor space of all buildings completed in the reference period, it is calculated according to the building design and the content of the budget regulation.

Projects under Construction refer to projects with construction and installation activities undertaken in the reference period. The number of projects under construction can reflect the actual size of investment in fixed assets during a given period, and when compared with the number of projects completed and put into use during the same period, it demonstrates the results of investment in fixed assets from the angle of the speed of the construction. Depending on the nature of construction activities, projects under construction can also be classified into projects beginning construction in current year, winding-up projects in current year and stopped or suspended projects in previous years (with resumption of work in current year).

Projects Completed and Put into Use refers to the construction projects which have been completed the main work and responding supporting facilities which has built up the productivity or project benefit in accordance with the design documents, have been checked and accepted after relevant examination; and have been formally delivered for use in the reference period.

Newly Increased Production Capacity (or Project Efficiency) refers to the increase in design capacity (or project efficiency) through investment in fixed assets, which reflects the accomplishment of investment in fixed assets in physical form, and its calculating coverage is the construction which can produce the production capacity and project efficiency independently and has been appraised and accepted (or come up to the designed standards)and has been transferred to use formally when it is completed.

Sources of Funds for Investment in Fixed Assets are categorized as surplus fund from the year-end of preceding year and source of funds this year ,depending on the sources of investment. Source of funds this year are categorized as follows:

(1)Fund from the State budget consists of budgetary appropriation includes central budget funds and local budget funds.central budget funds includes funds from the budget of the central government, capital construction fund (operation fund and non-operational fund), special expenses (e.g. expenses on substituting petroleum with coal), loans from repayment, discount fund, expenses on innovation and trial production of new products, expenses on urban construction, expenses on temporary construction from business departments, development fund for less developed areas, as well as local budgetary fund transferred from the central budget.

(2)Domestic loans refer to loans of various forms borrowed by investing units from banks and non-bank financial institutions during the reference period for the purpose of investment in fixed assets, including loans issued by banks from their self-owned funds and deposit, loans appropriated by higher authorities, special loans by government, loans arranged by local government from special funds, domestic reserve loan, and working loan.

(3)Bond refers to the funds raised by enterprises (corporations) or financial institutions through bonds issue and used for the investment in fixed assets, including the key enterprises bond and fundamental construction bond issued by banks deputized for national professional investment corporations.

(4)Foreign investment refers to foreign funds received during the reference period for the construction and purchase of investment in fixed assets (covering equipment, materials and technology). In calculating the utilization of foreign capital, foreign currencies are converted into Chinese Renminbi applying the current exchange rate when the foreign capitals are actually used.

(5)Self-raised funds refer to extra-budgetary funds for investment in fixed assets received during the reference period by investing units from central government ministries, local governments, enterprises and institutions, including their self-raised funds.

(6)Others refer to funds for investment in fixed assets received from sources other than those listed above, including capital raised through issuing bonds by enterprises or financial institutions, funds raised from individuals and through donations, and funds transferred from other units.

Chapter 4

四、城乡市场消费
Urban and Rural Consumption

4-1 全省流通业基本情况（2015-2020年）
Basic Statistics on Circulation of Commodities of Yunnan Province（2015-2020）

类 别	Category	2015	2016	2017	2018	2019	2020
全省限额以上法人企业（个）	**Corporate Enterprises above Designated Size(unit)**	**3 989**	**4 372**	**4 506**	**4 851**	**5 303**	**5 743**
批发和零售业	Wholesale and Retail Trades	3 077	3 286	3 356	3 581	3 953	4 202
住宿业	Hotels	537	593	611	659	717	771
餐饮业	Catering Services	375	493	539	611	633	770
全省限额以上单位从业人员（万人）	**Employed Persons in Enterprises above Designated Size (10 000 person)**	**35.70**	**35.58**	**34.15**	**34.36**	**32.92**	**32.92**
批发和零售业	Wholesale and Retail Trades	24.10	23.85	22.74	23.11	22.21	22.42
住宿业	Hotels	7.02	6.99	6.77	6.67	6.49	5.87
餐饮业	Catering Services	4.58	4.74	4.63	4.59	4.22	4.64
全省批发和零售业（亿元）	**Wholesale and Retail Trade (100 million yuan)**						
商品购进总额	Total Purchases	6 597.49	7 122.67	7 955.98	8 806.90	9 757.61	10 820.90
商品销售总额	Total Sales	14 417.16	16 571.64	19 154.36	21 532.21	24 222.33	23 881.58
商品库存总额	Total Inventory	781.15	750.78	742.84	718.68	745.26	1 038.39
全省社会消费品零售总额（亿元）	**Total Retail Sales of Consumer Goods (100 million yuan)**	**6 390.83**	**7 222.73**	**8 194.79**	**9 197.26**	**10 158.23**	**9 792.87**
按销售单位所在地分	**Grouped by Location of Marketing Establishments**						
城 镇	Urban Areas	5 581.25	6 304.05	7 149.24	8 017.42	8 853.03	8 530.70
#城 区	Cities	3 770.56	4 239.56	4 783.49	5 384.79	5 940.83	5 603.58
乡 村	Rural Areas	809.58	918.68	1 045.55	1 179.84	1 305.20	1 262.17
按消费形态分	**by Consumption Pattern**						
商品零售	Commodity Retail	5 517.93	6 231.59	7 060.52	7 906.35	8 725.73	8 503.37
餐饮收入	Food & Beverage Revenue	872.90	991.14	1 134.27	1 290.91	1 432.50	1 289.50

注：1. 从业人员的统计口径包括达到限额以上标准的法人企业、个体户和非同业产业活动单位。
2. 商品销售总额含限额以上及限额以下单位，而商品购进总额及商品库存总额仅包含限额以上法人企业。
3. 2015-2019年社会消费品零售总额相关数据根据第四次全国经济普查资料进行了修订。

Note: a.The statistical caliber of Employed Persons,Total Purchases,Total Inventory including Corporate Enterprises Designated above Size and self-employed Designated Size
b.Data of total sales include that of enterprises below and above designated size,while total purchases and total inventory data only include that of enterprises above designated size.
c.From 2015 to 2019, the data of total retail sales of consumer goods were revised according to the results of the Fourth National Economic Census.

4-2 社会消费品零售总额（1978-2020年）

Total Retail Sales of Consumer Goods (1978-2020)

单位：亿元 (100 million yuan)

年份 Year	社会消费品零售总额 Total Retail Sales of Consumer Goods	城镇 Urban Areas	城区 Cities	乡村 Rural Areas	按消费形态分 By Consumption Pattern: 商品零售 Commodity Retail	餐饮收入 Food & Beverage Revenue
1978	28.38	18.74	6.93	9.64		
1979	32.60	20.36	8.49	12.24		
1980	37.96	24.35	10.79	13.61		
1981	42.04	26.33	10.24	15.71		
1982	44.54	27.71	11.89	16.84		
1983	55.19	34.21	14.66	20.97		
1984	65.58	41.25	21.01	24.34		
1985	84.45	54.38	31.54	30.07		
1986	91.91	58.08	30.35	33.83		
1987	102.55	65.76	33.94	36.79		
1988	135.57	89.13	46.24	46.44		
1989	142.15	94.10	49.98	48.05		
1990	145.59	97.58	52.44	48.02		
1991	163.75	111.73	59.90	52.02		
1992	204.60	144.05	81.00	60.55		
1993	264.47	197.33	118.49	67.14		
1994	310.98	233.80	144.16	77.18		
1995	380.53	286.64	176.16	93.89		
1996	430.67	322.73	197.83	107.94		
1997	490.42	372.85	236.16	117.57		
1998	530.24	408.02	267.87	122.22		
1999	577.06	445.30	298.41	131.76	515.28	61.78
2000	630.53	488.54	328.11	141.99	554.91	75.62
2001	699.63	543.63	367.01	155.99	607.71	91.92
2002	784.16	612.49	414.09	171.67	674.32	109.85
2003	871.13	681.35	461.25	189.78	741.42	129.71
2004	1 033.33	811.61	545.20	221.72	891.90	141.43
2005	1 187.43	934.90	625.57	252.53	1 021.24	166.19
2006	1 387.48	1 096.26	731.61	291.22	1 193.14	194.34
2007	1 654.37	1 311.54	879.00	342.84	1 397.82	256.55
2008	2 072.93	1 653.88	1 109.15	419.05	1 737.34	335.59
2009	2 433.96	2 001.12	1 460.14	432.84	2 075.90	358.06
2010	3 057.12	2 608.31	1 877.93	448.82	2 623.45	433.67
2011	3 746.37	3 280.83	2 452.31	465.55	3 240.17	506.20
2012	4 380.22	3 833.90	2 850.11	546.31	3 796.27	583.95
2013	5 053.71	4 420.21	3 019.70	633.50	4 351.91	701.80
2014	5 744.42	5 024.86	3 425.60	719.56	4 965.47	778.95
2015	6 390.83	5 581.25	3 770.56	809.58	5 517.93	872.90
2016	7 222.73	6 304.05	4 239.56	918.68	6 231.59	991.13
2017	8 194.79	7 149.24	4 783.49	1 045.55	7 060.52	1 134.27
2018	9 197.26	8 017.42	5 384.79	1 179.84	7 906.35	1 290.91
2019	10 158.23	8 853.03	5 940.83	1 305.20	8 725.73	1 432.50
2020	9 792.87	8 530.70	5 603.58	1 262.17	8 503.37	1 289.50

注：1.本表1993-2019年数据根据第四次全国经济普查资料进行了修订。
2.因统计口径和方法调整，表中分城乡及消费形态数据增长速度不能简单与上年相比计算获取。

Note: a.Data from 1993 to 2019 have been adjusted according to the Fourth National Economic Census.
b.The growth rate of urban areas and rural areas and consumption patterns cannot be calculated simply, because statistical calibre and method adjustment.

4-3 各州市社会消费品零售总额（2020年）

Total Retail Sales of Consumer Goods by Region (2020)

单位：亿元 (100 million yuan)

州　市	Region	社会消费品零售总额 Total Retail Sales of Consumer Goods
全　省	**Yunnan**	**9 792.87**
昆　明	Kunming	3 070.44
曲　靖	Qujing	934.86
玉　溪	Yuxi	790.29
保　山	Baoshan	427.84
昭　通	Zhaotong	435.56
丽　江	Lijiang	233.57
普　洱	Pu'er	292.29
临　沧	Lincang	317.02
楚　雄	Chuxiong	518.66
红　河	Honghe	883.01
文　山	Wenshan	578.16
西双版纳	Xishuangbanna	272.52
大　理	Dali	607.63
德　宏	Dehong	328.18
怒　江	Nujiang	36.62
迪　庆	Diqing	66.22

4-4 限额以上批发和零售业商品销售情况（2019-2020年）
Total Sales of Enterprises above Designated Size in Wholesale and Retail Trades by Category of Commodities (2019-2020)

单位：亿元 (100 million yuan)

类别	Category	商品销售额 Sales		批发额 Wholesale		零售额 Retail	
		2019	2020	2019	2020	2019	2020
合计	**Total**	**10 707.49**	**12 379.50**	**8 254.20**	**10 003.96**	**2 453.29**	**2 375.54**
粮油、食品类	Oil and Food	729.65	1 269.67	486.39	1 001.24	243.26	268.43
饮料类	Beverages	135.72	142.86	95.03	101.84	40.69	41.03
烟酒类	Tobacco and Liquor	756.10	770.46	715.93	730.53	40.17	39.93
服装、鞋帽、针、纺织品类	Clothing,Footwear,Headgear, Knitting and Textiles	94.39	81.40	25.65	20.46	68.73	60.94
#服装类	Clothing	46.54	40.80	3.69	4.01	42.85	36.79
化妆品类	Cosmetics	33.61	31.69	4.10	2.59	29.51	29.10
金银珠宝类	Gold,Silver and Jewelry	26.72	43.04	5.59	19.20	21.12	23.84
日用品类	Articles for Daily Use	83.53	79.74	22.61	19.81	60.92	59.93
五金、电料类	Hardware and Electrical Materials	12.64	13.56	7.41	7.50	5.22	6.06
体育、娱乐用品类	Sports and Recreation Articles	4.60	4.61	0.70	1.75	3.90	2.86
书报杂志类	Newspapers and Magazines	72.39	66.79	35.15	29.65	37.24	37.14
电子出版物及音像制品类	E-journals and Audio-visual Products	1.16	0.87	0.45	0.40	0.71	0.47

4-4 续表 continued

单位：亿元 (100 million yuan)

类 别	Category	商品销售额 Sales 2019	2020	批发额 Wholesale 2019	2020	零售额 Retail 2019	2020
家用电器和音像器材类	Household Appliances and Audio-visual Equipment	143.25	125.85	79.93	68.72	63.32	57.13
中西药品类	Traditional Chinese and Western Medicines	691.75	751.04	516.48	562.12	175.27	188.92
#西药类	Western Medicine	559.15	607.90	412.48	451.88	146.67	156.02
中草药及中成药类	Herbal Medicine and Traditional Chinese Medicines Products	96.33	101.55	81.57	85.19	14.76	16.36
文化办公用品类	Cultural Goods and Office Stationery	63.42	123.59	37.24	97.25	26.18	26.34
家具类	Furniture	13.39	13.15	0.07	0.11	13.31	13.04
通讯器材类	Communication Equipment	237.90	247.38	203.69	212.33	34.21	35.04
煤炭及制品类	Coal and Related Products	462.70	520.14	456.92	514.12	5.78	6.02
木材及制品类	Timber and Related Products	9.74	32.45	9.74	32.45		
石油及制品类	Petroleum and Related Products	1 913.01	1 686.21	1 108.95	972.01	804.06	714.19
化工材料及制品类	Chemical Industrial Materials and Related Products	809.59	863.70	809.59	863.70		
#化肥类	Fertilizer	421.53	477.75	421.53	477.75		
金属材料类	Metal Materials	2 255.72	3 202.95	2 255.72	3 202.95		
建筑及装潢材料类	Building and Decoration Materials	398.91	473.38	372.83	449.16	26.08	24.22
机电产品及设备类	Mechanical and Electric Products and Equipment	78.50	86.13	68.44	75.74	10.06	10.39
汽车类	Automobiles	730.84	715.08	21.94	19.44	708.90	695.64
种子饲料类	Seeds and Forage	31.05	40.98	31.05	40.98		
棉麻类	Cotton and Hemp	2.43	2.55	2.30	2.52	0.13	0.03
其他类	Others	901.95	990.22	867.44	955.42	34.51	34.81

注：因年度限额以上单位数量及填报的数据均有变化，上年同期数以今年填报数为准，与历史统计年鉴数据有区别。
Note: Because the number of enterprises above designated size changed, The data are different from historical Statistical Yearbook. Data of last year is subject to submitted data.

4-5 限额以上批发和零售业法人企业商品购进、销售、库存总额（2020年）

单位：亿元

类别	Category	法人企业数（个）Number of Corporate Enterprises (unit)	从业人员数（万人）Number of Employed Persons (10 000 persons)
批发和零售业	**Wholesale Trade and Retail Trade**	**4 202**	**21.43**
批发业	**Wholesale Trade**	**1 733**	**8.40**
按登记注册类型分	**Grouped by Status of Registration**		
内资企业	Domestic-funded Enterprises	1 716	8.23
国有企业	State-owned Enterprises	39	1.91
集体企业	Collective-owned Enterprises	10	0.03
股份合作企业	Joint Stock Cooperative Enterprises	1	0.00
联营企业	Joint Ownership Enterprises	1	0.00
有限责任公司	Limited Liability Companies	318	1.78
股份有限公司	Incorporated Corporations	38	0.86
私营企业	Private Enterprises	1 270	3.60
其他企业	Other Enterprises	39	0.04
港、澳、台商投资企业	Enterprises Invested by Hong Kong, Macao and Taiwan	5	0.08
外商投资企业	Foreign-funded Enterprises	12	0.09
按国民经济行业分	**Grouped by Sector**		
农、林、牧、渔产品批发	Wholesale of Farm, Forestry, Livestock and Fishery Products	157	0.38
食品、饮料及烟草制品批发	Wholesale of Food, Beverages and Tobaccos	367	3.39
#米、面制品及食用油批发	Wholesale of Rice, Flour and Edible Oil	56	0.19
果品、蔬菜批发	Fruits and Vegetables	191	0.89
酒、饮料及茶叶批发	Wholesale of Liquor，Beverages and Tea	37	0.27
烟草制品批发	Wholesale of Tobaccos	19	1.78
纺织、服装及家庭用品批发	Wholesale of Textiles, Garments and Daily Consumer Articles	55	0.17
文化、体育用品及器材批发	Wholesale of Culture, Sports Appliances and Equipments	22	0.08
医药及医疗器材批发	Wholesale of Medicines and Medical Appliances	147	1.68
#西药批发	Wholesale of Western Medical	101	1.41
中药批发	Wholesale of Chinese herbal Medical	23	0.18
矿产品、建材及化工产品批发	Wholesale of Mineral Products, Building Materials and Chemical Products	789	1.99
#煤炭及制品批发	Wholesale of Coal and Related Products	111	0.15
石油及制品批发	Wholesale of Petroleum and Related Products	43	0.59
金属及金属矿批发	Wholesale of Metal Materials	205	0.41
建材批发	Wholesale of Building Materials	225	0.32
化肥批发	Wholesale of Chemical Fertilizer	92	0.27
机械设备、五金产品及电子产品批发	Wholesale of Machinery, Hardware and Electronic Products	149	0.63
贸易经纪与代理	Trade Broker and Agency	7	0.01
其他批发业	Other Wholesale Trades	40	0.08

Total Purchases, Sales and Inventory of Corporate Enterprises above Designated Size of Wholesale and Retail Trades (2020)

(100 million yuan)

商品购进总额 Total Purchases of Goods	进口 Imports of Goods	商品销售总额 Total Sales of Goods	批发 Wholesale	出口 Outputs	零售 Retail	年末库存总额 Inventory at Year-end	年末零售营业面积(万平方米) Retail Operating Area at Year-end (10 000 sq.m)
10 820.90	**395.66**	**12 261.94**	**9 901.61**	**287.99**	**2 348.58**	**1 038.39**	**1 058.02**
9 006.22	**346.34**	**9 978.18**	**9 643.23**	**264.77**	**323.27**	**844.30**	**209.43**
8 909.89	332.00	9 865.39	9 530.62	262.76	323.08	826.96	208.88
986.59	0.08	1 414.68	1 397.56	0.10	17.12	214.33	1.59
9.28	1.00	9.88	8.99	0.00	0.90	1.45	1.40
0.21		0.34	0.28		0.06	0.17	2.79
12.05		11.45	11.45			0.31	
5 252.84	196.74	5 429.95	5 382.47	75.83	38.53	188.60	37.63
886.49	1.33	1 070.79	857.40	6.75	213.39	315.63	75.54
1 744.46	132.86	1 909.37	1 853.69	180.08	52.98	106.25	89.57
17.96		18.92	18.80		0.09	0.22	0.36
41.40		42.91	42.72		0.19	14.28	0.01
54.94	14.33	69.89	69.89	2.02		3.06	0.54
175.77	18.26	199.38	194.36	5.94	4.75	29.34	5.32
1 560.05	17.42	2 028.30	2 004.66	125.73	23.61	280.77	38.97
96.46	0.81	97.14	91.90	0.02	5.24	29.95	7.86
263.81	9.06	297.47	289.09	101.35	8.35	2.28	23.62
54.50	1.35	65.15	62.09	4.13	3.06	13.78	4.94
887.27	1.40	1 303.29	1 297.50	16.83	5.78	215.24	0.58
120.61	34.90	132.05	131.18	15.83	0.59	7.49	0.72
58.71	0.04	61.13	60.93		0.20	6.02	1.19
529.59	4.09	638.16	601.08	0.76	36.97	67.81	32.84
472.00	1.75	521.42	489.21		32.09	56.26	29.66
32.51	2.19	85.59	81.00	0.76	4.59	8.03	2.11
6 232.26	259.24	6 572.33	6 317.92	68.48	243.57	427.57	117.39
201.10	2.87	212.95	208.55	2.80	2.96	5.88	12.08
823.21		1 018.23	791.44	0.37	226.79	12.73	76.22
3 187.04	74.15	3 238.37	3 223.82	6.05	5.60	356.02	4.17
743.05	0.55	760.85	757.69	1.44	3.16	13.79	13.47
984.31	59.10	1 034.15	1 030.29	54.27	3.85	29.94	8.10
266.68	9.59	281.28	269.34	47.98	11.78	22.37	8.24
3.68	0.78	3.43	3.43	0.05		2.17	1.20
58.87	2.02	62.12	60.33		1.79	0.76	3.55

4-5 续表1

单位：亿元

类　别	Category	法人企业数（个）Number of Corporate Enterprises (unit)	从业人员数（万人）Number of Employed Persons (10 000persons)
零售业	**Retail Trade**	**2 469**	**13.03**
按登记注册类型分	**Grouped by Status of Registration**		
内资企业	Domestic Funded Enterprises	2 427	11.89
国有企业	State-owned Enterprises	23	0.18
集体企业	Collective-owned Enterprises	18	0.05
股份合作企业	Joint Stock Cooperative Enterprises	14	0.05
联营企业	Joint Ownership Enterprise	1	0.00
有限责任公司	Limited Liability Companies	371	2.80
股份有限公司	Incorporated Corporations	30	0.46
私营企业	Private Enterprises	1 949	8.33
其他企业	Other Enterprises	21	0.03
港、澳、台商投资企业	Enterprises Invested by Hong Kong, Macao and Taiwan	16	0.33
外商投资企业	Foreign-funded Enterprises	26	0.81
按国民经济行业分	**Grouped by Sector**		
综合零售	Integrated Retail	447	3.32
#百货零售	Retail of General Merchandise	211	0.90
超级市场零售	Retail of Supermarkets	168	2.15
食品、饮料及烟草制品专门零售	Retail of Food, Beverages and Tobaccos	362	0.99
#粮油零售	Retail of Food and Edible Oil	72	0.22
果品、蔬菜零售	Fruits and Vegetables	139	0.37
肉、禽、蛋、奶及水产品零售	Meat,Poultry,Egg,Milk and Aquatic Products	47	0.14
酒、饮料及茶叶零售	Retail of Liquor、Beverages and Tea	43	0.13
纺织、服装及日用品专门零售	Retail of Textiles, Garments and Daily Consumer Articles	60	0.36
#服装零售	Retail of Garments	30	0.17
文化、体育用品及器材专门零售	Retail of Culture, Sports Appliances and Equipments	118	0.58
#图书、报刊零售	Retail of Books and Papers	27	0.39
珠宝首饰零售	Retail of Jewels	27	0.06
医药及医疗器材专门零售	Retail of Medicines and Medical Equipments	105	3.10
#西药零售	Retail of Western Medicines	93	2.65
中药零售	Retail of Traditional Chinese Medicine	7	0.45
汽车、摩托车、零配件和燃料及其他动力销售	Retail of Motor Vehicles, Motorcycles, Fuel and Parts	996	3.81
#汽车新车零售	Retail of New Motor Vehicles	645	2.42
机动车燃油零售	Retail of Fuel of Motor Vehicles	256	1.15
家用电器及电子产品专门零售	Special Retail of Household Electric Appliances and Electronic Products	186	0.57
#日用家电零售	Retail of Household Appliances	47	0.08
计算机、软件及辅助设备零售	Retail of Computer, Software and Assistant Appliances	70	0.21
通信设备零售	Retail of Communication Equipments	29	0.10
五金、家具及室内装饰材料专门零售	Special Retail of Hardware, Furniture and Decoration Materials	100	0.15
#家具零售	Furniture Merchandise	33	0.04
货摊、无店铺及其他零售业	Non-shop and Other Retails	95	0.16
按零售业态分	**Grouped by Retail Form**		
有店铺零售	Retail Sales by Shop	2 195	12.64
#超市	Supermarket	262	1.60
#大型超市	Hypermarket	41	1.28
百货店	Department Store	130	0.51
专业店	Specialty Store	799	5.78
专卖店	Exclusive Shop	762	2.86
无店铺零售	Retail Sales without Shop	140	0.39

continued

(100 million yuan)

商品购进总额 Total Purchases of Goods	进口 Imports of Goods	商品销售总额 Total Sales of Goods	批发 Wholesale	出口 Outputs	零售 Retail	年末库存总额 Inventory at Year-end	年末零售营业面积（万平方米） Retail Operating Area at Year-end (10 000 sq.m)
1 814.68	**49.32**	**2 283.76**	**258.38**	**23.22**	**2 025.31**	**194.08**	**848.59**
1 631.62	30.71	2 055.23	251.36	23.22	1 803.81	173.72	783.15
48.51	0.01	50.71	1.20		49.52	3.81	32.02
6.87		7.26	1.19	0.84	6.07	0.27	4.31
19.23		19.79	7.93		11.86	0.92	5.43
0.27		0.29			0.29	0.00	0.05
546.22	14.95	628.89	98.75		530.13	47.98	248.13
80.28		311.87	70.80		241.07	2.45	59.95
926.60	15.75	1 032.35	71.34	22.38	960.95	118.15	430.95
3.65		4.07	0.15		3.92	0.14	2.32
76.35	10.40	98.16	0.80		97.36	6.92	15.69
106.70	8.20	130.37	6.23		124.14	13.44	49.75
298.04	0.56	333.98	37.68	23.05	296.31	31.04	188.63
72.59	0.19	88.38	3.89	0.00	84.50	8.72	67.55
190.96	0.37	210.27	24.09	22.21	186.19	20.04	103.33
103.17	1.31	115.45	10.48	0.16	104.97	10.37	65.15
21.03	0.18	21.58	3.90		17.68	5.81	23.35
48.02		52.09	3.03	0.16	49.07	1.11	30.75
11.88	0.00	13.57	1.28		12.29	0.53	3.54
12.41	0.02	16.56	1.45		15.11	2.00	2.75
22.79	0.23	36.40	6.66		29.74	4.27	12.67
10.12		22.86			22.86	2.65	11.40
61.34	0.41	64.16	1.01		63.16	5.92	30.29
40.30		40.30	0.42		39.89	4.21	23.08
16.22	0.23	17.91	0.12		17.79	1.00	2.78
99.02	0.00	166.10	11.66		154.44	20.35	86.08
98.11	0.00	141.59	11.64		129.95	19.98	73.33
0.62		24.21	0.01		24.20	0.30	12.01
1 114.33	46.58	1 433.46	177.89		1 255.51	107.36	409.39
642.60	44.72	693.13	15.42		677.65	85.77	153.19
406.30		672.28	162.38		509.90	13.61	239.90
86.25	0.00	99.67	7.32		92.35	11.54	40.13
13.80		15.28	2.12		13.16	1.18	7.28
28.36		31.40	1.29		30.10	5.72	2.40
13.08	0.00	13.95	2.37		11.58	2.52	6.26
16.27	0.23	18.37	3.83		14.54	2.54	11.85
2.71		2.80	0.10		2.71	0.68	4.48
13.46		16.16	1.85		14.31	0.69	4.41
1 767.81	49.32	2 231.62	252.78	23.22	1 978.78	190.27	833.28
92.62	0.37	103.30	4.93		98.37	13.21	64.87
147.29	0.36	158.16	24.38	22.21	133.78	12.86	72.59
54.95	1.16	73.98	7.04	0.85	66.94	5.82	44.64
752.68	11.83	1 080.94	163.92		917.02	75.82	398.54
650.34	35.59	740.67	42.82		697.79	73.62	208.41
46.86		52.14	5.61		46.53	3.82	15.31

4–5 续表2

单位：亿元

类别	Category	法人企业数（个）Number of Corporate Enterprises (unit)	从业人员数（万人）Number of Employed Persons (10 000 persons)
批发业按地区分组	**Whole Trade by Region**		
昆明	Kunming	407	2.89
曲靖	Qujing	158	0.83
玉溪	Yuxi	156	0.92
保山	Baoshan	74	0.43
昭通	Zhaotong	45	0.29
丽江	Lijiang	16	0.21
普洱	Pu'er	49	0.25
临沧	Lincang	63	0.23
楚雄	Chuxiong	139	0.44
红河	Honghe	156	0.43
文山	Wenshan	66	0.36
西双版纳	Xishuangbanna	39	0.11
大理	Dali	144	0.57
德宏	Dehong	210	0.31
怒江	Nujiang	5	0.02
迪庆	Diqing	6	0.10
零售业按地区分组	**Retail Trade by Region**		
昆明	Kunming	366	5.71
曲靖	Qujing	302	0.98
玉溪	Yuxi	153	0.76
保山	Baoshan	141	0.40
昭通	Zhaotong	99	0.36
丽江	Lijiang	65	0.30
普洱	Pu'er	118	0.61
临沧	Lincang	109	0.32
楚雄	Chuxiong	303	0.65
红河	Honghe	251	0.74
文山	Wenshan	149	0.59
西双版纳	Xishuangbanna	59	0.40
大理	Dali	225	0.82
德宏	Dehong	88	0.25
怒江	Nujiang	17	0.06
迪庆	Diqing	24	0.07

continued

(100 million yuan)

商品购进总额 Total Purchases of Goods	进口 Imports of Goods	商品销售总额 Total Sales of Goods	批发 Wholesale	出口 Outputs	零售 Retail	年末库存总额 Inventory at Year-end	年末零售营业面积（万平方米） Retail Operating Area at Year-end (10 000 sq.m)
5 964.10	83.11	6 293.41	6 245.81	72.94	47.41	561.74	44.00
449.33		546.50	469.00		68.02	49.79	38.30
509.23	2.31	545.09	498.09	90.98	45.87	22.25	19.96
152.45	4.26	166.82	156.43	0.66	10.38	17.89	11.36
101.33		126.86	123.50		3.36	10.48	3.45
30.39		53.97	52.44		1.53	9.09	4.24
73.88	7.70	148.15	125.23	0.59	22.84	18.26	4.85
56.65	6.55	126.53	107.82	3.27	18.71	15.28	25.99
155.96		239.84	206.19	0.74	33.54	24.98	19.47
311.07	8.98	351.00	348.55	21.09	2.05	32.45	6.87
137.54		145.89	144.79	0.99	1.07	3.02	4.48
140.76	21.80	146.32	143.78	0.92	2.54	6.63	1.42
261.25		383.71	324.90		58.82	30.16	18.14
631.16	210.30	662.25	655.55	72.59	6.42	32.72	5.95
5.83		8.06	8.05		0.00	0.59	0.04
25.30	1.33	33.78	33.08		0.70	8.97	0.91
825.03	35.95	1 093.29	149.34		943.95	96.60	347.05
122.07	6.40	127.53	7.32		120.21	15.50	50.89
139.23	2.80	159.76	33.31	23.05	126.46	10.41	63.31
56.47	0.23	91.77	5.80		85.97	6.47	25.22
79.92		120.55	10.90		109.64	6.65	24.80
30.81	0.00	48.57	6.51		42.06	6.71	23.72
41.62		45.80	1.95		43.85	5.80	24.38
39.00	0.02	42.65	1.14		41.51	4.95	27.87
76.81	0.05	79.56	2.25		77.31	6.44	41.13
133.84	0.77	152.75	12.07		140.68	8.44	67.12
79.31	0.18	94.30	13.94	0.17	80.36	5.40	41.07
33.40		49.48	2.78		46.65	3.32	26.13
103.30	1.93	111.00	4.80		106.20	12.92	46.04
38.54	0.98	42.99	2.60		40.39	3.25	14.83
3.07		10.28	2.13		8.14	0.16	7.85
12.26		13.49	1.55		11.94	1.06	17.17

4–6 限额以上批发和零售业法人企业财务状况（2020年）

单位：亿元

类　　别	Category	法人企业数（个） Number of Corporate Enterprises (unit)	资产总计 Total Assets
批发和零售业	**Wholesale Trade and Retail Trade**	**4 202**	**6 212.26**
批发业	**Wholesale Trade**	**1 733**	**5 117.64**
按登记注册类型分	**Grouped by Status of Registration**		
内资企业	Domestic-funded Enterprises	1 716	5 014.63
国有企业	State-owned Enterprises	39	979.45
集体企业	Collective-owned Enterprises	10	2.22
股份合作企业	Joint Stock Cooperative Enterprises	1	0.77
联营企业	Joint Ownership Enterprises	1	1.35
有限责任公司	Limited Liability Companies	318	2 968.97
股份有限公司	Incorporated Corporations	38	271.89
私营企业	Private Enterprises	1270	787.52
其他企业	Other Enterprises	39	2.46
港、澳、台商投资企业	Enterprises Invested by Hong Kong, Macao and Taiwan	5	23.20
外商投资企业	Foreign-funded Enterprises	12	79.81
按国民经济行业分	**Grouped by Sector**		
农、林、牧、渔产品批发	Wholesale of Farm,Forestry,Livestock and Fishery Products	157	96.45
食品、饮料及烟草制品批发	Wholesale of Food, Beverages and Tobaccos	367	1 263.34
米、面制品及食用油批发	Wholesale of Rice, Flour and Edible Oil	56	102.51
果品、蔬菜批发	Fruits and Vegetables	191	77.92
酒、饮料及茶叶批发	Wholesale of Liquor，Beverages and Tea	37	76.76
烟草制品批发	Wholesale of Tobaccos	19	879.33
纺织、服装及家庭用品批发	Wholesale of Textiles, Garments and Daily Consumer Articles	55	136.24
文化、体育用品及器材批发	Wholesale of Culture, Sports Appliances and Equipments	22	51.05
医药及医疗器材批发	Wholesale of Medicines and Medical Appliances	147	387.13
西药批发	Wholesale of Western Medical	101	317.97
中药批发	Wholesale of Chinese herbal Medical	23	47.08
矿产品、建材及化工产品批发	Wholesale of Mineral Products,Building Materials and Chemical Products	789	3 017.93
煤炭及制品批发	Wholesale of Coal and Related Products	111	105.63
石油及制品批发	Wholesale of Petrolem and Related Products	43	176.45
金属及金属矿批发	Wholesale of Metal Materials	205	1 484.18
建材批发	Wholesale of Building Materials	225	283.83
化肥批发	Wholesale of Chemical Fertilizer	92	846.30
机械设备、五金产品及电子产品批发	Wholesale of Machinery, Hardware and Electronic Products	149	137.46
贸易经纪与代理	Trade Broker and Agency	7	6.77
其他批发业	Other Wholesale Trades	40	21.27

Financial Indicators of Enterprises above Designated Size of Wholesales and Retail Trades (2020)

(100 million yuan)

流动资产合计 Total Current Assets	负债合计 Total Liabilities	所有者权益合计 Total Owners' Equities	营业收入 Revenue from Business	营业成本 Cost of Business	税金及附加 Taxes and Other Charges	营业利润 Profits from Business
4 290.14	**3 650.62**	**2 559.68**	**11 157.86**	**10 322.11**	**98.02**	**314.53**
3 605.69	**2 932.74**	**2 183.55**	**9 060.51**	**8 469.25**	**93.33**	**270.48**
3 541.72	2 884.20	2 129.07	8 957.00	8 372.88	93.18	261.82
857.41	261.23	718.22	1 264.74	931.79	78.64	208.16
1.51	1.84	0.38	9.60	9.28	0.01	0.07
0.43	0.51	0.25	0.24	0.21	0.00	- 0.01
1.35	1.01	0.34	11.45	11.39	0.00	0.03
1 844.33	1 835.07	1 133.43	4 945.13	4 827.96	3.75	28.71
177.24	164.78	107.11	947.09	915.19	0.74	7.52
657.59	618.61	168.04	1 759.86	1 659.30	10.03	16.52
1.86	1.15	1.31	18.90	17.76	0.01	0.81
14.24	15.45	7.75	39.37	37.21	0.03	0.33
49.73	33.09	46.72	64.15	59.16	0.11	8.33
77.89	70.77	25.74	187.45	180.11	0.35	2.06
1 047.08	392.16	871.15	1 855.46	1 484.75	79.19	221.56
69.50	76.49	26.02	93.64	93.78	0.14	- 0.47
57.26	51.11	26.82	293.81	280.02	0.13	3.73
69.02	46.32	30.44	60.69	51.54	0.15	3.56
756.88	128.84	750.49	1 161.45	821.47	78.59	213.70
133.36	132.95	3.30	123.10	120.24	0.04	0.01
30.64	24.09	26.96	56.81	51.49	0.08	4.25
347.11	274.30	112.76	569.50	513.38	1.08	13.55
286.96	224.15	93.74	466.16	421.67	0.82	10.35
40.14	35.78	11.30	75.43	69.22	0.18	1.26
1 827.95	1 910.51	1 106.39	5 948.51	5 815.78	12.08	27.49
64.42	48.40	56.82	194.91	186.37	0.39	8.95
80.05	113.59	62.86	898.01	870.09	0.66	4.97
895.20	829.07	654.87	2 941.22	2 902.83	1.74	5.26
265.60	244.45	38.99	681.43	663.10	0.76	5.83
435.13	587.77	258.53	949.31	919.72	0.54	- 1.70
118.97	106.80	30.37	261.09	246.52	0.21	1.52
5.86	6.17	0.61	3.07	2.83	0.01	- 0.01
16.82	15.00	6.28	55.52	54.15	0.29	0.05

4-6 续表1

单位：亿元

类 别	Category	法人企业数(个) Number of Corporate Enterprises (unit)	资产总计 Total Assets
零售业	**Retail Trade**	**2 469**	**1 094.62**
按登记注册类型分	**Grouped by Status of Registration**		
内资企业	Domestic Funded Enterprises	2 427	974.96
国有企业	State-owned Enterprises	23	26.05
集体企业	Collective-owned Enterprises	18	1.79
股份合作企业	Joint Stock Cooperative Enterprises	14	1.95
联营企业	Joint Ownership Enterprise	1	0.27
有限责任公司	Limited Liability Companies	371	297.13
股份有限公司	Incorporated Corporations	30	115.29
私营企业	Private Enterprises	1 949	530.24
其他企业	Other Enterprises	21	2.24
港、澳、台商投资企业	Enterprises Invested by Hong Kong, Macao and Taiwan	16	53.49
外商投资企业	Foreign-funded Enterprises	26	66.17
按国民经济行业分	**Grouped by Sector**		
综合零售	Integrated Retail	447	159.51
百货零售	Retail of General Merchandise	211	47.37
超级市场零售	Retail of Supermarkets	168	101.99
食品、饮料及烟草制品专门零售	Retail of Food, Beverages and Tobaccos	362	80.59
粮油零售	Retail of Food and Edible Oil	72	24.93
果品、蔬菜零售	Fruits and Vegetables	139	17.48
肉、禽、蛋、奶及水产品零售	Meat,Poultry,Egg,Milk and Aquatic Products	47	9.69
酒、饮料及茶叶零售	Retail of Liquor、Beverages and Tea	43	18.15
纺织、服装及日用品专门零售	Retail of Textiles, Garments and Daily Consumer Articles	60	22.32
服装零售	Retail of Garments	30	16.66
文化、体育用品及器材专门零售	Retail of Culture, Sports Appliances and Equipments	118	48.71
图书、报刊零售	Retail of Books and Papers	27	34.31
珠宝首饰零售	Retail of Jewels	27	8.18
医药及医疗器材专门零售	Retail of Medicines and Medical Equipments	105	115.35
西药零售	Retail of Western Medicines	93	102.70
中药零售	Retail of Traditional Chinese Medicine	7	12.16
汽车、摩托车、零配件和燃料及其他动力销售	Retail of Motor Vehicles, Motorcycles,Fuel and Parts	996	588.90
汽车新车零售	Retail of Motor Vehicles	645	291.80
机动车燃油零售	Retail of Fuel of Motor Vehicles	256	257.62
家用电器及电子产品专门零售	Special Retail of Household Electric Appliances and Electronic Products	186	55.41
日用家电零售	Retail of Household Appliances	47	8.41
计算机、软件及辅助设备零售	Retail of Computer, Software and Assistant Appliances	70	19.00
通信设备零售	Retail of Communication Equipments	29	6.65
五金、家具及室内装饰材料专门零售	Special Retail of Hardware, Furniture and Decoration Materials	100	10.14
家具零售	Furniture Merchandise	33	2.14
货摊、无店铺及其他零售业	Non-shop and Other Retails	95	13.69
按零售业态分	**Grouped by Retail Form**		
有店铺零售	Retail Sales by Shop	2 195	1 065.16
#超市	Supermarket	262	48.12
#大型超市	Hypermarket	41	75.45
百货店	Department Store	130	45.99
专业店	Specialty Store	799	511.18
专卖店	Exclusive Shop	762	342.41
无店铺零售	Retail Sales without Shop	140	29.46

continued

(100 million yuan)

流动资产合计 Total Current Assets	负债合计 Total Liabilities	所有者权益合计 Total Owners' Equities	营业收入 Revenue from Business	营业成本 Cost of Business	税金及附加 Taxes and Other Charges	营业利润 Profits from Business
684.46	**717.88**	**376.13**	**2 097.35**	**1 852.86**	**4.69**	**44.05**
604.57	650.89	323.46	1 887.40	1 672.07	4.08	34.42
13.44	15.70	10.35	44.17	38.62	0.10	0.99
1.14	1.18	0.61	6.66	6.22	0.01	- 0.06
1.19	1.21	0.74	17.03	15.71	0.01	0.09
0.21	0.21	0.06	0.29	0.27	0.00	0.00
176.08	208.99	87.95	572.09	498.57	1.35	13.94
21.10	53.05	62.06	274.44	252.80	0.58	5.01
390.67	369.87	160.13	968.67	856.48	2.03	14.20
0.74	0.68	1.56	4.04	3.40	0.00	0.26
32.96	30.86	22.63	88.37	78.96	0.32	3.44
46.93	36.13	30.04	121.57	101.83	0.29	6.19
117.67	108.24	50.92	313.12	265.97	0.73	6.26
32.31	30.80	16.41	82.50	68.52	0.34	1.62
78.69	70.75	31.20	199.26	169.50	0.35	4.71
50.60	52.57	27.89	111.56	99.47	0.19	1.29
14.91	17.50	7.42	21.09	19.40	0.04	- 0.68
9.07	7.57	9.86	51.28	47.92	0.04	1.09
5.31	6.70	2.98	13.06	11.20	0.02	0.21
13.83	15.14	3.01	15.03	11.68	0.05	0.23
19.85	14.94	7.47	35.18	25.24	0.14	0.86
14.61	11.12	5.64	22.31	17.97	0.05	0.27
29.56	19.89	28.76	59.43	42.65	0.28	5.13
20.83	13.49	20.81	36.82	24.07	0.17	4.08
5.35	4.20	3.97	17.15	14.29	0.07	0.77
83.72	56.10	59.24	160.08	113.22	0.39	9.18
72.48	50.43	52.26	135.41	96.10	0.34	7.28
10.78	5.37	6.79	24.31	16.82	0.04	1.90
316.86	406.64	182.12	1 294.61	1 198.42	2.70	20.75
232.54	223.33	68.34	641.45	598.27	1.32	6.31
60.74	156.26	101.36	591.73	542.60	1.21	12.78
50.35	44.96	10.45	89.34	80.48	0.16	- 1.53
6.75	7.07	1.34	13.79	12.28	0.02	- 0.15
18.16	16.46	2.53	28.63	25.75	0.06	0.30
6.37	5.76	0.88	13.01	11.82	0.01	- 0.23
8.53	5.78	4.34	17.83	13.88	0.05	1.77
1.51	1.35	0.79	2.71	2.07	0.02	0.13
7.31	8.77	4.93	16.20	13.53	0.04	0.35
664.71	698.82	365.80	2 048.71	1 810.32	4.61	43.22
33.48	35.53	12.46	94.23	80.61	0.23	0.59
60.24	50.44	25.01	151.60	130.53	0.25	4.01
31.38	30.18	15.69	67.33	53.66	0.27	1.76
274.20	315.67	195.39	988.69	869.49	2.18	22.47
236.37	239.98	102.42	676.39	618.06	1.48	12.12
19.75	19.06	10.33	48.64	42.55	0.08	0.83

4-6 续表2

单位：亿元

类 别	Category	法人企业数（个）Number of Corporate Enterprises (unit)	资产总计 Total Assets	流动资产合计 Total Current Assets
批发业按地区分组	**Whole Trade by Region**			
昆 明	Kunming	407	3 340.29	2 145.40
曲 靖	Qujing	158	252.08	207.02
玉 溪	Yuxi	156	233.22	188.54
保 山	Baoshan	74	92.33	69.48
昭 通	Zhaotong	45	126.99	116.34
丽 江	Lijiang	16	29.34	24.54
普 洱	Pu'er	49	82.61	62.63
临 沧	Lincang	63	65.42	53.10
楚 雄	Chuxiong	139	121.90	96.07
红 河	Honghe	156	215.55	179.09
文 山	Wenshan	66	130.21	103.17
西双版纳	Xishuangbanna	39	67.81	55.06
大 理	Dali	144	160.79	129.37
德 宏	Dehong	210	144.46	126.67
怒 江	Nujiang	5	2.77	2.42
迪 庆	Diqing	6	51.86	46.79
零售业按地区分组	**Retail Trade by Region**			
昆 明	Kunming	366	570.43	357.94
曲 靖	Qujing	302	55.68	42.23
玉 溪	Yuxi	153	60.92	38.95
保 山	Baoshan	141	37.46	22.52
昭 通	Zhaotong	99	41.02	19.76
丽 江	Lijiang	65	20.64	10.22
普 洱	Pu'er	118	22.45	17.02
临 沧	Lincang	109	27.82	20.46
楚 雄	Chuxiong	303	38.39	25.53
红 河	Honghe	251	64.95	35.50
文 山	Wenshan	149	46.07	28.22
西双版纳	Xishuangbanna	59	26.96	14.96
大 理	Dali	225	53.75	37.84
德 宏	Dehong	88	15.19	8.98
怒 江	Nujiang	17	3.16	1.39
迪 庆	Diqing	24	9.71	2.93

continued

(100 million yuan)

负债合计 Total Liabilities	所有者权益合计 Total Owners' Equities	营业收入 Revenue from Business	营业成本 Cost of Business	税金及附加 Taxes and Other Charges	营业利润 Profits from Business
1 998.87	1 341.40	5 721.84	5 511.57	29.01	74.11
91.08	160.68	490.52	407.89	9.88	45.84
115.45	117.45	487.41	441.79	4.42	20.67
37.38	54.95	141.44	121.99	4.02	15.43
88.60	38.39	114.97	91.20	6.78	8.10
7.58	21.75	47.21	32.49	2.70	8.80
36.50	46.21	134.96	114.83	4.08	15.12
39.98	25.44	110.91	90.84	3.40	9.74
39.73	81.72	212.90	175.34	4.53	20.37
116.50	98.68	328.65	289.53	6.99	19.45
74.38	55.74	131.80	126.07	4.24	4.39
61.62	6.19	130.42	125.02	2.75	0.60
81.26	79.65	346.14	304.17	6.16	18.93
116.78	27.69	622.78	604.25	2.74	6.99
1.05	1.72	7.15	5.28	0.82	0.46
25.97	25.89	31.42	26.98	0.80	1.48
381.82	188.55	1 000.34	872.01	2.38	21.41
35.57	20.10	120.02	106.76	0.28	2.58
47.50	13.42	150.92	139.98	0.25	0.70
23.20	14.27	85.49	76.24	0.21	2.09
23.75	17.26	110.91	101.76	0.15	2.26
12.97	7.67	43.65	38.33	0.10	0.85
16.26	6.14	41.90	34.83	0.11	0.80
18.61	9.19	40.08	33.90	0.10	2.20
21.55	16.63	72.55	64.02	0.21	2.00
37.27	27.67	135.44	122.37	0.27	1.95
30.03	15.70	83.43	73.97	0.16	3.21
16.83	10.14	44.53	38.00	0.12	0.95
36.41	17.32	106.11	96.16	0.22	1.58
10.79	4.50	39.57	35.03	0.08	0.96
1.46	1.70	8.99	7.71	0.02	0.33
3.84	5.87	13.40	11.77	0.04	0.18

4-7 限额以上住宿和餐饮业法人企业经营情况（2020年）

单位：亿元

类　别	Category	法人企业数（个）Number of Corporate Enterprises (unit)	从业人员数（万人）Number of Employed Persons (10 000 persons)	营业额 Turnover	客房收入 Hotels
住宿和餐饮业	**Hotels and Catering Services**	**1 541**	**7.82**	**138.49**	**49.82**
住宿业	**Hotels**	**771**	**4.80**	**73.89**	**48.12**
按登记注册类型分	**Grouped by Status of Registration**				
内资企业	Domestic-funded Enterprises	752	4.58	70.53	45.99
国有企业	State-owned Enterprises	34	0.43	5.85	2.54
集体企业	Collective-owned Enterprises	3	0.02	0.50	0.28
联营企业	Joint Ownership Enterprises	1	0.01	0.10	0.06
有限责任公司	Limited Liability Companies	139	1.35	21.78	12.21
股份有限公司	Incorporated Corporations	6	0.07	0.81	0.48
私营企业	Private Enterprises	569	2.69	41.49	30.42
港、澳、台商投资企业	Enterprises Invested by Hong Kong, Macao and Taiwan	11	0.15	2.13	1.30
外商投资企业	Foreign-funded Enterprises	8	0.07	1.23	0.84
按住宿业行业分	**By Hotels**				
旅游饭店	Tourist Hotel	371	3.09	47.21	28.25
一般旅馆	Fonda	360	1.52	23.94	18.08
民宿服务	Homestay Service	10	0.03	0.35	0.25
其他住宿业	Others	30	0.17	2.39	1.54
按星级分	**Grouped by Stars Level**				
五星	Five - star	36	0.65	10.59	6.55
四星	Four - star	88	1.00	14.61	7.34
三星	Three - star	108	0.57	8.32	5.00
二星	Two- star	19	0.06	0.82	0.59
其他	Others	520	2.52	39.56	28.64

Basic Statistics of Corporate Enterprises above Designated Size of Hotel Industry and Catering Services (2020)

(100 million yuan)

餐费收入 Catering Services	商品销售收入 Retail Sales of Commodities	其他收入 Other	客房数（万间） Number of Hotel Rooms (10 000 units)	床位数（万个） Number of Hotel Beds (10 000 units)	餐位数（万位） Number of Dining Seats (10 000 units)	年末餐饮营业面积（万平方米） Catering Services Operational Area at Year-end (10 000 sq.m)
76.48	**4.21**	**7.98**	**19.27**	**31.74**	**71.28**	**403.44**
17.72	**1.60**	**6.45**	**18.77**	**30.86**	**30.04**	**272.35**
16.78	1.58	6.19	18.35	30.16	29.33	263.51
1.72	0.13	1.45	1.30	2.00	2.52	14.86
0.22	0.00	0.01	0.03	0.05	0.09	1.34
0.04		0.01	0.02	0.03	0.02	0.70
6.12	0.98	2.48	3.62	6.19	8.18	55.82
0.19	0.01	0.13	0.20	0.32	0.19	3.28
8.50	0.45	2.12	13.19	21.57	18.33	187.51
0.61	0.01	0.20	0.28	0.44	0.45	5.75
0.33	0.00	0.06	0.14	0.26	0.25	3.09
12.77	1.22	4.97	10.71	17.53	18.73	158.31
4.37	0.38	1.12	7.62	12.62	10.85	100.79
0.03	0.00	0.06	0.08	0.14	0.07	1.87
0.54	0.00	0.30	0.36	0.57	0.39	11.37
3.24	0.04	0.76	1.21	1.98	3.04	21.01
4.00	0.91	2.37	3.42	6.18	7.81	47.82
2.21	0.13	0.97	1.62	2.64	4.82	50.82
0.14	0.00	0.08	0.20	0.35	0.39	7.78
8.13	0.52	2.26	12.32	19.71	13.98	144.92

4-7 续表1

单位：亿元

类　别	Category	法人企业数（个）Number of Corporate Enterprises (unit)	从业人员数（万人）Number of Employed Persons (10 000 persons)	营业额 Turnover	客房收入 Hotels
餐饮业	**Catering Services**	**770**	**3.02**	**64.59**	**1.69**
按登记注册类型分	**Grouped by Status of Registration**				
内资企业	Domestic-funded Enterprises	764	2.52	55.89	1.69
国有企业	State-owned Enterprises	4	0.03	0.43	0.09
集体企业	Collective-owned Enterprises	3	0.03	0.32	0.11
有限责任公司	Limited Liability Companies	73	0.45	8.17	0.18
股份有限公司	Incorporated Corporations	2	0.00	0.18	
私营企业	Private Enterprises	680	2.00	46.64	1.31
其他企业	Other Enterprises	2	0.01	0.14	
港、澳、台商投资企业	Enterprises Invested by Hong Kong,Macao and Taiwan	2	0.09	1.71	
外商投资企业	Foreign-funded Enterprises	4	0.41	6.99	
按餐饮业行业分	**By Catering Services**				
正餐服务	Restaurant	733	2.23	49.47	1.68
快餐服务	Fast Food	10	0.49	9.34	
饮料及冷饮服务	Beverages and Cold Drinks	8	0.08	1.62	
餐饮配送及外卖送餐服务	Catering Distribution and Take out service	11	0.19	3.69	0.01
其他餐饮业	Others	8	0.03	0.48	

continued

(100 million yuan)

			客房数 (万间) Number of Hotel Rooms (10 000 units)	床位数 (万个) Number of Hotel beds (10 000 units)	餐位数 (万位) Number of Dining Seats (10 000 units)	年末餐饮营业面积 (万平方米) Catering Services Operational Area at the Year-end (10 000 sq.m)
餐费收入 Catering Services	商品销售收入 Retail Sales of Commodities	其他收入 Other				
58.76	**2.61**	**1.53**	**0.49**	**0.88**	**41.24**	**131.10**
50.66	2.59	0.94	0.49	0.88	40.28	127.71
0.34	0.00	0.00	0.03	0.05	0.33	1.45
0.19	0.00	0.02	0.05	0.09	0.15	4.19
6.87	0.75	0.37	0.08	0.12	5.56	23.11
0.18					0.02	0.15
42.94	1.84	0.56	0.34	0.62	34.07	98.65
0.14					0.15	0.16
1.43		0.28			0.07	0.40
6.67	0.02	0.30			0.90	2.99
44.73	2.23	0.82	0.49	0.87	38.93	124.49
9.06	0.00	0.28			1.73	4.62
1.56	0.03	0.03			0.26	0.73
2.93	0.35	0.40	0.01	0.01	0.03	0.39
0.48	0.00				0.30	0.86

4−7 续表2

单位：亿元

类　别	Category	法人企业数（个）Number of Corporate Enterprises (unit)	从业人员数（万人）Number of Employed Persons (10 000 persons)	营业额 Turnover	客房收入 Hotels
住宿业按地区分组	**Hotel Trade by Region**				
昆　明	Kunming	185	1.53	23.38	13.78
曲　靖	Qujing	55	0.32	6.08	4.49
玉　溪	Yuxi	34	0.20	2.90	1.44
保　山	Baoshan	32	0.34	3.99	2.66
昭　通	Zhaotong	42	0.22	3.54	2.35
丽　江	Lijiang	59	0.36	5.32	3.83
普　洱	Pu'er	26	0.12	1.60	1.28
临　沧	Lincang	19	0.11	1.39	1.02
楚　雄	Chuxiong	80	0.22	6.36	4.60
红　河	Honghe	38	0.23	3.48	1.96
文　山	Wenshan	25	0.11	1.41	0.95
西双版纳	Xishuangbanna	22	0.27	4.19	2.46
大　理	Dali	96	0.50	6.47	4.65
德　宏	Dehong	27	0.14	1.70	1.26
怒　江	Nujiang	10	0.05	0.58	0.47
迪　庆	Diqing	21	0.08	1.50	0.92
餐饮业按地区分组	**Catering Trade by Region**				
昆　明	Kunming	176	1.60	31.30	0.48
曲　靖	Qujing	57	0.16	6.18	0.14
玉　溪	Yuxi	41	0.09	1.74	0.04
保　山	Baoshan	24	0.07	1.50	0.04
昭　通	Zhaotong	23	0.09	1.98	0.14
丽　江	Lijiang	12	0.09	1.61	0.01
普　洱	Pu'er	10	0.02	0.48	0.04
临　沧	Lincang	18	0.05	1.11	0.02
楚　雄	Chuxiong	199	0.31	9.49	0.52
红　河	Honghe	33	0.10	2.33	0.08
文　山	Wenshan	22	0.06	1.03	0.10
西双版纳	Xishuangbanna	10	0.03	0.65	
大　理	Dali	90	0.21	3.15	0.04
德　宏	Dehong	41	0.09	1.50	0.03
怒　江	Nujiang	5	0.02	0.20	
迪　庆	Diqing	9	0.03	0.34	0.01

continued

(100 million yuan)

餐费收入 Catering Services	商品销售收入 Retail Sales of Commodities	其他收入 Other	客房数 (万间) Number of Hotel Rooms (10 000 units)	床位数 (万个) Number of Hotel beds (10 000 units)	餐位数 (万位) Number of Dining Seats (10 000 units)	年末餐饮营业面积(万平方米) Catering Services Operational Area at the Year-end (10 000 sq.m)
5.95	0.70	2.95	6.48	10.48	5.73	73.51
1.42	0.03	0.15	1.59	2.88	4.65	24.68
1.00	0.09	0.36	1.34	2.74	5.28	19.26
0.98	0.12	0.22	0.58	1.01	1.21	13.05
0.80	0.11	0.28	1.51	2.38	0.74	8.78
1.05	0.02	0.42	1.80	2.95	1.23	16.23
0.24	0.00	0.07	0.29	0.46	0.73	8.79
0.14	0.04	0.20	0.23	0.41	0.38	9.41
1.41	0.14	0.22	0.71	1.24	1.91	19.80
1.07	0.05	0.40	0.46	0.79	2.76	12.98
0.35	0.01	0.11	0.25	0.39	0.21	7.13
1.12	0.20	0.41	0.57	0.99	1.23	3.54
1.38	0.02	0.42	2.04	2.87	2.88	33.70
0.30	0.01	0.12	0.40	0.65	0.71	10.12
0.07	0.00	0.04	0.11	0.18	0.09	2.28
0.44	0.03	0.09	0.40	0.44	0.33	9.09
28.76	0.98	1.09	0.13	0.27	14.23	51.99
5.88	0.13	0.03	0.06	0.09	6.33	12.74
1.61	0.09	0.00	0.01	0.02	1.98	6.28
1.40	0.03	0.03	0.01	0.02	0.84	2.83
1.62	0.19	0.03	0.05	0.09	1.46	4.09
1.02	0.39	0.19	0.01	0.01	0.44	2.46
0.38	0.04	0.03	0.01	0.02	0.73	2.85
1.07	0.01	0.01	0.03	0.04	0.98	5.28
8.42	0.53	0.02	0.09	0.14	6.53	17.63
2.10	0.14	0.02	0.03	0.05	2.08	4.54
0.91	0.02	0.01	0.02	0.03	0.66	3.60
0.65					0.21	0.53
3.04	0.06	0.02	0.02	0.04	3.45	8.72
1.40	0.02	0.06	0.01	0.02	1.02	6.56
0.20					0.05	0.36
0.32	0.01	0.00	0.01	0.01	0.26	0.63

4-8 限额以上住宿和餐饮业企业法人财务状况（2020年）

单位：亿元

类 别	Category	法人企业数（个） Number of Corporate Enterprises (unit)	资产总计 Total Assets
住宿和餐饮业	**Hotels and Catering Services**	**1 541**	**431.61**
住宿业	**Hotels**	**771**	**354.15**
按登记注册类型分	**Grouped by Status of Registration**		
内资企业	Domestic-funded Enterprises	752	326.96
国有企业	State-owned Enterprises	34	20.32
集体企业	Collective-owned Enterprises	3	0.58
联营企业	Joint Ownership Enterprises	1	0.17
有限责任公司	Limited Liability Companies	139	127.76
股份有限公司	Incorporated Corporations	6	1.72
私营企业	Private Enterprises	569	176.41
港、澳、台商投资企业	Enterprises Invested by Hong Kong, Macao and Taiwan	11	19.25
外商投资企业	Foreign-funded Enterprises	8	7.94
按住宿业行业分	**By Hotels**		
旅游饭店	Tourist Hotel	371	265.03
一般旅馆	Fonda	360	75.76
民宿服务	Homestay Service	10	3.60
其他住宿业	Others	30	9.76
按星级分	**Grouped by Stars Level**		
五星	Five - star	36	84.88
四星	Four - star	88	60.25
三星	Three - star	108	26.71
二星	Two- star	19	3.10
其他	Others	520	179.22

Financial Indicators of Corporate Enterprises above Designated Size of Hotel Industry Catering Services by Region (2020)

(100 million yuan)

流动资产合计 Total Current Assets	负债合计 Total Liabilities	所有者权益 Total Owners' Equities	营业收入 Revenue from Business	营业成本 Cost of Business	税金及附加 Taxes and Other Charges	营业利润 Profits from Business
175.53	**296.23**	**133.75**	**134.41**	**78.33**	**1.24**	**-6.98**
130.92	**251.66**	**100.91**	**71.69**	**37.32**	**0.82**	**-9.53**
122.38	239.76	85.62	68.43	36.24	0.74	-8.85
6.33	7.05	13.27	5.77	3.11	0.06	-0.94
0.23	0.20	0.38	0.49	0.25	0.01	0.00
0.06	0.03	0.13	0.10	0.02	0.00	-0.01
41.74	103.06	23.12	21.03	10.36	0.27	-4.09
0.48	0.51	1.21	0.83	0.53	0.01	-0.19
73.54	128.91	47.50	40.22	21.96	0.39	-3.62
6.74	6.58	12.67	2.03	0.47	0.04	-0.51
1.79	5.31	2.63	1.23	0.61	0.04	-0.18
96.22	191.31	72.15	45.39	22.91	0.55	-7.88
30.00	49.66	26.08	23.62	13.03	0.26	-1.28
1.72	2.79	0.82	0.34	0.12	0.00	-0.18
2.98	7.91	1.86	2.34	1.26	0.01	-0.20
29.67	52.58	32.30	10.37	4.01	0.24	-2.60
25.76	37.76	20.90	13.62	7.15	0.16	-1.50
9.22	15.44	11.27	7.70	4.62	0.07	-0.64
0.67	1.45	1.65	0.77	0.59	0.02	-0.08
65.59	144.43	34.79	39.23	20.94	0.34	-4.71

4–8 续表1

单位：亿元

类　别	Category	法人企业数（个） Number of Corporate Enterprises (unit)	资产总计 Total Assets
餐饮业	**Catering Services**	**770**	**77.46**
按登记注册类型分	**Grouped by Status of Registration**		
内资企业	Domestic-funded Enterprises	764	73.18
国有企业	State-owned Enterprises	4	0.31
集体企业	Collective-owned Enterprises	3	0.14
有限责任公司	Limited Liability Companies	73	9.53
股份有限公司	Incorporated Corporations	2	0.07
私营企业	Private Enterprises	680	63.13
其他企业	Other Enterprises	2	0.00
港、澳、台商投资企业	Enterprises Invested by Hong Kong, Macao and Taiwan	2	1.33
外商投资企业	Foreign-funded Enterprises	4	2.95
按餐饮业行业分	**By Catering Services**		
正餐服务	Restaurant	733	68.02
快餐服务	Fast Food	10	5.11
饮料及冷饮服务	Beverages and Cold Drinks	8	0.68
餐饮配送及外卖送餐服务	Catering Distribution and Take out service	11	2.95
其他餐饮业	Others	8	0.70

continued

(100 million yuan)

流动资产合计 Total Current Assets	负债合计 Total Liabilities	所有者权益 Total Owners' Equities	营业收入 Revenue from Business	营业成本 Cost of Business	税金及附加 Taxes and Other Charges	营业利润 Profits from Business
44.61	**44.57**	**32.84**	**62.72**	**41.01**	**0.42**	**2.55**
42.03	41.95	31.18	54.55	35.86	0.41	2.16
0.17	0.17	0.14	0.40	0.30	0.00	-0.02
0.12	0.18	-0.04	0.31	0.11	0.00	0.02
4.09	5.30	4.23	7.99	5.75	0.04	-0.09
0.01	0.00	0.07	0.18	0.14	0.00	0.02
37.63	36.29	26.78	45.53	29.44	0.37	2.23
0.00	0.00	0.00	0.14	0.13	0.00	0.00
1.15	0.57	0.76	1.46	1.25	0.01	-0.14
1.44	2.05	0.90	6.71	3.90	0.00	0.53
39.32	38.88	29.09	48.35	32.49	0.40	1.82
2.59	2.94	2.16	8.92	4.33	0.00	0.76
0.25	0.69	-0.01	1.56	1.04	0.00	0.02
2.04	1.65	1.31	3.42	2.86	0.01	-0.09
0.42	0.41	0.29	0.48	0.29	0.01	0.05

4-8 续表2

单位：亿元

类　别	Category	法人企业数（个） Number of Corporate Enterprises (unit)	资产总计 Total Assets	流动资产合计 Total Current Assets
住宿业按地区分组	**Hotel Trade by Region**			
昆　明	Kunming	185	105.72	40.74
曲　靖	Qujing	55	14.36	5.84
玉　溪	Yuxi	34	10.38	3.27
保　山	Baoshan	32	21.88	6.68
昭　通	Zhaotong	42	7.15	3.26
丽　江	Lijiang	59	37.05	15.64
普　洱	Pu'er	26	9.53	4.23
临　沧	Lincang	19	8.43	4.28
楚　雄	Chuxiong	80	13.84	4.09
红　河	Honghe	38	16.72	4.96
文　山	Wenshan	25	8.76	2.24
西双版纳	Xishuangbanna	22	30.66	10.34
大　理	Dali	96	35.17	18.19
德　宏	Dehong	27	17.08	1.90
怒　江	Nujiang	10	3.27	1.81
迪　庆	Diqing	21	14.16	3.44
餐饮业按地区分组	**Catering Trade by Region**			
昆　明	Kunming	176	49.64	33.48
曲　靖	Qujing	57	2.73	1.28
玉　溪	Yuxi	41	0.97	0.50
保　山	Baoshan	24	1.87	0.71
昭　通	Zhaotong	23	0.95	0.57
丽　江	Lijiang	12	2.27	0.84
普　洱	Pu'er	10	1.50	0.36
临　沧	Lincang	18	1.20	0.49
楚　雄	Chuxiong	199	8.52	2.26
红　河	Honghe	33	1.87	1.47
文　山	Wenshan	22	1.40	0.26
西双版纳	Xishuangbanna	10	0.30	0.17
大　理	Dali	90	1.92	1.18
德　宏	Dehong	41	1.70	0.72
怒　江	Nujiang	5	0.09	0.03
迪　庆	Diqing	9	0.54	0.31

continued

(100 million yuan)

负债合计 Total Liabilities	所有者权益 Total Owners' Equities	营业收入 Revenue from Business	营业成本 Cost of Business	税金及附加 Taxes and Other Charges	营业利润 Profits from Business
69.37	36.34	23.26	11.21	0.21	-2.87
8.97	5.39	5.92	2.40	0.12	0.01
6.62	3.75	2.76	1.84	0.02	-0.37
19.24	2.65	3.91	2.25	0.06	-0.53
4.93	2.22	3.48	2.21	0.04	0.03
22.04	14.64	5.15	1.84	0.06	-1.03
6.46	3.07	1.54	1.01	0.01	-0.27
6.67	1.75	1.29	0.62	0.02	-0.23
4.50	9.34	5.31	3.44	0.04	0.32
11.16	5.56	3.44	2.16	0.02	-0.15
7.36	1.42	1.39	0.56	0.01	-0.16
33.53	-4.09	3.92	2.07	0.10	-2.00
29.83	5.34	6.44	3.14	0.04	-0.74
11.93	5.15	1.81	1.50	0.03	-0.76
2.76	0.51	0.57	0.28	0.01	-0.04
6.30	7.86	1.51	0.79	0.03	-0.76
32.27	17.37	30.30	17.18	0.20	0.52
1.06	1.68	5.84	4.79	0.06	0.22
0.47	0.50	1.72	1.24	0.01	0.10
0.44	1.44	1.49	0.91	0.01	-0.04
0.37	0.58	1.89	1.35	0.01	0.12
0.92	1.35	1.57	1.14	0.01	-0.02
1.06	0.44	0.48	0.35	0.01	0.07
0.31	0.89	1.10	0.70	0.01	0.17
3.05	5.42	9.31	7.14	0.07	0.88
1.03	0.84	2.22	1.61	0.02	0.17
1.37	0.03	1.01	0.69	0.01	0.02
0.15	0.15	0.63	0.45	0.00	0.07
0.72	1.20	3.12	2.21	0.01	0.18
1.11	0.59	1.48	0.96	0.01	0.04
0.05	0.04	0.20	0.11	0.01	0.00
0.22	0.32	0.34	0.19	0.00	0.04

主要统计指标解释

批发业 指向其他批发或零售单位（含个体经营者）及其他企事业单位、机关团体等批量销售生活用品、生产资料的活动，以及从事进出口贸易和贸易经纪与代理的活动，包括拥有货物所有权，并以本单位（公司）的名义进行交易活动，也包括不拥有货物的所有权，收取佣金的商品代理、商品代售活动；还包括各类商品批发市场中固定摊位的批发活动，以及以销售为目的的收购活动。

零售业 指百货商店、超级市场、专门零售商店、品牌专卖店、售货摊等主要面向最终消费者（如居民等）的销售活动，以互联网、邮政、电话、售货机等方式的销售活动，还包括在同一地点，后面加工生产，前面销售的店铺（如面包房）；谷物、种子、饲料、牲畜、矿产品、生产用原料、化工原料、农用化工产品、机械设备（乘用车、计算机及通信设备除外）等生产资料的销售不作为零售活动；多数零售商对其销售的货物拥有所有权，但有些则是充当委托人的代理人，进行委托销售或以收取佣金的方式进行销售。

批发和零售业商品购进、销售、库存额 指各种登记注册类型的批发和零售业企业（单位）以本企业（单位）为总体的，从国内、国外市场购进的商品总量，销售和出口的商品总量，库存的商品总量等情况。该指标可以反映商品流转过程中商品的购进、销售、库存之间的比例关系和存在的问题。

商品购进额 指从本企业以外的单位和个人购进（包括从国外直接进口）作为转卖或加工后转卖的商品金额（含增值税）。本指标反映批发和零售业从国内外市场上购进商品的总价。

商品购进包括：（1）从工农业生产者、批发和零售业企业、住宿和餐饮业企业、出版社或报社的出版发行部门和其他服务业企业购进的商品；（2）从机关团体、事业单位购进的商品；（3）从海关、市场管理部门购进的缉私和没收的商品；（4）从居民收购的废旧商品等。

商品购进不包括：（1）企业为本单位自身经营用，不是作为转卖而购进的商品，如材料物资、包装物、低值易耗品、办公用品等；（2）未通过买卖行为而收入的商品，如接受其他部门移交的商品、借入的商品、收入代其他单位保管的商品、其他单位赠送的样品、加工回收的成品等；（3）经本单位介绍，由买卖双方直接结算，本单位只收取手续费的业务；（4）销售退回和买方拒付货款的商品；（5）商品溢余；（6）期货交易商品。

商品销售额 指对本单位以外的单位和个人出售的商品金额（包括售给本单位消费用的商品，含增值税）。在批发和零售业中，本指标反映在国内市场上销售商品以及出口商品的总价。

商品销售包括：（1）售给个人和社会集团消费用的商品；（2）售给农业、工业、建筑业、服务业等国民经济各行业用于生产、经营用的商品，包括售予批发和零售业作为转卖或加工后转卖的商品；（3）对国（境）外直接出口的商品。

商品销售不包括：（1）未通过买卖行为付出的商品，如机构变动移交给其他企业单位的商品、借出的商品、归还受其他单位委托代保管的商品、付出的加工原料和赠送给其他单位的样品等；（2）促销返券所销售的、不计入营业收入的商品；（3）经本单位介绍，由买卖双方直接结算，本单位只收取手续费的业务；（4）未发生所有权转移的商品预付卡销售，如加油卡；（5）汽车维修、电话卡销售等服务性经济活动；（6）购货退回的商品；（7）商品损耗和损失；（8）出售本单位自用的废旧物资；（9）期货交易商品；（10）自来水供应企业、电力企业、天然气供应企业提供的水、电、气。

商品库存额 对于批发和零售业法人单位和个体经营户，是指报告期末取得所有权的全部商品金额（含增值税）；对于批发和零售业产业活动单位，是指报告期末实际在库且归属法人具有所有权的全部商品金额（含增值税）。这个指标反映批发和零售业的商品库存情况，以及对市场商品供应的保证程度。

库存商品包括：（1）存放在本单位（如门市部、批发站、采购站、经营处）的仓库、货场、货柜和货架中的商品；（2）挑选、整理、包装中的商品；（3）已记入购进而尚未运到本单位的商品，即发货单或银行承兑凭证已到而货未到的商品；（4）寄放他处的商品，如因购货方拒绝付款而暂时存在购货方的商品；（5）委托其他单位代销（未作销售或调出）尚未售出的商品；（6）代其他单位购进尚未交付的商品。

商品库存不包括：所有权不属于本单位的商品；委托外单位加工的商品；外贸企业代理其他单位从国外进口，尚未付给订货单位的商品；代国家储备部门保管的商品。

社会消费品零售总额 指企业（单位、个体户）通过交易直接售给个人、社会集团非生产、非经营用的实物商品金额，以及提供餐饮服务所取得的收入金额。个人包括城乡居民和入境人员，社会集团包括机关、社会团体、部队、学校、企事业单位、居委会或村委会等。

住宿业 指为旅行者提供短期留宿场所的活动，有些单位只提供住宿，也有些单位提供住宿、饮食、商务、娱乐一体的服务，不包括主要按月或按年长期出租房屋住所的活动。

餐饮业 指通过即时制作加工、商业销售和服务性劳动等，向消费者提供食品和消费场所及设施的服务。

营业额 指住宿和餐饮业单位在经营活动中，因提供服务或销售商品等取得的全部收入（含增值税）。包括：客房收入、餐费收入、商品销售额和其他收入。其中，客房收入指住宿和餐饮业单位在经营活动中因提供住宿服务取得的收入（含增值税）。餐费收入指本单位为顾客提供就餐服务取得的收入（含增值税），包括：经烹饪、调制加工后出售的各种食品，如主食、炒菜、凉拌菜等的收入。

Explanatory Notes on Main Statistical Indicators

Wholesale Trade refers to the activities of selling wholesale commodities for daily use and capital goods to enterprises of wholesale and retail trades (including self-employed individuals) and other enterprises, institutions and government organs and organizations, and the activities of engaging in import and export and acting as a trade agent. The wholesaler may have the ownership of the commodities for wholesale and trade in the name of its own (a company), and the wholesaler can act as commission agent or commodity broker without the ownership of commodities. Also included are the wholesale activities at the fixed stalls in wholesale market and the acquisition for sales purpose.

Retail Trade refers to the activities of department store, supermarket, franchised store, brand store, retail stall and on-the-spot-making-selling store selling commodities to the final consumers (residents) by any means including internet, post, telephone, sales machine. It also includes shops with sales and production located in the same places (such as bakeries). Retail trade excludes the activities of sales of capital goods such as grain, seed, feed, livestock, mineral products, raw material for production, industrial chemicals, chemical products for agricultural use, machine and equipment (excluding vehicles, computers and communication equipment). Most retailers have the ownership of commodities to sell, but some are acting as agents or brokers to make transactions for a commission.

Purchase, Sales and Stock of Commodities by Wholesale and Retail Trades refer to the total volume of commodities purchased, total volume of sales and exports, and the stock of commodities by wholesale and retail enterprises (establishments) of different status of registration from domestic and overseas markets. This indicator reflects the relationship among purchase, sales and stock of commodities in the circulation of goods and reveals the existing problems

Total Purchases of Commodities refer to the total value of purchases of commodities by enterprises (establishments) from other establishments or individuals (including direct import from abroad) for the purpose of re-selling, either with or without further processing of the commodities purchased. This indicator is used to show the total value of purchases of retail and wholesale commodities from domestic and overseas markets. The commodities include (1) commodities purchased from agricultural and industrial producer, wholesaler, retailer, publishing house and other service business; (2) commodities purchased from institutions and government departments; (3) confiscated goods purchased from the customs authorities or market management agencies; (4) second-hand goods and wastes purchased from residents; The commodities exclude (1) commodities purchased by enterprises (establishments) for use in their own business operation, commodities obtained without buying or selling procedures such as materials, consumable goods of low value, office appliance, etc. (2) received goods without trading, such as goods handed over from others, borrowed goods, preserved goods for others, donated goods from others, processed and retrieved goods, etc. (3) goods of direct settlement between buyer and seller with handling fees introduced by others, (4) goods returned or refused to pay by the buyer, (5) excessive goods.(6) futures traded commodity.

Total Sales of Commodities refer to value of commodities sold by the establishments to other establishments and individuals (including goods sold for self consumption, including the value-added tax). In the wholesale and retail trade, this indicator reflects the total price of goods sold on the domestic market and exported.

The commodities include (1) commodities sold to individuals and social groups for their consumption; (2) commodities sold to establishments in all industries for their production and operation, including agriculture, industry, construction, and catering services including commodities sold to wholesale and retail establishments for re-selling, with or without further processing; (3) commodities for direct export to abroad.

Excluded are (1) extended commodities without trading, such as goods handed over to other enterprises and institutions because of the change of organizations, lent goods, returned goods preserved for others, extended processing materials and samples donated to others; (2)The goods sold by the promotional coupons and not included in the operating income; (3) goods of direct settlement between buyer and seller with handling fees introduced by others; (4) the sale of prepaid CARDS, such as fuel CARDS, without transfer of ownership; (5) service economic activities such as automobile maintenance and sales of telephone CARDS; (6) goods returned after purchase; (7) damaged and spoiled goods; (8) waste and used goods of self use; (9) commodities traded in futures; (10) water supply enterprises, electric power enterprises and natural gas supply enterprises provide water, electricity and gas.

Total Stock of Commodities For the legal entities and self-employed individuals engaged in wholesale and retail trade, it refers to total value (including VAT) of commodities possessed at the end of the reference period; and for wholesale and retail establishments, it refers to the value (including VAT) of all commodities actually in stock and owned by their legal persons at the end of reference period. This indicator shows the commodity inventory in wholesale and retail trades, and to what extent the commodities will be supplied to the market. The commodities in stock includes: (1) commodities located in storage, garages, counters, and shelves of operating places of wholesale and retail trades (such as sale stores, wholesale centres, procurement stations and operating offices); (2) commodities in the process of being selected, sorted, and packed; (3) commodities not arrived but recorded as purchase in the account, i.e. commodities not arrived but payment receipts for the commodities from the sellers or the banks arrived; (4) commodities deposited in other places rather than places mentioned above, for instance: commodities in the hold of purchasers temporarily due to the refusal of payment; (5) commodities entrusted to other units to sell but not sold yet; (6) commodities purchased for other units but not delivered yet. Commodities not included as stock are those not owned by the enterprises (units), commodities on commission for processing, imported commodities of agency of foreign trade enterprise but not yet delivered to ordering units and finally those put in stock on behalf of the state reserves units.

Total Retail Sales of Consumer Goods refer to the amount obtained by enterprises (units, self-employed individuals) through direct sales of non-production and non-business physical commodity to individuals, social institutions, and revenue from providing catering services. Individuals include rural and urban households, population from abroad, social institutions include government agencies, social organizations, military units, schools, institutions, neighbourhood (village) committees.

Hotel Services refer to the accommodation services provided to visitors. Some units may provide only accommodation while others provide a combination of accommodation, meals, business services and/or recreational facilities. It excludes activities related to the provision of long-term primary residences in facilities such as apartments typically leased on a monthly or annual basis.

Catering Services refer to the activities of providing foods, serving locations and facilities to customers through instant processing, commercial sales and service-type labor.

Business Revenue refers to revenue of hotels and catering services received from providing services or selling commodities through business activities, including the total income (including value-added tax) from hotels, from catering services, from selling of commodities (including VAT) and from other services. Income (including value-added tax) from hotels refers to income of hotels and catering services by providing lodging services through business activities. Income (including value-added tax) from catering services refers to income from providing catering services, including selling of cooked or prepared foods, such as staple food, cooked dishes, or cold dishes.

Chapter 5

五、公共财政
Public Finance

5-1 地方一般公共预算收支额（1981-2020年）

General Public Budgetary Revenue and Expenditure of Local Government (1981-2020)

单位：亿元 (100 million yuan)

年 份 Year	地方一般公共预算收入 Public Budgetary Revenue of Local Government	增值税 Value Added Tax	营业税 Business Tax	企业所得税 Enterprise Income Tax	地方一般公共预算支出 Public Budgetary Expenditure of Local Government	农业支出 Expenditure for Agriculture	文教科卫事业费 Expenditure for Culture, Education, Science and Health	行政管理费 Expenditure for Government Administration	社会保障补助支出 Expenditure for Social Security
1981	12.69				15.73	2.46	4.30	2.21	
1982	15.66				18.80	3.15	5.14	2.47	
1983	17.17				24.23	3.68	6.55	2.98	
1984	19.73				30.77	4.41	8.15	4.54	
1985	27.41			5.98	36.70	4.18	9.38	4.92	
1986	30.01			4.50	47.31	5.71	11.29	5.75	
1987	37.49			4.78	53.86	6.66	12.59	6.29	
1988	50.53			7.59	64.84	8.39	15.56	6.45	
1989	63.27			9.19	81.89	11.62	18.15	7.50	
1990	77.43			7.21	90.76	13.20	21.32	8.88	
1991	99.78			8.09	110.82	15.91	24.08	10.56	
1992	109.32			5.17	121.59	18.53	28.76	13.86	
1993	204.94			4.99	200.62	23.82	37.36	16.73	
1994	76.70	22.52	11.75	6.72	203.73	25.06	48.91	21.40	
1995	98.35	23.28	15.40	7.87	235.10	28.28	54.06	24.47	
1996	130.01	26.54	21.21	9.42	270.39	32.51	69.04	30.22	
1997	150.42	27.84	25.36	9.70	313.20	33.82	75.01	30.58	
1998	168.23	30.57	29.76	14.47	328.00	34.66	80.50	32.07	2.71
1999	172.67	31.06	33.94	14.95	378.05	36.59	89.86	33.47	7.33
2000	180.75	31.37	36.00	20.17	414.11	39.20	98.70	37.24	15.89
2001	191.28	33.62	36.68	26.29	496.43	45.26	116.70	44.76	26.21
2002	206.76	34.42	41.41	25.78	526.89	46.35	132.37	49.36	25.67
2003	229.00	39.11	45.17	21.50	587.35	48.99	143.99	55.43	42.30
2004	263.36	45.56	56.57	27.78	663.64	71.90	170.60	67.76	33.31
2005	321.65	56.02	67.64	33.35	766.31	73.50	192.06	78.12	29.03
2006	379.97	67.50	89.49	41.30	893.58	83.86	236.16	95.21	34.15
2007	486.71	85.72	112.47	55.71	1 135.22	127.60	300.55	187.01	170.48
2008	614.05	99.41	136.63	66.03	1 470.24	177.77	392.19	217.12	224.72
2009	698.25	97.53	175.79	65.29	1 952.34	267.28	510.84	237.22	304.10
2010	871.19	112.78	237.26	82.28	2 285.72	327.21	615.46	246.50	304.69
2011	1 111.16	136.64	277.71	110.61	2 929.60	409.80	793.63	282.05	386.50
2012	1 338.15	148.00	340.54	135.82	3 572.66	518.60	1 036.48	338.16	439.06
2013	1 611.30	158.22	418.84	146.65	4 096.51	538.97	1 090.49	394.77	505.45
2014	1 698.06	186.11	396.31	159.63	4 437.98	594.45	1 126.71	399.48	584.08
2015	1 808.15	190.25	367.68	147.44	4 712.83	641.52	1 300.34	388.51	648.69
2016	1 812.29	369.93	167.23	148.76	5 018.86	712.92	1 462.91	476.98	692.38
2017	1 886.17	522.56		161.19	5 712.97	674.82	1 670.04	609.83	750.33
2018	1 994.35	609.35		180.67	6 075.03	842.20	1 779.99	643.28	846.23
2019	2 073.56	606.35		200.68	6 770.09	1117.20	1 815.26	650.86	915.00
2020	2 116.69	563.05		217.62	6 974.02	1100.13	2 031.38	604.15	978.77

注：1.本表中1994年以来的财政收支及分组口径调整，与历史资料不可比。
2.2006年以前农业支出包括农业支出、林业支出、水利气象支出和农林水利气象部门事业费。
3.2007年以后财政支出科目调整，对应关系为：农业支出对应农林水事务，文教科卫事业费对应文教科卫支出，行政管理费对应一般公共服务，社会保障补助支出对应社会保障和就业。
4.自2016年6月1日全面实施营改增后，取消了营业税。

Note: a.Since 1994,the local government revenue and expenditure and the grouping standard in this table are not comparable with the previous years.
b.Before 2006,the expenditure for agriculture included the spending on agriculture,forestry,water conservancy and meteorology and operating expenses for agriculture,forestry,water conservancy and meteorology.
c.After 2007, the local government expenditure category changed,the corresponding relationships are as follows:operating expense for agriculture refers to the expenditure for agriculture,forestry and water conservancy,operating expense for culture,education,science and technology and health care refers to expenditure for culture,education,science and technology and health care,operating expense for government administration refers to the expenditure for public service, operating expense for social security refers to the expenditure for social security and employment.
d.Since June 1,2016,the full implementation of replacing business tax with VAT,the business tax has been abolished.

5-2 地方一般公共预算收入（2019-2020年）
General Public Budgetary Revenue of Local Government (2019-2020)

单位：亿元 (100 million yuan)

类 别	Category	2019	2020	2020年比2019年增长(%) Increase rate in 2020 over 2019(%)
地方一般公共预算收入	**Public Budgetary Revenue of Local Government**	**2 073.56**	**2 116.69**	**2.1**
税收收入	**Tax Revenue**	**1 450.63**	**1 453.07**	**0.2**
#增值税	Value-added Tax	606.35	563.05	-7.1
企业所得税	Enterprise Income Tax	200.68	217.62	8.4
个人所得税	Personal Income Tax	48.91	49.96	2.2
资源税	Resource Tax	29.62	31.54	6.5
城市维护建设税	Tax on City Maintenance and Construction	132.79	129.97	-2.1
房产税	Tax on Real Estates	47.49	50.55	6.4
印花税	Stamp Tax	23.24	31.02	33.5
城镇土地使用税	Holding Tax on Urban and County Land	39.80	42.83	7.6
土地增值税	Land Value Added Tax	86.92	103.57	19.2
车船税	Tax on Vehicles and Their Registration	23.79	26.38	10.9
耕地占用税	Farmland Occupation Tax	33.32	25.19	-24.4
契　税	Contract Tax	118.66	120.74	1.8
烟叶税	Tobacco Leaf Tax	53.42	53.20	-0.4
其他税收收入	Others	0.67	1.58	135.6
非税收入	**Non-tax Revenue**	**622.93**	**663.62**	**6.5**
#专项收入	Specific Revenue	178.42	177.55	-0.5
行政性收费收入	Income from Administrative Fees	97.07	121.31	25.0
罚没收入	Penalty and Confiscatory Income	64.18	102.06	59.0
国有资源(资产)有偿使用收入	Revenue of Compensable Use of State-owned Resources(Assets)	186.02	184.45	-0.8
其他收入	Others	24.13	15.31	-36.5

5-3 地方一般公共预算支出（2019-2020年）

General Public Budgetary Expenditure of Local Government (2019-2020)

单位：亿元 (100 million yuan)

类　别	Item	2019	2020	2020年比2019年增长(%) Increase rate in 2020 over 2019 (%)
地方一般公共预算支出	**Public Budgetary Expenditure of Local Government**	**6 770.09**	**6 974.02**	**3.0**
一般公共服务	General Public Service	650.86	604.15	-7.2
公共安全	Public Security	382.83	388.91	1.6
教　育	Education	1 069.85	1 162.02	8.6
科学技术	Science and Technology	59.00	64.94	10.1
文化体育与传媒	Culture, Sports and Media	77.90	93.08	19.5
社会保障和就业	Social Security and Employment	915.00	978.77	7.0
卫生健康	Health	608.50	711.34	16.9
节能环保	Expenditure for Environment Protection	205.16	163.97	-20.1
城乡社区事务	Urban and Rural Community Affairs	554.02	363.78	-34.3
农林水事务	Farming, Forestry and Irrigation Affairs	1 117.20	1 100.13	-1.5
交通运输	Transport	542.81	628.49	15.8
工业商业金融等事务	Industrial,Commercial and Financial Affairs	86.21	159.63	85.2
其他各项支出	Others	500.75	554.82	10.8

5-4 各州市地方一般公共预算收入（2019-2020年）

General Public Budgetary Revenue of Local Government by Region (2019-2020)

单位：亿元　　(100 million yuan)

州　市	Region	2019	2020	2020年比2019年增长(%) Increase Rate in 2020 over 2019 (%)
全　省	**Yunnan**	**2 073.56**	**2 116.69**	**2.1**
昆　明	Kunming	630.03	650.47	3.2
曲　靖	Qujing	149.07	155.05	4.0
玉　溪	Yuxi	133.20	134.53	1.0
保　山	Baoshan	67.22	65.54	-2.5
昭　通	Zhaotong	81.81	85.01	3.9
丽　江	Lijiang	45.41	43.15	-5.0
普　洱	Pu'er	49.84	51.31	2.9
临　沧	Lincang	46.47	47.92	3.1
楚　雄	Chuxiong	87.61	90.28	3.0
红　河	Honghe	148.06	151.25	2.2
文　山	Wenshan	63.72	65.66	3.1
西双版纳	Xishuangbanna	34.74	35.81	3.1
大　理	Dali	103.27	108.48	5.0
德　宏	Dehong	40.10	42.31	5.5
怒　江	Nujiang	13.08	15.08	15.3
迪　庆	Diqing	14.10	15.01	6.4

5-5 各州市地方一般公共预算支出（2019-2020年）

General Public Budgetary Expenditure of Local Government by Region (2019-2020)

单位：亿元 (100 million yuan)

州 市	Region	2019	2020	2020年比2019年增长(%) Increase Rate in 2020 over 2019 (%)
全 省	**Yunnan**	**6 770.09**	**6 974.02**	**3.0**
昆 明	Kunming	820.86	875.05	6.6
曲 靖	Qujing	541.58	532.24	-1.7
玉 溪	Yuxi	292.69	301.57	3.0
保 山	Baoshan	270.92	270.94	0.0
昭 通	Zhaotong	640.64	625.92	-2.3
丽 江	Lijiang	172.98	175.60	1.5
普 洱	Pu'er	301.43	323.55	7.3
临 沧	Lincang	274.11	276.88	1.0
楚 雄	Chuxiong	279.56	293.61	5.0
红 河	Honghe	505.60	532.03	5.2
文 山	Wenshan	373.09	384.38	3.0
西双版纳	Xishuangbanna	139.93	133.87	-4.3
大 理	Dali	390.90	391.19	0.1
德 宏	Dehong	165.46	182.75	10.4
怒 江	Nujiang	175.73	163.18	-7.1
迪 庆	Diqing	171.31	159.47	-6.9

主要统计指标解释

地方一般公共预算收入 是指按照一定的形式和程序，由地方各级财政部门组织并纳入地方财政一般预算管理的各项收入。主要包括：

1. **税收收入：**包括国内增值税、企业所得税、个人所得税、资源税、城市维护建设税、各银行总行、各保险公司总公司集中交纳的部分、房产税、印花税、城镇土地使用税、土地增值税、车船税、耕地占用税、契税、烟叶税等。

2. **非税收入：**包括专项收入、行政事业性收费、罚没收入、国有资本经营收入、国有资源（资产）有偿使用收入和其他收入。

地方一般公共预算支出 是指地方各级财政部门对所集中的预算收入有计划地分配和使用而安排的支出。主要包括：

1. **一般公共服务：**指政府提供基本公共管理与服务的支出，包括人大事务、政协事务、政府办公厅（室）及相关机构事务、发展与改革事务、统计信息事务、财政事务、税收事务、审计事务、海关事务、人力资源事务、纪检监察事务、人口与计划生育事务、商贸事务、知识产权事务、工商行政管理事务、国土资源事务、海洋管理事务、测绘事务、地震事务、气象事务、民族事务、宗教事务、港澳台侨事务、档案事务、共产党事务、民主党派事务及工商联事务、群众团体事务、彩票事务等。

2. **公共安全：**指政府维护社会公共安全方面的支出，包括武装警察、公安、国家安全、检察、法院、司法行政、监狱、劳教、国家保密、缉私警察等。

3. **教育：**指政府教育事务支出，包括教育行政管理、学前教育、小学教育、初中教育、普通高中教育、普通高等教育、初等职业教育、中专教育、技校教育、职业高中教育、高等职业教育、广播电视教育、留学生教育、特殊教育、干部继续教育、教育机关服务等。

4. **科学技术：**指用于科学技术方面的支出，包括科学技术管理事务、基础研究、应用研究、技术研究与开发、科技条件与服务、社会科学、科学技术普及、科技交流与合作等。

5. **文化教育与传媒：**指政府在文化、文物、体育、广播影视、新闻出版等方面的支出。

6. **社会保障和就业：**指政府在社会保障与就业方面的支出，包括社会保障和就业管理事务、民政管理事务、财政对社会保险基金的补助、补充全国社会保障基金、行政事业单位离退休、企业改革补助、就业补助、抚恤、退役安置、社会福利、残疾人事业、城市居民最低生活保障、其他城镇社会救济、农村社会救济、自然灾害生活救助、红十字事务等。

7. **城乡社区事务：**指政府城乡社区事务支出，包括城乡社区管理事务支出、城乡社区规划与管理支出、城乡社区公共设施支出、城乡社区住宅支出、城乡社区环境卫生支出、建设市场管理与监督支出等。

8. **农林水事务：**指政府农林水事务支出，包括农业支出、林业支出、水利支出、扶贫支出、农业综合开发支出等。

9. **交通运输：**指政府交通运输和邮政业方面的支出，包括公路运输支出、水路运输支出、铁路运输支出、民用航空运输支出、邮政业支出等。

10. **工业商业金融等事务：**指政府对工业、商业及金融等方面的支出，包括采掘业支出、制造业支出、建筑业支出、工业和信息产业监管支出、国有资产监管支出、商业流通事务支出、金融业监管支出、旅游业管理与服务支出等。

Explanatory Notes on Main Statistical Indicators

Local Government Budgetary Revenue refers to incomes which were organized and managed by the financial departments of local governments at all levels according to certain forms and procedures.

The contents of the local government budgetary revenue include the following main items:

a.Tax Revenues, including domestic value added tax (VAT), VAT and consumption tax from imports, VAT and consumption tax rebate for exports, business tax, corporate income tax, individual income tax, resource tax, city maintenance and construct tax, house property tax, stamp tax, urban land use tax, land appreciation tax, tax on vehicles and boat operation, ship tonnage tax, vehicle purchase tax, tariffs, farm land occupation tax, deed tax, and tobacco leaf tax, etc.

b.Non-tax revenue, including special program receipts, charge of administrative and institutional units, penalty receipts and others non-tax receipts.

Local Government Budgetary Expenditure refers to the planned distribution and use of the raised budgetary revenue by the financial departments of local government at all levels.

It includes the following main items:

a.Expenditure for general public services: It refers to the spending on the basic public management and services which provided by governments, including the expense on affairs of People's Congress, affairs of People's Political Consultative Conference, affairs of government general office and relative institutions, affairs of development and reform, affairs of statistics, affairs of finance, affairs of taxation, affairs of audit, affairs of customs, affairs of human resources and social security, affairs of discipline inspection and supervision, affairs of population and family planning, affairs of commerce and trade, affairs of intellectual property, affairs of administration for industry and commerce, affairs of land and resources, affairs of oceanic administration, affairs of surveying and mapping, affairs of earthquake, ethnic affairs, religious affairs, affairs of Hong Kong, Macao, Taiwan, and Overseas Chinese, affairs of archives administration, affairs of Chinese Communist Party, affairs of democratic parties and federation of industry and commerce, affairs of mass organization, and affairs of lottery, etc.

b.Expenditure for public security: It refers to the spending of government on maintaining social and public security, including the expense on armed police force, public security, state security, prosecution, courts, justice, prison, labour education and rehabilitation, protection of state secrecy, anti-smuggling police, etc.

c.Expenditure for education: It refers to the spending of government on education, including the expense on the administration of education, pre-primary education, primary education, secondary education, high school education, regular higher education, primary vocational education, secondary vocational education, technical school education, vocational high school education and higher vocational education, radio and television education, student abroad education, special education, on the job training of cadres, education authorities services, etc.

d.Expenditure for Science and Technology: It refers to the spending of government on science and technology (S&T), including the expense on the administration of S&T, basic research, applied research, research and development, conditions and services of S&T, popularization of social science, science and technology, exchanges and cooperation of S&T, etc.

e.Expenditure for Culture, Sport and Media: It refers to the spending of government on culture, cultural heritage, sports, radio, film, television, press and publication, etc.

f.Expenditure for Social Safety Net And Employment Effort: It refers to the spending of government on social safety net and employment, including the expense on administration of social safety net and employment, civil affairs, budgetary subsidy on the social insurance funds, subsidy on National Social Security Fund, retirees of administrative units and institutions, subsidy on enterprise reform, subsidy on employment effort, pension, placement of ex-serviceman, social welfare, the handicapped undertakings, the system of cost of living allowances for urban residents, other urban social relief, rural social relief, living relief of natural disasters, affairs of Red Cross Society, etc.

g.Expenditure for Urban and Rural Community Affairs: It refers to the spending of government on urban and rural community affairs, including the expense on administration of urban and rural community, planning and management of urban and rural community, public facilities of urban and rural community, housing of urban and rural community, sanitation of urban and rural community, management and supervision on the construction market, etc.

h.Expenditure for Agriculture, Forestry and Irrigation Affairs: It refers to the spending of government on agriculture, forestry and irrigation affairs, including the expense on agriculture, forestry, irrigation affairs, poverty alleviation, comprehensive agricultural development, etc.

i.Expenditure for Transportation: It refers to the spending of government on transportation and postal services, including the expense on road transportation, waterway transportation, railway transportation, civil aviation transportation, and postal services.

j.Expenditure for Industry, Commerce and Banking: It refers to the spending of government on industry, commerce and banking, including the expense on mining, manufacturing, construction, industry and information technology supervision and administration, State-owned assets supervision and administration, commerce and circulation affairs, financial intermediation supervision and administration, tourism administration and service, etc.

Chapter 6

六、对外经济贸易
Foreign Trade

6-1 进出口贸易总额（1980-2020年）

Total Value of Import and Export Trade (1980-2020)

单位：亿美元 (USD 100 million)

年份 Year	进出口总额 Total Value of Export and Import	出口额 Exports	进口额 Imports	差额 Balance
1980	1.10	0.96	0.14	0.82
1981	1.35	1.03	0.31	0.72
1982	1.36	1.09	0.27	0.82
1983	1.47	1.19	0.29	0.90
1984	1.51	1.11	0.39	0.72
1985	2.10	1.29	0.81	0.48
1986	2.65	1.69	0.96	0.72
1987	3.42	2.62	0.80	1.82
1988	4.44	3.42	1.02	2.40
1989	5.48	3.74	1.73	2.01
1990	5.48	4.34	1.14	3.21
1991	5.51	4.01	1.50	2.51
1992	6.71	4.67	2.04	2.63
1993	8.40	5.23	3.17	2.06
1994	13.44	9.10	4.34	4.76
1995	18.96	12.15	6.81	5.35
1996	19.22	10.96	8.26	2.70
1997	19.37	11.72	7.65	4.08
1998	19.03	11.74	7.30	4.44
1999	16.60	10.34	6.25	4.09
2000	18.13	11.75	6.38	5.37
2001	19.89	12.44	7.45	4.99
2002	22.26	14.30	7.97	6.33
2003	26.77	16.77	9.91	6.85
2004	37.48	22.39	15.09	7.30
2005	47.38	26.42	20.97	5.45
2006	62.32	33.91	28.40	5.51
2007	87.80	47.36	40.44	6.92
2008	95.99	49.87	46.12	3.75
2009	80.19	45.14	35.05	10.09
2010	133.68	76.06	57.62	18.43
2011	160.53	94.73	65.80	28.93
2012	210.05	100.18	109.87	-9.69
2013	258.29	159.59	98.70	60.88
2014	296.22	188.02	108.20	79.82
2015	245.27	166.26	79.01	87.25
2016	199.99	115.82	84.17	31.65
2017	233.94	114.30	119.64	-5.33
2018	298.95	128.12	170.83	-42.71
2019	336.92	150.22	186.70	-36.48
2020	389.46	221.40	168.06	53.34

6-2 主要贸易方式进出口总额（1980-2020年）

Total Value of Main Trade Modes of Import and Export (1980-2020)

单位：亿美元 (USD 100 million)

年 份 Year	进出口总额 Total Value of Export and Import	出口额 Exports	#一般贸易 Ordinary Trade	边境小额贸易 Small-scale Border Trade	进口额 Imports	#一般贸易 Ordinary Trade	边境小额贸易 Small-scale Border Trade
1980	1.10	0.96			0.14		
1981	1.35	1.03			0.31		
1982	1.36	1.09			0.27		
1983	1.47	1.19			0.29		
1984	1.51	1.11			0.39		
1985	2.10	1.29		0.21	0.81		0.23
1986	2.65	1.69		0.28	0.96		0.31
1987	3.42	2.62		0.61	0.80		0.64
1988	4.44	3.42		1.31	1.02		1.01
1989	5.48	3.74		1.66	1.73		0.90
1990	5.48	4.34		1.28	1.14		0.75
1991	5.51	4.01		1.03	1.50		0.53
1992	6.71	4.67		1.55	2.04		0.75
1993	8.40	5.23		2.08	3.17		0.77
1994	13.44	9.10		1.46	4.34		1.11
1995	18.96	12.15		1.18	6.81		1.13
1996	19.22	10.96		0.45	8.26		0.91
1997	19.37	11.72		0.42	7.65		0.32
1998	19.03	11.31	9.25	0.89	5.22	3.60	0.42
1999	16.60	10.34	7.23	2.32	6.25	4.71	0.56
2000	18.13	11.75	7.84	2.78	6.38	4.21	0.78
2001	19.89	12.44	8.66	2.30	7.45	5.25	1.16
2002	22.26	14.29	10.57	2.31	7.97	5.25	1.37
2003	26.77	16.76	12.82	2.53	9.92	6.97	1.66
2004	37.48	22.39	16.73	3.09	15.04	11.27	2.15
2005	47.38	26.42	18.24	3.86	20.97	15.21	2.69
2006	62.32	33.91	22.34	4.65	28.40	20.28	3.11
2007	87.80	47.36	34.54	5.68	40.44	30.15	4.43
2008	95.99	49.87	39.96	5.72	46.12	37.51	6.29
2009	80.19	45.14	35.85	7.07	35.05	27.74	5.54
2010	133.68	76.03	44.34	9.88	57.62	47.23	7.47
2011	160.53	94.73	67.98	12.16	65.80	53.32	7.88
2012	210.05	100.18	48.33	13.95	109.87	64.45	7.54
2013	258.29	159.59	102.13	18.47	98.70	39.98	14.87
2014	296.22	188.02	130.75	21.79	108.20	50.29	14.00
2015	245.27	166.26	136.50	16.75	79.01	40.26	8.16
2016	199.99	115.82	86.36	17.51	84.17	37.71	11.96
2017	233.94	114.30	78.86	19.32	119.64	56.09	14.90
2018	298.95	128.12	90.05	19.23	170.83	104.56	13.52
2019	336.92	150.22	107.09	21.18	186.70	122.12	10.90
2020	389.46	221.40	166.56	17.63	168.06	108.70	11.80

6-3 边境贸易进出口总额（1997-2020年）
Total Value of Imports and Exports of Border Trade (1997-2020)

单位：亿美元 (USD 100 million)

年份 Year	边境贸易进出口总额 Total Value of Export and Import Of Border Trade	出口额 Exports	进口额 Imports
1997	0.74	0.42	0.32
1998	1.31	0.89	0.42
1999	2.78	2.32	0.56
2000	3.56	2.78	0.78
2001	3.46	2.30	1.16
2002	3.68	2.31	1.37
2003	4.19	2.53	1.66
2004	5.24	3.09	2.15
2005	6.55	3.86	2.69
2006	7.76	4.65	3.11
2007	10.11	5.68	4.43
2008	12.01	5.72	6.29
2009	12.61	7.07	5.54
2010	17.36	9.88	7.47
2011	20.05	12.16	7.88
2012	21.49	13.95	7.54
2013	33.34	18.47	14.87
2014	35.79	21.79	14.00
2015	24.91	16.75	8.16
2016	29.47	17.51	11.96
2017	34.23	19.32	14.90
2018	32.75	19.23	13.52
2019	31.08	20.18	10.90
2020	29.43	17.63	11.80

6-4 各州市进出口总额（2020年）

Total Value of Import and Export by Region (2020)

单位：亿美元 (USD 100 million)

州市	Region	进出口总额 Total Value of Import and Export	出口额 Exports	2020年比2019年增长(%) Increase Rate in 2020 Over 2019(%)	进口额 Imports	2020年比2019年增长(%) Increase Rate in 2020 Over 2019(%)	2020年比2019年增长(%) Increase Rate in 2020 Over 2019(%)
全省	**Yunnan**	**389.46**	**221.40**	**47.4**	**168.06**	**-10.0**	**15.6**
昆明	Kunming	160.59	77.45	114.8	83.15	-13.2	21.8
曲靖	Qujing	13.99	13.73	16.0	0.26	58.2	16.5
玉溪	Yuxi	36.35	34.65	15.0	1.71	160.8	18.1
保山	Baoshan	5.89	1.32	-30.4	4.57	-10.5	-15.9
昭通	Zhaotong	0.28	0.28	81.1			82.2
丽江	Lijiang	0.46	0.45	-9.7	0.01		-6.5
普洱	Pu'er	9.91	2.55	-1.1	7.37	-10.2	-8.0
临沧	Lincang	7.94	2.81	0.7	5.14	-15.0	-10.0
楚雄	Chuxiong	14.47	14.40	43.0	0.06	97.7	43.1
红河	Honghe	58.71	35.95	58.4	22.75	-8.8	23.2
文山	Wenshan	2.59	0.48	17.5	2.11	-30.4	-24.7
西双版纳	Xishuangbanna	17.70	4.93	89.2	12.77	-13.8	1.6
大理	Dali	1.76	1.69	0.1	0.05	-54.1	-3.5
德宏	Dehong	57.47	30.45	14.8	27.01	-0.9	6.8
怒江	Nujiang	1.28	0.20	-6.2	1.08	121.5	82.4
迪庆	Diqing	0.05	0.05	-15.0			-21.2

6-5 引进利用外资概况（1987-2020年）
Utilization of Foreign Capital (1987-2020)

年　份 Year	协议利用外资 Utilization of Foreign Capital		对 外 借 款 Foreign Borrowings		外商直接投资 Foreign Direct Investment		外商其他投资 Other Foreign Investment	
	项 目 (个) Number of Projects (unit)	金 额 (亿美元) Value (USD 100 million)	项 目 (个) Number of Projects (unit)	金 额 (亿美元) Value (USD 100 million)	项 目 (个) Number of Projects (unit)	金 额 (亿美元) Value (USD 100 million)	项 目 (个) Number of Projects (unit)	金 额 (亿美元) Value (USD 100 million)
签订利用外资协议(合同)额 Total Amount of Contracted Foreign Capital								
1987	9	0.14			9	0.11		0.04
1988	9		1		8			
1989	10	0.04			10	0.03		0.01
1990	16				11			
1991	31	0.60		0.34	22	0.16	6	0.10
1992	202				202			
1993	509	5.64			509	5.01		0.63
1994	262				262			
1995	277		8		269			
1996	159		6		153			
1997	135	3.25	8	0.57	127	2.67		
1998	122		3		119			
1999	140		2		138			
2000	110		4		106			
2001	140	2.94			140	2.94		
2002	150				150			
2003	167	5.44			167	5.44		
2004	167				167			
2005	152	4.36			152	4.36		
2006	204				204			
2007	170	9.66			170	9.66		
2008	228				228			
2009	190	16.82			190	16.82		
2010	163				163			
2011	163	21.54			163	21.54		
2012	121	10.95			121	10.95		
2013	116	12.14			116	12.14		
2014	132	10.82			132	10.82		
2015	142	22.58			142	22.58		
2016	134	26.54			134	26.54		
2017	215	51.61			215	51.61		
2018	182	82.79			182	82.79		
2019	236	55.45			236	55.45		
2020	267	36.76			267	36.76		

注：从1991年起实际利用外资额中对外借款从国家外汇管理局云南分局取得数字，1990年以前是从中国银行昆明分行取得数字。1994年后对外借款从云南省发改委外经处取得数字。

Note:Since 1991,data of borrowings in the foreign investment actually used have been obtained from Yunnan Branch of State Foreign Exchange Admistration Bureau,Before 1990,they were obtained from Kunming Branch of Bank of China. Since 1994, data of foreign exchange borrowings have been obtained from Foreign Trade Section of Provincial Development and Reform Commission.

6-5 续表 continued

年 份 Year	协议利用外资 Utilization of Foreign Capital		对外借款 Foreign Borrowings		外商直接投资 Foreign Direct Investment		外商其他投资 Other Foreign Investment	
	项目（个） Number of Projects (unit)	金额（亿美元） Value (USD 100 million)	项目（个） Number of Projects (unit)	金额（亿美元） Value (USD 100 million)	项目（个） Number of Projects (unit)	金额（亿美元） Value (USD 100 million)	项目（个） Number of Projects (unit)	金额（亿美元） Value (USD 100 million)
实际利用外资金额 Total Amount of Foreign Capital Actually Used								
1987								
1988		0.08				0.03		0.05
1989								
1990				0.04		0.03		0.05
1991								
1992		0.50		0.21		0.23		0.06
1993								
1994		3.14		1.11		2.03		
1995			27					
1996		3.38		1.58		1.80		
1997								
1998		2.98		1.52		1.46		
1999								
2000								
2001								
2002		2.84		1.72		1.12		
2003								
2004		2.14		0.73		1.42		
2005								
2006		4.29		1.27		3.02		
2007								
2008		9.36		1.59		7.77		
2009								
2010		13.29				13.29		
2011		17.38				17.38		
2012		21.89				21.89		
2013		25.15				25.15		
2014		27.06				27.06		
2015		29.92				29.92		
2016		8.67				8.67		
2017		9.63				9.63		
2018		10.56				10.56		
2019		7.23				7.23		
2020		7.59				7.59		

注：2016年起实际利用外资数据为新口径
Note: The data of actually utilization of foreign capital are new caliber since 2016.

6-6 分行业利用外商直接投资情况（2020年）

Utilization of Foreign Direct Investment by Sector (2020)

单位：亿美元 (USD 100 million)

国民经济行业	National Economic Sector	协议投资 Contracted Investment		实际投资金额 Actual Investment Amount
		项目(个) Number of Projects(unit)	金额 Value	
全　省	**Yunnan**	**267**	**36.76**	**7.59**
农、林、牧、渔业	Farming,Forestry,Animal Husbandry and Fishery	19	2.72	0.11
采矿业	Mining and Quarrying	2	0.19	–
制造业	Manufacturing	12	0.79	0.68
电力、煤气及水生产和供应业	Production and Supply of Electricity,Gas and Water	3	1.31	0.11
建筑业	Construction	4	1.63	–
地质勘查、水利管理业	Geological Prospecting and Water Conservancy	–		–
交通运输、仓储及邮电通信业	Transport,Storage,Postal and Telecommunication Services	4	0.02	0.60
批发和零售贸易餐饮业	Wholesale and Retail Trade and Food Services	119	15.45	2.98
房地产业	Real Estate	12	1.89	1.72
社会服务业	Social Services	92	12.73	1.37
卫生体育和社会福利业	Health Care,Sports and Social Welfare	–	–	–
教育、文化艺术和广播电影电视业	Education,Culture and Arts,Broadcasting,Film and Television	–	–	–
科学研究和综合技术服务业	Scientific Research and Polytechnic Services	–	–	–
其他行业	Others	–	–	–

6-7 各州市利用外商直接投资情况（2019-2020年）
Utilization of Foreign Direct Investment by Region (2019-2020)

单位：亿美元 (USD 100 million)

州市	Region	协议投资 Contracted Investment				实际投资金额 Actual Investment	
		项目(个) Number of Projects (unit)		金额 Value			
		2019	2020	2019	2020	2019	2020
全省	**Yunnan**	**236**	**267**	**55.45**	**36.76**	**7.23**	**7.59**
昆明	Kunming	116	165	29.32	17.99	6.49	6.62
曲靖	Qujing	9	4	0.32	10.02	0.03	0.12
玉溪	Yuxi	6	7	0.50	0.11	0.10	0.02
保山	Baoshan	5	4	0.35	3.62	0.04	0.19
昭通	Zhaotong	3	4	0.06	0.12		0.01
丽江	Lijiang	10	8	0.47	0.24	0.11	
普洱	Pu'er	1		0.17	0.96	0.07	
临沧	Lincang	1					
楚雄	Chuxiong	16	7	0.38	0.28	0.03	0.05
红河	Honghe	13	19	16.27	3.48	0.08	0.36
文山	Wenshan	3	2	0.05	0.20		
西双版纳	Xishuangbanna	4	14	0.04	0.14	0.12	0.06
大理	Dali	13	14	0.07	0.28	0.04	
德宏	Dehong	27	19	0.28	0.28	0.08	0.10
怒江	Nujiang	3		0.15			
迪庆	Diqing	2			-0.99		
省直	Those Directly under Provincial Government	4		7.00			

6-8 实际利用外资额（2015-2020年）

Foreign Investment Actually Utilized (2015-2020)

单位：亿美元 (USD 100 million)

项　　目	Item	2015	2016	2017	2018	2019	2020
全　省	**Yunnan**	**29.92**	**8.67**	**9.63**	**10.56**	**7.23**	**7.59**
外商直接投资	Foreign Direct Investment	29.92	8.67	9.63	10.56	7.23	7.59
合资经营企业	Joint Ventures	7.45	2.71	1.03	3.88	1.09	
合作经营企业	Cooperative Enterprises	3.64	0.03	0.04	0.04		
独资企业	Sole Proprietorship Enterprises	17.51	3.47	5.05	4.18	6.13	
外商投资股份制企业	Foreign-funded Joint Stock Enterprises	1.32	2.46	3.51	2.46		

6–9 对外承包工程和劳务合作（1991–2020年）
Contracted Projects and Labor Cooperation with Foreign Countries (1991-2020)

单位：亿美元 (USD 100 million)

年 份 Year	合同份数（份） Number of Contracts (unit)	合同金额 Contracted Value	完成营业额 Value of Business Fulfilled
承包工程 Contracted Projects			
1991	19	0.11	0.08
1992	6	0.15	0.15
1993	3	0.40	0.26
1994	15	1.02	0.21
1995	46	2.20	1.01
1996	25	0.78	1.22
1997	47	0.77	0.91
1998	72	3.06	0.99
1999	120	2.50	1.25
2000	162	2.96	1.53
2001	60	1.53	1.45
2002	107	2.94	2.25
2003	71	3.07	2.44
2004	83	3.16	3.36
2005	131	5.34	3.87
2006	85	6.04	4.33
2007	96	7.00	4.99
2008	94	7.80	6.17
2009	63	9.24	7.38
2010	22	9.71	9.85
2011	47	11.21	11.45
2012	52	12.77	15.48
2013	55	12.81	18.17
2014	44	13.44	20.70
2015	95	12.86	23.42
2016	48	19.19	25.75
2017	99	13.63	17.03
2018	87	14.25	17.27
2019	51	15.30	13.14
2020	17	7.25	9.70
劳务合作 Labor Consultation Service			
1991	4	0.01	
1992	3	0.01	
1993	9	0.01	
1994	7	0.03	0.01
1995	7	0.02	0.01
1996	9	0.02	0.01
1997	13	0.10	0.03
1998	11	0.04	0.01
1999	14	0.02	0.03
2000	8	0.04	0.02
2001	9	0.02	0.01
2002	2		0.01
2003	2	0.01	
2004	2		0.01
2005	1		
2006			
2007	2	0.01	0.02
2008	6	0.15	0.04
2009	26	0.06	0.04
2010	16	0.05	0.05

注：从2009年起承包工程统计包括设计咨询在内。
Note: Since 2009, statistics of design consultation had been included in that of construction projects under contract.

6-10 云南省对主要国家或地区出口总额（2019-2020年）
Total Value of Provincial Exports to Major Countries and Regions (2019-2020)

单位：万美元

(USD 10 thousand)

国家或地区	Country or Region	2019	2020	2020年比2019年增长(%) Increase Rate in 2020 Over 2019 (%)
亚洲小计	**Asia**	**1 251 592**	**1 560 660**	**24.7**
阿富汗	Afghanistan	240	187	- 22.1
孟加拉国	Bangladesh	5 879	10 045	70.9
文　莱	Brunei	116	295	154.3
缅　甸	Myanmar	334 797	373 752	11.6
柬埔寨	Cambodia	3 243	7 325	125.8
朝　鲜	The Democratic People's Republic of Korea	4	–	–
中国香港	Hong Kong,China	254 269	236 322	- 7.1
中国澳门	Macao, China	1 109	406	- 63.4
中国台湾	Taiwan,China	8 818	10 012	13.5
印　度	India	66 411	76 893	15.8
印度尼西亚	Indonesia	43 844	40 361	- 7.9
伊　朗	Iran	8 033	6 833	- 14.9
以色列	Israel	862	6 064	603.5
日　本	Japan	17 439	39 179	124.6
约　旦	Jordan	390	1 036	165.6
科威特	Kuwait	152	2 528	1 563.2
老　挝	Laos	40 043	25 273	- 36.9
黎巴嫩	Lebanon	154	460	198.7
马来西亚	Malaysia	25 775	47 266	83.4
尼泊尔	Nepal	1 681	–	–
阿　曼	Oman	151	2 320	1 436.4
巴基斯坦	Pakistan	3 571	6 588	84.5
菲律宾	Philippines	15 469	25 291	63.5
沙特阿拉伯	Saudi Arabia	1 811	34 620	1 811.7
新加坡	Singapore	20 114	54 031	168.6
韩　国	Korea	13 365	28 734	115.0
斯里兰卡	Sri Lanka	2 061	2 954	43.3
叙利亚	Syria	264	166	- 37.1
泰　国	Thailand	89 480	103 925	16.1
土耳其	Turkey	3 008	5 805	93.0
阿联酋	United Arab Emirates	6 310	18 623	195.1
越　南	Vietnam	278 524	383 991	37.9
非洲小计	**Africa**	**11 960**	**35 588**	**197.4**
阿尔及利亚	Algeria	412	979	137.6
埃　及	Egypt	1 984	6 882	246.9
埃塞俄比亚	Ethiopia	101	295	192.1
肯尼亚	Kenya	244	2 293	839.8
毛里求斯	Mauritius	36	706	1 861.1
摩洛哥	Morocco	723	1 604	121.9

6—10 续表1 continued

单位：万美元 (USD 10 thousand)

国家或地区	Country or Region	2019	2020	2020年比2019年增长(%) Increase Rate in 2020 Over 2019(%)
尼日尔	Niger	10		
尼日利亚	Nigeria	1 557	3 824	145.6
南非(阿扎尼亚)	South Africa (Azania)	1 387	5 804	318.5
多　哥	Togo	182	575	215.9
津巴布韦	Zimbabwe	38	20	-47.4
欧洲小计	**Europe**	**105 415**	**204 332**	**93.8**
比利时	Belgium	11 258	20 737	84.2
丹　麦	Denmark	331	904	173.1
英　国	United Kingdom	19 316	45 623	136.2
德　国	Germany	18 005	29 428	63.5
法　国	France	5 271	9 891	87.6
爱尔兰	Ireland	64	274	328.1
意大利	Italy	9 747	27 552	182.7
荷　兰	Netherlands	15 445	24 882	61.1
希　腊	Greece	2 440	7 110	191.4
葡萄牙	Portugal	726	1 337	84.2
西班牙	Spain	6 925	10 114	46.1
奥地利	Austria	13	36	176.9
保加利亚	Bulgaria	73	51	-30.1
芬　兰	Finland	234	205	-12.4
匈牙利	Hungary	34	171	402.9
马耳他	Malta	300	388	29.3
挪　威	Norway	106	236	122.6
波　兰	Poland	6 279	6 251	-0.6
罗马尼亚	Romania	650	1 623	149.7
瑞　典	Sweden	474	1 591	235.7
瑞　士	Switzerland	430	477	10.9
拉脱维亚	Latvia	47	58	23.4
立陶宛	Lithuania	174	330	89.7
俄罗斯联邦	Russia	4 284	9 037	110.9
乌克兰	Ukraine	535	2 235	317.8
南斯拉夫	Yugoslavia			
斯洛文尼亚	Slovenia	1 151	1 189	3.3
捷　克	Czech	231	678	193.5
拉丁美洲小计	**Latin America**	**40 977**	**78 006**	**90.4**
阿根廷	Argentina	6 812	13 731	101.6
巴　西	Brazil	17 502	20 428	16.7
智　利	Chile	3 066	7 645	149.3
哥伦比亚	Colombia	553	3 792	585.7
多米尼克	Dominica			

6–10 续表2 continued

单位：万美元 (USD 10 thousand)

国家或地区	Country or Region	2019	2020	2020年比2019年增长(%) Increase Rate in 2020 Over 2019 (%)
古 巴	Cuba	133	80	- 39.8
多米尼加共和国	Republic of Dominican	137	715	421.9
海 地	Haiti	57	138	142.1
墨西哥	Mexico	5 862	14 482	147.0
巴拿马	Panama	847	4 607	443.9
巴拉圭	Paraguay	77	133	72.7
秘 鲁	Peru	2 879	6 201	115.4
波多黎各	Puerto Rico	14	118	742.9
圣卢西亚岛	Saint Lucia			
萨尔瓦多	El Salvador	82	132	61.0
乌拉圭	Uruguay	2 116	1 983	- 6.3
委内瑞拉	Venezuela	62	489	688.7
北美洲小计	**North America**	**63 890**	**283 712**	**343.1**
加拿大	Canada	11 284	39 955	254.1
美 国	United States	52 605	243 757	362.1
大洋洲小计	**Oceanica**	**28 360**	**51 737**	**82.4**
澳大利亚	Australia	26 977	47 867	77.4
斐 济	Fiji	16	222	1 287.5
新西兰	New Zealand	1 260	3 196	153.4
巴布亚新几内亚	Papua New Guinea	35	142	305.7
合计中：东南亚国家联盟	**Total of ASEAN**	**851 407**	**1 061 509**	**24.7**
合计中：欧洲联盟	**Total of European Union**	**98 572**	**145 234**	**81.2**

6-11 云南省对主要国家或地区进口总额（2019-2020年）

Total Value of Provincial Imports from Major Countries and Regions (2019-2020)

单位：万美元 (USD 10 thousand)

国家或地区	Country or Region	2019	2020	2020年比2019年增长(%) Increase Rate in 2020 Over 2019 (%)
亚洲小计	**Asia**	**1 458 824**	**1 247 331**	**- 14.5**
缅　甸	Myanmar	478 088	439 208	- 8.1
中国香港	Hong Kong,China	566	474	- 16.3
中国澳门	Macao,China			
中国台湾	Taiwan,China	86 601	101 437	17.1
印　度	India	4 513	6 793	50.0
印度尼西亚	Indonesia	1 000	9 496	849.6
伊　朗	Iran	27 940	428	- 98.5
以色列	Israel	1 160	955	- 17.7
日　本	Japan	6 886	5 313	- 22.8
科威特	Kuwait	51 345	74 779	45.6
老　挝	Laos	86 019	87 476	1.8
马来西亚	Malaysia	1 324	2 139	62.2
菲律宾	Philippines	1 044	47	- 95.8
卡塔尔	Qatar	9 274	14 166	52.7
沙特阿拉伯	Saudi Arabia	266 109	163 276	- 38.6
新加坡	Singapore	1 350	2 482	83.9
韩　国	Korea	1 533	5 750	275.1
泰　国	Thailand	68 650	57 731	- 15.9
阿联酋	United Arab Emirates	74 339	70 541	- 5.1
越　南	Vietnam	168 731	125 122	- 25.9

6-11 续表 continued

单位：万美元 (USD 10 thousand)

国家或地区	Country or Region	2019	2020	2020年比2019年增长(%) Increase Rate in 2020 Over 2019 (%)
非洲小计	**Africa**	**19 601**	**50 539**	**160.7**
南非(阿扎尼亚)	South Africa	7 186	20 637	180.1
坦桑尼亚	Tanzania	53	16	- 69.8
欧洲小计	**Europe**	**81 797**	**94 345**	**15.1**
比利时	Belgium	442	628	42.1
丹　麦	Denmark	223	72	- 67.7
英　国	United Kingdom	847	2 537	199.5
德　国	Federal Republic of Germany	8 155	5 044	- 38.1
法　国	France	2 463	2 480	0.7
爱尔兰	Ireland	43		
意大利	Italy	2 391	16 539	591.7
荷　兰	Netherlands	7 577	5 360	- 29.3
西班牙	Spain	12 499	9 525	- 24.5
奥地利	Austria	1 138	533	- 53.2
芬　兰	Finland	469	163	- 65.2
罗马尼亚	Romania	41	496	1 109.8
瑞　典	Sweden	1 425	3 175	122.8
瑞　士	Switzerland	491	544	10.8
哈萨克斯坦	Kazakhstan			
俄罗斯联邦	Russia	24 444	38 113	55.4
乌克兰	Ukraine	19	316	1 563.2
拉丁美洲小计	**Latin America**	**257 647**	**247 836**	**- 3.8**
阿根廷	Argentina	591	783	32.5
巴　西	Brazil	63 233	71 561	13.4
智　利	Chile	90 326	41 094	- 54.5
圭亚那	Guyana			
墨西哥	Mexico	15 199	43 020	184.6
秘　鲁	Peru	82 089	75 594	- 7.8
北美洲小计	**North America**	**14 921**	**12 858**	**- 13.9**
加拿大	Canada	8 472	2 878	66.1
美　国	United States	6 448	9 980	54.8
大洋洲小计	**Oceanica**	**33 085**	**26 644**	**- 19.1**
澳大利亚	Australia	31 096	25 106	- 18.8
新西兰	New Zealand	1 139	570	- 50.0
东南亚国家联盟	**Total of ASEAN**	**806 207**	**723 706**	**- 10.2**
欧洲联盟	**Total of European Union**	**38 774**	**44 594**	**17.0**

6-12 实际利用外商直接投资额（按国别或地区分）（2019-2020年）
Actually Utilized Foreign Direct Investment by Country and Region (2019-2020)

单位：万美元 (USD 10 thousand)

国家或地区	Country or Region	2019	2020
总　计	**Total**	**72 262**	**75 854**
亚 洲	**Asia**		
#中国香港	Hong Kong,China	63 136	70 608
中国台湾	Taiwan,China	61	93
中国澳门	Macao,China	13	100
菲律宾	Philippines		
泰　国	Thailand	422	28
新加坡	Singapore	7 668	3 246
马来西亚	Malaysia	7	
日　本	Japan		202
韩　国	Korea	338	9
缅　甸	Myanmar		
非 洲	**Africa**		
欧 洲	**Europe**		
#德　国	Germany		
法　国	France		4
意大利	Italy		
荷　兰	Netherlands	14	
英　国	United Kingdom	13	192
比利时	Belgium		
丹　麦	Denmark		
爱尔兰	Ireland		
希　腊	Greece		
葡萄牙	Portugal		
西班牙	Spain		
芬　兰	Finland		
瑞　士	Switzerland		
俄罗斯联邦	Russia		
拉丁美洲	**Latin America**		
#巴　西	Brazil		
维尔京群岛	Virgin Islands	15	
开曼群岛	Cayman Islands		
北美洲	**North America**		
#加拿大	Canada		
美　国	United States	139	164
大洋洲	**Oceanica**		
#澳大利亚	Australia	37	
新西兰	New Zealand		
其　他	**Others**		

主要统计指标解释

货物进出口总额 指实际进出我国国境的货物总金额。包括对外贸易实际进出口货物，来料加工装配进出口货物，国家间、联合国及国际组织无偿援助物资和赠送品，华侨、港澳台同胞和外籍华人捐赠品，租赁期满归承租人所有的租赁货物，进料加工进出口货物，边境地方贸易及边境地区小额贸易进出口货物(边民互市贸易除外)，中外合资企业、中外合作经营企业、外商独资经营企业进出口货物和公用物品，到、离岸价格在规定限额以上的进出口货样和广告品(无商业价值、无使用价值和免费提供出口的除外)，从保税仓库提取在中国境内销售的进口货物，以及其他进出口货物。该指标可以观察一个国家在对外贸易方面的总规模。我国规定出口货物按离岸价格统计，进口货物按到岸价格统计。

商品经营单位所在地进、出口额 指在所在地海关注册登记的有进出口经营权的企业实际进、出口额。

商品目的地进口额和商品货源地出口额 目的地进口额指进口货物的消费、使用或最终抵运地的实际进口额；货源地出口额指出口货物的产地或原始发货地的实际出口额。

服务进出口 指常住单位与非常住单位之间相互提供的服务。包括运输服务、旅游服务、通信服务、建筑服务、保险服务、金融服务、计算机和信息服务、咨询服务、广告宣传服务、电影音像服务、专有权利使用费和特许费、其他商务服务。不包括政府服务。

外商直接投资 是指外国投资者在我国境内通过设立外商投资企业、合伙企业、与中方投资者共同进行石油资源的合作勘探开发以及设立外国公司分支机构等方式进行投资。外国投资者可以用现金、实物、无形资产、股权等投资，还可以用从外商投资企业获得的利润进行再投资。

外商其他投资 指除对外借款和外商直接投资以外的各种利用外资的形式。包括企业在境内外股票市场公开发行的以外币计价的股票发行价总额，国际租赁进口设备的应付款，补偿贸易中外商提供的进口设备、技术、物料的价款，加工装配贸易中外商提供的进口设备、物料的价款。

对外直接投资 指我国企业、团体等(简称境内投资主体)在国外及港澳台地区以现金、实物、无形资产等方式投资，并以控制国(境)外企业的经营管理权为核心的经济活动。对外直接投资的内涵主要体现在一经济体通过投资于另一经济体而实现其持久利益的目标。

对外承包工程 根据《对外承包工程管理条例》，对外承包工程是指中国的企业或者其他单位承包境外建设工程项目的活动。

对外劳务合作 指组织劳务人员赴其他国家或地区为国外的企业或机构工作的经营性活动。

Explanatory Notes on Main Statistical Indicators

Total Import and Export of Goods refer to the real value of commodities imported and exported across the border of China. They include the actual imports and exports through foreign trade, imported and exported goods under the processing and assembling trades and materials, supplies and gifts as aid given gratis between governments and by the United Nations and other international organizations, and contributions donated by overseas Chinese, compatriots in Hong Kong and Macao and Chinese with foreign citizenship, leasing commodities owned by tenant at the expiration of leasing period, the imported and exported commodities processed with imported materials, commodities trading in border areas (excluding mutual exchange goods), the imported and exported commodities and articles for public use of the Sino-foreign joint ventures, cooperative enterprises and ventures with sole foreign investment. Also included is import or export of samples and advertising goods for which CIF or FOB value are beyond the permitted ceiling (excluding goods of no trading or use value and free commodities for export), imported goods sold in China from bonded warehouses and other imported or exported goods. The indicator of the total imports and exports at customs can be used to observe the total size of external trade in a country. In accordance with the stipulation of the Chinese government, imports are calculated at CIF, while exports are calculated at FOB.

Import or Export Value by Location of China's Foreign Trade Managing Units refers to actual value of imports and exports carried out by corporations which have been registered by the local Customs house and are vested with right to run import export business.

Import Value of Commodities by Place of Destination and Export Value of Commodities by Place of Origin in China The former indicator refers to the value of import commodities of the places of their consumption, utilization or the places of their final destination. The latter indicator refers to the value of export commodities of the places of their origin or the places of the commodities dispatched.

Import and Export of Services refers to services provided between resident and non-resident units, including services on transportation, tourism, communications, construction, insurance, banking, computer and information, consultancy, advertising and publicity, as well as film, audio and video services, royalty for patents, trade marks and other special rights, other commercial services, but excluding government services.

Foreign Direct Investment refers to foreign investment in China through the establishment of foreign invested enterprises, cooperative exploration and development of petroleum resources with domestic investors and the establishment of branch organizations of foreign enterprises. Foreign investment can be made in forms of cash, physical investment, intangible assets and equity, in addition with reinvestment of the foreign enterprises with the profits gained from the investment.

Other Foreign Investment refers to all forms of utilization of foreign capitals other than foreign borrowings and foreign direct investment. It includes the total value of stock shares in foreign currencies issued by enterprises at domestic or foreign stock exchanges, rent payable for the imported equipment through international leasing arrangement, cost of imported equipment, technology and materials provided by foreign counterparts in compensation trade and processing and assembly trade.

Overseas Direct Investment refers to investment made by domestic enterprises and organizations (referred to as domestic investors) in foreign countries and Hong Kong SAR, Macao SAR and Taiwan province in forms of cash, physical investment and intangible assets, and the economic activities centring on operation and management of those enterprises are under the control of domestic investors. The content of overseas direct investment mainly reflects one economic entity by investing in another economic entity to achieve its goal of lasting interest.

Overseas Contracted Projects refer to activities of contracting overseas construction projects by Chinese enterprises or any other units, which are stipulated in the Regulations on Administration of Foreign Contracted Project.

Overseas Labour Services refer to operational activities of organizing labour force to go abroad providing services to foreign enterprises or agencies.

Chapter 7

七、农业和农村
Agriculture and Country

7-1 主要农业机械拥有量（1978-2020年）

Number of Major Agricultural Machinery Owned (1978-2020)

年份 Year	农业机械总动力（万千瓦） Total Power of Agricultural Machinery (10 000 kW)	拖拉机(万台) Tractor (10 000 units)	拖拉机配套农具（万部） Tractors . Towing Farm Machinery (10 000 units)	水稻插秧机（台） Rice Planter (unit)	节水灌溉类（万台、万套） Water-saving Irrigation (10 000 units)	谷物联合收割机（台） Grain Combine Harvesters (unit)	机动脱粒机（万台） Power-driver Shellers (10 000 units)
1978	243					215	4.19
1979	292					201	5.07
1980	295					184	5.36
1981	328					156	5.28
1982	335					170	4.84
1983	369					93	4.22
1984	407					68	3.97
1985	439					53	3.38
1986	475					53	3.13
1987	513					42	3.17
1988	579					60	3.74
1989	612					124	3.39
1990	649					120	3.66
1991	710					154	4.14
1992	754					125	4.59
1993	788					197	5.05
1994	850					126	5.44
1995	906					134	5.92
1996	1 003					101	8.01
1997	1 104					171	9.70
1998	1 177					257	10.22
1999	1 255					360	9.24
2000	1 301					450	11.10
2001	1 398					484	11.57
2002	1 460					483	11.58
2003	1 543					652	11.24
2004	1 608					817	11.57
2005	1 666					1 150	12.40
2006	1 755					1 570	14.82
2007	1 862					2 168	17.67
2008	2 014					2 537	21.80
2009	2 159					3 016	24.31
2010	2 411					3 496	27.10
2011	2 628					4 299	31.85
2012	2 874					5 075	33.92
2013	3 070					5 803	35.00
2014	3 215					6 596	36.93
2015	3 333					7 214	40.22
2016	3 440					8 051	41.90
2017	3 535					8 275	45.42
2018	2 694	38.46	36.98	2 462	5.36	8 455	48.44
2019	2 714	36.42	36.00	2 538	6.62	8 408	52.84
2020	2 787	36.29	36.06	2 630	7.75	8 754	56.16

注：由于统计指标变化，表中2018年以后农业机械总动力与历史数据不可比较。

Note: Because of the change of statistical indicators,data of total power of agricultural machinery since 2018 cannot be compared with historical data.

7-2 各州市农村基本情况及农业生产条件（2020年）
Basic Conditions of Rural Areas and Agricultural Production by Region (2020)

州 市	Region	自来水受益村数（个）Villages with Tap Water Supply (unit)	通有线电视村数（个）Villages with Wire Television (unit)	通宽带村数（个）Villages with Band (unit)	农村用电量（亿千瓦时）Rural Consumption of Electricity (100 million kWh)
全 省	**Yunnan**	**12 905**	**11 218**	**12 986**	**123.99**
昆 明	Kunming	1 126	952	1 122	12.52
曲 靖	Qujing	1 575	1 249	1 549	14.77
玉 溪	Yuxi	664	653	665	21.71
保 山	Baoshan	847	782	868	7.56
昭 通	Zhaotong	1 211	821	1 189	9.88
丽 江	Lijiang	422	336	457	2.62
普 洱	Pu'er	993	742	993	4.90
临 沧	Lincang	891	820	943	3.39
楚 雄	Chuxiong	966	966	966	5.82
红 河	Honghe	1 128	983	1 140	13.40
文 山	Wenshan	964	857	977	8.74
西双版纳	Xishuangbanna	258	258	258	2.26
大 理	Dali	1 076	1 076	1 076	12.36
德 宏	Dehong	336	302	336	1.64
怒 江	Nujiang	259	257	259	1.30
迪 庆	Diqing	189	164	188	1.12

7-3 各州市农田水利情况（2020年）

Basic Conditions of Farmland Water Conservancy by Region (2020)

州　市	Region	水库座数（座）Number of Reservoirs (unit)	水库总库容（亿立方米）Capacity of Reservoirs (100 million cu.m)	耕地灌溉面积（万公顷）Effective Irrigated Area (10 000 hectares)
全　省	**Yunnan**	**6 811**	**142.35**	**197.81**
昆　明	Kunming	847	28.19	14.39
曲　靖	Qujing	1 010	23.68	21.46
玉　溪	Yuxi	608	7.56	7.26
保　山	Baoshan	405	5.80	16.12
昭　通	Zhaotong	208	10.49	13.65
丽　江	Lijiang	151	4.00	8.42
普　洱	Pu'er	339	7.59	15.64
临　沧	Lincang	284	6.09	14.73
楚　雄	Chuxiong	1 129	12.81	11.80
红　河	Honghe	511	11.46	18.53
文　山	Wenshan	342	6.71	17.31
西双版纳	Xishuangbanna	193	3.64	5.46
大　理	Dali	690	8.93	17.02
德　宏	Dehong	75	3.08	12.31
怒　江	Nujiang	11	0.47	1.70
迪　庆	Diqing	8	1.85	2.01

7-4 水库库容量（2005—2020年）
Storage Capacity of Reservoirs (2005-2020)

年份 Year	水 库（座） Number of Reservoirs (unit)				水库库容量（亿立方米） Reservoir Capacity (100 million cu.m)				比上年增长（%） Increase Rate Over Last Year(%)	
	总计 Total	大型水库 Large Reservoirs	中型水库 Medium Size Reservoirs	小型水库 Small Reservoirs	总计 Total	大型水库 Large Reservoirs	中型水库 Medium Size Reservoirs	小型水库 Small Reservoirs	水 库 Number of Reservoirs	水库库容量 Capacity of Reservoirs
2005	5 368	5	169	5 194	98.87	16.79	48.68	33.40	0.8	1.9
2006	5 399	6	171	5 222	104.36	21.62	48.98	33.76	0.6	5.5
2007	5 403	6	173	5 224	106.23	21.62	50.33	34.28	0.1	1.8
2008	5 474	6	178	5 290	106.98	21.62	50.94	34.42	1.3	0.7
2009	5 514	6	183	5 325	108.30	21.63	52.01	34.67	0.7	1.2
2010	5 555	7	188	5 360	111.04	22.69	53.46	34.89	0.7	2.5
2011	5 590	7	201	5 382	114.19	22.69	56.15	35.35	0.6	2.8
2012	5 631	9	211	5 411	122.00	28.25	57.86	35.83	0.7	6.8
2013	5 964	10	215	5 739	123.97	29.79	58.14	36.04	5.9	1.6
2014	6 000	10	221	5 769	125.39	29.79	58.22	37.38	0.6	1.2
2015	6 126	10	230	5 886	127.57	29.79	59.63	38.15	2.1	1.7
2016	6 271	10	237	6 024	130.42	29.79	61.30	39.33	2.4	2.2
2017	6 384	10	246	6 128	132.42	29.79	62.61	40.02	1.8	1.5
2018	6 590	10	252	6 328	134.27	29.79	63.61	40.87	3.2	1.4
2019	6 650	10	262	6 378	136.61	29.79	64.93	41.89	0.9	1.7
2020	6 811	12	268	6 413	142.35	33.19	66.38	42.78	2.4	0.7

7-5 各州市农用化肥及农用薄膜施用量（2020年）
Quantity of Chemical Fertilizers and Chemical Film Used for Farming by Region (2020)

单位：万吨 (10 000 tons)

州市	Region	化肥施用量 Consumption of Chemical Fertilizer	氮肥 Nitrogenous Fertilizer	磷肥 Phosphate Fertilizer	钾肥 Potash Fertilizer	复合肥 Compound Fertilizer	农用塑料薄膜使用量 Plastic Film	地膜使用量 Mulching Film	农药使用量 Compound Fertilizer
全省	**Yunnan**	**196.65**	**94.43**	**27.05**	**22.72**	**52.45**	**12.16**	**9.42**	**4.48**
昆明	Kunming	17.02	8.03	2.84	1.22	4.92	1.39	0.93	0.37
曲靖	Qujing	29.79	14.26	5.31	2.94	7.29	2.34	2.13	0.46
玉溪	Yuxi	7.91	3.98	1.01	2.26	0.66	1.04	0.79	0.44
保山	Baoshan	10.63	5.67	1.13	1.71	2.12	0.67	0.56	0.40
昭通	Zhaotong	13.66	7.71	2.03	1.49	2.42	0.60	0.52	0.12
丽江	Lijiang	8.03	2.99	1.75	0.94	2.33	0.34	0.32	0.12
普洱	Pu'er	8.45	5.67	0.70	0.90	1.18	0.57	0.40	0.34
临沧	Lincang	19.84	7.37	0.65	1.50	10.32	0.46	0.32	0.21
楚雄	Chuxiong	14.62	8.03	2.67	0.70	3.22	1.17	0.69	0.28
红河	Honghe	23.92	10.70	3.48	3.23	6.50	1.58	0.99	0.80
文山	Wenshan	17.41	8.12	2.56	1.94	4.79	0.81	0.72	0.25
西双版纳	Xishuangbanna	5.58	2.27	0.39	1.18	1.74	0.10	0.07	0.26
大理	Dali	10.37	4.15	1.40	1.42	3.40	0.67	0.57	0.28
德宏	Dehong	7.23	4.62	0.72	1.22	0.66	0.31	0.30	0.13
怒江	Nujiang	0.81	0.31	0.07	0.01	0.42	0.05	0.05	0.01
迪庆	Diqing	1.40	0.54	0.34	0.06	0.46	0.06	0.05	0.02

注：化肥施用量按折纯计算。

Note: Consumption of chemical fertilizers is calculated according to the volume of effective component of the chemical fertilizers.

7-6 农、林、牧、渔业总产值（2019-2020年）
Gross Output Value of Farming, Forestry, Animal Husbandry and Fishery (2019-2020)

单位：亿元 (100 million yuan)

项　　目	Item	按当年价格计算 At Current Prices	
		2019	2020
农、林、牧、渔业总产值	**Gross Output Value of Farming, Forestry,Animal Husbandry and Fishery**	**4 935.73**	**5 920.52**
农业产值	**Gross Output Value of Farming**	**2 680.16**	**2 902.24**
谷物及其他作物	Cereals and Other Crops	852.78	903.39
#谷物	Corn Cereals	394.22	399.01
薯类	Tubers	67.32	85.22
油料	Oil-bearing Crops	31.04	30.58
豆类	Beans and Peas	53.83	51.55
糖料	Sugar Crops	66.71	73.47
烟草	Tobacco	238.36	261.61
蔬菜园艺作物	Vegetables and Horticultural Crops	826.18	976.27
水果、坚果、饮料和香料作物	Fruits，Nuts, Beverages and Spiceberry Crops	555.86	588.17
中药材	Traditional Chinese Medicinal Materials	445.34	434.41
林业产值	**Gross Output Value of Animal Husbandry**	**395.54**	**429.50**
林木的培育和种植	Cultivation of Forest Trees	78.85	83.89
竹木采运	Logging and Transport of Timber and Bamboo	112.01	84.65
林产品	Forest Products	204.68	260.96
牧业产值	**Gross Output Value of Animal Husbandry**	**1 600.73**	**2 315.41**
牲畜饲养	Livestock Raising	494.87	708.42
生猪	Hogs	861.64	1 376.87
家禽	Poultry	210.66	191.36
狩猎和捕捉动物	Hunting	0.05	0.06
其他畜牧业	Others	33.52	38.70
渔业产值	**Gross Output Value of Fishery**	**105.38**	**103.98**
农、林、牧、渔服务业产值	**Output Value of Services in Support of Farming, Forestry, Animal Husbandry and Fishery**	**153.92**	**169.40**

7-7 农、林、牧、渔业总产值（1978-2020年）
Historical Total Output Value of Farming, Forestry, Animal Husbandry and Fishery (1978-2020)

(按当年价格计算) (calculated at current prices)
单位：亿元 (100 million yuan)

年 份 Year	农业总产值 Historic Total Output Value of Farming	农 业 Farming	林 业 Forestry	牧 业 Animal Husbandry	渔 业 Fishery	农、林、牧、渔服务业 Services in Support of Agriculture,Forestry, Animal Husbandry and Fishery
1978	40.02	28.58	2.48	7.08	0.08	1.80
1979	44.71	31.03	3.17	8.27	0.09	2.15
1980	48.20	33.02	2.94	10.22	0.19	1.83
1981	55.20	38.32	3.77	10.74	0.20	2.17
1982	61.84	41.90	3.87	12.79	0.21	3.07
1983	65.68	42.30	4.73	13.84	0.24	4.57
1984	77.36	48.78	5.97	15.79	0.27	6.55
1985	88.88	52.02	7.90	20.33	0.40	8.23
1986	96.01	51.80	7.40	26.14	0.71	9.96
1987	111.25	61.75	8.85	29.42	0.95	10.28
1988	135.39	76.11	10.05	37.01	1.56	10.66
1989	152.68	84.30	12.97	41.68	1.93	11.80
1990	211.72	119.63	18.27	54.01	1.39	18.42
1991	222.93	130.67	18.69	55.68	1.37	16.52
1992	250.35	146.70	22.84	61.54	2.02	17.25
1993	281.21	179.39	25.39	72.89	3.54	
1994	356.78	228.99	30.41	92.13	5.25	
1995	474.46	299.48	40.53	127.19	7.26	
1996	567.51	369.36	43.21	146.03	8.91	
1997	612.01	397.09	40.40	163.93	10.59	
1998	620.02	381.26	41.77	184.83	12.16	
1999	642.48	394.96	45.60	188.82	13.10	
2000	680.86	416.36	49.75	201.49	13.26	
2001	703.53	431.31	47.21	210.63	14.38	
2002	737.55	445.35	53.52	223.49	15.19	
2002(新口径)	743.75	414.89	59.27	223.49	15.19	
2003	799.33	433.91	73.17	242.53	16.56	33.16
2004	965.22	516.92	86.40	305.42	19.14	35.19
2005	1 068.58	559.32	105.53	339.68	22.97	41.08
2006	1 209.76	630.19	142.59	362.89	26.30	44.78
2007	1 414.79	707.15	156.27	459.63	35.73	56.00
2008	1 641.46	790.87	183.60	570.01	38.12	58.86
2009	1 706.19	850.65	196.13	557.76	41.96	59.69
2010	1 810.53	925.58	184.23	588.81	48.06	63.85
2011	2 306.49	1 124.72	245.67	808.20	55.93	71.98
2012	2 680.22	1 398.18	225.83	912.97	63.10	80.14
2013	3 056.04	1 639.40	293.25	962.55	70.41	90.43
2014	3 261.30	1 805.06	303.25	974.98	78.35	99.66
2015	3 383.09	1 840.61	317.52	1 031.48	81.67	111.80
2016	3 704.69	1 888.83	330.37	1 286.06	76.39	123.04
2017	3 872.93	1 982.52	381.53	1 289.45	87.70	131.72
2018	4 108.88	2 234.74	396.88	1 237.12	98.25	141.89
2019	4 935.73	2 680.16	395.54	1 600.73	105.38	153.92
2020	5 920.52	2 902.24	429.50	2 315.41	103.98	169.40

注：1. "农林牧渔服务业"1992年及以前年份为"副业"。
2. 从2003年开始，按新国民经济行业分类标准，农业总产值中取消"农民家庭兼营的商品性工业"；"木材采运"改为全社会口径；增加"农林牧渔服务业"。"农林牧渔服务业"包含在"农业总产值"中(下同)。

Note: a. Services in Support of farming, forestry,animal husbandry and fishery was called sideline production before 1992.
b. According to the new standards for the classification of National Economy,subsidiary commercial industry operated by farmers has been deleted from the output value of agriculture since 2003. The Statistical Coverage of logging and transport of timber has been changed to the whole society. Services in support of farming, forestry,animal husbandry and fishery are added.Services of farming, forestry,animal husbandry and fishery are included in the output value of agriculture (The same as below).

7-8 农、林、牧、渔业总产值指数（1978-2020年）
Indices of Historical Gross Output Value of Farming，Forestry, Animal Husbandry and Fishery (1978-2020)

(1952年=100) (1952=100)

年 份 Year	农业总产值指数 Indices of Historic Gross Output Value of Farming	农 业 Farming	林 业 Forestry	牧 业 Animal Husbandry	渔 业 Fishery	农、林、牧、渔服务业 Services in Support of Agriculture,Forestry, Animal Husbandry and Fishery
1978	249.2	233.0	13 119.8	410.2	1 296.6	103.5
1979	235.2	213.5	14 288.8	404.3	1 619.3	103.9
1980	251.2	231.3	14 938.3	418.3	1 759.0	104.9
1981	273.6	255.7	16 118.2	439.9	1 886.9	105.7
1982	302.9	274.1	16 885.3	525.0	1 946.7	150.0
1983	319.7	274.8	19 622.1	568.2	2 225.7	222.2
1984	368.3	303.7	25 504.0	645.6	2 500.9	321.5
1985	391.8	308.2	29 241.5	700.0	3 058.1	404.4
1986	382.6	288.0	25 449.1	717.4	3 599.1	489.3
1987	406.0	315.8	24 428.5	738.9	4 402.0	504.9
1988	432.8	339.7	25 935.5	781.7	5 771.3	524.1
1989	445.3	346.4	27 366.2	821.8	5 091.1	530.0
1990	474.5	366.1	29 995.2	882.9	5 318.0	566.6
1991	501.1	398.6	30 756.4	929.5	5 702.4	514.0
1992	523.0	416.5	33 893.6	968.5	6 181.4	503.7
1993	538.8	422.1	40 280.4	991.9	7 462.5	479.0
1994	555.4	426.3	42 959.2	1 050.2	9 256.1	
1995	591.2	457.0	43 946.1	1 112.7	11 177.8	
1996	634.9	490.8	46 714.7	1 195.0	13 223.3	
1997	686.9	530.1	49 941.7	1 303.4	14 728.1	
1998	718.1	533.2	52 506.4	1 467.9	18 282.1	
1999	753.7	555.6	53 943.5	1 571.6	20 274.7	
2000	802.7	589.3	56 155.9	1 705.5	20 850.3	
2001	831.5	611.7	54 154.9	1 800.6	22 289.4	
2002	870.0	633.3	59 030.7	1 892.0	24 368.0	
2003	927.8	663.1	67 532.6	2 027.4	25 600.1	105.1
2004	990.7	703.8	70 033.8	2 204.5	28 027.2	116.6
2005	1 059.1	734.0	76 196.7	2 431.6	31 222.3	121.1
2006	1 148.5	791.1	86 271.6	2 610.6	36 558.9	132.5
2007	1 232.3	844.1	94 553.7	2 767.3	44 309.4	146.7
2008	1 329.7	899.8	105 521.9	3 016.3	47 278.1	152.1
2009	1 407.2	938.0	112 529.3	3 255.4	52 293.3	153.9
2010	1 472.9	972.1	119 348.5	3 440.4	57 204.7	158.6
2011	1 562.2	1 038.5	133 935.2	3 527.5	62 460.7	170.5
2012	1 672.1	1 094.5	147 321.8	3 803.6	71 248.7	184.5
2013	1 788.7	1 166.4	165 132.5	4 018.6	81 035.5	201.9
2014	1 897.8	1 235.2	179 829.3	4 235.6	88 814.9	217.2
2015	2 011.7	1 310.5	197 272.8	4 405.0	96 630.6	239.2
2016	2 129.2	1 391.0	219 145.5	4 534.6	107 345.4	260.3
2017	2 257.6	1 477.2	242 527.8	4 733.6	117 446.4	276.2
2018	2 399.5	1 577.3	266 596.9	4 934.0	129 003.6	293.1
2019	2 534.7	1 713.9	270 884.3	5 010.7	134 106.2	310.7
2020	2 680.5	1 834.1	288 177.5	5 191.5	138 689.6	329.5

注：1.本表按可比价格计算。
2."农林牧渔业"1993年及以前年份为"副业"。
3.农林牧渔服务业产值指数从2003年开始计算，为新农业发展速度口径。

Note: a. The data in this table are calculated at comparable prices.
b. Farming，forestry,animal husbandry and fishery in 1993 and years before 1993 were called sideline production.
c. The indices of services in support of agriculture,forestry,animal husbandry and fishery has been calculated according to the new calculating coverage of agriculture developing speed since 2003.

7-9 各州市农、林、牧、渔业总产值（2020年）
Gross Output Value of Farming, Forestry, Animal Husbandry and Fishery by Region (2020)

(按当年价格计算)　　(calculated at current prices)
单位：亿元　　(100 million yuan)

州　市	Region	农业总产值 Gross Output Value of Farming	农　业 Farming	林　业 Forestry	牧　业 Animal Husbandry	渔　业 Fishery	农、林、牧、渔服务业 Services in Support of Agriculture,Forestry, Animal Husbandry and Fishery
全　省	**Yunnan**	**5 920.52**	**2 902.24**	**429.50**	**2 315.41**	**103.98**	**169.40**
昆　明	Kunming	519.50	299.58	22.54	170.88	8.12	18.39
曲　靖	Qujing	911.13	326.38	28.16	520.49	14.05	22.05
玉　溪	Yuxi	343.53	240.15	10.22	82.03	2.71	8.42
保　山	Baoshan	385.41	170.09	37.80	163.16	5.43	8.92
昭　通	Zhaotong	342.34	168.65	13.50	145.18	5.15	9.85
丽　江	Lijiang	135.62	65.25	6.55	57.40	2.50	3.91
普　洱	Pu'er	385.88	177.88	73.99	108.30	16.75	8.97
临　沧	Lincang	377.09	208.34	17.48	131.07	7.24	12.95
楚　雄	Chuxiong	441.12	233.49	38.13	148.83	4.47	16.20
红　河	Honghe	564.39	259.42	35.44	247.25	7.63	14.64
文　山	Wenshan	396.05	189.47	23.70	164.72	6.53	11.63
西双版纳	Xishuangbanna	230.10	124.91	67.76	20.18	10.95	6.30
大　理	Dali	618.35	284.40	21.53	285.13	7.55	19.73
德　宏	Dehong	192.48	125.83	18.54	38.60	4.41	5.10
怒　江	Nujiang	47.08	16.62	8.53	20.68	0.08	1.17
迪　庆	Diqing	30.46	11.78	5.62	11.51	0.40	1.16

7-10 各州市农、林、牧、渔业总产值指数（2020年）
Indices of Gross Output Value of Agriculture, Forestry, Animal Husbandry and Fishery by Region (2020)

(上年=100)　(preceding year = 100)
单位：%　(%)

州 市	Region	指 数 Indices of Gross Output Value of Agriculture	农 业 Farming	林 业 Forestry	牧 业 Animal Husbandry	渔 业 Fishery	农、林、牧、渔服务业 Services in Support of Agriculture,Forestry, Animal Husbandry and Fishery
全 省	**Yunnan**	**105.8**	**107.0**	**106.4**	**103.6**	**103.4**	**106.0**
昆 明	Kunming	105.7	108.5	100.6	100.2	101.2	107.8
曲 靖	Qujing	105.9	104.3	112.6	107.0	100.4	105.9
玉 溪	Yuxi	105.8	105.3	88.5	110.3	92.7	106.7
保 山	Baoshan	105.6	109.1	109.2	109.0	102.2	104.9
昭 通	Zhaotong	105.7	105.8	110.6	106.0	85.5	106.2
丽 江	Lijiang	105.5	107.0	107.1	103.7	101.8	106.6
普 洱	Pu'er	105.8	106.4	106.8	104.8	101.1	105.5
临 沧	Lincang	105.7	105.3	100.1	107.8	102.9	105.0
楚 雄	Chuxiong	105.8	105.9	105.4	105.6	106.7	107.0
红 河	Honghe	105.9	108.5	105.0	103.5	90.8	106.3
文 山	Wenshan	105.4	103.8	89.3	111.9	95.1	106.3
西双版纳	Xishuangbanna	106.0	108.6	101.6	103.9	109.6	106.0
大 理	Dali	105.7	101.9	115.0	112.0	92.3	105.9
德 宏	Dehong	105.7	106.0	104.5	106.3	101.9	103.5
怒 江	Nujiang	105.2	106.7	107.9	102.6	104.7	105.9
迪 庆	Diqing	105.6	102.1	108.1	110.3	92.4	104.8

注：本表数据按可比价格计算。
Note : The data in the table are calculated at comparable prices.

7-11 各州市农、林、牧、渔业总产值构成（2020年）
Composition of Gross Output Value of Farming, Forestry, Animal Husbandry and Fishery by Region (2020)

(按当年价格计算)
单位：%

(calculated at current prices)
(%)

州 市	Region	构 成 Composition	农 业 Farming	林 业 Forestry	牧 业 Animal Husbandry	渔 业 Fishery	农、林、牧、渔服务业 Services in Support of Agriculture,Forestry, Animal Husbandry and Fishery
全 省	**Yunnan**	**100.00**	**49.02**	**7.25**	**39.11**	**1.76**	**2.86**
昆 明	Kunming	100.00	57.67	4.34	32.89	1.56	3.54
曲 靖	Qujing	100.00	35.82	3.09	57.13	1.54	2.42
玉 溪	Yuxi	100.00	69.91	2.97	23.88	0.79	2.45
保 山	Baoshan	100.00	44.13	9.81	42.34	1.41	2.31
昭 通	Zhaotong	100.00	49.26	3.94	42.41	1.51	2.88
丽 江	Lijiang	100.00	48.11	4.83	42.33	1.84	2.89
普 洱	Pu'er	100.00	46.10	19.17	28.06	4.34	2.32
临 沧	Lincang	100.00	55.25	4.64	34.76	1.92	3.44
楚 雄	Chuxiong	100.00	52.93	8.64	33.74	1.01	3.67
红 河	Honghe	100.00	45.97	6.28	43.81	1.35	2.59
文 山	Wenshan	100.00	47.84	5.98	41.59	1.65	2.94
西双版纳	Xishuangbanna	100.00	54.29	29.45	8.77	4.76	2.74
大 理	Dali	100.00	45.99	3.48	46.11	1.22	3.19
德 宏	Dehong	100.00	65.37	9.63	20.05	2.29	2.65
怒 江	Nujiang	100.00	35.30	18.11	43.93	0.17	2.49
迪 庆	Diqing	100.00	38.66	18.44	37.79	1.31	3.80

7-12 各州市农、林、牧、渔业中间消耗（2020年）
Intermediate Consumption of Farming, Forestry, Animal Husbandry and Fishery by Region (2020)

(按当年价格计算)　　(calculated at current prices)
单位：亿元　　(100 million yuan)

州市	Region	农业中间消耗 Intermediate Consumption of Farming	农业 Farming	林业 Forestry	牧业 Animal Husbandry	渔业 Fishery	农、林、牧、渔服务业 Services in Support of Agriculture，Forestry, Animal Husbandry and Fishery
全省	**Yunnan**	**2 246.06**	**974.35**	**144.81**	**977.36**	**42.93**	**106.62**
昆明	Kunming	200.32	105.96	6.87	72.27	3.65	11.56
曲靖	Qujing	351.56	107.16	8.60	212.81	6.98	16.01
玉溪	Yuxi	146.37	92.45	3.07	44.37	0.99	5.49
保山	Baoshan	136.48	53.96	10.55	65.43	1.97	4.57
昭通	Zhaotong	111.26	45.57	2.72	54.78	2.11	6.08
丽江	Lijiang	55.51	26.65	2.14	23.28	1.05	2.39
普洱	Pu'er	147.10	68.82	19.70	45.70	7.56	5.32
临沧	Lincang	130.26	60.42	5.47	53.21	3.08	8.08
楚雄	Chuxiong	164.32	65.78	23.36	63.78	1.42	9.98
红河	Honghe	211.08	90.54	12.30	95.96	3.09	9.19
文山	Wenshan	152.62	61.77	7.84	73.11	2.49	7.41
西双版纳	Xishuangbanna	82.38	38.60	28.73	7.65	3.27	4.13
大理	Dali	265.75	105.70	7.53	137.28	3.24	12.00
德宏	Dehong	64.93	41.84	2.83	15.24	1.87	3.15
怒江	Nujiang	15.38	4.87	2.51	7.43	0.02	0.56
迪庆	Diqing	10.74	4.27	0.61	5.05	0.12	0.70

7-13 各州市农林牧渔业中间消耗占总产值比重（2020年）
Proportion of Intermediate Consumption of Farming, Forestry, Animal Husbandry and Fishery to Gross Output Value by Region (2020)

(按当年价格计算)　　(calculated at current prices)

单位：亿元　　(100 million yuan)

州　市	Region	农、林、牧、渔业总产值 Gross Output Value Animal Husbandry and Fishery	中间消耗 Intermediate Consumption	
			绝对数 Absolute value	比重（%） Proportion（%）
全　省	**Yunnan**	**5 920.52**	**2 246.06**	**37.94**
昆　明	Kunming	519.50	200.32	38.56
曲　靖	Qujing	911.13	351.56	38.59
玉　溪	Yuxi	343.53	146.37	42.61
保　山	Baoshan	385.41	136.48	35.41
昭　通	Zhaotong	342.34	111.26	32.50
丽　江	Lijiang	135.62	55.51	40.93
普　洱	Pu'er	385.88	147.10	38.12
临　沧	Lincang	377.09	130.26	34.54
楚　雄	Chuxiong	441.12	164.32	37.25
红　河	Honghe	564.39	211.08	37.40
文　山	Wenshan	396.05	152.62	38.54
西双版纳	Xishuangbanna	230.10	82.38	35.80
大　理	Dali	618.35	265.75	42.98
德　宏	Dehong	192.48	64.93	33.73
怒　江	Nujiang	47.08	15.38	32.67
迪　庆	Diqing	30.46	10.74	35.25

7-14 主要农产品产量（1978-2020年）
Output of Major Farm Products （1978-2020）

单位：万吨 (10 000 tons)

年 份 Year	粮 食 Grain	稻 谷 Rice	小 麦 Wheat	玉 米 Corn	豆 类 Beans	大 豆 Soybeans	薯 类（折粮）Tubers	油 料 Oil-bearing Crops	花 生 Peanuts	油菜籽 Rapeseeds	烟 叶 Tobacco	烤 烟 Flue-cured Tobacco
1978	864.05	411.60	85.95	233.10		9.70	48.65	5.51	2.05	3.18		12.26
1979	792.90	382.50	70.55	225.05		6.50	46.90	4.61	1.63	2.74		10.59
1980	865.55	387.60	78.55	263.05		7.05	53.60	6.48	1.83	4.18		10.38
1981	917.09	436.20	73.81	269.79		7.86	53.40	10.71	2.63	7.25		16.36
1982	945.90	463.90	67.20	278.20		8.70	56.00	13.81	3.00	9.95		25.10
1983	954.35	456.90	86.60	268.95		8.80	55.90	13.80	2.57	10.63		14.44
1984	1 005.00	500.90	82.00	273.95		10.00	60.55	12.37	3.06	8.37		27.50
1985	935.00	482.95	61.90	248.75		9.60	63.00	11.81	3.60	7.17		41.00
1986	870.00	440.00	43.50	257.80		9.50	64.70	10.98	3.44	6.70		28.60
1987	934.84	457.96	74.58	249.81		8.42	64.29	13.52	2.88	10.03		33.56
1988	940.72	458.32	82.72	250.37		9.37	60.75	11.89	2.77	8.57		50.73
1989	998.41	467.54	80.40	292.79		10.18	66.31	10.32	2.93	6.72		45.67
1990	1 061.21	509.44	106.79	280.56		10.12	67.51	13.31	2.93	9.65	44.70	43.60
1991	1 093.00	516.87	115.11	300.15		10.10	69.64	17.16	3.14	13.07		58.18
1992	1 070.40	503.39	127.57	272.20		8.82	66.50	18.85	2.96	14.88		77.80
1993	1 085.24	479.31	135.58	289.12		10.08	73.89	13.37	3.37	9.04		87.44
1994	1 146.47	510.23	124.07	332.36		11.14	78.55	13.95	4.11	9.06		59.23
1995	1 188.91	515.77	138.50	341.83		13.13	79.48	19.58	4.33	14.29	76.83	76.07
1996	1 246.30	535.15	145.39	365.03		12.02	82.72	18.81	4.32	13.61	90.19	88.39
1997	1 271.90	533.77	166.14	365.63		12.54	85.10	17.43	3.82	12.80	110.16	109.28
1998	1 319.50	540.86	152.22	420.72		12.95	87.58	17.46	4.55	11.95	57.29	56.37
1999	1 399.25	534.34	153.47	463.44		13.43	98.86	20.62	4.78	14.54	62.66	60.95
2000	1 467.80	536.29	151.19	473.30		13.99	145.46	26.98	5.35	19.11	65.57	64.61
2001	1 486.30	595.87	137.88	477.30		15.97	148.96	27.66	5.40	20.42	61.47	60.08
2002	1 424.74	543.20	134.11	461.50		15.89	153.88	27.52	5.37	20.52	71.80	66.15
2003	1 471.01	635.89	124.35	399.93		14.81	172.29	29.70	5.34	22.75	65.49	63.68
2004	1 509.50	639.40	121.67	425.66		20.62	191.39	33.41	5.59	26.23	70.75	69.24
2005	1 514.93	646.34	106.86	449.31		17.39	193.60	36.22	5.75	29.02	79.09	77.22
2006	1 457.60	612.90	93.00	478.00	93.80	10.90	157.40	39.01	5.80	31.57	77.73	75.78
2007	1 460.70	589.70	91.20	498.60	80.10	17.90	162.20	36.65	6.11	29.07	79.12	76.68
2008	1 518.59	621.01	83.05	529.55	112.12	26.16	169.76	40.38	6.70	32.10	86.38	83.97
2009	1 576.92	636.23	92.30	542.67	130.36	29.06	172.18	50.16	7.13	41.41	91.69	88.03
2010	1 650.00	492.75	40.52	741.29	84.51	26.54	226.08	34.23	7.01	25.98	99.14	95.40
2011	1 755.38	509.20	85.81	704.80	113.01	46.53	250.02	60.75	7.04	51.84	105.57	101.82
2012	1 827.84	483.82	79.99	787.78	118.96	30.00	260.04	62.84	7.49	53.50	115.00	111.05
2013	1 897.61	495.00	77.28	836.42	120.02	31.18	269.03	60.68	7.99	50.69	107.55	103.85
2014	1 940.82	488.59	81.06	873.63	117.90	31.22	272.15	64.68	8.15	54.93	98.35	94.50
2015	1 969.79	479.95	81.20	902.14	123.07	31.43	274.83	65.92	8.20	56.07	92.76	90.34
2016	1 815.10	524.10	71.50	892.30	117.00	43.10	145.40	56.34	6.30	47.51	90.74	87.89
2017	1 843.40	529.20	73.70	912.90	118.30	43.50	157.00	56.26	6.24	47.52	86.23	83.85
2018	1 860.54	527.70	74.28	926.00	118.08	43.51	160.74	60.98	6.96	52.52	84.47	82.29
2019	1 870.03	534.00	71.90	920.00	122.33	46.00	168.30	62.51	6.76	54.10	83.54	81.00
2020	1 895.86	524.91	69.70	938.00	123.33	46.40	185.03	63.09	7.61	54.23	84.30	81.60

注：1.1991-2009年粮食产量为抽样调查数，2010-2015年为全面统计数，2016年以后为抽样调查数。
2.2008-2009年畜牧业数据为抽样调查数，2010-2015年为全面统计数，2016年以后为抽样调查数。
3.2016-2017年主要农产品及水产品数据为根据第三次全国农业普查结果核定和修订的数据。

Note:a.Data of grain output from 1991 to 2009 are sampling survey data,from 2010 to 2015 are comprehensive statistics.,since 2016,those are sampling survey data.
b.Data of animal husbandry from 2008 to 2009 are sampling survey data,from 2010 to 2015 are comprehensive statistics.,since 2016,those are sampling survey data.
c.Data of output of major farm products and aquatic products from 2016 to 2017 are verified and revised according to the Third National Agricultural Census.

7-14 续表 continued

单位：万吨 (10 000 tons)

年 份 Year	糖 料 Sugar Crops	甘 蔗 Sugarcane	茶 叶 Tea	水 果 Fruits	猪牛羊肉 Pork, Beef and Mutton	禽 蛋 Poultry Eggs	水产品 Aquatic Products	麻 类 Fiber Crops	棉 花 Cotton
1978	160.04	160.01	1.78	11.62	29.23		1.12		
1979	181.46	181.44	1.49	9.74	30.01		1.40		
1980	184.59	184.45	1.78	11.63	30.91		1.52		
1981	224.95	224.74	2.04	13.90	35.92		1.63		
1982	307.44	307.12	2.28	14.12	37.84	2.59	1.69		
1983	354.60	354.15	2.57	16.77	46.91	2.78	1.93		
1984	378.01	377.76	2.82	22.64	51.54	3.97	2.17		
1985	480.13	479.77	3.11	21.18	56.82	3.90	2.65		
1986	529.85	529.49	3.41	27.49	56.73	3.84	3.12		
1987	558.80	558.47	3.92	31.63	59.62	4.04	3.81		
1988	584.29	583.83	4.28	33.96	64.55	4.09	4.13		
1989	551.82	551.28	4.27	34.32	68.34	4.59	4.41		
1990	662.32	661.88	4.48	31.97	74.74	4.90	4.60	0.22	0.04
1991	821.29	820.74	4.77	36.74	81.27	5.13	4.94		
1992	907.20	906.89	2.29	42.83	87.28	4.82	5.37		
1993	900.03	899.92	6.10	47.72	96.16	5.17	5.83		
1994	928.46	928.00	6.38	50.14	107.68	6.42	6.85		
1995	1 056.31	1 055.92	6.40	55.71	120.45	6.85	8.44	0.22	0.07
1996	1 143.36	1 143.08	6.82	59.01	133.37	7.41	10.20	0.30	0.06
1997	1 435.18	1 434.92	7.08	66.02	148.95	8.51	11.89	0.23	0.07
1998	1 598.09	1 597.71	7.75	68.07	166.21	8.70	13.84	0.22	0.08
1999	1 526.89	1 526.53	7.51	73.83	180.35	9.83	15.53	0.21	0.06
2000	1 420.61	1 420.29	7.94	76.95	191.51	10.63	16.62	0.19	0.05
2001	1 481.49	1 481.10	8.07	79.29	203.84	11.80	18.02	0.49	0.05
2002	1 733.66	1 733.36	8.36	85.63	218.74	13.16	19.26	2.33	0.04
2003	1 695.24	1 694.96	8.59	96.53	234.53	14.39	20.43	4.49	0.03
2004	1 688.80	1 688.49	9.51	115.52	257.10	16.49	22.05	13.66	0.03
2005	1 415.89	1 415.50	11.59	136.63	277.32	20.35	23.85	14.10	0.02
2006	1 679.06	1 678.73	13.82	162.56	296.13	20.54	29.24	5.88	0.02
2007	1 938.81	1 938.67	16.99	202.37	238.60	18.00	33.39	2.42	0.03
2008	1 898.88	1 898.75	17.15	266.18	257.18	19.41	39.37	2.28	0.04
2009	1 761.42	1 761.31	18.29	342.74	270.88	20.75	43.06	1.84	0.04
2010	1 750.97	1 750.92	20.73	397.91	474.82	37.78	48.17	0.56	0.04
2011	1 898.78	1 898.78	23.83	476.43	517.44	40.98	54.88	1.05	0.04
2012	2 043.78	2 043.78	27.17	581.12	578.18	47.40	68.01	1.02	0.07
2013	2 146.25	2 146.25	30.17	634.52	597.48	56.51	78.16	0.79	0.04
2014	2 110.40	2 110.40	33.55	669.02	627.46	60.59	87.01	0.36	0.03
2015	1 930.05	1 930.05	36.58	726.54	627.03	72.23	93.74	0.05	0.01
2016	1 523.77	1 523.77	37.30	797.77	369.60	71.22	60.15	0.05	0.01
2017	1 516.15	1 516.15	39.30	783.90	374.10	73.62	63.12	0.02	
2018	1 640.08	1 640.08	42.33	813.35	378.47	32.72	63.75	0.02	
2019	1 569.69	1 569.69	43.72	860.32	346.58	35.80	63.65	0.09	
2020	1 597.17	1 597.17	46.32	961.58	353.28	41.75	64.40	2.92	

7−15 粮食播种面积和产量（1978−2020年）

Sown Areas and Grain Yields (1978-2020)

单位：万吨、万公顷 (10 000 tons, 10 000 hectares)

年份 Year	粮食产量 Total Yield of Grain	夏收粮 Summer Harvest Grain		秋收粮 Autumn Harvest Grain	
		面积 Area	产量 Grain Yield	面积 Area	产量 Grain Yield
1978	864.05	105.26	134.79	262.52	729.26
1979	792.90	103.81	107.27	264.93	685.63
1980	865.55	93.99	126.64	265.28	738.91
1981	917.10	88.24	124.01	265.75	793.09
1982	945.90	82.72	111.59	264.67	834.31
1983	954.35	84.86	140.28	262.22	814.07
1984	1005.00	85.43	135.28	258.70	869.72
1985	935.00	84.55	109.23	247.30	825.77
1986	870.00	84.42	75.48	248.87	794.52
1987	934.84	85.87	133.89	250.58	800.95
1988	940.72	92.86	138.49	248.92	802.23
1989	998.41	97.85	132.19	254.86	866.22
1990	1061.21	102.87	170.02	259.36	891.19
1991	1 093.00	104.41	184.25	257.48	908.75
1992	1 070.40	105.62	196.00	252.58	874.40
1993	1 085.24	106.54	211.24	246.17	874.00
1994	1 146.47	113.62	201.36	253.26	945.11
1995	1 188.91	112.69	228.18	251.59	960.73
1996	1 246.30		234.30		1 012.00
1997	1 271.90		254.70		1 017.20
1998	1 319.50		240.15		1 079.35
1999	1399.25	130.09	234.49	274.12	1 164.76
2000	1467.80	126.48	241.00	272.69	1 226.80
2001	1486.30	133.00	233.86	300.90	1 252.44
2002	1424.74	121.82	240.85	294.24	1 183.89
2003	1471.01	119.45	244.55	287.39	1 226.46
2004	1509.50	117.67	236.32	298.17	1 273.18
2005	1514.93	118.89	222.31	306.50	1 292.62
2006	1457.60	110.55	220.60	291.66	1 237.00
2007	1460.70	109.72	223.40	289.73	1 237.30
2008	1518.59	110.17	207.58	299.42	1 311.01
2009	1576.92	112.83	236.47	307.18	1 340.45
2010	1650.00	116.23	139.44	313.67	1 484.98
2011	1755.38	118.00	237.22	318.45	1 441.40
2012	1827.84	117.27	270.11	324.51	1 557.73
2013	1897.61	121.39	273.25	323.63	1 623.91
2014	1940.82	69.38	169.75	247.29	1 370.69
2015	1969.79	120.17	272.10	324.88	1 671.44
2016	1815.10				
2017	1843.40				
2018	1860.54	97.71	241.98	315.83	1 596.66
2019	1870.03	97.41	243.60	315.24	1 604.73
2020	1895.86	96.78	249.54	319.96	1 646.32

注：2020年秋收粮包含早稻。
Note：Autumn Harvest Grain of 2020 Including Early Season Rice.

7-16 各州市主要农作物播种面积（2020年）

Total Sown Areas of Major Farm Crops by Region (2020)

单位：万公顷 (10 000 hectares)

州市	Region	总播种面积 Total Sown Area	粮食播种面积 Sown Area of Grain Crops	稻谷 Rice	小麦 Wheat	玉米 Corn	豆类 Beans	薯类 Tubers
全省	**Yunnan**	**701.01**	**416.74**	**81.89**	**32.00**	**180.25**	**48.46**	**54.39**
昆明	Kunming	43.81	23.34	1.46	2.37	8.58	3.93	3.75
曲靖	Qujing	112.90	63.04	5.96	3.64	23.15	6.41	18.94
玉溪	Yuxi	28.84	11.08	1.63	1.17	5.78	1.30	0.50
保山	Baoshan	41.56	26.34	5.39	0.88	10.79	3.63	2.13
昭通	Zhaotong	70.61	50.41	2.53	2.34	22.53	4.44	17.85
丽江	Lijiang	18.71	12.78	1.21	0.98	4.62	2.38	2.09
普洱	Pu'er	51.28	34.22	7.15	2.57	18.85	3.30	1.50
临沧	Lincang	46.16	28.81	4.32	3.21	15.32	3.55	1.94
楚雄	Chuxiong	43.95	24.55	5.85	3.86	8.08	4.21	0.83
红河	Honghe	67.12	38.52	8.81	2.68	14.30	5.03	4.21
文山	Wenshan	78.81	44.48	7.52	3.66	20.22	7.22	3.90
西双版纳	Xishuangbanna	14.67	8.54	2.53		5.65	0.13	0.09
大理	Dali	42.36	29.68	5.06	1.50	13.17	4.57	1.81
德宏	Dehong	25.80	12.91	5.69	0.15	4.37	0.59	2.08
怒江	Nujiang	8.25	5.81	0.36	0.51	2.14	1.42	0.87
迪庆	Diqing	6.17	4.28	0.22	0.59	1.80	0.43	0.46

注：全省粮食分品种面积数据为抽样调查数据，分州市面积数据为全面调查数据。
Note: Data of whole province are sampling survey data,and data of regions are comprehensive statistics.

7-16 续表 continued

单位：万公顷 (10 000 hectares)

州 市	Region	油料播种面积 Oil-bearing Crops	花 生 Peanuts	油菜籽 Rapeseeds	甘 蔗 Sugarcane	烤烟播种面积 Flue-cured Tobacco	蔬菜播种面积 Vegetables and Melon	其他作物 Other Farm Crops
全 省	**Yunnan**	**31.12**	**4.34**	**25.77**	**23.57**	**39.58**	**122.37**	**38.29**
昆 明	Kunming	0.79	0.07	0.68		3.43	11.54	3.08
曲 靖	Qujing	8.45	0.06	8.32		7.71	18.00	12.33
玉 溪	Yuxi	1.44	0.08	1.32	0.84	3.96	10.14	0.91
保 山	Baoshan	2.97	0.09	2.85	1.67	2.87	4.67	1.11
昭 通	Zhaotong	2.48	0.46	1.96	0.06	1.59	9.85	5.12
丽 江	Lijiang	0.53	0.07	0.41	0.01	1.42	2.00	0.47
普 洱	Pu'er	1.47	0.81	0.64	4.34	2.47	4.05	2.80
临 沧	Lincang	1.27	0.18	1.03	6.79	1.99	3.95	1.96
楚 雄	Chuxiong	2.51	0.10	2.35	0.09	3.99	10.32	1.51
红 河	Honghe	1.71	0.74	0.92	1.60	3.46	15.63	4.14
文 山	Wenshan	5.43	1.49	3.52	2.25	2.51	19.70	2.41
西双版纳	Xishuangbanna	0.09	0.09		1.36		2.38	0.27
大 理	Dali	1.19	0.04	1.13	0.01	3.18	5.54	0.43
德 宏	Dehong	0.40	0.05	0.35	4.53	0.94	3.30	1.20
怒 江	Nujiang	0.19	0.02	0.08	0.02		0.97	0.17
迪 庆	Diqing	0.23		0.21		0.07	0.32	0.39

7-17 橡胶、咖啡和香料作物面积和产量（2005-2020年）

Areas and Output of Rubber, Coffee and Perfume plants (2005-2020)

单位：万公顷、万吨 (10 000 hectare,10 000 tons)

年份 Year	橡胶 Rubber 年末实有面积 Real Area at Year-end	收获面积 Harvest Area	总产量 Total Output	咖啡 Coffee 年末实有面积 Real Area at Year-end	收获面积 Harvest Area	总产量 Total Output	香料作物(折香料油) Perfume Plants (perfume oil) 年末实有面积 Real Area at Year-end	收获面积 Harvest Area	总产量 Total Output
2005	29.90	13.96	24.03	1.72	1.53	2.16	1.00	0.77	0.12
2006	33.41	15.33	26.42	1.84	1.42	2.54	0.70	0.53	0.09
2007	39.65	16.66	28.22	2.04	1.49	2.96	0.52	0.40	0.09
2008	43.58	17.35	25.72	2.43	1.62	3.29	0.45	0.38	0.10
2009	46.14	48.67	18.46	3.66	2.24	4.76	0.48	0.34	0.11
2010	48.67	21.04	33.06	4.31	2.50	4.94	0.60	0.52	0.08
2011	53.03	22.25	36.34	6.13	2.94	6.51	0.60	0.51	0.11
2012	55.64	24.95	38.98	9.23	3.76	9.18	0.50	0.40	0.07
2013	55.43	26.26	42.56	11.91	4.94	11.66	0.56	0.45	0.09
2014	57.10	28.12	43.33	12.21	6.12	13.71	0.68	0.58	0.33
2015	57.34	30.74	43.93	11.80	6.97	13.91	0.59	0.52	0.09
2016	59.17	32.19	44.86	11.70	8.05	15.84	0.48	0.43	0.08
2017	57.73	32.85	43.79	11.07	8.34	16.47	0.42	0.39	0.07
2018	57.14	33.08	45.48	9.96	7.79	15.12	0.45	0.43	0.07
2019	57.14	34.11	45.85	9.25	7.26	14.50	0.45	0.38	0.06
2020	56.37	36.19	47.21	8.91	7.08	13.51	0.42	0.37	0.07

7-18　茶叶、水果生产情况（2005-2020年）

Planting Areas and Output of Tea and Fruits (2005-2020)

单位：万公顷、万吨　　　　(10 000 hectares,10 000 tons)

年 份 Year	茶 叶 Tea		水 果 Fruits		香 蕉 Bananas		苹 果 Apples		柑 橘 Citrus	
	面 积 Area	产 量 Output	面 积 Area	产 量 Output	面 积 Area	产 量 Output	面 积 Area	产 量 Output	面 积 Area	产 量 Output
2005	21.85	11.59	22.48	136.63	2.24	24.52	3.15	15.94	2.79	21.11
2006	24.75	13.82	24.20	162.56	2.46	33.81	3.03	20.20	2.91	24.36
2007	30.29	16.99	26.51	202.37	3.62	54.00	3.11	23.49	3.21	28.08
2008	33.57	17.15	28.90	266.18	5.09	94.85	2.99	26.80	3.29	32.72
2009	35.46	18.29	32.72	342.74	5.85	115.59	3.05	26.93	3.41	38.31
2010	36.77	20.73	31.52	397.91	6.32	133.58	3.09	25.79	3.43	41.66
2011	38.00	23.83	37.69	476.43	7.98	168.74	3.19	25.29	3.65	45.04
2012	38.96	27.17	42.02	581.12	9.13	218.29	4.06	32.24	3.95	51.73
2013	40.06	30.17	43.17	634.52	9.24	240.50	4.19	33.65	4.05	56.61
2014	40.94	33.55	45.79	669.02	9.36	236.96	4.54	38.74	4.20	53.59
2015	42.48	36.58	50.27	726.54	10.23	258.83	4.69	41.38	4.47	59.49
2016	42.21	37.30	57.57	797.77	7.98	210.20	6.93	57.40	5.91	76.90
2017	43.79	39.30	59.43	783.90	7.35	176.80	7.07	59.70	7.57	88.80
2018	46.66	42.33	62.42	813.35	8.57	203.47	5.20	51.94	7.53	98.11
2019	48.09	43.72	65.33	860.32	8.45	211.40	5.48	54.96	8.43	108.57
2020	49.35	46.32	69.89	961.58	8.24	197.64	5.46	60.58	9.76	135.85

注：2016-2017年主要农产品数据为根据第三次全国农业普查结果核定和修订的数据。
Note: Data of output of major farm products from 2016 to 2017 are verified and revised by the Third National Agricultural Census.

7-18 续表 continued

单位：万公顷、万吨 (10 000 hectares,10 000 tons)

年 份 Year	梨 Pears		葡 萄 Grapes		菠 萝 Pineapple		瓜 果 Melon and Fruit		#西 瓜 Watermelon	
	面 积 Area	产 量 Output	面 积 Area	产 量 Output	面 积 Area	产 量 Output	面 积 Area	产 量 Output	面 积 Area	产 量 Output
2005	3.97	19.70	0.56	6.97	0.34	2.21				
2006	4.17	21.69	0.63	9.01	0.37	1.95				
2007	4.34	24.05	0.70	9.38	0.38	2.49	2.22	49.60	1.88	42.62
2008	4.69	28.69	0.79	12.84	0.41	2.89	1.83	47.26	1.49	39.32
2009	4.83	27.87	0.96	16.71	0.43	3.65	1.78	38.89	1.40	31.36
2010	5.16	33.2	1.23	20.6	0.38	3.62	2.49	56.27	2.11	48.22
2011	4.89	36.41	1.92	35.61	0.41	3.63	2.84	71.04	2.39	60.28
2012	5.22	41.63	2.71	54.35	0.40	5.51	2.77	70.40	2.21	59.26
2013	5.32	47.17	2.82	65.94	0.39	4.40	2.52	63.06	1.81	48.86
2014	5.26	48.14	3.56	80.55	0.43	6.85	2.63	63.74	2.08	51.22
2015	5.46	50.88	3.88	85.16	0.57	7.71	3.04	70.21	2.47	60.59
2016	6.59	60.30	5.79	136.50	0.53	7.33	2.68	62.07	2.14	52.46
2017	6.44	63.60	5.55	126.50	0.57	8.96	2.43	58.51	1.83	47.42
2018	6.14	57.62	4.10	101.26	0.62	10.14	2.44	56.21	1.71	43.75
2019	5.97	57.33	3.95	95.09	0.72	11.67	2.49	57.59	1.58	41.49
2020	5.84	65.41	3.90	97.51	0.74	11.58	3.37	81.16	1.80	48.15

7-19 各州市营造林生产情况

Forestry Production by Region

单位：万公顷 (10 000 hectares)

年份 州市	Year Region	人工造林面积 Area of Artificial afforestation	人工更新造林面积 Area of Reforested Slash	森林抚育作业面积 Area of Cultivating Growth	成林抚育面积 Area of Cultivating Mature Forest	零星(四旁)植树(万株) Number of Four-side Tree Planting(10 000 trees)	育苗面积(公顷) Area of Growing Seedings (hectare)	无林地新封山育林面积 Area of afforestation without Forest
2002					5.64	11 226	2 579	
2003					3.12	11 972	3 303	
2004					3.02	10 990	3 098	
2005					1.65	11 687	3 748	
2006					6.11	10 112	2 040	
2007					3.96	8 650	1 911	
2008					2.42	8 891	3 627	
2009					3.84	9 166	4 332	
2010					4.86	9 261	5 823	
2011					12.73	9 323	4 358	
2012					14.02	10 740	6 449	
2013					14.82	9 855	115 997	
2014					14.14	9 885	9 491	
2015		35.05	0.56	18.07		9 614	6 895	3.66
2016		30.84		16.40		9 817	6 352	2.31
2017		27.77		14.33		9 554	15 151	1.79
2018		26.11		16.99		11 511	13 286	1.25
2019		26.12	0.03	7.05				2.29
2020		25.42	0.02	6.63				1.33
昆　明	Kunming	0.72		1.35				
曲　靖	Qujing	1.74		0.01				0.40
玉　溪	Yuxi	1.20		0.33				
保　山	Baoshan	1.15		0.57				0.04
昭　通	Zhaotong	8.01		0.33				0.39
丽　江	Lijiang	1.20		0.23				0.03
普　洱	Pu'er	1.86	0.01	0.71				
临　沧	Lincang	1.51	0.01					
楚　雄	Chuxiong	0.91		0.63				0.11
红　河	Honghe	1.40		0.93				0.03
文　山	Wenshan	3.38						0.28
西双版纳	Xishuangbanna	0.58		0.27				
大　理	Dali	0.64		0.05				0.03
德　宏	Dehong	0.22		0.98				
怒　江	Nujiang	0.56						
迪　庆	Diqing	0.33		0.21				0.05

注：零星(四旁)植树是指在路、沟旁、渠旁、宅旁植树。

Note: Scattered (four-side)Planting Trees refer to trees planted by the roadside,near the ditch,canal and house.

7–20 各州市主要林产品产量（2020年）

Output of Major Forest Products by Region (2020)

单位：万吨 (10 000 tons)

州 市	Region	橡 胶 Rubber	松 脂 Pine Resin	油桐籽 Tung-oil Seeds	油茶籽 Rapeseeds	核 桃 Walnuts	板 栗 Chestnuts	紫 胶 Shellac
全 省	**Yunnan**	**47.21**	**9.13**	**1.69**	**2.66**	**112.50**	**11.01**	**0.20**
昆 明	Kunming				0.01	1.31	4.29	
曲 靖	Qujing			0.75	0.58	2.04	0.47	
玉 溪	Yuxi		0.03		0.01	1.67	1.22	
保 山	Baoshan		0.43	0.01	0.13	16.36	0.39	0.01
昭 通	Zhaotong			0.13		3.30	0.25	
丽 江	Lijiang					2.20	0.11	
普 洱	Pu'er	8.09	7.79		0.01	2.19	0.17	0.08
临 沧	Lincang	4.90	0.57	0.05	0.01	26.89	0.09	0.06
楚 雄	Chuxiong		0.26			7.18	2.94	
红 河	Honghe	2.44			0.02	0.90	0.30	0.05
文 山	Wenshan	0.01	0.02	0.71	1.44	0.44	0.11	
西双版纳	Xishuangbanna	31.20	0.01			0.01	0.00	
大 理	Dali		0.02	0.02		42.56	0.49	
德 宏	Dehong	0.58		0.01	0.44	2.74	0.07	
怒 江	Nujiang			0.02	0.01	1.18	0.03	
迪 庆	Diqing					1.53	0.07	

7−21 各州市畜产品产量（2020年）

Output of Livestock Products by Region (2020)

单位：万吨 (10 000 tons)

州　市	Region	畜产品产量 Output of Livestock Products	猪肉 Pork	牛肉 Beef	羊肉 Mutton	牛奶 Cow Milk	禽蛋 Eggs
全　省	**Yunnan**	**353.28**	**291.57**	**40.94**	**20.77**	**67.29**	**41.75**
昆　明	Kunming	18.69	14.66	2.34	1.69	14.11	5.75
曲　靖	Qujing	89.13	75.17	8.55	5.41	4.46	3.79
玉　溪	Yuxi	11.25	8.91	1.60	0.74	0.92	7.61
保　山	Baoshan	30.53	26.73	2.61	1.19	1.21	1.12
昭　通	Zhaotong	27.97	24.98	2.03	0.96		1.59
丽　江	Lijiang	8.92	7.07	0.83	1.02	0.41	0.29
普　洱	Pu'er	17.14	15.27	1.34	0.53	0.02	1.11
临　沧	Lincang	23.28	20.74	1.75	0.79	0.07	0.69
楚　雄	Chuxiong	24.11	18.71	3.31	2.09	0.05	1.01
红　河	Honghe	35.45	29.19	4.62	1.64	7.65	9.21
文　山	Wenshan	22.45	16.65	4.79	1.01	0.21	1.69
西双版纳	Xishuangbanna	2.72	2.34	0.35	0.03		0.41
大　理	Dali	30.10	22.31	4.88	2.91	35.69	6.87
德　宏	Dehong	4.91	3.44	1.30	0.17	0.24	0.40
怒　江	Nujiang	3.69	2.98	0.27	0.44	0.01	0.15
迪　庆	Diqing	2.94	2.42	0.37	0.15	2.21	0.07

7-22　各州市水产品产量及养殖面积（2020年）

Output of Aquatic Products and Aquaculture Areas by Region (2020)

单位：万吨、万公顷　　(10 000 tons,10 000 hectare)

州　市	Region	水产品产量 Output of Aquatic Products	养殖产量 Artificially Cultured	捕捞产量 Naturally Grown	鱼类 Fish	虾蟹类 Shrimps, Prawns and Crabs	贝类 Shellfish	其他 Others	水产养殖面积 Aquiculture Area
全　省	**Yunnan**	**64.40**	**61.45**	**2.94**	**63.32**	**0.54**	**0.15**	**0.39**	**10.58**
昆　明	Kunming	3.60	3.54	0.06	3.60				0.60
曲　靖	Qujing	9.95	8.93	1.02	9.60	0.33		0.01	1.09
玉　溪	Yuxi	1.43	0.95	0.47	1.42			0.01	0.23
保　山	Baoshan	4.27	4.09	0.18	4.23	0.03			1.18
昭　通	Zhaotong	4.00	4.00		3.99	0.01			0.47
丽　江	Lijiang	1.85	1.61	0.24	1.78			0.07	0.32
普　洱	Pu'er	16.06	11.50	4.56	15.63	0.18	0.04	0.20	0.85
临　沧	Lincang	12.77	11.42	1.35	12.63	0.05	0.06	0.03	1.13
楚　雄	Chuxiong	4.16	4.14	0.02	4.14	0.01		0.01	0.99
红　河	Honghe	4.70	4.52	0.18	4.60	0.03		0.06	0.64
文　山	Wenshan	6.03	5.26	0.77	5.92	0.08	0.01	0.01	1.17
西双版纳	Xishuangbanna	8.96	8.65	0.31	8.83	0.03	0.01	0.09	0.57
大　理	Dali	5.93	4.57	1.36	5.85	0.08			0.55
德　宏	Dehong	4.41	4.19	0.22	4.31	0.01	0.08		0.72
怒　江	Nujiang	0.07	0.07		0.07				0.01
迪　庆	Diqing	0.29	0.29		0.29				0.05

注：2020年全省数据为核定数，州（市）数据为年报数。

Note: In 2020, data of the whole province are verified, and the data by region are annual reports.

7-23 各州市主要蔬菜产品产量（2020年）

Output of Major Vegetable Products by Region (2020)

单位：万吨 (10 000 tons)

州 市	Region	蔬菜产量 Yield of Vegetable	叶菜类 Leaf Vegetables	白菜类 Chinese Cabbage	甘蓝类 Wild Cabbage	根茎类 Rhizome	瓜菜类 Melon Vegetables	豆类 Soybeans	茄果类 Eggplant Vegetables	葱蒜类 Onion and Garlic Vegetables	水生菜类 Aquatic Vegetables
全 省	**Yunnan**	**2 507.89**	**324.77**	**560.06**	**146.24**	**377.67**	**168.46**	**202.92**	**282.50**	**257.59**	**34.14**
昆 明	Kunming	332.46	71.77	106.31	22.34	23.45	20.26	14.26	23.95	15.38	3.90
曲 靖	Qujing	341.16	37.31	125.27	9.92	77.65	10.84	9.85	25.04	11.35	4.27
玉 溪	Yuxi	290.16	22.47	40.96	45.90	39.76	11.55	32.77	21.09	48.82	2.19
保 山	Baoshan	99.72	7.75	9.36	1.94	9.54	11.98	26.35	22.14	4.38	3.08
昭 通	Zhaotong	158.85	13.54	73.42	7.54	29.07	8.63	5.72	10.70	6.71	0.94
丽 江	Lijiang	33.43	3.05	7.55	0.49	5.64	1.74	2.15	2.65	5.56	2.79
普 洱	Pu'er	61.91	10.78	11.13	2.96	9.65	8.82	6.37	7.32	2.85	0.15
临 沧	Lincang	86.39	8.00	10.19	2.61	10.61	9.51	20.70	18.03	3.29	0.61
楚 雄	Chuxiong	266.37	45.52	54.54	13.26	44.81	21.04	27.19	37.32	14.30	1.04
红 河	Honghe	420.27	47.42	67.43	25.15	54.38	32.22	21.85	55.77	91.81	12.24
文 山	Wenshan	163.27	23.78	25.60	7.94	45.30	11.57	6.47	32.47	4.91	0.65
西双版纳	Xishuangbanna	39.96	2.84	2.41	1.49	2.44	6.36	12.17	7.52	1.39	0.62
大 理	Dali	152.89	22.55	21.63	3.14	17.97	7.55	12.48	13.46	44.40	1.56
德 宏	Dehong	46.34	5.93	2.19	1.01	3.55	4.37	4.08	2.97	1.35	0.09
怒 江	Nujiang	9.01	1.65	1.22	0.26	2.38	1.64	0.40	0.76	0.53	
迪 庆	Diqing	5.72	0.41	0.87	0.31	1.47	0.36	0.11	1.30	0.57	

7-24 各州市特种作物生产情况（2020年）

Output of Special Crops by Region (2020)

州市	Region	鲜切花 (亿枝) Fresh Cut Flowers (100 million branches)	药材 (万吨) Medicinal Materials (10 000 tons)	食用菌 (万吨) Edible Mushrooms (10 000 tons)
全省	**Yunnan**	**146.57**	**63.08**	**11.88**
昆明	Kunming	91.93	3.84	0.20
曲靖	Qujing	8.38	11.54	4.90
玉溪	Yuxi	17.47	2.33	0.22
保山	Baoshan	0.03	9.01	0.36
昭通	Zhaotong	0.06	2.18	0.18
丽江	Lijiang	0.56	4.39	0.03
普洱	Pu'er	0.30	1.70	0.50
临沧	Lincang	0.09	0.82	0.36
楚雄	Chuxiong	17.86	3.32	1.32
红河	Honghe	9.26	5.52	0.30
文山	Wenshan	0.04	2.15	1.23
西双版纳	Xishuangbanna	0.44	0.30	0.68
大理	Dali	0.11	9.11	0.46
德宏	Dehong	0.01	1.99	1.02
怒江	Nujiang	0.00	0.42	0.01
迪庆	Diqing	0.02	4.47	0.09

主要统计指标解释

农、林、牧、渔业总产值 指以货币形式表现的农林渔业全部产品总量和对农、林、牧、渔业生产活动进行的各种支持性服务活动的价值。它反映了一定时期（通常指一年）农、林、牧、渔业生产及其服务的总成果和总规模。

1957 年以前的农业总产值包括了厩肥和农民自给性手工业（如农民自制衣服、鞋、袜，自己从事粮食初步加工等）。1958 年及以后的农业总产值，林业中增加了村及村以下竹木采伐产值；牧业中取消了厩肥产值；副业中取消了农民自给性手工业产值，增加了村及村以下的工业产值；渔业中增加了机械化捕鱼产值。1980 年及以后农业总产值，在副业中增加了农民商品性家庭手工业的产值。从 1984 年起村及村以下办工业产值划归工业。1993 年取消副业产值，农业总产值改为农、林、牧、渔业总产值。原副业产值的采集野生植物和农民家庭兼营商品性工业划归农业产值；捕猎野兽野禽划归牧业产值。2003 年开始，增加农林牧渔服务业产值，同时取消农民家庭兼营商品性工业，竹木采运由村及村以下扩大到全社会口径。

农、林、牧、渔业中间消耗 指各种经济类型的农业生产单位和农户在农业生产经营过程中投入（或消耗）的各种物质产品和劳务价值的总和。包括中间物质消耗和中间劳务消耗两个部分。计入中间消耗必须具备以下两个条件：一是与总产出相对应的生产过程中消耗的物质产品和劳务活动；二是本期投入并一次性消耗的不属于固定资产的非耐用品。

自来水受益村数 包括取水、净水、输配水三部分组成的自来水供给的，或由取水和输配水两部分的符合饮用卫生标准的简易自来水年末实际受益的村委会个数。

通汽车村数 指拥有乡级以上公路通过，并通达客运或货运汽车的村委会个数。

粮食产量 指全社会的产量。包括国营农场等全民所有制经营的、集体统一经营的和农民家庭经营的粮食产量，还包括工矿企业家属办的农场和其他生产单位的产量。粮食除包括稻谷、小麦、玉米、高粱、谷子及其他杂粮外，还包括薯类和大豆。其产量计算方法，豆类按去豆荚后的干豆计算；薯类（包括甘薯和马铃薯，不包括芋头和木薯）1963 年以前按每 4 公斤鲜薯折 1 公斤粮食计算，从 1964 年以后按 5 公斤鲜薯折 1 公斤粮食计算。其他粮食一律按脱粒后的原粮计算。

谷物 指稻谷、小麦、玉米、谷子、高粱和其他谷物，不包括薯类和豆类。其他谷物指除稻谷、小麦、玉谷、高粱以外的一些子实主要用作粮食的作物，包括大麦、元麦（青稞）、莜麦、荞麦、糜子等。

油料产量 指全部油料作物的生产量。包括花生、油菜籽、芝麻、向日葵子、胡麻子（亚麻子）和其他油料。不包括大豆、木本油料和野生油料。花生以带壳干花生计算。

水产品产量 指人工养殖的水产品天然生长的水产品的捕捞量。包括海水的鱼类、虾蟹类、贝类和藻类以及淡水的鱼类、虾蟹类、贝类，不包括淡水水生植物。

猪、牛、羊产量 指当年的猪、牛、羊的肉产量。即屠宰后除去头、蹄、下水后带骨肉（即胴体重）的重量。

期初（末）畜禽存栏头（只）数 指报告期初（末）农村各种合作经济组织和国营农场、农民个人、机关、团体、学校、工矿企业、部队等单位以及城镇居民饲养的大牲畜、猪、羊、家禽等畜禽的存栏数。数据上报方式及数据调整情况同猪、牛、羊肉产量。

耕地灌溉面积 指具有一定的水源，地块比较平整，灌溉工程或设备已经配套，在一般年景下当年能够正常灌溉的耕地面积。在一般情况下，耕地灌溉面积应等于灌溉工程或设备已经配套，能够正常灌溉的水田和水浇地面积之和。它是反映我国农田水利建设的重要指标。

农作物播种面积 指日历年度内收获农作物在全部土地（耕地或非耕地）上的播种或移植面积。凡是本年内收获的农作物，无论是本年还是上年播种，都算为播种面积，但不包括本年播种，下年收获的农作物面积。

农用化肥施用量 指本年内实际用于农业生产的化肥数量，包括氮肥、磷肥、钾肥和复合肥。化肥施用量要求按折纯量计算数量。折纯量是指把氮肥、磷肥、钾肥分别按含氮、含五氧化二磷、含氧化钾的百分之百成分进行折算后的数量。复合肥按其所含主要成分折算。公式为：

折纯量 = 实物量 × 某种化肥有效成分含量的百分比

农业机械总动力 指主要用于农、林、牧、渔业的各种动力机械的动力总和。包括耕作机械、排灌机械、收获机械、农用运输机械、植物保护机械、牧业机械、林业机械、渔业机械和其他农业机械（内燃机按引擎马力折成瓦（特）计算、电动机按功率折成瓦（特）计算）。不包括专门用于乡、镇、村、组办工业、基本建设、非农业运输、科学试验和教学等非农业生产方面用的动力机械与作业机械。这个指标的统计数据主要来源于农机部门。

Explanatory Notes on Main Statistical Indicators

Gross Output Value of Farming, Forestry, Animal Husbandry and Fishery refers to the total value of products of farming, forestry, animal husbandry and fishery and the value of support services for production of farming, forestry, animal husbandry and fishery, which reflects the total scale and result of agricultural production and services during a given period (generally one year).

The gross agricultural output value before 1957 included output value of barnyard manure and farmers' self-supporting handicraft industry (e.g., self-made clothing, shoes, socks, initial grain processing, etc.). Since 1958, output value of felling timber and bamboo by villages and organizations has been included in below village that of forestry; output value of barnyard manure has been excluded from that of animal husbandry; output value of farmers' self-supporting handicraft industry has been excluded from that of sideline production, while output value of industries run by villages and organizations had been included in it; output value of mechanized fishing has been included in that of fishery. Since 1980, output value of farmers' commercial household handicraft industry has been added to that of sideline production. Since 1984, output value of industries run by villages or organizations below village has been classified into that of industry. Since 1993, output value of sideline production has been cancelled and gross agricultural output value has been changed to gross output value of farming, forestry, animal husbandry and fishery; output value of wild plants gathering and commercial industry run by rural households has been incorporated to agricultural output value; output value of animal and bird hunting has been classified into that of animal husbandry. Since 2003, output value of services of farming, forestry, animal husbandry and fishery has been added while farmers' commercial household industry has been cancelled, and transporting and felling timber and bamboo by villages and organizations below village has been expanded to all levels.

Intermediate Consumption of Farming, Forestry, Animal Husbandry and Fishery refers to the total value of material products and labor input (or consumed) by various agricultural production entities and rural households in the process of agricultural production and operation. It is composed of intermediate material consumption and intermediate labor consumption. Items calculated into intermediate consumption should satisfy the following two conditions: first, they are material products and labor consumed in the process of production against total output; second, they are is non-durable goods that do not belong to fixed assets but input and consumed up one time in the present phase.

Number of Villages Accessible to Motor Vehicle refers to the number of villages with town-level road passing through and transport service.

Grain Yield refers to the total yield in the whole country including grain produced by state farms, collective entities, rural households, industrial enterprises and mines. Grain includes rice, wheat, maize, sorghum, millet and other cereals as well as tubers and soybeans. Output of beans refers to dry beans without pods. Output of tubers (sweet potatoes and potatoes, not including taros and cassava) was converted into that of grain at the ratio 4:1, i.e. 4 kilograms of fresh tubers was equivalent to 1 kilogram of grain up to 1963. Since 1964 the ratio for conversion has been 5:1. Tubers supplied as vegetables (such as potatoes) in cities and suburbs are calculated as fresh vegetables and their output is not included in the output of grain. Other kinds of grain are calculated as husked grain.

Cereals refer to rice, wheat, maize millet, sorghum and other kinds of grain, but tubers and beans are not included. Other kinds of grain refer to some crops whose seeds are mainly used for food such as barley, highland barley, naked oats, buckwheat, broom corn millet, etc.

Output of Oil-bearing Crops refers to the total production of oil-bearing crops of various kinds, including peanuts (dry, in shell), rapeseeds, sesame, sunflower seeds, flax seeds, and other oil-bearing crops. Soybeans, oil-bearing woody plants, and wild oil-bearing crops are not included.

Output of Aquatic Products refers to catches of both artificially cultured and naturally grown aquatic products, including fish, shrimps, crabs and shellfish in sea and inland water as well as seaweed. Freshwater plants are not included.

Output of Pork, Beef, and Mutton refers to the weight of the meat of slaughtered hogs, cattle, sheep and goats with head, feet, and offal taken away.

Number of Livestock or Poultry in Stock at Beginning (or End) of Period refers to the total number of large animals, pigs, sheep, fowls, etc. raised by rural cooperative organizations, State farms, rural individuals, government agencies, schools, industrial and mining enterprises, army, and urban residents at the beginning (or end) of the reference period. Data reporting system and data adjustment are the same as that in the output of pork, beef and mutton.

Irrigated Area of cultivated land refers to area of land that are effectively irrigated, i.e. relatively level land, where there are water sources or complete sets of irrigation facilities to lift and move adequate water for irrigation purpose under normal conditions. Under normal situations, irrigated area of cultivated land is the sum of watered fields and irrigated fields where irrigation systems or equipment have been installed for regular irrigation purpose. It is an important indicator to reflect the farmland water conservancy construction in China.

Sown Area of Crops refers to area of all land (cultivated or non-cultivated area) sown or transplanted with crops that are harvested within the calendar yaer. All Crops harvested within the yaer are counted as sown area, regardless of being sown in this year or the previous year. Crops sown this year but will be harvested in the coming year are excluded.

Consumption of Chemical Fertilizers in Agriculture refers to the quantity of chemical fertilizers applied in agriculture in the year, including nitrogenous fertilizer, phosphate fertilizer, potash fertilizer, and compound fertilizer. The consumption of chemical fertilizers is calculated in terms of volume of effective components by means of converting the gross weight of the respective fertilizers into weight containing effective component (e.g. nitrogen content in nitrogenous fertilizer, phosphorous pentoxide contents in phosphate fertilizer, and potassium oxide contents in potash fertilizer). Compound fertilizer is converted in regard to its major components. The formula is:

Volume of effective component=physical quantity×effective component of certain chemical fertilizer(%)

Total Power of Agricultural Machinery refers to total mechanical power of machinery used in agriculture, forestry, animal husbandry and fishery, including machinery for ploughing, irrigation and drainage, harvesting, transport, plant protection, animal husbandry, forestry and fishery and other agricultural machineries. (For the power of internal combustion engines, it is converted from its horsepower into watts while for electric motors the output power is converted into watts.) Machinery employed for non-agricultural purposes, such as the machines used in township-run and village-run industry, construction, non-agricultural transport, scientific experiments and teaching, are not included. Data are mainly from agricultural machinery agencies.

Chapter 8

八、工业和能源
Industry and Energy

8-1 工业总产值及其构成（1978-2020年）

Gross Industrial Output Value by Light and Heavy Industry (1978-2020)

单位：亿元 (100 million yuan)

年份 Year	工业总产值 Gross Industrial Output Value	轻工业 Light Industry	重工业 Heavy Industry	占全部工业总产值的比重(%) Share in Gross Industrial Output Value(%) 轻工业 Light Industry	重工业 Heavy Industry
1978	55.43	23.84	31.60	43.0	57.0
1979	62.38	26.26	36.12	42.1	57.9
1980	65.35	29.54	35.81	45.2	54.8
1981	72.54	35.18	37.36	48.5	51.5
1982	83.60	41.30	42.30	49.4	50.6
1983	95.11	47.37	47.75	49.8	50.2
1984	112.27	55.13	57.15	49.1	50.9
1985	136.26	65.93	70.33	48.4	51.6
1986	147.02	67.71	79.31	46.1	53.9
1987	181.85	85.53	96.32	47.0	53.0
1988	244.63	121.64	122.99	49.7	50.3
1989	304.91	154.61	150.30	50.7	49.3
1990	345.26	181.14	164.12	52.5	47.5
1991	393.63	203.85	189.78	51.8	48.2
1992	477.07	240.85	236.22	50.5	49.5
1993	690.08	333.28	356.79	48.3	51.7
1994	948.71	514.69	434.02	54.3	45.7
1995	1 230.01	656.60	573.41	53.4	46.6
1996	1 291.38	695.56	595.82	53.9	46.1
1997	1 440.11	751.15	688.96	52.2	47.8
1998	1 503.23	774.72	728.52	51.5	48.5
1999	1 561.08	793.88	767.20	50.9	49.1
2000	1 589.36	802.70	786.66	50.5	49.5
2001	1 675.11	863.76	811.35	51.6	48.4
2002	1 850.46	954.27	896.19	51.6	48.4
2003	2 176.40	1 014.70	1 161.69	46.6	53.4
2004	2 479.07	917.21	1 561.86	37.0	63.0
2005	3 249.84	1 120.47	2 129.37	34.5	65.5
2006	4 110.25	1 269.63	2 840.61	30.9	69.1
2007	5 137.30	1 830.16	3 307.14	35.6	64.4
2008	5 738.81	1 447.80	4 291.01	25.2	74.8
2009	6 261.75	1 930.88	4 330.87	30.8	69.2
2010	7 880.70	2 317.95	5 562.75	29.4	70.6
2011	9 595.15	2 779.50	6 815.66	29.0	71.0
2012	11 641.46	3 555.22	8 086.24	30.5	69.5
2013	12 756.98	3 911.54	8 845.44	30.7	69.3
2014	12 840.64	4 017.84	8 822.80	31.3	68.7
2015	12 169.67	4 257.51	7 912.16	35.0	65.0
2016	12 823.21	4 650.60	8 172.61	36.3	63.7
2017	13 112.95	4 563.72	8 549.23	34.8	65.2
2018	14 607.31	4 671.10	9 936.21	32.0	68.0
2019	16 784.52	5 117.95	11 666.57	30.5	69.5
2020	16 975.20	5 056.80	11 918.40	29.8	70.2

注：本表总产值按当年价格计算。
Note: Gross output values in this table are calculated at current prices.

8-2 规模以上工业增加值（2016-2020年）

单位：亿元

工业行业	Industrial Sector	2016 增加值 Industrial Added Value	2016 比上年增长(%) Increase Rate over Last Year (%)
全　省	**Yunnan**	**3 668.28**	**6.5**
轻工业	Light Industry	1 798.76	2.1
重工业	Heavy Industry	1 869.52	10.9
按行业类别分	**Grouped by Industry Sector**		
采矿业	**Mining**	**328.93**	**17.3**
煤炭开采和洗选业	Mining and Washing of Coal	124.37	26.1
石油和天然气开采业	Extraction of Petroleum and Natural Gas		
黑色金属矿采选业	Mining and Processing of Ferrous Metal Ores	52.93	10.3
有色金属矿采选业	Mining and Processing of Non-Ferrous Metal Ores	109.15	19.3
非金属矿采选业	Mining and Processing of Nonmetal Ores	42.48	-1.8
开采辅助活动	Mining Auxiliary Activities		
其他采矿业	Other Minerals Mining		
制造业	**Manufacturing Industry**	**2 683.34**	**5.6**
农副食品工业	Processing of Food from Agricultural Products	149.01	17.3
食品制造业	Manufacture of Foods	57.22	21.6
酒、饮料和精制茶制造业	Beverage Manufacturing	107.74	18.5
烟草制品业	Manufacture of Tobacco	1 183.50	-4.3
纺织业	Manufacture of Textile	5.82	17.5
纺织服装、服饰业	Textile,Clothing, Footwear Production	5.64	34.0
皮革、毛皮、羽毛及其制品和制鞋业	Feather, Furs, Down, Related Products and Footwear	2.79	10.5
木材加工及木、竹、藤、棕、草制品业	Processing of Timber,Manufacture of Wood,Bamboo,Rattan,Palm and Straw Products	23.76	5.4
家具制造业	Manufacture of Furniture	2.19	45.3
造纸及纸制品业	Manufacture of Paper and Paper Products	26.15	22.8
印刷业和记录媒介的复制	Printing, Reproduction of Recording Media	24.42	0.4
文教、工美、体育和娱乐用品制造业	Manufacture of Culture,Education,Industrial Arts,Sports and Entertainment Goods	45.76	9.8
石油加工、炼焦及核燃料工业	Processing of Petroleum, Coking, Processing of Nuclear Fuel	15.63	6.2
化学原料及化学制品制造业	Manufacture of Raw Chemical Materials and Chemical Products	156.16	3.3
医药制造业	Manufacture of Medicines	113.07	16.9
化学纤维制造业	Manufacture of Chemical Fibers	5.48	-2.8
橡胶和塑料制品业	Rubber and Plastic Products	24.37	7.2
非金属矿物制品业	Manufacture of Non-metallic Mineral Products	144.45	21.6
黑色金属冶炼及压延工业	Smelting and Pressing of Ferrous Metals	64.42	-5.3
有色金属冶炼及压延工业	Smelting and Pressing of Non-ferrous Metals	315.97	6.9
金属制品业	Manufacture of Metal Products	28.29	36.2
通用设备制造业	Manufacture of General Purpose Machinery	36.10	8.7
专用设备制造业	Manufacture of Special Purpose Machinery	20.21	10.8
汽车制造业	Automotive Industry	35.38	27.4
铁路、船舶、航空航天和其他运输设备制造业	Manufacture of Trnmsport Equipment for Railway,Boats and Aerospace and Other Transport Equipments	15.14	38.2
电气机械及器材制造业	Manufacture of Electrical Machinery and Equipment	19.02	1.2
计算机、通信和其他电子设备制造业	Computers,Communication Equipment and Other Computers and Other Electronic Equipment	47.16	506.9
仪器仪表制造业	Instrument Industry	1.23	2.7
其他制造业	Others	1.02	3.8
废弃资源综合利用业	Comprehensive Utilization of Discarded Resources and Waste	5.87	29.9
金属制品、机械和设备修理业	Manufacture of Metal Products, Machinery and Equipment Repairing	0.34	62.6
电力、热力、燃气及水生产和供应业	**Production and Supply of Electricity, Heat ,Gas and Water**	**656.01**	**4.9**
电力、热力生产和供应业	Production and Supply of Electric Power and Heat Power	615.90	5.2
燃气生产和供应业	Production and Supply of Gas	22.64	-3.7
水的生产和供应业	Production and Supply of Water	17.47	4.5

注：本表绝对数按当年价格计算，增幅按可比价计算。

Added Value of Industry Above Designated Size (2016-2020)

(100 million yuan)

2017		2018		2019		2020	
增加值 Industrial Added Value	比上年增长(%) Increase Rate over Last Year (%)	比上年增长 Industrial Added Value	占 比 (%) Percentage	比上年增长(%) Increase Rate over Last Year (%)	占 比 (%) Percentage	比上年增长(%) Increase Rate over Last Year (%)	占 比 (%) Percentage
3 876.34	**10.6**	**11.8**	**100.0**	**8.1**	**100.0**	**2.4**	**100.0**
1 905.33	4.4	3.6	45.3	2.8	39.6	-1.2	39.2
1 971.01	17.5	19.8	54.7	11.8	60.4	4.7	60.8
316.35	**9.3**	**6.6**	**7.1**	**8.1**	**8.8**	**0.8**	**8.4**
85.40	7.7	5.5	2.1	14.8	3.5	-1.6	3.3
56.36	12.4	4.5	1.1	8.6	1.1	6.6	1.2
129.95	11.3	11.5	3.1	4.2	3.3	4.1	3.1
44.64	4.1	-3.8	0.8	-0.6	1.0	-8.5	0.8
				-36.6	0.0	9.6	0.0
						-100.0	0.0
2 827.82	**8.5**	**10.9**	**75.0**	**6.5**	**71.4**	**1.6**	**70.7**
164.77	11.7	10.1	3.9	6.2	3.6	-5.8	3.2
63.14	10.4	2.9	1.4	9.3	1.5	-6.0	1.3
113.52	11.4	6.1	2.6	7.8	2.8	-10.0	2.7
1 220.48	0.5	1.3	29.1	1.1	24.7	0.8	25.8
6.91	8.8	0.4	0.1	0.3	0.1	-3.4	0.1
5.26	4.5	14.6	0.1	11.3	0.1	-18.8	0.1
3.09	4.7	6.0	0.1	2.0	0.1	10.5	0.0
23.68	5.0	4.0	0.5	10.2	0.4	-12.9	0.3
4.28	52.9	11.7	0.1	-21.6	0.04	-14.2	0.0
29.61	14.6	1.0	0.7	7.4	0.6	-4.9	0.5
24.28	2.4	12.0	0.6	3.9	0.5	-5.1	0.4
45.88	1.7	14.3	1.2	3.7	1.0	-10.9	0.7
66.82	534.3	145.7	4.7	8.3	4.8	-10.2	3.8
151.70	3.6	8.0	4.1	0.7	4.3	-0.3	4.0
139.60	13.5	5.6	3.3	4.9	3.0	-4.3	2.7
6.11	4.9	-3.8	0.1	-2.0	0.1	-2.3	0.1
24.33	-0.7	12.1	0.6	0.2	0.5	5.2	0.5
189.75	15.2	6.8	5.3	10.9	5.6	3.0	5.6
95.08	8.2	11.0	3.5	18.1	3.9	11.8	3.6
230.96	6.5	12.4	6.9	4.9	7.3	11.5	8.7
27.08	-8.8	17.9	0.8	3.5	0.7	1.1	0.6
20.18	-2.0	-8.4	0.2	-0.5	0.2	13.8	0.3
24.92	11.3	-0.9	0.3	2.6	0.3	-10.0	0.3
43.63	30.6	4.8	0.9	-30.1	0.6	-42.2	0.4
8.79	-39.8	-9.0	0.1	6.1	0.2	-16.4	0.1
23.02	5.7	4.5	0.5	9.5	0.5	-1.0	0.5
58.76	127.4	75.5	2.5	67.0	3.3	43.1	3.7
3.12	74.6	33.0	0.1	44.6	0.2	-30.8	0.1
0.89	-4.6	-42.5	0.0	-6.5	0.0	97.8	0.0
7.72	60.3	41.5	0.3	19.6	0.2	15.5	0.2
0.47	-0.7	2 914.3	0.4	3.2	0.4	0.7	0.4
732.17	**19.5**	**17.7**	**17.8**	**12.8**	**19.7**	**5.5**	**21.0**
661.39	19.6	18.3	15.8	12.8	18.0	6.5	19.1
50.14	24.3	17.0	1.4	11.2	1.2	-1.8	1.3
20.63	6.2	1.8	0.6	15.0	0.6	-8.7	0.5

Note: Absolute figures in this table are calculated at current prices while increase rates are calculated at comparable prices.

8-3 规模以上工业发展指数（2010-2020年）

(按可比价格计算，上年=100)

工业行业	Industrial Sector	2010	2011
全　省	**Yunnan**	**115.0**	**118.0**
轻工业	Light Industry	115.0	117.9
重工业	. Heavy Industry	115.0	118.0
按行业类别分	**Grouped by Industry Sector**		
采矿业	**Mining**		
煤炭开采和洗选业	Mining and Washing of Coal	114.8	129.0
石油和天然气开采业	Extraction of Petroleum and Natural Gas	44.7	
黑色金属矿采选业	Mining and Processing of Ferrous Metal Ores	114.7	133.8
有色金属矿采选业	Mining and Processing of Non-Ferrous Metal Ores	105.7	118.2
非金属矿采选业	Mining and Processing of Nonmetal Ores	109.2	118.9
开采辅助活动	Mining Auxiliary Activities		
其他采矿业	Other Minerals Mining		
制造业	**Manufacturing Industry**		
农副食品加工业	Processing of Food from Agricultural Products	109.7	119.7
食品制造业	Manufacture of Foods	127.1	127.2
酒、饮料和精制茶制造业	Beverage Manufacturing	122.6	125.1
烟草制品业	Manufacture of Tobacco	116.0	117.5
纺织业	Manufacture of Textile	117.7	105.6
纺织服装、服饰业	Textile,Clothing, Footwear Production	114.9	98.1
皮革、毛皮、羽毛及其制品和制鞋业	Feather, Furs, Down, Related Products and Footwear	111.3	
木材加工及木、竹、藤、棕、草制品业	Processing of Timber,Manufacture of Wood,Bamboo,Rattan,Palm and Straw Products	139.2	107.6
家具制造业	Manufacture of Furniture	139.8	86.0
造纸及纸制品业	Manufacture of Paper and Paper Products	102.8	115.3
印刷业和记录媒介的复制	Printing, Reproduction of Recording Media	108.8	110.6
文教、工美、体育和娱乐用品制造业	Manufacture of Culture,Education,Industrial Arts,Sports and Entertainment Goods		
石油加工、炼焦及核燃料加工业	Processing of Petroleum, Coking, Processing of Nuclear Fuel	115.8	103.5
化学原料及化学制品制造业	Manufacture of Raw Chemical Materials and Chemical Products	117.1	122.1
医药制造业	Manufacture of Medicines	112.0	122.7
化学纤维制造业	Manufacture of Chemical Fibers	97.6	101.1
橡胶制品业	Manufacture of Rubber	148.1	124.5
塑料制品业	Manufacture of Plastics	109.6	114.7
橡胶和塑料制品业	Rubber and Plastic Products		
非金属矿物制品业	Manufacture of Non-metallic Mineral Products	118.9	120.1
黑色金属冶炼及压延加工业	Smelting and Pressing of Ferrous Metals	118.7	112.6
有色金属冶炼及压延加工业	Smelting and Pressing of Non-ferrous Metals	111.0	116.7
金属制品业	Manufacture of Metal Products	104.2	111.6
通用设备制造业	Manufacture of General Purpose Machinery	142.7	115.7
专用设备制造业	Manufacture of Special Purpose Machinery	109.8	99.8
交通运输设备制造业	Manufacture of Transport Equipment	99.9	109.6
汽车制造业	Automotive Industry		
铁路、船舶、航空航天和其他运输设备制造业	Manufacture of Transport Equipment for Railway,Boats and Aerospace and Other Transport Equipments		
电气机械及器材制造业	Manufacture of Electrical Machinery and Equipment	104.7	105.6
计算机、通信和其他电子设备制造业	Computers,Communication Equipment and Other Computers and Other Electronic Equipment	154.2	128.2
仪器仪表制造业	Instrument Industry	110.2	105.6
其他制造业	Others	71.0	104.6
废弃资源综合利用业	Comprehensive Utilization of Discarded Resources and Waste	103.7	128.6
金属制品、机械和设备修理业	Manufacture of Metal Products, Machinery and Equipment Repairing		
电力、热力、燃气及水生产和供应业	**Production and Supply of Electricity, Heat ,Gas and Water**		
电力、热力生产和供应业	Production and Supply of Electric Power and Heat Power	119.9	118.3
燃气生产和供应业	Production and Supply of Gas	139.1	86.4
水的生产和供应业	Production and Supply of Water	96.9	95.6
昆　明	Kunming	115.8	116.6
曲　靖	Qujing	115.1	115.9
玉　溪	Yuxi	115.9	116.6
保　山	Baoshan	115.2	125.6
昭　通	Zhaotong	116.8	122.9
丽　江	Lijiang	124.4	132.7
普　洱	Pu'er	114.0	126.8
临　沧	Lincang	104.6	124.2
楚　雄	Chuxiong	114.4	116.2
红　河	Honghe	110.1	117.1
文　山	Wenshan	116.1	124.2
西双版纳	Xishuangbanna	110.1	118.8
大　理	Dali	115.8	124.7
德　宏	Dehong	128.1	119.1
怒　江	Nujiang	93.2	101.1
迪　庆	Diqing	115.1	111.9

Development Indices of Industry above Designated Size by Sector (2010-2020)

(Data in this table are calculated at comparable prices,preceding year=100)

2012	2013	2014	2015	2016	2017	2018	2019	2020
115.6	**112.3**	**107.3**	**106.7**	**106.5**	**110.6**	**111.8**	**108.1**	**102.4**
117.1	107.4	110.1	106.5	102.1	104.4	103.6	102.8	98.8
114.4	116.3	104.9	106.9	110.9	117.5	119.8	111.8	104.7
	115.90	**82.20**	**110.6**	**117.3**	**109.3**	**106.6**	**108.1**	**100.8**
118.2	119.2	62.0	117.0	126.1	107.7	105.5	114.8	98.4
114.8	120.4	98.5	95.6	110.3	112.4	104.5	108.6	106.6
123.2	110.7	112.4	114.0	119.3	111.3	111.5	104.2	104.1
135.3	105.6	90.5	108.2	98.2	104.1	96.2	99.4	91.5
							63.4	109.6
	110.00	**110.00**	**106.0**	**105.6**	**108.5**	**110.9**	**106.5**	**101.6**
129.2	115.1	113.5	110.4	117.3	111.7	110.1	106.2	94.2
129.3	118.2	120.5	111.2	121.6	110.4	102.9	109.3	94.0
127.2	126.8	119.0	110.4	118.5	111.4	106.1	107.8	90.0
113.2	103.9	108.5	104.4	95.7	100.5	101.3	101.1	100.8
151.1	92.9	117.4	114.6	117.5	108.8	100.4	100.3	96.6
198.4	155.8	138.2	141.6	134.0	104.5	114.6	111.3	81.2
158.2	110.2	145.8	116.1	110.5	104.7	106.0	102.0	110.5
181.9	122.6	119.4	105.8	105.4	105.0	104.0	110.2	87.1
94.5	93.3	187.6	105.4	145.3	152.9	111.7	78.4	85.8
124.3	96.7	104.0	107.5	122.8	114.6	101.0	107.4	95.1
107.1	104.2	96.4	102.5	100.4	102.4	112.0	103.9	94.9
240.5	134.8	127.0	141.5	109.8	101.7	114.3	103.7	89.1
96.3	111.6	95.2	83.4	106.2	634.3	245.7	108.3	89.8
109.6	102.6	105.7	106.8	103.3	103.6	108.0	100.7	99.7
126.6	116.0	108.6	107.0	116.9	113.5	105.6	104.9	95.7
99.8	111.5	101.5	95.6	97.2	104.9	96.2	98.0	97.7
148.9	167.5	109.8	107.5	107.2	99.3	112.1	100.2	105.2
117.1	120.5	110.4	103.4	121.6	115.2	106.8	110.9	103.0
105.6	114.6	96.6	80.8	94.7	108.2	111.0	118.1	111.8
119.7	115.2	118.9	114.2	106.9	106.5	112.4	104.9	111.5
149.1	117.8	107.6	130.5	136.2	91.2	117.9	103.5	101.1
88.9	121.9	129.3	114.8	108.7	98.0	91.6	99.5	113.8
117.9	122.2	113.7	105.6	110.8	111.3	99.1	102.6	90.0
117.9	118.0	117.7	103.2	127.4	130.6	104.8	69.9	57.8
93.7	102.7	100.5	106.3	138.2	60.2	91.0	106.1	83.6
110.3	118.5	112.6	116.5	101.2	105.7	104.5	109.5	99.0
129.9	102.1	120.1	119.9	606.9	227.4	175.5	167.0	143.1
119.7	104.5	113.7	120.6	102.7	174.6	133.0	144.6	69.2
141.9	191.6	116.5	109.9	103.8	95.4	57.5	93.5	197.8
79.1	107.0	216.3	132.6	129.9	160.3	141.5	119.6	115.5
136.8	175.4	111.4	87.3	162.6	99.3	3 014.3	103.2	100.7
	122.70	**116.80**	**107.5**	**104.9**	**119.5**	**117.7**	**112.8**	**105.5**
110.1	123.6	117.2	107.9	105.2	119.6	118.3	112.8	106.5
114.2	99.1	97.8	96.6	96.3	124.3	117.0	111.2	98.2
106.6	105.2	119.3	105.0	104.5	106.2	101.8	115.0	91.3
115.6	111.0	107.0	105.4	104.5	110.4	114.0	104.8	100.9
115.7	115.5	99.3	104.5	107.9	111.0	111.9	112.0	106.8
117.2	106.8	108.1	106.4	102.6	107.2	108.1	106.0	99.7
112.5	118.0	113.2	115.2	112.2	114.1	114.0	112.9	103.4
120.1	124.0	101.0	104.9	103.9	109.3	111.9	108.5	101.2
126.9	127.5	97.2	108.9	106.0	113.0	118.0	115.5	109.5
124.3	127.5	108.0	106.0	112.1	112.1	106.8	107.0	95.5
120.5	119.6	114.4	110.6	112.3	113.1	113.8	110.5	95.7
120.5	110.3	113.1	110.0	110.3	112.2	113.5	111.6	107.2
116.0	112.0	107.2	110.2	110.9	114.0	113.5	110.8	106.1
116.5	122.7	118.1	112.3	111.5	114.5	115.1	117.4	109.6
121.9	122.5	120.6	112.0	102.2	107.1	106.0	112.4	97.6
114.1	114.0	109.0	107.8	106.2	111.3	112.3	101.7	92.4
119.1	108.9	106.9	102.0	109.7	115.2	105.8	105.8	110.2
114.2	110.6	109.4	105.6	109.6	113.8	129.0	122.0	101.7
102.8	123.2	108.5	102.1	105.1	116.1	117.2	136.0	110.1

8-4 规模以上工业企业主要经济数据

单位：亿元

年 份 类 别	Year Item	企业单位数（个）Number of Enterprises (unit)	亏损企业 Loss-making Enterprises
2000		2 124	862
2001		2 031	853
2002		2 072	911
2003		1 995	846
2004		2 407	856
2005		2 362	829
2006		2 601	813
2007		2 698	744
2008		3 320	1 056
2009		3 489	1 036
2010		3 599	832
2011		2 773	599
2012		3 211	805
2013		3 551	939
2014		3 797	1 147
2015		3 876	1 207
2016		4 194	1 005
2017		4 186	824
2018		4 260	830
2019		4 366	924
2020		4 401	1 066
按登记注册类型分	**Grouped by Registration Status**		
国有企业	State-owned Enterprises	82	23
集体企业	Collective-owned Enterprises	20	4
股份合作企业	Share Holding Enterprises	5	
股份制企业	Joint-stock Enterprises	3 986	966
外商及港澳台投资企业	Industry Enterprises with Funds from Hong Kong,Macao,Taiwan and Foreign Funds	150	26
其他企业	Other Enterprises		
在总计中：亏损企业	Of which: Lossmaking Enterprises	1 066	1 066
在总计中：国有控股企业	Of which: State-holding Enterprises	666	180
按企业规模分	**Grouped by Size of Enterprises**		
大型企业	Large Enterprises	90	10
中型企业	Medium-sized Enterprises	409	108
小型企业	Small Enterprises	3 346	788
微型企业	Microenterprise	556	160
按门类分	**Grouped by Sector**		
采矿业	Mining	471	152
制造业	Manufacturing Industry	3 523	815
电力、热力、燃气及水生产和供应业	Production and Supply of Electricity, Heat, Gas and Water	407	99

注：1. 2019-2020年年报表中无“工业销售产值”“出口交货值”两个指标；
2. 工业部分表中的合计数和部分计算数据因小数取舍而产生的误差，均未作机械调整。

Main Economic Indicators of Industrial Enterprises above Designated Size

(100 million yuan)

工业总产值 Gross Industrial Output Value	工业销售产值 Industrial Sale Output Value	出口交货值 Delivery Value of Exports	资产合计 Total Assets	产成品 Finished Goods
1 063.36	1 050.45		2 310.22	75.61
1 157.40	1 141.31		2 585.06	80.17
1 320.62	1 307.43		2 722.14	82.86
1 557.17	1 547.14		3 033.50	131.01
2 093.98	2 061.84	94.04	3 567.17	116.54
2 596.21	2 577.47	89.63	3 964.32	146.72
3 393.09	3 338.22	115.76	4 808.98	186.21
4 298.29	4 225.66	159.26	5 834.12	219.13
5 144.58	4 896.85	116.03	7 185.11	259.64
5 178.21	4 962.99	99.14	7 674.88	266.08
6 464.63	6 247.87	115.14	9 611.09	317.04
7 780.83	7 527.74	114.19	11 053.93	417.82
9 224.81	8 783.33	125.59	13 076.97	513.52
10 289.07	9 831.22	130.91	15 854.90	518.55
10 521.79	10 022.04	153.60	17 458.16	565.88
10 155.67	9 667.86	172.95	18 180.58	559.16
10 609.75	10 084.35	269.81	19 474.18	540.81
11 559.51	11 150.77	269.46	20 241.46	574.40
13 157.59	12 634.59	369.03	20 562.12	559.21
14 299.47			21 439.45	535.93
14 640.16			24 673.74	600.92
392.21			655.68	54.40
41.86			27.36	4.37
1.76			1.81	0.02
13 591.64			22 967.78	511.38
464.70			816.02	23.95
2 160.73			3 833.84	126.09
7 430.49			17 055.54	212.20
5 818.61			9 959.18	127.34
3 519.22			5 177.04	175.22
4 827.12			8 633.09	268.36
475.22			904.42	30.01
951.34			1 875.57	44.41
11 816.90			13 010.30	551.01
1 871.91			9 787.87	5.51

Note:a. There is no "Industrial Sale Output Value" and "Delivery Value of Exports" in the 2019 and 2020 annual report.

b. There is no mechanical adjustment for the errors caused by the total count and partial calculation data in some tables.

8-4 续表1

单位：亿元

年 份 类 别	Year Item	负债合计 Total Liabilities	主营业务收入 Revenue from Principal Business
2000		1 280.62	1 058.91
2001		1 399.56	1 161.38
2002		1 475.14	1 313.29
2003		1 664.86	1 537.37
2004		1 878.60	2 052.46
2005		2 068.42	2 569.71
2006		2 638.14	3 357.53
2007		3 173.66	4 306.61
2008		4 168.36	4 961.12
2009		4 382.48	4 968.08
2010		5 735.24	6 356.24
2011		6 763.81	7 621.91
2012		8 255.51	8 942.15
2013		10 223.00	10 040.21
2014		10 991.96	10 358.22
2015		11 782.30	9 829.69
2016		12 431.16	10 149.03
2017		12 555.54	11 684.53
2018		12 479.36	13 227.39
2019		12 342.49	14 322.44
2020		14 289.32	14 510.63
按登记注册类型分	**Grouped by Registration Status**		
国有企业	State-owned Enterprises	394.72	366.90
集体企业	Collective-owned Enterprises	7.04	40.52
股份合作企业	Share Holding Enterprises	1.10	0.52
股份制企业	Joint-stock Enterprises	13 406.39	13 525.44
外商及港澳台投资企业	Industry Enterprises with Funds from Hong Kong,Macao,Taiwan	339.18	453.04
其他企业	Other Enterprises		
在总计中:亏损企业	Of which:Lossmaking Enterprises	3 211.20	2 082.67
在总计中:国有控股企业	Of which:State-holding Enterprises	10 030.39	7 904.07
按企业规模分	**Grouped by Size of Enterprises**		
大型企业	Large Enterprises	4 731.68	6 186.59
中型企业	Medium-sized Enterprises	2 931.97	3 432.73
小型企业	Small Enterprises	5 964.71	4 472.79
微型企业	Microenterprise	660.96	418.52
按门类分	**Grouped by Sector**		
采矿业	Mining	1 150.80	802.42
制造业	Manufacturing Industry	6 355.02	11 846.70
电力、热力、燃气及水生产和供应业	Production and Supply of Electricity, Heat ,Gas and Water	6 783.50	1 861.50

continued

(100 million yuan)

主营业务税金及附加 Taxes and Other Charges on Principal Business	销售费用 Selling Expenses	管理费用 Administration Expenses	利润总额 Total Profits	亏损企业亏损总额 Total Losses of Loss-making Enterprises	利税总额 Total Tax and Profits	本年应交增值税 Value Added Tax Payable	全部从业人员年均人数(万人) Employed Persons at Year-end (10 000 persons)
174.86	26.58	86.12	69.75	23.15	333.13	88.52	11.63
171.03	36.40	94.09	82.19	20.15	347.40	94.18	2.22
192.48	52.00	102.95	73.16	30.04	371.47	105.83	0.79
207.08	57.37	119.55	108.06	29.44	439.03	123.90	0.10
227.08	64.86	144.36	215.47	24.63	593.76	151.21	27.05
245.62	76.28	154.21	227.91	31.18	651.22	177.68	9.83
278.24	90.70	179.26	310.18	32.78	806.86	218.45	35.15
327.11	108.45	208.88	388.61	28.21	996.13	280.41	0.46
389.51	133.66	275.17	310.14	99.67	1 005.52	305.87	2.12
442.36	150.01	282.10	360.25	59.77	1 094.18	291.57	3.25
507.41	198.84	371.07	599.34	38.14	1 444.33	337.57	92.60
619.98	214.50	402.02	639.70	57.08	1 664.48	404.80	90.62
706.73	245.99	431.81	586.52	130.29	1 758.58	463.85	101.04
786.38	274.62	468.02	630.63	163.97	1 896.76	478.02	103.32
824.19	267.73	463.00	516.08	228.59	1 821.02	472.75	99.24
836.99	275.24	450.86	465.53	298.25	1 758.24	446.16	93.45
766.12	280.90	460.75	334.98	440.42	1 545.48	434.75	90.54
849.50	334.73	485.31	782.65	185.27	2 133.18	487.20	87.10
958.75	382.89	503.15	925.21	162.62	2 428.07	523.21	82.99
	400.31	480.28	950.80	180.45	2 489.38	491.32	84.58
	388.51	504.84	1115.02	162.71	2 584.97	440.12	79.39
	11.34	15.87	25.88	3.95	39.95	8.86	2.66
	1.13	4.66	4.25	0.04	4.91	0.42	0.31
	0.04	0.19	0.11		0.16	0.04	0.02
	338.51	453.00	1021.59	150.13	2 451.21	413.05	70.64
	34.45	22.00	50.35	7.29	67.79	13.11	3.81
	44.35	76.67	- 162.71	162.71	30.26	43.27	16.13
	116.30	276.12	587.01	106.16	1 893.96	321.84	31.11
	140.17	217.58	562.67	9.95	1 642.60	250.16	26.37
	120.42	123.32	260.14	77.19	519.09	92.12	22.80
	123.98	155.94	262.98	69.14	387.72	93.25	29.47
	3.94	7.99	29.23	6.43	35.55	4.59	0.75
	24.40	56.10	104.00	20.83	166.28	35.57	9.27
	356.68	406.40	820.86	89.28	2 117.98	311.29	60.14
	7.43	42.34	190.17	52.60	300.71	93.27	9.98

8-4 续表2

单位：亿元

类　　别	Item	企业单位数(个) Number of Enterprises (unit)
按行业类别分	**Grouped by Industry Sector**	
采矿业	**Mining**	**471**
煤炭开采和洗选业	Coal Mining and Dressing	227
石油和天然气开采业	Petroleum & Natural Gas Extraction	
黑色金属矿采选业	Mining & Dressing of Ferrous Metals	45
有色金属矿采选业	Mining and Processing of Non-Ferrous Metal Ores	108
非金属矿采选业	Mining and Processing of Nonmetal Ores	90
开采辅助活动	Assitant Activities of Mining	1
其他采矿业	Mining of Other Ores	
制造业	**Manufacturing Industry**	**3 523**
农副食品加工业	Processing of Food from Agricultural Products	602
食品制造业	Manufacture of Foods	162
酒、饮料和精制茶制造业	Manufacture of Wine, Beverage and Refined Tea	235
烟草制品业	Manufacture of Tobacco	9
纺织业	Manufacture of Textile	32
纺织服装、服饰业	Manufacture of Textile Wearing Apparel and Dress Adornment	20
皮革、毛皮、羽毛及其制品和制鞋业	Manufacture of Leather. Fur, Feather and Related Products	8
木材加工和木、竹、藤、棕、草制品业	Processing of Timber, Manufacture of Wood, Bamboo, Rattan, Palm and Straw Products	83
家具制造业	Manufacture of Furniture	12
造纸和纸制品业	Manufacture of Paper and Paper Products	79
印刷和记录媒介复制业	Printing, Reproduction of Recording Media	67
文教、工美、体育和娱乐用品制造业	Manufacture of Articles for Culture, Education, Arts, Sport Activities and Entertainment	30
石油加工、炼焦和核燃料加工业	Processing of Petroleum, Coking, Processing of Nuclear Fuel	31
化学原料和化学制品制造业	Manufacture of Raw Chemical Materials and Chemical Products	325
医药制造业	Manufacture of Medicines	160
化学纤维制造业	Manufacture of Chemical Fibers	3
橡胶和塑料制品业	Manufacture of Rubber and Plastics	146
非金属矿物制品业	Manufacture of Non-metallic Mineral Products	644
黑色金属冶炼和压延加工业	Smelting and Pressing of Ferrous Metals	93
有色金属冶炼和压延加工业	Smelting and Pressing of Non-ferrous Metals	205
金属制品业	Manufacture of Metal Products	135
通用设备制造业	Manufacture of General Purpose Machinery	61
专用设备制造业	Manufacture of Special Purpose Machinery	65
汽车制造业	Manufacture of Cars	37
铁路、船舶、航空航天和其他运输设备制造业	Manufacture of Railways, Boats, Aerospace and Other Transport Equipment	9
电气机械和器材制造业	Manufacture of Electrical Machinery and Equipment	108
计算机、通信和其他电子设备制造业	Manufacture of Computer, Communication Equipment and Electronic Equipment	86
仪器仪表制造业	Manufacture of Measuring Instruments and Machinery	24
其他制造业	Other Manufacturing Industry	4
废弃资源综合利用业	Comprehensive Utilization of Waste	45
金属制品、机械和设备修理业	Manufacture of Metal Products, Machinery and Equipment Repairing	3
电力、热力、燃气及水生产和供应业	**Production and Supply of Electricity, Heat, Gas and Water**	**407**
电力、热力生产和供应业	Production and Supply of Electric Power and Heat Power	326
燃气生产和供应业	Production and Supply of Gas	39
水的生产和供应业	Production and Supply of Water	42

continued

(100 million yuan)

亏损企业 Loss-making Enterprises	工业总产值 Gross Industrial Output Value	资产合计 Total Assets	产成品 Finished Goods
152	**951.34**	**1 875.57**	**44.41**
83	354.32	655.13	18.23
13	146.08	189.94	5.27
35	339.52	823.63	10.39
21	111.17	206.79	10.52
	0.25	0.09	
815	**11 816.90**	**13 010.30**	**551.01**
120	929.72	600.43	43.62
23	284.95	259.55	15.99
41	332.55	463.03	50.29
	1 602.59	2 335.95	73.35
8	30.76	24.35	2.87
7	18.98	42.73	0.82
2	2.85	2.59	1.13
33	71.57	53.14	5.70
4	6.64	12.17	2.43
16	88.82	109.98	6.66
13	81.85	225.31	7.75
2	113.69	57.87	8.29
14	662.87	440.32	14.89
95	943.27	1 000.32	58.03
38	404.22	969.78	28.23
1	15.07	11.19	0.55
29	147.45	102.34	9.81
115	962.43	1 133.19	29.58
33	1 392.35	1 007.19	48.84
74	2 073.13	2 525.14	64.00
29	216.14	160.08	10.05
17	74.50	81.27	6.15
15	81.13	118.03	5.05
17	173.94	319.49	16.40
3	27.97	91.70	1.88
23	165.52	158.94	16.51
28	764.84	575.68	18.28
1	33.10	49.69	1.49
	3.83	2.31	0.02
13	109.18	62.55	2.34
1	1.00	13.99	
99	**1 871.91**	**9 787.87**	**5.51**
77	1 718.89	8 787.31	1.30
8	107.87	539.21	0.27
14	45.15	461.36	3.94

8-4 续表3

单位：亿元

类别	Item	负债合计 Total Liabilities
按行业类别分	**Grouped by Industry Sector**	
采矿业	**Mining**	**1 150.80**
煤炭开采和洗选业	Coal Mining and Dressing	421.89
石油和天然气开采业	Petroleum & Natural Gas Extraction	
黑色金属矿采选业	Mining & Dressing of Ferrous Metals	134.32
有色金属矿采选业	Mining and Processing of Non-Ferrous Metal Ores	470.64
非金属矿采选业	Mining and Processing of Nonmetal Ores	123.95
开采辅助活动	Assitant Activities of Mining	
其他采矿业	Mining of Other Ores	
制造业	**Manufacturing Industry**	**6 355.02**
农副食品加工业	Processing of Food from Agricultural Products	360.96
食品制造业	Manufacture of Foods	118.24
酒、饮料和精制茶制造业	Manufacture of Wine, Beverage and Refined Tea	264.24
烟草制品业	Manufacture of Tobacco	307.03
纺织业	Manufacture of Textile	13.14
纺织服装、服饰业	Manufacture of Textile Wearing Apparel and Dress Adornment	27.04
皮革、毛皮、羽毛及其制品和制鞋业	Manufacture of Leather, Fur, Feather and Related Products	2.32
木材加工和木、竹、藤、棕、草制品业	Processing of Timber, Manufacture of Wood, Bamboo, Rattan, Palm and Straw Products	29.36
家具制造业	Manufacture of Furniture	10.06
造纸和纸制品业	Manufacture of Paper and Paper Products	61.52
印刷和记录媒介复制业	Printing, Reproduction of Recording Media	49.58
文教、工美、体育和娱乐用品制造业	Manufacture of Articles for Culture,Education,Arts,Sport Activities and Entertainment	12.84
石油加工、炼焦和核燃料加工业	Processing of Petroleum, Coking, Processing of Nuclear Fuel	254.71
化学原料和化学制品制造业	Manufacture of Raw Chemical Materials and Chemical Products	643.75
医药制造业	Manufacture of Medicines	379.94
化学纤维制造业	Manufacture of Chemical Fibers	1.78
橡胶和塑料制品业	Manufacture of Rubber and Plastics	58.84
非金属矿物制品业	Manufacture of Non-metallic Mineral Products	692.55
黑色金属冶炼和压延加工业	Smelting and Pressing of Ferrous Metals	684.81
有色金属冶炼和压延加工业	Smelting and Pressing of Non-ferrous Metals	1 425.39
金属制品业	Manufacture of Metal Products	104.37
通用设备制造业	Manufacture of General Purpose Machinery	60.67
专用设备制造业	Manufacture of Special Purpose Machinery	71.06
汽车制造业	Manufacture of Cars	236.46
铁路、船舶、航空航天和其他运输设备制造业	Manufacture of Railways,Boats,Aerospace and Other Transport Equipment	28.70
电气机械和器材制造业	Manufacture of Electrical Machinery and Equipment	80.80
计算机、通信和其他电子设备制造业	Manufacture of Computer,Communication Equipment and Electronic Equipment	305.84
仪器仪表制造业	Manufacture of Measuring Instruments and Machinery	28.10
其他制造业	Other Manufacturing Industry	1.08
废弃资源综合利用业	Comprehensive Utilization of Waste	29.50
金属制品、机械和设备修理业	Manufacture of Metal Products, Machinery and Equipment Repairing	10.34
电力、热力、燃气及水生产和供应业	**Production and Supply of Electricity, Heat, Gas and Water**	**6 783.50**
电力、热力生产和供应业	Production and Supply of Electric Power and Heat Power	6 221.01
燃气生产和供应业	Production and Supply of Gas	264.31
水的生产和供应业	Production and Supply of Water	298.18

continued

(100 million yuan)

主营业务收入 Revenue from Principal Business	税金及附加 Taxes and Other Charges	销售费用 Selling Expenses	管理费用 Administration Expenses	利润总额 Total Profit	亏损企业亏损总额 Total Losses of Loss-Making Enterprises	利税总额 Total Tax and Profit	本年应交增值税 Value Added Tax Payable	全部从业人员年均人数(万人) Employed Persons Average Number of (10 000 persons)
802.42	**26.72**	**24.40**	**56.10**	**104.00**	**20.83**	**166.28**	**35.57**	**9.27**
301.99	11.44	10.57	25.19	28.28	8.32	54.37	14.65	5.11
122.21	3.29	3.64	5.54	18.05	0.50	26.50	5.16	0.70
256.73	7.60	2.64	17.83	47.64	11.14	66.30	11.07	2.60
121.25	4.39	7.56	7.54	10.04	0.87	19.10	4.68	0.85
0.25			0.01			0.01	0.01	0.02
11 846.70	**985.84**	**356.68**	**406.40**	**820.86**	**89.28**	**2 117.98**	**311.29**	**60.14**
831.60	2.30	19.45	21.82	37.45	5.17	46.92	7.16	6.14
255.15	1.14	25.39	11.24	22.21	1.17	28.29	4.94	2.65
364.29	5.42	38.26	15.13	39.65	2.62	54.82	9.75	3.86
1 621.83	798.59	19.59	101.16	192.13		1 144.83	154.11	2.21
23.41	0.08	0.31	0.85	0.51	0.33	0.71	0.12	0.46
15.32	0.15	0.23	1.44	1.18	0.27	1.73	0.40	0.41
2.77		0.06	0.12	0.07	0.01	0.07		0.10
54.79	0.21	1.08	1.59	2.89	0.81	4.12	1.01	0.91
4.70	0.03	0.21	0.22	0.08	0.15	0.14	0.03	0.09
77.40	0.64	2.39	3.24	0.94	2.52	3.45	1.87	0.93
78.21	0.59	1.72	5.37	7.81	0.39	10.56	2.17	1.06
98.59	0.99	1.49	13.93	10.44	0.02	11.61	0.19	0.75
637.31	138.66	6.88	11.54	- 17.26	23.78	140.08	18.68	1.24
897.08	4.60	41.05	36.84	51.61	9.08	71.83	15.62	5.82
341.81	3.12	86.85	23.36	119.17	4.36	138.30	16.02	3.10
15.27	0.11	0.10	0.86	4.11	0.01	4.91	0.70	0.05
128.86	0.48	2.66	3.49	6.52	0.53	8.75	1.75	1.23
900.44	8.14	34.99	36.90	104.37	5.98	143.08	30.57	6.81
1 405.08	3.67	22.41	17.89	16.65	7.56	31.60	11.28	5.02
2 445.41	8.77	12.95	47.13	90.69	8.41	112.44	12.97	7.47
213.81	0.63	3.50	5.45	4.96	1.32	7.55	1.96	1.39
72.04	0.37	2.12	3.43	1.75	1.24	4.16	2.05	0.78
70.67	0.58	2.30	6.16	3.72	0.93	5.95	1.65	1.04
162.75	0.77	5.12	7.08	- 5.34	8.59	- 3.95	0.62	1.15
32.19	0.31	0.92	1.78	1.92	0.04	2.40	0.17	0.35
151.55	0.76	4.56	6.38	4.60	1.00	7.82	2.46	1.43
799.73	4.03	18.42	18.19	111.80	2.14	123.19	7.36	2.87
35.10	0.18	0.74	1.45	2.99		3.55	0.38	0.36
3.93	0.01	0.07	0.16	0.19		0.23	0.04	0.03
104.65	0.51	0.89	2.12	3.07	0.84	8.82	5.24	0.39
0.96	0.01		0.07	- 0.01	0.03	0.02	0.02	0.04
1 861.50	**17.27**	**7.43**	**42.34**	**190.17**	**52.60**	**300.71**	**93.27**	**9.98**
1 718.83	16.08	3.05	33.43	174.34	48.11	278.89	88.47	8.79
99.24	0.56	1.84	4.21	14.38	0.17	18.01	3.08	0.52
43.44	0.63	2.54	4.70	1.45	4.32	3.81	1.73	0.67

8-5 各州市规模以上工业企业主要经济数据（2020年）

Main Economic Indicators of Industry above Designated Size by Region (2020)

单位：个 (unit)

州市	Region	企业单位数 Number of Enterprises	大型企业 Large Enterprises	中型企业 Medium-sized Enterprises	小型企业 Small Enterprises	微型企业 Mini Enterprises	亏损企业数 Number of Loss-making Enterprises
全　省	**Yunnan**	**4 401**	**90**	**409**	**3 346**	**556**	**1 066**
昆　明	Kunming	997	31	95	801	70	219
曲　靖	Qujing	656	15	88	451	102	169
玉　溪	Yuxi	428	10	44	337	37	122
保　山	Baoshan	272	3	27	197	45	41
昭　通	Zhaotong	145	3	21	100	21	41
丽　江	Lijiang	50	2		44	4	13
普　洱	Pu'er	166	1	14	128	23	59
临　沧	Lincang	177	2	15	128	32	53
楚　雄	Chuxiong	348	5	15	285	43	55
红　河	Honghe	442	9	43	325	65	106
文　山	Wenshan	179	4	16	128	31	44
西双版纳	Xishuangbanna	112	1	7	93	11	38
大　理	Dali	244	2	13	192	37	56
德　宏	Dehong	145	1	9	102	33	42
怒　江	Nujiang	19	1		17	1	
迪　庆	Diqing	21		2	18	1	8

8-5 续表1 continued

单位：亿元 (100 million yuan)

州 市	Region	国有企业 State-owned Enterprise		集体企业 Collective-owned Enterprise		股份合作制企业 Corporations Enterprise		工业总产值 Gross Industrial Output Value
		单位数（个） Number of Enterprises (unit)	总产值（亿元） Gross Output Value (100 million yuan)	单位数（个） Number of Enterprises (unit)	总产值（亿元） Gross Output Value (100 million yuan)	单位数（个） Number of Enterprises (unit)	总产值（亿元） Gross Output Value (100 million yuan)	
全 省	**Yunnan**	**82**	**392.21**	**20**	**41.86**	**5**	**1.76**	**14 640.16**
昆 明	Kunming	21	132.81	2	1.07	1	0.20	4 334.77
曲 靖	Qujing	20	37.62	11	14.00			2 070.85
玉 溪	Yuxi	3	7.93	5	4.11			1 845.66
保 山	Baoshan	4	2.21	1	21.83	1	0.47	606.23
昭 通	Zhaotong	2	1.29					594.63
丽 江	Lijiang							205.53
普 洱	Pu'er	2	6.35					253.86
临 沧	Lincang	2	1.09					302.88
楚 雄	Chuxiong	6	101.85	1	0.86			1 200.83
红 河	Honghe	13	39.47			2	1.08	1 550.74
文 山	Wenshan	5	59.43			1		460.30
西双版纳	Xishuangbanna	**1**	**0.74**					211.11
大 理	Dali	2	1.10					635.76
德 宏	Dehong	1	0.32					189.81
怒 江	Nujiang							81.46
迪 庆	Diqing							95.72

8-5 续表2 continued

单位：亿元 (100 million yuan)

州 市	Region	资产合计 Total Assets	产成品 Finished Goods	流动资产 Current Assets	负债合计 Total Liabilities
全 省	**Yunnan**	**24 673.74**	**600.92**	**8 815.16**	**14 289.32**
昆 明	Kunming	7 515.38	204.82	3 256.62	4 374.01
曲 靖	Qujing	2 476.09	82.97	900.66	1 396.44
玉 溪	Yuxi	2 046.26	54.50	1 055.21	777.11
保 山	Baoshan	920.19	40.93	379.07	553.20
昭 通	Zhaotong	1 606.53	8.26	328.63	848.04
丽 江	Lijiang	803.85	4.22	207.68	603.41
普 洱	Pu'er	894.00	14.26	154.77	604.78
临 沧	Lincang	610.49	19.91	178.93	400.53
楚 雄	Chuxiong	1 740.01	28.84	418.02	1 187.50
红 河	Honghe	2 233.80	51.31	878.99	1 300.16
文 山	Wenshan	873.37	12.69	269.44	428.51
西双版纳	Xishuangbanna	348.11	35.20	160.47	197.61
大 理	Dali	1 421.84	25.38	424.14	854.16
德 宏	Dehong	394.30	14.59	145.30	252.14
怒 江	Nujiang	352.81	1.53	25.26	215.29
迪 庆	Diqing	436.69	1.51	31.98	296.42

8-5 续表3 continued

单位：亿元 (100 million yuan)

州 市	Region	主营业务收入 Revenue from Principal Business	税金及附加 Taxes and Other Charge	销售费用 Selling Expenses	管理费用 Administration Expenses
全 省	**Yunnan**	**14 510.63**	**1 029.82**	**388.51**	**504.84**
昆 明	Kunming	4 909.12	342.60	166.33	150.27
曲 靖	Qujing	1 986.66	129.45	38.41	69.65
玉 溪	Yuxi	1 721.18	283.36	37.10	61.99
保 山	Baoshan	538.53	4.23	12.87	30.30
昭 通	Zhaotong	586.54	49.41	10.92	23.18
丽 江	Lijiang	203.09	1.73	2.50	3.11
普 洱	Pu'er	231.71	2.53	6.21	9.35
临 沧	Lincang	244.86	1.86	4.20	7.55
楚 雄	Chuxiong	1 042.62	60.77	18.41	28.16
红 河	Honghe	1 501.91	107.18	33.84	63.67
文 山	Wenshan	307.22	3.64	9.36	15.29
西双版纳	Xishuangbanna	233.83	1.29	6.10	6.12
大 理	Dali	644.68	36.91	36.29	20.32
德 宏	Dehong	183.10	1.06	4.17	6.42
怒 江	Nujiang	81.52	1.53	0.35	5.99
迪 庆	Diqing	94.04	2.27	1.47	3.47

8-5 续表4 continued

单位：亿元 (100 million yuan)

州市	Region	利税总额 Total Tax and Profits	本年应交增值税 Value Added Tax Payable	利润总额 Total Profit	亏损企业亏损总额 Total Losses of Loss-making Enterprises	全部从业人员年均人数(万人) Average Number of Employed Persons at Year-end (10 000 persons)
全　省	**Yunnan**	**2 584.97**	**440.12**	**1 115.02**	**162.71**	**79.39**
昆　明	Kunming	805.24	127.11	335.53	57.46	19.64
曲　靖	Qujing	267.52	54.90	83.17	28.23	13.07
玉　溪	Yuxi	474.28	72.84	118.08	6.66	8.56
保　山	Baoshan	68.17	10.13	53.81	4.84	4.01
昭　通	Zhaotong	174.13	33.60	91.12	6.90	3.16
丽　江	Lijiang	39.78	11.22	26.83	1.89	1.01
普　洱	Pu'er	34.76	10.93	21.30	8.86	3.59
临　沧	Lincang	25.77	7.50	16.40	5.34	2.23
楚　雄	Chuxiong	163.21	23.87	78.57	3.80	4.33
红　河	Honghe	274.72	40.04	127.50	14.11	8.94
文　山	Wenshan	34.07	1.06	29.38	6.88	3.10
西双版纳	Xishuangbanna	32.05	5.62	25.14	1.59	1.40
大　理	Dali	132.36	24.08	71.37	6.60	3.30
德　宏	Dehong	18.58	4.66	12.86	2.03	1.76
怒　江	Nujiang	17.61	5.28	10.80		0.84
迪　庆	Diqing	22.70	7.28	13.16	7.53	0.46

8-6 主要工业产品产量（2020年）

Output of Major Industrial Products (2020)

单位：万吨 (10 000 tons)

名 称	Item	生产量 Output
原 煤	Coal	5 265.63
洗精煤(用于炼焦)	Washed Coal （Used For Coking)	540.28
焦 炭	Coke	1 093.32
发电量（亿千瓦小时）	Electricity (100 million kWh)	3 451.17
#水电	Thermal Power	2 763.45
火电	Hydro Power	409.81
铁矿石原矿量	Ironstone in Original Iron Ores	2 170.30
锰矿石成品矿	Manganese Ore	59.75
铜选矿产品含铜量	Copper Content of Copper Dressing Products	26.05
铅选矿产品含铅量	Lead Content of Lead Dressing Products	12.88
锌选矿产品含锌量	Zinc Content of Zinc Dressing Products	51.30
锡选矿产品含锡量	Stannum Content of Stannum Dressing Products	6.34
钨精矿折含量	tungsten ores & concentrates	0.58
硫铁矿（折S 35%）	Pyrite Ore(converted into 35% sulphur)	58.65
磷矿石（折P_2O_3 30%）	Rock Phosphate (converted into 30% P_2O_3)	1 807.52
生 铁	Pig Iron	1 873.25
粗 钢	Crude Steel	2 233.02
钢 材	Rolled Steel	2 640.72
中小型型钢	Medium and Small Rolled Steel	92.62
棒 材	Steel Bar	254.33
钢 筋	Corrugated Steel Bar	1 174.36
盘 条（线材）	Wire Rod(Wire Stock)	518.88
中 板	Medium Steel Plate	
铁合金	Ferroalloy	53.69
十种有色金属	Ten Kinds of Nonferrous Metals	511.41
#铜	Copper	69.93
原铝	Primary Aluminum	259.21
铅	Lead	41.51
锌	Zinc	129.44
锡	Stannum	9.46
锑	Stibium	0.95
硫 酸（折100%）	Sulfuric Acid(Converted into 100% H_2SO_4)	1 566.39
烧 碱（折100%）	Caustic Soda (Converted into 100% Sodium Hydroxide)	22.87
电 石（折合量）	Calcium Carbide(Reduced Quantity)	61.30
黄 磷	Yellow Phosphorus	55.04
纯 碱	Soda Ash	9.54
初级形态塑料	Plastic	34.52
合成氨	Synthetic Ammonia	239.24
化 肥(折100%)	Chemical Fertilizer(Converted into 100% Nitrogen,Phosphorus and Kalium)	213.77
#氮肥	Nitrogen Fertilizer	89.35
磷肥	Phosphate Fertilizer	123.94
农用薄膜	Agriculture Plastic Film	11.60
小型拖拉机（万台）	Agricultural Transport Machinery(10 000 units)	1.62
饲料	Forage	553.80
复烤烟叶	Flue-cured Tobacco	59.22
卷烟(亿支)	Cigarettes(100 million pieces)	3 515.88
成品糖	Sugar of Finished Product	261.22
发酵酒精（折96度)(万升)	Fermenting Alcohol (Converted into 96% alc.)(10 kiloliters)	18 393.46
精制茶叶	Refined Tea	14.50

注：本表统计范围为规模以上工业法人单位。
Note: The coverage of statistics are industrial enterprises above designated size in this table.

8-6 续表 continued

单位：万吨 (10 000 tons)

名 称	Item	生产量 Output
原 盐	Salt	160.30
饮料酒（亿升）	Liquor (100 million liters)	8.13
#白酒（折65度)(亿升)	White Spirit (Converted into 65% alc.)(100 million liters)	0.91
啤酒(亿升)	Beer (100 million liters)	6.96
葡萄酒(亿升)	Wine(100 million liters)	0.11
软饮料	Soft Drinks	477.36
罐 头	Canned Food	1.47
乳制品	Milk Products	62.17
糖 果	Candy	1.83
化学纤维	Chemical Fiber	4.01
纱	Yarn	1.23
布（万米）	Cloth (10 000 m)	
#纯棉布(万米)	#Cotton Cloth (10 000 m)	
印染布（万米）	Printed Fabric (10 000 m)	
丝（吨）	Silk (ton)	3 126.64
服 装（万件）	Garments (10 000 pieces)	1 265.69
塑料制品	Plastic Products	62.79
自来水生产量（万立方米）	Tap Water Output (10 000 cu.m)	98 988.48
合成洗涤剂	Synthetic Detergents	10.22
卫生陶瓷器（万件）	Ceramics for Daily Use (10 000 units)	204.63
日用玻璃制品	Glass Products for Daily Use	1.61
纸 浆	Paper Pulp	34.42
机制纸及纸板	Machine-made Paper and Cardboard	74.29
大 米	Rice	33.31
小麦粉	Wheat Flour	26.29
食用植物油	Edible Vegetable Oil	43.46
水 泥	Cement	12 984.71
平板玻璃（万重量箱）	Plate Glass (10 000 weight boxes)	2 449.25
大理石板材（万平方米）	Marble Building Block (10 000 sq.m)	218.03
商品混凝土（万立方米）	Concrete (10 000 cu.m)	7 746.75
人造板（万立方米）	Manmade Plates (10 000 cu.m)	355.00
复合地板（万平方米）	Engineered Floor(10 000 sq.m)	398.01
松 香	Rosin	17.02
矿山设备	Mining Equipment	5.19
金属轧制设备	Metal Shaping Equipment	0.25
起重机	Lifting Equipment	1.65
发电设备（万千瓦）	Power Equipment (10 000 kW)	40.08
交流电动机（万千瓦）	Alternating Current Motor (10 000 kW)	36.15
变压器（万千伏安）	Transformer (10 000 KVA)	2 228.60
金属切削机床（万台）	Metal-cutting Machine Tools (10 000 units)	3.49
汽 车（万辆）	Motor Vehicles (10 000 units)	2.05
发动机（万千瓦）	Internal Combustion Engines (10 000 kW)	4 658.96
电力电缆（万公里）	Electric Power Cable (10 000km)	46.90
轴 承（万套）	Bearing (10 000 units)	
打印机（万台）	Printers (10 000 units)	1.66
单色印刷（万令）	Single-color Printing (10 000 reams)	79.38
化学药品原药	Chemical Medicine	0.10
中成药	Chinese Traditional Patent Medicine	6.11
光学仪器(万台、个)	Optical Instrument (10 000 units, unit)	824.25

8-7 按三次产业划分能源消费量（1997−2020年）
Total Consumption of Energy by Industry (1997-2020)

单位：万吨标准煤 (10 000 tons of SCE)

年份 Year	能源消费总量 Total Consumption of Energy	第一产业 Primary Industry	第二产业 Secondary Industry	#工业 Industry	第三产业 Tertiary Industry	居民生活消费 Household Consumption
1997	3 428.98	182.86	2 466.80	2 429.07	240.75	538.57
1998	3 364.49	179.42	2 420.41	2 383.39	236.22	528.44
1999	3 287.97	282.40	2 261.68	2 224.42	275.50	468.40
2000	3 468.33	297.89	2 385.74	2 346.44	290.61	494.09
2001	3 741.03	271.83	2 518.84	2 481.69	404.99	545.37
2002	4 131.31	264.90	2 840.50	2 796.86	473.48	552.43
2003	4 449.97	239.17	3 180.70	3 132.01	525.53	504.57
2004	5 209.81	216.33	3 859.73	3 802.21	616.96	516.79
2005	6 023.97	228.12	4 468.59	4 390.68	734.12	593.14
2006	6 620.57	225.14	4 975.84	4 883.00	791.77	627.81
2007	7 132.63	237.90	5 395.98	5 300.98	848.27	650.47
2008	7 510.82	205.26	5 714.25	5 597.96	910.28	681.03
2009	8 032.06	215.93	5 999.71	5 868.90	971.21	845.21
2010	8 674.17	177.49	6 461.17	6 301.64	1 214.52	820.99
2011	9 540.28	194.55	7 130.56	6 939.30	1 392.31	822.86
2012	10 433.68	184.21	7 780.95	7 591.39	1 558.60	909.91
2013	10 072.09	180.25	7 426.06	7 241.02	1 533.74	932.04
2014	10 454.83	198.08	7 471.46	7 269.69	1 718.02	1 067.27
2015	10 424.69	233.68	7 150.41	6 934.91	1 862.16	1 178.44
2016	10 725.95	225.18	7 324.03	7 091.53	1 999.92	1 176.82
2017	11 163.57	225.56	7 695.43	7 449.99	2 063.15	1 179.43
2018	11 590.02	228.77	7 903.86	7 632.21	2 199.19	1 258.20
2019	12 157.65	232.89	8 274.42	7 969.85	2 378.85	1 271.50
2020	12 981.94	239.78	9 104.64	8 809.99	2 300.41	1 337.11

注：采用数据为等价热值，2005至2008年数据根据云南省第二次全国经济普查数据修正；2013至2014年数据根据云南省第三次全国经济普查数据修正，2015至2018年的数据根据云南省第四次全国经济普查数据修正。

Note: Data used in this table are equivalent caloricity. Data from 2005 to 2008 are regulated according to that of the second national economic census. Data from 2013 to 2014 have been adjusted according to the third national economic census. Data from 2015 to 2018 have been adjusted according to the Forth national economic census.

8-8 全省综合能源平衡表（2020年）

项　目	Sector	能源消费总量（万吨标准煤）Total Energy Consumption (10 000 tons of SCE)
可供本地区消费的能源量	**Total Energy Available for Consumption**	**12 981.94**
年初库存量	Stock in Early Year	726.37
一次能源生产量	Primary Energy Output	13 731.13
外省(区、市)调入量	Quantity of Fold	7 437.41
进口量	Imports	295.05
境内轮船和飞机在境外加油量	Fueling Charge in Foreign Countries of Domestic Motorship Engine	
本省(区、市)调出量(-)	Quantity of Call-out (-)	-8 389.69
出口量(-)	Exports(-)	-90.82
境外轮船和飞机在境内加油量(-)	Fueling Charge in Foreign Countries of Foreign Motorship Engine(-)	
年末库存量(-)	Stock at Year-end(-)	- 727.52
加工转换投入(-)产出(+)量	**Input(-) and Output(+) Processing and Transformation**	**357.95**
损失量	**Losses**	**424.61**
终端消费量	**Final Energy Consumption**	**12 915.28**
第一产业	Primary Industry	239.78
第二产业	Secondary Industry	9 037.98
第三产业	Tertiary Industry	2 300.41
农、林、牧、渔业	Farming,Forestry,Animal Husbandry,Fishery	239.78
工业	Industry	8 743.33
建筑业	Construction	294.65
交通运输、仓储和邮政业	Transport, Storage, Post and Telecommunication Services	1 361.27
批发、零售业和住宿、餐饮业	Wholesale and Retail Trades, Hotels and Catering Services	392.61
其他	Others	546.54
生活消费	Residential Consumption	1 337.11
城镇	Urban Areas	572.92
乡村	Rural Areas	764.19
平衡差额（+、-）	**Balance(+、-)**	
消费量合计	**Total Consumption of Energy**	**12 981.94**

注：本表为等价热值。

Balance Sheet of Overall Energy (2020)

原　煤 (万　吨) Coal (10 000 tons)	焦　炭 (万　吨) Coke (10 000 tons)	石油及石油制品 (万　吨) Petroleum and Related Products (10 000 tons)	天 然 气 (亿立方米) Natural Gas (100 million cu.m)	电　力 (亿千瓦小时) Electricity (100 million kWh)
7 712.43	**123.64**	**1 536.36**	**19.09**	**1 610.55**
526.02	52.80	133.77		
5 529.73				3 259.86
4 403.06	288.74	2 280.21	0.48	0.03
			18.63	14.97
-2 034.90	-141.95	-754.69		-1 636.22
				-28.09
-711.48	-75.95	-122.93	- 0.02	
-3 892.98	**1 093.32**	**-24.52**	**- 2.27**	**414.58**
				131.33
3 819.45	**1 216.96**	**1 511.84**	**16.82**	**1 893.80**
210.13	2.45	32.96	0.01	25.03
3 187.63	1 214.51	355.45	14.87	1 355.74
151.50		935.23	0.34	247.20
210.13	2.45	32.96	0.01	25.03
3 154.72	1 214.51	286.31	14.86	1 303.35
32.91		69.14	0.01	52.39
		839.37	0.17	40.48
98.27		49.66	0.13	71.06
53.23		46.21	0.04	135.66
270.19		188.21	1.60	265.83
7.46		89.89	1.54	126.88
262.73		98.32	0.06	138.95
7 712.43	**1 216.96**	**1 536.36**	**18.70**	**2 025.13**

Note: Data used in this table are equivalent caloricity.

8-9 主要年份能源生产和消费总量及其构成
Total Production and Consumption of Energy and Their Composition in Significant Years

单位：万吨标准煤 (10 000 tons of SCE)

年 份 Year	能源生产总量 Total Production of Energy	占能源生产总量的比重(%) Percentage to Total Production (%)		能源消费总量 Total Consumption of Energy	占能源消费总量的比重(%) Percentage to Total Consumption (%)			
		原 煤 Coal	一次电 Hydro Power		煤 炭 Coal	石 油 Petroleum	天 然 气 Natural Gas	一 次 电 Hydro Power
1957	114.30	96.00	4.00	119.20	92.00	4.10		3.90
1962	224.70	93.50	6.50	256.30	89.30	4.50		6.20
1965	326.10	93.90	6.10	348.70	87.80	6.50		5.70
1970	555.60	91.80	8.20	591.50	86.20	6.10		7.70
1975	861.10	85.60	14.40	920.30	80.10	6.40		13.50
1976	751.20	85.40	14.60	797.00	79.40	6.80		13.80
1977	893.20	86.30	13.70	931.10	79.60	7.30		13.10
1978	1 002.60	84.50	15.50	1 065.90	78.20	7.20		14.60
1979	933.90	82.70	17.30	1 072.20	72.00	7.50	5.40	15.10
1980	841.90	79.60	20.40	946.10	67.00	9.00	5.70	18.30
1981	872.50	77.90	22.10	948.40	65.90	8.60	5.90	19.60
1982	930.20	81.90	18.10	1 020.60	69.70	8.30	4.90	17.10
1983	966.30	83.30	16.70	1 094.70	72.20	8.50	4.60	14.70
1984	1 076.30	81.50	18.50	1 226.30	71.20	8.30	4.20	16.30
1985	1 162.80	80.40	19.60	1 298.33	69.60	8.50	4.40	17.50
1986	1 220.30	79.50	20.50	1 399.07	69.70	8.40	4.10	17.80
1987	1 355.30	91.10	8.90	1 533.22	72.20	8.40	3.50	15.90
1988	1 404.50	83.50	16.50	1 622.52	75.70	6.90	3.10	14.30
1989	1 522.79	81.80	18.20	1 706.87	72.30	8.10	3.20	16.40
1990	1 594.50	79.80	20.20	1 954.18	71.70	7.20	2.80	18.30
1991	1 649.02	75.30	24.70	1 961.92	67.00	8.50	2.80	21.70
1992	1 763.66	77.10	22.90	2 016.61	69.40	8.00	2.70	19.90
1993	1 811.57	76.70	24.30	2 089.80	70.00	8.00	2.70	19.30
1994	2 073.79	71.50	28.50	2 282.80	66.00	7.70	2.50	23.80
1995	2 313.65	69.20	30.80	2 640.55	66.10	6.90	2.20	24.80
1996	2 556.85	68.60	31.40	2 819.43	64.50	6.90	2.50	26.10
1997	2 619.97	71.85	28.15	3 428.98	71.38	6.01	2.01	20.60
1998	2 451.49	71.99	28.01	3 364.49	71.31	6.52	1.76	20.41
1999	2 267.97	67.06	32.94	3 287.97	68.22	7.18	1.88	22.72
2000	2 471.77	64.03	32.11	3 468.33	62.61	7.46	1.81	25.39
2001	2 611.54	65.48	30.53	3 741.03	62.33	10.62	1.72	22.57
2002	3 259.95	67.19	29.41	4 131.31	61.04	11.12	1.51	23.70
2003	3 608.45	64.24	30.78	4 449.97	60.85	11.64	1.53	22.01
2004	4 455.68	68.13	27.04	5 209.81	63.30	11.13	1.34	20.16
2005	5 353.36	68.93	26.61	6 023.97	62.48	11.14	1.35	21.11
2006	6 075.09	75.29	22.42	6 620.57	67.70	11.52	1.09	17.62
2007	6 546.65	73.82	23.70	7 132.63	66.47	12.37	1.02	17.93
2008	7 595.31	68.87	29.48	7 510.82	60.83	12.81	0.93	23.79
2009	7 851.21	68.65	28.59	8 032.06	62.62	12.74	0.75	21.22
2010	8 822.03	66.60	32.05	8 674.17	56.73	15.11	0.56	23.98
2011	9 752.64	63.97	35.03	9 540.28	55.97	14.88	0.53	27.72
2012	10 577.62	59.33	39.15	10 433.68	53.16	14.93	0.50	29.87
2013	12 531.99	54.50	44.38	10 072.09	50.63	14.36	0.53	33.05
2014	9 805.49	26.63	72.28	10 454.83	43.07	14.71	0.54	40.66
2015	11 004.66	30.17	68.71	10 424.69	40.99	16.20	0.75	40.87
2016	11 381.56	24.65	74.15	10 725.95	39.93	16.68	0.89	41.22
2017	12 060.40	23.57	75.17	11 163.57	38.06	17.25	1.05	42.27
2018	12 618.75	20.77	77.97	11 590.02	36.30	17.04	1.33	43.96
2019	13 751.11	23.39	75.32	12 157.65	34.57	17.63	1.80	44.55
2020	13 731.13	21.61	76.76	12 981.94	34.87	16.75	1.91	44.74

注：采用数据为等价热值，2005至2008年数据根据云南省第二次全国经济普查数据修正，2013至2014年数据根据云南省第三次全国经济普查数据修正，2015至2018年的数据根据云南省第四次全国经济普查数据修正。

Note: Data used in this table are equivalent caloricity. Data from year 2005 to 2008 are regulated according to that of the second national economic census.Data from 2013 to 2014 have been adjusted according to the third national economic census.Data from 2015 to 2018 have been adjusted according to the Forth national economic census.

8-10 全省能源生产弹性系数（1980-2020年）

Elasticity Ratio of Energy Production at Current Year (1980-2020)

年 份 Year	当年能源生产增长(%) Growth Rate of Energy Production at Current Year (%)	当年电力生产增长(%) Growth Rate of Electricity Production at Current Year (%)	当年生产总值增长(%) Growth Rate of Gross Regional Product of Yunnan Province at Current Year (%)	当年能源生产弹性系数 Elasticity Ratio of Energy Production at Current Year	当年电力生产弹性系数 Elasticity Ratio of Electricity Production at Current Year
1980	-9.85	1.63	8.5	-1.16	0.19
1981	3.63	6.17	7.8	0.47	0.79
1982	6.61	3.96	15.5	0.43	0.26
1983	3.88	-0.63	8.4	0.46	-0.07
1984	11.38	14.00	14.5	0.78	0.97
1985	8.04	7.37	13.0	0.62	0.57
1986	4.94	12.02	4.3	1.15	2.80
1987	11.06	11.61	12.3	0.90	0.94
1988	3.63	8.41	16.0	0.23	0.53
1989	8.42	11.60	5.8	1.45	2.00
1990	4.71	10.22	8.7	0.54	1.17
1991	3.42	11.98	6.6	0.52	1.82
1992	6.95	10.58	10.9	0.64	0.97
1993	2.72	10.48	11.1	0.24	0.94
1994	14.47	18.22	12.2	1.19	1.49
1995	11.57	12.29	11.7	0.99	1.05
1996	10.51	11.05	11.1	0.95	1.00
1997	2.47	-0.20	9.7	0.25	-0.02
1998	-6.43	4.54	8.1	-0.79	0.56
1999	-7.49	12.69	7.3	-1.03	1.74
2000	8.99	6.46	7.5	1.20	0.86
2001	5.65	13.25	6.8	0.83	1.95
2002	24.83	18.76	9.0	2.76	2.08
2003	10.69	11.20	8.8	1.21	1.27
2004	23.48	15.43	11.3	2.08	1.37
2005	20.15	13.89	9.0	2.26	1.56
2006	13.48	20.74	11.6	1.16	1.79
2007	7.76	20.02	12.2	0.64	1.64
2008	16.02	14.93	10.6	1.51	1.41
2009	3.37	12.91	12.1	0.28	1.07
2010	12.37	16.27	12.3	1.01	1.32
2011	10.55	13.94	13.7	0.77	1.02
2012	8.46	12.24	13.0	0.65	0.94
2013	18.48	24.92	12.1	1.53	2.07
2014	-21.76	16.95	8.1	-2.69	2.09
2015	10.25	0.13	8.7	1.18	0.01
2016	3.42	5.45	8.7	0.39	0.63
2017	5.96	9.75	9.5	0.63	1.03
2018	4.63	9.72	8.9	0.52	1.09
2019	8.97	6.89	8.1	1.11	0.85
2020	-0.15	6.03	4.0	-0.04	1.51

注：2005至2008年数据根据云南省第二次全国经济普查数据修正，2013至2014年数据根据云南省第三次全国经济普查数据修正，2015至2018年的数据根据云南省第四次全国经济普查数据修正。

Note: Data from year 2005 to 2008 are regulated according to that of the second national economic census.
Data from 2013 to 2014 have been adjusted according to the third national economic census.
Data from 2015 to 2018 have been adjusted according to the Forth national economic census.

8-11 全省能源消费弹性系数（1980-2020年）

Elasticity Ratio of Energy Consumption at Current Year (1980-2020)

年 份 Year	当年能源消费增长(%) Growth Rate of Energy Consumption at Current Year (%)	当年电力消费增长(%) Growth Rate of Electricity Consumption at Current Year (%)	当年生产总值增长(%) Growth Rate of Gross Regional Product at Current Year of Yunnan Province (%)	当年能源消费弹性系数 Elasticity Ratio of Energy Consumption at Current Year	当年电力消费弹性系数 Elasticity Ratio of Electricity Consumption at Current Year
1980	- 11.76	5.07	8.5	-1.38	0.60
1981	0.24	3.42	7.8	0.03	0.44
1982	7.61	4.47	15.5	0.49	0.29
1983	7.26	-0.21	8.4	0.86	-0.02
1984	12.02	13.15	14.5	0.83	0.91
1985	5.87	9.05	13.0	0.45	0.70
1986	7.76	17.69	4.3	1.81	4.12
1987	9.59	4.44	12.3	0.78	0.36
1988	5.82	20.80	16.0	0.36	1.30
1989	5.20	4.74	5.8	0.90	0.82
1990	14.49	12.60	8.7	1.67	1.45
1991	0.40	13.26	6.6	0.06	2.01
1992	2.79	9.79	10.9	0.26	0.90
1993	3.63	26.98	11.1	0.33	2.43
1994	9.24	-0.58	12.2	0.76	-0.05
1995	15.67	14.41	11.7	1.34	1.23
1996	6.77	12.82	11.1	0.61	1.16
1997	21.62	4.56	9.7	2.23	0.47
1998	-1.88	2.44	8.1	-0.23	0.30
1999	-2.27	9.75	7.3	-0.31	1.34
2000	5.49	6.93	7.5	0.73	0.92
2001	7.86	9.40	6.8	1.16	1.38
2002	10.43	13.37	9.0	1.16	1.48
2003	7.71	4.15	8.8	0.88	0.47
2004	17.08	15.96	11.3	1.51	1.41
2005	15.63	17.27	8.9	1.74	1.94
2006	9.90	15.86	11.6	0.85	1.37
2007	7.73	15.47	12.2	0.63	1.27
2008	5.30	11.26	10.6	0.50	1.06
2009	6.94	7.44	12.1	0.57	0.62
2010	7.99	22.04	12.3	0.65	1.79
2011	9.98	19.90	13.7	0.73	1.45
2012	9.36	9.28	13.0	0.72	0.71
2013	8.47	10.94	12.1	0.70	0.91
2014	3.80	4.77	8.1	0.47	0.59
2015	- 0.94	- 5.94	8.7	-0.11	-0.68
2016	2.89	- 1.95	8.7	0.33	-0.22
2017	4.08	9.05	9.5	0.43	0.95
2018	3.82	9.17	8.9	0.43	1.03
2019	4.90	7.92	8.1	0.60	0.98
2020	6.78	11.78	4.0	1.70	2.95

注：2005至2008年数据根据云南省第二次全国经济普查数据修正，2013至2014年数据根据云南省第三次全国经济普查数据修正，2015至2018年的数据根据云南省第四次全国经济普查数据修正。

Note: Data from year 2005 to 2008 are regulated according to that of the second national economic census.
Data from 2013 to 2014 have been adjusted according to the third national economic census.
Data from 2015 to 2018 have been adjusted according to the Forth national economic census.

8-12 全省规模以上工业企业能源消费与库存（2020年）

Total Consumption and Inventory of Energy of Industrial Enterprises above Designated Size (2020)

单位：万吨

名　称	Item	年初库存 Stock in Early Year	消费 Consumption	年末库存 Stock at Year-end
原　煤	Raw Coal	454.06	6 704.45	471.52
洗精煤（用于炼焦）	Well Washed Coal （Used For Coking)	93.80	1 457.58	85.07
其他洗煤	Other Washed Coal	12.56	192.58	11.98
煤制品	Manufacture of Coal	0.04	1.32	0.04
焦　炭	Coke	34.43	1034.35	43.87
其他焦化产品	Other Coked Products	0.14	0.22	0.07
焦炉煤气（亿立方米）	Coal Gas of Coking Furnace (100 million cu.m)		15.73	
高炉煤气（亿立方米）	Coal Gas of Furnace (100 million cu.m)		297.58	
其他煤气（亿立方米）	Other Coal Gas (100 million cu.m)		23.94	
天然气（亿立方米）	Natural Gas (100 million cu.m)	0.01	18.33	0.02
液化天然气	Liquefied Natural Gas		3.95	
原　油	Raw Oil	37.10	1026.09	27.67
汽　油	Gasoline	0.06	2.36	0.06
煤　油	Kerosene		0.05	
柴　油	Diesel Oil	1.39	39.01	1.50
燃料油	Fuel Oil			
液化石油气	Liquefied Petroleum Gas	0.29	31.13	0.07
炼厂干气	Gas of Metallurgical Plant		20.86	
其他石油制品	Other Petroleum Products	0.33	30.65	0.28
热　力（万百万千焦）	Heat (10 000 million kilo-joule)		1501.36	
电　力（亿千瓦小时）	Electricity (100 million kWh)		1287.92	
其他燃料(万吨标准煤)	Other Fuel (10 000 tons of SCE)	0.26	15.99	0.22

8-13 主要年份能源利用经济效益指标（一）

Indicators on Economic Benefits from Energy Utilization in Significant Years (I)

（按当年价格计算）

(Calculated at current prices)

年份 Year	能源消费量（万吨标准煤） Total Consumption of Energy (10 000 tons of SCE)	工业部门消费 Industrial Consumption	万元工业产值耗能（吨标准煤/万元） Energy Consumption of Industrial Output Value per 10 000 yuan (ton of SCE/10 000 yuan)	万元生产总值耗能（吨标准煤/万元） Energy Consumption of Gross Regional Product per 10 000 yuan (ton of SCE/10 000 yuan)	吨能创造工业产值(万元) Industrial Output Value Created by Energy per Ton (10 000 yuan)	吨能创造生产总值(万元) Gross Regional Product Created by Energy per Ton (10 000 yuan)
1957	119.20	72.70	10.65	5.29	0.09	0.19
1962	256.30	166.60	17.72	10.46	0.06	0.10
1965	348.70	226.70	17.17	10.37	0.06	0.10
1970	591.50	390.40	19.19	15.36	0.05	0.07
1975	920.30	607.40	21.74	16.95	0.05	0.06
1976	797.00	494.10	24.45	16.18	0.04	0.06
1977	931.10	605.20	20.14	16.67	0.05	0.06
1978	1 065.9	692.80	19.23	15.44	0.05	0.06
1979	1 072.2	696.90	17.19	13.96	0.06	0.07
1980	946.10	615.50	14.48	11.23	0.07	0.09
1981	948.40	612.60	13.07	10.08	0.08	0.10
1982	1 020.60	668.20	12.21	9.27	0.08	0.11
1983	1 094.70	651.30	11.51	9.12	0.09	0.11
1984	1 226.30	709.70	10.92	8.79	0.09	0.11
1985	1 298.33	761.10	9.53	7.87	0.11	0.13
1986	1 399.07	875.00	9.52	7.68	0.11	0.13
1987	1 533.22	937.80	8.43	6.69	0.12	0.15
1988	1 622.52	991.50	6.63	5.39	0.15	0.19
1989	1 706.87	1 037.10	5.60	4.70	0.18	0.21
1990	1 954.18	1 143.60	5.66	4.33	0.18	0.23
1991	1 961.92	1 143.40	4.98	3.79	0.20	0.26
1992	2 016.61	1 189.10	4.23	3.26	0.24	0.31
1993	2 089.80	1 282.00	3.03	2.68	0.33	0.37
1994	2 282.80	1 402.70	2.41	2.34	0.42	0.43
1995	2 640.55	1 948.65	2.48	2.19	0.40	0.46
1996	2 819.43	2 036.82	2.55	1.89	0.39	0.53
1997	3 428.98	2 429.07	2.77	2.09	0.36	0.48
1998	3 364.49	2 383.39	2.40	1.88	0.42	0.53
1999	3 287.97	2 224.42	2.20	1.77	0.45	0.56
2000	3 468.33	2 346.44	1.48	1.72	0.68	0.58
2001	3 741.03	2 481.69	1.48	1.75	0.67	0.57
2002	4 131.31	2 796.86	1.51	1.79	0.66	0.56
2003	4 449.97	3 132.01	1.44	1.74	0.69	0.57
2004	5 209.81	3 802.21	1.53	1.69	0.65	0.59
2005	6 023.97	4 390.68	1.35	1.74	0.74	0.57
2006	6 620.57	4 883.00	1.19	1.66	0.84	0.60
2007	7 132.63	5 300.98	1.03	1.49	0.97	0.67
2008	7 510.82	5 597.96	0.98	1.32	1.03	0.76
2009	8 032.06	5 868.90	0.94	1.30	1.07	0.77
2010	8 674.17	6 088.39	0.90	1.20	1.11	0.83
2011	9 540.28	6 939.30	0.87	1.09	1.15	0.92
2012	10 433.68	7 591.39	0.83	1.01	1.20	0.99
2013	10 072.09	7 241.02	0.71	0.85	1.42	1.17
2014	10 454.83	7 269.69	0.70	0.82	1.43	1.23
2015	10 424.69	6 934.91	0.69	0.70	1.45	1.44
2016	10 725.95	7 091.53	0.66	0.66	1.52	1.53
2017	11 163.57	7 449.99	0.61	0.60	1.65	1.66
2018	11 590.02	7 632.21	0.58	0.56	1.72	1.80
2019	12 157.65	7 969.85	0.56	0.52	1.80	1.91
2020	12 981.94	8 809.99	1.61	0.53	0.62	1.89

注：1.能源综合数据按等价热值计算。
2.生产总值、工业总产值按当年价计算。
3.2005至2008年能源消费量根据云南省第二次全国经济普查数据进行了调整，2013至2014年数据根据云南省第三次全国经济普查数据修正，2015至2018年的数据根据云南省第四次全国经济普查数据修正。

Note: a.Comprehensive data of energy were calculated according to equivalent caloricity
b.Total output value and gross value of industrial output were calculated according to the prices of their respective years.
c.The energy consumption volume of year 2005 to 2008 were regulated according to the materials of the second national economic Census. Data from 2013 to 2014 have been adjusted according to the third national economic census. Data from 2015 to 2018 have been adjusted according to the Forth national economic census.

8-14 主要年份能源利用经济效益指标（二）

Indicators on Economic Benefits from Energy Utilization in Significant Years (Ⅱ)

年 份 Year	能源消费总量（万吨标准煤）Total Consumption of Energy (10 000 tons of SCE)		规模以上工业综合能耗（万吨标准煤）Comprehensive Energy Consumption of the Industrial Enterprises above Designated Size (10 000 tons of SCE)	万元生产总值耗能（吨标准煤/万元）Energy Consumption of Gross Regional Product per 10 000 yuan (tons of SCE/10 000 yuan)		规模以上万元工业增加值能耗（吨标准煤/万元）Energy Consumption per 10 000 yuan of Industrial Added Value above Designated Size (ton of SCE/10 000 yuan)
	等价热值 Equivalent Caloricity	当量热值 Equivalent Heat Value	当量热值 Equivalent Heat Value	按等价热值 Equivalent Caloricity	按当量热值 Equivalent Heat Value	按当量热值 Equivalent Heat Value
	按2000年可比价计算(calculated at comparable prices of 2000)					
2000	3 468.33	2 940.74		1.72	1.46	
2001	3 741.03	3 240.39		1.74	1.51	
2002	4 131.31	3 576.86		1.76	1.53	
2003	4 449.97	3 861.70		1.75	1.52	
2004	5 209.81	4 576.79	3 338.83	1.83	1.61	4.35
2005	6 023.97	5 219.55	3 546.35	1.95	1.69	4.26
	按2005年可比价计算(calculated at comparable prices of 2005)					
2005	6 023.97	5 219.55	3 546.35	1.74	1.51	3.55
2006	6 620.57	5 976.53	4 095.81	1.71	1.55	3.40
2007	7 132.63	6 487.79	4 269.52	1.65	1.50	3.16
2008	7 510.82	6 534.34	4 212.50	1.57	1.37	2.85
2009	8 032.06	7 222.76	4 446.47	1.49	1.34	2.74
2010	8 674.17	7 655.60	4 607.10	1.44	1.26	2.47
	按2010年可比价计算(calculated at comparable prices of 2010)					
2010	8 674.17	7 655.60	4 607.10	1.20	1.06	2.05
2011	9 540.28	8 121.85	4 974.14	1.16	0.99	1.88
2012	10 433.68	8 730.66	5 298.34	1.12	0.94	1.73
2013	10 072.09	8 387.50	5 732.85	0.97	0.81	1.67
2014	10 454.83	8 116.71	5 432.34	0.93	0.72	1.47
2015	10 424.69	7 994.22	4 837.34	0.80	0.62	1.23
	按2015年可比价计算(calculated at comparable prices of 2015)					
2016	10 725.95	8 135.67	4 858.25	0.66	0.50	1.32
2017	11 163.57	8 424.22	5 096.56	0.63	0.47	1.31
2018	11 590.02	8 668.79	5 252.49	0.60	0.45	1.27
2019	12 157.65	9 076.54	5 569.44	0.58	0.43	1.14
2020	12 981.94	9 754.20	6 093.60	0.60	0.40	1.22

注：2005至2008年数据根据云南省第二次全国经济普查数据修正，2013至2014年数据根据云南省第三次全国经济普查数据修正，2015至2018年的数据根据云南省第四次全国经济普查数据修正。

Note:Data from 2005 to 2008 are regulated according to that of the second national economic census. Data from 2013 to 2014 have been adjusted according to the third national economic census.Data from 2015 to 2018 have been adjusted according to the Forth national economic census.

8-15 主要国民经济行业能源消费总量和构成（2016-2020年）

单位：万吨标准煤

国民经济行业	National Economic Sector	2016	
		能源消费量 Total Consumption of Energy	构 成 (%) Percentage (%)
工 业	**Industry**	**7 091.53**	**100.00**
轻工业	Light Industry	357.70	5.04
重工业	Heavy Industry	6 733.82	94.96
采矿业	**Mining**	**442.93**	**6.25**
煤炭开采和洗选业	Coal Mining and Dressing	253.86	3.58
石油和天然气开采业	Petroleum and Natural Gas Extraction		
黑色金属矿采选业	Ferrous Metals Mining and Dressing	66.15	0.93
有色金属矿采选业	Nonferrous Metals Mining and Dressing	76.87	1.08
非金属矿采选业	Nonmetal Minerals Mining and Dressing	46.06	0.65
其他采矿业	Other Mining		
制造业	**Manufacturing**	**5 916.24**	**83.43**
农副食品加工业	Agricultural Non-staple Food Processing	114.60	1.62
食品制造业	Food Manufacturing	36.78	0.52
饮料制造业	Beverage Manufacturing	46.09	0.65
烟草制品业	Tobacco Production	33.82	0.48
纺织业	Textile	8.23	0.12
纺织服装、鞋、帽制造业	Textile,Clothing, Footwear Production	0.60	0.01
皮革、毛皮、羽绒及其制造业	Leather, Furs, Down and Related Products	0.85	0.01
木材加工及竹、藤、棕、草制造业	Timber Processing, Bamboo, Cane, Palm Fiber and Straw Products	23.60	0.33
家具制造业	Furniture Manufacturing	0.17	0.00
造纸及纸制造业	Papermaking and Paper Products	71.88	1.01
印刷业	Printing	4.99	0.07
文教体育用品制造业	Cultural, Educational and Sports Goods	1.03	0.01

注：采用数据按等价热值计算，2015至2018年的数据根据云南省第四次全国经济普查数据修正。

Total Energy Consumption of Main National Economic Sectors and Its Composition (2016-2020)

(10 000 tons of SCE)

2017		2018		2019		2020	
能源消费量 Total Consumption of Energy	构 成 (%) Percentage (%)	能源消费量 Total Consumption of Energy	构 成 (%) Percentage (%)	能源消费量 Total Consumption of Energy	构 成 (%) Percentage (%)	能源消费量 Total Consumption of Energy	构 成 (%) Percentage (%)
7 449.99	**100.00**	**7 632.21**	**100.00**	**7 969.85**	**100.00**	**8 809.99**	**100.00**
408.80	5.49	421.66	5.52	355.06	4.46	434.49	4.93
7 041.19	94.51	7 210.56	94.48	7 614.79	95.54	8 375.50	95.07
534.86	**7.18**	**427.68**	**5.60**	**338.51**	**4.25**	**393.37**	4.47
249.30	3.35	151.20	1.98	161.75	2.03	147.91	1.68
0.36	0.00	0.24	0.00			0.39	0.00
62.54	0.84	47.66	0.62	44.53	0.56	42.71	0.48
140.70	1.89	148.70	1.95	75.42	0.95	124.33	1.41
64.09	0.86	66.51	0.87	56.81	0.71	66.23	0.75
0.23	0.00	13.38	0.18			11.80	0.13
6 324.91	**84.90**	**6 553.28**	**85.86**	**6 619.38**	**83.06**	**7 636.25**	86.68
112.73	1.51	125.11	1.64	109.26	1.37	136.46	1.55
40.85	0.55	45.92	0.60	52.42	0.66	49.98	0.57
43.83	0.59	28.09	0.37	27.92	0.35	28.93	0.33
36.13	0.48	40.57	0.53	29.88	0.37	33.87	0.38
7.18	0.10	4.76	0.06	4.88	0.06	3.02	0.03
1.16	0.02	0.90	0.01	0.69	0.01	0.80	0.01
0.56	0.01	0.99	0.01	0.30	0.00	0.68	0.01
19.55	0.26	27.01	0.35	17.23	0.22	25.03	0.28
0.21	0.00	3.43	0.04	0.14	0.00	3.70	0.04
86.50	1.16	87.60	1.15	91.29	1.15	90.89	1.03
7.19	0.10	7.31	0.10	5.97	0.07	7.03	0.08
1.83	0.02	1.53	0.02	2.16	0.03	1.14	0.01

Note: Data used in this table are equivalent caloricity.Data from 2015 to 2018 have been adjusted according to the Forth national economic census.

8-15 续表

单位：万吨标准煤

国民经济行业	National Economic Sector	2016 能源消费量 Total Consumption of Coal	2016 构成(%) Percentage (%)
石油加工、炼焦及核燃料加工业	Petroleum Processing,Coking and Nuclear Fuel Processing	144.27	2.03
化学原料及化学品制造业	Raw Chemical Materials and Chemical Products	1 411.30	19.90
医药制造业	Medical and Pharmaceutical Products	24.96	0.35
化学纤维制造业	Chemical Fiber	4.88	0.07
橡胶和塑料制品业	Rubber and plastic Products Manufacturing	21.50	0.30
非金属矿物制品业	Nonmetal Mineral Products	1 397.96	19.71
黑色金属冶炼及压延加工业	Smelting and Pressing of Ferrous Metals	1 302.45	18.37
有色金属冶炼及压延加工业	Smelting and Pressing of Nonferrous Metals	1 196.83	16.88
金属制品业	Metal Products Manufacturing	14.16	0.20
通用设备制造业	General-purpose Machinery Manufacturing	3.40	0.05
专用设备制造业	Special Purposes Equipment Manufacturing	3.58	0.05
交通运输设备制造业	Transport Equipment Manufacturing	8.02	0.11
电气机械及器材制造业	Electric Equipment and Machinery Manufacturing	7.18	0.10
通信设备、计算机及其他电子设备制造业	Communication Equipment,Computers and Other Electronic Equipment Production	2.59	0.04
仪器仪表、文化办公用机械制造业	Instruments, Meters, Cultural and Clerical Machinery Manufacturing	0.45	0.01
工艺品及其他制造业	Handicraft Articles and Other Goods Production	8.82	0.12
废弃资源和废旧材料回收加工业	Recycling and Disposal of Waste	21.25	0.30
电力、热力、燃气及水生产和供应业	**Production and Supply of Electricity, Heat, Gas and Water**	**732.35**	**10.33**
电力、热力生产和供应业	Production and Supply of Electric Power and Heat	710.73	10.02
燃气生产和供应业	Gas Production and Supply	8.34	0.12
水的生产和供应业	Water Production and Supply	13.28	0.19
建筑业	**Construction**	**232.48**	
交通运输、仓储及邮电通信业	**Transport, Storage and Post Services**	**1 197.12**	

continued

(10 000 tons of SCE)

2017		2018		2019		2020	
能源消费量 Total Consumption of Coal	构　成 (%) Percentage (%)	能源消费量 Total Consumption of Coal	构　成 (%) Percentage (%)	能源消费量 Total Consumption of Coal	构　成 (%) Percentage (%)	能源消费量 Total Consumption of Coal	构　成 (%) Percentage (%)
326.66	4.38	320.16	4.19	340.73	4.28	470.12	5.34
1 206.50	16.19	1 149.45	15.06	1 085.04	13.61	1 204.73	13.67
31.06	0.42	28.58	0.37	24.50	0.31	26.42	0.30
3.81	0.05	4.19	0.05	4.88	0.06	4.03	0.05
42.14	0.57	46.04	0.60	22.37	0.28	45.58	0.52
1 672.43	22.45	1 659.47	21.74	1 585.92	19.90	1 808.43	20.53
1 284.31	17.24	1 444.53	18.93	1 582.08	19.85	1 586.77	18.01
1 274.99	17.11	1 382.86	18.12	1 514.63	19.00	1 909.40	21.67
34.06	0.46	41.88	0.55	17.05	0.21	42.27	0.48
4.46	0.06	7.90	0.10	5.30	0.07	5.21	0.06
3.76	0.05	4.79	0.06	2.11	0.03	4.16	0.05
12.01	0.16	8.30	0.11	11.45	0.14	10.92	0.12
10.83	0.15	12.49	0.16	7.97	0.10	20.80	0.24
5.14	0.07	1.55	0.02	51.00	0.64	38.32	0.43
0.15	0.00	1.89	0.02	0.34	0.00	2.13	0.02
35.76	0.48	42.67	0.56	0.76	0.01	47.53	0.54
19.10	0.26	21.18	0.28	21.08	0.26	26.22	0.30
590.22	**7.92**	**651.26**	**8.53**	**1 011.97**	**12.70**	**780.37**	**8.86**
565.04	7.58	605.43	7.93	949.41	11.91	726.80	8.25
4.01	0.05	23.10	0.30	43.92	0.55	16.89	0.19
21.17	0.28	22.72	0.30	18.64	0.23	36.68	0.42
245.48		**271.63**		**304.57**		**294.65**	
1 233.08		**1 303.26**		**1 423.63**		**1 361.27**	

8-16 主要国民经济行业原煤消费量和构成（2016-2020年）

单位：万吨

国民经济行业	National Economic Sector	2016 原煤消费量 Total Consumption of Coal	2016 构成(%) Percentage (%)
工　业	**Industry**	**7 978.99**	**100.00**
轻工业	Light Industry	251.78	3.16
重工业	Heavy Industry	7 727.21	96.84
采矿业	**Mining**	**3 154.45**	**39.53**
煤炭开采和洗选业	Coal Mining and Dressing	3 105.54	38.92
石油和天然气开采业	Petroleum and Natural Gas Extraction		
黑色金属矿采选业	Ferrous Metals Mining and Dressing	13.75	0.17
有色金属矿采选业	Nonferrous Metals Mining and Dressing	0.70	0.01
非金属矿采选业	Nonmetal Minerals Mining and Dressing	34.45	0.43
其他采矿业	Other Mining		
制造业	**Manufacturing**	**3 807.72**	**47.72**
农副食品加工业	Agricultural Non-staple Food Processing	43.46	0.54
食品制造业	Food Manufacturing	24.94	0.31
饮料制造业	Beverage Manufacturing	40.92	0.51
烟草制品业	Tobacco Production	15.07	0.19
纺织业	Textile Industry	8.09	0.10
纺织服装、鞋、帽制造业	Textile,Clothing, Footwear Production	0.16	0.00
皮革、毛皮、羽绒及其制品业	Leather, Furs, Down and Related Products	0.30	0.00
木材加工及竹、藤、棕、草制品业	Timber Processing, Bamboo, Cane, Palm Fiber and Straw Products	1.32	0.02
家具制造业	Furniture Manufacturing		
造纸及纸制品业	Papermaking and Paper Products	61.65	0.77
印刷业	Printing	0.79	0.01
文教体育用品制造业	Cultural, Educational and Sports Goods		

注：2015至2018年的数据根据云南省第四次全国经济普查数据修正。

Total Consumption Of Coal of Main National Economic Sectors and Its Composition (2016-2020)

(10 000 tons)

2017		2018		2019		2020	
原煤消费量 Total Consumption of Coal	构　成 (%) Percentage (%)	原煤消费量 Total Consumption of Coal	构　成 (%) Percentage (%)	原煤消费量 Total Consumption of Coal	构　成 (%) Percentage (%)	原煤消费量 Total Consumption of Coal	构　成 (%) Percentage (%)
7 675.50	**100.00**	**7 062.72**	**100.00**	**7 033.89**	**100.00**	**7 047.70**	**100.00**
222.04	2.89	203.59	2.88	197.19	2.80	165.48	2.35
7 453.46	97.11	6 859.13	97.12	6 836.70	97.20	6 882.22	97.65
2 865.77	**37.34**	**2 139.10**	**30.29**	**2 099.97**	**29.86**	**1 603.95**	**22.76**
2 812.45	36.64	2 091.67	29.62	2 045.89	29.09	1 554.70	22.06
11.46	0.15	5.70	0.08	8.82	0.13	0.78	0.01
0.66	0.01	0.51	0.01	0.46	0.01	0.68	0.01
41.20	0.54	41.22	0.58	44.80	0.64	47.79	0.68
3 771.45	**49.14**	**3 460.77**	**49.00**	**3382.86**	**48.09**	**3 264.02**	**46.31**
46.63	0.61	41.57	0.59	34.35	0.49	29.11	0.41
22.28	0.29	36.58	0.52	39.45	0.56	39.78	0.56
42.51	0.55	19.54	0.28	18.96	0.27	15.52	0.22
10.96	0.14	7.81	0.11	3.97	0.06	2.96	0.04
6.02	0.08	3.85	0.05	2.43	0.03	1.58	0.02
0.14	0.00	0.09	0.00	0.01	0.00	0.01	0.00
0.21	0.00	0.05	0.00				
0.55	0.01	0.40	0.01	0.14	0.00	0.10	0.00
56.93	0.74	52.30	0.74	62.39	0.89	61.35	0.87
0.69	0.01	0.33	0.00	0.38	0.01	0.19	0.00
0.28	0.00	0.46	0.01	0.83	0.01	0.54	0.01

Note: Data from 2015 to 2018 have been adjusted according to the Forth national economic census.

8-16 续表

单位：万吨

国民经济行业	National Economic Sector	2016 原煤消费量 Total Consumption of Energy	构成 (%) Percentage (%)
石油加工、炼焦及核燃料加工业	Petroleum Processing,Coking and Nuclear Fuel Processing	413.63	5.18
化学原料及化学品制造业	Raw Chemical Materials and Chemical Products	1 201.29	15.06
医药制造业	Medical and Pharmaceutical Products	18.85	0.24
化学纤维制造业	Chemical Fiber	5.26	0.07
橡胶和塑料制品业	Rubber and plastic Products Manufacturing	7.70	0.10
非金属矿物制品业	Nonmetal Mineral Products	1 430.94	17.93
黑色金属冶炼及压延加工业	Smelting and Pressing of Ferrous Metals	248.17	3.11
有色金属冶炼及压延加工业	Smelting and Pressing of Nonferrous Metals	237.74	2.98
金属制品业	Metal Products Manufacturing	5.40	0.07
通用设备制造业	General-purpose Machinery Manufacturing	0.22	0.00
专用设备制造业	Special Purposes Equipment Manufacturing	0.01	0.00
交通运输设备制造业	Transport Equipment Manufacturing	0.56	0.01
电气机械及器材制造业	Electric Equipment and Machinery Manufacturing	0.51	0.01
通信设备、计算机及其他电子设备制造业	Communication Equipment, Computers and Other Electronic Equipment Production		
仪器仪表、文化办公用机械制造业	Instruments, Meters, Cultural and Clerical Machinery Manufacturing		
工艺品及其他制造业	Handicraft Articles and Other Goods Production	32.30	0.40
废弃资源和废旧材料回收加工业	Recycling and Disposal of Waste	8.45	0.11
电力、热力、燃气及水生产和供应业	**Production and Supply of Electricity, Heat ,Gas and Water**	**1 016.82**	**12.74**
电力、热力的生产和供应业	Production and Supply of Electric Power and Heat	1 015.24	12.72
燃气生产和供应业	Gas Production and Supply	1.58	0.02
水的生产和供应业	Water Production and Supply		
建筑业	**Construction**	**36.88**	
交通运输、仓储及邮电通信业	**Transport, Storage and Post Services**	**15.15**	

注：能源综合消费量按等价热值计算。

continued

(10 000 tons)

2017		2018		2019		2020	
原煤消费量 Total Consumption of Energy	构　成 (%) Percentage (%)	原煤消费量 Total Consumption of Energy	构　成 (%) Percentage (%)	原煤消费量 Total Consumption of Energy	构　成 (%) Percentage (%)	原煤消费量 Total Consumption of Energy	构　成 (%) Percentage (%)
331.06	4.31	188.51	2.67	181.72	2.58	245.52	3.48
1 099.84	14.33	906.77	12.84	758.49	10.78	650.80	9.23
17.44	0.23	12.91	0.18	12.17	0.17	3.61	0.05
4.79	0.06	4.53	0.06	4.55	0.06	4.39	0.06
8.15	0.11	7.30	0.10	4.85	0.07	4.99	0.07
1 566.78	20.41	1 525.07	21.59	1 652.38	23.49	1 619.69	22.98
254.12	3.31	328.64	4.65	313.11	4.45	306.85	4.35
275.40	3.59	279.61	3.96	261.83	3.72	256.45	3.64
4.76	0.06	5.24	0.07	3.72	0.05	3.52	0.05
0.04	0.00	0.03	0.00	0.03	0.00		
0.01	0.00					0.20	0.00
0.15	0.00						
0.15	0.00	0.03	0.00				
						0.02	0.00
13.16	0.17	23.57	0.33	17.70	0.25	6.44	0.09
8.40	0.11	15.58	0.22	9.40	0.13	10.40	0.15
1 038.28	**13.53**	**1 462.84**	**20.71**	**1 551.06**	**22.05**	**2 179.73**	**30.93**
1 038.28	13.53	1 458.77	20.65	1 541.18	21.91	2 151.63	30.53
		4.07	0.06	9.88	0.14	28.10	0.40
37.73		**36.31**		**34.13**		**32.91**	
12.74		**12.41**		**11.42**			

Note: The energy consumption volume was calculated according to the equivalent caloricity.

8-17 主要国民经济行业焦炭消费量和构成（2016-2020年）

单位：万吨

国民经济行业	National Economic Sector	2016 焦炭消费量 Total Consumption of Coke	2016 构成(%) Percentage (%)
工　业	**Industry**	**904.26**	**100.00**
轻工业	Light Industry		
重工业	Heavy Industry	904.26	100.00
采矿业	**Mining**	**2.87**	**0.32**
煤炭开采和洗选业	Coal Mining and Dressing		
石油和天然气开采业	Petroleum and Natural Gas Extraction		
黑色金属矿采选业	Ferrous Metals Mining and Dressing	2.13	0.24
有色金属矿采选业	Nonferrous Metals Mining and Dressing	0.74	0.08
非金属矿采选业	Nonmetal Minerals Mining and Dressing		
其他采矿业	Other Mining		
制造业	**Manufacturing**	**901.39**	**99.68**
农副食品加工业	Agricultural Non-staple Food Processing		
食品制造业	Food Manufacturing		
饮料制造业	Beverage Manufacturing		
烟草制品业	Tobacco Production		
纺织业	Textile Industry		
纺织服装、鞋、帽制造业	Textile,Clothing, Footwear Production		
皮革、毛皮、羽绒及其制品业	Leather, Furs, Down and Related Products		
木材加工及竹、藤、棕、草制品业	Timber Processing, Bamboo, Cane, Palm Fiber and Straw Products		
家具制造业	Furniture Manufacturing		
造纸及纸制品业	Papermaking and Paper Products		
印刷业	Printing		
文教体育用品制造业	Cultural, Educational and Sports Goods		

注：2015至2018年的数据根据云南省第四次全国经济普查数据修正。

Total Consumption of Coke of Main National Economic Sectors and Its Composition (2016-2020)

(10 000tons)

2017		2018		2019		2020	
焦炭消费量 Total Consumption of Coke	构 成 (%) Percentage (%)	焦炭消费量 Total Consumption of Coke	构 成 (%) Percentage (%)	焦炭消费量 Total Consumption of Coke	构 成 (%) Percentage (%)	焦炭消费量 Total Consumption of Coke	构 成 (%) Percentage (%)
949.45	**100.00**	**1 062.03**	**100.00**	**1117.69**	**100.00**	**1214.51**	**100.00**
949.45	100.00	1 062.03	100.00	1117.69	100.00	1214.51	100.00
2.57	**0.27**	**1.24**	**0.12**	**0.67**	**0.06**	**0.28**	**0.02**
2.24	0.24	0.86	0.08	0.23	0.02		
0.33	0.03	0.38	0.04	0.44	0.04	0.28	0.02
946.88	**99.73**	**1 060.79**	**99.88**	**1117.02**	**99.94**	**1214.23**	**99.98**

Note: Data from 2015 to 2018 have been adjusted according to the Forth national economic census.

8-17 续表

单位：万吨

国民经济行业	National Economic Sector	2016 焦炭消费量 Total Consumption of Coke	构成(%) Percentage (%)
石油加工、炼焦及核燃料加工业	Petroleum Processing,Coking and Nuclear Fuel Processing		
化学原料及化学品制造业	Raw Chemical Materials and Chemical Products	164.39	18.18
医药制造业	Medical and Pharmaceutical Products		
化学纤维制造业	Chemical Fiber		
橡胶和塑料制品业	Rubber and plastic Products Manufacturing		
非金属矿物制品业	Nonmetal Mineral Products	1.68	0.19
黑色金属冶炼及压延加工业	Smelting and Pressing of Ferrous Metals	698.35	77.23
有色金属冶炼及压延加工业	Smelting and Pressing of Nonferrous Metals	32.33	3.58
金属制品业	Metal Products Manufacturing	0.49	0.05
通用设备制造业	General-purpose Machinery Manufacturing	0.81	0.09
专用设备制造业	Special Purposes Equipment Manufacturing	0.15	0.02
交通运输设备制造业	Transport Equipment Manufacturing	0.02	0.00
电气机械及器材制造业	Electric Equipment and Machinery Manufacturing	0.04	0.00
通信设备、计算机及其他电子设备制造业	Communication Equipment,Computers and Other Electronic Equipment Production		
仪器仪表、文化办公用机械制造业	Instruments, Meters, Cultural and Clerical Machinery Manufacturing		
工艺品及其他制造业	Handicraft Articles and Other Goods Production		
废弃资源和废旧材料回收加工业	Recycling and Disposal of Waste	3.10	0.34
电力、热力、燃气及水生产和供应业	**Production and Supply of Electricity, Heat ,Gas and Water**		
电力、热力生产和供应业	Production and Supply of Electric Power and Heat		
燃气生产和供应业	Gas Production and Supply		
水的生产和供应业	Water Production and Supply		
建筑业	**Construction**		
交通运输、仓储及邮电通信业	**Transport, Storage and Post Services**		

continued

10 000 tons

2017		2018		2019		2020	
焦炭消费量 Total Consumption of Coke	构　成 (%) Percentage (%)	焦炭消费量 Total Consumption of Coke	构　成 (%) Percentage (%)	焦炭消费量 Total Consumption of Coke	构　成 (%) Percentage (%)	焦炭消费量 Total Consumption of Coke	构　成 (%) Percentage (%)
				0.03		0.11	0.01
144.55	15.22	143.19	13.48	113.35	10.14	154.49	12.72
3.13	0.33	0.99	0.09	0.65	0.06	0.42	0.03
769.95	81.09	894.86	84.26	985.61	88.18	1 015.83	83.64
25.13	2.65	15.49	1.46	12.65	1.13	33.61	2.77
0.24	0.03	2.55	0.24	0.81	0.07	6.95	0.57
0.92	0.10	1.18	0.11	1.46	0.13	0.32	0.03
0.01	0.00						
0.05	0.01	0.04	0.00				
2.90	0.31	2.49	0.23	2.46	0.22	2.50	0.21

8-18 主要国民经济行业石油消费量和构成（2016-2020年）

单位：万吨

国民经济行业	National Economic Sector	2016 石油消费量 Total Consumption of Petroleum	2016 构成(%) Percentage (%)
工业	**Industry**	**136.12**	**100.00**
轻工业	Light Industry	6.82	5.01
重工业	Heavy Industry	129.30	94.99
采矿业	**Mining**	**21.48**	**15.78**
煤炭开采和洗选业	Coal Mining and Dressing	4.88	3.59
石油和天然气开采业	Petroleum and Natural Gas Extraction		
黑色金属矿采选业	Ferrous Metals Mining and Dressing	2.31	1.70
有色金属矿采选业	Nonferrous Metals Mining and Dressing	8.35	6.14
非金属矿采选业	Nonmetal Minerals Mining and Dressing	5.93	4.36
其他采矿业	Other Mining		
制造业	**Manufacturing**	**112.74**	**82.83**
农副食品加工业	Agricultural Non-staple Food Processing	1.10	0.81
食品制造业	Food Manufacturing	1.16	0.85
饮料制造业	Beverage Manufacturing	2.66	1.95
烟草制品业	Tobacco Production	0.45	0.33
纺织业	Textile	0.07	0.05
纺织服装、鞋、帽制造业	Textile,Clothing, Footwear Production	0.01	0.01
皮革、毛皮、羽绒及其制品业	Leather, Furs, Down and Related Products	0.01	0.01
木材加工及竹、藤、棕、草制品业	Timber Processing, Bamboo, Cane, Palm Fiber and Straw Products	0.32	0.23
家具制造业	Furniture Manufacturing		
造纸及纸制品业	Papermaking and Paper Products	0.44	0.32
印刷业	Printing	0.19	0.14
文教体育用品制造业	Cultural, Educational and Sports Goods	0.09	0.07

注：2015至2018年的数据根据云南省第四次全国经济普查数据修正。

Total Consumption of Petroleum of Main National Economic Sectors and Its Composition (2016-2020)

(10 000 tons)

2017		2018		2019		2020	
石油消费量 Total Consumption of Petroleum	构　成 (%) Percentage (%)	石油消费量 Total Consumption of Petroleum	构　成 (%) Percentage (%)	石油消费量 Total Consumption of Petroleum	构　成 (%) Percentage (%)	石油消费量 Total Consumption of Petroleum	构　成 (%) Percentage (%)
223.40	**100.00**	**212.22**	**100.00**	**237.05**	**100.00**	**310.83**	**100.00**
3.75	1.68	3.36	1.59	3.18	1.34	2.27	0.73
219.65	98.32	208.85	98.41	233.87	98.66	308.56	99.27
21.03	**9.41**	**21.45**	**10.11**	**19.91**	**8.40**	**20.97**	**6.75**
3.95	1.77	4.09	1.93	3.60	1.52	6.44	2.07
2.15	0.96	1.96	0.92	1.76	0.74	1.32	0.42
8.20	3.67	8.70	4.10	6.90	2.91	6.59	2.12
6.73	3.01	6.70	3.16	7.65	3.23	6.62	2.13
200.68	**89.83**	**188.75**	**88.94**	**214.83**	**90.63**	**287.13**	**92.38**
0.92	0.41	0.73	0.34	0.72	0.30	0.31	0.10
1.21	0.54	1.05	0.49	1.01	0.43	0.87	0.28
0.36	0.16	0.27	0.13	0.29	0.12	0.25	0.08
0.38	0.17	0.34	0.16	0.32	0.13	0.19	0.06
		0.01	0.00	0.01	0.00		
		0.02	0.01	0.03	0.01		
0.28	0.13	0.20	0.09	0.21	0.09	0.18	0.06
						0.01	0.00
0.35	0.16	0.41	0.20	0.32	0.13	0.25	0.08
0.17	0.08	0.24	0.11	0.14	0.06	0.13	0.04
0.07	0.03	0.06	0.03	0.05	0.02	0.02	0.01

Note: Data from 2015 to 2018 have been adjusted according to the Forth national economic census.

8-18 续表

单位：万吨

国民经济行业	National Economic Sector	2016 石油消费量 Total Consumption of Petroleum (10 000 tons)	2016 构成(%) Percentage (%)
石油加工、炼焦及核燃料加工业	Petroleum Processing,Coking and Nuclear Fuel Processing	0.16	0.12
化学原料及化学品制造业	Raw Chemical Materials and Chemical Products	0.09	0.07
医药制造业	Medical and Pharmaceutical Products	0.28	0.21
化学纤维制造业	Chemical Fiber		
橡胶和塑料制品业	Rubber and plastic Products Manufacturing	0.40	0.29
非金属矿物制品业	Nonmetal Mineral Products	45.99	33.79
黑色金属冶炼及压延加工业	Smelting and Pressing of Ferrous Metals	24.15	17.74
有色金属冶炼及压延加工业	Smelting and Pressing of Nonferrous Metals	32.03	23.53
金属制品业	Metal Products Manufacturing	0.82	0.60
通用设备制造业	General-purpose Machinery Manufacturing	0.10	0.07
专用设备制造业	Special Purposes Equipment Manufacturing	0.64	0.47
交通运输设备制造业	Transport Equipment Manufacturing	0.67	0.49
电气机械及器材制造业	Electric Equipment and Machinery Manufacturing	0.27	0.20
通信设备、计算机及其他电子设备制造业	Communication Equipment,Computers and Other Electronic Equipment Production	0.01	0.01
仪器仪表、文化办公用机械制造业	Instruments, Meters, Cultural and Clerical Machinery Manufacturing	0.02	0.02
工艺品及其他制造业	Handicraft Articles and Other Goods Production	0.36	0.27
废弃资源和废旧材料回收加工业	Recycling and Disposal of Waste	0.24	0.18
电力、热力、燃气及水生产和供应业	**Production and Supply of Electricity, Heat ,Gas and Water**	**1.90**	**1.40**
电力、热力的生产和供应业	Production and Supply of Electric Power and Heat	1.64	1.21
燃气生产和供应业	Gas Production and Supply	0.19	0.14
水的生产和供应业	Water Production and Supply	0.07	0.05
建筑业	**Construction**	**66.17**	
交通运输、仓储及邮电通信业	**Transport, Storage and Post Services**	**743.90**	

continued

(10 000 tons)

2017		2018		2019		2020	
石油消费量 Total Consumption of Petroleum (10 000 tons)	构　成 (%) Percentage (%)	石油消费量 Total Consumption of Petroleum (10 000 tons)	构　成 (%) Percentage (%)	石油消费量 Total Consumption of Petroleum (10 000 tons)	构　成 (%) Percentage (%)	石油消费量 Total Consumption of Petroleum (10 000 tons)	构　成 (%) Percentage (%)
73.40	32.86	39.85	18.78	60.93	25.70	34.42	11.07
10.92	4.89	26.41	12.44	21.91	9.24	99.99	32.17
0.29	0.13	0.23	0.11	0.29	0.12	0.24	0.08
0.33	0.15	0.30	0.14	0.21	0.09	0.15	0.05
51.41	23.01	56.82	26.77	93.62	39.49	109.98	35.38
25.31	11.33	9.05	4.27	8.32	3.51	8.72	2.81
33.46	14.98	50.97	24.02	25.01	10.55	29.40	9.46
0.43	0.19	0.51	0.24	0.34	0.14	0.37	0.12
0.06	0.03	0.10	0.05	0.06	0.03	0.04	0.01
0.46	0.21	0.14	0.07	0.13	0.05	0.12	0.04
0.62	0.28	0.70	0.33	0.55	0.23	1.05	0.34
0.13	0.06	0.19	0.09	0.21	0.09	0.29	0.09
		0.02	0.01	0.02	0.01		
0.01	0.00	0.01	0.00	0.01	0.00	0.02	0.01
0.12	0.05	0.11	0.05	0.12	0.05	0.13	0.04
1.69	**0.76**	**2.02**	**0.95**	**2.31**	**0.97**	**2.73**	**0.88**
1.48	0.66	1.70	0.80	1.73	0.73	2.49	0.80
0.16	0.07	0.26	0.12	0.52	0.22	0.16	0.05
0.05	0.02	0.06	0.03	0.06	0.03	0.08	0.03
67.66		**69.05**		**71.71**		**69.14**	
759.42		**801.09**		**873.71**		**839.37**	

8-19 主要国民经济行业电力消费量和构成（2016-2020年）

单位：亿千瓦小时

国民经济行业	National Economic Sector	2016 电力消费量 Total Consumption of Electricity	2016 构成(%) Percentage (%)
工业	**Industry**	**1 002.86**	**100.00**
轻工业	Light Industry	35.01	3.49
重工业	Heavy Industry	967.85	96.51
采矿业	**Mining**	**44.48**	**4.44**
煤炭开采和洗选业	Coal Mining and Dressing	9.36	0.93
石油和天然气开采业	Petroleum and Natural Gas Extraction		
黑色金属矿采选业	Ferrous Metals Mining and Dressing	11.35	1.13
有色金属矿采选业	Nonferrous Metals Mining and Dressing	18.44	1.84
非金属矿采选业	Nonmetal Minerals Mining and Dressing	5.33	0.53
其他采矿业	Other Mining		
制造业	**Manufacturing**	**749.77**	**74.76**
农副食品加工业	Agricultural Non-staple Food Processing	9.54	0.95
食品制造业	Food Manufacturing	4.55	0.45
饮料制造业	Beverage Manufacturing	3.23	0.32
烟草制品业	Tobacco Production	4.92	0.49
纺织业	Textile	0.79	0.08
纺织服装、鞋、帽制造业	Textile,Clothing, Footwear Production	0.13	0.01
皮革、毛皮、羽绒及其制品业	Leather, Furs, Down and Related Products	0.21	0.02
木材加工及竹、藤、棕、草制品业	Timber Processing, Bamboo, Cane, Palm Fiber and Straw Products	4.58	0.46
家具制造业	Furniture Manufacturing	0.05	0.00
造纸及纸制品业	Papermaking and Paper Products	6.91	0.69
印刷业	Printing	1.16	0.12
文教体育用品制造业	Cultural, Educational and Sports Goods	0.26	0.03

注：2015至2018年的数据根据云南省第四次全国经济普查数据修正。

Total Consumption of Electricity of Main National Economic Sectors and Its Composition (2016-2020)

(100 million kwh)

2017		2018		2019		2020	
电力消费量 Total Consumption of Electricity	构 成 (%) Percentage (%)	电力消费量 Total Consumption of Electricity	构 成 (%) Percentage (%)	电力消费量 Total Consumption of Electricity	构 成 (%) Percentage (%)	电力消费量 Total Consumption of Electricity	构 成 (%) Percentage (%)
1 084.80	**100.00**	**1 174.21**	**100.00**	**1 253.01**	**100.00**	**1 434.68**	**100.00**
54.47	5.02	60.47	5.15	44.40	3.54	65.70	4.58
1 030.33	94.98	1 113.74	94.85	1 208.61	96.46	1 368.98	95.42
78.77	**7.26**	**80.37**	**6.84**	**46.22**	**3.69**	**73.57**	**5.13**
13.97	1.29	13.67	1.16	9.78	0.78	12.75	0.89
0.11	0.01	0.07	0.01			0.12	0.01
11.13	1.03	10.70	0.91	10.24	0.82	11.42	0.80
38.31	3.53	40.56	3.45	19.65	1.57	35.09	2.45
9.90	0.91	11.35	0.97	6.55	0.52	10.54	0.73
0.07	0.01	4.01	0.34			3.65	0.25
834.32	**76.91**	**908.48**	**77.37**	**910.95**	**72.70**	**1 126.03**	**78.49**
11.42	1.05	12.29	1.05	11.34	0.91	14.03	0.98
6.43	0.59	6.18	0.53	8.38	0.67	7.64	0.53
3.80	0.35	3.54	0.30	3.13	0.25	4.01	0.28
6.31	0.58	7.81	0.66	5.09	0.41	6.76	0.47
0.97	0.09	0.65	0.06	1.05	0.08	0.60	0.04
0.31	0.03	0.22	0.02	0.17	0.01	0.22	0.02
0.14	0.01	0.29	0.02	0.09	0.01	0.21	0.01
4.41	0.41	6.66	0.57	3.68	0.29	6.17	0.43
0.06	0.01	1.03	0.09	0.04	0.00	1.14	0.08
8.10	0.75	8.65	0.74	9.17	0.73	8.97	0.63
1.85	0.17	1.84	0.16	1.50	0.12	1.80	0.13
0.46	0.04	0.34	0.03	0.46	0.04	0.19	0.01

Note: Data from 2015 to 2018 have been adjusted according to the Forth national economic census.

8-19 续表

单位：亿千瓦小时

国民经济行业	National Economic Sector	2016	
		电力消费量 Total Consumption of Electricity	构 成 (%) Percentage (%)
石油加工、炼焦及核燃料加工业	Petroleum Processing,Coking and Nuclear Fuel Processing	6.94	0.69
化学原料及化学品制造业	Raw Chemical Materials and Chemical Products	163.68	16.32
医药制造业	Medical and Pharmaceutical Products	2.70	0.27
化学纤维制造业	Chemical Fiber	0.49	0.05
橡胶和塑料制品业	Rubber and plastic Products Manufacturing	4.63	0.46
非金属矿物制品业	Nonmetal Mineral Products	104.40	10.41
黑色金属冶炼及压延加工业	Smelting and Pressing of Ferrous Metals	139.09	13.87
有色金属冶炼及压延加工业	Smelting and Pressing of Nonferrous Metals	279.61	27.88
金属制品业	Metal Products Manufacturing	2.10	0.21
通用设备制造业	General-purpose Machinery Manufacturing	0.69	0.07
专用设备制造业	Special Purposes Equipment Manufacturing	0.72	0.07
交通运输设备制造业	Transport Equipment Manufacturing	1.83	0.18
电气机械及器材制造业	Electric Equipment and Machinery Manufacturing	1.89	0.19
通信设备、计算机及其他电子设备制造业	Communication Equipment,Computers and Other Electronic Equipment Production	0.75	0.07
仪器仪表、文化办公用机械制造业	Instruments, Meters, Cultural and Clerical Machinery Manufacturing	0.12	0.01
工艺品及其他制造业	Handicraft Articles and Other Goods Production	0.08	0.01
废弃资源和废旧材料回收加工业	Recycling and Disposal of Waste	3.72	0.37
电力、热力、燃气及水生产和供应业	**Production and Supply of Electricity, Heat ,Gas and Water**	**208.61**	**20.80**
电力、热力的生产和供应业	Production and Supply of Electric Power and Heat	203.53	20.29
燃气生产和供应业	Gas Production and Supply	1.24	0.12
水的生产和供应业	Water Production and Supply	3.83	0.38
建筑业	**Construction**	**29.47**	
交通运输、仓储及邮电通信业	**Transport, Storage and Post Services**	**27.67**	

continued

(100 million kwh)

2017		2018		2019		2020	
电力消费量 Total Consumption of Electricity	构 成 (%) Percentage (%)	电力消费量 Total Consumption of Electricity	构 成 (%) Percentage (%)	电力消费量 Total Consumption of Electricity	构 成 (%) Percentage (%)	电力消费量 Total Consumption of Electricity	构 成 (%) Percentage (%)
12.63	1.16	19.87	1.69	19.28	1.54	22.07	1.54
127.60	11.76	142.61	12.15	149.91	11.96	147.90	10.31
4.67	0.43	4.80	0.41	3.45	0.28	5.23	0.36
0.24	0.02	0.32	0.03	0.53	0.04	0.28	0.02
11.00	1.01	12.33	1.05	5.74	0.46	13.07	0.91
169.62	15.64	176.32	15.02	123.04	9.82	193.95	13.52
125.98	11.61	132.57	11.29	140.58	11.22	127.72	8.90
306.85	28.29	334.68	28.50	395.06	31.53	510.95	35.61
8.53	0.79	10.15	0.86	3.45	0.28	9.76	0.68
1.01	0.09	1.96	0.17	1.12	0.09	1.46	0.10
0.90	0.08	1.32	0.11	0.54	0.04	1.19	0.08
3.29	0.30	1.64	0.14	2.43	0.19	1.88	0.13
3.15	0.29	3.64	0.31	2.29	0.18	6.22	0.43
1.54	0.14	0.46	0.04	15.47	1.23	11.76	0.82
0.04	0.00	0.56	0.05	0.10	0.01	0.65	0.05
9.71	0.90	12.51	1.07			14.62	1.02
3.30	0.30	2.61	0.22	3.86	0.31	5.06	0.35
171.71	**15.83**	**185.36**	**15.79**	**295.84**	**23.61**	**235.08**	**16.39**
164.26	15.14	176.08	15.00	282.58	22.55	221.78	15.46
1.13	0.10	2.50	0.21	7.62	0.61	1.99	0.14
6.32	0.58	6.79	0.58	5.64	0.45	11.31	0.79
34.55		**42.53**		**52.96**		**52.39**	
33.46		**36.32**		**41.46**		**40.48**	

主要统计指标解释

工业 指从事自然资源的开采，对采掘品和农产品进行加工和再加工的物质生产部门。具体包括：

1. 对自然资源的开采，如采矿、晒盐等(但不包括禽兽捕猎和水产捕捞)

2. 对农副产品的加工、再加工，如粮油加工、食品加工、缫丝、纺织、制革等；

3. 对采掘品的加工、再加工，如炼铁、炼钢、化工生产、石油加工、机器制造、木材加工等，以及电力、燃气及水的生产和供应等。

4. 对工业品的修理、翻新，如机器设备的修理等。

1984 年以前农村的村及村以下办工业归属农业，1984 年及以后划归工业。

工业统计调查单位为工业法人单位。

工业法人单位 指从事工业生产经营活动的法人单位。工业法人单位应同时具备以下条件：①依法成立，有自己的名称、组织机构和场所，能够独立承担民事责任；②独立拥有(或授权)使用资产，承担负债，有权与其他单位签订合同；③具有包括资产负债表在内的帐户，或者能够根据需要编制帐户。

规模以上工业 从 2011 年开始，为年主营业务收入 2000 万元及以上的工业法人单位。

国有企业 指企业全部资产归国家所有，并按《中华人民共和国企业法人登记管理条例》规定登记注册的非公司制的经济组织。不包括有限责任公司中的国有独资公司。

集体企业 指企业资产归集体所有，并按《中华人民共和国企业法人登记管理条例》规定登记注册的经济组织。

股份合作企业 指以合作制为基础，由企业职工共同出资入股，吸收一定比例的社会资产投资组建，实行自主经营，自负盈亏，共同劳动，民主管理，按劳分配与按股分红相结合的一种集体经济组织。

股份制企业 指两个或两个以上的利益主体，以集股经营的方式自愿结合的一种企业组织形式。

其他企业 指上述企业之外的其他内资经济组织。

港澳台商投资企业 是指港、澳、台地区投资者依照中国法律，以合资、合作或独资的形式在内地开办的企业。

外商投资企业 是指外国投资者根据中华人民共和国有关涉外经济的法律、法规，以合资、合作或独资的形式在中国内地开办企业而形成的一种经济组织。

大、中、小和微型企业 企业规模的划分标准执行《统计上大中小微型企业划分办法（2017）》，按照企业从业人员、主营业务收入，将企业划分为大型、中型、小型和微型。

工业总产值 指工业企业在报告期内生产的以货币形式表现的工业最终产品和提供工业劳务活动的总价值量。它包括：在本企业内不再进行加工，经检验、包装入库的成品价值、对外加工费收入、自制半成品、在制品期末期初差额价值。工业总产值采用“工厂法”计算，即以工业企业作为一个整体，按企业工业生产活动的最终成果计算，企业内部不允许重复计算，不能把企业内部各个车间（分厂）生产的成果相加。但在企业之间、行业之间、地区之间存在重复计算。

工业总产值计算遵循以下规定：

1. 凡用自备原材料生产的产品，不论其加工的繁简程度如何，一律按全价，即工业总产值包括自备原材料的价值。

2. 凡承接来料加工生产的产品，加工企业只收取加工费，加工企业一律按财务上结算的加工费计算工业总产值，即不包括订货者来料的价值。

3. 自制半成品、在制品期末期初差额价值，原则上应计入工业总产值，但如果会计产品成本核算中不计算自制半成品、在制品成本，则不计入工业总产值；如果会计产品成本核算中计算自制半成品、在制品成本的，则计入工业总产值。

4. 成品价值按成品实物量乘以报告期不含应交增值税（销项税额）的产品实际销售平均单价计算。

资产总计 指企业过去的交易或者事项形成的、由企业拥有或者控制的、预期会给企业带来经济利益的资源。资产一般按流动性分为流动资产和非流动资产。其中流动资产可分为货币资金、交易性金融资产、应收票据、应收账款、预付款项、其他应收款、存货等；非流动资产可分为长期股权投资、固定资产、无形资产及其他非流动资产等。

全员劳动生产率 指根据产品的价值量指标的平均每一职工在单位时间内的产品生产量。目前我国的全员劳动生产率是用工业总产值或工业增加值除以同一时期全部职工的平均人数来计算的。计算公式为：

全员劳动生产率 = 工业总产值 / 全部职工平均人数 ×12/ 累计月份

或 = 工业增加值 / 全部职工平均人数 ×12/ 累计月份

工业产品销售率 指报告期工业销售产值与同期全部工业总产值之比，反映工业产品生产已实现销售的程度。计算公式为：

工业产品销售率（%）= 报告期现价工业销售产值 / 报告期现价工业总产值 ×100%

工业成本费用利润率 指报告期实现利润总额与成本费用之比，反映降低成本的经济效益。计算公式为。

工业成本费用利润率（%）= 报告期实现利润总额 / 报告期成本费用总额 ×100%

成本费用是产品销售成本、产品销售费用、管理费用、财务费用之和

流动资产周转率 指一定时期内流动资产完成的周转次数，反映流动资产的周转速度。计算公式为：

流动资产周转率 = 报告期止累计产品销售收入 / 报告期平均流动资产 ×12/ 累计月数

资产负债率 又称债务比率，该比率反映在企业资产总额中有多少资产是通过借债而得到的。是反映企业长期偿债能力的指标之一，也可以用于衡量企业利用债权人提供资金进行经营活动的能力以及企业在清算时保护债权人利益的程度。计算公式为：

资产负债率 = 负债总额 ÷ 资产总额 ×100%

总资产贡献率 是反映全部资产的获利能力，是企业管理水平和经营业绩的集中体现。计算公式为：

总资产贡献率（%）= 利润总额＋利息支出 / 平均资产总额 ×12/ 累计月数 ×100%

平均资产总额为资产总计期初、期末之和的算术平均值。即：

平均资产总额 =（期初资产总额＋期末资产总额）÷2

资本保值增值率 反映企业资产的变动状况，是企业发展能力的集中体现。计算公式为：

资产保值增值率（%）= 期末所有者权益 / 期初所有者权益 ×100%

能源生产总量 指一定时期内全国（地区）一次能源生产量的总和，是观察全国（地区）能源生产水平、规模、过程构成和发展速度的总量指标。一次能源生产量包括原煤、原油、天然气、水电、核电及其他动力能（如风能、地热能等）发电量，不包括低热值燃料生产量、太阳热能等的利用和由一次能源加工转换而成的二次能源产量。

能源消费总量 指一定时期内全国（地区）国民经济各行业和居民家庭在一定时期消费的各种能源的总和。能源消费总量分为三部分，即终端能源消费量、能源加工转换损失量和能源损失量。

1. 终端能源消费量 指一定时期内全国（地区）各行业和居民生活消费的各种能源数量在扣除了用于加工转换二次能源消费量和损失量以后的数量。

2. 能源加工转换损失量 指一定时期内全国（地区）投入加工转换的各种能源数量之和与产出各种能源产品之和的差额。它是观察能源在加工转换过程中损失量变化的指标。

3. 能源损失量 指一定时期内能源在输送、分配、储存过程中发生的损失和由客观原因造成的各种损失量。不包括各种气体能源放空、放散量。

能源生产弹性系数 是研究能源生产增长速度与国民经济增长速度之间的关系的指标。其计算公式为：

能源生产弹性系数 = 能源生产总量年平均增长速度 / 国民经济年平均增长速度

国民经济年平均增长速度，可根据不同的目的或需要，用工农业总产值、生产总值等指标来计算，本资料是采用生产总值指标计算的。

电力生产弹性系数 是研究电力生产增长速度与国民经济增长速度之间关系的指标。计算公式为：

电力生产弹性系数 = 电力生产量年平均增长速度 / 国民经济年平均增长速度

能源消费弹性系数 是反映能源消费增长速度与国民经济增长速度之间比例关系的指标。计算公式为：

能源消费弹性系数 = 能源消费总量年平均增长速度 / 国民经济年平均增长速度

能源节约量 指在满足相等需求，达到相等目标的条件下节约和少用的能源数量。它是评价和考核节约能源工作好坏的重要指标。包括由于提高管理水平和技术水平，使单位产品能耗降低而节约能源的数量，以及由于调整产业结构、产品结构等使产值能耗降低而少用的能源数量。

能源节约率 是反映能源节约程度的综合性指标。能源节约率一般按年计算，如果要研究一个时期内能源节约程度的一般水平，可计算平均能源节约率指标。计算公式为：

能源节约率 =（报告期单位能源消费量 / 基期单位能源消费量－ 1）× 100%

年平均节能率 =（n 报告期单位能源消费量 / 基期单位能源消费源 -1）× 100%

公式中：单位能源消费量可以按生产总值、国民收入或工业总产值等计算

n 为基期与报告期间隔的年份数。

能源加工转换效率 指一定时期内能源经过加工转换后，产出的各种能源产品的数量与投入加工转换的各种能源数量的比率。它是观察能源加工转换装置和生产工艺先进与落后、管理水平高低等的重要指标。计算公式：

能源加工转换效率＝加工转换产出量 / 加工转换投入量 × 100%

能源折算标准 各种能源由于原始计算单位不同，热值也不一样。因此，必须折算成同一标准计算单位，才能进行汇总、对比和分析。国际上习惯采用两种标准计算单位：一种为标准煤，另一种为标准油。目前我国采用标准煤为能源的计算单位。标准煤亦称煤当量，就是将不同品种、不同含热量的能源按各自不同的含热量折合成为一种标准含量的统一计量单位的能源。各类能源折算标准煤是按 1 公斤标准煤的热值为 7000 千卡进行折算的。

当量热值 热值又称理论热值（或实际发热值），是指某种能源一个度量单位本身所含热量。其热值的计算可根据试样在充氧的弹筒中（放有浸没氧弹的水的容器）完全燃烧所放出的热量（用燃烧后水温升高计算出来的）进行实测。

等价热值 是指加工转换产出的某种二次能源与相应投入的一次能源的当量，即获得一个度量单位的某种二次能源所消耗的，以热值表示的一次能源量。也就是消耗一个度量单位的某种二次能源，就等价于

消耗了以热值表示的一次能源量。等价热值是个变动值，随着能源加工转换工艺的提高和能源管理工作的加强，转换损失逐渐减少，等价热值会不断降低。等价热值是对二次能源及消耗工质而言，因此一次能源不存在折算问题，因此也无所谓等价热值。

等价热值 = 二次能源具有的能量 ÷ 转换效率

转换效率 = 二次能源产出标准量 ÷ 加工转换投入能源标准量

原材料、能源消费量 指在报告期内实际使用的原材料、能源的数量，包括企业主营活动和附营活动实际使用的数量。消费的核算原则为 “谁消费谁统计”，即按使用权来统计。核算方法为当进入第一道生产工序，改变原来的形态或性能、或已实际投入使用，即作消费统计。

原材料、能源库存量 指在报告期期初、期末实际结存的原材料、能源数量。库存的核算原则为“谁支配，谁统计”，即按所有权来统计。核算方法是指企业有权支配动用的某一时点实际结存的原材料、能源的数量。

Explanatory Notes on Main Statistical Indicators

Industry refers to the material production sector which is engaged in the extraction of natural resources and processing and reprocessing of minerals and agricultural products,including

1.Extraction of natural resources, such as mining, salt production, but not including hunting, fishing and logging;

2.Processing and reprocessing of farm and sideline produces, such as rice husking, food processing, flour milling, wine making, oil pressing, cotton ginning, silk reeling, spinning and weaving, and leather making;

3.Manufacturing of extracted products, such as steel making, iron smelting, chemicals manufacturing, petroleum processing, machine building, timber processing; water and gas production and electricity generation and supply;

4.repairing and renovating of industrial products such as the machinery.

Prior to 1984, the rural industry run by villages and cooperative organizations under village was classified into agriculture. Since 1984, it has been grouped into industry.

In industrial survey,the units of enquiry are industrial corporate units.

Industrial corporate units refer to corporate units engaging in industrial production and operation activities, which meet the following requirements:

1.They are established legally,having their own names,organizations,location,and are able to take civil liability independently;

2.They possess (or are authorized to use)assets independently,assume liabilities and are entitled to sign contracts with other units;

3.They have accounts including the balance sheets or can compile the accounts according to the need.

Industrial Enterprises above Designated Size refer to industrial enterprises with main business revenue reaches and exceeds 20 million yuan every year since 2011.

State-owned Enterprises refers to non-corporate economic organizations whose assets are owned by the state and registered in accordance with the regulations of the People's Republic of China for controlling the registration of enterprises as legal persons. Exclusive of a wholly state-owned company in a limited liability company.

Collective-owned Enterprises refers to economic organizations whose assets are owned by the collective and registered in accordance with the regulations of the People's Republic of China for controlling the registration of enterprises as legal persons.

Joint-stock Cooperative Enterprises refers to a kind of collective economy organization that established by a foundation with cooperative system, investment of enterprises workers and a certain proportion investment of the social assets. It executes independent management, self-financing profit and loss, joint labor, democratic management, distribution according to work and joint dividend by share.

Joint-stock Enterprises refers to a form of enterprise organization in which two or more interest subjects are voluntarily combined in the form of stock collection.

Other Enterprises refers to other domestic economic organizations other than the above-mentioned enterprises.

Hong Kong, Macao and Taiwan Investment Enterprises refers to Hong Kong, Macao and Taiwan investors in accordance with Chinese law, established in the mainland in the form of joint venture, cooperation or sole proprietorship.

Foreign-invested Enterprises refers to a kind of economic organization established by foreign investors, according to the relevant foreign-related economic laws, regulations of the People's Republic of China, established in the mainland in the form of joint venture, cooperation or sole proprietorship.

Large, Medium, Small and Microenterprises Since the bulletin of 2011,the standard of grouping the enterprises' scale has been changed according to Statistical Method of Classing Large, Medium, Small and Mini-sized Enterprises established by Ministry of Information and Industry, State Statistical Bureau, National Development and Reform Commission, Ministry of Finance. According to partitioning standards are number of employees, main operation revenue, enterprises are classified into large-sized, medium-sized, small-sized and microenterprises.

Gross Industry Output Value refers to the total value of final industrial products produced and industrial services provided during the reporting period. It is the total volume of industrial products produced during a given period in monetary terms, which reflects the total achievements and overall scale of industrial production. It includes value of finished products, which are not to be further processed in the enterprises and have been inspected, packed and put in storage, income from external processing, and differential value of self-made semi-finished products and products in process at the end and beginning of the report period. The gross industrial output value is calculated by the "factory method", i.e. an industrial enterprise is treated as the basic amounting unit in calculating the gross industrial output value; no double calculations are to be made within the same enterprise, e.g. the output value of the different workshops (branch factories) of an enterprises should not be added, however, this method does not exclude the possibility of double counting among different enterprises, industries and regions.

Calculation of gross Industry output value according to the following rules:

1.Products produced with self-prepared raw material are calculated at all-round price in reporting the gross industrial output value, irrespective complexity of simplicity of production, i.e., the gross industrial output value includes the value of self-prepared raw material.

2. Products processed with supplied materials are calculated, processing enterprises only charge processing fees, according to processing charges financially settled in reporting the gross industrial output value, i.e., the gross industrial output value excludes the value of orders' material.

3. The value of change in semi-finished products should be included in the gross industrial output value if it is included in the accounting record of the enterprise,otherwise it should not be included.

4. Value of finished product is calculated by the quantity of the finished products multiplied by the average unit price at which products are sold(excluding value-added tax).

Total Assets refer to all resources that are owned or controlled by enterprises through previous trades or transactions with expectation of making economic profits. Classified by the degree of liquidity,total assets include current assets, ad non-current assents.Current assets can be classified into monetary assets,trading financial assets,notes receivable,accounts receivable,advanced payment, other prepaid money and inventories.Non-current assets can be divided into long-term equity investment, fixed assets,intangible assets and other non-current assets.

Overall Labor Productivity refers to the average output per employed person of industrial enterprises in unit time in value terms. At present, gross industrial output value or added value of industry and average number of staff and workers of an industrial enterprise in a given period are used to calculate overall labor productivity. The formula used is as follows:

Overall Labor Productivity = Gross Industrial Output Value/Average Number of Staff and Workers× 12/ Accumulated Months = Added Value of Industry/Average Number of Staff and Workers×12/Accumulated Months

Ratio of Sales to Gross Output Value refers to the ratio of industrial sales value in the report period to gross industrial output value in the same period, which reflects the linkage between the industrial production and the realized sales. The formula is as follows:

Ratio of Sales to Gross Output Value = (Industrial Sales Value at Current Price in the Report Period/Gross Industrial Output Value at Current Price in the Report Period)×100%

Ratio of Profits to Total Costs and Expenses refers to the ratio of profits realized in the report period to the total costs and expenses in the same period, which reflects the economic efficiency of cost reduction. It is calculated as follows:

Ratio of Profits to Total Costs and Expenses (%) = (Total Profits Realized in the Report Period/Total Costs and Expenses in the Report Period)×100%

Costs and expenses are the sum of product sales cost, product sales expenses and financial expenses.

Turnover Rate of Current Assets refers to the number of times of turnover of current assets in a given period of time, which reflects the speed of the turnover of current assets. It is calculated as follows:

Turnover Rate of Current Assets (%) = (Accumulated Sales Revenue of Products by the End of Report Period/ Average Current Assets in the Report Period) ×12/Accumulated Months

Ratio of Debts to Assets reflects the proportion of assets obtained by borrowing in the total assets of an enterprise. It is one of the indicators reflecting the debt repaying capability of an enterprise in the long run and can also be used to measure the operating capability of an enterprise with the capital from creditors and the degree to which an enterprise can protect the interest of creditor during liquidation. The formula is as follows:

Ratio of Debts to Assets (%) = (Total Debts/Total Assets) ×100%

Contribution Rate of Total Assets reflects the profit-making capability of all assets and it is a key indicator manifesting the performance and management level of an enterprise. The formula is as follows: Contribution Rate of Total Assets (%) = [(Total Profits and Tax + Interest Payment)/Total Average Assets] × 12/Accumulated Months×100%

Total average assets refer to the arithmetic average value of total assets at the beginning and end of period, i.e. Total Average Assets = (Total Assets at the Beginning of Period + Total Assets at the End of Period) ÷2.

Rate of Asset Hedge and Increment reflects the variation of assets of an enterprise and manifests the development capability of an enterprise. The formula is as follows:

Rate of Asset Hedge and Increment (%) = (Owner's Equity at the End of Period/ Owner's Equity at the Beginning of Period) ×100%

Total Energy Production Volume refers to the total production volume of primary energy by all energy production enterprises in the country in a given period of time. It is a comprehensive indicator to show the capacity, scale, composition and development of energy production of the country. The production volume of primary energy includes that of coal, crude oil, natural gas, hydro-power and electricity generated by nuclear energy and other means such as wind power and geothermal power, but excludes that of fuels of low calorific value, bio-energy, solar energy and the secondary energy converted from the primary energy.

Total Domestic Energy Consumption refers to the total consumption of energy of various kinds by the production and the households in the country(region) in a given period of time. Total energy consumption can be divided into three parts: end-use energy consumption ; loss during the process of energy conversion ; and energy loss.

1.End-use energy consumption It refers to the total energy consumption by the production sectors and households in the country(region) in a given period of time.It does not include the consumption during the conversion of primary energy into the secondary energy and the loss in the process of energy conversion.

2.Loss during the process of energy conversion It refers to the total input of various kinds of energy for conversion, minus the total output of various kinds of energy in the country(region) in a given period of time. It is an indicator to show the loss that occurs during the process of energy conversion.

3.Energy loss It refers to the total of the loss of energy during the course of energy transport, distribution and storage and the loss caused by any objective reason in a given period of time. The loss of various kinds of gas due to gas discharges and stocktaking is not include.

Elasticity Ratio of Energy Production is an indicator to show the relationship between the growth rate of energy production and that of the national economy. The formula is as follows:

Elasticity Ratio of Energy Production = Average Annual Growth Rate of Energy Production/Average Annual Growth Rate of National Economy.

The average annual growth rate of the national economy can be calculated by gross output value of industry and agriculture, gross output value or other indicators, depending upon the purposes or needs. Gross output value is used in calculation of the ratio in this chapter.

Elasticity Ratio of Electricity Production is an indicator to show the relationship between the growth rate of electricity production that of the national economy. The formula is as follows:

Elasticity Ratio of Electricity Production = Average Annual Growth Rate of Electricity Production/Average Annual Growth Rate of National Economy.

Elasticity Ratio of Energy Consumption is an indicator to show the relationship between the growth rate of energy consumption and that of the national economy. The formula is as follows:

Elasticity Ratio of Energy Consumption = Average Annual Growth Rate of Energy Consumption/Average Annual Growth Rate of National Economy.

Quantity of Energy Conservation refers to the quantity of energy saved and less used in a certain period. It is an important indicator to appraise and examine the work of energy conservation. It includes the quantity of energy saved in unit product by improving management level and technology level and the quantity of energy less used due to the adjustment of industrial structure and product structure.

Ratio of Energy Conservation is a comprehensive indicator reflecting the degree of energy conservation. Ratio of energy conservation is usually calculated annually. The indicator of average ratio of energy conservation can be calculated for the study of the energy conservation in a certain period. The formula is as follows:

Ratio of Energy Conservation = [(Unit Energy Consumption in the Report Period/Unit Energy Consumption in the Base Period) – 1] ×100%

Annual Average Ratio of Energy Conservation = the N-the Root of [(Unit Energy Consumption in the Report Period/Unit Energy Consumption in the Base Period) – 1] ×100%

In which: The unit energy consumption can be calculated according to gross output value, national product or gross industrial output value, etc.

The n represents the number of years between base period and report period.

Efficiency of Energy Processing and Conversion refers to the ratio of the total output of energy products of various kinds after processing and conversion to the total input of energy of various kinds for processing and conversion in the same report period. It is an important indicator to show the current conditions of energy processing and conversion equipment, production technique and management. The formula is as follows:

Efficiency of Energy Processing and Conversion=output of process conversion /input of process conversion×100%

Energy Conversion Standard Different units are often used to compute different caloric value of various energy sources, so a uniform standard computing unit has to be conversed to summarize, compare and analyze energy. There are two standard computing units practiced internationally: one is standard coal and the other is standard oil. Currently, standard coal is adopted as the computing unit in China for energy calculation, Standard coal also call calorie value equivalent, it refers a uniform standard energy of communistically unit is converted into by differed kinds, different caloric value of various energy .Every kind of energy is converted into standard coal according to one kilogram standard coal quail caloric of 7,000 kilocalories.

Equivalent Caloricity also called theoretic caloricity (or actual calorific value) refers to the heat value contained in one measurement unit of certain energy. The calculation of the heat value is according to the actual measurement of the heat released by complete burning of the test specimen in the cylinder filled with oxygen (container with the oxygen bomb immersed by water).

Equivalent Heat Value refers to certain secondary energy produced by conversion and its equivalent value of corresponding input of the primary energy, which means the quantity of the primary energy expressed by heat value and consumed to obtain one measurement unit of certain secondary energy. It is variation value. With the advancement of the energy conversion technology and the improvement of the energy management, the conversion loss becomes less and less, and the equivalent heat value will reduce gradually. Equivalent heat value is specific to secondary energy and consumed actuating medium, so when it comes into primary energy, there is no equivalent heat value.

Equivalent Heat Value = Energy Content of Secondary Energy÷Conversion Efficiency

Conversion Efficiency = Output Standardized Quantity of Secondary Energy ÷ Energy Standardized Quantity Input by Conversion

Consumption of Raw Materials and Energy refers to the quantity of raw materials and energy actually used in the report period. It includes the volume actually used in the main business line and sideline activities of an enterprise. The calculation principle of consumption is: "The one who consumes energy is responsible for conducting statistics on its consumption", i.e., statistics is made according to the use right. The calculation method is that when raw materials or energy enter the first production sequence and the original form or property is changed or they are put into actual use, they are treated as consumption statistics.

Inventory of Raw Materials and Energy refers to the quantity of raw materials and energy actually stored in the beginning and end of the report period. The calculation principle of inventory is, "The one who disposes energy is responsible for conducting statistics on its inventory", i.e., statistics is made according to the ownership. The calculation method refers to the quantity of raw materials and energy actually stored at a certain time that can be disposed by an enterprise.

Chapter 9

九、建筑业和房地产业
Construction and Real Estate

9-1 主要年份建筑施工企业数、人数和施工产值

Number of Construction Enterprises, Employed Persons and Their Output Value in Significant Years

年份 Year	全省 Yunnan	国有企业 State-owned Construction Enterprises	集体企业 Collective-owned Construction Enterprises	其他 Others
施工企业数(个) Number of Enterprises (unit)				
1985	2 522	144	2 378	
1990	3 010	123	2 887	
1995	2 657	140	2 517	2 663
2000	1 564	201	854	509
2001	1 583	190	713	680
2002	1 317	152	440	725
2003	1 231	129	330	772
2004	1 663	122	325	1 216
2005	1 648	111	258	1 279
2006	1 796	110	243	1 443
2007	1 903	107	232	1 564
2008	2 150	105	230	1 815
2009	2 117	100	212	1 805
2010	2 176	99	198	1 879
2011	2 227	99	197	1 931
2012	2 362	106	196	2 060
2013	2 483	97	174	2 212
2014	2 520	91	149	2 280
2015	2 651	92	142	2 417
2016	2 760	96	134	2 530
2017	2 772	101	129	2 542
2018	3 036	93	111	2 832
2019	3 456	103	114	3 239
2020	3 647	98	103	3 446
施工企业人数(万人) Number of Employed Persons (10 000 persons)				
1985	46.64	16.70	29.95	
1990	47.61	16.10	31.56	
1995	64.65	18.10	46.39	0.10
2000	53.55	15.90	25.38	12.30
2001	55.58	14.15	22.30	19.12
2002	51.77	12.45	17.03	22.28
2003	57.37	15.35	13.60	28.42
2004	50.30	10.56	10.28	29.46
2005	55.31	9.47	8.63	37.21
2006	63.32	10.53	9.01	43.78
2007	64.77	11.64	7.42	45.71
2008	65.81	11.49	6.86	47.46
2009	70.99	13.44	6.05	51.50
2010	78.64	12.45	5.69	60.50
2011	89.44	9.34	5.28	74.82
2012	91.44	19.24	5.81	66.39
2013	103.25	11.81	6.51	84.93
2014	107.86	23.80	11.20	72.86
2015	113.73	10.02	5.58	98.13
2016	132.32	17.28	5.42	109.62
2017	150.85	15.34	7.50	128.01
2018	174.80	19.83	5.65	149.32
2019	181.66	21.60	4.02	156.04
2020	187.35	25.66	3.54	158.14
建筑业总产值(亿元) Gross Output Value (100 million yuan)				
1985	21.28	10.00	11.01	
1990	36.68	19.00	18.09	
1995	181.22	74.00	107.14	0.34
2000	311.34	131.00	108.83	72.00
2001	345.51	127.83	100.46	117.23
2002	358.24	121.88	77.76	158.59
2003	396.97	132.23	68.24	196.50
2004	448.50	136.31	66.41	245.78
2005	539.59	138.96	58.03	342.60
2006	672.88	183.95	63.78	425.16
2007	763.32	205.86	64.12	493.33
2008	907.58	227.54	71.47	608.57
2009	1 196.86	304.28	77.84	814.74
2010	1 511.85	364.41	83.04	1 064.00
2011	1 869.65	478.01	99.91	1 291.73
2012	2 386.64	532.27	152.15	1 702.22
2013	2 888.82	569.67	177.19	2 141.96
2014	3 059.62	440.42	142.00	2 477.20
2015	3 275.64	435.01	143.75	2 696.88
2016	3 891.65	694.28	147.06	3 050.31
2017	4 726.36	882.95	150.88	3 692.53
2018	5 458.52	1 208.19	108.68	4 141.65
2019	6 122.09	1 535.46	120.37	4 466.26
2020	6 724.82	1 572.27	107.24	5 045.32

注：1. 1996年起各种经济类型的，具有资质等级证书的建筑企业均纳入国家统计。
2. 2013年起施工企业人数和建筑业总产值数据不含劳务分包企业。

Note: a.Since 1996, the state statistical coverage has included the construction enterprises of various types of ownership with credentials.
b. Number of employed persons of construction enterprises and total output value of construction industry doesn't include those of labor subcontracting enterprises since 2013.

9-2 总承包专业承包建筑施工企业生产情况（2020年）

单位：亿元

类别	Category	企业个数（个）Number of Enterprises (unit)	建筑业总产值 Gross Output Value of Construction	建筑工程 Output Value of Construction Projects	安装工程 Output Value of Installation Projects	竣工产值 Value of Construction Completed
全省	**Yunnan**	**3 449**	**6 724.82**	**6 090.92**	**369.78**	**2 262.48**
按企业控股情况分	**Grouped by Share Holding**					
国有控股	State-controlled	188	3 322.25	3 086.34	132.54	526.80
集体控股	Collective-controlled	154	214.69	196.53	15.31	100.18
私人控股	Private-controlled	2 994	3 050.06	2 692.94	204.57	1 562.97
按国民经济行业分	**Grouped by Sector**					
房屋建筑业	Building Construction Industry	2 018	4 170.89	3 882.12	102.83	1 716.04
土木工程建筑业	Civil Engineering Construction Industry	807	2 195.44	2 033.60	113.60	397.80
建筑安装业	Construction Installation	293	211.49	63.48	137.76	68.27
建筑装饰和其他建筑业	Architectural Decoration and Other Construction Industry	331	147.00	111.72	15.60	80.37
按企业资质等级分	**Grouped by Qualification Criteria**					
施工总承包	Construction Contract	2 672	6 254.99	5 770.87	254.43	2 077.04
特级	Special Grade	9	1 505.51	1 497.86	4.67	273.77
一级	First Grade	98	1 717.02	1 612.07	94.54	296.43
二级	Second Grade	645	1 349.72	1 244.87	55.85	688.40
专业承包	Professional Contract	777	469.83	320.05	115.35	185.43
一级	First Grade	138	215.32	168.52	35.38	65.15
二级	Second Grade	295	95.62	63.39	26.58	47.10
按州市分	**Grouped by Region**					
昆明	Kunming	1 253	3 829.00	3 463.63	228.03	841.61
曲靖	Qujing	286	588.65	542.25	22.75	308.53
玉溪	Yuxi	252	287.87	265.61	13.25	137.52
保山	Baoshan	152	226.53	219.57	2.90	110.65
昭通	Zhaotong	107	125.54	112.45	11.15	35.78
丽江	Lijiang	92	58.76	54.67	1.33	38.28
普洱	Pu'er	169	176.88	157.04	13.64	115.92
临沧	Lincang	93	107.67	90.36	6.04	57.49
楚雄	Chuxiong	204	374.40	342.76	17.42	218.13
红河	Honghe	228	462.17	405.24	25.92	195.71
文山	Wenshan	121	139.51	118.06	13.40	48.79
西双版纳	Xishuangbanna	60	39.76	37.98	1.59	10.05
大理	Dali	256	182.19	165.51	6.50	75.75
德宏	Dehong	118	87.58	79.07	5.00	40.49
怒江	Nujiang	27	21.64	21.47	0.05	15.87
迪庆	Diqing	31	16.68	15.24	0.80	11.92

Construction Situation of Construction Enterprises of General Contractors and Professional Contractors (2020)

(100 million yuan)

房屋施工面积(万平方米) Floor Space under Construction (10 000 sq.m)	本年新开工面积 Newly Started Building Area in This Year	房屋竣工面积(万平方米) Floor Space Completed (10 000 sq.m)	房屋建筑面积竣工率(%) Ratio of Floor Space Completed (%)	计算建筑业劳动生产率的平均人数(万人) Average Persons of calculating the Labor Productivity (10 000 persons)	年末从业人数(万人) Number of Employed Persons at Year-end (10 000 persons)	全员劳动生产率(万元/人) Overall Labor Productivity of Construction Enterprises (10 000 yuan/person)
20 128.75	**7 514.10**	**6 238.39**	**31.0**	**187.35**	**135.75**	**35.9**
7 851.57	1 877.31	1 177.28	15.0	68.54	40.74	48.5
722.92	385.01	347.13	48.0	6.28	5.70	34.2
11 276.81	5 158.29	4 573.83	40.6	108.97	85.30	28.0
18 840.36	6 940.30	5 647.60	30.0	105.30	91.30	39.6
759.35	347.49	228.35	30.1	57.11	35.92	38.4
334.78	137.58	190.90	57.0	20.08	4.19	10.5
194.27	88.73	171.54	88.3	4.86	4.34	30.3
19 549.98	7 279.34	5 849.84	29.9	159.84	125.28	39.1
4 189.94	1 043.33	621.38	14.8	36.24	15.93	41.5
4 541.08	1 425.99	891.89	19.6	36.46	31.39	47.1
6 322.69	2 175.18	1 988.69	31.5	39.89	35.35	33.8
578.77	234.76	388.55	67.1	27.50	10.48	17.1
250.20	57.21	123.50	49.4	5.76	3.58	37.4
230.12	122.96	205.41	89.3	17.36	2.98	5.5
10 328.22	2 393.22	1 987.72	19.2	111.34	63.16	34.4
2 207.59	1 411.32	1 098.13	49.7	14.02	13.62	42.0
1 148.63	649.29	446.86	38.9	8.07	10.72	35.7
603.64	149.58	251.66	41.7	7.22	7.03	31.4
420.01	103.84	111.81	26.6	2.72	3.26	46.2
192.27	106.41	115.29	60.0	1.69	1.57	34.7
638.08	300.70	357.11	56.0	5.02	4.04	35.2
289.71	173.98	134.78	46.5	2.96	2.63	36.4
1 046.16	613.20	659.12	63.0	9.90	8.40	37.8
1 427.98	763.10	623.31	43.7	13.04	11.24	35.4
443.45	199.70	161.30	36.4	3.18	2.53	43.8
305.24	127.57	24.66	8.1	0.75	0.65	52.7
653.27	310.32	136.25	20.9	4.38	4.15	41.6
330.58	152.74	68.31	20.7	2.17	1.96	40.4
60.25	35.84	34.11	56.6	0.46	0.42	46.7
33.64	23.29	27.99	83.2	0.44	0.37	38.3

9-3 总承包专业承包建筑施工企业财务状况（2020年）

单位：亿元

类　　别	Item	资产合计 Total Assets	固定资产净值 Net Fixed Assets	负债合计 Total Liabilities	流动负债 Liquid Liabilities
全　省	**Yunnan**	**8 485.24**		**5 373.90**	**4 649.33**
按企业控股情况分	**Grouped by Share Holding**				
国有控股	State-controlled	5 668.85		3 629.31	3 085.52
集体控股	Collective-controlled	153.18		98.94	81.36
私人控股	Private-controlled	2 512.80		1 535.17	1 385.58
按国民经济行业分	**Grouped by Sector**				
房屋建筑业	Building Construction Industry	5 226.50		3 166.79	2 799.54
土木工程建筑业	Civil Engineering Construction Industry	2 831.79		1 924.49	1 628.88
建筑安装业	Construction Installation	283.04		194.49	140.91
建筑装饰和其他建筑业	Architectural Decoration and Other Construction Industry	143.91		88.14	79.99
按企业资质等级分	**Grouped by Qualification Criteria**				
施工总承包	Construction Contract	8 026.66		5 074.75	4 369.81
特　级	Special Grade	3 372.26		1 881.04	1 659.35
一　级	First Grade	2 140.45		1 652.86	1 492.25
二　级	Second Grade	1 126.24		697.79	642.31
专业承包	Professional Contract	458.58		299.15	279.52
一　级	First Grade	197.22		139.31	135.65
二　级	Second Grade	100.13		59.34	55.83
劳务分包	Labor Subcontract				
按州市分	**Grouped by Region**				
昆　明	Kunming	6 395.75		4 047.72	3 585.64
曲　靖	Qujing	314.55		165.58	154.13
玉　溪	Yuxi	324.02		234.23	116.00
保　山	Baoshan	193.54		120.42	108.48
昭　通	Zhaotong	130.91		100.37	89.14
丽　江	Lijiang	60.01		33.65	30.98
普　洱	Pu'er	132.94		94.55	85.28
临　沧	Lincang	63.76		34.88	31.64
楚　雄	Chuxiong	112.57		61.92	54.51
红　河	Honghe	249.08		153.85	112.44
文　山	Wenshan	153.72		98.15	88.83
西双版纳	Xishuangbanna	18.21		13.05	12.19
大　理	Dali	208.57		133.86	112.79
德　宏	Dehong	92.94		64.87	58.16
怒　江	Nujiang	15.56		9.60	3.52
迪　庆	Diqing	19.11		7.20	5.60

Financial Indicators of Construction Enterprises of General Contractors and Professional Contractors (2020)

(100 million yuan)

所有者权益 Owners' Equity	实收资本 Paid-in Capitals	主营业务收入 Revenue from Business	主营业务成本 Cost of Business	主营业务税金及附加 Taxes and Other Charges on Principal Business	营业利润 Profits of Business	经营费用 Operation Expenses	管理费用 Management Expenses	税金 Tax	财务费用 Financial Expenses
3 111.34	**2 049.18**	**5 405.23**	**4 911.53**	**46.29**	**256.08**	**17.32**	**153.79**		**66.11**
2 039.53	1 429.35	2 836.00	2 597.29	8.45	153.54	1.30	54.67		49.65
54.23	28.25	134.18	120.14	5.00	3.43	0.61	8.75		1.58
977.63	569.74	2 346.19	2 113.35	31.76	96.81	15.15	86.24		13.84
2 059.71	1 549.72	3 113.96	2 867.53	34.39	131.49	10.13	81.67		41.75
907.31	412.32	1 937.20	1 726.13	9.13	117.62	4.28	51.55		20.63
88.55	49.73	203.23	185.40	0.93	4.09	1.49	11.21		1.19
55.77	37.40	150.84	132.47	1.84	2.88	1.41	9.36		2.54
2 951.91	1 945.28	4 970.31	4 528.52	42.83	241.36	13.93	127.15		61.76
1 491.22	1 195.85	1 435.32	1 320.71	4.31	90.33	0.15	17.43		30.82
487.59	223.86	1 537.04	1 407.61	5.69	70.79	0.55	31.12		17.66
428.45	251.53	899.87	812.74	15.99	33.58	5.07	31.82		7.03
159.43	103.90	434.92	383.01	3.46	14.72	3.39	26.64		4.36
57.91	33.92	202.06	185.15	0.80	5.05	0.95	8.48		1.42
40.79	32.02	96.42	87.28	0.79	0.24	0.81	7.09		0.39
2 348.03	1 651.96	3 498.32	3 190.27	13.57	178.45	5.25	88.15		52.09
148.97	74.24	433.49	390.09	8.05	23.43	2.49	9.85		1.15
89.79	39.84	187.31	172.21	2.52	6.32	1.88	6.67		2.06
73.12	33.03	140.89	132.02	1.21	5.12	0.27	3.36		0.30
30.54	18.83	80.76	75.01	0.73	1.69	0.23	3.73		1.09
26.36	13.90	49.72	44.14	0.96	2.37	0.46	1.84		0.50
38.39	26.85	108.58	101.04	1.25	1.11	0.66	4.52		0.68
28.89	15.38	101.76	89.89	3.70	6.28	0.36	3.48		0.43
50.65	28.31	166.60	149.07	3.71	6.20	1.69	5.86		0.99
95.23	33.91	308.80	265.07	7.15	16.03	3.10	13.58		3.70
55.58	29.71	100.57	92.69	1.28	5.01	0.13	3.04		0.66
5.15	5.01	25.98	24.35	0.22	0.25	0.05	1.03		0.04
74.70	46.04	118.42	109.08	1.10	1.78	0.48	5.27		2.04
28.07	20.37	56.41	52.30	0.27	1.10	0.07	2.27		0.35
5.96	5.23	14.55	12.93	0.09	0.18	0.03	0.57		0.03
11.91	6.56	13.08	11.36	0.46	0.76	0.19	0.57		0.03

9−3　续表

单位：亿元

类　别	Item	利润总额 Total Profits
全　省	**Yunnan**	**253.37**
按企业控股情况分	**Grouped by Share Holding**	
国有控股	State-controlled	153.52
集体控股	Collective-controlled	2.60
私人控股	Private-controlled	94.66
按国民经济行业分	**Grouped by Sector**	
房屋建筑业	Building Construction Industry	130.25
土木工程建筑业	Civil Engineering Construction Industry	115.89
建筑安装业	Construction Installation	4.30
建筑装饰和其他建筑业	Architectural Decoration and Other Construction Industry	2.94
按企业资质等级分	**Grouped by Qualification Criteria**	
施工总承包	Construction Contract	237.62
特　级	Special Grade	89.18
一　级	First Grade	70.57
二　级	Second Grade	31.63
专业承包	Professional Contract	15.75
一　级	First Grade	5.10
二　级	Second Grade	0.78
劳务分包	Labor Subcontract	
按州市分	**Grouped by Region**	
昆　明	Kunming	176.03
曲　靖	Qujing	23.70
玉　溪	Yuxi	6.50
保　山	Baoshan	5.50
昭　通	Zhaotong	1.71
丽　江	Lijiang	2.34
普　洱	Pu'er	0.66
临　沧	Lincang	6.33
楚　雄	Chuxiong	6.23
红　河	Honghe	15.76
文　山	Wenshan	4.83
西双版纳	Xishuangbanna	0.19
大　理	Dali	1.59
德　宏	Dehong	1.07
怒　江	Nujiang	0.17
迪　庆	Diqing	0.75

continued

(100 million yuan)

企业总收入 Total Revenue	上缴税金 Tax Payment	应交增值税 Value-added Tax Payable	产值利税率(%) Ratio of Profits & Taxes to Output Value(%)	资产利税率(%) Ratio of Profits and Taxes to Assets(%)
5 630.62	**198.62**	**144.30**	**6.7**	**5.3**
2 979.86	59.29	49.94	6.4	3.8
136.77	9.97	4.41	5.9	8.2
2 415.10	125.07	86.79	7.2	8.7
3 253.88	136.37	97.38	6.4	5.1
1 999.24	48.41	38.29	7.5	5.8
215.26	5.57	4.56	4.7	3.5
162.25	8.26	4.07	7.6	7.8
5 175.11	181.54	133.56	6.7	5.2
1 527.61	27.33	22.74	7.7	3.5
1 579.17	46.21	39.24	6.8	5.5
933.31	49.09	32.73	6.0	7.2
455.51	17.07	10.74	7.0	7.2
215.10	7.37	4.20	5.8	6.3
100.25	3.95	2.70	5.0	4.7
3 665.89	94.39	76.20	7.1	4.2
444.77	25.43	17.31	8.3	15.6
191.38	7.80	5.24	5.0	4.4
145.89	6.71	5.00	5.4	6.3
92.36	3.75	2.98	4.4	4.2
50.79	2.92	1.87	9.0	8.8
109.94	4.95	3.35	3.2	4.2
105.36	7.44	3.58	12.8	21.6
168.47	9.88	6.09	4.3	14.3
309.88	20.26	11.45	7.8	14.5
108.65	5.36	3.99	7.3	6.6
26.38	1.28	0.76	3.7	8.1
124.70	5.42	4.28	3.9	3.4
57.40	1.40	1.13	2.8	2.7
15.03	0.42	0.30	2.7	3.8
13.73	1.21	0.74	11.8	10.3

9-4 全省房地产业发展情况（2020年）

单位：亿元

类　别	Category	房地产开发投资 Investment in Real Estate Development	国　有 State-owned Economy
本年固定资产投资完成额	**Investment in Fixed Assets Completed This Year**	**4 505.19**	**168.93**
按构成分	**Grouped by Use of Funds**		
建筑工程	Construction	3 239.58	136.62
安装工程	Installation	137.08	2.28
设备工器具购置	Purchase of Equipment and Instruments	19.01	0.39
其他费用	Others	1 109.51	29.64
#旧建筑物购置费	Purchase of Used Building	11.43	
土地购置费	Purchase of Land	974.00	27.52
按工程用途分	**Grouped by Use of Buildings**		
住　宅	Residential Buildings	3 317.55	125.57
#90平方米以下住房	Residential Buildings below 90 sq.m	563.14	19.39
别墅、高档公寓	Villas and Upper-scale Apartments		
办公楼	Office Buildings	153.04	6.44
商业营业用房	Buildings for Business	494.51	14.32
其　他	Others	540.08	22.60
本年新增固定资产	**Newly Increased Fixed Assets**	**712.01**	**49.68**
本年资金来源合计	**Total Funds of All Sources**		
上年末结余资金	Fund Left from Last Year	1 558.09	44.06
本年资金来源小计	Fund of All Sources in Current Year	4 086.07	139.05
国内贷款	Domestic Loans	294.97	4.05
#银行贷款	From Banks	244.86	3.30
非银行金融机构贷款	From Other Financial Institutions	50.10	0.75
利用外资	Foreign Investment	18.71	1.47
#外商直接投资	Foreign Direct Investment		
自筹资金	Self-Raising Funds	1 197.16	27.75
#自有资金	Self-owned Funds		
定金及预收款	Earnest Money and Advance Charge	1 379.76	37.52
个人按揭贷款	Mortgage Loans	974.24	30.15
其他资金来源	Others	2 575.24	38.11
本年各项应付款合计	**Account Payable**	**1 573.57**	**70.21**
#工程款	Payment for Construction	965.14	47.87
待开发土地面积（万平方米）	**Space of Land to be Developed (10 000 sq.m)**	**1 751.27**	**16.63**
本年购置土地面积（万平方米）	**Space of Land Purchased in Current Year (10 000 sq.m)**	**1 055.27**	**46.86**
本年土地成交价款	**Value of Commercial Land**	**361.06**	**15.03**

Basic Statistics on Real Estate Development (2020)

(100 million yuan)

集　体 Collective-owned Economy	私营个体 Private and Individuals	股份制 Share Holding Economy	外　商 Foreign Funded Economy	港澳台 Economy with Funds from HongKong, Macao and Taiwan	其　他 Others
1.58	**1 770.21**	**104.81**	**41.64**	**73.41**	**2 344.61**
0.23	1 338.38	78.72	24.75	54.29	1 606.60
	66.51	1.09	2.03	6.44	58.73
	12.13	0.99		0.89	4.61
1.35	353.20	24.01	14.85	11.80	674.68
	1.18				10.25
1.35	322.02	22.16	14.11	9.89	576.95
0.23	1 328.74	85.76	24.37	54.68	1 698.19
	214.94	7.98	1.88	8.77	310.19
	30.76	1.18	0.56	3.55	110.55
	210.21	8.08	12.52	8.52	240.86
1.35	200.50	9.78	4.18	6.66	295.01
	359.73	**11.97**	**15.51**	**9.09**	**266.03**
0.02	434.28	16.83	17.36	15.62	1 029.92
1.40	1 609.15	72.97	27.81	96.93	2 138.76
	65.01	1.52	5.68	8.42	210.29
	53.45	1.52	5.68	8.42	172.49
	11.56				37.80
		0.73	0.40	6.79	9.32
0.10	561.31	35.59	6.56	23.63	542.22
	532.28	17.09	11.35	29.39	752.13
	371.52	12.62	3.76	22.57	533.62
1.30	79:04	5.42	0.06	6.13	2 445.18
1.40	**674.20**	**78.55**	**4.27**	**16.87**	**728.08**
	413.72	26.36	3.30	14.05	459.84
6.75	**530.83**	**41.49**		**103.05**	**1 052.52**
6.75	**454.80**	**20.45**	**19.19**	**45.28**	**461.94**
1.29	**190.25**	**3.07**	**5.02**	**15.81**	**130.60**

9-5 全省房地产开发企业财务状况（2020年）

单位：亿元

类　别	Category	房地产企业 Real Estate	国　有 State-owned Economy
年初存货	**Inventory at Beginning of Current Year**	**9 005.08**	**404.99**
年末资产负债	**Property debt at Year-end**		
流动资产合计	Total Liquid Liabilities	20 034.85	1 281.37
#存　货	Inventory	10 973.62	611.03
固定资产原价	Fixed Asset Value	596.41	73.26
累计折旧	Accumulated Depreciation	129.37	7.13
#本年折旧	in Current Year	26.75	1.57
资产总计	Assets	25 357.53	2 205.88
负债总计	Liabilities	21 385.38	1 481.93
所有者权益合计	Owners' Equity	3 972.15	723.95
#实收资本	Paid-up Capital	2 279.54	157.90
损益及分配	**Net Income or Loss and Distribution**		
主营业务收入	Operating Income	2 120.80	35.91
#土地转让收入	Revenues from Land Transfer	11.02	1.52
商品房屋销售收入	Revenues from Commercial Housing Sales	2 005.31	25.45
房屋出租收入	Housing Rental Income	27.20	2.45
其他收入	Others	66.13	5.57
主营业务成本	Main Business Cost	1 602.83	28.42
主营业务税金及附加	Main Business Tax & Additional	129.81	2.88
其他业务利润	Other Operating Profits	1.51	- 0.25
销售费用	Sales Expenses	142.05	2.37
管理费用	Management Expenses	111.02	6.08
#税　金	Taxes		
财务费用	Financial Expenses	140.37	6.70
#利息支出	Interests	106.87	7.62
营业利润	Business Profits	104.29	5.17
营业外收入	Non-operating Income	12.50	2.37
营业外支出	Non-operating Expenses	42.44	0.67
利润总额	Total Profits	70.45	6.87
应缴所得税	Income Tax Payable	74.55	1.68
本年应付工资总额	Wages Payable in Current Year	92.05	3.83

Financial Status of Real Estate Investment and Development Enterprises (2020)

(100 million yuan)

集　体 Collective-owned Economy	私　营 Individuals	股份制 Share Holding Economy	外　商 Foreign Funded Economy	港澳台 Economy with Funds from Hong Kong,Macao and Taiwan	其　他 Others
0.85	**3 200.52**	**108.29**	**161.84**	**226.45**	**4 902.15**
1.95	6 481.10	559.35	265.91	737.09	10 708.08
0.85	3 930.25	119.13	179.43	222.69	5 910.24
0.12	221.00	4.96	26.31	104.16	166.60
0.11	66.52	1.65	6.10	12.12	35.74
0.00	12.80	0.27	0.92	4.88	6.31
1.98	7 485.27	735.54	297.05	1 226.56	13 405.25
2.11	6 992.84	670.80	200.31	960.72	11 076.68
- 0.13	492.43	64.74	96.75	265.84	2 328.57
0.05	557.99	38.22	66.30	201.13	1 257.96
0.02	739.32	33.26	55.31	66.39	1 190.59
	6.12	0.06			3.33
	697.59	27.00	54.14	60.90	1 140.24
	15.47	0.79	0.06	2.17	6.26
0.02	17.16	5.41	1.00	0.39	36.58
0.01	572.42	24.47	43.27	58.57	875.67
0.00	42.82	1.38	2.84	6.09	73.79
0.00	1.65		0.00	0.05	0.06
	55.78	0.71	2.18	3.14	77.87
0.02	50.93	2.21	1.31	4.65	45.83
0.02	36.51	10.50	0.96	8.16	77.52
0.00	28.80	1.61	0.90	6.55	61.39
- 0.03	- 5.91	- 1.77	6.43	4.94	95.46
0.00	5.05	0.34	0.09	0.53	4.12
	17.60	0.66	0.06	0.19	23.26
- 0.02	- 20.75	- 2.00	6.48	5.29	74.59
	15.51	0.45	2.10	0.70	54.11
0.21	40.64	1.80	1.21	2.46	41.90

9-6 房地产开发企业（单位）施工、销售和待售情况（2020年）

类　别	Category	房地产企业 Enterprises Real Estate	住 宅 Residential Buildings
房屋施工面积(万平方米)	**Floor Space Under Construction (10 000 sq.m)**	**25 801.30**	**17 482.38**
#新开工面积	Newly-started Projects	7 538.09	5 286.82
房屋竣工面积(万平方米)	**Floor Space Completed (10 000 sq.m)**	**1 637.76**	**1 163.01**
#不可销售面积	Space of Floor not Ready for Sale	72.52	5.87
商品住宅竣工套数(万套)	**Number of Commercial Buildings Completed (10 000 units)**		**8.13**
竣工房屋价值（亿元）	**Value of Buildings Completed (100 million yuan)**	**515.37**	**370.38**
出租房屋面积(万平方米)	**Floor Space of Buildings to Lease (sq.m)**	**55.14**	**41.07**
商品房销售面积(万平方米)	**Floor Space of Commercial Buildings Sold (10 000 sq.m)**	**4 857.26**	**4 175.88**
#现房销售面积	Floor Space of Complete Apartment	414.97	285.14
期房销售面积	Floor Space of Forward Delivery Housing	4 442.29	3 890.74
商品房销售额(亿元)	**Total Sale of Commercial Buildings (100 million yuan)**	**3 969.91**	**3 452.00**
#现房销售额	Sale of Complete Apartment	286.45	184.23
期房销售额	Sale of Forward Delivery Housing	3 683.46	3 267.77
商品住宅销售套数(万套)	**Number of Commercial Buildings Sold (10 000 units)**		**33.73**
#现房销售套数	Complete Apartment		2.12
期房销售套数	Forward Delivery Housing		31.61
待售面积(万平方米)	**Floor Space of Commercial Buildings Unoccupied (10 000 sq.m)**	**1 159.47**	**470.76**
#待售1-3年(含1年)	Unoccupied from 1 to 3 Years	348.03	163.00
待售3年及以上	Unoccupied for More Than 3 Years	349.14	96.42

Basic Statistics on Construction,Sale and Vacancy of Buildings Built of Real Estate Enterprises (2020)

#90平方米及以下 below 90 sq.m	144平方米及以上 Above 144 sq.m	办公楼 Office Buildings	商业营业用房 Buildings for Business	其他 Others
3 216.12	**5 333.42**	**855.66**	**2 959.76**	**4 503.51**
786.23	1 621.65	224.29	686.57	1 340.41
110.58	**526.68**	**29.16**	**185.67**	**259.92**
0.99	0.05	0.54	14.18	51.94
1.82	**2.31**			
31.20	**176.24**	**14.21**	**61.30**	**69.47**
41.07		**1.49**	**6.28**	**6.30**
531.72	**1 339.47**	**63.21**	**292.27**	**325.90**
39.75	131.23	21.41	58.91	49.51
491.97	1 208.24	41.80	233.36	276.39
456.92	**1 060.10**	**66.99**	**309.61**	**141.31**
26.08	90.83	24.79	52.73	24.71
430.84	969.27	42.20	256.88	116.60
7.35	**7.05**			
0.56	0.62			
6.79	6.42			
78.60	**226.87**	**41.53**	**369.34**	**277.84**
25.38	65.64	13.99	90.27	80.77
15.85	54.06	10.47	149.03	93.22

主要统计指标解释

建筑业统计单位 指从事房屋、构筑物建造和设备安装活动的法人企业。建筑业法人企业应具有建筑业资质并能够独立核算，同时还应具备以下条件：①依法成立，有自己的名称、组织机构和场所，能够承担民事责任；②独立拥有和使用资产，承担负债，有权与其他单位签订合同；③独立核算盈亏，能够编制资产负债表。

建筑业总产值 是以货币形式表现的建筑业企业在一定时期内生产的建筑业产品和提供服务的总和。

建筑业总产值包括：

（1）建筑工程产值：指列入建筑工程预算内的各种工程价值。

（2）安装工程产值：指设备安装工程价值，不包括被安装设备本身的价值。

（3）其他产值：建筑业总产值中除建筑工程、安装工程以外的产值。包括房屋构筑物修理产值、非标准设备制造产值、总包企业向分包企业收取的管理费，以及不能明确划分的施工活动所完成的产值。

a. 房屋构筑物修理产值：指房屋和构筑物修理所完成的产值，但不包括被修理房屋、构筑物本身价值和生产设备的修理价值。

b. 非标准设备制造产值：指加工制造没有定型的非标准生产设备的加工费和原材料价值（如化工厂、炼油厂用的各种罐、槽，矿井生产统一使用的各种漏斗、三角槽、阀门等）以及附属加工厂为本企业承担工程制作的非标准设备的价值。

房屋施工面积 指在报告期内施工的全部房屋建筑面积，包括本期新开工的房屋面积、上期施工跨入本期继续施工的房屋面积、上期停缓建在本期恢复施工的房屋面积、本期竣工的房屋面积及本期施工后又停缓建的房屋面积。

房屋竣工面积 指在报告期内房屋建筑按照设计要求全部完工，达到了住人和使用条件，经验收鉴定合格，正式移交使用单位的房屋建筑面积。

营业收入 指企业经营主要业务和其他业务所确认的收入总额。包括主营业务收入与其他业务收入。

主营业务收入 指企业确认的销售商品、提供服务等主营业务收入。

利润总额 指企业在一定会计期间的经营成果，是生产经营过程中各种收入扣除各种耗费后的盈余，反映企业在报告期内实现的盈亏总额。

产值利税率 是指报告期内企业实现的利润总额与上缴税金的和占同期建筑业总产值的百分比。

房地产开发投资 指各种登记注册类型的房地产开发法人单位统一开发的住宅、厂房、仓库、饭店、宾馆、度假村、写字楼、办公楼等房屋建筑物，配套的服务设施，土地开发工程（如道路、给水、排水、供电、供热、通讯、平整场地等基础设施工程）和土地购置的投资；不包括单纯的土地开发和交易活动。

商品房销售面积 指报告期内出售商品房屋的合同总面积（即双方签署的正式买卖合同中所确定的建筑面积）。商品房销售面积由现房销售建筑面积和期房销售建筑面积两部分组成。

商品房销售额 指报告期内出售商品房屋的合同总价款（即双方签署的正式买卖合同中所确定的合同总价）。该指标与商品房销售面积同口径，由现房销售额和期房销售额两部分组成。

不可销售面积 指报告期房地产公司竣工的用于拆迁还建的房屋面积；接受委托、定向开发建设，并收取一定的管理费所建设的统建代建房屋竣工面积；竣工的学校、幼儿园、派出所、居委会、商店等公益设施建筑面积。

待售面积 指报告期末已竣工的可供销售或出租的商品房屋建筑面积中，尚未销售或出租的商品房屋建筑面积，包括以前年度竣工和本期竣工的房屋面积，但不包括报告期已竣工的拆迁还建、统建代建、公共配套建筑、房地产公司自用及周转房等不可销售或出租的房屋面积。按照商品房待售时间的长短可以划分为待售一年以下、待售一至三年（含一年）和待售三年以上（含三年）。

Explanatory Notes on Main Statistical Indicators

Statistical Unit in Construction Industry refers to a corporate enterprise engaged in the construction of buildings and structures and in the installation of equipment. A corporate construction enterprise should have qualification certificates with independent accounting system, and should meet the following 3 requirements: ① being set up in line with relevant legal basis, having its full name, organization and location, and capable of taking civil liabilities; ② independently possessing and using its assets and assuming its liabilities, and entitled to sign contracts with other institutions; ③ making independent accounts of its profits and losses, and capable of compiling its own balance sheet.

Gross Output Value of Construction refers to total of construction products and services, expressed in money terms, produced or rendered by construction and installation enterprises during a given period of time. It includes:

Output value of construction projects: the value of projects covered by the project budgets;

Output value of installation projects: the value of the installation of equipment (excluding the value of the equipment to be installed);

Other output values: the output value of construction industry apart from that of construction projects and installation projects. It includes: output value of repair of buildings and structures; output value of non-standard equipment manufacturing; overhead expenses received by contracted enterprises from the sub-contracted enterprises and the completed output value of construction activities for which there is no clear definition.

a.Output value of repair of buildings and structures: the value created through the repair of building or structures. It does not include the value of buildings or structures being repaired and the value of the repair of production equipment.

b.Output value of manufactured non-standard equipment: the value of non-standard production equipment,including raw materials and manufacturing cost, made for the construction project(i.e., chemical plant; kettles or tanks used by refineries; various fillers, triangle tanks, valve used by mine). It also includes the output value of equipment manufactured by subsidiary workshops.

Floor Space of Buildings Under Construction refers to the floor space of buildings under construction during the report period, including newly started buildings, buildings started in the preceding period and continued during the current period, and buildings suspended in the preceding period but restarted in the current period, buildings completed during the current period, and buildings under construction and then suspended during the current period.

Floor Space of Buildings Completed refers to the floor space of buildings that are completed in the report period in accordance with the requirements of the design, up to the standard of putting them into use, and have been checked and accepted by concerned departments as qualified ones.

Operating Revenue refers to the sum of income from principal business and other business of enterprises, including income from settlement of projects and other operating income.

Main Business Income refers to the income recognized by an enterprise from main business such as sale of commodities and rendering of service.

Total Profits refer to the operating result of an enterprise in certain accounting period. It is the surplus of all revenues deducting all costs in its production and operation, reflecting its total profit and loss realized in the reporting period.

Ratio of Profit to Output Value to profit and tax refers to the ratio of the total profits and tax to the gross output value of construction in the report period.

Investment in Real Estate Development refers to investment by real estate development companies, commercialized buildings construction companies and other real estate development units of various types of ownership in the construction of buildings, such as residential buildings, factory buildings, warehouses, hotels, guesthouses, holiday villages, office buildings, and the complementary service facilities and land development projects, such as roads, water supply, water drainage, power supply, heating supply, telecommunications, land leveling and other infrastructural projects. It does not include activities in pure land transactions.

Area of Commercialized Housing Sold refers to total contracted area of commercialized housing (i.e. area of floor space as designated in the formal contracts signed by both sides) during the reference time.Area of commercialized housing sold constitutes floor space of completed housing and floor space of future housing.

Value of Commercialized Housing Sold refers to the total contracted value (i.e. value of sales/purchase for selling/purchase of commercialized housing as designated in the contract signed by both sides) during the reference time.This indicator has the same coverage as the area of commercialized housing sold, which constitutes floor space of completed housing and floor space of housing yet to be completed.

Non-Marketable Area refers to the building area used for removal and rebuilding which completed by real estate companies in reference period; completed building area of unified construction and acting construction which constructed by accepting commission, orientating development construction and charging certain management overhead; building area of completed schools, kindergartens, police stations, neighborhood committees, stores and such public utility constructions.

Floor Space of Vacant Building refers to the area of commercialized buildings haven't been sold or rent in the area of completed marketable and rentable commercialized buildings in the reference period, including the completed building area in the former years and in the current period, while excluding the completed removal and rebuilding buildings, unified and deputized construction buildings, public matched installations buildings and area of the buildings for self-use and revolving buildings of the real estate companies which are unmarketable or can't be rented. According to the vacant time, the buildings can be categorized as follows: buildings vacant less than one year, vacant for one to three years (including one year), vacant more than three years (including three years).

Chapter 10

十、交通运输、通信和服务业
Transport,Communication and Service Industry

10-1 主要年份年末交通运输线路长度
Length of Transport Routes at Year-end in Significant Years

单位：万公里 (10 000 km)

年 份 Year	铁路营业里程 Length of Railways in Operation	公路通车里程 Total Length of Highways	内河航道里程 Length of Navigable Inland Waterways	民用航空航线里程 Length of Civil Aviation Routes	国际航线 International Lines
1980	0.17	4.41	0.10	0.10	
1985	0.17	4.95	0.10	2.27	0.13
1988	0.16	5.25	0.11	2.37	0.31
1989	0.17	5.47	0.11	2.27	0.31
1990	0.17	5.65	0.11	2.66	0.31
1991	0.17	5.81	0.11	3.08	0.31
1992	0.17	6.00	0.11	4.73	0.41
1993	0.16	6.31	0.11	4.51	0.70
1994	0.16	6.56	0.13	6.42	0.95
1995	0.16	6.82	0.13	5.16	0.95
1996	0.16	7.03	0.13	7.06	0.67
1997	0.20	7.38	0.13	8.98	0.67
1998	0.20	7.70	0.13	12.87	1.63
1999	0.20	10.24	0.15	13.31	3.37
2000	0.20	16.36	0.16	11.97	2.04
2001	0.20	16.40	0.18	13.51	2.07
2002	0.20	16.49	0.18	14.81	2.91
2003	0.20	16.61	0.18	14.55	2.09
2004	0.19	16.71	0.25	13.78	2.43
2005	0.19	19.45	0.28	13.54	2.44
2006	0.19	19.85	0.28	13.68	2.24
2007	0.19	20.03	0.28	12.99	2.63
2008	0.19	20.38	0.28	11.21	1.47
2009	0.19	20.60	0.28	15.20	2.39
2010	0.19	20.92	0.29	18.28	4.96
2011	0.21	21.45	0.32	18.56	5.39
2012	0.24	21.91	0.34	22.85	4.84
2013	0.24	22.29	0.36	29.44	7.06
2014	0.26	23.04	0.36	33.15	10.65
2015	0.27	23.60	0.41	31.69	9.99
2016	0.34	23.81	0.43	26.70	8.45
2017	0.37	24.25	0.43	27.48	9.29
2018	0.38	24.88	0.43	29.74	9.02
2019	0.40	26.24	0.45	33.27	9.15
2020	0.41	29.25	0.51	36.79	7.56

10-2 公路运输线路长度

Length of Highways

单位：公里 (km)

年 份 Year 州 市 Region	公路通车里程 Total Length of Highways	等级公路 Expressway Total	高 速 Highway	一 级 First class	二 级 Second Class	三 级 Third Class	四 级 Fourth Class	等外公路 Highway Below Class IV
1980	44 149							
1985	49 541							
1988	52 534	43 911			99	6 209	37 683	8 543
1989	54 732	46 296			126	6 252	39 902	8 436
1990	56 536	48 244			195	6 484	41 524	8 292
1991	58 123	49 917			199	6 718	42 959	8 206
1992	60 045	52 007			211	6 811	44 900	8 038
1993	63 086	55 317			587	7 056	47 633	7 769
1994	65 578	57 992			615	7 302	50 034	7 586
1995	68 236	60 777			917	7 571	52 248	7 459
1996	70 279	62 936			1 066	7 862	53 922	7 343
1997	73 821	66 561	45	71	1 301	8 080	57 064	7 260
1998	76 957	69 783	205	61	1 311	8 420	59 786	7 174
1999	102 405	95 354	405	72	1 435	8 702	84 740	7 051
2000	109 636	102 626	517	153	1 722	8 798	91 436	7 010
2001	163 953	106 396	517	164	2 106	9 787	93 822	57 557
2002	164 853	107 617	746	164	2 192	9 969	94 546	57 236
2003	166 134	109 302	1 064	230	2 677	10 057	95 274	56 832
2004	167 050	110 876	1 291	237	3 089	10 062	96 197	56 174
2005	167 678	111 961	1 424	287	3 325	9 918	97 007	55 717
2006	198 496	99 834	1 549	279	3 696	9 513	84 797	98 662
2007	200 333	104 771	2 507	600	4 370	9 469	87 825	95 562
2008	203 753	124 526	2 512	633	4 859	9 563	106 959	79 227
2009	206 028	138 150	2 512	628	4 973	9 518	120 519	67 878
2010	209 230	158 119	2 630	733	5 771	9 329	139 656	51 111
2011	214 524	165 843	2 746	842	9 553	8 407	144 295	48 681
2012	219 052	171 960	2 943	974	10 299	8 372	149 371	47 092
2013	222 940	178 371	3 200	1 003	10 307	8 354	155 508	44 568
2014	230 398	189 481	3 255	1 068	10 596	8 409	166 153	40 917
2015	236 007	197 071	4 006	1 152	10 860	8 286	172 768	38 936
2016	238 052	200 898	4 134	1 196	11 752	8 618	175 198	37 154
2017	242 546	208 526	5 022	1 354	11 941	8 937	181 272	34 020
2018	252 929	220 555	5 184	1 443	12 222	9 715	191 991	32 374
2019	262 409	231 741	6 003	1 546	12 770	10 265	201 158	30 668
2020	292 479	272 273	8 406	1 649	13 021	9 779	239 418	20 206
昆 明 Kunming	21 350	20 069	1 153	255	1 199	471	16 992	1 280
曲 靖 Qujing	27 860	26 521	1 070	221	769	724	23 737	1 338
玉 溪 Yuxi	17 750	17 750	559	118	670	865	15 538	
保 山 Baoshan	20 876	20 223	405	63	1 017	200	18 538	654
昭 通 Zhaotong	25 241	23 668	707	110	1 071	837	20 943	1 573
丽 江 Lijiang	10 231	9 819	321	43	534	434	8 487	413
普 洱 Pu'er	27 779	25 611	566	22	1 104	850	23 069	2 168
临 沧 Lincang	19 874	18 349	157	52	1 221	159	16 759	1 525
楚 雄 Chuxiong	21 825	17 508	545	155	447	812	15 549	4 316
红 河 Honghe	25 558	24 055	1 083	117	975	1 235	20 644	1 503
文 山 Wenshan	17 517	16 125	562	77	851	1 023	13 611	1 392
西双版纳 Xishuangbanna	8 156	7 802	330	41	446	316	6 668	354
大 理 Dali	23 761	21 224	547	302	996	976	18 402	2 537
德 宏 Dehong	9 530	8 888	283	58	566	175	7 805	642
怒 江 Nujiang	6 685	6 345	37		449	236	5 624	340
迪 庆 Diqing	8 485	8 315	79	16	704	466	7 050	170

10–3 铁路里程和机车拥有量（2015–2020年）
Length of Railways and Number of Railway Locomotives Owned (2015-2020)

指　　标	Item	2015	2016	2017	2018	2019	2020
铁路里程	**Length of Railways in Operation**						
正线延长里程(公里)	Length of Railways in Trunk Line (km)	3 159.23	4 532.73	4 912.07	4 971.04	5 201.09	5 316.46
营业里程(公里)	Length of Railways in Operation (km)	2 660.08	3 374.78	3 681.68	3 847.90	3 974.21	4 141.59
高速铁路（公里）	High-speed Railway	–	698.78	698.78	873.63	1 051.13	1 051.13
准　轨(公里)	Standard Tracks (km)	2 004.05	2 712.62	3 022.36	3 194.70	3 321.01	3 488.39
米　轨(公里)	Meter Tracks (km)	656.03	662.16	659.32	653.20	653.20	653.20
内燃机车牵引里程(公里)	Length of Diesel Engine Routes (km)	1 058.37	1 058.39	1 086.33	1 077.70	1 077.70	1 077.70
占营业里程比重(%)	As Percentage of Railways in Operation (%)	39.78	31.36	29.50	28.01	27.12	26.02
无缝线路里程(公里)	Length of Continuous Welded Rail (km)	1 585.98	3 960.28	4 126.10	4 558.01	4 793.53	5 057.05
占营业里程比重(%)	As Percentage of Railways in Operation (%)	59.62	63.05	65.59	67.19	67.97	70.58
营业线路主要车站(个)	Railways Station of in Operation (unit)	120	120	120	128	131	141
铁路机车拥有量(台)	**Number of Railway Locomotives(unit)**	**533**	**562**	**561**	**578**	**575**	**523**
内燃机车	Diesel Locomotives	193	199	204	208	193	192
电力机车	Electric Locomotives	340	363	357	370	382	331
动车组（按车型分）		–	**34**	**49**	**78**	**109**	**119**
CRH2A		–	21	21	30	30	30
CRH380A		–	13	28	43	51	53
CRH2G		–	–	–	5	11	19
CR200J		–	–	–	–	17	17

10-4 铁路客货车拥有量（2019-2020年）
Number of Railway Passenger Coaches and Freight Cars Owned (2019-2020)

指 标	Item	2019	2020
客车合计(辆)	**Passenger Coaches (unit)**	**1 538**	**1 531**
软卧车	Soft Berth Coaches	112	107
硬卧车	Hard berth Coaches	708	708
硬座车	Hard Seat Coaches	487	487
餐 车	Dining Cars	78	78
行李邮政车	Luggage and Post Cars	73	69
货车合计(辆)	**Freight Cars (unit)**	**953**	**953**
按车型分	Grouped by Type		
棚 车	Covered Cars	163	163
敞 车	Open cars	662	662
平 车	Flat Cars	58	58
罐 车	Tank Cars	70	70
其 他	Others		
按载重量分	Grouped by Capacity		
40吨及以下	40 Tons and Below	953	953
货车总载重(万吨)	Total Loading Capacity of Freight Cars (10 000 tons)	5.10	5.10
平均每辆车载重量(吨)	Average Marked Loading Capacity Per Car (ton)	45	45

注：由于统计口径不同，铁路客车不含动车组。
Note: Due to different statistical caliber, railway passenger cars do not contain D-Series High-Speed Train.

10-5(1) 各州市民用车辆拥有量（按类型分组）（2020年）

Possession of Civil Vehicles by Region (Grouped by Vehicles Types) (2020)

单位：万辆、万人 (10 000 units, 10 000 persons)

州市	Region	民用车辆拥有量 Civilian Vehicle	汽车合计 Total	摩托车 Motors	拖拉机 Tractors	挂车 Trailers	其他类型车 Others	机动车驾驶员 Number of Motor Drivers	汽车驾驶员 Automobile Drivers
全省	**Yunnan**	**1 579.89**	**803.42**	**756.45**	**16.80**	**3.22**		**1 626.09**	**1 184.97**
昆明	Kunming	297.80	263.19	33.33	0.77	0.52		368.39	345.60
曲靖	Qujing	130.59	84.23	45.48	0.43	0.45		171.56	143.02
玉溪	Yuxi	95.22	49.81	43.75	1.02	0.63		99.66	79.04
保山	Baoshan	94.93	32.20	60.55	2.09	0.10		86.71	48.30
昭通	Zhaotong	112.43	43.37	65.91	3.04	0.11		116.96	74.85
丽江	Lijiang	37.96	21.81	14.59	1.51	0.04		38.07	29.24
普洱	Pu'er	120.06	32.28	87.14	0.58	0.06		94.84	46.37
临沧	Lincang	100.48	25.00	74.48	0.97	0.04		81.65	35.00
楚雄	Chuxiong	79.17	33.12	45.33	0.46	0.25		88.54	59.87
红河	Honghe	133.24	59.93	72.78	0.12	0.41		128.19	92.94
文山	Wenshan	108.36	43.91	63.78	0.53	0.14		99.83	63.80
西双版纳	Xishuangbanna	55.02	22.21	29.62	3.19	0.00		49.35	34.87
大理	Dali	118.67	53.75	63.53	1.06	0.34		113.53	78.42
德宏	Dehong	64.74	23.41	41.29	0.00	0.04		61.37	35.93
怒江	Nujiang	14.92	5.32	9.51	0.08	0.01		14.26	7.93
迪庆	Diqing	14.06	8.55	4.48	0.95	0.09		13.17	9.78

10-5(2) 各州市汽车拥有量（2020年）

Possession of Vehicles by Region (2020)

单位：万辆 (10 000 units)

州　市	Region	汽车拥有量合计 Total	载客汽车 Passenger Vehicles	轿　车 Cars	载货汽车 Trucks	其他汽车 Others
全　省	**Yunnan**	**803.42**	**681.18**	**346.52**	**118.67**	**3.57**
昆　明	Kunming	263.19	241.88	138.34	20.06	1.25
曲　靖	Qujing	84.23	73.36	34.71	10.57	0.30
玉　溪	Yuxi	49.81	40.03	22.40	9.51	0.28
保　山	Baoshan	32.20	25.11	12.71	6.96	0.12
昭　通	Zhaotong	43.37	34.13	14.87	9.03	0.21
丽　江	Lijiang	21.81	18.14	8.65	3.58	0.09
普　洱	Pu'er	32.28	24.79	10.33	7.35	0.13
临　沧	Lincang	25.00	18.54	9.11	6.37	0.09
楚　雄	Chuxiong	33.12	28.05	12.80	4.90	0.17
红　河	Honghe	59.93	49.09	22.53	10.61	0.23
文　山	Wenshan	43.91	36.05	16.77	7.73	0.14
西双版纳	Xishuangbanna	22.21	17.77	8.74	4.36	0.08
大　理	Dali	53.75	43.90	20.76	9.56	0.29
德　宏	Dehong	23.41	18.37	9.39	4.95	0.10
怒　江	Nujiang	5.32	4.16	1.42	1.14	0.02
迪　庆	Diqing	8.55	6.56	2.50	1.93	0.05

10−5(3) 各州市私人车辆拥有量（2020年）

Number of Private Motor Vehicles by Region (2020)

单位：万辆 (10 000 units)

州　市	Region	私人车辆拥有量 Private Cars	载客汽车 Passenger Vehicles	载货汽车 Trucks	摩托车 Motors
全　省	**Yunnan**	**1 496.07**	**637.50**	**101.55**	**754.11**
昆　明	Kunming	271.71	222.09	15.72	33.21
曲　靖	Qujing	125.24	70.08	9.38	45.43
玉　溪	Yuxi	90.41	38.14	8.17	43.67
保　山	Baoshan	91.04	23.92	6.52	60.46
昭　通	Zhaotong	106.70	32.32	8.47	65.75
丽　江	Lijiang	34.87	16.97	3.28	14.56
普　洱	Pu'er	117.26	23.47	6.73	86.96
临　沧	Lincang	97.98	17.44	6.08	74.39
楚　雄	Chuxiong	76.39	26.60	4.33	45.27
红　河	Honghe	126.54	46.42	7.39	72.62
文　山	Wenshan	103.54	34.49	5.29	63.69
西双版纳	Xishuangbanna	50.47	16.87	4.04	29.52
大　理	Dali	114.09	41.53	8.79	63.42
德　宏	Dehong	63.23	17.39	4.58	41.20
怒　江	Nujiang	14.26	3.73	1.04	9.48
迪　庆	Diqing	12.34	6.02	1.76	4.46

10−5(4) 各州市载客汽车拥有量（2020年）

Possession of Passenger Vehicles by Region (2020)

单位：万辆 (10 000 units)

州 市	Region	载客汽车拥有量 Passenger Vehicles	大 型 Large	中 型 Medium	小 型 Small	微 型 Miniature
全 省	**Yunnan**	**681.18**	**3.15**	**1.97**	**671.78**	**4.28**
昆 明	Kunming	241.88	1.30	0.36	238.54	1.68
曲 靖	Qujing	73.36	0.20	0.14	72.68	0.33
玉 溪	Yuxi	40.03	0.16	0.07	39.20	0.60
保 山	Baoshan	25.11	0.11	0.08	24.79	0.13
昭 通	Zhaotong	34.13	0.13	0.08	33.73	0.19
丽 江	Lijiang	18.14	0.17	0.11	17.76	0.10
普 洱	Pu'er	24.79	0.09	0.09	24.55	0.07
临 沧	Lincang	18.54	0.05	0.07	18.35	0.07
楚 雄	Chuxiong	28.05	0.11	0.12	27.63	0.19
红 河	Honghe	49.09	0.20	0.15	48.44	0.30
文 山	Wenshan	36.05	0.10	0.12	35.71	0.12
西双版纳	Xishuangbanna	17.77	0.11	0.09	17.51	0.06
大 理	Dali	43.90	0.19	0.24	43.24	0.24
德 宏	Dehong	18.37	0.08	0.08	18.08	0.13
怒 江	Nujiang	4.16	0.03	0.02	4.09	0.01
迪 庆	Diqing	6.56	0.07	0.05	6.37	0.07

10−5(5) 各州市载货汽车拥有量（2020年）

Possession of Freight Vehicles by Region (2020)

单位：万辆 (10 000 units)

州　市	Region	载货汽车拥有量 Trucks	重　型 Heavy	中　型 Medium	轻　型 Light	微　型 Miniature	三轮汽车 Three-wheel	低速货车 Four-wheel
全　省	**Yunnan**	**118.67**	**18.14**	**4.21**	**95.04**	**0.01**	**0.21**	**1.05**
昆　明	Kunming	20.06	3.54	0.53	15.98	0.00		0.00
曲　靖	Qujing	10.57	2.30	0.28	7.87	0.00	0.04	0.08
玉　溪	Yuxi	9.51	2.72	0.36	6.42		0.00	0.00
保　山	Baoshan	6.96	0.71	0.16	6.06	0.00	0.00	0.04
昭　通	Zhaotong	9.03	0.89	0.29	7.65	0.00	0.00	0.20
丽　江	Lijiang	3.58	0.35	0.17	2.91	0.00	0.03	0.12
普　洱	Pu'er	7.35	0.62	0.49	6.12	0.00	0.02	0.10
临　沧	Lincang	6.37	0.49	0.28	5.55	0.00		0.06
楚　雄	Chuxiong	4.90	0.92	0.18	3.77	0.00		0.04
红　河	Honghe	10.61	2.09	0.40	8.08		0.00	0.03
文　山	Wenshan	7.73	0.71	0.17	6.63	0.00	0.12	0.10
西双版纳	Xishuangbanna	4.36	0.16	0.13	4.06	0.00	0.00	0.00
大　理	Dali	9.56	1.55	0.34	7.46	0.00	0.00	0.20
德　宏	Dehong	4.95	0.56	0.25	4.10	0.00	0.00	0.03
怒　江	Nujiang	1.14	0.08	0.05	0.97		0.00	0.05
迪　庆	Diqing	1.93	0.43	0.12	1.38	0.00	0.00	0.01

10–5(6) 各州市摩托车和拖拉机拥有量（2020年）
Possession of Motorcycles and Tractors by Region (2020)

单位：万辆　　　　(10 000 units)

州　市	Region	摩托车拥有量 Motors	普　通 Common	轻　便 Convenient	拖拉机拥有量 Tractors	轮式拖拉机 Wheeled Tractors	手扶拖拉机 Walking Tractors	履带拖拉机 Crawler Tractors	轮式拖拉机运输机组 Transport unit of Wheeled Tractors	手扶拖拉机运输机组 Transport unit of Walking Tractors
全　省	**Yunnan**	**754.11**	**722.07**	**32.04**	**16.80**	**2.82**	**0.49**	**0.00**	**8.93**	**4.56**
昆　明	Kunming	33.21	30.84	2.37	0.77	0.22		0.00	0.31	0.24
曲　靖	Qujing	65.75	64.05	1.70	1.02	0.79	0.00	0.00	0.20	0.03
玉　溪	Yuxi	45.43	42.51	2.92	3.04	0.05			2.39	0.60
保　山	Baoshan	45.27	43.08	2.19	0.53	0.14	0.25		0.08	0.06
昭　通	Zhaotong	43.67	40.93	2.74	0.43	0.04	0.00		0.39	
丽　江	Lijiang	72.62	68.86	3.75	1.06	0.03			0.87	0.16
普　洱	Pu'er	63.69	60.95	2.74	0.97	0.06			0.01	0.90
临　沧	Lincang	86.96	85.91	1.05	0.95	0.08	0.01		0.48	0.37
楚　雄	Chuxiong	29.52	28.01	1.51	2.09	0.15	0.02	0.00	1.81	0.11
红　河	Honghe	63.42	60.01	3.41	1.51	0.27			1.13	0.12
文　山	Wenshan	60.46	58.04	2.42	0.58	0.24	0.00		0.30	0.05
西双版纳	Xishuangbanna	41.20	38.04	3.16	0.46	0.16	0.12	0.00	0.13	0.05
大　理	Dali	14.56	14.08	0.48	0.12	0.12		0.00		0.00
德　宏	Dehong	9.48	9.41	0.07	3.19	0.44	0.08		0.81	1.85
怒　江	Nujiang	4.46	4.44	0.02	0.00	0.00				
迪　庆	Diqing	74.39	72.91	1.48	0.08	0.03			0.03	0.02

10-6 民用机动运输船舶年末实有数（2015-2020年）
Number of Civil Transport Vessels at Year-end (2015-2020)

类　　型	Type	2015	2016	2017	2018	2019	2020
全　省	**Yunnan**						
艘　数（艘）	Number (unit)	1 033	1 092	1 236	1 241	1 239	1 236
净载重量（万吨位）	Net Weight Tonnage (10 000 tons)	12.92	13.32	15.63	16.86	17.29	19.02
载客量（万客位）	Passenger Capacity (10 000 seats)	2.26	2.44	2.88	3.11	3.02	2.88
功　率（万千瓦）	Drawing Power (10 000 kW)	10.70	11.49	12.50	13.38	13.20	14.01
客　船	**Passenger Boat**						
艘　数（艘）	Number (unit)	761	833	933	1 000	1 036	1 012
载客量（万客位）	Passenger Capacity (10 000 seats)	2.02	2.19	2.63	3.00	2.93	0.99
功　率（万千瓦）	Drawing Power (10 000 kW)	4.23	5.11	5.92	6.23	6.40	5.44
客货船	**Passenger Boat and Cargo Vessel**						
艘　数（艘）	Number (unit)	94	87	136	57	37	31
净载重量（吨位）	Net Weight Tonnage (ton)	1 314	1 322	1 930	879	570	578
载客量（万客位）	Passenger Capacity (10 000 seats)	0.24	0.24	0.24	0.11	0.08	0.07
功　率（万千瓦）	Drawing Power (10 000 kW)	0.30	0.34	0.52	0.31	0.28	0.31
货　船	**Cargo Vessel**						
艘　数（艘）	Number (unit)	176	167	164	180	162	186
净载重量（万吨位）	Net Weight Tonnage (10 000 tons)	11.80	12.17	14.23	15.40	15.89	17.94
功　率（万千瓦）	Drawing Power (10 000 kW)	6.13	5.97	5.99	6.75	6.43	8.19
拖　船	**Tugboat**						
艘　数（艘）	Number (unit)	2	3	3	4	4	3
功　率（千瓦）	Drawing Power (kW)	500	756	756	896	896	676
驳　船	**Barge**						
艘　数（艘）	Number (unit)	2	2	4	5	5	4
净载重量（吨位）	Net Weight Tonnage (ton)	187	162	300	371	371	326

10－7 主要年份交通运输客运量

Passenger Traffic in Significant Years

单位：亿人 (100 million persons)

年份 Year	全省客运量 Passenger Traffic	铁路 Railways	公路 Highways	水运 Waterways	民用航空(万人) Civil Aviation(10 000 persons)
1978	0.39	0.13	0.25		8.9
1980	0.53	0.15	0.36	0.01	17.2
1985	0.94	0.15	0.77	0.01	23.0
1987	1.01	0.14	0.86	0.01	39.0
1988	1.06	0.14	0.89	0.02	32.0
1989	1.04	0.13	0.89	0.01	31.0
1990	1.07	0.10	0.95	0.02	34.0
1991	1.11	0.10	0.99	0.01	50.0
1992	1.06	0.11	0.93	0.01	83.0
1993	1.11	0.13	0.95	0.02	127.0
1994	2.52	0.14	2.35	0.01	145.8
1995	2.17	0.13	2.01	0.01	211.0
1996	2.39	0.11	2.24	0.01	253.0
1997	2.50	0.11	2.34	0.01	288.3
1998	2.99	0.13	2.80	0.02	331.1
1999	3.30	0.15	3.08	0.02	435.4
2000	3.37	0.15	3.16	0.02	345.0
2001	4.00	0.14	3.79	0.03	380.0
2002	3.89	0.14	3.67	0.04	393.0
2003	3.52	0.14	3.30	0.04	377.0
2004	3.89	0.15	3.65	0.04	464.0
2005	4.11	0.16	3.85	0.05	495.0
2006	4.38	0.18	4.09	0.05	599.1
2007	4.63	0.21	4.29	0.06	672.3
2008	3.48	0.24	3.12	0.06	599.4
2009	3.66	0.24	3.28	0.07	721.4
2010	4.04	0.27	3.62	0.07	753.8
2011	4.60	0.30	4.14	0.08	758.5
2012	4.96	0.30	4.48	0.09	848.7
2013	5.19	0.33	4.66	0.09	1 000.0
2013（新口径）	4.88	0.33	4.34	0.10	1 000.0
2014	5.01	0.34	4.45	0.11	1 104.1
2015	4.98	0.38	4.37	0.12	1 210.3
2016	4.88	0.51	4.12	0.13	1 183.1
2017	4.70	0.60	3.86	0.13	1 193.0
2018	4.41	0.68	3.46	0.13	1 348.2
2019	4.13	0.80	3.07	0.11	1 472.3
2020	2.59	0.52	1.92	0.05	956.5

注：1.公路客运量1993年前为运输系统统计数，1994年起为全社会统计数。
2.2008年公路客运量为全国专项调查数，与2007年口径不一致。
3.铁路客运量从2008年起调整口径。
4.2014年起交通部门调整了公路、水路客运量计算口径。
5.由于统计口径不同，铁路不含动车组

Note: a. Before 1993,the data of highways passenger traffic were transportation system data, and since 1994, whole society statistics.
b.The data of highways passenger traffic of 2008 were the data of national special survey and the coverage is different from that of 2007.
c. The data of the railways passenger traffic statistics has been changed since 2008.
d.Transport sector has adjusted the coverage of highway and waterway transport volume.
e. Due to different statistical caliber, railway passenger cars do not contain D-Series High-Speed Train.

10-8 主要年份交通运输旅客周转量

Passenger-kilometers in Significant Years

单位：亿人公里 (100 million persons-km)

年份 Year	全省旅客周转量 Passenger Traffic of Yunnan Province	铁路 Railways	公路 Highways	水运 Waterways	民用航空 Civil Aviation
1978	24.25	9.92	13.89	0.12	0.32
1980	33.74	12.86	20.30	0.26	0.32
1985	72.84	19.56	52.53	0.32	0.43
1987	88.41	23.20	59.92	0.55	4.74
1988	93.46	23.91	64.81	0.57	4.17
1989	94.01	21.92	67.66	0.42	4.01
1990	87.67	17.22	65.77	0.46	4.22
1991	95.86	17.95	71.83	0.37	5.72
1992	99.98	20.29	69.89	0.34	9.46
1993	111.90	22.86	73.38	0.37	15.29
1994	146.87	24.41	101.77	0.33	20.36
1995	137.93	23.03	93.10	0.35	21.45
1996	149.94	20.57	102.40	0.37	26.61
1997	172.37	22.73	119.47	0.38	29.78
1998	189.85	24.76	131.80	0.58	32.71
1999	237.99	32.82	164.20	0.64	40.34
2000	237.94	31.35	171.20	0.78	34.57
2001	304.20	31.79	232.76	0.82	38.83
2002	281.60	30.50	210.10	0.90	40.10
2003	263.45	30.07	192.87	0.88	39.60
2004	317.76	37.30	227.21	0.91	52.34
2005	331.60	41.04	233.12	1.05	56.39
2006	362.40	47.22	247.71	1.17	66.30
2007	393.40	52.63	265.80	1.21	73.76
2008	411.89	66.61	272.98	1.54	70.76
2009	448.45	63.37	302.22	1.55	81.31
2010	523.64	80.73	352.10	1.78	89.03
2011	610.78	91.91	424.57	1.96	92.34
2012	670.22	91.99	470.20	2.02	106.01
2013	720.33	99.70	493.00	2.23	125.40
2013（新口径）	550.43	99.34	323.10	2.23	125.40
2014	573.63	103.22	321.06	2.37	146.98
2015	599.49	111.38	330.21	2.50	155.40
2016	585.55	110.92	319.99	2.70	151.93
2017	596.70	131.90	308.27	2.88	153.66
2018	595.88	150.99	269.63	3.02	172.23
2019	632.51	181.95	251.27	2.30	196.99
2020	375.63	117.39	138.47	0.74	119.03

注：1.公路旅客周转量1993年前为运输系统统计数，1994年起为全社会统计数。
2.2008年公路旅客周转量为全国专项调查数，与2007年口径不一致。
3.铁路旅客周转量从2008年起调整口径。
4.2014年起交通部门调整了公路、水路客运量计算口径。

Note: a. Before 1993,the data of highways passenger-kilometers were transportation system data, and since 1994, whole society statistics.
b.The data of highways passenger-kilometers of 2008 were the data of national special survey and the coverage is different from that of 2007.
c. The coverage of the railways passenger traffic statistics has been changed since 2008.
d.Transport sector has adjusted the coverage of highway and waterway transport volume since 2014.

10−9　主要年份交通运输货运量

Freight Traffic in Significant Years

单位：亿吨　　(100 million tons)

年　份 Year	全省货运量 Passenger Traffic	铁　路 Railways	公　路 Highways	水　运(万吨) Waterways (10 000 tons)	民用航空(万吨) Civil Aviation (10 000 tons)
1978	0.50	0.19	0.30	93	0.16
1980	0.48	0.21	0.26	65	0.22
1985	2.00	0.20	1.80	52	0.40
1987	2.16	0.23	1.92	91	0.50
1988	2.30	0.24	2.05	91	0.60
1989	3.08	0.25	2.82	91	1.00
1990	3.83	0.26	3.57	104	0.43
1991	3.08	0.26	2.82	91	0.63
1992	4.28	0.27	4.00	105	1.00
1993	3.57	0.27	3.29	115	1.84
1994	3.79	0.28	3.49	168	2.00
1995	3.84	0.28	3.54	123	2.40
1996	4.29	0.29	3.97	245	3.50
1997	4.68	0.29	4.37	157	5.60
1998	4.84	0.31	4.52	141	7.27
1999	5.08	0.33	4.74	118	7.75
2000	5.25	0.35	4.88	134	7.82
2001	5.32	0.39	4.92	142	8.63
2002	5.50	0.43	5.05	146	6.70
2003	5.87	0.46	5.39	160	6.10
2004	5.96	0.51	5.43	221	7.50
2005	6.22	0.53	5.67	236	7.93
2006	6.64	0.55	6.06	247	8.56
2007	7.18	0.60	6.55	262	8.74
2008	4.56	0.61	3.91	339	7.56
2009	4.71	0.59	4.08	345	7.74
2010	5.23	0.63	4.57	402	8.74
2011	6.63	1.17	5.42	439	6.79
2012	7.55	1.18	6.32	465	6.96
2013	8.39	1.19	7.15	484	8.80
2013（新口径）	11.11	1.19	9.87	508	8.80
2014	11.59	1.21	10.32	560	9.35
2015	11.43	1.17	10.20	602	9.17
2016	12.19	1.18	10.95	646	9.03
2017	13.74	1.26	12.41	667	8.43
2018	14.91	1.31	13.53	687	7.60
2019	16.01	1.42	14.51	696	8.75
2020	13.04	1.42	11.56	519	6.23

注：1.公路货运量从1984年起为国家统计局统一口径的全社会运量数。
2.2008年公路货运量为全国专项调查数，与2007年口径不一致。
3.铁路货运量从2008年起调整口径。
4.2014年起交通部门调整了公路、水路货运量计算口径。

Note: a. Since 1984, the approach in computation of freight-traffic of highways has been included in total social count according to National Bureau of Statistics of China .
b.The data of highways freight traffic of 2008 were the data of national special survey and the coverage is different from that of 2007.
c.The coverage of the railways passenger traffic statistics has been changed since 2008.
d.Transport sector has adjusted the coverage of highway and waterway transport volume since 2014.

10−10 主要年份交通运输货物周转量

Freight Ton-kilometers in Significant Years

单位：亿吨公里 (100 million tons-km)

年 份 Year	全省货物周转量 Passenger Traffic of Yunnan Province	铁 路 Railways	公 路 Highways	水 运 Waterways	民用航空 Civil Aviation
1978	62.34	43.52	18.57	0.24	0.01
1980	68.76	50.59	17.84	0.32	0.01
1985	154.11	64.83	88.73	0.50	0.05
1987	195.89	79.77	115.35	0.69	0.08
1988	208.05	82.78	124.44	0.75	0.08
1989	225.21	88.00	136.10	1.04	0.07
1990	260.67	93.91	166.10	0.59	0.07
1991	233.12	96.07	136.42	0.55	0.08
1992	275.85	100.92	173.92	0.88	0.13
1993	241.61	106.23	134.06	1.08	0.24
1994	295.08	107.86	185.99	0.98	0.26
1995	307.71	114.24	192.10	1.06	0.31
1996	352.44	122.24	228.53	1.23	0.44
1997	384.94	129.00	253.96	1.21	0.76
1998	416.18	141.08	273.12	0.96	1.02
1999	443.09	152.64	288.14	0.92	1.11
2000	479.52	180.76	296.65	0.98	1.13
2001	517.31	196.58	318.49	0.99	1.25
2002	551.20	215.80	333.20	1.20	1.00
2003	595.88	235.79	357.64	1.54	0.90
2004	628.39	260.01	365.08	2.12	1.18
2005	656.49	270.37	381.96	2.93	1.23
2006	692.21	277.21	409.46	4.22	1.32
2007	770.96	314.23	450.83	4.59	1.31
2008	811.15	336.20	468.63	5.16	1.16
2009	843.67	340.95	496.14	5.42	1.16
2010	915.04	358.31	548.53	6.91	1.29
2011	996.20	369.70	617.27	8.19	1.04
2012	1 092.09	379.75	702.51	8.71	1.12
2013	1 202.23	390.24	801.04	9.52	1.43
2013（新口径）	1 325.30	390.24	921.98	11.65	1.43
2014	1 407.63	390.59	1 002.35	13.09	1.60
2015	1 465.30	371.83	1 077.89	14.08	1.51
2016	1 569.20	379.44	1 173.06	15.20	1.50
2017	1 798.67	420.62	1 360.37	16.21	1.46
2018	1 943.85	436.08	1 489.23	17.33	1.21
2019	1 524.03	489.86	1 015.20	17.44	1.54
2020	1 551.07	441.38	1 101.54	7.18	0.97

注：1.公路货物周转量从1984年起为国家统计局统一口径的全社会数。
2.2008年公路货物周转量为全国专项调查数，与2007年口径不一致。
3.铁路货物周转量从2008年起调整口径。
4.2014年起交通部门调整了公路、水路货运量计算口径。

Note: a. Since 1984, the approach in computation of freight-kilometers of highways has been included in total social count according to National Bureau of Statistics of China .
b.The data of highways freight ton-kilometers of 2008 were the data of national special survey and the coverage is different from that of 2007.
c.The coverage of the railways passenger traffic statistics has been changed since 2008.
d.Transport sector has adjusted the coverage of highway and waterway transport volume since 2014.

10-11 全省铁路货物运输量（2019-2020年）

Railway Freight Traffic of Yunnan Province (2019-2020)

(按货类分) (by category of cargo)

品 种	Item	2019 货运量（万吨）Freight Traffic (10 000 tons)	2019 货物周转量（亿吨公里）Freight Ton-kilometers (100 million tons-km)	2019 平均运距（公里）Average Transport Distance (km)	2020 货运量（万吨）Freight Traffic (10 000 tons)	2020 货物周转量（亿吨公里）Freight Ton-kilometers (100 million tons-km)	2020 平均运距（公里）Average Transport Distance (km)
全 省	**Yunnan**	**14 224**	**489.86**	**345**	**14 214**	**441.38**	**311**
煤	Coal	2 340	78.36	335	2 284	61.94	271
焦 炭	Coke	343	10.11	295	398	10.35	260
石 油	Petroleum	750	19.58	261	601	16.14	268
钢铁及有色金属	Steel and Nonferrous metal	1 467	52.88	361	1 381	47.20	342
金属矿石	Metal Ores	2 338	92.49	396	1 854	64.08	346
非金属矿石	Nonmetal Materials	169	4.67	276	101	3.27	324
磷矿石	Phosphate Mineral	386	9.63	250	358	7.84	219
矿物性建筑材料	Mineral Building Materials	177	5.70	322	262	5.29	202
水 泥	Cement	12	0.65	530	19	0.98	508
木 材	Timber	57	1.87	327	33	1.06	322
化肥农药	Chemical Fertilizers and pesticide	973	35.39	364	962	32.98	343
粮 食	Grain	568	21.48	378	465	16.52	355
棉 花	Cotton	0.18	0.01	457	0.16	0.01	365
盐	Salt	42	1.17	276	32	0.83	260
农副土特产品	Farm Crops	12	0.36	300	11	0.32	294
鲜活易腐货物	Goods of Live Animal and Putrescence	5	0.13	276	4	0.12	280
其 他	Others	388	13.49	348	372	12.67	341

10-12 全省民用航空运输基本情况（2015-2020年）

Principal Statistics on Civil Aviation of Yunnan Province (2015-2020)

指 标	Item	2015	2016	2017	2018	2019	2020
旅客发运量（万人）	**Passenger Traffic (10 000 persons)**	**1 210.32**	**1 183.08**	**1 193.02**	**1 348.35**	**1 472.23**	**956.51**
国际航线（万人）	International Routes (10 000 persons)	103.48	109.33	135.73	154.32	176.50	22.74
国内航线（万人）	Domestic Routes (10 000 persons)	1 106.84	1 073.75	1 057.29	1 194.02	1 295.73	933.77
地区航线（万人）	Regional Routes (10 000 persons)	16.75	21.26	20.21	17.84	18.90	0.90
货邮发运量（万吨）	**Freight Traffic (10 000 tons)**	**9.17**	**9.03**	**8.43**	**7.60**	**8.75**	**6.23**
国际航线（万吨）	International Routes (10 000 tons)	0.75	0.68	0.92	0.69	1.04	0.19
国内航线（万吨）	Domestic Routes (10 000 tons)	8.42	8.35	7.51	6.91	7.70	6.04
地区航线（万吨）	Regional Routes (10 000 tons)	0.17	0.26	0.20	0.05	0.05	0.00
旅客周转量（亿人公里）	Passenger-tons(100 million persons-km)	155.40	151.93	153.66	174.30	197.01	119.03
货邮周转量（亿吨公里）	Freight Ton-kilometers (100 million tons-km)	1.51	1.50	1.46	1.22	1.54	0.97
总周转量（亿吨公里）	Total Air Traffic Ton-kilometers (100 million tons-km)	15.28	14.97	15.16	16.61	18.92	11.52
起飞架次（万架次）	Number of Flying Aircrafts (10 000 units)	11.44	10.73	10.99	11.93	12.90	9.53
飞行里程（万公里）	Distance of Flying (10 000 km)	12 892	12 212	12 447	13 825	15 546	10 952
飞行小时（万小时）	Hours of Flying (10 000 hours)	22.24	21.15	21.94	24.16	26.68	19.08
飞行生产率（吨公里/小时）	Productivity of Flying (ton-km/h)	6 873	7 074	6 909	6 874	7 093	6 037
正班载运率（%）	Carry Rate of Aircrafts (%)	74.1	75.7	75.1		72.9	66.8
正班客座率（%）	Utilization Rate of Seats (%)	80.6	81.1	79.4	80.6	79.9	70.1

10-13 全省电信业务基本情况（2000-2020年）

单位：万户

年　份 Year	电信业务总量(亿元) Business Volume of Telecommunication Services (100 million yuan)	移动短信业务量(亿条) Short Message Services (100 million messages)	移动电话年末用户 Number of Mobile Telephone Subscribers at Year-end
2000	82.43		200.90
2001	93.40		338.50
2002	118.50	10.70	502.30
2003	151.45	24.90	628.40
2004	200.80	33.00	732.40
2005	253.60	55.90	898.80
2006	327.70	77.90	1 068.90
2007	458.30	134.00	1 346.40
2008	594.28	169.80	1 635.90
2009	655.25	222.06	1 936.38
2010	754.10	270.00	2 244.50
2011	299.90	310.86	2 589.51
2012	344.34	367.44	2 895.78
2013	379.23	384.12	3 395.76
2014	539.28	356.11	3 748.54
2015	756.25	187.22	3 789.77
2016	500.98	145.93	3 942.79
2017	1 144.02	131.91	4 228.40
2018	2 477.03	178.45	4 659.05
2019	4 186.02	352.67	4 863.01
2020	5 647.82	364.77	4 953.38

注：1.电信业务总量按照不同的不变价计算，2001-2010年按2000年不变价格计算，2011-2015年按2010年不变价格计算。2017年以来，执行工业和信息化部统一制定的“2015年不变单价”标准。
2.2018年及以前移动短信业务不含公益短信。

Basic Conditions of Telecommunication Services of Yunnan Province (2000-2020)

(10 000 subscribers)

3G移动电话用户 3G Wireless Subscribers	4G移动电话用户 4G Wireless Subscribers	5G移动电话用户 5G Wireless Subscribers	(固定)互联网宽带接入用户 Internet Broadband Users	固定电话年末用户 Number of Fixed Telephone Subscribers at Year-end	城市用户 Number of Urban Fixed Subscribers	农村用户 Number of Rural Fixed Subscribers
				288.90	221.90	67.00
				359.90	276.20	83.70
				437.20	357.40	79.60
				483.20	226.50	114.90
				547.20	232.30	121.40
				597.70	444.00	153.80
				644.20	441.70	202.60
				628.70	237.90	210.00
				616.30	248.60	221.00
				583.12	267.29	205.38
88.76			224.10	562.50	357.70	204.80
234.16			306.52	540.11	361.43	178.68
571.79			375.52	524.29	364.68	159.61
1 084.63			405.97	485.41	346.92	138.49
1 286.54			424.88	429.82	312.34	117.48
822.96			455.03	370.94	287.56	83.38
448.07			655.31	335.01	267.14	67.87
320.30			812.60	301.10	247.00	54.10
284.22	3 375.48		1 019.43	275.24	229.39	45.85
72.04	3 699.97	7.10	1 156.08	287.78		
37.02	3 834.53	779.75	1 278.12	274.56		

Note:a.The business volume of telecommunication services were calculated at the different constant prices, and were calculated at 2000 constant prices from 2001 to 2010, and were calculated at 2010 from 2011 to 2015. Since 2017, business volume of telecommunication service is calculated to the constant price of 2015 stipulated by Ministry of Industry and Information.

b. Before 2018 (including 2018), mobile SMS service does not include public service SMS.

10-14 全省主要年份邮政业务基本情况

年份 州市	Year Region	营业网点（处）Number of Postal Offices (unit)	信筒信箱（个）Number of Postal Boxes (unit)	邮路总长度（万公里）Length of Postal Routes (10 000 km)	汽车邮路 Highway Routes	铁路邮路 Railway Routes
1978		1 698	2 359	26.08	25 494	5 101
1980		1 680	3 929	25.58	27 241	4 812
1985		1 684	4 647	5.00	29 261	5 395
1990		1 696	4 500	5.64	31 299	5 398
1995		1 779	4 786	6.56	34 948	5 106
2000		1 930	4 436	12.98	44 420	4 638
2001		1 893	4 538	13.53	51 427	4 666
2002		1 884	4 471	13.65	53 013	4 666
2003		1 891	4 487	13.64	52 855	4 638
2004		1 895	4 292	14.05	58 347	4 666
2005		1 879	4 013	14.60	66 382	4 666
2006		1 853	3 857	14.62	66 777	4 638
2007		1 794	3 936	16.87	67 477	10 375
2008		1 789	3 266	17.57	71 103	13 403
2009		1 736	3 315	17.27	70 151	13 533
2010		1 722	2 927	17.14	79 701	15 170
2011		1 765	2 875	19.48	83 012	21 279
2012		4 410	1 820	50.28	74 136	
2013		4 909	1 817	79.21	73 966	31 422
2014		5 269	1 804	73.41	85 547	3 212
2015		4 802	1 885	67.17	94 867	11 308
2016		6 306	1 904	61.80	96 513	14 482
2017		7 970	1 909	29.10	108 176	13 839
2018		9 100	1 909	29.18	115 437	14 391
2019		10 250	1 900	33.60	139 134	10 819
2020		11 746	1 880	17.76	121 635	10 269
昆明	Kunming	3 115	290	5.27	42 420	10 269
曲靖	Qujing	892	148	0.56	5 648	-
玉溪	Yuxi	510	94	0.35	3 481	-
保山	Baoshan	584	106	0.60	5 120	-
昭通	Zhaotong	687	165	1.06	10 586	-
丽江	Lijiang	431	72	4.53	2 955	-
普洱	Pu'er	593	126	1.00	9 918	-
临沧	Lincang	509	99	0.61	6 062	-
楚雄	Chuxiong	547	143	0.75	7 534	-
红河	Honghe	778	184	0.71	7 074	-
文山	Wenshan	473	126	0.44	4 377	-
西双版纳	Xishuangbanna	381	51	0.37	3 658	-
大理	Dali	1 254	141	0.63	6 276	-
德宏	Dehong	649	73	0.36	2 984	-
怒江	Nujiang	185	31	0.12	1 168	-
迪庆	Diqing	158	31	0.30	2 374	-

注：1.邮路总长度1980年及以前是邮路及农村投递线路总长度之和。
2.营业网点不含代办点，1998年及以前年份的为邮电支局所(已剔除独立的电信局所)。
3.1990年及以前年份没有单独核算邮政业务量。
4.2012年以后营业网点和邮路总长度是邮政企业和快递企业的汇总数。
5.汽车邮路长度是邮政企业的汇总数。

Basic Conditions of Postal Services of Yunnan Province in Significant Years

快递业务量 (万件) Express Business Volume (10 000 pieces)	农村投递路线长度 (万公里) Rural Delivery Routes (10 000 km)	邮政业务总量 (亿元) Business Volume of Postal Services (100 million yuan)	函 件 (万 件) Number of Letters (10 000 pieces)	报刊期发数 (万份) Issue of Newspaper and Magazines (10 000 copies)
			5 571.57	224.08
			7 023.68	364.22
	18.05		9 496.54	639.24
	17.13		8 957.46	471.20
	17.09	2.17	16 024.08	484.57
	16.69	3.21	10 001.50	421.30
	16.47	7.60	8 876.10	459.20
	16.43	8.30	12 344.10	410.80
	16.52	8.52	9 969.30	328.90
	16.38	8.18	8 386.70	339.10
	16.55	8.60	7 957.40	317.60
	16.05	9.92	7 299.80	342.80
	16.14	11.10	6 695.60	264.50
	16.09	12.71	7 442.82	279.69
	15.99	14.74	6 516.11	305.00
	15.96	15.09	5 498.61	300.76
1 031.86	15.86	16.32	4 119.53	318.51
3 774.37	16.94	18.25	5 250.00	316.01
6 870.32	16.90	23.38	7 231.00	321.00
8 546.08	16.50	27.95	9 550.00	299.00
11 109.14	17.04	35.30	6 664.72	327.66
17 445.80	17.09	50.05	3 647.56	264.92
22 775.76	16.98	66.24	1 777.82	259.34
33 999.10	17.19	90.43	2 449.98	251.69
43 160.83	19.26	118.32	1 864.91	240.78
62 974.08	18.96	158.10	876.52	236.62
42 073.11	1.64	92.99	302.66	54.28
1 981.13	1.86	6.63	227.74	17.70
1 416.66	0.81	3.89	59.51	10.81
1 153.02	1.19	3.59	42.80	12.54
1 355.60	1.72	5.03	14.13	16.30
1 002.79	0.64	2.95	10.01	8.72
1 092.55	1.44	3.26	21.79	11.82
673.13	1.21	2.27	6.75	9.81
1 085.47	1.81	3.59	21.32	15.22
2 507.92	2.01	8.69	62.81	19.88
1 295.02	1.60	5.05	15.43	13.85
1 455.56	0.32	3.95	41.35	7.75
2 164.59	1.48	7.19	23.44	18.22
3 505.54	0.56	7.90	17.96	8.79
84.07	0.33	0.50	5.71	6.09
127.93	0.31	0.61	3.11	4.84

Note: a.Length of postal routes in 1980 and before refers to the length of postal routes and rural delivery routes.
b.Number of postal offices excluded the number of post sub-stations, while in and before 1998,the number of postal offices referred to postal and telecommunications offices (has excluded the independent telecommunications offices)
c.In and before 1990,the business volume of postal services was not calculated independently.
d.Number of post offices and length of postal routes are those of postal and express enterprises after 2012.
e.Number of mail car length is that of postal enterprises

10－15　规模以上服务业企业财务状况（2019－2020年）

单位：亿元

类　别	Category	企业数（个）Number of Enterprises (unit)	营业收入 Total Business Revenue		营业成本 Operating Cost	
			2019	2020	2019	2020
全　省	**Yunnan**	**1 974**	**2 860.97**	**2 143.13**	**2 258.49**	**1 747.70**
按国民经济行业分	**Grouped by Sector**					
交通运输、仓储和邮政业	Transport, Storage and Post	315	1 555.96	794.42	1 368.05	792.64
铁路运输业	Railway Transport	2	243.74	194.71	249.35	228.44
道路运输业	Highway Transport	193	902.79	252.46	744.27	199.57
水上运输业	Waterway Transport					
航空运输业	Air Transport	14	306.18	165.70	285.43	201.03
管道运输业	Pipeline Transport	1	6.55	5.99	2.44	1.77
多式联运和运输代理业	Multimodal Transport and Forwarding Agencies	37	20.30	50.29	17.37	44.56
装卸搬运和仓储业	Lording,Unlording,Carrying and Storage	44	22.98	59.02	21.54	57.72
邮 政 业	Post	24	53.42	66.25	47.64	59.54
信息传输、软件和信息技术服务业	Information Transmission,Software and Information Technology	197	484.37	508.08	313.62	325.02
电信、广播电视和卫星传输服务	Telecommunication, Videocast and Satellite Transmissions Service	77	408.76	429.11	255.28	264.53
互联网和相关服务	Network and Related Services	26	14.79	13.50	9.33	9.51
软件和信息技术服务业	Software and Information Technology Services	94	60.82	65.47	49.01	50.98
房地产业(不含房地产开发经营)	Real Estate(Exclude Real Estate Exploitation)	140	67.89	75.46	47.55	52.34
物业管理	Property Management Services	112	57.39	63.35	43.50	47.08
房地产中介服务	Real Estate Intermediary Services	6	2.25	2.74	1.33	1.36
房地产租赁经营	Real Estate Tenancy Management	22	8.25	9.38	2.71	3.89
其他房地产业	Other Real Estate					

Financial Statistics of Above Designated Size Service Industry (2019-2020)

(100 million yuan)

税金及附加 Taxes and other Charges		营业费用、管理费用财务费用和研发费用合计 Expenses on business, Management，Finance and R&D		营业利润 Profits from Business		利润总额 Total Profits		应付职工薪酬 Wages Payable for Employee		平均用工人数（万人） Average Number Of Employees (10 000 Persons)
2019	2020	2019	2020	2019	2020	2019	2020	2019	2020	2020
16.67	**11.46**	**479.11**	**421.49**	**197.10**	**91.06**	**204.10**	**99.76**	**489.90**	**460.98**	**48.25**
6.19	3.43	218.45	164.87	15.32	-80.32	19.38	-75.33	242.46	203.85	14.92
0.27	0.26	14.19	9.50	-17.11	-30.24	-18.79	-30.15	75.53	76.08	3.79
3.68	1.25	150.95	114.89	33.07	-21.80	37.50	-18.41	84.80	49.69	6.24
1.67	1.27	38.43	24.08	-1.42	-46.13	-0.27	-45.32	60.16	50.61	2.45
0.04	0.05	1.06	0.84	3.22	3.56	3.25	3.56	0.41	0.48	0.03
0.09	0.17	2.70	3.82	0.09	16.39	0.08	16.74	2.30	3.16	0.41
0.07	0.09	3.65	3.77	-0.44	-1.20	-0.06	-0.59	2.86	3.06	0.36
0.37	0.33	7.47	7.96	-2.08	-0.90	-2.33	-1.16	16.41	20.78	1.64
1.42	1.31	80.43	83.85	89.05	99.82	88.61	98.66	59.57	60.71	4.22
1.09	0.98	67.13	69.29	85.14	95.60	84.20	93.97	45.34	46.79	3.01
0.10	0.09	3.44	2.79	1.93	1.26	2.01	1.57	1.95	2.47	0.19
0.23	0.24	9.86	11.77	1.97	2.96	2.40	3.12	12.28	11.44	1.02
1.45	1.40	14.13	13.43	6.21	10.41	6.27	10.57	22.17	22.07	4.46
0.49	0.58	9.30	8.12	4.33	7.93	4.37	8.08	20.71	20.10	4.25
0.02	0.01	0.93	1.09	-0.03	0.28	-0.03	0.29	0.33	0.53	0.06
0.95	0.81	3.90	4.21	1.91	2.21	1.93	2.20	1.12	1.43	0.15

10-15 续表

单位：亿元

类　别	Category	企业数(个) Number of Enterprises (unit)	营业收入 Total Business Revenue 2019	2020	营业成本 Operating Cost 2019	2020
租赁和商务服务业	Leasing Trade and Business Service	432	273.49	227.00	197.85	170.18
租赁业	Leasing Trade	14	3.18	4.22	3.29	3.89
商务服务业	Commercial Serive	418	270.32	222.78	194.55	166.29
科学研究和技术服务业	Scientific Research, Technology Service	240	206.54	264.16	156.18	205.28
研究和试验发展	R & D	11	3.85	4.38	2.47	2.11
专品技术服务业	Professional Technology Service	219	198.36	256.44	150.63	200.91
科技推广和应用服务业	Technology Promotion and Application Service	10	4.32	3.35	3.08	2.27
水利、环境和公共设施管理业	Water Conservancy, Administration of Environment and Public Facilities	81	78.86	90.08	54.93	79.53
水利管理业	Water Conservancy Administration	2	0.57	0.73	0.29	0.33
生态保护和环境治理业	Conservatory Ecology and Administration of Environment	8	9.39	9.98	6.53	7.91
公共设施管理业	Administration of Public Facilities	69	56.43	40.89	37.46	35.62
土地管理业	Land Management	2	12.47	38.48	10.65	35.67
居民服务、修理和其他服务业	Services to Households,Repair and Other Service	166	36.47	31.22	22.08	19.55
居民服务业	Services to Households	78	23.59	19.02	12.59	10.50
机动车、电子产品和日用产品修理业	Repair Services of Motor Vehicle,Electronics and Daily Products	64	8.30	7.71	6.50	6.00
其他服务业	Other Service	24	4.59	4.49	2.99	3.05
教　育	Education	64	19.99	20.67	13.73	13.66
卫生和社会工作	Health Care, Social Works	137	73.36	80.24	49.31	56.39
卫　生	Health Care	136	73.36	80.13	49.31	56.29
社会工作	Social Works	1		0.11		0.11
文化、体育和娱乐业	Culture, Sports and Entertainment	202	64.03	51.80	35.20	33.11
新闻和出版业	News and Publishing	13	18.20	18.28	13.85	13.22
广播、电视、电影和影视录音制作业	Broadcast, Television,Filmdom and Audio & Video Production	54	10.82	6.86	6.31	5.09
文化艺术业	Culture and Arts	56	16.57	12.48	6.12	5.46
体育	Sports	11	3.54	3.30	1.30	1.13
娱乐业	Entertainment	68	14.91	10.88	7.62	8.20

continued

税金及附加 Taxes and othe Charges		营业费用、管理费用财务费用和研发费用合计 Expenses on business, Management，Finance and R&D		营业利润 Profits from Business		利润总额 Total Profits		应付职工薪酬 Wages Payable for Emploee		平均用工人数（万人） Average Number Of Employees (10 000 Persons)
2019	2020	2019	2020	2019	2020	2019	2020	2019	2020	2020
2.75	2.08	56.27	50.41	39.39	22.90	41.97	25.59	54.48	55.20	11.78
0.02	0.03	0.56	0.92	- 0.76	- 0.28	- 0.80	- 0.27	1.01	0.87	0.12
2.73	2.05	55.71	49.48	40.15	23.18	42.76	25.86	53.47	54.32	11.65
1.20	1.44	33.95	39.05	20.63	21.97	21.27	22.64	46.96	56.30	3.69
0.06	0.07	2.17	3.21	2.26	- 0.84	2.29	- 0.86	1.42	1.80	0.10
1.11	1.34	30.38	34.78	18.29	22.52	18.70	23.17	44.24	53.66	3.51
0.03	0.03	1.40	1.06	0.08	0.30	0.28	0.33	1.30	0.84	0.07
1.99	0.54	18.31	14.66	9.07	5.61	8.15	5.46	15.53	12.98	2.14
0.01	0.01	0.08	0.20	0.22	0.21	0.22	0.21	0.13	0.14	0.01
0.03	0.03	1.23	1.16	3.47	5.89	3.52	5.89	0.91	0.73	0.07
1.45	0.27	16.66	12.71	4.05	- 5.59	3.09	- 5.56	14.28	11.87	2.05
0.50	0.23	0.34	0.59	1.33	5.10	1.32	4.92	0.21	0.23	0.01
0.32	0.24	11.14	8.89	3.03	2.66	3.38	3.10	10.69	8.48	1.86
0.25	0.18	8.39	6.28	2.41	2.05	2.75	2.46	7.07	4.96	1.01
0.04	0.04	1.48	1.40	0.28	0.31	0.25	0.32	1.29	1.24	0.23
0.03	0.02	1.27	1.21	0.34	0.30	0.38	0.32	2.33	2.28	0.62
0.19	0.16	5.06	5.42	0.92	3.35	1.02	3.51	5.93	7.28	1.06
0.17	0.15	19.89	22.36	3.67	0.89	3.41	0.82	19.61	23.08	2.78
0.17	0.15	19.89	22.35	3.67	0.90	3.41	0.83	19.61	23.06	2.77
			0.02		- 0.01		- 0.01		0.02	0.01
0.99	0.72	21.47	18.56	9.83	3.77	10.63	4.74	12.52	11.05	1.35
0.11	0.14	2.05	2.46	4.60	6.14	4.63	6.09	3.12	3.08	0.16
0.15	0.09	2.50	1.71	2.00	- 0.01	2.44	0.16	1.41	1.16	0.18
0.23	0.13	5.57	5.41	5.26	1.98	5.40	2.01	3.09	2.41	0.34
0.23	0.23	2.85	3.46	- 0.84	- 1.50	- 0.82	- 1.46	1.37	1.41	0.18
0.27	0.13	8.50	5.52	- 1.20	- 2.84	- 1.01	- 2.06	3.53	2.99	0.49

10-16 各州市规模以上服务业企业财务状况
Financial Indicators of Above Designated Size Service Industry by Region

单位：亿元 (100 million yuan)

州 市	Region	企业数(个) Number of Enterprises (unit)	营业收入 Total Business Revenue		营业成本 Cost of Business		税金及附加 Taxes and Other Charges	
			2019	2020	2019	2020	2019	2020
全　省	**Yunnan**	**1 974**	**2 860.97**	**2 143.13**	**2 258.49**	**1 747.70**	**16.67**	**11.46**
昆　明	Kunming	943	2 135.10	1 434.39	1 744.81	1 217.65	10.62	8.13
曲　靖	Qujing	115	68.15	73.19	47.70	52.30	0.29	0.30
玉　溪	Yuxi	98	81.53	70.68	45.64	54.22	0.45	0.36
保　山	Baoshan	73	50.12	51.47	36.10	37.57	0.32	0.32
昭　通	Zhaotong	64	48.70	53.39	30.68	34.49	0.26	0.22
丽　江	Lijiang	77	55.97	39.85	36.03	29.59	0.43	0.20
普　洱	Pu'er	62	47.53	47.41	34.15	34.43	0.20	0.18
临　沧	Lincang	28	27.37	28.37	17.36	17.68	0.11	0.11
楚　雄	Chuxiong	89	43.83	45.82	35.60	38.22	0.27	0.19
红　河	Honghe	108	89.98	87.37	73.91	70.33	0.36	0.29
文　山	Wenshan	61	40.26	41.30	27.69	27.49	0.17	0.14
西双版纳	Xishuangbanna	60	33.46	32.44	22.74	22.44	1.17	0.13
大　理	Dali	106	73.73	75.29	54.23	60.86	1.63	0.58
德　宏	Dehong	44	43.77	44.26	36.16	35.53	0.22	0.18
怒　江	Nujiang	13	6.93	7.06	5.35	5.08	0.05	0.04
迪　庆	Diqing	33	14.54	10.84	10.33	9.82	0.13	0.09

10-16 续表 continued

单位：亿元 (100 million yuan)

州 市	Region	营业费用、管理费用财务费用和研发费用合计 Expenses on business, Management，Finance and R&D		营业利润 Profits from Business		利润总额 Total Profits		应付职工薪酬 Wages Payable for Employee		平均用工人数（万人） Average Number Of Employees (10 000 Persons)
		2019	2020	2019	2020	2019	2020	2019	2020	2020
全 省	**Yunnan**	**479.11**	**421.49**	**197.10**	**91.06**	**204.10**	**99.76**	**489.90**	**460.98**	**48.25**
昆 明	Kunming	338.67	283.05	109.57	30.64	113.23	35.27	362.24	335.63	29.32
曲 靖	Qujing	13.08	12.60	7.95	8.56	8.45	9.56	11.98	12.42	1.90
玉 溪	Yuxi	10.42	9.28	25.85	7.96	26.13	8.40	12.24	13.02	2.23
保 山	Baoshan	9.13	8.72	5.06	5.30	5.40	5.43	9.76	9.68	1.43
昭 通	Zhaotong	8.94	9.09	8.74	10.14	8.90	10.48	8.93	9.19	1.32
丽 江	Lijiang	10.23	7.68	9.92	3.29	8.41	3.50	8.92	7.50	1.05
普 洱	Pu'er	10.99	12.46	2.75	0.60	2.83	0.93	9.36	9.53	1.49
临 沧	Lincang	5.48	5.70	4.38	4.91	4.41	5.10	4.95	4.90	0.57
楚 雄	Chuxiong	6.71	6.60	10.44	15.89	11.76	16.43	8.59	8.55	1.42
红 河	Honghe	19.00	18.49	0.32	0.16	2.29	0.46	12.43	12.23	1.79
文 山	Wenshan	6.64	7.00	5.91	6.97	6.27	7.09	8.24	8.29	1.27
西双版纳	Xishuangbanna	7.89	8.08	4.26	1.95	4.36	2.15	7.01	6.05	0.90
大 理	Dali	17.98	19.17	2.42	-3.32	2.35	-3.39	14.51	13.91	2.09
德 宏	Dehong	7.19	7.19	0.68	1.36	0.63	1.23	5.89	5.64	0.93
怒 江	Nujiang	1.68	1.69	-0.22	0.25	-0.21	0.44	1.57	1.58	0.21
迪 庆	Diqing	5.08	4.69	-0.94	-3.59	-1.09	-3.32	3.29	2.87	0.33

主要统计指标解释

铁路营业里程 又称营业长度（包括正式营业和临时营业里程），指办理客货运输业务的铁路正线总长度。凡是全线或部分建成双线及以上的线路，以第一线的实际长度计算；复线、站线、段管线、岔线和特殊用途线以及不计算运费的联络线都不计算营业里程。该指标可以反映铁路运输业基础设施的发展水平，也是计算客货周转量、运输密度和机车车辆运用效率等指标的基础资料。

公路里程 指在一定时期内实际达到《公路工程技术标准 JTG B01-2003》规定的技术等级的公路，并经公路主管部门正式验收交付使用的公路里程数。包括大、中城市的郊区公路，以及公路通过小城镇（指县城、集镇）街道的公路里程和公路桥梁长度、隧道长度、渡口的宽度以及分期修建的公路已验收交付使用的里程，不包括大、中城市的街道、厂矿、林区生产用道和农业生产用道的里程。两条或多条公路共同经由同一路段，只计算一次，不得重复计算里程长度。按公路技术等级分为等级公路和等外公路，其中等级公路分为高速公路、一级公路、二级公路、三级公路和四级公路。

内河航道里程 内河航道通航里程指在一定时期内，能通航运输船舶及排筏的天然河流、湖泊水库、运河及通航渠道的长度。包括全年季节性通航累计三个月以上的航道，不包括仅供零散流放竹、木排的河道。两省以河为界的航道里程，双方均按一半计算，以免重复。该指标可以反映内河水运网的规模、水平和发展。

民用航空航线里程 指统计期间内全部民用航空航线的航线总长度。航线长度指民用航空航线的计费距离。计算航线里程可按重复和不重复两种方法，前者是指各航线长度相加的总和；后者则要扣除各航线之间相同航段重复计算的部分。

货（客）运量 指在一定时期内，各种运输工具实际运送的货物（旅客）数量。该指标是反映运输业为国民经济和人民生活服务的数量指标，也是制订和检查运输生产计划、研究运输发展规模和速度的重要指标。货运按吨计算，客运按人计算。货物不论运输距离长短、货物类别，均按实际重量统计。旅客不论行程远近或票价多少，均按一人一次客运量统计；半价票、小孩票也按一人统计。

货物（旅客）周转量 指在一定时期内，由各种运输工具运送的货物（旅客）数量与其相应运输距离的乘积之总和。该指标可以反映运输业生产的总成果，也是编制和检查运输生产计划，计算运输效率、劳动生产率以及核算运输单位成本的主要基础资料。计算货物周转量通常按发出站与到达站之间的最短距离，也就是计费距离计算。计算公式为：

货物（旅客）周转量 =Σ（货物（旅客）运输量 × 运输距离）

邮电业务总量 指以货币形式表示的邮电企业为社会提供各类邮电服务的总数量，是用于观察邮电业务发展变化总趋势的综合性总量指标。分别按邮政业务总量和电信业务总量统计。邮电业务总量是以各类业务的实物量分别乘以相应的不变单价，得出各类业务的货币量再加总求得。

移动电话用户 指报告期末通过移动电话交换机进入移动电话网的全部电话用户。包括各类签约用户、智能网预付费用户、无线上网卡用户（包括 2G 和 3G 无线上网卡用户）等。

固定电话用户 指在电信企业登记注册，且在报告期末实际已经接入电信企业固定电话网（包括局用电话交换机、接入网设备、软交换用户接入设备、无线市话设备）上的全部电话用户。包括普通电话用户、无线接入电话用户、公用电话用户、窄带综合业务数字网 (N-ISDN) 用户、集中用户交换机 (CENTREX) 用户、模拟中继线用户等。

Explanatory Notes on Main Statistical Indicators

Length of Railways in Operation refers to the total length of the trunk line under passenger and freight transportation (including both full operation and temporary operation). The calculation is based on the actual length of the first line even if this line has a full or partial double track or more tracks, excluding double tracks, station sidings, tracks under the charge of stations, branch lines, special purpose lines and the non payable connecting lines. The length of railways in operation is an important indicator to show the development of the infrastructure for the railway transport, and also the essential data to calculate volume of passenger freight transport, traffic density and utilization efficiency of the locomotives and carriages.

Length of Highways refers to the length of highways which have actually reached the technical level specified in the technical standard JTG B01-2003 in a certain period of time and have been formally checked and accepted by the department of highway and put into use. The length of highway includes that of the suburb highways at large and medium-sized cities,highways passing through streets at small cities and towns,and also the length of bridge and ferries. It does not include the length of streets in big and medium-sized cities and highways built for the production purpose at factories, mines, forest areas and agricultural areas. If two more highways go the same section of the way, the length of the section is only calculated for once and no duplication is allowed. It is divided into grade highway and grade external highway by highway technology grade, among which grade highway is divided into expressway, grade one highway, grade two highway, grade three highway and grade four highway.

Length of Navigable Inland Waterways it is an indicator reflecting the size and development of inland water network, it refers to the length of the natural rivers, lakes, reservoirs, canals, and ditches open to navigation during a given period, which enables the transport by ships and rafts. It includes the channels open to navigation for over an accumulative 3 months in a year, yet this does not include the river courses, which are only used to float odd logs and bamboo rafts.The distance between the two provinces is calculated in half to avoid duplication. This indicator can reflect the scale, level and development situation of the inland waterway network.

Length of Civil Aviation Routes refers to the length of all routes for regular civil aviation flights, which is used to account the freight, during the period of statistics. There are usually two ways to calculate the route length: duplicated calculation and non-duplicated calculation, the former is the sum of length of all civil aviation routes, and latter should deduct the duplication length of same route among all routes.

Freight (Passenger) Traffic refers to the volume of freight (passenger) transported with various means. The freight (passenger)traffic provides a quantitative measure to show how the transport industry serves the national economy and people, and is also an important indicator for planning the transport industry and for studying the development scale and speed of the transport industry. Freight transport is calculated in tons and passenger traffic is calculated in the number of persons. Despite the type of freight and traveling distance, the freight transport is calculated in the actual weight of the goods, and despite the traveling distance and ticket price, the passenger traffic is calculated by the principle that one person can be counted only once in one travel. The passengers who travel with a half price ticket or a child ticket is also calculated as one person.

Freight Ton-kilometres (Passenger-kilometres) refer to the sum of the products of the volume of transported cargo (passengers) multiplying by the transport distance. It is an important indicator to reflect the achievement of transportation industry. Normally, the shortest distance between the departure station and the destination station (i.e., the payable distance) is the basis to calculate the freight ton-kilometers. This is an important indicator to show the total results of the transport industry, to prepare and examine the transport plan and to measure the efficiency, the labour productivity and the unit cost of transport. The formula is as follows:

$$\text{Freight ton-kilometres (passenger-kilometres)} = \sum \text{freight (passenger) traffic} \times \text{distance of transportation}$$

Business Volume of Post and Telecommunications refers to the total amount of post and telecommunication services, expressed in value terms, provided by the post and telecommunications departments for the society. This indicator reflects the overall results of development of postal and telecommunication services. It can be classified as postal services and telecommunication services. Business Volume of Post and Telecommunications is the sum of all services in kind multiplying with the unit price (constant price) to get the total business value.

Mobile Telephone Subscribers refer to all telephone users who enter the mobile phone network through a mobile phone exchange at the end of the report. It includes all kinds of subscribers, prepaid users of smart networks, and users of wireless CARDS (including 2G and 3G wireless CARDS) and so on.

Local Telephone Subscribers refers to all telephone users registered in telecom enterprises and actually connected to the fixed telephone network of telecom enterprises at the end of the report (including the local telephone exchange, access network equipment, soft exchange user access equipment and wireless local telephone equipment). It includes general subscribers, wireless local telephone subscribers, public telephones subscribers, N-ISDN subscribers, CENTREX users, analog relay users and so on.

Chapter 11

十一、金融和保险业
Banking and Insurance

11-1 金融机构存贷款年末余额（1978-2020年）

Loans and Deposits of Financial Institutions Year-end (1978-2020)

单位：亿元 (100 million yuan)

年 份 Year	存款年末余额 The balance of deposits at Year-end	非金融企业存款 Deposits of non-financial Enterprises	住户存款 Household deposits	贷款年末余额 The balance of Loans at Year-end	非金融企业及机关团体贷款 Loans of non-financial Enterprises	住户贷款 Household Loans
1978	28.51	8.36	3.24			
1979	34.48	9.60	3.91			
1980	39.95	11.14	5.43			
1981	48.25	12.92	7.22			
1982	59.61	17.88	12.36			
1983	68.81	20.28	16.17			
1984	81.45	25.43	22.24			
1985	99.67	40.93	29.83			
1986	128.58	53.80	39.76			
1987	156.64	54.98	55.46			
1988	190.41	70.51	63.84			
1989	218.26	79.89	86.45			
1990	292.19	105.81	117.89			
1991	365.81	136.82	152.28			
1992	466.72	172.79	195.82			
1993	593.56	203.41	251.23			
1994	841.15	319.19	351.40			
1995	1 187.24	478.89	500.13			
1996	1 539.59	650.80	671.20			
1997	1 829.40	825.24	805.99			
1998	2 076.06	910.64	912.89			
1999	2 254.38	940.79	1 028.93			
2000	2 465.68	1 038.40	1 138.22			
2001	2 779.71	1 082.52	1 298.53			
2002	3 121.28	1 106.12	1 500.24			
2003	3 747.46	1 344.70	1 766.51			
2004	4 404.36	1 688.81	2 052.12			
2005	5 140.50	1 773.63	2 430.28			
2006	6 131.25	2 066.50	2 854.86			
2007	7 170.87	2 578.84	3 046.40			
2008	8 418.94	2 882.69	3 783.78			
2009	11 119.64	3 942.38	4 668.61			
2010	13 411.49	4 462.42	5 719.55	10 568.78	8 123.83	2 444.94
2011	15 416.70	5 449.03	6 693.67	12 114.59	9 187.77	2 926.82
2012	18 008.04	6 131.96	7 848.64	13 848.10	10 283.40	3 564.70
2013	20 767.77	6 446.34	9 163.61	15 782.46	11 395.29	4 387.17
2014	22 456.26	6 354.69	9 923.95	17 978.74	12 819.60	5 159.14
2015	25 035.09	6 863.46	10 736.62	20 842.86	15 043.53	5 726.30
2016	27 726.10	7 983.61	11 935.78	23 056.28	1 6856.13	6 134.67
2017	29 963.85	8 707.45	13 164.69	25 398.93	18 425.84	6 912.24
2018	30 518.85	7 781.40	14 459.15	28 042.02	19 884.66	8 098.53
2019	32 791.37	8 082.52	15 888.28	31 140.08	21 274.53	9 811.74
2020	35 474.99	8 661.13	17 675.38	34 651.14	23 128.68	11 464.05

注：本表资料1981年及以前为国有商业银行数据，1982年后为全部金融机构数据，2010年及以前非金融企业存款为企业存款，住户存款为储蓄存款，变更后的指标口径不同,不具有可比性。

Note: The data in this table are obtained from National Commercial Bank before 1981,while after 1982,all data are obtained from financial institutions.Before2010,Deposits of non-financial Enterprises is Deposits of Enterprises,Household deposits is Savings Deposits,The Changed Statistical caliber is different and isn't comparable.

11-2 各州市金融机构存贷款余额（2020年）

Loans and Deposits of Financial Institutions by Region (2020)

单位：亿元 (100 million yuan)

州 市	Region	各项存款 Total Deposits		住户存款 Household deposits		各项贷款 Total Loans	
		余 额 Balance at Year-end	比年初增减额(±) Increase over Year Beginning(±)	余 额 Balance at Year-end	比年初增减额(±) Increase over Year Beginning(±)	余 额 Balance at Year-end	比年初增减额(±) Increase over Year Beginning(±)
全 省	**Yunnan**	**35 474.99**	**2 683.62**	**17 675.38**	**1 787.10**	**34 651.14**	**3 511.06**
昆 明	Kunming	16 295.36	1 416.02	5 962.63	607.38	19 673.62	1 880.13
曲 靖	Qujing	2 765.60	280.62	1 721.99	216.77	1 793.91	139.00
玉 溪	Yuxi	2 010.91	54.10	1 053.89	87.85	1 512.61	172.04
保 山	Baoshan	1 086.37	26.01	781.73	70.04	1 050.86	123.21
昭 通	Zhaotong	1 874.05	101.57	1 047.37	95.26	1 305.44	250.29
丽 江	Lijiang	805.75	37.38	494.16	34.14	589.89	24.83
普 洱	Pu'er	1 012.93	84.89	637.96	69.00	973.68	122.76
临 沧	Lincang	798.15	106.48	482.35	65.79	629.85	60.93
楚 雄	Chuxiong	1 343.85	75.21	829.65	80.71	1 039.32	115.49
红 河	Honghe	2 264.26	117.61	1 485.71	140.55	1 634.93	140.04
文 山	Wenshan	1 158.89	77.00	752.86	71.98	1 073.96	126.36
西双版纳	Xishuangbanna	750.22	61.52	465.41	36.60	529.35	69.46
大 理	Dali	1 946.83	166.78	1 208.65	133.62	1 698.77	217.65
德 宏	Dehong	715.36	56.87	483.79	52.61	549.59	58.07
怒 江	Nujiang	270.44	5.23	119.08	10.45	214.85	36.14
迪 庆	Diqing	375.69	16.46	147.81	14.48	314.95	40.59

11-3 金融机构人民币信贷情况（2020年）

Credit Funds of RMB Operation Condition of Financial Institution (2020)

单位：亿元 (100 million yuan)

项　目	Item	全　省 Yunnan	比年初增长（%） Increase Rate over year Beginning (%)
各项存款余额	**Deposits in Various Forms**	**35 474.99**	**8.2**
#非金融企业存款	Deposits of non-financial Enterprises	8 661.13	7.2
活期存款	Savings Deposits	4 774.25	2.6
定期及其他存款	Time and other Deposits	3 886.89	13.4
住户存款	Household deposits	17 675.38	11.3
活期存款	Savings Deposits	8 083.75	8.5
定期及其他存款	Time and other Deposits	9 591.63	13.7
财政性存款	Financial Deposits	988.10	9.1
机关团体存款	Temporary Deposits	7 315.09	-0.3
各项贷款余额	**Loans in Various Forms**	**34 651.14**	**11.3**
#短期贷款	Short-term Loans	6 573.80	9.3
中长期贷款	Medium & Long-term Loans	25 017.45	12.6

11−4 全省保险费收入和赔款给付（1999−2020年）

Premium Income and Expenditure for Claim and Payment (1999-2020)

单位：亿元 (100 million yuan)

年份 Year	保险费收入 Premium Income	赔款及给付支出 Expenditure for Claim and Payment	简单赔付率(%) Rate of Simple Claim and Payment (%)
1999	37.46	14.03	37.5
2000	39.72	16.71	42.1
2001	42.70	18.97	44.4
2002	55.44	19.18	34.6
2003	73.75	20.35	27.6
2004	74.22	25.91	34.9
2005	81.03	24.01	29.6
2006	95.29	28.90	30.3
2007	111.86	47.75	42.7
2008	165.39	63.40	38.3
2009	180.08	65.12	36.2
2010	235.68	66.31	28.1
2011	241.10	79.89	33.1
2012	271.30	100.11	36.9
2013	320.77	122.06	38.1
2014	375.99	150.88	40.1
2015	434.60	173.23	39.9
2016	529.37	206.10	38.9
2017	613.28	218.05	35.6
2018	667.99	248.60	37.2
2019	742.10	260.65	35.1
2020	756.45	277.68	36.7

11-5 保险业务经济技术指标（2020年）

Economic and Technical Indicators of Insurance Companies (2020)

单位：亿元 (100 million yuan)

项　目	Item	保险金额 Premium	原保险保费收入 Original Insurance Premium Income	各项赔款和给付 Claim and Payment
全　省	**Yunnan**	**999 573.32**	**756.45**	**277.68**
财产保险公司	**Property Insurance Companies**	**844 730.74**	**342.21**	**182.87**
企业财产保险	Enterprise Property Insurance	15 438.25	6.90	2.77
家庭财产保险	Family Property Insurance	4 375.00	1.45	0.74
机动车辆保险	Motor Vehicle Insurance	89 628.18	234.63	114.32
工程保险	Engineering Insurance	2 402.88	4.67	2.24
责任保险	Liability Insurance	316 705.47	14.02	7.68
信用保险	Export Credit Insurance	296.16	0.75	0.36
保证保险	Guarantee Insurance	348.71	13.55	10.62
船舶保险	Ship Insurance	8.03	0.04	0.01
货物运输保险	Freight Transport	6 572.88	1.09	0.48
特殊风险保险	Special Risk Insurance	1 177.70	0.39	0.16
农业保险	Agricultural Insurance	1 533.41	17.67	14.32
健康险	Health Insurance	144 859.06	30.82	23.48
意外伤害保险	Accident Injury Insurance	218 870.49	15.57	5.57
其他险	Other Insurance	42 514.53	0.67	0.12
人身保险公司	**Life Insurance Companies**	**154 842.57**	**414.24**	**94.81**
人寿保险	Life Insurance	6 084.05	285.55	49.59
健康保险	Health Insurance	113 897.06	117.93	42.28
意外伤害保险	Personal Accident Injury Insurance	34 861.46	10.76	2.93

11-6 云南省辖区证券市场基本情况（2015-2020年）

Basic Statistics on Securities Markets of Yunnan Province (2015-2020)

项　　目	Item	2015	2016	2017	2018	2019	2020
上市公司数（家）	**Number of Listed Companies (unit)**	**30**	**32**	**34**	**33**	**36**	**37**
发行A股公司数	A Shares	30	32	34	33	36	37
发行B股公司数	B Shares						
A、B股均发行公司数	A Shares and B Shares						
境外发行公司数	Overseas-listed Companies	1					
境内、外均发行公司数	Companies of Overseas-listed and Domestic	1					
ST公司数	ST Listed Companies	3	3	3	2	2	3
证券公司数（家）	**Number of Securities Companies(unit)**	**2**	**2**	**2**	**2**	**2**	**2**
证券营业部数（家）	**Number of Securities Business Department (unit)**	**148**	**174**	**189**	**187**	**183**	**183**
证券投资咨询机构数（家）	**Number of Securities Investment Consultative Institutions (unit)**	**1**	**1**	**1**	**1**	**1**	**1**
证券投资者资金开户数(累计数)(万户)	**Number Of Opening Account of Securities Investors (Cumulative Number) (10 000 households)**	**160.75**	**186.60**	**210.75**	**234.63**	**262.43**	**290.99**
上市公司当年境内募集资金总额(扣除发行费)(亿元)	**Total Volume of Domestic Raise Capital by Listed Companies in current year (after deducting issuance fee)(100 million yuan)**	**242.15**	**279.78**	**238.98**	**393.49**	**644.27**	**169.20**
首次公开发行	IPO	3.55	10.23	42.21		26.15	8.75
配股	Share Right Issued		42.98			10.22	
增发	Adding the Share Issue	107.00	117.57	131.77	66.59	565.27	96.02
可转债及公司债	Transferable Loans	131.60	109.00	65.00	326.90	323.80	64.43
市价总值（亿元）	**Total Market Value (100 million yuan)**	**3 881.62**	**3 928.65**	**5 125.98**	**3 554.55**	**5 743.70**	**7 544.26**
证券经营机构证券累计成交量(亿元)	**Trading Volume of Securities Managerial (100 million yuan)**	**42 636.40**	**22 911.42**	**26 403.60**	**20 563.09**	**27 555.35**	**35 336.37**

注：证券分支机构包括证券分公司和证券营业部。
Note: The securities branch includes branch companies and securities business departments.

主要统计指标解释

存款 指企业、机关、团体或居民根据资金必须收回的原则，把货币资金存入银行或其他信贷机构保管并取得一定利息的一种信用活动形式。根据存款对象或性质的不同可划分为住户存款、非金融企业存款、政府存款、非银行业金融机构存。它是银行信贷资金的主要来源。

贷款 指银行或其他信贷机构根据资金必须归还的原则，按一定利率，为企业、个人等提供资金的一种信用活动形式。我国银行贷款分为短期贷款、中长期贷款、融资租赁、票据融资、各项垫款、境外贷款等。

保险金额 指保险人承担赔偿或者给付保险金责任的最高限额。

保费 指投保人为取得保险人在约定范围内所承担赔偿责任而支付给保险人的费用。

赔款 指保险人根据保险公司合同的规定，向被保险人支付的赔偿保险责任损失的金额。

Explanatory Notes on Principle Statistical Indicators

Deposit is a form of credit by which enterprises, institutions, organizations or households can put money into banks and other credit institutions for safekeeping and interest earning under the principle of free withdrawal. It can be divided into household deposits, non-financial corporate deposits, government deposits and non-banking financial institutions deposits according to the different objects or nature of deposits. Deposits are major sources of the credit funds of banks.

Loan is a form of credit by which banks and other credit institutions provide funds at certain interest rate to enterprises and individuals in the light of the principle of unconditional repayment. Loans from Chinese banks include short-term loan, medium-term and long-term loans, financial lease, bill financing, various money advanced, foreign loans.

Amount Insured refers to the maximum amount that the insurant will get for the claim of the case insured.

Premium is the fee paid by the insurant to the insurer to obtain the obligation of compensation from the insurance within the agreed terms.

Settled Claim is the compensation paid by the insurer to the insurant in accordance with the insurance contract.

Chapter 12

十二、旅游业
Tourism

12—1 全省旅游业发展情况（2015—2020年）

Basic Statistics on Tourism Development (2015-2020)

项 目	Item	2015	2016	2017	2018	2019	2020
游客总人数(万人次)	**Number of Tourists (10 000 person-times)**	**32 914.03**	**43 119.71**	**57 339.81**	**68 847.80**	**80 716.79**	**52 944.72**
国内游客（万人次）	**Domestic Tourists (10 000 person-times)**	**32 343.95**	**42 519.33**	**56 672.12**	**68 141.72**	**79 977.77**	**52 887.07**
过夜游客	Overnight Tourists	17 430.55	20 584.47	28 286.16	31 670.11	35 185.17	21 597.98
一日游游客	One-day Tourists	14 913.40	21 934.85	28 385.95	36 471.61	44 792.60	31 289.09
入境过夜游客（万人次）	**Overseas Tourists (10 000 person-times)**	**570.08**	**600.38**	**667.69**	**706.08**	**739.02**	**57.65**
外国人	Foreigners	420.00	450.69	507.52	549.94	586.50	51.36
港澳台同胞	Compatriots from Hong Kong,Macao and Taiwan	150.08	149.69	160.17	156.14	152.52	6.29
入境游客(万人次)	**Number of Overseas Visitor Arrivals (10 000 person-times)**	**1 075.32**	**1 199.42**	**1 364.66**	**1 416.46**	**1 484.93**	**148.69**
旅游总收入（亿元）	**Total Tourism Revenue (100 million yuan)**	**3 281.79**	**4 726.25**	**6 922.23**	**8 991.44**	**11 035.20**	**6 477.03**
国内旅游收入（亿元）	Domestic Tourism Revenue (100 million yuan)	3 104.37	4 536.54	6 682.58	8 698.97	10 679.51	6 449.21
过夜游客收入	Revenue from Overnight Tourists	2 494.77	3 521.79	5 171.55	6 597.76	7 889.83	4 609.46
一日游收入	Revenue from One-day Tourists	609.60	1 014.75	1 511.03	2 101.21	2 789.69	1 839.74
国际旅游收入(亿美元)	Foreign Exchange Earning from International tourism（100 million USD）	28.76	30.75	35.50	44.18	51.47	4.03
折合人民币（亿元）	Equivalent Amount Converted into RMB (100 million yuan)	177.42	189.71	239.65	292.47	355.68	27.82

注：本表入境游客含口岸入境一日游游客。

Note: In this table, data of entry tourists include the port entry day tourists.

12-2 边境口岸入境一日游游客数及外汇收入（2020年）
Number of One-day Entry Tourists and Earnings in Foreign Exchange in Border Areas (2020)

拥有边境口岸州市	Region with Border Port	口岸入境一日游人数（万人次）Number of One-day Entry Tourists (10 000 person-times)	2020年比2019年增长(%) Increase Rate over 2019 (%)	口岸入境一日游外汇收入(万美元) Earnings in Foreign Exchange from One-day Entry Tourists (USD 10 thousand)	2020年比2019年增长(%) Increase Rate over 2019 (%)
保　山	Baoshan	0.61	-94.1	49.95	-94.11
普　洱	Pu'er	2.29	-89.1	186.75	-89.06
临　沧	Lincang	8.41	-82.2	685.02	-82.20
红　河	Honghe	11.29	-93.7	918.78	-93.69
文　山	Wenshan	8.38	-91.5	682.23	-91.53
西双版纳	Xishuangbanna	5.21	-93.3	424.15	-93.33
德　宏	Dehong	53.82	-82.1	4 381.28	-82.10
怒　江	Nujiang	1.03	-90.5	83.76	-90.54

12-3 各州市旅游业发展情况（2020年）

Tourism Development by Region (2020)

州 市 Region		旅游总收入 (亿元) Total Tourism Revenue (100 million yuan)	旅游外汇收入 (亿美元) Foreign Exchange Earnings (USD 100 million)	国内旅游人数 (万人次) Domestic Tourists (10 000 person-times)	海外旅游者 (万人次) Overseas Tourists (10 000 person-times)
全 省	**Yunnan**	**6 477.03**	**4.03**	**52 887.07**	**57.65**
昆 明	Kunming	1 900.57	0.59	13 631.43	9.91
曲 靖	Qujing	367.68	0.03	3 249.46	0.44
玉 溪	Yuxi	266.21	0.00	3 213.84	0.08
保 山	Baoshan	267.03	0.05	2 609.55	1.15
昭 通	Zhaotong	205.48	0.00	2 718.93	0.00
丽 江	Lijiang	510.41	0.33	2 620.10	5.01
普 洱	Pu'er	211.91	0.08	2 059.31	1.23
临 沧	Lincang	185.31	0.30	1 869.81	3.93
楚 雄	Chuxiong	459.53	0.06	4 681.60	0.78
红 河	Honghe	465.69	0.17	4 234.13	0.70
文 山	Wenshan	366.93	0.10	3 608.51	1.16
西双版纳	Xishuangbanna	369.97	0.24	1 977.97	2.28
大 理	Dali	604.60	0.31	3 916.80	4.42
德 宏	Dehong	189.80	1.57	1 400.80	23.62
怒 江	Nujiang	25.09	0.02	246.51	0.20
迪 庆	Diqing	80.80	0.15	848.32	2.73

注：本表旅游外汇收入包括口岸一日游创汇收入。

Note: In this table, the data of foreign exchange earning is included part of Revenue from one-day tourists in port .

12-4 按国别分外国入境游客及港澳台游客（2015-2020年）
Number of Overseas Visitor Arrivals by Country and Visitor Arrivals from Hong Kong and Macao (2015-2020)

单位：万人次　　(10 000 person-times)

国家或地区	Country and Territory	2015	2016	2017	2018	2019	2020
海外和港澳台	**Tourists from Overseas and Hong Kong, Macao & Taiwan**	**570.08**	**600.38**	**667.69**	**706.08**	**739.02**	**57.65**
外国旅游者	**Foreigners**	**420.00**	**450.69**	**507.52**	**549.94**	**586.50**	**51.36**
亚洲	**Asia**	**292.84**	**325.07**	**371.92**	**427.69**	**466.98**	**45.33**
日本	Japan	12.56	13.61	11.31	17.28	16.43	1.09
新加坡	Singapore	25.18	26.57	28.02	27.91	18.73	0.62
泰国	Thailand	50.34	52.40	59.33	55.65	55.47	2.26
马来西亚	Malaysia	25.76	24.20	22.85	21.16	24.60	1.44
蒙古	Mongolia	0.66	0.29	0.60	3.76	5.05	0.09
印度	India	5.72	5.29	5.63	6.21	6.07	0.26
其他	Others	172.62	202.71	244.17	295.72	298.22	39.58
美洲	**America**	**27.82**	**32.14**	**32.62**	**34.35**	**34.37**	**1.80**
美国	United States	18.86	22.20	22.15	23.33	21.38	1.26
加拿大	Canada	6.56	7.57	7.68	7.35	8.78	0.36
其他	Others	2.40	2.37	2.79	3.67	4.22	0.18
欧洲	**Europe**	**83.09**	**76.36**	**83.95**	**67.36**	**65.97**	**3.28**
英国	United Kingdom	12.54	13.05	15.76	13.02	12.61	0.65
德国	Germany	12.45	12.03	12.52	10.56	8.75	0.52
法国	France	15.09	14.84	15.76	13.46	13.04	0.71
意大利	Italy	9.11	9.04	9.90	7.95	7.47	0.22
瑞士	Switzerland	9.27	8.46	7.54	4.26	5.02	0.16
瑞典	Sweden	5.73	5.14	5.13	3.66	3.79	0.15
西班牙	Spain	3.56	3.39	3.26	2.58	3.28	0.17
俄罗斯	Russia	3.74	3.24	4.31	4.37	5.44	0.21
其他	Others	11.60	7.17	9.77	7.50	6.56	0.50
大洋洲	**Oceanic**	**11.17**	**11.86**	**12.75**	**14.14**	**13.48**	**0.61**
澳大利亚	Australia	8.52	8.99	9.27	10.28	8.54	0.39
新西兰	New Zealand	2.05	2.23	2.67	2.76	3.14	0.15
其他	Others	0.59	0.64	0.81	1.10	1.80	0.08
非洲	**Africa**	**0.64**	**0.68**	**0.90**	**1.17**	**1.03**	**0.08**
其他国家	**Others**	**4.45**	**4.59**	**5.38**	**5.22**	**4.68**	**0.25**
港澳台同胞	**Compatriots from Hong Kong, Macao and Taiwan**	**150.08**	**149.69**	**160.17**	**156.64**	**152.52**	**6.29**

主要统计指标解释

入境游客 指报告期内来中国（大陆）观光、度假、探亲访友、就医疗养、购物、参加会议或从事经济、文化、体育、宗教活动的外国人、港澳台同胞等游客（即入境旅游人数）。入境旅游人数包括入境过夜游客和入境一日游游客。

出境人数（出境游客） 指中国（大陆）居民因公或因私出境前往其他国家、中国香港特别行政区、澳门特别行政区和台湾省观光、度假、探亲访友、就医疗养、购物、参加会议或从事经济、文化、体育、宗教活动的人数（即出境游客）。

国内游客 指报告期内在中国（大陆）观光游览、度假、探亲访友、就医疗养、购物、参加会议或从事经济、文化、体育、宗教活动的中国（大陆）居民人数，其出游的目的不是通过所从事的活动谋取报酬。

国际旅游（外汇）收入 指入境游客在中国（大陆）境内旅行、游览过程中用于交通、参观游览、住宿、餐饮、购物、娱乐等全部花费。

国内旅游收入 指国内游客在国内旅行、游览过程中用于交通、参观游览、住宿、餐饮、购物、娱乐等全部花费。

Explanatory Notes on Main Statistical Indicators

Overseas Visitor Arrivals refer to the number of tourists of foreigners, Chinese compatriots from Hong Kong, Macao and Taiwan who come to China (mainland) within the reference period for sight-seeing, vacation, visiting relatives, medical treatment, shopping, attending conference, or to engage in economic, cultural, sports and religious activities (namely the number of overseas visitor arrivals). The number of overseas visitor arrivals includes inbound overnight tourists and one-day tourists.

Number of Chinese Residents Going Abroad (Chinese Outbound Visitors) refers to the number of Chinese (mainland) residents going to other countries, Hong Kong Special Administrative region, Macao Special Administrative region and Taiwan for on official or private purposes, for sight-seeing, vacation, visiting relatives, medical treatment, shopping, attending conference, or to engage in economic, cultural, sports and religious activities (namely the Chinese outbound visitors).

Number of Domestic Tourists refers to the number of Chinese (mainland) residents who travel within China (mainland) for sight-seeing, vacation, visiting relatives, medical treatment, shopping, attending conference, or to engage in economic, cultural, sports and religious activities.

Foreign Exchange Earnings from International Tourism refer to the total expenditure of foreigners, overseas Chinese, Chinese compatriots from Hong Kong, Macao and Taiwan during their stay in the mainland of China on transportation, sighting, accommodation, food, shopping and entertainment.

Income from Domestic Tourism refer to expenditure of domestic tourists on transportation, sighting, accommodation, food, shopping and entertainment while they travel.

Chapter 13

十三、教育、科技和文化
Education,Science,Technology and Culture

13-1 主要年份各级各类教育学校数
Number of Schools by Level and Type in Significant Years

单位：所 (unit)

年份 Year	普通高等教育学校 Regular Institutions of Higher Education	中等教育学校 Secondary Schools					普通小学 Primary Schools	幼儿园 Kindergartens
		普通中等教育专业学校 Regular Secondary Specialized Schools	普通教育中学 Regular Secondary Schools	高中 Senior Secondary Schools	初中 Junior Secondary Schools	职业教育中学 Vocational Secondary Schools		
1978	15	70	1 476	841	635		66 672	371
1980	18	100	1 435	610	825	59	59 499	591
1985	26	111	1 765	528	1 237	179	58 484	1 981
1986	26	118	1 825	520	1 305	185	57 786	1 728
1987	26	127	1 885	518	1 367	197	57 055	1 798
1988	26	130	1 946	518	1 431	208	55 154	1 760
1989	26	138	1 994	506	1 488	215	54 145	1 522
1990	26	138	2 030	503	1 527	228	53 556	1 434
1991	26	139	2 068	497	1 571	216	30 231	1 097
1992	26	142	2 120	496	1 624	228	28 124	1 054
1993	26	142	2 178	789	1 699	234	26 376	1 093
1994	26	142	2 182	469	1 723	231	25 007	1 323
1995	26	143	2 225	455	1 770	233	24 612	1 340
1996	26	144	2 242	442	1 800	217	24 078	1 501
1997	26	146	2 240	431	1 809	217	23 724	1 412
1998	26	142	2 245	419	1 826	211	23 249	1 500
1999	24	136	2 225	407	1 818	209	22 705	1 568
2000	24	127	2 236	418	1 818	199	22 151	1 770
2001	28	121	2 276	419	1 857	209	21 315	1 530
2002	31	121	2 267	411	1 856	193	20 595	1 711
2003	34	113	2 275	421	1 854	181	20 296	1 862
2004	43	99	2 280	429	1 851	177	19 725	2 103
2005	44	96	2 257	443	1 814	172	18 747	2 247
2006	50	93	2 266	452	1 814	168	18 127	2 495
2007	51	93	2 281	465	1 816	182	17 163	2 760
2008	59	94	2 272	460	1 812	182	16 573	3 085
2009	61	94	2 248	457	1 791	191	15 826	3 381
2010	61	91	2 183	451	1 732	198	14 059	3 790
2011	64	89	2 144	444	1 700	193	13 320	4 257
2012	66	87	2 124	444	1 680	192	13 020	4 768
2013	67	82	2 114	440	1 674	188	12 845	5 326
2014	67	83	2 113	446	1 667	175	12 608	6 129
2015	69	81	2 144	465	1 679	171	12 413	6 540
2016	72	81	2 150	480	1 670	166	11 673	7 310
2017	77	82	2 175	509	1 666	165	11 186	8 286
2018	79	86	2 196	519	1 677	162	10 900	10 156
2019	81	87	2 234	547	1 687	162	10 789	12 085
2020	82	88	2 290	601	1 689	163	10 688	13 385

13-2 各级各类学校专任教师数（1978-2020年）
Number of Full-time Teachers by Level and Type of School （1978-2020）

单位：万人 (10 000 persons)

年份 Year	普通高等教育学校 Regular Institutions of Higher Education	中等教育学校 Secondary Schools					普通小学 Primary Schools	幼儿园 Kindergartens
		普通中等教育专业学校 Regular Secondary Specialized Schools	普通教育中学 Regular Secondary Schools	高中 Senior Secondary Schools	初中 Junior Secondary Schools	职业教育中学 Vocational Secondary Schools		
1978	0.37	0.22	5.90	1.16	4.74	0.02	16.41	0.25
1979	0.44		5.35				16.54	
1980	0.44	0.33	5.27	0.89	4.37	0.03	17.54	0.35
1981	0.45		4.83				17.96	
1982	0.50		4.77				17.62	
1983	0.53		4.82				17.75	
1984	0.56		4.86				17.15	
1985	0.64	0.46	5.21	1.07	4.14	0.19	17.16	0.81
1986	0.75	0.52	5.45	1.11	4.33	0.22	17.22	0.94
1987	0.78	0.60	5.86	1.16	4.70	0.25	17.23	0.94
1988	0.80	0.65	6.23	1.19	5.04	0.29	17.26	1.01
1989	0.80	0.69	6.58	1.21	5.37	0.34	17.40	1.09
1990	0.78	0.71	6.92	1.23	5.69	0.37	17.42	1.20
1991	0.76	0.71	7.25	1.27	5.98	0.44	17.44	1.24
1992	0.75	0.74	7.52	1.28	6.24	0.46	17.53	1.40
1993	0.72		7.66				17.59	
1994	0.73		7.85				17.84	
1995	0.74	0.79	8.02	1.27	6.75	0.55	18.14	1.63
1996	0.75	0.82	8.38	1.30	7.09	0.57	18.43	1.73
1997	0.77	0.84	8.81	1.31	7.51	0.60	18.91	1.89
1998	0.81	0.84	9.27	1.30	7.97	0.63	19.39	1.83
1999	0.83	0.83	9.89	1.35	8.54	0.69	20.11	1.86
2000	0.92	0.78	10.56	1.46	9.10	0.71	21.05	1.96
2001	1.00	0.77	10.97	1.60	9.37	0.71	21.77	1.31
2002	1.12	0.76	11.49	1.84	9.65	0.72	22.29	1.45
2003	1.22	0.73	12.02	2.15	9.87	0.72	22.16	1.53
2004	1.52	0.61	12.47	2.51	9.96	0.72	21.90	1.70
2005	1.68	0.63	13.17	2.98	9.96	0.75	21.92	1.80
2006	1.94	0.61	13.85	3.40	10.44	0.80	22.20	1.96
2007	2.12	0.63	14.31	3.68	10.63	0.89	22.27	2.13
2008	2.33	0.71	14.86	3.83	11.03	0.91	22.68	2.32
2009	2.49	0.74	15.52	3.97	11.55	0.96	23.38	2.53
2010	2.65	0.73	16.10	4.12	11.98	1.02	23.75	2.92
2011	2.95	0.76	16.21	4.29	11.92	1.05	23.48	3.27
2012	3.13	0.75	16.59	4.52	12.07	1.07	23.37	3.56
2013	3.44	0.76	16.91	4.73	12.18	1.07	23.02	4.01
2014	3.54	0.78	17.20	4.95	12.25	1.06	22.59	4.47
2015	3.69	0.76	17.53	5.15	12.38	1.08	22.48	4.90
2016	3.89	0.76	18.04	5.39	12.65	1.08	22.70	5.37
2017	3.93	0.78	18.56	5.66	12.90	1.08	22.73	5.89
2018	4.01	0.82	19.14	5.91	13.23	1.05	22.84	6.56
2019	4.15	0.76	19.63	6.25	13.38	1.04	23.08	7.29
2020	5.81	0.95	24.20	11.20	13.00	1.21	23.57	13.50

13-3 各级各类学校招生数（1978−2020年）
Number of New Students Enrollment by Level and Type of School (1978-2020)

单位：万人 (10 000 persons)

年份 Year	普通高等教育学校 Regular Institutions of Higher Education	中等教育学校 Secondary Schools: 普通中等教育专业学校 Regular Specialized Secondary Schools	普通教育中学 Regular Secondary Schools	高中 Senior Secondary Schools	初中 Junior Secondary Schools	职业教育中学 Vocational Secondary Schools	普通小学 Primary Schools
1978	0.71	1.28	51.55	10.42	41.13		109.34
1980	0.50	1.48	34.97	6.27	28.70	0.35	111.97
1985	1.26	1.97	36.58	6.32	30.26	1.95	103.58
1986	1.22	2.22	38.34	6.02	32.32	2.02	89.49
1987	1.32	2.45	39.22	5.91	33.31	2.21	79.96
1988	1.45	2.51	41.02	6.27	33.75	3.04	78.84
1989	1.27	2.29	41.49	6.05	35.44	2.97	78.46
1990	1.30	2.29	44.40	6.51	37.89	3.28	79.99
1991	1.34	2.36	45.15	6.46	38.69	5.80	81.75
1992	1.56	2.67	45.65	6.40	39.25	6.61	85.43
1993	1.64	3.04	44.50	6.00	38.50	7.07	84.32
1994	1.58	3.30	45.21	6.25	38.96	6.68	86.78
1995	1.65	3.51	47.66	6.54	41.12	6.56	87.93
1996	1.72	3.70	48.77	5.84	42.93	6.13	87.52
1997	1.83	3.96	52.52	6.25	46.27	6.31	85.27
1998	2.04	3.94	56.30	6.56	49.74	7.31	75.80
1999	2.75	3.65	62.94	7.43	55.51	7.77	70.99
2000	3.20	3.76	69.84	8.82	61.02	6.42	70.20
2001	4.25	4.67	72.20	10.67	61.54	6.20	72.36
2002	5.04	4.81	77.74	12.44	65.30	6.17	73.71
2003	6.22	4.54	81.59	13.84	67.75	5.35	73.11
2004	6.67	5.17	80.13	16.73	63.40	5.00	73.25
2005	7.45	5.97	82.31	19.00	63.31	5.80	73.34
2006	9.07	6.60	86.04	20.47	65.57	6.67	76.03
2007	9.92	6.92	88.59	20.33	68.26	8.73	75.46
2008	11.71	8.34	91.51	21.20	70.31	8.44	72.91
2009	13.24	9.79	91.74	22.03	69.70	10.71	69.50
2010	14.25	13.57	93.56	22.90	70.66	14.32	66.93
2011	16.13	10.18	93.00	24.38	68.62	8.23	65.38
2012	14.63	10.96	93.53	26.13	67.40	7.23	62.29
2013	16.83	10.95	94.90	26.74	68.16	6.86	61.35
2014	17.59	11.13	93.94	26.81	67.13	6.30	60.93
2015	18.98	11.25	92.74	27.45	65.29	6.25	63.41
2016	20.17	11.51	92.43	28.82	63.61	6.83	64.46
2017	23.28	11.92	93.18	29.79	63.39	6.75	63.48
2018	25.58	11.60	91.50	30.25	61.25	6.73	66.44
2019	30.55	10.47	93.78	33.05	60.73	6.26	66.97
2020	34.57	9.99	96.40	36.00	60.40	5.80	64.91

13-4 各级各类学校在校学生数（1978-2020年）
Number of Students Enrolled by Level and Type of School （1978-2020）

单位：万人 (10 000 persons)

年份 Year	普通高等教育学校 Regular Institutions of Higher Education	中等教育学校 Secondary Schools: 普通中等教育专业学校 Regular Specialized Secondary Schools	普通教育中学 Regular Secondary Schools	高中 Senior Secondary Schools	初中 Junior Secondary Schools	职业教育中学 Vocational Secondary Schools	普通小学 Primary Schools	幼儿园 Kindergartens
1978	1.59	2.66	128.54	23.78	104.76	0.39	436.03	4.08
1979	1.86		108.47				427.32	
1980	1.81	4.02	96.86	14.67	82.20	0.54	424.39	10.32
1981	2.17		86.56				424.86	
1982	1.93		86.82				435.72	
1983	2.09		85.90				457.89	
1984	2.49		93.91				497.55	
1985	3.23	5.01	101.99	17.49	84.50	4.07	514.66	19.68
1986	3.77	5.58	110.52	18.22	92.30	4.84	512.13	20.35
1987	4.10	6.15	117.35	18.20	99.15	5.03	499.38	22.91
1988	4.50	6.79	119.38	18.13	101.25	6.04	480.40	23.32
1989	4.51	7.18	119.53	17.69	101.84	6.48	457.42	25.86
1990	4.35	7.38	123.95	18.06	105.89	6.82	446.86	30.06
1991	4.31	7.36	128.84	18.41	110.44	9.43	442.57	34.20
1992	4.54	7.75	131.66	18.66	113.01	10.26	445.43	40.26
1993								
1994								
1995	5.14	10.26	127.25	17.78	109.47	12.54	462.41	51.74
1996	5.40	10.97	133.43	17.61	115.82	9.78	473.12	53.35
1997	5.74	11.68	142.31	17.76	124.55	11.38	483.71	53.72
1998	6.24	12.24	152.15	17.84	134.31	12.51	485.45	54.37
1999	7.39	11.95	167.44	19.42	148.02	15.78	480.80	57.75
2000	9.04	11.92	185.97	22.21	163.76	15.85	472.06	60.35
2001	11.90	12.86	200.46	26.50	173.96	15.26	460.50	62.70
2002	14.34	13.89	215.14	31.55	183.58	14.64	450.93	66.85
2003	17.53	14.84	228.46	36.33	192.13	13.14	441.88	70.66
2004	20.06	14.76	235.06	41.98	193.09	13.21	440.65	75.37
2005	23.21	15.56	238.88	48.31	190.58	14.08	441.23	77.27
2006	26.81	17.35	244.70	54.54	190.16	16.21	452.26	82.38
2007	30.21	18.63	251.77	57.64	194.12	19.64	453.31	86.31
2008	34.35	20.53	259.48	59.47	200.01	21.28	451.04	89.57
2009	38.95	23.37	264.97	61.15	203.82	24.10	444.14	92.17
2010	43.69	29.00	270.63	63.28	207.35	28.64	435.21	98.69
2011	48.76	30.15	270.90	66.03	204.87	27.62	424.08	108.59
2012	51.22	31.56	265.95	70.62	195.33	24.96	406.70	112.23
2013	54.86	30.13	261.07	73.74	187.33	18.81	392.08	119.02
2014	57.70	30.84	266.55	76.85	189.70	17.83	382.69	124.58
2015	61.46	30.97	267.60	78.28	189.32	17.35	377.78	129.40
2016	65.66	31.25	267.78	80.58	187.20	17.30	376.61	131.50
2017	70.59	32.12	270.69	83.41	187.28	17.79	375.21	139.43
2018	76.47	31.97	272.64	86.49	186.15	18.24	379.51	143.10
2019	86.40	30.81	275.45	90.91	184.54	17.55	385.10	149.87
2020	96.42	29.53	279.53	97.16	182.37	16.85	389.22	167.27

13-5 各级各类学校毕业生数（1978-2020年）
Number of Graduates by Level and Type of School （1978-2020）

单位：万人 (10 000 persons)

年份 Year	普通高等教育学校 Regular Institutions of Higher Education	中等教育学校 Secondary Schools 普通中等教育专业学校 Regular Specialized Secondary Schools	普通教育中学 Regular Secondary Schools	高中 Senior Secondary Schools	初中 Junior Secondary Schools	职业教育中学 Vocational Secondary Schools	普通小学 Primary Schools
1978	0.33	0.99	44.60	9.19	35.41	0.11	56.76
1980	0.53	1.59	27.90	8.12	19.78	0.09	48.27
1985	0.54	1.23	24.32	4.63	19.69	0.58	51.90
1986	0.67	1.65	26.35	5.00	21.35	0.95	57.34
1987	0.98	1.92	28.83	5.58	23.25	1.55	60.99
1988	1.05	1.87	32.72	5.92	26.80	1.67	61.22
1989	1.27	1.88	33.96	5.81	28.15	2.12	62.58
1990	1.45	2.07	33.99	5.57	28.42	2.63	64.59
1991	1.32	2.34	33.32	5.56	27.77	2.21	61.95
1992	1.33	2.27	34.76	5.47	29.29	2.07	59.60
1993							
1994							
1995	1.63	2.63	35.71	5.55	30.16	2.83	56.03
1996	1.45	2.96	34.03	5.25	28.78	2.90	57.98
1997	1.49	3.20	37.03	5.48	31.55	2.97	61.25
1998	1.53	3.30	40.17	5.82	34.35	3.17	61.80
1999	1.58	3.50	42.80	5.15	37.65	3.50	65.61
2000	1.62	3.77	47.54	5.65	41.89	4.61	72.15
2001	1.94	3.69	52.50	5.93	46.56	4.94	76.04
2002	2.56	3.69	58.80	7.11	51.70	4.49	77.52
2003	3.13	3.94	63.94	8.45	55.49	4.30	77.15
2004	3.26	4.87	67.88	9.94	57.94	3.55	72.13
2005	4.49	4.88	73.10	11.60	61.50	4.07	69.32
2006	5.58	4.34	76.29	12.77	63.52	3.98	68.69
2007	6.61	5.07	76.21	15.33	60.88	4.51	71.46
2008	7.28	5.46	77.91	17.39	60.52	5.13	73.23
2009	8.36	6.31	80.45	18.38	62.08	5.58	73.31
2010	9.34	6.45	82.60	18.44	64.16	6.55	73.69
2011	10.73	6.93	86.00	19.23	66.77	5.97	72.91
2012	11.89	8.24	86.11	19.62	66.49	8.02	72.28
2013	12.79	10.72	83.48	21.00	62.48	10.21	71.38
2014	14.20	8.57	78.89	22.16	56.73	5.84	69.28
2015	14.60	9.24	81.76	24.07	57.69	5.45	67.22
2016	15.24	9.33	84.91	24.90	60.01	5.39	65.11
2017	17.53	9.14	85.75	25.22	60.53	5.19	64.55
2018	18.81	9.13	87.09	25.70	61.39	5.00	61.92
2019	19.65	9.12	89.10	27.24	61.86	5.66	61.06
2020	23.52	9.54	90.88	28.37	62.51	5.35	60.80

13-6 培养研究生数（1985-2020年）
Number of Postgraduates（1985-2020）

单位：万人 (10 000 persons)

年 份 Year	招生数 New Students Enrollment	在校人数 Total Enrollment		毕业生数 Graduates	
		攻读硕士学位 Master's Degree	攻读博士学位 Doctor's Degree	攻读硕士学位 Master's Degree	攻读博士学位 Doctor's Degree
1985	0.04	0.07		0.01	
1986	0.04	0.10		0.01	
1987	0.03	0.10		0.03	
1988	0.02	0.09		0.05	
1989	0.02	0.07		0.04	
1990	0.02	0.05		0.02	
1991	0.01	0.05		0.02	
1992	0.02	0.05		0.01	
1993	0.03	0.06		0.02	
1995	0.03	0.09	0.01	0.02	
1996	0.04	0.10	0.02	0.03	
1997	0.06	0.14	0.02	0.03	
1998	0.06	0.15	0.02	0.04	0.01
1999	0.08	0.18	0.02	0.05	0.01
2000	0.12	0.24	0.03	0.05	
2001	0.18	0.34	0.04	0.06	0.01
2002	0.23	0.48	0.05	0.07	0.01
2003	0.33	0.67	0.07	0.11	0.01
2004	0.45	0.93	0.09	0.16	0.01
2005	0.55	1.22	0.11	0.21	0.02
2006	0.62	1.49	0.13	0.30	0.02
2007	0.65	1.68	0.15	0.40	0.02
2008	0.69	1.84	0.17	0.49	0.03
2009	0.83	2.03	0.19	0.55	0.03
2010	0.93	2.32	0.21	0.57	0.03
2011	0.95	2.58	0.23	0.62	0.04
2012	0.99	2.68	0.24	0.80	0.04
2013	1.04	2.80	0.26	0.85	0.04
2014	1.05	2.88	0.22	0.86	0.04
2015	1.08	2.97	0.23	0.93	0.03
2016	1.12	3.06	0.25	0.96	0.04
2017	1.40	3.39	0.27	0.99	0.04
2018	1.52	3.80	0.31	1.00	0.04
2019	1.67	4.31	0.35	1.04	0.04
2020	2.12	5.06	0.41	1.25	0.04

13-7 各级各类成人学校基本情况（2020年）
Basic Statistics on Adult Schools by Level and Type of School (2020)

单位：所、万人 (unit, 10 000 persons)

项　目	Item	学校数 Schools	毕业生数 Graduates	招生数 New Student Enrollment	在校学生数 Student Enrollment	教职工合计 Faculty	专任教师 Full-time Teachers
成人高等教育	**Adult Education Schools**	**1**	**6.45**	**8.78**	**26.48**	**0.01**	**0.01**
按办学形式	**Grouped by Form of Running a School**		**6.45**	**8.78**	**26.48**		
函　授	Correspondence Schools		4.06	6.15	17.73		
业　余	Sparetime Schools		2.12	2.55	8.42		
脱　产	Full-time Schools		0.28	0.08	0.33		
成人中专	**Secondary Specialized Schools for Adults**	**120**	**0.21**	**10.72**	**13.55**	**0.22**	**0.20**
成人小学	**Primary Schools for Adults**	**802**	**8.06**		**7.17**	**0.14**	**0.08**
小学班	Primary Courses	627	6.66		6.35	0.06	0.02

13-8 各级各类学校师生比（2010-2020年）

Student-teacher Ratio by Level and Type of School (2010-2020)

单位：% (教师数=1) | (%) (Number Of Teacher=1)

年 份	普通高等院校 Regular Institutions of Higher Education	普通中专 Regular Secondary Specialized Schools	成人中专 Specialized Secondary Schools for Adult	普通高中 Regular Senior Secondary Schools	职业高中 Vocational Senior Secondary Schools	普通初中 Regular Junior Secondary Schools	职业初中 Vocational Junior Secondary Schools	小 学 Primary Schools	幼儿园 Kindergartens
2010	20.46	39.62	2.31	20.06	28.35	17.31	20.81	18.32	33.79
2011	19.40	39.70	1.70	15.40	26.20	17.20	37.40	18.60	33.20
2012	21.50	31.92	2.41	15.60	23.10	16.18	10.22	17.95	31.54
2013	18.40	28.46	0.60	15.60	18.10	15.40	10.00	17.00	29.66
2014	18.90	26.44	0.60	15.53	16.61	15.49	10.64	16.94	27.90
2015	19.30	25.90	0.25	15.20	15.60	15.30	13.00	16.80	26.40
2016	19.40	25.11	0.11	14.96	15.28	14.80	22.96	16.59	24.48
2017	20.70	24.01	0.23	14.74	15.84	14.52	1.13	16.51	23.68
2018	21.90	21.09	0.35	14.62	16.92	14.07	0.71	16.62	21.80
2019	23.90	20.77	0.58	14.55	18.62	13.79	—	16.69	20.58
2020	25.14	22.81	0.54	13.31	20.69	13.09		16.40	21.08

注：普通高等学校师生比按教育部新标准测算。

Note: The data in this table are calculated according to the new standards of educational departments.

13-9 主要年份小学学龄儿童入学率

Enrollment Rate of School-age Children in Primary Schools in Significant Years

单位：万人 (10 000 persons)

年 份 Year	学龄儿童人数 School-Age Children	已入学学龄儿童数 School-Age Children Enrolled in Schools	入学率(%) Enrollment Rate (%)		
			总计 Total	男生 Boys	女生 Girls
1980	400.79	349.54	87.20		
1985	421.61	384.14	93.10		
1990	342.40	324.06	94.60		
1995	427.81	416.79	97.40		
1997	452.05	446.64	98.40		
1998	454.13	448.37	98.37		
1999	449.02	444.52	99.00		
2000	438.41	434.10	99.02	99.11	98.90
2001	429.62	426.92	99.37	99.69	99.06
2002	421.63	419.86	99.58	99.56	99.60
2003	412.87	396.92	96.14	96.35	95.89
2004	416.06	400.02	96.15	96.28	96.00
2005	420.31	404.77	96.30	96.42	96.17
2006	427.83	413.17	96.57	96.69	96.44
2007	425.09	414.84	97.59	97.67	97.50
2008	420.32	413.15	98.29	98.30	98.28
2009	415.57	408.45	98.29	98.32	98.25
2010	402.01	400.82	99.71	99.69	99.71
2011	392.23	390.72	99.61	99.63	99.59
2012	370.61	369.03	99.57	99.61	99.53
2013	354.70	352.94	99.50	99.54	99.46
2014	349.56	347.83	99.51	99.54	99.47
2015	345.12	344.01	99.68	99.69	99.66
2016	346.41	345.47	99.73	99.75	99.70
2017	347.69	347.06	99.82	99.83	99.80
2018	352.03	351.55	99.86	99.88	99.85
2019	358.84	358.21	99.83	99.82	99.83
2020	370.65	370.17	99.87	99.87	99.88

13-10 初中、高中、高等教育毛入学率（2000-2020年）
The Gross Enrollment Rate of the Junior Middle School, Senior Secondary Education and Higher Education（2000-2020）

单位：%　　(%)

年 份 Year	初中阶段毛入学率 Gross Enrollment Rate of Junior Middle School			高中阶段毛入学率 Gross Enrollment Rate of Senior Secondary Education	高等教育毛入学率 Gross Enrollment Rate of Higher Education
	总计 Total	男生 Boys	女生 Girls		
2000	82.77	84.37	81.00	24.93	4.91
2001	84.95	86.64	83.09	25.99	6.11
2002	87.50	89.14	85.68	27.30	8.64
2003	90.79	92.00	89.44	28.00	11.00
2004	93.29	94.06	92.43	29.85	11.15
2005	95.35	96.27	94.31	33.66	12.65
2006	98.19	98.81	97.49	39.34	14.00
2007	99.63	100.19	98.99	45.71	14.61
2008	102.21	102.08	102.31	52.00	16.17
2009	103.12	103.00	103.18	58.60	17.57
2010	104.36	104.73	103.95	65.00	20.02
2011	105.24	105.74	104.69	70.00	23.00
2012	106.04	106.11	105.96	71.20	24.30
2013	106.56	106.52	106.60	72.10	25.80
2014	107.81	107.87	107.74	75.30	28.30
2015	106.36	106.44	106.28	80.10	30.20
2016	106.91	106.89	106.93	82.60	32.60
2017	106.89	106.68	107.13	76.05	37.70
2018	107.41	107.39	107.43	78.43	41.73
2019	108.02	107.84	108.22	84.33	46.05
2020	106.68	107.00	106.33	90.98	50.05

13–11 主要年份科学技术奖获奖统计

Statistics on Prizes of Science and Technology awards in Significant Years

单位：项 (unit)

年份 Year	获奖数 Number of Prize-wining	云南省科学技术奖 Science and Technology awards of Yunnan Province				
		杰出贡献奖和科学技术合作奖 Outstanding Contribution Award & Science and Technology Cooperation Award	自然科学奖、技术发明奖和科学技术进步奖			
			特等奖 Special award	一等奖 Grade I	二等奖 Grade II	三等奖 Grade III
2000	249	1		10	41	197
2001	204	2		10	37	155
2002	211	1		16	41	153
2003	239			12	44	183
2004	221			12	42	167
2005	244	2		15	50	177
2006	231	1		12	46	172
2007	228	1		15	45	167
2008	212	1		22	42	147
2009	199	1		18	40	140
2010	180	2	1	17	35	125
2011	193	1	2	19	40	131
2012	195	1	2	18	41	133
2013	181	1	2	12	37	129
2014	180	1	1	12	38	128
2015	180	2	4	20	38	116
2016	198	1	3	20	39	135
2017	196	1	4	20	40	131
2018	193	3	4	20	37	129
2019	154	1	4	20	35	94
2020	175	3	4	20	40	108

注：杰出贡献奖、科学技术合作奖在2009年前分别叫突出贡献奖、国际科学技术合作奖。

Note: Before 2009, the award of Excellent Contribution & Science and Technology Cooperation were named Outstanding Contribution & International Science and Technology Cooperation respectively.

13-12 主要年份自然科学研究机构数（独立科研机构）
Number of Research Institutions of Natural Science in Significant Years (Independent Research Institutions)

单位：个 (unit)

年 份 Year	中国科学院 Chinese Academy of Sciences	国务院各部委直属 Directly under Departments of State Council	省业务局直属 Directly under Provincial Departments	州(市)直属 Directly under Prefecture (municipal) Departments	年 份 Year	中国科学院 Chinese Academy of Sciences	国务院各部委直属 Directly under Departments of State Council	省业务局直属 Directly under Provincial Departments	州(市)直属 Directly under Prefecture (municipal) Departments
1980	5	12	54	83	2007	3	4	21	58
1985	4	15	57	72	2008	3	5	19	59
1990	4	14	55	80	2009	3	5	19	58
1995	4	12	54	79	2010	3	5	18	60
1996	4	12	54	79	2011	3	5	18	61
1997	4	12	54	78	2012	3	5	19	57
1998	4	12	53	77	2013	3	5	19	56
1999	4	12	51	73	2014	3	5	19	60
2000	4	9	55	67	2015	4	3	21	59
2001	4	9	55	65	2016	4	4	20	61
2002	4	9	55	64	2017	4	5	25	60
2003	3	8	55	64	2018	4	5	24	59
2004	3	5	24	62	2019	4	5	24	57
2005	3	4	23	61	2020	4	8	37	56
2006	3	4	22	60					

13-13 主要年份分行业自然科学独立研究机构数
Number of Independent Research Institutions of Natural Science by Sector in Significant Years

单位：个 (unit)

年 份 Year	全 省 Yunnan	农 业 Farming	工 业 Industry	建筑业 Construction	交通运输邮电通信业 Transport, Postal and Telecommunication Services	社会服务业 Social Services	卫生、体育和社会福利业 Health Care, Sports and Social Welfare	科学研究与综合技术服务业 Scientific Research and Polytechnic Services	地质普查及勘探业 Geological Prospecting
1985	149	59	44	2	3		16	24	1
1990	153	79	35	2	3	3	12	17	2
1994	150	77	32	2	3	3	12	19	2
1995	149	76	32	2	3	3	12	19	2
1996	149	61	36	2	3	5	11	28	3
1997	148	57	48	2	3	7	12	16	3
1998	146	57	46	2	3	7	12	16	3
1999	140	56	44	2	3	7	11	14	1
2000	135	67	25	1	3	4	5	29	1
2001	133	67	22	1	3	4	6	29	1
2002	132	70	22	1	3	4	6	25	1
2003	130	70	27	2	2	4	6	19	
2004	94	57	10	1	1	6	7	12	
2005	91	56	9	1	1	5	7	11	1
2006	89	56	8	1	1	5	7	10	1
2007	86	56	7	1	1	5	6	9	1
2008	86	56	7	1	1	4	6	10	1
2009	85	56	7		1	4	6	10	1
2010	86	55	8		1	4	7	10	1
2011	87	56	8		1	4	7	11	
2012	84	55	7		1	4	8	9	
2013	83	53	8		1	4	8	9	
2014	87	53	7	1	1	4	8	13	
2015	87	53	5	1		4	8	16	
2016	89	54	7	1		4	7	16	
2017	94	55	6	1		4	7	21	
2018	92	54	5	1		4	6	22	
2019	90	52	5	1		4	6	22	
2020	101	57	5	1		4	6	28	

注：从1991年起不包括国防科工委系统的机构数。

Note: Units under committee of science, technology and industry for national defense have not been included since 1991.

13-14 主要年份分行业自然科学独立研究机构科技活动人员数
Number of Scientific and Technical Personnel in Independent Research Institutions of Natural Science by Sector in Significant Years

单位：人 (person)

年份 Year	全省 Yunnan	农业 Farming	工业 Industry	建筑业 Construction	交通运输邮电通信业 Transport, Postal and Telecommunication Services	社会服务业 Social Services	卫生、体育和社会福利业 Health Care, Sports and Social Welfare	科学研究与综合技术服务业 Scientific Research and Polytechnic Services	地质普查及勘探业 Geological Prospecting
1985	8 012	1 956	3 522	60	193		845	1 340	96
1990	11 008	2 801	5 006	89	190	98	814	1 890	120
1994	8 875	2 818	2 746	72	187	105	876	1 948	123
1995	8 722	2 821	2 606	67	175	115	875	1 943	120
1996	8 260	2 572	2 523	64	170	331	562	1 895	143
1997	8 135	2 524	2 724	53	172	411	592	1 532	127
1998	7 863	2 305	2 619	62	154	400	623	1 482	128
1999	7 606	2 528	2 306	98	160	409	522	1 443	58
2000	7 160	2 819	1 754	82	152	258	321	1 726	48
2001	7 224	2 978	1 609	82	138	220	406	1 748	43
2002	6 965	3 060	1 574	85	157	201	407	1 433	48
2003	6 573	3 033	1 578	164	116	156	352	1 174	
2004	5 229	3 281	293	50	45	317	413	830	
2005	5 151	3 192	298	50	46	277	413	811	64
2006	5 517	3 497	343	60	35	285	406	826	65
2007	5 467	3 452	373	55	35	292	334	865	61
2008	5 471	3 465	323	55	38	279	333	917	61
2009	5 657	3 476	302		47	283	292	1 196	61
2010	5 774	3 527	309		44	291	312	1 230	61
2011	5 856	3 589	307		45	269	328	1 318	
2012	6 088	3 598	344		40	261	444	1 401	
2013	6 324	3 860	307		44	227	496	1 390	
2014	6 326	3 593	327	14	43	282	498	1 569	
2015	6 967	3 821	205	15		265	565	2 096	
2016	7 266	3 888	350	15		246	580	2 187	
2017	7 622	3 477	375	15		296	606	2 853	
2018	7 488	3 479	320	16		278	430	2 879	
2019	7 457	3 515	411	9		229	431	2 862	
2020	7 554	3 039	478	9		249	302	3 477	

注：从1991年起不包括国防科工委系统的人员数。

Note:Number Of committee of science, technology and industry for national defense have not been included since 1991.

13-15 各州市自然科学机构中从事科技人员数（2020年）
Number of Scientific and Technical Personnel in Natural Science Institutions by Region (2020)

单位：人 (person)

州 市	Region	科技人员数 Scientists and Technicians	高级技术人员 Senior Technicians	中级技术人员 Middle Technicians	其他 Others
全 省	**Yunnan**	**7 554**	**2 899**	**2 405**	**2 250**
昆 明	Kunming	4 275	1 734	1 322	1 219
曲 靖	Qujing	65	38	13	14
玉 溪	Yuxi	48	18	20	10
保 山	Baoshan	244	93	70	81
昭 通	Zhaotong	93	39	27	27
丽 江	Lijiang	118	49	36	33
普 洱	Pu'er	206	66	62	78
临 沧	Lincang	109	45	52	12
楚 雄	Chuxiong	239	76	75	88
红 河	Honghe	529	156	154	219
文 山	Wenshan	195	70	66	59
西双版纳	Xishuangbanna	891	348	314	229
大 理	Dali	252	81	88	83
德 宏	Dehong	233	64	84	85
怒 江	Nujiang	21	7	7	7
迪 庆	Diqing	36	15	15	6

13-16 各州市独立研究与开发机构情况（2019-2020年）
Basic Statistics on Independent Scientific Research and Development Institutions by Region (2019-2020)

单位：个、人 (unit, person)

州 市	Region	2019				2020			
		合 计 Total		自然科学 Natural Science		合 计 Total		自然科学 Natural Science	
		机 构 Institutions	人 员 Employees	机 构 Institutions	人 员 Employees	机 构 Institutions	人 员 Employees	机 构 Institutions	人 员 Employees
全 省	**Yunnan**	**110**	**10 129**	**90**	**9 287**	**121**	**10 371**	**101**	**9 545**
昆 明	Kunming	40	5 982	30	5 277	44	5 807	40	5 572
曲 靖	Qujing	1	54	1	54	2	65	2	65
玉 溪	Yuxi	3	73	1	43	2	59	1	48
保 山	Baoshan	5	255	5	255	4	244	4	244
昭 通	Zhaotong	3	111	2	94	3	110	2	93
丽 江	Lijiang	5	138	4	123	5	137	4	120
普 洱	Pu'er	6	262	5	244	6	259	5	241
临 沧	Lincang	6	120	5	110	6	119	5	109
楚 雄	Chuxiong	6	277	5	249	6	272	5	243
红 河	Honghe	7	566	7	566	7	559	7	559
文 山	Wenshan	4	376	4	376	4	400	4	400
西双版纳	Xishuangbanna	8	1 344	8	1 344	8	1 286	8	1 286
大 理	Dali	3	257	3	257	4	267	4	267
德 宏	Dehong	7	261	6	251	7	252	6	241
怒 江	Nujiang	3	24	2	19	3	26	2	21
迪 庆	Diqing	3	29	2	25	3	40	2	36

13-17 独立研究与开发机构基本情况（2015-2020年）

Basic Statistics on Independent Research and Development Institutions (2015-2020)

单位：个、人 (unit, person)

指 标	Item	2015	2016	2017	2018	2019	2020
机构合计	**Total Institutions**	**108**	**112**	**116**	**113**	**110**	**121**
人员合计	**Total Employees**	**8 986**	**9 808**	**9 978**	**10 078**	**10 129**	**10 371**
自然科学技术领域	Field of Natural Sciences and Technology						
机构数	Number of Institutions	87	89	94	92	90	101
人员数	Number of Employees	8 171	8 950	9 141	9 246	9 287	9 545
#大学本科及以上学历	Bachelor Degree and above	5 385	5 761	5 920	5 944	–	–
社会、人文科学技术领域	Field of Social Sciences and Humanities						
机构数	Number of Institutions	9	11	10	9	9	9
人员数	Number of Employees	506	541	517	516	519	515
#大学本科及以上学历	Bachelor Degree and above	433	460	439	439	–	–
科技情报和文献机构	Scientific-Technological Information and Literature Institutions						
机构数	Number of Institutions	12	12	12	12	11	11
人员数	Number of Employees	309	317	320	316	323	311
#大学本科及以上学历	Bachelor Degree and above	253	266	262	245	–	–

13-18 主要年份专利申请和批准数

Number of Patents Applications Approved and Granted in Significant Years

单位：件 (unit)

年 份 Year	专利申请数（件） Applications for patent	发 明 Invention	实用新型 Utility Models	外观设计 Design	专利批准数（件） Applications Granted	发 明 Invention	实用新型 Utility Models	外观设计 Design
1985	135	66	65	4				
1990	461	77	326	58	362	24	312	26
1993	729	164	485	80	686	35	568	83
1994	883	171	499	213	439	25	367	47
1995	959	195	476	288	569	35	346	188
1996	1 290	266	665	359	602	33	336	233
1997	1 108	163	612	333	692	20	362	310
1998	1 136	163	579	394	832	45	477	310
1999	1 246	198	609	438	1 185	73	695	417
2000	1 710	341	737	632	1 216	139	606	417
2001	1 793	344	807	642	1 347	113	662	572
2002	1 780	448	722	610	1 128	83	522	523
2003	1 976	574	797	605	1 213	172	521	513
2004	1 710	341	737	632	1 216	139	606	471
2005	2 556	776	905	875	1 381	306	563	512
2006	3 085	1 005	1 076	1 004	1 637	355	689	593
2007	3 108	1 014	1 100	994	2 139	368	1 017	754
2008	4 089	1 474	1 389	1 226	2 021	383	1 038	600
2009	4 633	1 637	1 825	1 171	2 923	476	1 338	1 109
2010	5 645	2 333	2 212	1 100	3 823	652	2 026	1 145
2011	7 150	2 796	3 175	1 179	4 199	1 006	2 217	976
2012	9 260	3 324	4 482	1 454	5 853	1 301	3 456	1 096
2013	11 512	3 961	5 705	1 846	6 804	1 312	4 322	1 170
2014	13 343	4 732	6 508	2 103	8 124	1 423	5 438	1 263
2015	17 603	6 301	9 147	2 155	11 658	2 079	7 437	2 142
2016	23 709	7 907	13 549	2 253	12 032	2 125	8 063	1 844
2017	28 695	7 801	17 867	3 027	14 230	2 259	10 085	1 886
2018	36 515	9 606	23 655	3 254	20 340	2 297	15 573	2 470
2019	35 240	9 024	22 765	3 451	22 324	2 174	17 405	2 745
2020	/	/	/	/	28 943	2 458	23 095	3 390

注：国家市场监督管理局暂未公布2020年专利申请相关数据。

Note:The data of patent applications for 2020 has not yet released by The State Administration for Market Regulation.

13−19 文化事业机构数（1978−2020年）

Number of Cultural Institutions （1978-2020）

单位：个 (unit)

年 份 Year	文化艺术事业 Culture and Art		图书出版社 Publishing Houses	博物馆 Museums	公共图书馆 Public Libraries
	表演团体 Art Performance Troupes	艺术表演场馆 Art Performance Places			
1978	149	3	2	4	16
1979	154			3	66
1980	154	26	2	4	80
1981	159			3	84
1982	157	15	4	3	149
1983	157			5	142
1984	158			10	149
1985	154			16	149
1986	147			17	148
1987	147			17	148
1988	141			17	148
1989	137			20	148
1990	137	46	7	20	148
1991	137			21	148
1992	136			22	148
1993	136			22	148
1994	135	44	8	22	148
1995	134	44	8	22	148
1996	133	42	8	23	148
1997	132	40	8	26	148
1998	131	40	8	27	148
1999	130	39	8	27	147
2000	129	40	8	30	148
2001	128	41	8	30	147
2002	124	38	8	30	148
2003	123	39	8	30	149
2004	116	40	8	31	149
2005	135	38	8	32	149
2006	126	33	8	33	149
2007	131	31	8	36	149
2008	127	31	8	36	150
2009	146	34	8	113	150
2010	142	36	8	120	150
2011	161	27	8	84	152
2012	220	60	8	85	152
2013	259	18	8	84	152
2014	284	17	8	86	151
2015	276	40	8	86	151
2016	221	30	8	90	151
2017	316	45	8	125	151
2018	268	27	8	137	151
2019	304	50	8	147	151
2020	99	12	8	161	151

13-19 续表 continued

单位：个 (unit)

年 份 Year	群众文化事业 Mass Culture		广播事业 Broadcasting and Television Stations	
	群众艺术馆及文化馆 Mass Art Centers and Cultural Centers	文 化 站 Cultural Stations	中短波发射台 Medium and Short Wave Transmitting Station	县级以上广播电台 Broadcasting Stations above County Level
1978	145	2	5	3
1980	148	388	5	4
1985	148	1 456	12	5
1990	147	1 477	24	12
1994	147	1 591	15	13
1995	147	1 567	30	14
1996	147	1 582	30	14
1997	147	1 577	44	13
1998	147	1 593	44	13
1999	147	1 580	44	13
2000	147	1 551	44	14
2001	146	1 586	28	14
2002	147	1 576	27	11
2003	148	1 582	17	12
2004	149	1 577	33	14
2005	149	1 535	33	15
2006	148	1 400	33	15
2007	148	1 375	56	15
2008	148	1 376	56	16
2009	148	1 365	56	16
2010	148	1 369	57	16
2011	148	1 371	60	17
2012	148	1 378	60	12
2013	148	1 398	60	6
2014	148	1 410	60	9
2015	148	1 416	61	7
2016	149	1 434	60	7
2017	149	1 444	51	9
2018	149	1 445	52	9
2019	149	1 450	50	/
2020	148	1 434	50	/

注：因机构改革，2019年全省电视台与广播电台基本合并，故无广播电台数据。
Note: There is no data of Broadcasting Stations in 2019, due to institutional reform that TV stations and Broadcasting stations were merged .

13-20 艺术、群众文化发展情况（1978-2020年）
Basic Statistics on Artist and Mass Cultural Development (1978-2020)

年 份 Year	艺术活动 Artist Activities		群众文化活动 Mass Cultural Activities	
	演出场次(万场) Number of Performances (10 000 shows)	国内观众人次(万人次) Number of Domestic Spectators (10 000 person-times)	办展览(万个) Number of Exhibitions (10 000 units)	培训人次(万人次) Number of Training (10 000 person-times)
1978	0.68	975.60	0.06	
1979				
1980	1.61	1 528.80	0.10	1.16
1981	1.50	1 376.40	0.09	1.29
1982	1.68	1 569.50	0.09	1.63
1983	1.74	1 481.60	0.07	2.21
1984	1.22	1 230.20	0.09	6.81
1985	0.91	886.40	0.08	2.02
1986	0.76	638.20	0.12	2.50
1987	0.82	694.40	0.09	2.82
1988	0.84	782.90	0.07	2.75
1989	0.80	840.20	0.23	2.30
1990	0.91	1 064.50	0.25	2.40
1991	0.92	926.60	0.24	2.86
1992	0.40	322.00	0.20	8.24
1993	0.60	773.00	0.23	8.01
1994	1.13	859.60	0.26	8.04
1995	1.45	1 295.40	0.21	7.03
1996				
1997				
1998				
1999	1.02	1 206.60	0.31	19.20
2000	1.01	1 329.20	0.34	17.80
2001	1.10	1 220.90	0.30	16.70
2002	0.89	1 111.30	0.31	20.80
2003	0.90	1 029.80	0.33	21.60
2004	1.03	1 320.00	0.53	21.88
2005	0.82	1 113.70	0.43	22.60
2006	0.89	1 227.70	1.15	23.10
2007	1.50	1 254.70	0.31	43.90
2008	0.96	1 122.60	0.33	47.30
2009	2.37	2 069.60	0.42	58.60
2010	2.10	1 740.70	0.42	63.81
2011	2.04	1 549.80	0.32	85.94
2012	2.66	2 226.98	0.39	128.56
2013	3.82	2 305.28	1.13	263.61
2014	5.28	2 605.57	0.52	146.09
2015	5.75	2 079.85	0.52	135.21
2016	5.52	4 101.46	0.53	144.03
2017	5.60	2 854.58	0.46	141.04
2018	4.98	2 569.95	0.44	123.68
2019	7.57	3 539.40	0.52	142.87
2020	2.49	1 298.97	0.59	152.32

13-21 图书馆、博物馆利用情况（1978-2020年）
Facilities and Services of Libraries and Museums (1978-2020)

年 份 Year	图书馆 Library		博物馆 Museum	
	借阅册次（万册次）Number of Books Borrowed by the Readers (10 000 volume-times)	借阅人次（万人次）Number of Circulation Borrowing People (10 000 person-times)	陈列、展览（个）Number of Displays and Exhibitions (unit)	参观人数（万人次）Number of Visitors (10 000 person-times)
1978	55.20	35.80		
1979				
1980	338.40	288.90	19	4.00
1981	460.60	336.40	19	22.90
1982	607.90	412.10	10	6.30
1983	655.00	620.70	9	6.00
1984	746.50	696.40	16	13.70
1985	539.90	463.00	99	47.30
1986	483.00	466.00	48	33.20
1987	649.50	525.80	60	67.20
1988	683.00	507.00	59	42.10
1989	680.00	499.00	82	45.00
1990	710.00	517.00	85	50.60
1991	519.30	1 131.30	70	48.00
1992	630.50	349.60	68	46.00
1993	560.00	608.50	64	44.70
1994	552.10	510.10	64	38.90
1995	528.50	558.60	112	88.70
1996				
1997				
1998				
1999	742.60	403.00	146	143.70
2000	680.30	383.40	145	106.60
2001	687.70	372.90	156	111.20
2002	641.40	341.50	109	123.40
2003	618.10	342.20	98	58.00
2004	585.00	276.60	131	126.60
2005	700.50	351.90	139	137.10
2006	631.20	317.10	221	181.50
2007	607.10	396.50	131	151.40
2008	568.00	276.90	299	234.10
2009	767.00	389.70	598	932.60
2010	702.40	402.60	2 681	1 529.10
2011	982.18	415.50	509	1 020.50
2012	759.77	473.99	524	1 078.36
2013	869.58	506.69	365	1 238.43
2014	892.14	529.94	452	1 678.70
2015	1 071.66	534.13	466	1 700.37
2016	972.72	534.04	507	1 912.32
2017	958.49	519.58	781	2 342.31
2018	1 142.38	562.00	867	2 322.63
2019	1 055.93	485.98	882	2 407.49
2020	793.10	351.82	1 075	1 061.83

13–22 图书、杂志、报纸出版发行情况（1978–2020年）
Publication of Books, Magazines and Newspapers (1978-2020)

年份 Year	出版总数(种) Number of Publications (kind)			出版印数 Printed Copies		
	图书 Books Published	杂志 Magazines Published	报纸 Newspapers Published	图书(万册) Books Published (10 000 copies)	杂志(万册) Magazines Published (10 000 copies)	报纸(亿份) Newspapers Published (100 million copies)
1978	333	31	7	6 753	75	
1979				6 293	96	
1980	336	87	11	8 106	739	1.76
1981				7 082	890	1.72
1982				8 332	850	1.73
1983				8 810	1 141	0.99
1984				12 229	1 152	2.96
1985	568	65	43	11 411	1 161	3.21
1986				10 111	1 103	3.58
1987				11 877	1 491	2.40
1988				12 288	1 266	2.60
1989				13 072	1 072	2.05
1990	804	68	41	12 330	954	2.23
1991				12 568	1 117	2.37
1992				13 027	1 305	0.26
1993				11 667	1 453	2.72
1994				11 248	1 391	2.23
1995	1 452	99	44	11 889	1 604	2.59
1996				13 489	1 495	2.74
1997				15 413	1 566	3.44
1998				14 281	1 599	2.87
1999				17 151	1 811	2.96
2000	1 644	125	70	13 414	2 877	3.60
2001				13 471	3 186	3.68
2002				12 687	2 755	3.93
2003				14 687	2 745	4.26
2004				15 052	2 379	4.72
2005	2 337	124	61	12 898	2 308	4.97
2006	2 471	124	61	17 388	2 898	5.33
2007	3 117	126	63	15 962	2 793	5.59
2008	3 336	126	63	17 485	3 265	5.89
2009	3 541	125	63	17 068	3 086	6.72
2010	4 598	126	64	15 084	3 538	6.41
2011	6 110	125	64	16 952	3 326	6.52
2012	7 901	127	63	16 736	3 890	6.54
2013	7 730	127	64	17 162	4 157	6.51
2014	6 958	127	63	15 307	4 000	6.14
2015	8 465	127	62	19 020	3 792	4.61
2016	8 563	127	42	15 244	3 387	4.00
2017	7 972	128	42	16 423	2 830	3.56
2018	7 496	128	62	10 512	3 127	3.33
2019	6 711	128	59	10 833	2 218	3.26
2020	5 879	128	59	17 017	1 869	3.13

13-23 各州市文化、文物事业建设情况（2020年）

Basic Statistics on Development of Culture and Cultural Relics by Region (2020)

州 市	Region	公共图书馆(个) Public Libraries (unit)	公共图书馆藏书量(万册) Number of books in Public Libraries (10 000 volumes)	艺术表演团体(个) Numbers of Art Performance Troupes(unit)	艺术表演场馆(个) Arts Performance Places (unit)	群众艺术馆及文化馆(个) Mass Art and Cultural Centers (unit)	文化站(个) Cultural Centers (unit)	文物事业费(亿元) Total Expenditures on Cultural Relics (100 million yuan)	博物馆(个) Museums (unit)
全 省	**Yunnan**	**151**	**1 733.30**	**99**	**12**	**149**	**1 454**	**31.03**	**161**
省本级	Provincial Level	1	371.88	4	1	1	—	1.02	2
昆 明	Kunming	16	289.16	3	3	15	141	4.72	35
曲 靖	Qujing	11	137.10	4	2	10	138	1.93	12
玉 溪	Yuxi	10	125.34	7	2	10	75	2.09	9
保 山	Baoshan	7	66.94	5		6	81	4.36	21
昭 通	Zhaotong	12	80.77	10		12	146	1.74	3
丽 江	Lijiang	6	57.77	1		6	65	0.89	6
普 洱	Pu'er	11	82.96	8		11	105	1.75	8
临 沧	Lincang	9	53.21	9		10	84	0.83	3
楚 雄	Chuxiong	11	115.00	10	2	11	103	1.54	7
红 河	Honghe	14	178.54	6		14	139	2.99	16
文 山	Wenshan	9	67.80	7		9	105	1.77	3
西双版纳	Xishuangbanna	4	21.17	4	1	4	44	1.41	2
大 理	Dali	13	112.13	7		14	112	1.78	20
德 宏	Dehong	8	51.51	7		7	58	1.24	7
怒 江	Nujiang	5	38.26	5		5	29	0.91	2
迪 庆	Diqing	4	24.75	2	1	5	29	1.07	5

13-24 广播电视业发展情况（2008-2020年）

Basic Statistics on Development of Radio and Television (2008-2020)

年份 Year	广播电台、电视台、广播电视台 (座) Number of Radio stations, Television stations, Media groups (unit)	职工人数 (万人) Number of Staff and Workers (10 000 persons)	广播人口覆盖率 (%) Radio Coverage of Population (%)	电视人口覆盖率 (%) Television Coverage of Population (%)
2008	16	1.50	93.1	94.3
2009	16	1.55	94.3	95.1
2010	17	1.63	95.4	96.4
2011	17	1.75	95.7	96.7
2012	12	1.83	96.0	97.0
2013	11	1.80	96.3	97.3
2014	10	1.91	96.5	97.5
2015	10	1.85	96.7	97.7
2016	10	1.92	97.4	98.2
2017	10	1.97	98.4	98.7
2018	149	1.90	98.7	98.9
2019	141	2.10	99.0	99.1
2020	137	2.07	99.3	99.4

注：“广播电台、电视台、广播电视台”指标中2017年及以前数据仅包含“广播电台”座数，2018年该指标数据包含广播电台（9座）、电视台（15座）、广播电视台（125座）三类。2019年机构改革，广播电台和电视台基本合并，数据包含广播电台（0座）、电视台（11座）、广播电视台（130座）。

Note: Before 2017,data of "Radio stations, Television stations,and Media groups" included radio stations only.In 2018, it included radio stations (9 units),television stations (15 units) and media groups (125 units).In 2019,with the institutional reforms,radio stations and television stations almost merged ,it included radio stations （0 units),television stations (11 units) and media groups (130 units).

13-25 规模以上工业企业科技活动基本情况（2015-2020年）
Basic Statistics on Science and Technology Activities of Industrial Enterprises above Designated Size（2015-2020）

指 标	Item	2015	2016	2017	2018	2019	2020
企业基本情况	**Industrial Enterprises**						
有R&D活动企业数(个)	Number of Enterprises Having R&D Activities (unit)	744	879	1 003	1 003	1 243	1 206
有R&D活动企业所占比重(%)	Percentage of Enterprises Having R&D Activities to Total Number of Enterprises (%)	19.21	20.98	23.97	22.76	28.47	27.40
R&D活动情况	**R&D Activities**						
R&D人员全时当量(万人年)	**Full-time Equivalent of R&D Personnel (10 000 person-years**	**1.60**	**1.72**	**2.14**	**2.40**	**2.94**	**2.89**
R&D经费内部支出(亿元)	Intramural Expenditure on R&D (100 million yuan)	61.96	74.18	88.56	107.02	129.77	145.15
R&D经费内部支出与主营业务收入之比(%)	Percentage of Intramural Expenditure on R&D to Sales Revenue (%)	0.63	0.73	0.76	0.80	0.91	1.00
R&D项目数(项)	Projects of R&D (item)	3 017	3 441	4 122	4 216	6 286	6 065
R&D项目经费内部支出(亿元)	Intramural Expenditure on R&D Projects (100 million yuan)	58.79	73.97	88.34	101.13	130.78	151.64
企业办科技机构情况	**R&D Institutions**						
机构数(个)	Number of R&D Institutions (unit)	479	554	648	542	538	488
机构人员数(万人)	R&D Personnel (10 000 persons)	1.45	1.46	1.80	1.54	1.61	1.68
机构经费支出(亿元)	Expenditure on R&D (100 million yuan)	33.52	36.45	49.06	52.01	66.43	59.07
新产品开发及生产情况	**New Products Development and Production**						
新产品开发项目数(项)	Number of New Products (unit)	2 503	3 834	4 208	4 150	5 661	5 532
新产品开发经费支出(亿元)	Expenditure on New Products Development (100 million yuan)	63.20	88.43	102.67	96.54	122.77	115.37
新产品销售收入(亿元)	Sales Revenue of New Products (100 million yuan)	513.20	628.45	808.62	928.83	939.55	1 216.09
#新产品出口	Export	19.89	30.25	36.46	21.59	38.24	16.41
专利情况	**Patent**						
专利申请数(件)	Patent Applications (unit)	3 751	4 942	5 389	6 190	7 611	9 451
#发明专利	Inventions	1 493	1 878	1 891	2 038	2 665	3 131
有效发明专利数(件)	Number of Patents In Force (unit)	4 605	5 880	6 510	6 466	10 131	9 515
技术获取和技术改造情况(亿元)	**Technology Acquisition and Technology Reconstruction (100 million yuan)**						
引进境外技术经费支出	Expenditure for Acquisition of Technology	0.47	1.54	1.26	3.12	8.33	0.78
引进境外技术消化吸收经费支出	Expenditure for Assimilation of Technology	2.50	0.22	0.08	0.18	0.10	0.02
购买境内技术经费支出	Expenditure for Purchase of Domestic Technology	0.63	4.90	4.44	6.90	11.67	7.56
技术改造经费支出	Expenditure for Technical Renovation	34.80	28.77	35.35	40.33	70.00	65.01

13－26 按登记注册类型分规模以上工业企业研究与试验发展(R&D)活动情况（2020年）
Basic Statistics on R&D Activities of Industrial Enterprises above Designated Size by Registration Status (2020)

登记注册类型	Status of Registration	R&D人员全时当量（人年）Full-time Equivalent of R&D Personnel (person-year)	R&D经费（亿元）Expenditure on R&D (100 million yuan)
全　省	**Yunnan**	**28 894**	**145.15**
内资企业	**Domestic Funded Enterprises**	**27 556**	**138.89**
国有企业	State-owned Enterprises	625	3.37
集体企业	Collective-owned Enterprises	82	0.31
股份合作企业	Cooperative Enterprises		
联营企业	Joint Ownership Enterprises		
国有联营企业	State Joint Ownership Enterprises		
有限责任公司	Limited Liability Corporations	9 990	62.22
国有独资公司	State Sole Funded Corporations	1 650	13.08
股份有限公司	Share-holding Corporations Ltd.	4 141	23.10
私营企业	Private Enterprises	12 718	49.89
其他企业	Other Enterprises		
港澳台商投资企业	**Enterprises with Funds from Hong Kong,Macao & Taiwan**	**814**	**3.93**
合资经营企业	Joint-venture Enterprises	416	1.44
合作经营企业	Cooperative Enterprises	26	0.02
独资经营企业	Enterprises with Sole Fund	70	0.53
投资股份有限公司	Share-holding Corporations Ltd.	302	1.94
外商投资企业	**Foreign Funded Enterprises**	**524**	**2.32**
中外合资经营企业	Joint-venture Enterprises	222	1.03
中外合作经营企业	Cooperation Enterprises	30	0.36
外资企业	Enterprises with Sole Fund	218	0.63
外商投资股份有限公司	Share-holding Corporations Ltd.	55	0.30

13-27 按行业分规模以上工业企业研究与试验发展(R&D)活动情况（2020年）
Basic Statistics on R&D Activities of Industrial Enterprises above Designated Size by Industrial Sector (2020)

行业	Sector	R&D人员全时当量(人年) Full-time Equivalent of R&D Personnel (person-year)	R&D经费(亿元) Expenditure on R&D (100 million yuan)
全省	**Yunnan**	**28 894**	**145.15**
采矿业	**Mining**	**1 042**	**5.23**
煤炭开采和洗选业	Mining and Washing of Coal	156	0.55
黑色金属矿采选业	Mining and Dressing of Ferrous Metal Ores	190	1.26
有色金属矿采选业	Mining and Dressing of Nonferrous Metals Ores	562	2.87
非金属矿采选业	Mining and Dressing of Nonmetal Ores	134	0.55
制造业	**Manufacturing Industry**	**27 494**	**136.97**
农副食品加工业	Processing of Farm and Sideline Food	1 676	7.71
食品制造业	Manufacture of Food	992	3.87
酒、饮料和精制茶制造业	Manufacture of Wine,Beverage and Refined Tea	694	2.71
烟草制品业	Tobacco Products Manufacturing	744	6.84
纺织业	Textile Industry	90	0.30
纺织服装、服饰业	Manufacture of Textile Garments and Dress Accessory	97	0.15
皮革、毛皮、羽毛及其制品和制鞋业	Feather, Furs, Down, Related Products and Footwear Manufacturing	16	0.07
木材加工和木、竹、藤、棕、草制品业	Timber Processing,Bamboo,Cane,Palm Fiber & Straw Products Manufacturing	107	0.59
家具制造业	Manufacture of Furniture	22	0.16
造纸和纸制品业	Papermaking and Paper Products Manufacturing	566	1.85
印刷和记录媒介复制业	Printing and Record Medium Reproduction	745	2.07
文教、工美、体育和娱乐用品制造业	Manufacture of Culture,Education,Industrial Arts,Sports and Entertainment Goods	46	0.14
石油加工、炼焦和核燃料加工业	Petroleum Refining, Coking and Nuclear Fuel Processing	328	2.65
化学原料和化学制品制造业	Manufacture of Raw Chemical Materials and Chemica Products	3 117	17.13
医药制造业	Manufacture of Medicines	1 677	6.59
化学纤维制造业	Chemical Fiber Manufacturing	1	0.00
橡胶和塑料制品业	Rubber and Plastic Products Manufacturing	405	2.16
非金属矿物制品业	Nonmetal Mineral Products Manufacturing	1 499	7.89
黑色金属冶炼和压延加工业	Smelting and Pressing of Ferrous Metals	2 963	18.45
有色金属冶炼和压延加工业	Smelting and Pressing of Nonferrous Metals	4 681	29.37
金属制品业	Metal Products Manufacturing	520	2.21
通用设备制造业	Manufacture of General Purpose Equipment	503	1.77
专用设备制造业	Manufacture of Special Purpose Equipment	707	1.91
汽车制造业	Automotive Industry	338	3.60
铁路、船舶、航空航天和其他运输设备制造业	Manufacture of Transport Equipment for Railway,Boats and Aerospace and Other Transport Equipments	319	1.65
电气机械和器材制造业	Electric Equipment and Machinery Manufacturing	1 185	4.74
计算机、通信和其他电子设备制造业	Communication Equipment,Computers and Other Electronic Equipment Production	2 675	7.87
仪器仪表制造业	Instrument Industry	619	1.68
其他制造业	Other Goods Production	38	0.25
废弃资源综合利用业	Comprehensive Utilization of Discarded Resources and Waste	125	0.57
金属制品、机械和设备修理业	Manufacture of Metal Products, Machinery and Equipment Repairing		
电力、热力、燃气及水生产和供应业	**Production and Supply of Electricity, Heat ,Gas and Water**	**357**	**2.95**
电力、热力生产和供应业	Production and Supply of Electric Power and Heat Power	272	2.61
燃气生产和供应业	Production and Supply of Gas	33	0.13
水的生产和供应业	Production and Supply of Tap Water	53	0.20

13－28 按州市分规模以上工业企业研究与试验发展(R&D)活动情况（2020年）
Basic Statistics on R&D Activities of Industrial Enterprises above Designated Size by Region（2020）

州 市	Region	有R&D活动的单位数（个）Number of enterprises with R&D activities (unit)	R&D人员全时当量（人年）Full-time Equivalent of R&D Personnel (person-year)	R&D经费（亿元）Expenditure on R&D (100 million yuan)
全　省	**Yunnan**	**1 206**	**28 894**	**145.15**
昆　明	Kunming	320	9 196	45.45
曲　靖	Qujing	193	4 184	26.31
玉　溪	Yuxi	183	4 717	20.84
保　山	Baoshan	91	1 521	5.54
昭　通	Zhaotong	18	472	3.88
丽　江	Lijiang	9	350	1.78
普　洱	Pu'er	41	482	2.00
临　沧	Lincang	29	304	1.49
楚　雄	Chuxiong	65	699	3.52
红　河	Honghe	141	4 393	20.21
文　山	Wenshan	39	658	4.83
西双版纳	Xishuangbanna	14	162	2.08
大　理	Dali	48	1 147	5.78
德　宏	Dehong	10	103	0.44
怒　江	Nujiang	1	488	0.50
迪　庆	Diqing	4	18	0.51

13−29 按登记注册类型分规模以上工业企业新产品开发及生产情况（2020年）
New Products Development and Production of Industrial Enterprises above Designated Size by Registration Status (2020)

单位：亿元 (100 million yuan)

登记注册类型	Status of Registration	新产品项目数(项) New Products (unit)	开发新产品经费 Expenditure on New Products Development	新产品销售收入 Sales Revenue of New Products	出口 Exports
全　省	**Yunnan**	**5 532**	**115.37**	**1 216.10**	**16.41**
内资企业	**Domestic Funded Enterprises**	**5 202**	**108.98**	**1 178.39**	**12.90**
国有企业	State-owned Enterprises	163	2.20	4.49	0.17
集体企业	Collective-owned Enterprises	16	0.18	2.05	
股份合作企业	Cooperative Enterprises				
联营企业	Joint Ownership Enterprises				
国有联营企业	State Joint Ownership Enterprises				
有限责任公司	Limited Liability Corporations	2 024	48.47	605.74	3.34
国有独资公司	State Sole Funded Corporations	652	10.78	61.25	1.36
股份有限公司	Share-holding Corporations Ltd.	893	20.79	249.46	3.78
私营企业	Private Enterprises	2 106	37.34	316.64	5.61
其他企业	Other Enterprises				
港澳台商投资企业	**Enterprises with Funds from Macao & Taiwan**	**221**	**4.34**	**19.85**	**2.67**
合资经营企业	Joint-venture Enterprises	119	1.52	12.88	
合作经营企业	Cooperative Enterprises	4	0.03	0.10	0.10
独资经营企业	Enterprises with Sole Fund	16	0.52	3.15	1.03
投资股份有限公司	Share-holding Corporations Ltd.	82	2.27	3.72	1.53
外商投资企业	**Foreign Funded Enterprises**	**109**	**2.05**	**17.85**	**0.84**
中外合资经营企业	Joint-venture Enterprises	48	0.86	8.53	0.69
中外合作经营企业	Cooperation Enterprises	8	0.35		
外资企业	Enterprises with Sole Fund	28	0.45	6.21	0.16
外商投资股份有限公司	Share-holding Corporations Ltd.	25	0.39	3.11	

13-30 按行业分规模以上工业企业新产品开发及生产情况（2020年）

New Products Development and Production of Industrial Enterprises above Designated Size by Industrial Sector (2020)

单位：亿元

行业	Sector	新产品项目数（项）New Products (unit)	开发新产品经费 Expenditure on New Products Development	新产品销售收入 Sales Revenue of New Products	出口 Exports
全省	**Yunnan**	**5 532**	**115.37**	**1 216.10**	**16.41**
采矿业	**Mining**	**108**	**3.14**	**16.50**	
煤炭开采和洗选业	Mining and Washing of Coal	3	0.03	0.33	
黑色金属矿采选业	Mining and Dressing of Ferrous Metal Ores	14	0.90	2.50	
有色金属矿采选业	Mining and Dressing of Nonferrous Metals Ores	81	1.86	13.33	
非金属矿采选业	Mining and Dressing of Nonmetal Ores	10	0.36	0.35	
制造业	**Manufacturing Industry**	**4 906**	**106.80**	**1 196.30**	**16.41**
农副食品加工业	Processing of Farm and Sideline Food	409	9.13	54.18	0.34
食品制造业	Manufacture of Food	217	3.55	29.61	2.97
酒、饮料和精制茶制造业	Manufacture of Wine,Beverage and Refined Tea	204	3.46	14.47	0.04
烟草制品业	Tobacco Products Manufacturing	198	6.57	7.45	
纺织业	Textile Industry	24	0.26	1.87	0.32
纺织服装、服饰业	Manufacture of Textile Garments and Dress Accessory	5	0.17	1.60	
皮革、毛皮、羽毛及其制品和制鞋业	Feather,Furs,Down,Related Products and Footwear Manufacturing				
木材加工和木、竹、藤、棕、草制品业	Timber Processing,Bamboo,Cane,Palm Fiber & Straw Products Manufacturin	21	0.58	2.20	
家具制造业	Manufacture of Furniture	5	0.14	0.05	
造纸和纸制品业	Papermaking and Paper Products Manufacturing	111	1.92	14.74	0.00
印刷和记录媒介复制业	Printing and Record Medium Reproduction	105	1.71	26.62	0.14
文教、工美、体育和娱乐用品制造业	Manufacture of Culture,Education,Industrial Arts,Sports and Entertainment Goods	4	0.17	0.19	
石油加工、炼焦和核燃料加工业	Petroleum Refining, Coking and Nuclear Fuel Processing	20	0.71	6.79	
化学原料和化学制品制造业	Manufacture of Raw Chemical Materials and Chemical Products	536	12.69	92.07	1.42
医药制造业	Manufacture of Medicines	600	7.14	43.65	1.11
化学纤维制造业	Chemical Fiber Manufacturing	5	0.01		
橡胶和塑料制品业	Rubber and Plastic Products Manufacturing	115	2.32	19.92	0.28
非金属矿物制品业	Nonmetal Mineral Products Manufacturing	232	6.31	35.89	0.20
黑色金属冶炼和压延加工业	Smelting and Pressing of Ferrous Metals	126	5.71	123.31	1.57
有色金属冶炼和压延加工业	Smelting and Pressing of Nonferrous Metals	485	17.53	154.73	1.39
金属制品业	Metal Products Manufacturing	166	2.66	21.62	0.18
通用设备制造业	Manufacture of General Purpose Equipment	169	2.35	17.00	0.68
专用设备制造业	Manufacture of Special Purpose Equipment	186	2.22	16.16	0.78
汽车制造业	Automotive Industry	224	3.46	95.25	
铁路、船舶、航空航天 和其他运输设备制造业	Manufacture of Transport Equipment for Railway,Boats and Aerospace and Other Transport Equipments	91	1.82	5.77	1.70
电气机械和器材制造业	Electric Equipment and Machinery Manufacturing	327	5.05	60.51	0.40
计算机、通信和其他电子设备制造业	Communication Equipment,Computers and Other Electronic Equipment Production	164	6.82	333.18	1.22
仪器仪表制造业	Instrument Industry	132	1.80	15.83	1.66
其他制造业	Other Goods Production	13	0.31	1.26	
废弃资源综合利用业	Comprehensive Utilization of Discarded Resources and Waste	12	0.21	0.39	
电力、热力、燃气及水生产和供应业	**Production and Supply of Electricity, Heat ,Gas and Water**	**518**	**5.43**	**3.29**	
电力、热力生产和供应业	Production and Supply of Electric Power and Heat Power	504	5.23	3.29	
燃气生产和供应业	Production and Supply of Gas	6	0.08		
水的生产和供应业	Production and Supply of Tap Water	8	0.11		

13−31 按州市分规模以上工业企业新产品开发及生产情况（2020年）
New Products Development and Production of Industrial Enterprises above Designated Size by Region (2020)

单位：亿元 (100 million yuan)

州 市	Region	新产品项目数(项) New Products (unit)	开发新产品经费 Expenditure on New Products Development	新产品销售收入 Sales Revenue of New Products	出口 Exports
全 省	**Yunnan**	**5 532**	**115.37**	**1 216.10**	**16.41**
昆 明	Kunming	2 861	48.17	566.32	8.09
曲 靖	Qujing	643	18.40	154.55	3.26
玉 溪	Yuxi	639	12.35	192.13	2.53
保 山	Baoshan	164	3.13	81.08	0.27
昭 通	Zhaotong	114	2.89	70.98	0.29
丽 江	Lijiang	23	1.81	30.96	0.08
普 洱	Pu'er	91	1.56	4.11	0.01
临 沧	Lincang	45	1.71	5.97	0.48
楚 雄	Chuxiong	160	3.28	17.04	0.19
红 河	Honghe	333	10.09	40.05	1.04
文 山	Wenshan	144	3.19	5.30	
版 纳	Xishuangbanna	76	2.63	9.11	
大 理	Dali	185	4.93	37.89	0.15
德 宏	Dehong	22	0.26	0.56	0.02
怒 江	Nujiang	1			
迪 庆	Diqing	31	0.93		

13—32 按登记注册类型分规模以上工业企业专利情况（2020年）
Statistics on Patent of Industrial Enterprises above Designated Size by Registration Status (2020)

单位：件 (piece)

登记注册类型	Status of Registration	专利申请数 Patent Applications	发明专利 Invention Patents	有效发明专利数 Number of Patents in Force
全　省	**Yunnan**	**9 451**	**3 131**	**9 515**
内资企业	**Domestic Funded Enterprises**	**8 993**	**2 990**	**8 937**
国有企业	State-owned Enterprises	167	62	137
集体企业	Collective-owned Enterprises	9	5	22
股份合作企业	Cooperative Enterprises			14
联营企业	Joint Ownership Enterprises			
国有联营企业	State Joint Ownership Enterprises			
有限责任公司	Limited Liability Corporations	5 084	1 917	4 313
国有独资公司	State Sole Funded Corporations	1 958	1 004	1 330
股份有限公司	Share-holding Corporations Ltd.	1 027	477	1 412
私营企业	Private Enterprises	2 706	529	3 039
其他企业	Other Enterprises			
港澳台商投资企业	**Enterprises with Funds from Macao & Taiwan**	**308**	**116**	**424**
合资经营企业	Joint-venture Enterprises	144	41	219
合作经营企业	Cooperative Enterprises	3	3	11
独资经营企业	Enterprises with Sole Fund	13	1	78
投资股份有限公司	Share-holding Corporations Ltd.	148	71	116
外商投资企业	**Foreign Funded Enterprises**	**150**	**25**	**154**
中外合资经营企业	Joint-venture Enterprises	88	7	50
中外合作经营企业	Cooperation Enterprises			20
外资企业	Enterprises with Sole Fund	23	2	65
外商投资股份有限公司	Share-holding Corporations Ltd.	39	16	19

13–33 按行业分规模以上工业企业专利情况（2020年）
Statistics on Patent of Industrial Enterprises above Designated Size by Industrial Sector (2020)

单位：件 (piece)

国民经济行业	Sector	专利申请数 Patent Applications	发明专利 Invention Patents	有效发明专利数 Number of Patents In Force
全 省	**Yunnan**	**9 451**	**3 131**	**9 515**
采矿业	**Mining**	**240**	**68**	**231**
煤炭开采和洗选业	Mining and Washing of Coal	7		
黑色金属矿采选业	Mining and Dressing of Ferrous Metal Ores	49	6	47
有色金属矿采选业	Mining and Dressing of Nonferrous Metals Ores	149	44	125
非金属矿采选业	Mining and Dressing of Nonmetal Ores	35	18	59
制造业	**Manufacturing Industry**	**7 183**	**1 999**	**8 120**
农副食品加工业	Processing of Farm and Sideline Food	483	69	310
食品制造业	Manufacture of Food	255	76	298
酒、饮料和精制茶制造业	Manufacture of Wine,Beverage and Refined Tea	138	29	244
烟草制品业	Tobacco Products Manufacturing	1 742	610	992
纺织业	Textile Industry	13	8	25
纺织服装、服饰业	Manufacture of Textile Garments and Dress Accessory	6	2	4
皮革、毛皮、羽毛及其制品和制鞋业	Feather,Furs,Down,Related Products and Footwear Manufacturing			
木材加工和木、竹、藤、棕、草制品业	Timber Processing,Bamboo,Cane,Palm Fiber & Straw Products Manufacturing	24	5	18
家具制造业	Manufacture of Furniture	3		
造纸和纸制品业	Papermaking and Paper Products Manufacturing	116	23	191
印刷和记录媒介复制业	Printing and Record Medium Reproduction	197	36	173
文教、工美、体育和娱乐用品制造业	Manufacture of Culture,Education,Industrial Arts,Sports and Entertainment Goods			13
石油加工、炼焦和核燃料加工业	Petroleum Refining, Coking and Nuclear Fuel Processing	38	1	11
化学原料和化学制品制造业	Manufacture of Raw Chemical Materials and Chemical Products	698	195	875
医药制造业	Manufacture of Medicines	379	115	983
化学纤维制造业	Chemical Fiber Manufacturing	12	10	78
橡胶和塑料制品业	Rubber and Plastic Products Manufacturing	172	33	130
非金属矿物制品业	Nonmetal Mineral Products Manufacturing	311	64	245
黑色金属冶炼和压延加工业	Smelting and Pressing of Ferrous Metals	247	61	415
有色金属冶炼和压延加工业	Smelting and Pressing of Nonferrous Metals	605	198	983
金属制品业	Metal Products Manufacturing	202	47	270
通用设备制造业	Manufacture of General Purpose Equipment	187	42	288
专用设备制造业	Manufacture of Special Purpose Equipment	328	73	271
汽车制造业	Automotive Industry	103	30	265
铁路、船舶、航空航天和其他运输设备制造业	Manufacture of Transport Equipment for Railway,Boats and Aerospace and Other Transport Equipments	165	75	124
电气机械和器材制造业	Electric Equipment and Machinery Manufacturing	352	47	486
计算机、通信和其他电子设备制造业	Communication Equipment, Computers and Other Electronic Equipment Production	230	106	226
仪器仪表制造业	Instrument Industry	134	35	171
其他制造业	Other Goods Production	23	1	3
废弃资源综合利用业	Comprehensive Utilization of Discarded Resources and Waste	20	8	28
电力、热力、燃气及水生产和供应业	**Production and Supply of Electricity, Heat ,Gas and Water**	**2 028**	**1 064**	**1 164**
电力、热力生产和供应业	Production and Supply of Electric Power and Heat Power	2 014	1 062	1 140
燃气生产和供应业	Production and Supply of Gas	7		13
水的生产和供应业	Production and Supply of Tap Water	7	2	11

13－34　按州市分规模以上工业企业专利情况（2020年）
Statistics on Patent of Industrial Enterprises above Designated Size by Region (2020)

单位：件　　(piece)

州　市	Region	专利申请数 Patent Applications	发明专利 Invention Patents	有效发明专利数 Number of Patents in Force
全　省	**Yunnan**	**9 451**	**3 131**	**9 515**
昆　明	Kunming	6 265	2 426	5 621
曲　靖	Qujing	714	159	914
玉　溪	Yuxi	774	150	1080
保　山	Baoshan	89	17	133
昭　通	Zhaotong	114	18	134
丽　江	Lijiang	32	3	60
普　洱	Pu'er	85	18	117
临　沧	Lincang	61	23	73
楚　雄	Chuxiong	520	130	435
红　河	Honghe	288	96	360
文　山	Wenshan	184	40	154
西双版纳	Xishuangbanna	58	17	75
大　理	Dali	175	24	316
德　宏	Dehong	44	3	26
怒　江	Nujiang	17	2	2
迪　庆	Diqing	31	5	15

主要统计指标解释

普通高等学校 指通过国家普通高等教育招生考试，招收高中毕业生为主要培养对象，实施高等学历教育的全日制大学、独立设置的学院、独立学院和高等专科学校、高等职业学校及其他普通高教机构。

大学、独立设置的学院主要实施本科及本科层次以上的教育。独立学院主要实施本科层次的教育。高等专科学校、高等职业学校实施专科层次的教育。其他普通高教机构是指承担国家普通招生计划任务不计校数的机构，包括普通高等学校分校、大专班等。

成人高等学校 指通过国家成人高等教育招生考试，招收具有高中毕业或同等学力的人员为主要培养对象，利用函授、业余、脱产等多种形式，对其实施高等学历教育的学校。包括：职工高等学校、农民高等学校、管理干部学院、教育学院、独立函授学院、广播电视大学、其他成人高教机构等。其他成人高教机构是指承担国家成人招生计划任务不计校数的机构。

小学学龄儿童净入学率 指调查范围内已入小学学习的学龄儿童占校内外学龄儿童总数（包括弱智儿童在内，但不包括盲聋哑儿童）的比重。

研究与试验发展 (R&D) 指在科学技术领域，为增加知识总量，以及运用这些知识去创造新的应用进行的系统的创造性的活动，包括基础研究、应用研究、试验发展三类活动。国际上通常采用 R&D 活动的规模和强度指标反映一国的科技实力和核心竞争力。

R&D 人员 指参与研究与试验发展项目研究、管理和辅助工作的人员，包括项目 (课题) 组人员，企业科技行政管理人员和直接为项目 (课题) 活动提供服务的辅助人员。反映投入从事拥有自主知识产权的研究开发活动的人力规模。

R&D 人员全时当量 指全时人员数加非全时人员按工作量折算为全时人员数的总和。例如：有两个全时人员和三个非全时人员 (工作时间分别为 20%、30% 和 70%)，则全时当量为 2+0.2+0.3+0.7=3.2 人年。为国际上比较科技人力投入而制定的可比指标。

R&D 经费支出合计 指调查单位用于内部开展 R&D 活动（基础研究、应用研究和试验发展）的实际支出。包括用于 R&D 项目（课题）活动的直接支出，以及间接用于 R&D 活动的管理费、服务费、与 R&D 有关的基本建设支出以及外协加工费等。不包括生产性活动支出、归还贷款支出以及与外单位合作或委托外单位进行 R&D 活动而转拨给对方的经费支出。

新产品销售收入 指报告期企业销售新产品实现的销售收入。新产品是指采用新技术原理、新设计构思研制、生产的全新产品，或在结构、材质、工艺等某一方面比原有产品有明显改进，从而显著提高了产品性能或扩大了使用功能的产品。既包括经政府有关部门认定并在有效期内的新产品，也包括企业自行研制开发，未经政府有关部门认定，从投产之日起一年之内的新产品。

专利 是专利权的简称，是对发明人的发明创造经审查合格后，由专利局依据专利法授予发明人和设计人对该项发明创造享有的专有权。包括发明、实用新型和外观设计。反映拥有自主知识产权的科技和设计成果情况。

发明（专利） 指对产品、方法或者其改进所提出的新的技术方案。是国际通行的反映拥有自主知识产权技术的核心指标。

实用新型（专利） 指对产品的形状、构造或者其结合所提出的适于实用的新的技术方案。反映具有一定技术含量的技术成果情况。

外观设计（专利） 指对产品的形状、图案、色彩或者其结合所作出的富有美感并适于工业上应用的新设计。反映拥有自主知识产权的外观设计成果情况。

Explanatory Notes on Main Statistical Indicators

Regular Institutions of Higher Education refer to educational establishments recruiting graduates from senior secondary schools as the main target through National Matriculation TEST. They include full-time universities, independently established colleges, colleges, and institutions of higher professional education, institutions of higher vocational education and other institutions of higher education.

Universities and independently established colleges primarily provide undergraduate and above courses; colleges mainly impart undergraduate courses, institutions of higher professional education and institutions of higher vocational education primarily provide professional trainings; and other institutions of higher education refer to educational establishments, which are responsible for enrolling higher education students under the State Plan but not enumerated in the total number of schools, including: branch schools of universities and colleges and junior colleges.

Institutions of Higher Education for Adults refer to educational establishments, enrolling personnel with senior secondary school or equivalent education through National Matriculation TEST for Adult, and providing higher education courses in forms of correspondence, spare time, or full time for adults. Institutions of higher learning for adults include schools of higher education for staff and workers, schools of higher education for peasants, colleges for management cadres, pedagogical colleges, independent correspondence colleges, radio and television universities and other educational establishments of higher education for adult. Other educational establishments of higher education for adult refer undertakings to enrol adult students but not enumerated in the number of schools under the State Plan.

Enrollment Rate of Primary School-age Children refers to the proportion of school age children enrolled at primary schools to the total number of school age children both in and outside schools (including retarded children, but excluding blind, deaf and mute children).

Research and Development (R&D) refers to systematic and creative activities in the field of science and technology aiming at increasing the knowledge and using the knowledge for new application. R&D includes 3 categories of activities: basic research, applied research and experiments and development. The scale and intensity of R&D are widely used internationally to reflect the strength of S&T and the core competitiveness of a country in the world.

R&D Personnel refer to persons engaged in research, management and supporting activities of R & D, including persons in the project teams, persons engaged in the management of S&T activities of enterprises and supporting staff providing direct service to the research projects. This indicator reflects the size of personnel engaged in R&D activities with independent intellectual property.

Full-time Equivalent of R&D Personnel refers to the sum of the full-time persons and the full-time equivalent of part-time persons converted by workload. For instance, if there are 2 full-time persons and 3 part-time workers (20%, 30% and 70% of working hours respectively on R&D activities), the full-time equivalent are 2+0.2+0.3+0.7=3.2 person-years. This is an internationally comparable indicator of S&T manpower input.

Total Expenditure of Funds on R&D refers to the real expenditure of surveyed units on their own R&D activities (basic research, applied research, experiments and development) including direct expenditure on R&D activities, indirect expenditure of management and services on R&D activities, expenditure on capital construction and material processing by others. Excluding the expenditure on production activities, return of loan, and fees transferred to cooperated or entrusted agencies on R&D activities.

Sales Income of New Products refers to the sales income of new products of the enterprises at the reference period. New products refer to products developed and produced with new technologies and designs or improved in structure, material, process or other aspects so that their performance are improved or their functions expanded. New products include those affirmed by government authorities in their validity period and also those developed by enterprises without the affirmation of government authorities within one year after they are put into production.

Patent is an abbreviation for the patent right and refers to the exclusive right of ownership by the inventors or designers for the creation or inventions, given from the patent offices after due process of assessment and approval in accordance with the Patent Law. Patents are granted for inventions, utility models and designs. This indicator reflects the achievements of S&T and design with independent intellectual property.

Patented Inventions refer to new technical proposals to the products or methods or their modifications. This is universal core indicator reflecting the technologies with independent intellectual property.

Patented Utility Models refer to the practical and new technical proposals on the shape and structure of the product or the combination of both. This indicator reflects the condition of technological results with certain technical content.

Designs refer to the aesthetics and industrially applicable new designs for the shape, pattern and colour of the product, or their combinations. This indicator reflects the appearance design achievements with independent intellectual property.

Chapter 14

十四、卫生、体育和社会管理
Public Health,Sports and Social Management

14–1 卫生医疗机构数（1985–2020年）
Number of Health and Medical Institutions （1985-2020）

单位：个 (unit)

年份 Year	医院 Hospitals	门诊部 Clinics	疾病预防控制中心（含卫生防疫站） Center for Disease Control and Prevention (Including Epidemic Prevention Stations)	妇幼保健站 Women and Children Care Agencies
1985	1 813	3 846	159	145
1986	1 789	3 959	159	145
1987	1 802	4 018	158	144
1988	1 868	4 068	150	144
1989	1 884	4 041	150	143
1990	1 908	4 085	150	144
1991	1 928	4 091	150	144
1992	1 950	4 107	149	144
1993	1 969	3 772	157	143
1994	2 115	3 618	157	143
1995	2 108	3 522	158	145
1996	548	53	148	140
1997	589	46	149	140
1998	594	53	150	143
1999	603	51	151	140
2000	602	51	151	142
2001	590	37	152	142
2002	584	38	148	144
2003	566	52	153	151
2004	594	69	150	146
2005	648	73	153	148
2006	649	69	150	148
2007	668	73	150	148
2008	692	74	152	148
2009	720	66	152	147
2010	780	78	150	147
2011	845	101	150	148
2012	924	126	150	147
2013	997	150	150	147
2014	1 060	159	150	145
2015	1 101	208	150	145
2016	1 187	262	152	145
2017	1 252	290	153	145
2018	1 280	316	153	146
2019	1 376	385	153	147
2020	1 445	465	150	147

14-2 卫生医疗机构床位数（1985-2020年）

Number of Beds in Health and Medical Institutions（1985-2020）

年份 Year	机构病床数(万张) Number of beds in Health and Medical Institutions (10 000 units)	医院 Hospitals	乡镇卫生院 Township Health Centers	平均每万人口拥有医院床位数(张) Number of Hospital Beds per 10 000 Persons(unit)
1985	7.45	6.80	4.77	20.00
1986	7.53	8.63	4.72	19.90
1987	7.83	7.06	7.76	20.10
1988	8.27	7.49	4.88	20.80
1989	8.27	7.50	4.84	20.60
1990	8.45	7.61	4.83	20.40
1991	7.74	7.84	4.99	20.90
1992	9.10	8.09	5.05	21.10
1993	9.27	8.25	5.19	21.40
1994	9.37	8.34	4.98	21.20
1995	9.56	8.40	5.09	21.00
1996	9.08	6.08	3.07	15.10
1997	9.40	6.34	3.02	15.50
1998	9.60	6.40	2.97	15.50
1999	9.72	6.46	3.06	15.30
2000	9.75	6.61	3.12	15.60
2001	9.98	6.60	3.17	15.50
2002	9.66	6.75	3.19	15.60
2003	9.84	6.79	3.15	15.50
2004	10.22	7.12	3.23	16.10
2005	10.70	7.47	3.25	16.80
2006	11.05	7.74	3.43	17.30
2007	11.90	8.32		18.40
2008	12.78	9.04		19.90
2009	14.01	9.97		21.90
2010	15.71	11.25		24.50
2011	17.34	12.63	3.61	27.28
2012	19.47	14.35	3.98	30.81
2013	21.01	15.61	4.20	33.30
2014	22.49	16.97	4.35	36.00
2015	23.76	18.13	4.44	38.23
2016	25.36	19.47	4.62	40.82
2017	27.48	21.08	5.00	43.92
2018	29.12	22.33	5.29	46.23
2019	31.19	24.13	5.44	49.68
2020	32.52	25.25	5.49	53.48

14-3 卫生医疗机构人员数（1978-2020年）

Number of Employed Persons in Health and Medical Institutions（1978-2020）

年份 Year	卫生医疗机构人数(万人) Number of Employed Persons in Health and Medical Institutions (10 000 persons)	卫生技术人员 Medical Technical Personnel	执业（助理）医师 Doctors	每千人口拥有卫生技术人员或医生(人) Number of Medical Technical Personnel or Doctors per 1 000 Persons(person) 卫生技术人员 Medical Technical Personnel	执业（助理）医师 Doctors
1978	7.95	6.55	3.11	2.12	1.01
1979					
1980	8.91	7.14	3.34	2.25	1.28
1981	9.58	7.69	3.73	2.39	1.16
1982	9.86	7.96	3.01	2.43	1.16
1983	10.16	8.22	3.96	2.48	1.19
1984	10.47	8.46	4.09	2.52	1.22
1985	10.79	8.73	4.27	2.56	1.25
1986	11.13	8.98	4.37	2.60	1.27
1987	11.66	9.44	4.57	2.69	1.30
1988	11.99	9.75	5.12	2.71	1.43
1989	12.19	9.91	5.19	2.72	1.42
1990	12.55	10.16	5.39	2.72	1.44
1991	12.90	10.42	5.32	2.76	1.42
1992	13.18	10.56	5.35	2.76	1.40
1993	13.39	10.77	5.55	2.77	1.43
1994	13.72	11.09	5.77	2.82	1.46
1995	13.95	11.25	5.95	2.86	1.49
1996	13.87	11.16	5.64	2.76	1.40
1997	14.59	11.82	5.91	2.89	1.44
1998	14.72	11.92	5.91	2.88	1.43
1999	14.84	12.10	6.07	2.88	1.44
2000	15.16	12.41	6.26	2.93	1.48
2001	14.98	12.30	6.23	2.89	1.46
2002	13.32	10.97	5.17	2.56	1.20
2003	13.40	11.17	5.27	2.55	1.20
2004	13.67	11.39	5.32	2.58	1.21
2005	14.22	11.84	5.58	2.66	1.25
2006	14.56	12.14	5.65	2.71	1.26
2007	14.93	12.37	5.66	2.74	1.25
2008	15.19	12.62	5.73	2.78	1.26
2009	16.08	13.38	5.94	2.94	1.30
2010	17.00	14.17	6.21	3.08	1.35
2011	17.80	14.93	6.34	3.22	1.37
2012	19.61	16.48	6.69	3.54	1.44
2013	26.56	19.33	7.49	4.12	1.60
2014	28.28	20.89	7.54	4.43	1.60
2015	30.46	22.80	7.96	4.81	1.68
2016	33.04	25.02	8.59	5.25	1.80
2017	36.92	28.39	9.39	5.91	1.96
2018	39.02	30.20	9.97	6.25	2.06
2019	42.93	33.97	11.40	6.99	2.35
2020	45.89	36.65	12.26	7.76	2.60

注：2002年及以后医生数系执业(助理)医师数。
Note: Number of doctors refers to number of certified (assistant) doctors since 2002.

14-4 疾病预防控制中心、妇幼保健机构情况（1978-2020年）
Basic Statistics on Center for Disease Control and Prevention , Women and Children Care Agencies（1978-2020）

单位：个、人

(unit, person)

年 份 Year	疾病预防控制中心 Center for Disease Control and Prevention		妇幼保健机构 Women and Children Care Agencies		
	机构数 Number of Institutions	人员数 Number of Employed Persons	机构数 Number of Institutions	床位数 Number of Beds	人员数 Number of Employed Persons
1978	149	3 604	142	82	1 194
1979					
1985	159	4 931	145	524	2 108
1986	159	5 083	145	712	2 234
1987	158	5 286	144	770	2 401
1988	150	5 529	144	841	2 612
1989	150	5 737	143	872	2 808
1990	150	5 930	144	928	3 001
1991	150	6 146	144	1 021	3 252
1992	149	6 388	144	1 073	3 467
1993	157	6 606	143	1 244	3 669
1994	157	6 810	143	1 350	3 869
1995	158	6 962	145	1 510	4 197
1996	158	7 136	142	1 657	4 270
1997	159	7 344	142	1 836	4 559
1998	150	7 390	141	2 024	4 692
1999	151	7 493	140	2 252	4 822
2000	160	7 574	142	2 356	5 017
2001	175	7 810	142	2 588	5 124
2002	148	7 125	144	3 174	5 624
2003	153	7 241	151	3 341	5 650
2004	150	6 782	146	3 386	5 482
2005	153	7 590	148	3 521	5 641
2006	150	7 585	148	3 662	5 703
2007	150	7 844	148	3 954	5 782
2008	152	7 847	148	4 162	5 638
2009	152	7 734	147	4 398	6 031
2010	150	7 929	147	4 704	6 152
2011	150	7 942	148	4 927	6 393
2012	150	8 013	147	5 139	6 836
2013	150	8 134	147	5 579	7 403
2014	150	8 143	145	5 717	8 108
2015	150	8 225	145	5 834	9 359
2016	152	8 301	145	6 175	11 745
2017	153	8 473	145	6 894	14 397
2018	153	8 638	146	7 324	15 375
2019	153	8 915	147	8 587	18 773
2020	150	9 495	147	8 963	20 935

14-5 主要年份等级裁判员、运动员人数

Number of Referees and Athletes in Significant Years

单位：人

年 份 Year	等级裁判员 Number of Referees in Grades	国际级裁判 International Level Referees	一级裁判 First Grade Referees	二级裁判 Second Grade Referees	三级裁判 Third Grade Referees
1985	1 316		135	280	901
1990	1 920	1	145	455	1 320
1995	1 675		57	316	134
2000	2 229		40	519	1 663
2008	1 214	2	276	832	
2009	1 989		44	1 942	
2010	1 948		633	1 304	
2011	2 114	4	41	1 014	
2012	7 056		487	3 087	3 479
2013	9 133		289	3 480	5 363
2014	3 258		291	2 954	
2015	2 714		395	2 319	
2016	4 199		531	3 668	
2017	3 605		152	3 453	
2018	2 725		536	2 189	
2019	2 753	3	289	473	1 988
2020	6 090		114	2 593	3 413

14-5 续表 continued

单位：人

年 份 Year	等级运动员 Number of Athletes in Grades	#国际级健将 International level Master Sportsmen	运动健将 Master Sportsmen	#一级运动员 First Grade Sportsmen	二级运动员 Second Grade Sportsmen
1985	1 843			63	83
1990	1 379	4	36	38	352
1995	1 474	3	27	52	328
2000	1 187			12	353
2008	463	7	21	58	377
2009	1 457	8	21	43	1 385
2010	950	7	24	83	836
2011	622	4	21	163	434
2012	1 281	2	34	190	1 038
2013	1 259	2	18	158	1 068
2014	1 105		18	177	910
2015	1 139	2	23	305	809
2016	611		29	184	398
2017	730		37	192	501
2018	773	5	18	230	520
2019	1 081	2	20	401	658
2020	444	2	16	25	414

14-6 主要年份运动员参赛获奖情况
Prizes Won by Yunnan Athletes in Significant Years

单位：枚 (medal)

年 份 Year	金 牌 Gold Medal		银 牌 Silver Medal		铜 牌 Copper Medal	
	国 际 International Competitions	全 国 National Competitions	国 际 International Competitions	全 国 National Competitions	国 际 International Competitions	全 国 National Competitions
1978	1	4	1	9	14	8
1980	4	13	2	13		21
1985	11	24	13	13	9	18
1990	4	22		27	6	19
1995	9	27	3	29	4	31
2000	1	44		38	5	36
2005	1	34	1	30		32
2006	6	13	4	15	1	12
2007	2	13		15	1	15
2008	4	14	3	6	5	11
2009	3	17	2	16	10	22
2010	5	14	4	16	7	17
2011	6	13	3	5	5	15
2012	9	14	3	10	3	15
2013	4	15	3	21	4	12
2014	9	11	6	10	1	12
2015	3	15	5	16		14
2016	7	67	7	51	3	55
2017	7	68	2	82	5	58
2018	9	122	9	87	7	87
2019	18	178	9	156	9	147
2020	3	58	1	35		35

14－7 律师、公证工作机构人员情况（2015－2020年）
Basic Statistics on Lawyers and Notarization (2015-2020)

项　　目	Item	2015	2016	2017	2018	2019	2020
律师工作	**Lawyers work**						
律师事务所(个)	Number of Law Offices (unit)	709	790	858	916	950	989
国资所	State-owned	106	105	103	96	78	62
合作所	Cooperative						
合伙所	Partnership	398	434	457	499	476	627
个人发起所	Initiated by Individual	205	251	298	321	308	300
执业律师（人）	Number of Lawyers (person)	8 190	8 963	10 143	10 995	11 889	12 580
专职律师	Full-time Lawyers	7 385	8 030	9 110	9 502	10 141	10 306
兼职律师	Part-time Lawyers	222	218	508	231	244	301
特邀律师	Guest Lawyers						
公证工作	**Notarization**						
公证处(个)	Number of Notary Offices (unit)	140	140	140	140	140	140
公证员(人)	Notaries (person)	554	578	625	648	616	620
公证员助理（人）	Assistant Notaries (person)	440	518	470	615	553	562
办理各类公证事项(万件)	Number of Notarized Affairs (10 000 items)	38.93	43.69	51.38	58.13	51.57	47.59

14-8 主要年份提供住宿的社会服务机构基本情况

Basic Statistics on Social Service Agency with Accommodation in Significant Years

年 份 Year	单位数(个) Number of Institutions(unit)	床位数(万张) Number of Beds(10 000 units)	年末在院人数(万人) Persons under Care at Year-end (10 000 persons)	社会福利经费(亿元) Funds of Institution (100 million yuan)
1985	34		0.14	0.02
1990	45		0.15	0.03
1993	49		0.16	0.05
1994	49		0.17	0.10
1995	50		0.18	0.11
1996	50		0.18	0.11
1997	50		0.22	0.13
1998	50		0.22	0.16
1999	50		0.12	0.19
2000	75		0.25	0.21
2001	112		0.28	0.23
2002	754	1.78	1.00	0.25
2003	781	1.97	1.10	0.28
2004	748	1.91	1.07	0.32
2005	771	2.06	1.09	0.56
2006	583	1.42	0.81	0.92
2007	667	2.28	1.53	1.48
2008	702	2.98	2.09	1.58
2009	729	3.77	2.75	2.20
2010	757	4.39	3.33	4.52
2011	778	4.93	3.78	7.45
2012	806	5.99	4.53	11.58
2013	992	7.44	5.63	8.79
2014	1 060	8.17	4.44	6.49
2015	1 639	11.80	5.36	13.14
2016	2 139	14.36	5.31	12.19
2017	2 251	13.30	4.02	17.82
2018	2 400	12.20	3.83	16.90
2019	2 994	12.26	3.90	29.88
2020	3 658	12.85	3.93	32.60

14-9 社会服务业发展情况（2016-2020年）
Basic Statistics on Social Service Development (2016-2020)

项目	Item	2016	2017	2018	2019	2020
社会服务工作	**Social Service Work**					
提供住宿的社会服务机构情况	**Social Service Agency Providing Accommodation**					
单位数（个）	Number of Institutions(unit)	2 139	2 251	2 400	2 994	3 658
床位数（万张）	Number of Beds (10 000 sets)	14.36	13.30	12.20	12.26	12.85
收养人数（万人）	Number of People Adopted (10 000 persons)	5.31	4.02	3.83	3.9	3.93
不提供住宿的社会服务机构(个)	**Social Service Agency without Accommodation(unit)**					
福利彩票发行单位	Welfare Lottery Issuer	12	13	15	14	14
捐赠、救助等其他事业单位	Donation，Rescue and Other Government-sponsored Institutions	242	236	236	249	243
其他社会服务机构(个)	**Other Social Service Agencies(unit)**					
婚姻	**Marriage**					
婚姻登记服务类单位	Marriage Registration Service Agency	25	24	24	22	24
殡葬	**Funeral**					
殡仪馆	Funeral Home	77	78	77	80	100
公墓	Cemetery	23	23	22	22	21
殡葬管理单位	Administrative Office of Funeral	46	48	54	57	52
组织构成(个)	**Member Organization(unit)**					
社会组织	**Social Organization**	**22 552**	**23 184**	**23 723**	**23 640**	**23 294**
社会团体	Social Group	14 973	14 679	14 647	14 333	13 562
基金会	Foundation	98	112	116	117	110
民办非企业单位	Civilian-run Nonbusiness Unit	7 481	8 393	8 960	9 190	9 622
自治组织	**Self-governing Organization**	**14 299**	**14 378**	**14 416**	**14 501**	**14 648**
社区居委会	Residential Committee	2 328	2 473	2 551	2 632	2 823
村委会	Village Neighborhood Committee	11 971	11 905	11 865	11 869	11 825

14—10 社会救助情况（2015—2020年）

Basic Statistics on Social Assistance(2015-2020)

单位：万人 (10 000 persons)

项　　目	Item	2015	2016	2017	2018	2019	2020
社会救助	**Social Assistance**						
临时救助(万人次)	Person-times of Temporary Relief			57.71	94.00	135.29	109.96
本地户籍	Local domicile			57.57	93.64	133.45	108.04
非本地户籍	Non local household registration			0.14	0.36	1.84	1.92
城市居民最低生活保障人数	Urban Residents Received Subsistence Security Allowances	98.11	89.68	70.90	48.34	43.75	41.00
农村居民最低生活保障人数	Rural Residents Received Subsistence Security Allowances	455.28	422.94	329.90	254.95	251.10	244.90
农村五保供养人数	Rural Residents Enjoy the Five-guarantee System	20.71	17.35	13.80	11.76	11.36	11.62
农村集中供养五保人数	Rural Residents Enjoy the Concentrated Form of Five-guarantee System	4.17	2.85	1.58	1.17	1.36	1.48
农村分散供养五保人数	Rural Residents Enjoy the scattered Form of Five-guarantee System	16.55	14.50	12.22	10.59	10.00	10.14
农村传统救济人数	Rural Residents Supported by the Traditional Way of Relief	3.81	3.74	3.74	3.35	2.98	2.32

14-11 全省社会保险参保情况

Number of Persons Participating in Social Insurance

单位：万人 (10 000 persons)

年 份 Year	城镇职工基本养老保险 Number of Persons Participating in Basic Pension Insurance System for Urban Enterprises' Employees	城镇职工基本医疗保险 Number of Persons Participating in Basic Medical Insurance System for Urban Employees	城乡居民医疗保险 Medical insurance for urban and rural residents	城镇失业保险 Number of Persons Participating in Unemployment Insurance System	工伤保险 Number of Persons Participating in Employment Injury Insurance System	城镇职工生育保险 Number of Persons Participating in Child-bearing Insurance System for Urban Employees
1997	168.44			129.00	47.65	57.40
1998	208.92			129.00	101.75	97.43
1999	223.47	45.00		181.00	99.64	96.67
2000	252.28	69.48		196.03	99.14	95.47
2001	243.12	185.72		190.73	97.26	96.11
2002	252.13	238.40		183.23	88.96	86.87
2003	257.34	281.52		183.01	84.11	82.79
2004	255.26	302.34		173.20	150.93	142.33
2005	258.69	320.70		189.20	166.95	156.14
2006	267.42	331.54		189.36	173.85	159.51
2007	279.36	345.81	73.00	190.00	188.47	165.14
2008	293.72	356.82	261.38	195.60	202.47	168.38
2009	306.54	397.42	365.03	198.60	215.13	181.13
2010	317.42	414.77	405.71	209.61	227.37	210.23
2011	342.82	443.36	422.44	216.75	243.40	216.49
2012	364.47	452.22	430.17	224.00	295.26	239.22
2013	384.32	457.96	660.79	232.52	334.26	270.87
2014	397.89	462.60	673.34	236.87	341.71	279.26
2015	412.94	468.29	672.47	243.34	368.07	289.83
2016	581.80	479.13	684.50	251.16	372.75	295.91
2017	591.46	491.32	3 972.49	259.81	383.67	307.92
2018	616.22	506.88	4 014.04	273.12	403.30	339.52
2019	649.88	527.96	4 005.45	289.17	438.51	356.00
2020	701.34	548.42	4 032.83	307.39	498.81	374.96

注：本表城乡居民养老保险数据在2017年以前仅为城镇居民医疗保险，2017年以后新农保与城镇居民基本医疗保险合并为城乡居民基本医疗保险。

Note: Data of basic pension insurance system for urban and rural residents in this table were only medical insurance for urban residents before 2017, and after 2017, new rural insurance and urban residents' basic medical insurance were merged into basic medical insurance system for urban and rural residents.

14−12　城镇职工基本养老保险情况（2016−2020年）

Statistics on Basic Pension Insurance for Urban Employees (2016-2020)

类　　别	Item	2016	2017	2018	2019	2020
年末参保人数（万人）	**Number of People Insured at Year-end (10 000 persons)**	**581.80**	**591.46**	**616.22**	**649.88**	**701.34**
职工	Employed Persons	413.78	420.12	440.23	468.41	515.78
企业	Enterprises	292.41	297.34	316.56	343.38	388.20
离休、退休、退职人数	Retired and Resigned Persons	168.02	171.34	175.99	181.47	185.56
基金收支情况	**Fund Revenue and Expenses**					
基本养老保险费征缴收入(亿元)	Fund Revenue (100 million yuan)	453.81	875.33	692.82	693.55	574.76
基本养老保险基金支出(亿元)	Fund Expenses (100 million yuan)	497.52	958.29	677.14	764.47	804.57
企业退休人员社会化管理服务情况(%)	**Socialized Management of Enterprise Retirees（%）**	**88.01**	**88.09**	**88.15**	**88.20**	**88.25**
企业养老金实发人数(万人)	Number of People Receiving Pension Insurance (10 000 persons)	121.93	123.12	126.32	128.76	131.35

14–13 残疾人事业基本情况（2017–2020年）
Basic Statistics on the Work for Persons with Disabilities（2017-2020）

项　目	Item	2017	2018	2019	2020
康复（万人）	**Rehabilitation**				
视力残疾基本康复服务人数	Rehabilitation of Persons with Visual Disability (10 000 persons)	3.55	4.76	2.73	2.56
听力残疾基本康复服务人数	Rehabilitation of Persons with Hearing and Speech Disability (10 000 persons)	2.11	2.67	2.14	2.00
言语残疾基本康复服务人数	Rehabilitation of Persons with Speech Disabilities (10 000 persons)	0.22	0.32	0.17	0.17
肢体残疾基本康复服务人数	Rehabilitation of Persons with Physical Disability (10 000 persons)	14.07	20.56	12.78	11.47
智力残疾基本康复服务人数	Rehabilitation of Persons with Intellectual Disability (10 000 persons)	1.88	2.56	1.62	1.56
精神残疾基本康复服务人数	Prevention and Rehabilitation of Mental Illness (PRMI)(10 000 persons)	4.09	5.82	5.58	5.94
多重残疾基本康复服务人数	Rehabilitation of Persons with Multiple Disabilities (10 000 persons)	1.38	2.04	1.56	1.58
教育(人)	**Education (person)**				
残疾人中等职业教育在校生	Students at Secondary Vocational Schools for PWDs	819	1 545	968	1 039
普通高等院校录取残疾考生	Disable Students Admitted to Higher Education Institutions	917	773	934	1 098
社会保障(万人)	**Social Security (10 000 persons)**				
托养残疾人	Fostered PWDs	1.56	1.78	1.77	1.83
扶贫(万人次)	**Poverty Alleviation**				
残联系统开展农村残疾人实用技术培训	Vocational Skills Training for PWDs (10 000 person-times)	3.52	3.29	3.40	2.33
就业（万人）	Employment				
城镇残疾人就业总人数	Persons with Disabled Employed in Urban (10 000 persons)	45.00	44.94	42.18	42.24
集中就业人数	Concentrated Employment (10 000 persons)	0.77	0.76	0.69	0.69
按比例就业人数	Proportional employment (10 000 persons)	1.84	1.83	1.58	1.62
个体及其他形式就业人数	Individuals and Other Forms of Employment (10 000 persons)	42.39	42.36	39.91	39.94
维权(件)	**Rights Protection (case)**				
残疾人法律救助工作站（个）	**Legal Assistance Station for PWDs (unit)**	32	36	62	85
残疾人法律救助工作站办理的案件(件)	Case Handled by the Legal Assistance Station for PWDs (unit)	79	93	101	96
贫困残疾人家庭无障碍改造（户）	Barrier-free Renovation of Poor Families with Disabilities (householc	3 419	4 141	4 389	5 358
残疾人机动轮椅车燃油补贴（万人）	Fuel Subsidy for Disabled Motorized Wheelchairs (10 000 persons)	1.73	2.19	1.79	1.75
组织建设(万人)	**Organization Development**				
残疾人人口库持证残疾人	PWDs with Disability Certificate in the PWD Database (10 000 persons)	136.07	144.15	151.27	149.93

主要统计指标解释

卫生机构 指从卫生行政部门取得《医疗机构执业许可证》，或从民政、工商行政、机构编制管理部门取得法人单位登记证书，为社会提供医疗保健、疾病控制、卫生监督服务或从事医学科研和教育等工作的单位。卫生机构包括医院、疗养院、社区卫生服务中心（站）、卫生院、门诊部、诊所（卫生所、医务室）、急救中心（站）、采供血机构、妇幼保健院（所、站）、专科疾病防治院（所、站）、疾病预防控制中心（防疫站）、卫生监督所、卫生监督检验（监测、检测）机构、医学科研机构、医学在职培训机构、健康教育所（站）等其他卫生机构。

医疗机构 指从卫生行政部门取得《医疗机构执业许可证》的机构，包括医院、疗养院、社区卫生服务中心（站）、卫生院、门诊部、诊所（卫生所、医务室）、妇幼保健院（所、站）、专科疾病防治院（所、站）、急救中心（站）和临床检验中心。

卫生技术人员 包括执业（助理）医师、注册护士、药剂人员、检验和影像人员等卫生专业人员。不包括从事管理工作的卫生技术人员（一律计入管理人员）。

执业医师 指具有《医师执业证》及其“级别”为“执业医师”且实际从事医疗、预防保健工作的人员，不包括实际从事管理工作的执业医师。执业医师类别分为临床、中医、口腔和公共卫生。

执业助理医师 指具有《医师执业证》及其“级别”为“执业助理医师”且实际从事医疗、预防保健工作的人员，不包括实际从事管理工作的执业助理医师。执业助理医师类别同样分为临床、中医、口腔和公共卫生四类。

城镇职工基本养老保险

1.（参保）职工人数 指报告期末按照国家法律、法规和有关政策规定参加基本养老保险并在社保经办机构已建立缴费记录档案的职工人数，包括中断缴费但未终止养老保险关系的职工人数，不包括只登记未建立缴费记录档案的人数。

2.（参保）离退休人员人数 指报告期末参加基本养老保险的离休、退休和退职人员的人数。

3. 基本养老保险基金收入 指根据国家有关规定，由纳入基本养老保险范围的缴费单位和个人按国家规定的缴费基数和缴费比例缴纳的养老保险基金，以及通过其他方式取得的形成基金来源的收入。包括单位和职工个人缴纳的基本养老保险费、基本养老保险基金利息收入、上级补助收入、下级上解收入、转移收入、财政补贴和其他收入。

4. 基本养老保险基金支出 指按照国家政策规定的开支范围和开支标准从养老保险基金中支付给参加基本养老保险的个人的养老金、丧葬抚恤补助，以及由于保险关系转移、上下级之间调剂资金等原因而发生的支出。包括离休金、退休金、退职金、各种补贴、医疗费、死亡丧葬补助费、抚恤救济费、社会保险经办机构管理费、补助下级支出、上解上级支出、转移支出、其他支出等。

律师 指受聘参加法律顾问工作，担任法律顾问、刑（民）事代理人、刑事辩护人，办理非诉讼事件，解答法律询问，代写法律事务文书等主要从事律师业务的专职法律工作者和兼职律师。

公证人员 指在国家公证机关依法办理公证事务的司法人员，包括公证员、助理公证员和公证处公证的其他人员。

Explanatory Notes on Main Statistical Indicators

Health Care Institutions refer to the units which have been qualified the Certification of Health Care Institution by the administration of public health, or qualified the Certification of Corporate Unit by the civil affairs, administration for industry and commerce, commission office for public sector reform, and engaging in medical care, disease prevention and control, health supervision and inspection, medicine research and health education, etc., including: hospitals, sanatoriums, community health service centers (stations), health centers, clinics (health stations and infirmaries), first-aid centres (stations), blood gathering and supplying institutions, women and children care agencies (centres and stations), special disease prevention and curing agencies (centres and stations), disease prevention and control centres (epidemic prevention stations), health supervision and inspection agencies, sanitary inspection institutions, medicinal scientific research and on-job training institutions, health education centres and so on.

Medical Organizations refer to the institutions which have been qualified the Certification of Health Care Institution by the administration of public health, including: hospitals, sanatoriums, community health service centers (stations), health centers, clinics (health stations and infirmaries), women and children care agencies (centres and stations), special disease prevention and curing agencies (centres and stations), first-aid centres (stations) and clinic inspection centers.

Medical Technical Personnel refer to the professional staff engaged in health care, including licensed (assistant) doctors, registered nurse, pharmacists, laboratory technician, and imaging staff, excluding the medical technical personnel engaged in management job (included as the management staff).

Licensed Doctors refer to the medical workers who have obtained the licenses of qualified doctors and are employed in medical treatment, disease prevention or healthcare institutions, excluding the licensed doctors engaged in management job. The classification of licensed doctors is clinician, Chinese medicine, dentist and public health.

Licensed Assistant Doctors refer to the medical workers who have obtained the licenses of qualified assistant doctors and are employed in medical treatment, disease prevention or healthcare institutions, excluding the licensed assistant doctors engaged in management job. The classification of licensed assistant doctors is clinician, Chinese medicine, dentist and public health.

Basic Pension Insurance for Urban Employees

1.Number of staff and workers covered refers to staff and workers participating in the basic pension insurance programme according to national laws, regulations and related policies at the end of the reference period, who have already had payment records in social security management agencies, including those who have interrupt payment without terminating the insurance programme. Those who have registered in the programme but with no payment records are not included.

2. Number of retirees participating in the basic pension insurance programme refers to the number of retirees participating in basic pension insurance programmes by the end of the reference period.

3. Revenue of the basic pension insurance programme refers to payments made by employers and individuals participating in the pension insurance programme in accordance with the basis and proportion stipulated in State regulations, and income from other sources that become source of pension insurance fund, including the premium paid by employers and staff and workers, interest income, subsidies from higher level agencies, income as transfer from subordinate agencies, transferred income, government financial subsidies and other income.

4. Expenditure of basic pension insurance programme refers to payment made on pensions and funeral subsidies to those retired and resigned people covered in pension insurance programmes according to related national policies on scopeand standard of expenditure. Also included are expenditure which arises due to shift of the insurance relationship or adjustment of funds among agencies. More specifically, included are pensions for resigned people, pensions for retired people, pension for people quitting jobs, various subsidies, medical fees, funeral subsidies, compensation payments, management fees for social security agencies, expenses on subsidies to lower subordinates, expenses as transfer to agencies at higher level, transferred expenditure and other expenditure.

Lawyers refer to the full-time legal workers and the part-time lawyers engaged in the law practices, employed by legal counseling firms to act as legal advisers, agents in criminal or civil lawsuits and defenders in criminal lawsuits, to handle non-lawsuit legal matters, advise on matters of law and write legal papers for others.

Notary Personnel refer to the judicial officers who handle the notary affairs under the law in the national notary organs, including notaries, assistant notaries and other workers who handle the notary affairs in the notary offices.

Chapter 15

十五、人口与就业
Population and Employment

15-1 主要年份全省年末人口数
Historical Population at Year-end in Significant Years

单位：万人 (10 000 persons)

年 份 Year	总人口 Total Population	按性别分 By Sex 男 Male	 女 Female	按城乡分 By Residence 城镇人口 Urban	 乡村人口 Rural
1949	1 595.0				
1952	1 695.1			82.3	1 612.8
1957	1 896.8	941.9	954.8	237.1	1 659.7
1958	1 914.5	959.9	954.6	349.7	1 564.8
1960	1 894.6	937.8	956.7	305.2	1 589.4
1962	1 963.7	966.2	997.5	275.0	1 688.7
1965	2 160.4	1 075.3	1 085.1	261.4	1 899.0
1970	2 503.3	1 246.4	1 256.9	271.2	2 232.1
1973	2 746.9	1 369.7	1 377.2	323.9	2 423.0
1974	2 819.0	1 408.0	1 411.0	326.1	2 492.9
1975	2 884.3	1 441.8	1 442.5	335.9	2 548.4
1976	2 951.7	1 477.1	1 474.6	343.3	2 608.4
1977	3 024.6	1 515.0	1 509.6	351.7	2 672.9
1978	3 091.5	1 548.7	1 542.8	375.7	2 715.8
1979	3 134.8	1 569.1	1 565.6	388.3	2 746.5
1980	3 173.4	1 590.0	1 583.4	395.4	2 778.0
1981	3 222.8	1 622.2	1 600.6	416.5	2 806.3
1982	3 283.1	1 657.5	1 625.6	433.0	2 850.1
1983	3 330.8	1 683.1	1 647.7	472.0	2 858.8
1984	3 372.1	1 707.3	1 664.8	698.7	2 673.4
1985	3 418.1	1 733.7	1 684.4	904.6	2 513.5
1986	3 480.0	1 766.8	1 713.2	1 007.5	2 472.5
1987	3 534.0	1 797.7	1 736.3	996.2	2 537.8
1988	3 594.0	1 829.0	1 765.0	1 426.1	2 167.9
1989	3 648.0	1 861.2	1 786.8	1 524.5	2 123.5
1990	3 730.6	1 910.8	1 819.8	1 510.1	2 220.5
1991	3 782.1	1 939.1	1 843.0	1 555.2	2 226.9
1992	3 831.6	1 967.1	1 864.5	1 608.1	2 223.5
1993	3 885.2	1 997.0	1 888.2	1 664.0	2 221.2
1994	3 939.2	2 027.1	1 912.1	1 782.1	2 157.1
1995	3 989.6	2 055.2	1 934.4	1 821.3	2 168.3
1996	4 041.5	2 084.8	1 956.7	1 857.4	2 184.1
1997	4 094.0	2 112.9	1 981.1	1 937.3	2 156.7
1998	4 143.8	2 139.0	2 004.8	1 951.7	2 192.1
1999	4 192.4	2 165.8	2 026.6	1 991.3	2 201.1
2000	4 240.8	2 192.0	2 048.8	990.6	3 250.2
2001	4 287.4	2 217.4	2 070.0	1 066.0	3 221.4
2002	4 333.1	2 240.6	2 092.5	1 127.0	3 206.1
2003	4 375.6	2 263.6	2 112.0	1 163.9	3 211.7
2004	4 415.2	2 284.1	2 131.1	1 240.7	3 174.5
2005	4 450.4	2 302.2	2 148.2	1 312.9	3 137.5
2006	4 483.0	2 319.1	2 163.9	1 367.3	3 115.7
2007	4 514.0	2 335.1	2 178.9	1 426.4	3 087.6
2008	4 543.0	2 350.1	2 192.9	1 499.2	3 043.8
2009	4 571.0	2 364.6	2 206.4	1 554.1	3 016.9
2010	4 601.6	2 387.6	2 214.0	1 601.8	2 999.8
2011	4 620.0	2 389.9	2 230.1	1 689.5	2 930.5
2012	4 631.0	2 395.6	2 235.4	1 781.5	2 849.5
2013	4 641.0	2 400.7	2 240.3	1 855.9	2 785.1
2014	4 653.0	2 407.0	2 246.0	1 917.5	2 735.5
2015	4 663.0	2 412.1	2 250.9	2 001.8	2 661.2
2016	4 677.0	2 419.4	2 257.6	2 087.8	2 589.2
2017	4 693.0	2 427.6	2 265.4	2 172.4	2 520.6
2018	4 703.0	2 432.8	2 270.2	2 231.1	2 471.9
2019	4 714.0	2 438.5	2 275.5	2 294.3	2 419.7
2020	4 722.0	2 442.6	2 279.4	2 363.4	2 358.6

注：本表2011-2019年数据根据第七次全国人口普查结果进行了修订。
Note: Data from 2011 to 2019 in this table have been adjusted according to the seventh National Census.

15-2 各州市户数、人口数及构成（2020年）
Number of Households, Population and Its Composition by Region (2020)

州市	Region	总户数（万户）Family Households (10 000 households)	总人口（万人）Total Population (10 000 persons)	按性别分（万人）By Sex (10 000 persons)		按城乡分（万人）By Residence (10 000 persons)		人口密度（人/平方千米）Population Density (person/sq.km)
				男 Male	女 Female	城镇人口 Urban	乡村人口 Rural	
全省	**Yunnan**	**1 644.5**	**4 722.0**	**2 442.6**	**2 279.4**	**2 363.4**	**2 358.6**	**119.8**
昆明	Kunming	351.5	846.3	432.9	413.4	674.3	172.0	392.1
曲靖	Qujing	207.1	576.6	298.9	277.7	282.7	293.9	193.1
玉溪	Yuxi	78.8	225.0	115.5	109.4	121.1	103.9	147.2
保山	Baoshan	73.8	243.1	124.8	118.3	85.3	157.8	123.8
昭通	Zhaotong	165.5	509.3	267.2	242.1	201.3	308.0	221.2
丽江	Lijiang	42.2	125.5	64.7	60.8	59.8	65.7	59.1
普洱	Pu'er	82.7	240.5	126.5	114.0	97.5	143.0	53.0
临沧	Lincang	71.0	225.8	118.1	107.7	79.2	146.6	92.2
楚雄	Chuxiong	88.1	241.7	123.5	118.2	108.3	133.4	55.8
红河	Honghe	149.0	447.8	232.0	215.8	213.6	234.2	136.0
文山	Wenshan	104.4	350.3	182.5	167.8	130.3	220.0	108.7
西双版纳	Xishuangbanna	44.9	130.4	68.6	61.8	61.4	69.0	66.2
大理	Dali	110.9	333.8	169.3	164.4	143.1	190.7	113.3
德宏	Dehong	44.1	131.8	68.7	63.1	64.5	67.3	114.3
怒江	Nujiang	17.8	55.3	29.0	26.3	29.0	26.3	37.7
迪庆	Diqing	12.7	38.8	20.3	18.4	12.1	26.7	16.3

15-3 全省各民族人口数（2020年）
Provincial Population by Nationality (2020)

单位：万人、%　　(10 000 persons ,%)

民族	Nationality	人口数 Population	比重 Proportion	民族	Nationality	人口数 Population	比重 Proportion
全　省	**Yunnan**	**4722.00**	**100.0**	藏　族	Tibetan	14.80	0.3
汉　族	Han Nationality	3158.04	66.9	景颇族	Jingpo Nationality	14.64	0.3
彝　族	Yi Nationality	507.22	10.7	布朗族	Bulang Nationality	11.98	0.3
白　族	Bai Nationality	160.41	3.4	普米族	Pumi Nationality	4.31	0.1
哈尼族	Hani Nationality	163.34	3.5	怒　族	Nu Nationality	3.43	0.1
壮　族	Zhuang Nationality	121.01	2.6	阿昌族	Achang Nationality	4.00	0.1
傣　族	Dai Nationality	125.97	2.7	基诺族	Jinuo Nationality	2.53	0.1
苗　族	Miao Nationality	125.36	2.7	德昂族	De'ang Nationality	2.08	0.0
傈僳族	Lisu Nationality	70.54	1.5	蒙古族	Mongolian	2.52	0.1
回　族	Hui Nationality	73.77	1.6	独龙族	Dulong Nationality	0.67	0.0
拉祜族	Lahu Nationality	46.94	1.0	满　族	Manchu Nationality	1.96	0.0
佤　族	Wa Nationality	38.37	0.8	水　族	Shui Nationality	0.98	0.0
纳西族	Naxi Nationality	30.43	0.6	布依族	Buyi Nationality	6.82	0.1
瑶　族	Yao Nationality	21.89	0.5	其　他	Other Nationalities	8.01	0.2

15-4 全省户数、年平均人口数及人口密度（1978-2020年）
Number of Households, Annual Average Population and Population Density (1978-2020)

年 份 Year	户 数 (万户) Number of Households (10 000 households)	平均每户人数 (人／户) Average Households Size (person/household)	年均人口数 (万人) Annual Average Population (10 000 persons)	人口密度 (人／平方千米) Population Density (person/sq.km)
1978	571.8	5.4	3 058.0	78.5
1979	577.5	5.4	3 113.1	79.6
1980	590.9	5.4	3 154.1	80.5
1981	605.8	5.3	3 198.1	81.8
1982	617.5	5.3	3 252.9	83.3
1983	634.8	5.2	3 307.0	84.5
1984	649.6	5.2	3 351.5	85.6
1985	667.4	5.1	3 395.1	86.8
1986	690.6	5.0	3 449.5	90.9
1987	721.5	4.9	3 507.0	92.3
1988	752.6	4.8	3 564.0	93.8
1989	782.7	4.6	3 621.0	95.3
1990	812.0	4.5	3 689.3	94.7
1991	837.4	4.5	3 756.4	96.4
1992	857.8	4.4	3 806.9	97.7
1993	883.4	4.4	3 858.4	99.0
1994	902.4	4.3	3 912.2	100.4
1995	925.9	4.3	3 964.4	101.3
1996	946.1	4.2	4 015.6	103.1
1997	965.4	4.2	4 067.8	103.9
1998	991.3	4.2	4 118.9	105.2
1999	1 012.0	4.2	4 168.1	106.4
2000	1 030.6	4.1	4 216.6	107.6
2001	1 046.7	4.1	4 264.1	108.8
2002	1 063.3	4.1	4 310.3	109.8
2003	1 083.1	4.0	4 354.4	111.0
2004	1 117.1	4.0	4 395.4	112.0
2005	1 216.2	3.7	4 432.8	112.9
2006	1 183.9	3.8	4 466.7	113.8
2007	1 222.3	3.7	4 498.5	114.5
2008	1 252.9	3.7	4 528.5	115.3
2009	1 287.3	3.5	4 557.0	116.0
2010	1 323.5	3.5	4 586.3	116.6
2011	1 358.8	3.4	4 610.8	117.2
2012	1 362.1	3.4	4 625.5	117.5
2013	1 406.4	3.3	4 636.0	117.8
2014	1 410.0	3.3	4 647.0	118.1
2015	1 457.2	3.2	4 658.0	118.3
2016	1 461.6	3.2	4 670.0	118.7
2017	1 513.9	3.1	4 685.0	119.1
2018	1 567.7	3.0	4 698.0	119.3
2019	1 571.3	3.0	4 708.5	119.6
2020	1 644.5	2.9	4 718.0	119.8

15-5 七次全国人口普查全省人口基本情况
Basic Statistics on National Population Census in 1953,1964,1982,1990, 2000 , 2010and 2020

指　　标	Item	1953	1964	1982	1990	2000	2010	2020
全省总人口(万人)	**Total Population of Yunnan Province (10 000 persons)**	**1 713.3**	**2 051.0**	**3 255.4**	**3 697.3**	**4 235.9**	**4 596.6**	**4 720.9**
男	Male	846.0	1 024.7	1 650.0	1 899.6	2 219.9	2 385.0	2 442.1
女	Female	867.3	1 026.3	1 605.4	1 797.7	2 016.0	2 211.6	2 278.8
性别比（以女性为100）	Sex Ratio (female=100)	97.6	99.8	102.8	105.7	110.1	107.8	107.2
家庭户规模（人/户）	**Average Family Household Size (person/household)**		**4.7**	**5.2**	**4.5**	**3.7**	**3.5**	**2.9**
各年龄组人口构成(%)	Population by Age Group (%)							
0–14岁	0-14	34.5	39.2	39.2	31.7	26.0	20.7	19.6
15–64岁	15-64	58.1	58.2	56.4	61.2	68.0	71.7	69.7
65岁及以上	65 and Over	7.4	2.6	4.5	7.1	6.0	7.6	10.8
民族人口数	**Population by Ethnicity**							
汉族人口数(万人)	Han (10 000 persons)	1 178.8	1 410.7	2 223.4	2 462.8	2 820.7	3 062.9	3 157.3
占总人口比重(%)	Percentage to Total Population (%)	68.8	68.8	68.3	66.6	66.6	66.6	66.9
少数民族人口数(万人)	Ethnic Minorities (10 000 persons)	534.5	640.3	1 032.0	1 234.5	1 415.2	1 533.7	1 563.6
占总人口比重(%)	Percentage to Total Population(%)	31.2	31.2	31.7	33.4	33.4	33.4	33.1
每十万人拥有的各种受教育程度人口数(万人)	**Population with Various Education Attainments Per 100 000 Persons (10 000persons)**							
大专及以上	Junior College and Above		0.03	0.03	0.08	0.20	0.58	1.16
高中和中专	Senior Secondary School and Technical Secondary School		0.10	0.28	0.41	0.66	0.84	1.03
初中	Junior Secondary School		0.31	1.02	1.38	2.12	2.75	2.92
小学	Primary School		2.31	2.93	3.79	4.48	4.34	3.57
平均受教育年限(年)	Average Education Year (year)		2.2	3.6	4.8	6.3	7.6	8.8
文盲人口数及文盲率	**Illiterate Population and Illiterate Rate**							
文盲人口数(万人)	Illiterate Population (10 000 persons)		969.9	1 025.1	940.6	484.2	276.9	219.3
文盲率(%)	Illiterate Rate (%)		47.3	31.5	25.4	11.4	6.0	4.7
平均预期寿命(岁)	**Life Expectancy (year old)**			**60.8**	**63.5**	**65.5**	**69.5**	**-**
男	Male			59.9	62.1	64.2	67.1	-
女	Female			61.6	64.9	66.9	72.4	-

注：1.1953年总人口数据中包括了间接调查人口，而民族人口、城乡人口中未包括。
　　2.1964年文盲人口为12岁及12岁以上不识字人口，1982、1990、2000、2010、2020年文盲人口为15岁及以上不识字或识字很少人口。

Note:a.Total population of 1953 National Population Census includes the population from indirect survey,but it didn't include the ethnic minority population, urban and rural population.

b.Illiterate population of 1964 National Population Census referred to the population aged 12 and over who are unable to read. Illiterate population of 1982,1990,2000,2010 and 2020 National Population Censuses referred to the population aged 15 and over who are unable or have difficulty to read.

15-6　人口社会就业基本情况（2015-2020年）
Basic Statistics on Employment (2015-2020)

单位：万人　　(10 000 persons)

项　　目	Item	2015	2016	2017	2018	2019	2020
全省就业人员	**Number of Employed Persons**	**2 823.00**	**2 855.00**	**2 831.00**	**2 822.00**	**2 812.00**	**2 806.00**
按三次产业分就业人员	**Employed persons by Three Industries Persons**						
第一产业	Primary Industry	1 478.41	1 474.04	1 380.11	1 295.30	1 260.51	1 226.00
第二产业	Secondary Industry	400.87	415.97	437.11	459.99	469.95	497.00
第三产业	Tertiary Industry	943.73	964.99	1 013.78	1 066.72	1 081.54	1 083.00
就业人员构成(%)	**Composition of Employed Persons(%)**						
第一产业	Primary Industry	52.4	51.6	48.8	45.9	44.8	43.7
第二产业	Secondary Industry	14.2	14.6	15.4	16.3	16.7	17.7
第三产业	Tertiary Industry	33.4	33.8	35.8	37.8	38.5	38.6
按城乡分就业人员	**Number of Employed Persons by Urban and Rural Areas**						
城镇就业人员	Urban Employed Persons	917.87	1 017.09	1 062.67	1 152.11	1 231.04	1 292.00
乡村就业人员	Rural Employed Persons	1 905.13	1 837.91	1 768.33	1 669.89	1 580.96	1 514.00
城镇单位在岗职工人数	**Number of Staff and Workers in Urban Units**	**343.25**	**345.80**	**357.38**	**359.20**	**310.48**	**305.34**
国有单位	State-owned Units	165.18	165.54	160.88	155.84	150.30	155.04
城镇集体单位	Urban Collective-owned Units	10.62	9.17	8.65	6.83	7.05	6.08
其他单位	Units of Other Types of Ownership	167.45	171.08	187.85	196.53	153.13	144.22
城镇单位女性就业人员	**Number of Female Employment in Urban Units**	**144.15**	**146.13**	**155.22**	**160.28**	**149.67**	**152.11**
城镇登记失业人数	**Number of Registered Unemployed Persons in Urban Areas**	**19.47**	**20.58**	**19.81**	**20.88**	**22.93**	**31.86**
城镇登记失业率(%)	**Registered Unemployment Rate in Urban Areas (%)**	**3.96**	**3.60**	**3.20**	**3.40**	**3.25**	**3.92**

15-7 按三次产业分的年末就业人员数（1980-2020年）
Number of Employed Persons at Year-end by Type of Industry (1980-2020)

单位：万人 (10 000 persons)

年 份 Year	全 省 Yunnan	第一产业 Primary Industry	第二产业 Secondary Industry	第三产业 Tertiary Industry	构 成 Percentage (%) (total=100) 第一产业 Primary Industry	第二产业 Secondary Industry	第三产业 Tertiary Industry
1980	1 404.20	1 194.00	113.30	96.90	85.0	8.1	6.9
1981	1 479.80	1 246.10	124.10	109.60	84.2	8.4	7.4
1982	1 543.60	1 295.10	129.30	119.20	83.9	8.4	7.7
1983	1 583.20	1 315.40	133.40	134.40	83.1	8.4	8.5
1984	1 620.30	1 322.70	144.30	153.30	81.6	8.9	9.5
1985	1 672.30	1 329.20	172.00	171.10	79.5	10.3	10.2
1986	1 731.40	1 367.80	177.40	186.20	79.0	10.2	10.8
1987	1 777.50	1 411.10	182.90	183.50	79.4	10.3	10.3
1988	1 826.90	1 454.40	183.30	189.20	79.6	10.0	10.4
1989	1 880.70	1 503.20	183.90	193.60	79.9	9.8	10.3
1990	1 922.70	1 537.80	184.80	200.10	80.0	9.6	10.4
1991	1 989.50	1 588.80	191.70	209.00	79.9	9.6	10.5
1992	2 032.60	1 612.90	198.00	221.70	79.4	9.9	10.7
1993	2 071.50	1 630.90	203.60	237.00	78.7	9.9	11.4
1994	2 108.70	1 642.10	215.80	250.80	77.9	10.2	11.9
1995	2 149.00	1 656.10	216.60	276.30	77.1	10.1	12.9
1996	2 186.20	1 596.90	242.70	346.60	73.0	11.1	15.9
1997	2 223.50	1 653.20	236.00	334.30	74.4	10.6	15.0
1998	2 240.50	1 687.50	232.00	321.00	75.3	10.4	14.3
1999	2 244.00	1 720.40	197.50	326.10	76.7	8.8	14.5
2000	2 295.40	1 695.90	210.40	389.20	73.9	9.2	17.0
2001	2 322.50	1 710.40	207.90	404.20	73.7	9.0	17.4
2002	2 341.30	1 715.80	206.50	419.00	73.3	8.8	17.9
2003	2 353.30	1 709.30	209.90	434.10	72.6	8.9	18.5
2004	2 401.40	1 711.90	218.40	471.10	71.3	9.1	19.6
2005	2 461.30	1 709.20	245.10	507.00	69.4	10.0	20.6
2006	2 517.60	1 696.95	262.45	558.15	67.4	10.4	22.2
2007	2 573.80	1 684.70	279.80	609.30	65.4	10.9	23.7
2008	2 638.37	1 678.42	298.57	661.38	63.6	11.3	25.1
2009	2 684.80	1 672.50	321.30	691.00	62.3	12.0	25.7
2010	2 794.00	1 687.58	352.04	754.38	60.4	12.6	27.0
2011	2 844.00	1 689.34	372.56	782.10	59.4	13.1	27.5
2012	2 835.00	1 610.00	382.16	842.85	56.8	13.5	29.7
2013	2 835.00	1 559.25	388.40	887.36	55.0	13.7	31.3
2014	2 859.00	1 515.27	397.40	946.33	53.0	13.9	33.1
2015	2 823.00	1 478.41	400.87	943.73	52.4	14.2	33.4
2016	2 855.00	1 474.04	415.97	964.99	51.6	14.6	33.8
2017	2 831.00	1 380.11	437.11	1 013.78	48.8	15.4	35.8
2018	2 822.00	1 295.30	459.99	1 066.72	45.9	16.3	37.8
2019	2 812.00	1 260.51	469.95	1 081.54	44.8	16.7	38.5
2020	2 806.00	1 226.00	497.00	1 083.00	43.7	17.7	38.6

注：2000年起就业人员人数，按一、二、三产业划分的就业人员人数计算方法有调整，详见本篇末指标解释。
Note: Since 2000, the statistical method for employed persons in primary, secondary and tertiary industries is adjusted. The detail is explained in the explanatory notes at the end of this part.

15-8 按城乡分的年末就业人员数（1980-2020年）
Number of Employed Persons at Year-end by Residence in Urban and Rural Areas (1980-2020)

单位：万人 (10 000 persons)

年份 Year	就业人员 Employed Persons	城镇就业人员 Engaged Persons in Urban Private Enterprises and Self-employed Individuals	乡村就业人员 Rural Employed Persons
1980	1 404.20	0.81	1 173.40
1981	1 479.80	1.80	1 242.60
1982	1 543.60	2.53	1 298.70
1983	1 583.20	4.47	1 331.40
1984	1 620.30	8.26	1 355.40
1985	1 672.30	11.60	1 397.70
1986	1 731.40	11.94	1 450.80
1987	1 777.50	11.86	1 490.90
1988	1 826.90	13.51	1 533.30
1989	1 880.70	13.49	1 581.40
1990	1 922.65	13.75	1 617.03
1995	2 149.00	32.30	1 797.97
1998	2 240.50	57.50	1 878.80
1999	2 244.00	69.90	1 881.80
2000	2 295.40	66.40	1 948.80
2001	2 322.53	81.83	1 971.02
2002	2 341.25	92.54	1 990.68
2003	2 353.33	97.38	2 002.70
2004	2 401.39	125.45	2 029.99
2005	2 461.32	163.35	2 050.93
2006	2 517.60	159.28	2 099.10
2007	2 573.82	181.03	2 096.51
2008	2 638.37	222.13	2 112.74
2009	2 684.77	235.46	2 137.27
2010	2 794.00	661.07	2 132.93
2011	2 844.00	720.09	2 123.91
2012	2 835.00	796.66	2 038.34
2013	2 835.00	825.55	2 009.45
2014	2 859.00	860.84	1 998.16
2015	2 823.00	917.87	1 905.13
2016	2 855.00	1 017.09	1 837.91
2017	2 831.00	1 062.67	1 768.33
2018	2 822.00	1 152.11	1 669.89
2019	2 812.00	1 231.04	1 580.96
2020	2 806.00	1 292.00	1 514.00

注：本表2011-2019年数据根据第七次全国人口普查结果进行了修订。
Note: Data from 2011 to 2019 in this table have been adusted according to the seventh National Census.

15-9 各州市按城乡分的年末就业人员数（2020年）
Number of Employed Persons at Year-end by Residence in Urban and Rural Areas and by Region (2020)

单位：万人 (10 000 persons)

州 市	Region	就业人员 Number of Employed Persons	城镇就业人员 Urban Employed Persons	乡村就业人员 Rural Employed Persons
全 省	**Yunnan**	**2 806.00**	**1 292.00**	**1 514.00**
昆 明	Kunming	502.43	355.44	146.99
曲 靖	Qujing	341.04	157.38	183.66
玉 溪	Yuxi	147.10	79.04	68.06
保 山	Baoshan	149.97	51.84	98.12
昭 通	Zhaotong	280.80	91.73	189.07
丽 江	Lijiang	78.25	36.61	41.64
普 洱	Pu'er	149.30	58.83	90.47
临 沧	Lincang	136.90	47.48	89.42
楚 雄	Chuxiong	151.00	66.15	84.85
红 河	Honghe	268.15	126.58	141.57
文 山	Wenshan	200.81	64.54	136.27
西双版纳	Xishuangbanna	68.59	29.04	39.55
大 理	Dali	198.90	70.92	127.98
德 宏	Dehong	75.32	31.63	43.70
怒 江	Nujiang	32.16	12.63	19.53
迪 庆	Diqing	25.27	12.16	13.11

15-10 分行业城镇单位年末职工人数（2015-2020年）

Number of Staff and Workers in Urban Unit by Sector at Year-end (2015-2020)

单位：万人 (10 000 persons)

国民经济行业	Sector	2015	2016	2017	2018	2019	2020
城镇单位在岗职工人数	**Number of Staff and Workers in Urban Units**	**343.25**	**345.80**	**357.38**	**359.20**	**310.48**	**305.34**
农、林、牧、渔业	Farming,Forestry,Animal Husbandry and Fishery	5.48	5.03	4.19	3.55	2.89	2.06
采矿业	Mining	11.89	10.59	11.59	10.73	6.20	5.44
制造业	Manufacturing	49.79	48.22	55.72	55.52	37.84	36.44
电力、热力、燃气及水生产和供应业	Production and Supply of Electric Power, Heat, Gas and Water	8.82	9.06	9.41	9.47	11.38	10.71
建筑业	Construction	48.41	51.00	51.19	50.29	27.23	23.78
批发和零售业	Wholesale and Retail Trade	21.57	21.69	21.03	21.01	13.99	12.82
交通运输、仓储及邮政业	Transportation,Storage and Post	14.87	15.20	15.86	15.57	14.67	14.54
住宿和餐饮业	Hotel and Food Service	7.51	7.29	7.54	7.51	4.94	4.48
信息传输、软件和信息技术服务业	Information Transmission, Software and Information Technology Service	4.27	4.60	4.80	4.47	4.94	4.82
金融业	Banking	8.77	9.06	9.07	8.99	9.74	9.33
房地产业	Real Estate	9.65	9.72	10.69	11.94	9.07	8.97
租赁和商务服务业	Leasing Trade and Business Service	7.99	8.41	8.94	9.55	9.10	9.63
科学研究和技术服务业	Scientific Research, Technology Service and Geological Prospecting	8.94	9.09	9.35	9.02	8.22	8.65
水利、环境和公共设施管理业	Water Conservancy, Admistration of Environment and Public Facilities	5.63	5.62	5.41	5.41	4.54	4.76
居民服务、修理和其他服务业	Services to Households, Repair and Other Services	1.16	1.36	2.01	2.28	1.48	1.40
教育	Education	56.10	56.47	55.58	55.83	58.09	62.34
卫生和社会工作	Health Care, Social Works	21.59	21.88	22.33	22.98	24.35	27.76
文化、体育和娱乐业	Culture, Sports and Entertainment	2.98	3.10	3.32	3.44	3.34	3.42
公共管理、社会保障和社会组织	Common Administration and Social Organization	47.81	48.41	49.35	51.64	58.47	53.98

15-11 各州市分行业年末城镇单位就业人员数（2020年）

Number of Employed Persons in Urban Entities at Year-end by Sector and Region (2020)

单位：万人 (10 000 persons)

州 市	Region	就业人数 Employed Persons	农、林、牧、渔业 Farming, Forestry, Animal Husbandry and Fishery	采矿业 Mining	制造业 Manufacturing	电力、热力、燃气及水生产和供应业 Production and Supply of Electric Power,Heat,Gas and Water
全　省	**Yunnan**	**358.23**	**2.56**	**5.74**	**40.34**	**11.28**
昆　明	Kunming	112.64	0.49	0.79	13.46	7.58
曲　靖	Qujing	34.12	0.20	1.78	6.00	0.58
玉　溪	Yuxi	18.38	0.07	0.39	2.32	0.19
保　山	Baoshan	15.76	0.08	0.12	2.41	0.36
昭　通	Zhaotong	25.22	0.11	0.58	0.85	0.28
丽　江	Lijiang	7.92	0.05		0.36	0.11
普　洱	Pu'er	14.29	0.41	0.19	1.45	0.14
临　沧	Lincang	13.64	0.08	0.07	1.32	0.13
楚　雄	Chuxiong	17.55	0.10	0.27	1.80	0.16
红　河	Honghe	29.18	0.17	0.76	4.72	0.50
文　山	Wenshan	17.92	0.19	0.52	1.62	0.49
西双版纳	Xishuangbanna	8.30	0.44	0.01	0.99	0.10
大　理	Dali	20.95	0.10	0.07	1.49	0.26
德　宏	Dehong	9.15	0.02	0.01	0.84	0.17
怒　江	Nujiang	4.52	0.03	0.00	0.60	0.12
迪　庆	Diqing	4.77	0.01	0.18	0.12	0.11

注：1.不含城镇规模以下私营及个体就业人员，含乡村规模以上企业就业人员。
2.全省数含铁路部门数据。

Note: a. Employed persons in urban private and individual enterprises under designated size are excluded from employed persons in urban entities,while employed persons of rural enterprises above designated size are included.
b.Data of the whole province include the railway.

15-11 续表1 continued

单位：万人 (10 000 persons)

州 市	Region	建筑业 Construction	批发和零售业 Wholesale and Retail Trade	交通运输、仓储和邮政业 Transportation, Storage and Post	住宿和餐饮业 Hotel and Catering Service	信息传输、软件和信息技术服务业 Information Transmission,Software and Information Technology Service
全 省	**Yunnan**	**33.71**	**14.44**	**16.18**	**4.94**	**5.26**
昆 明	Kunming	14.49	6.28	7.06	2.56	2.58
曲 靖	Qujing	4.61	1.11	0.64	0.20	0.24
玉 溪	Yuxi	1.15	1.23	0.53	0.16	0.18
保 山	Baoshan	0.84	0.42	0.38	0.20	0.13
昭 通	Zhaotong	0.94	0.55	0.43	0.17	0.29
丽 江	Lijiang	0.44	0.32	0.25	0.37	0.10
普 洱	Pu'er	1.05	0.27	0.38	0.04	0.24
临 沧	Lincang	0.88	0.45	0.36	0.10	0.21
楚 雄	Chuxiong	2.12	0.53	0.43	0.14	0.20
红 河	Honghe	3.67	1.23	0.50	0.23	0.38
文 山	Wenshan	0.71	0.51	0.38	0.09	0.21
西双版纳	Xishuangbanna	0.24	0.29	0.15	0.18	0.11
大 理	Dali	1.61	0.81	0.43	0.29	0.19
德 宏	Dehong	0.45	0.22	0.12	0.08	0.09
怒 江	Nujiang	0.26	0.07	0.14	0.04	0.05
迪 庆	Diqing	0.25	0.15	0.09	0.10	0.06

15-11 续表2 continued

单位：万人 (10 000 persons)

州 市	Region	金融业 Banking	房地产业 Real Estate	租赁和商务服务业 Leasing Trade and Business Service	科学研究和技术服务业 Scientific Research, Technology Service and Geological Prospecting	水利、环境和公共设施管理业 Water Conservancy, Admistration of Environment and Public Facilities
全 省	**Yunnan**	**11.91**	**10.23**	**11.73**	**9.56**	**6.44**
昆 明	Kunming	4.08	4.27	5.05	4.62	1.92
曲 靖	Qujing	0.97	0.86	0.67	0.52	0.55
玉 溪	Yuxi	0.63	0.72	0.65	0.51	0.34
保 山	Baoshan	0.34	0.45	0.33	0.25	0.24
昭 通	Zhaotong	0.46	0.26	0.45	0.36	0.11
丽 江	Lijiang	0.34	0.18	0.25	0.18	0.27
普 洱	Pu'er	0.58	0.23	0.66	0.64	0.29
临 沧	Lincang	0.33	0.47	0.34	0.24	0.12
楚 雄	Chuxiong	0.69	0.63	0.58	0.35	0.30
红 河	Honghe	1.26	0.74	0.56	0.52	0.41
文 山	Wenshan	0.42	0.23	0.23	0.27	0.20
西双版纳	Xishuangbanna	0.31	0.29	0.17	0.35	0.43
大 理	Dali	0.91	0.66	1.05	0.50	0.54
德 宏	Dehong	0.37	0.18	0.52	0.21	0.03
怒 江	Nujiang	0.13	0.04	0.08	0.00	0.02
迪 庆	Diqing	0.09	0.03	0.15	0.04	0.67

15-11 续表3 continued

单位：万人 (10 000 persons)

州 市	Region	居民服务、修理和其他服务业 Services to Households, Repairand Other Services	教 育 Education	卫生和社会工作 Health Care, Social Security and Social Welfare	文化、体育和娱乐业 Culture, Sports and Entertainment	公共管理、社会保障和社会组织 Common Administration and Social Organization
全 省	**Yunnan**	**1.49**	**68.46**	**33.57**	**3.76**	**66.60**
昆 明	Kunming	0.74	14.68	7.82	1.50	12.67
曲 靖	Qujing	0.10	7.17	2.87	0.21	4.84
玉 溪	Yuxi	0.06	3.51	1.77	0.16	3.81
保 山	Baoshan	0.02	3.42	1.96	0.08	3.73
昭 通	Zhaotong	0.08	8.12	3.18	0.22	7.78
丽 江	Lijiang	0.01	1.78	0.89	0.15	1.88
普 洱	Pu'er	0.03	3.10	1.47	0.14	2.97
临 沧	Lincang	0.10	2.96	1.78	0.13	3.56
楚 雄	Chuxiong	0.07	3.21	1.95	0.20	3.83
红 河	Honghe	0.09	5.43	2.76	0.26	4.99
文 山	Wenshan	0.07	5.65	2.20	0.14	3.78
西双版纳	Xishuangbanna	0.03	0.95	1.07	0.21	1.98
大 理	Dali	0.04	4.93	2.35	0.18	4.53
德 宏	Dehong	0.02	1.78	1.16	0.07	2.82
怒 江	Nujiang	0.05	1.03	0.14	0.05	1.69
迪 庆	Diqing	0.01	0.75	0.19	0.05	1.73

15-12 各州市城镇单位分行业年末职工人数（2020年）
Number of Staff and Workers in Urban Entities at Year-end by Sector and Region (2020)

单位：万人 (10 000 persons)

州 市	Region	城镇单位职工人数 Number of Staff and Workers	农、林、牧、渔业 Farming,Forestry, Animal Husbandry and Fishery	采矿业 Mining	制造业 Manufacturing	电力、热力、燃气及水生产和供应业 Production and Supply of Electric Power,Heat,Gas and Water
全 省	**Yunnan**	**305.34**	**2.06**	**5.44**	**36.44**	**10.71**
昆 明	Kunming	93.68	0.44	0.75	12.22	7.24
曲 靖	Qujing	30.59	0.17	1.71	5.54	0.55
玉 溪	Yuxi	15.37	0.06	0.34	2.06	0.17
保 山	Baoshan	14.29	0.06	0.11	2.32	0.35
昭 通	Zhaotong	22.39	0.08	0.56	0.80	0.26
丽 江	Lijiang	6.83	0.04		0.34	0.11
普 洱	Pu'er	12.36	0.31	0.19	0.69	0.13
临 沧	Lincang	11.64	0.07	0.07	1.13	0.13
楚 雄	Chuxiong	14.74	0.09	0.24	1.73	0.14
红 河	Honghe	25.37	0.14	0.74	4.46	0.47
文 山	Wenshan	15.20	0.14	0.48	1.58	0.47
西双版纳	Xishuangbanna	7.30	0.33	0.01	0.80	0.09
大 理	Dali	17.23	0.08	0.07	1.35	0.22
德 宏	Dehong	7.67	0.02	0.01	0.70	0.16
怒 江	Nujiang	3.85	0.01	0.00	0.60	0.11
迪 庆	Diqing	3.26	0.01	0.16	0.12	0.10

15-12 续表1 continued

单位：万人 (10 000 persons)

州 市	Region	建筑业 Construction	批发和零售业 Wholesale and Retail Trade	交通运输、仓储和邮政业 Transportation, Storage and Post	住宿和餐饮业 Hotel and Catering Service	信息传输、软件和信息技术服务业 Information Transmission,Software and Information Technology Service
全 省	**Yunnan**	**23.78**	**12.82**	**14.54**	**4.48**	**4.82**
昆 明	Kunming	9.94	5.73	6.28	2.24	2.42
曲 靖	Qujing	3.40	1.04	0.61	0.20	0.23
玉 溪	Yuxi	0.96	0.99	0.46	0.15	0.17
保 山	Baoshan	0.64	0.40	0.35	0.20	0.12
昭 通	Zhaotong	0.68	0.50	0.35	0.16	0.22
丽 江	Lijiang	0.29	0.17	0.22	0.36	0.10
普 洱	Pu'er	0.88	0.26	0.36	0.04	0.23
临 沧	Lincang	0.62	0.43	0.34	0.09	0.17
楚 雄	Chuxiong	1.46	0.49	0.37	0.11	0.15
红 河	Honghe	2.81	1.03	0.47	0.20	0.37
文 山	Wenshan	0.38	0.39	0.32	0.09	0.14
西双版纳	Xishuangbanna	0.20	0.23	0.13	0.17	0.11
大 理	Dali	1.02	0.76	0.39	0.25	0.18
德 宏	Dehong	0.25	0.22	0.11	0.07	0.09
怒 江	Nujiang	0.12	0.05	0.12	0.03	0.05
迪 庆	Diqing	0.14	0.13	0.09	0.10	0.05

15-12 续表2 continued

单位：万人 (10 000 persons)

州 市	Region	金融业 Banking	房地产业 Real Estate	租赁和商务服务业 Leasing Trade and Business Service	科学研究和技术服务业 Scientific Research,Technology Service and Geological Prospecting	水利、环境和公共设施管理业 Water Conservancy, Administration of Environment and Public Facilities
全 省	**Yunnan**	**9.33**	**8.97**	**9.63**	**8.65**	**4.76**
昆 明	Kunming	3.72	3.68	3.98	4.00	1.58
曲 靖	Qujing	0.75	0.81	0.59	0.49	0.35
玉 溪	Yuxi	0.57	0.63	0.33	0.49	0.24
保 山	Baoshan	0.31	0.42	0.26	0.25	0.20
昭 通	Zhaotong	0.42	0.20	0.43	0.34	0.10
丽 江	Lijiang	0.20	0.18	0.23	0.17	0.23
普 洱	Pu'er	0.45	0.19	0.65	0.60	0.20
临 沧	Lincang	0.20	0.35	0.34	0.23	0.11
楚 雄	Chuxiong	0.38	0.57	0.48	0.31	0.27
红 河	Honghe	0.78	0.60	0.53	0.47	0.37
文 山	Wenshan	0.37	0.23	0.22	0.27	0.12
西双版纳	Xishuangbanna	0.17	0.28	0.16	0.33	0.31
大 理	Dali	0.57	0.60	0.81	0.47	0.49
德 宏	Dehong	0.23	0.16	0.49	0.21	0.03
怒 江	Nujiang	0.12	0.04	0.02	0.00	0.02
迪 庆	Diqing	0.09	0.02	0.10	0.04	0.15

15-12 续表3 continued

单位：万人 (10 000 persons)

州 市	Region	居民服务、修理和其他服务业 Services to Households, Repairand Other Services	教 育 Education	卫生和社会工作 Health Care, Social Security and Social Welfare	文化、体育和娱乐业 Culture, Sports and Entertainment	公共管理、社会保障和社会组织 Common Administration and Social Organization
全 省	**Yunnan**	**1.40**	**62.34**	**27.76**	**3.42**	**53.98**
昆 明	Kunming	0.69	12.66	5.78	1.35	8.96
曲 靖	Qujing	0.10	6.70	2.62	0.19	4.55
玉 溪	Yuxi	0.06	3.08	1.51	0.15	2.94
保 山	Baoshan	0.02	3.26	1.91	0.08	3.03
昭 通	Zhaotong	0.08	7.78	2.78	0.22	6.44
丽 江	Lijiang	0.01	1.67	0.59	0.15	1.79
普 洱	Pu'er	0.03	3.03	1.38	0.13	2.61
临 沧	Lincang	0.10	2.72	1.28	0.13	3.12
楚 雄	Chuxiong	0.06	2.85	1.71	0.19	3.14
红 河	Honghe	0.08	5.12	1.98	0.21	4.53
文 山	Wenshan	0.06	5.07	1.94	0.14	2.80
西双版纳	Xishuangbanna	0.03	0.95	1.03	0.20	1.77
大 理	Dali	0.02	4.32	2.02	0.16	3.43
德 宏	Dehong	0.01	1.70	0.99	0.06	2.18
怒 江	Nujiang	0.05	0.87	0.09	0.04	1.49
迪 庆	Diqing	0.01	0.55	0.14	0.04	1.21

15-13 全省分行业城镇单位年末职工人数（2020年）

Provincial Number of Staff and Workers in Urban Unit by Sector at Year-end (2020)

单位：万人 (10 000 persons)

国民经济行业	Sector	城镇单位职工 Number of Staff and Workers	国有单位 State-owned Entities	城镇集体单位 Urban Collective-owned Entities	其他单位 Other Ownership
城镇单位在岗职工人数	**Number of Staff and Workers in Urban Units**	**305.34**	**155.04**	**6.08**	**144.22**
农、林、牧、渔业	Farming,Forestry,Animal Husbandry and Fishery	2.06	1.19	0.05	0.82
采矿业	Mining	5.44	1.11	0.14	4.20
制造业	Manufacturing	36.44	0.97	0.36	35.11
电力、热力、燃气及水生产和供应业	Production and Supply of Electricity, Heat, Gas and Water	10.71	0.51	0.08	10.12
建筑业	Construction	23.78	1.16	2.05	20.57
批发和零售业	Wholesale and Retaile Trade	12.82	1.83	0.18	10.81
交通运输、仓储及邮政业	Transportation,Storage and Post	14.54	2.92	0.20	11.42
住宿和餐饮业	Hotel and Food Service	4.48	0.60	0.10	3.78
信息传输、软件和信息技术服务业	Information Transmission, Software and Information Technology Service	4.82	0.47	0.01	4.34
金融业	Banking	9.33	1.56	1.19	6.58
房地产业	Real Estate	8.97	0.29	0.08	8.60
租赁和商务服务业	Leasing Trade and Business Service	9.63	1.19	0.10	8.34
科学研究和技术服务业	Scientific Research, Technology Service and Geological Prospecting	8.65	5.28	0.11	3.27
水利、环境和公共设施管理业	Water Conservancy,Admistration of Environment and Public Facilities	4.76	2.23	0.03	2.50
居民服务、修理和其他服务业	Services to Households, Repair and Other Services	1.40	0.14	0.02	1.24
教育	Education	62.34	53.71	0.80	7.83
卫生和社会工作	Health Care, Social Works	27.76	24.11	0.46	3.19
文化、体育和娱乐业	Culture, Sports and Entertainment	3.42	2.17	0.02	1.23
公共管理、社会保障和社会组织	Common Administration and Social Organization	53.98	53.61	0.08	0.29

15-14 城镇单位全部就业人员数（2020年）

Number of Employed Persons in Urban Entities (2020)

单位：万人 (10 000 persons)

国民经济行业	National Economic Sector	就业人员 Number of Employed Persons	国有单位 State-owned Economy	城镇集体单位 Urban Collective-owned Entities	其他单位 Entities of Other Types of Ownership
全 省	**Yunnan**	**358.23**	**182.59**	**6.72**	**168.91**
按执行会计标准类别分组	**Category according to the Accounting Standards**				
企业	Enterprises	181.71	15.57	5.29	160.84
政府	Government	169.84	165.97	1.27	2.60
按国民经济行业分组	**Grouped by Industry Sector**				
农、林、牧、渔业	**Farming,Forestry,Animal Husbandry and Fishery**	**2.56**	**1.38**	**0.08**	**1.10**
农业	Farming	0.81	0.19	0.03	0.59
林业	Forestry	0.92	0.77	0.02	0.14
畜牧业	Animal Husbandry	0.21	0.05	0.02	0.15
渔业	Fishery	0.01	0.01	0.00	0.01
农、林、牧、渔服务业	Farming,Forestry,Animal Husbandry and Fishery Services	0.60	0.38	0.01	0.21
采矿业	**Mining**	**5.74**	**1.17**	**0.15**	**4.42**
煤炭开采和洗选业	Coal Mining and Dressing	3.06	1.14	0.10	1.83
石油和天然气开采业	Petroleum and Natural Gas Extraction	0.00			0.00
黑色金属矿采选业	Ferrous Metals Mining and Dressing	0.30	0.01	0.00	0.29
有色金属矿采选业	Nonferrous Metals Mining and Dressing	1.69	0.02	0.02	1.65
非金属矿采选业	Nonmetal Minerals Mining and Dressing	0.68	0.00	0.03	0.65
开采辅助活动	Mining Auxiliary Activities	0.00			
其他采矿业	Other Minerals Mining	0.00			
制造业	**Manufacturing**	**40.34**	**1.23**	**0.41**	**38.69**
农副食品加工业	Agricultural Non-staple Food Processing	3.01	0.07	0.02	2.92
食品制造业	Food Manufacturing	1.42	0.00	0.02	1.40
酒、饮料和精制茶制造业	Beverage Manufacturing	2.24	0.19	0.04	2.01
烟草制品业	Tobacco Production	2.22	0.05	0.06	2.11
纺织业	Textile Industry	0.29			0.29
纺织服装、服饰业	Textile,Clothing, Footwear Production	0.28	0.02	0.01	0.25
皮革、毛皮、羽毛及其制品和制鞋业	Feather, Furs, Down, Related Products and Footwear	0.05	0.01	0.00	0.04
木材加工和木、竹、藤、棕、草制品业	Timber Processing, Bamboo, Cane, Palm Fiber and Straw Products	0.37	0.06		0.31

注：不含城镇规模以下私营及个体就业人员，含乡村规模以上企业就业人员。
Note: Employed persons in urban private and individual enterprises under designated size are excluded.

15-14 续表1 continued

单位：万人 (10 000 persons)

国民经济行业	National Economic Sector	就业人员 Number of Employed Persons	国有单位 State-owned Economy	城镇集体单位 Urban Collective-owned Entities	其他单位 Entities of Other Types of Ownership
家具制造业	Furniture Manufacturing	0.05	0.02	0.00	0.04
造纸和纸制品业	Papermaking and Paper Products	0.58	0.01	0.04	0.53
印刷业和记录媒介复制业	Printing and Record Medium Reproduction	0.94	0.08	0.01	0.85
文教、工美、体育和娱乐用品制造业	Manufacture of Culture, Education,Industrial Arts,Sports and Entertainment Goods	0.64	0.00	0.06	0.58
石油加工、炼焦和核燃料加工业	Petroleum Processing,Coking and Nuclear Fuel Processing	1.08	–	0.00	1.08
化学原料和化学制品制造业	Raw Chemical Materials and Chemical Products	4.80	0.11	0.01	4.68
医药制造业	Medical and Pharmaceutical Products	2.54	0.11	0.02	2.41
化学纤维制造业	Chemical Fiber Manufacturing	0.04	–	–	0.04
橡胶和塑料制品业	Rubber and Plastic Products	0.52	0.01	0.01	0.51
非金属矿物制品业	Nonmetal Mineral Products	3.91	0.04	0.04	3.84
黑色金属冶炼和压延加工业	Smelting and Pressing of Ferrous Metals	3.24	0.12	-	3.12
有色金属冶炼和压延加工业	Smelting and Pressing of Nonferrous Metals	6.23	0.27	0.04	5.92
金属制品业	Metal Products	0.84	0.03	0.02	0.79
通用设备制造业	General-purpose Machinery Manufacturing	0.47	0.01	0.01	0.45
专用设备制造业	Special Purposes Equipment	0.49	0.01	0.00	0.48
汽车制造业	Automotive Industry	0.68	0.00	–	0.68
铁路、船舶、航空航天和其他运输设备制造业	Manufacture of Transport Equipment for Railway,Boats and Aerospace and Other Transport Equipments	0.31	–	–	0.31
电气机械和器材制造业	Electric Equipment and Machinery	0.84	0.02	0.00	0.81
计算机、通信和其他电子设备制造业	Computers,Communication Equipment and other Other Electronic Equipment Production	1.87	0.00	–	1.87
			–	–	
仪器仪表制造业	Instrument Industry	0.21	–	0.00	0.21
其他制造业	Other Goods Production	0.01	0.00	0.00	0.01
废弃资源综合利用业	Comprehensive Utilization of Discarded Resources and Waste	0.12	–	–	0.12
金属制品、机械和设备修理业	Metal Products,Machinery and Equipment Repairing	0.05	–	0.00	0.05
电力、热力、燃气及水生产和供应业	**Production and Supply of Electricity, Heat ,Gas and Water**	**11.28**	**0.56**	**0.08**	**10.64**
电力、热力生产和供应业	Production and Supply of Electric Power and Heat	9.34	0.18	0.03	9.13
燃气生产和供应业	Gas Production and Supply	0.58	0.03	–	0.55
水的生产和供应业	Water Production and Supply	1.36	0.35	0.05	0.96
建筑业	**Construction**	**33.71**	**1.69**	**2.25**	**29.77**
房屋建筑业	House Building	22.13	0.59	2.03	19.50
土木工程建筑业	Construction Industry of Civil Engineering	9.10	0.84	0.21	8.04
建筑安装业	Construction Installation	1.35	0.13	0.01	1.21
建筑装饰和其他建筑业	Building Decoration and Other Construction Industry	1.14	0.12	0.00	1.02
批发和零售业	**Wholesale and Retail Trade**	**14.44**	**2.24**	**0.19**	**12.01**
批发业	Wholesale	7.15	1.98	0.08	5.09
零售业	Retail Trade	7.29	0.26	0.11	6.92

15-14 续表2 continued

单位：万人 (10 000 persons)

国民经济行业	National Economic Sector	就业人员 Number of Employed Persons	国有单位 State-owned Economy	城镇集体单位 Urban Collective-owned Entities	其他单位 Entities of Other Types of Ownership
交通运输、仓储和邮政业	**Transport, Storage and Post**	**16.18**	**3.33**	**0.26**	**12.60**
铁路运输业	Railway transport	3.92	–	–	3.92
道路运输业	Highway Transport	7.37	1.61	0.03	5.73
水上运输业	Water Way Transport	0.02	0.00	–	0.02
航空运输业	Air Transport	2.65	0.90	–	1.76
管道运输业	Pipeline Transport	0.03	–	–	0.03
多式联运和运输代理业	Multimodal Transport and Forwarding Agencies	0.25	0.01	–	0.24
装卸搬运和仓储业	Lording, Unlording, Carrying and Storage	0.75	0.06	0.23	0.47
邮政业	Postal	1.19	0.75	–	0.44
住宿和餐饮业	**Hotel and Food Service**	**4.94**	**0.71**	**0.12**	**4.11**
住宿业	Hotel Service	3.34	0.67	0.09	2.59
餐饮业	Food Service	1.60	0.04	0.03	1.53
信息传输、软件和信息技术服务业	**Information Transmission,Software and Information Technology Service**	**5.26**	**0.58**	**0.01**	**4.67**
电信、广播电视和卫星传输服务	Telecommunication, Videocast and Satellite Transmissions Service	3.80	0.40	0.00	3.39
互联网和相关服务	Internet and Related Service	0.26	0.01	0.01	0.24
软件和信息技术服务业	Software and Information Technology service	1.21	0.17	0.00	1.04
金融业	**Finance and Insurance**	**11.91**	**1.60**	**1.25**	**9.06**
货币金融服务	Banking	7.09	1.51	1.25	4.33
资本市场服务	Securities Industry	0.22	0.01	–	0.22
保险业	Insurance	4.55	0.07	–	4.48
其他金融业	Other Financial Trade	0.04	0.01	–	0.03
房地产业	**Real Estate Trade**	**10.23**	**0.33**	**0.09**	**9.81**
房地产业	Real Estate Trade	10.23	0.33	0.09	9.81
租赁和商务服务业	**Leasing Treade and Business Service**	**11.73**	**1.32**	**0.11**	**10.30**
租赁业	Leasing Trade	0.24	0.02	0.00	0.21
商务服务业	Commercial Services	11.50	1.30	0.11	10.09
科学研究和技术服务业	**Scientific Research,Technology Service and Geological Prospecting**	**9.56**	**5.71**	**0.12**	**3.73**
研究与试验发展	R & D	0.98	0.71	0.01	0.26
专业技术服务业	Professional Technology Service	6.08	2.88	0.10	3.10
科技推广和应用服务业	Service Industry of Science and Technology Popularization and Application	2.50	2.12	0.01	0.37

15-14 续表3 continued

单位：万人 (10 000 persons)

国民经济行业	National Economic Sector	就业人员 Number of Employed Persons	国有单位 State-owned Economy	城镇集体单位 Urban Collective-owned Entities	其他单位 Entities of Other Types of Ownership
水利、环境和公共设施管理业	**Water Conservancy,Admistration of Environment and Public facilities**	**6.44**	**3.54**	**0.04**	**2.86**
水利管理业	Water Conservancy Admistrition	0.69	0.62	0.00	0.07
生态环境和环境治理业	Protection of Ecological Environment and Admistration of Environment	1.55	1.35	0.01	0.18
公共设施管理业	Admistration of Public Facilities	4.11	1.52	0.03	2.57
土地管理业	Land Management	0.10	0.05	0.00	0.05
居民服务、修理和其他服务业	**Services to Households and Other Services**	**1.49**	**0.17**	**0.04**	**1.28**
居民服务业	Services to Households	0.74	0.13	0.02	0.59
机动车、电子产品和日用产品修理业	Repair Industry of Automotive Vehicles,Electronic Products and Daily Products	0.28	0.01	0.01	0.26
其他服务业	Other Services	0.47	0.02	0.02	0.43
教 育	**Education**	**68.46**	**58.90**	**0.89**	**8.67**
教育	Education	68.46	58.90	0.89	8.67
卫生和社会工作	**Health Care, Social Work**	**33.57**	**29.58**	**0.52**	**3.47**
卫生	Health Care	32.78	29.05	0.50	3.23
社会工作	Social Work	0.79	0.54	0.01	0.24
文化、体育和娱乐业	**Culture, Sports and Entertainment**	**3.76**	**2.38**	**0.02**	**1.36**
新闻和出版业	News and Publishing	0.56	0.38	0.00	0.18
广播、电视、电影和影视录音制作业	Broadcast, Television,Filmdom and Audio & Video Production	0.86	0.69	0.01	0.17
文化艺术业	Culture and Arts	1.45	1.04	0.01	0.39
体育	Sports	0.37	0.20	0.00	0.16
娱乐业	Entertainment	0.53	0.07		0.46
公共管理、社会保障和社会组织	**Common Administration,Social Security and Social Organization**	**66.60**	**66.16**	**0.08**	**0.36**
中国共产党机关	Organs of Communist Party of China	4.01	4.01		0.00
国家机构	Government Agencies of Country	60.37	60.03	0.07	0.27
人民政协和民主党派	Chinese People's Political Consultative Conferences and Democracy Parties	0.64	0.64		
社会保障	Social Security	0.65	0.63	0.00	0.02
群众社团、社会团体和宗教组织	Mass Groups,Social Groups and Religion Organization	0.92	0.84	0.01	0.07

15-15 城镇单位女性就业人员数（2020年）

Number of Female Employed in Urban Entities (2020)

单位：万人 (10 000 persons)

国民经济行业	National Economic Sector	女性就业人员 Number of Female Employed Persons	国有单位 State-owned Economy	城镇集体单位 Urban Collective-owned Entities	其他单位 Entities of Other Types of Ownership
全 省	**Yunnan**	**152.11**	**88.75**	**2.48**	**60.88**
按执行会计标准类别分组	**Category according to the Accounting Standards**				
企业	Enterprises	62.78	5.78	1.61	55.40
政府	Government	84.56	82.34	0.77	1.44
按国民经济行业分组	**Grouped by Industry Sector**				
农、林、牧、渔业	**Farming,Forestry,Animal Husbandry and Fishery**	**0.96**	**0.41**	**0.01**	**0.53**
农业	Farming	0.43	0.08	0.01	0.34
林业	Forestry	0.26	0.20	0.00	0.06
畜牧业	Animal Husbandry	0.07	0.02	0.00	0.05
渔业	Fishery	0.00	0.00	0.00	0.00
农、林、牧、渔服务业	Farming,Forestry,Animal Husbandry and Fishery Services	0.19	0.11	0.00	0.08
采矿业	**Mining**	**1.08**	**0.28**	**0.01**	**0.79**
煤炭开采和洗选业	Coal Mining and Dressing	0.56	0.28	0.00	0.28
石油和天然气开采业	Petroleum and Natural Gas Extraction				
黑色金属矿采选业	Ferrous Metals Mining and Dressing	0.05	0.00	0.00	0.05
有色金属矿采选业	Nonferrous Metals Mining and Dressing	0.31	0.00	0.00	0.30
非金属矿采选业	Nonmetal Minerals Mining and Dressing	0.16	0.00	0.00	0.16
开采辅助活动	Mining Auxiliary Activities	0.00			
其他采矿业	Other Minerals Mining	0.00			
制造业	**Manufacturing**	**13.03**	**0.40**	**0.16**	**12.48**
农副食品加工业	Agricultural Non-staple Food Processing	1.27	0.03	0.00	1.24
食品制造业	Food Manufacturing	0.63	0.00	0.01	0.62
酒、饮料和精制茶制造业	Beverage Manufacturing	0.96	0.09	0.01	0.86
烟草制品业	Tobacco Production	0.64	0.02	0.03	0.59
纺织业	Textile Industry	0.22			0.22
纺织服装、服饰业	Textile,Clothing, Footwear Production	0.17	0.01	0.01	0.16
皮革、毛皮、羽毛及其制品和制鞋业	Feather, Furs, Down, Related Products and Footwear	0.03	0.00	0.00	0.03
木材加工和木、竹、藤、棕、草制品业	Timber Processing, Bamboo, Cane, Palm Fiber and Straw Products	0.14	0.02		0.12

15−15 续表1 continued

单位：万人 (10 000 persons)

国民经济行业	National Economic Sector	女性就业人员 Number of Female Employed Persons	国有单位 State-owned Economy	城镇集体单位 Urban Coll-ective-owned Entities	其他单位 Entities of Other Types of Ownership
家具制造业	Furniture Manufacturing	0.01	0.00	0.00	0.01
造纸和纸制品业	Papermaking and Paper Products	0.22	0.00	0.02	0.20
印刷业和记录媒介复制业	Printing and Record Medium Reproduction	0.37	0.04	0.00	0.33
文教、工美、体育和娱乐用品制造业	Manufacture of Culture, Education,Industrial Arts, Sports and Entertainment Goods	0.34	0.00	0.04	0.30
石油加工、炼焦和核燃料加工业	Petroleum Processing,Coking and Nuclear Fuel Processing	0.27	–	0.00	0.27
化学原料和化学制品制造业	Raw Chemical Materials and Chemical Products	1.48	0.03	0.01	1.45
医药制造业	Medical and Pharmaceutical Products	1.23	0.05	0.01	1.18
化学纤维制造业	Chemical Fiber Manufacturing	0.01	–	–	0.01
橡胶和塑料制品业	Rubber and Plastic Products	0.23	0.00	0.00	0.22
非金属矿物制品业	Nonmetal Mineral Products	0.91	0.01	0.01	0.89
黑色金属冶炼和压延加工业	Smelting and Pressing of Ferrous Metals	0.91	0.03	–	0.88
有色金属冶炼和压延加工业	Smelting and Pressing of Nonferrous Metals	1.36	0.05	0.01	1.30
金属制品业	Metal Products	0.19	0.01	0.00	0.18
通用设备制造业	General-purpose Machinery Manufacturing	0.09	0.00	0.00	0.08
专用设备制造业	Special Purposes Equipment	0.11	0.00	0.00	0.11
汽车制造业	Automotive Industry	0.12	0.00	–	0.12
铁路、船舶、航空航天和其他运输设备制造业	Manufacture of Transport Equipment for Railway,Boats and Aerospace and Other Transport Equipments	0.07	–	–	0.07
电气机械和器材制造业	Electric Equipment and Machinery	0.24	0.01	0.00	0.23
计算机、通信和其他	Computers,Communication Equipment and other	0.69	0.00	–	0.69
电子设备制造业	Other Electronic Equipment Production		–	–	
仪器仪表制造业	Instrument Industry	0.07	–	0.00	0.07
其他制造业	Other Goods Production	0.00	0.00	0.00	0.00
废弃资源综合利用业	Comprehensive Utilization of Discarded Resources and Waste	0.03	–	–	0.03
金属制品、机械和设备修理业	Metal Products,Machinery and Equipment Repairing	0.01	–	0.00	0.01
电力、热力、燃气及水生产和供应业	**Production and Supply of Electricity,Heat,Gas and Water**	**3.20**	**0.19**	**0.02**	**2.99**
电力、热力生产和供应业	Production and Supply of Electric Power and Heat	2.51	0.04	0.01	2.47
燃气生产和供应业	Gas Production and Supply	0.18	0.01	–	0.17
水的生产和供应业	Water Production and Supply	0.50	0.13	0.02	0.35
建筑业	**Construction**	**5.78**	**0.29**	**0.38**	**5.11**
房屋建筑业	House Building	3.61	0.12	0.34	3.15
土木工程建筑业	Construction Industry of Civil Engineering	1.64	0.13	0.04	1.47
建筑安装业	Construction Installation	0.28	0.02	0.00	0.26
建筑装饰和其他建筑业	Building Decoration and Other Construction Industry	0.25	0.02	0.00	0.23
批发和零售业	**Wholesale and Retail Trade**	**7.16**	**0.80**	**0.09**	**6.27**
批发业	Wholesale	2.96	0.66	0.03	2.27
零售业	Retail Trade	4.20	0.14	0.05	4.00

15-15 续表2 continued

单位：万人 (10 000 persons)

国民经济行业	National Economic Sector	女性就业人员 Number of Female Employed Persons	国有单位 State-owned Economy	城镇集体单位 Urban Collective-owned Entities	其他单位 Entities of Other Types of Ownership
交通运输、仓储和邮政业	**Transport, Storage and Post**	**4.93**	**1.16**	**0.11**	**3.66**
铁路运输业	Railway transport	0.71	–	–	0.71
道路运输业	Highway Transport	2.33	0.45	0.01	1.87
水上运输业	Water Way Transport	0.01	0.00	–	0.00
航空运输业	Air Transport	1.03	0.31	–	0.71
管道运输业	Pipeline Transport	0.01	–	–	0.01
多式联运和运输代理业	Multimodal Transport and Forwarding Agencies	0.06	0.00	–	0.06
装卸搬运和仓储业	Lording, Unlording, Carrying and Storage	0.24	0.02	0.11	0.11
邮政业	Postal	0.56	0.37	-	0.19
住宿和餐饮业	**Hotel and Food Service**	**2.95**	**0.41**	**0.06**	**2.48**
住宿业	Hotel Service	2.03	0.38	0.04	1.60
餐饮业	Food Service	0.92	0.02	0.02	0.88
信息传输、软件和信息技术服务业	**Information Transmission,Software and Information Technology Service**	**2.09**	**0.24**	**0.01**	**1.84**
电信、广播电视和卫星传输服务	Telecommunication, Videocast and Satellite Transmissions Service	1.57	0.19	–	1.38
互联网和相关服务	Internet and Related Service	0.11	0.01	0.00	0.10
软件和信息技术服务业	Software and Information Technology service	0.41	0.05	0.00	0.36
金融业	**Finance and Insurance**	**6.67**	**0.79**	**0.55**	**5.33**
货币金融服务	Banking	3.65	0.75	0.55	2.35
资本市场服务	Securities Industry	0.10	0.00	–	0.10
保险业	Insurance	2.90	0.03	–	2.87
其他金融业	Other Financial Trade	0.02	0.00	–	0.01
房地产业	**Real Estate Trade**	**4.16**	**0.13**	**0.03**	**3.99**
房地产业	Real Estate Trade	4.16	0.13	0.03	3.99
租赁和商务服务业	**Leasing Treade and Business Service**	**3.42**	**0.53**	**0.04**	**2.85**
租赁业	Leasing Trade	0.07	0.01	0.00	0.06
商务服务业	Commercial Serive	3.35	0.52	0.04	2.79
科学研究和技术服务业	**Scientific Research,Technology Service and Geological Prospecting**	**3.20**	**2.05**	**0.04**	**1.11**
研究与试验发展	R & D	0.41	0.30	0.00	0.10
专业技术服务业	Professional Technology Service	1.90	1.02	0.04	0.84
科技推广和应用服务业	Service Industry of Science and Technology Popularization and Application	0.89	0.72	0.00	0.16

15-15 续表3 continued

单位：万人 (10 000 persons)

国民经济行业	National Economic Sector	女性就业人员 Number of Female Employed Persons	国有单位 State-owned Economy	城镇集体单位 Urban Collective-owned Entities	其他单位 Entities of Other Types of Ownership
水利、环境和公共设施管理业	**Water Conservancy,Admistration of Environment and Public facilities**	**2.76**	**1.33**	**0.01**	**1.41**
水利管理业	Water Conservancy Admistrition	0.20	0.18	0.00	0.02
生态环境和环境治理业	Protection of Ecological Environment and Admistration of Environment	0.40	0.34	0.00	0.06
公共设施管理业	Admistration of Public Facilities	2.11	0.79	0.01	1.31
土地管理业	Land Management	0.04	0.02		0.02
居民服务、修理和其他服务业	**Services to Households and Other Services**	**0.78**	**0.06**	**0.02**	**0.70**
居民服务业	Services to Households	0.41	0.04	0.01	0.36
机动车、电子产品和日用产品修理业	Repair Industry of Automotive Vehicles,Electronic Products and Daily Products	0.08	0.00	0.00	0.07
其他服务业	Other Services	0.29	0.01	0.01	0.27
教　育	**Education**	**40.09**	**33.62**	**0.51**	**5.96**
教育	Education	40.09	33.62	0.51	5.96
卫生和社会工作	**Health Care, Social Work**	**24.63**	**21.73**	**0.38**	**2.52**
卫生	Health Care	24.12	21.40	0.37	2.36
社会工作	Social Work	0.51	0.33	0.01	0.17
文化、体育和娱乐业	**Culture, Sports and Entertainment**	**1.89**	**1.22**	**0.01**	**0.67**
新闻和出版业	News and Publishing	0.27	0.17	0.00	0.10
广播、电视、电影和影视录音制作业	Broadcast,Television,Filmdom and Audio & Video Production	0.41	0.33	0.00	0.08
文化艺术业	Culture and Arts	0.79	0.60	0.01	0.19
体育	Sports	0.16	0.08		0.08
娱乐业	Entertainment	0.27	0.03		0.23
公共管理、社会保障和社会组织	**Common Administration ,Social Security and Social Organization**	**23.33**	**23.12**	**0.03**	**0.18**
中国共产党机关	Organs of Communist Party of China	1.42	1.42		0.00
国家机构	Government Agencies of Country	20.83	20.68	0.02	0.13
人民政协和民主党派	Chinese People's Political Consultative Conferences and Democracy Parties	0.20	0.20		
社会保障	Social Security	0.39	0.38	0.00	0.01
群众社团、社会团体和宗教组织	Mass Groups, Social Groups and Religion Organization	0.50	0.45	0.01	0.04

15−16 城镇登记失业人数和登记失业率（1978−2020年）

Registered Urban Unemployed Persons and Unemployment Rate (1978-2020)

单位:万人 (10 000 persons)

年 份 Year	登记失业人数 Registered Urban Unemployed Persons	女 性 Female	长期失业者人数 Permanent Unemployed Persons	城镇登记失业率 (%) Urban Unemployment Rate (%)
1978	6.40			2.7
1979	9.90			4.3
1980	6.00			2.3
1981	6.16			3.1
1982	6.15			2.7
1983	5.83			2.0
1984	4.70			1.7
1985	4.21			2.5
1986	4.77			1.7
1987	5.85			2.0
1988	5.97			2.0
1989	7.07			2.4
1990	7.76			2.5
1991	7.63			2.3
1992	7.53			2.3
1993	7.34			2.3
1994	7.14			2.2
1995	8.10			2.3
1996	8.01			2.8
1997	7.84			2.7
1998	6.01	3.02		2.2
1999	6.20	3.10	3.10	2.5
2000	6.77	3.28	3.42	2.6
2001	8.00	3.89	3.64	3.3
2002	9.80	4.04	4.79	4.0
2003	12.12	5.94	5.64	4.1
2004	11.95	6.28	4.85	4.3
2005	12.97	6.12	5.17	4.3
2006	13.79	6.35	5.01	4.3
2007	14.02	6.37	4.20	4.2
2008	14.77	6.50	3.79	4.2
2009	15.63	6.73	3.44	4.3
2010	15.69	6.40	3.38	4.2
2011	15.99	6.80	2.56	4.1
2012	17.40	7.90	2.70	4.0
2013	18.09	8.05	2.46	4.0
2014	19.19	8.28	2.60	4.0
2015	19.47	8.31	2.90	4.0
2016	20.58	8.60	2.88	3.6
2017	19.81	8.50	3.40	3.2
2018	20.88	8.90	3.09	3.4
2019	22.93	10.03	2.69	3.3
2020	31.86	14.31	2.34	3.9

15−17 全部职工工资总额和指数（1978−2020年）

Total Wages of Staff and Workers and Related Indices (1978-2020)

单位：亿元、%　　　　(100 million yuan, %)

年份 Year	职工工资总额 Total Wages	国有单位 State-owned Entities	城镇集体单位 Urban Collective-owned Entities	其他单位 Other Ownership	工资总额指数 Indices of Total Wages	国有单位 State-owned Entities	城镇集体单位 Urban Collective-owned Entities	其他单位 Other Ownership
1978	12.68	11.42	1.26		115.3	117.4	99.6	
1979	14.26	12.84	1.42		112.4	112.4	112.7	
1980	17.16	15.46	1.69		120.3	120.4	119.6	
1981	17.97	16.13	1.84		104.7	104.3	108.5	
1982	19.05	17.05	2.01		106.0	105.7	109.3	
1983	20.28	18.11	2.17		106.4	106.2	107.9	
1984	25.43	22.23	3.17	0.03	125.4	122.8	146.4	
1985	30.13	26.30	3.79	0.05	118.5	118.3	119.4	180.6
1986	34.09	29.72	4.31	0.06	113.1	113.0	113.4	125.8
1987	38.68	33.82	4.78	0.08	113.5	113.8	110.9	137.4
1988	47.09	41.30	5.66	0.13	121.7	122.1	118.4	158.7
1989	60.12	53.56	6.42	0.14	111.8	111.5	113.4	110.4
1990	60.66	53.56	6.97	0.13	115.3	116.3	108.6	93.6
1991	68.66	60.27	8.23	0.17	113.2	112.5	118.1	128.6
1992	81.43	71.26	9.95	0.23	118.6	118.2	120.9	135.2
1993	97.02	84.12	12.50	0.39	119.1	118.1	125.6	174.8
1994	138.94	121.35	15.57	2.03	143.2	144.3	124.5	514.3
1995	158.96	137.81	18.22	2.93	114.4	113.6	116.7	144.5
1996	194.07	169.06	20.27	4.73	122.1	122.7	111.3	161.5
1997	219.08	190.75	21.05	7.28	112.9	112.8	103.8	154.0
1998	226.09	193.15	18.70	14.24	103.2	101.3	88.9	195.5
1999	235.93	195.97	17.57	22.39	104.4	101.5	94.0	157.2
2000	254.46	209.50	16.78	28.18	107.9	106.9	95.5	125.8
2001	275.98	225.33	14.37	36.28	108.5	107.6	85.7	128.7
2002	300.85	245.22	13.21	42.42	109.0	108.8	91.9	116.9
2003	314.98	246.24	12.34	56.40	104.7	100.4	93.4	132.9
2004	344.52	264.02	11.53	68.97	109.4	107.2	93.4	122.3
2005	377.16	283.30	10.80	83.05	109.5	107.3	93.7	120.4
2006	458.62	339.88	14.70	104.04	121.6	120.0	136.0	125.3
2007	566.49	398.49	16.32	151.68	123.5	117.2	111.0	145.8
2008	683.69	473.30	18.89	191.50	120.7	118.8	115.7	126.3
2009	788.38	546.72	21.61	220.05	115.3	115.5	114.4	114.9
2010	903.72	619.53	24.46	259.73	114.6	113.3	113.2	118.0
2011	1 111.38	709.16	32.46	369.76	123.0	114.5	132.7	142.4
2012	1 340.24	794.46	41.79	503.99	120.6	112.0	128.8	136.3
2013	1 630.67	797.61	54.29	778.77	121.7	100.4	129.9	154.5
2014	1 727.71	916.93	52.51	758.27	106.0	115.0	96.7	97.4
2015	1 958.70	1 065.57	58.98	834.15	113.4	116.2	112.3	110.0
2016	2 284.05	1 323.26	58.14	902.65	116.6	124.2	98.6	108.2
2017	2 636.42	1 565.96	60.23	1 010.23	115.4	118.3	103.6	111.9
2018	2 922.04	1 659.47	55.04	1 207.53	110.8	106.0	91.4	119.5
2019	2 905.61	1 648.62	55.21	1 201.79	99.4	99.3	100.3	99.5
2020	3 050.83	1 808.24	53.76	1 188.82	105.0	109.7	97.4	98.9

15–18 全部职工平均工资及指数（1978–2020年）

Average Wages of Staff and Workers and Related Indices (1978-2020)

单位：万元/人、%　　　　(10 000 yuan/person,%)

年份 Year	职工平均工资 Average Wages	国有单位 State-owned Entities	集体单位 Urban Collective-owned Entities	其他单位 Other Ownership	平均工资指数(上年=100，%) Indices of Average Wages (preceding year = 100 ,%) 货币工资 Money Wages	国有单位 State-owned Entities	集体单位 Urban Collective-owned Entities	其他单位 Other Ownership	实际工资 Real Wages	国有单位 State-owned Entities	城镇集体单位 Urban Collective-owned Entities	其他单位 Other Ownership
1978	0.06	0.06	0.05		112.0	108.5	128.8		112.0	108.5	128.8	
1979	0.07	0.07	0.05		108.6	109.0	106.7		107.7	108.1	105.8	
1980	0.08	0.08	0.06		115.2	115.2	114.2		106.5	106.5	105.6	
1981	0.08	0.08	0.06		102.6	102.3	105.8		101.8	101.5	105.0	
1982	0.08	0.08	0.07		103.3	103.1	105.8		101.6	101.4	104.0	
1983	0.08	0.09	0.07		104.2	103.9	106.4		103.6	103.3	105.7	
1984	0.10	0.10	0.08	0.11	120.7	122.4	114.5		117.7	119.3	111.6	
1985	0.12	0.12	0.10	0.11	115.5	115.1	117.9	97.0	103.2	102.8	105.3	86.7
1986	0.13	0.13	0.11	0.12	111.0	110.5	113.8	110.6	105.9	105.5	108.6	105.6
1987	0.14	0.15	0.12	0.13	110.7	111.2	107.6	105.7	103.1	103.5	100.2	98.4
1988	0.17	0.18	0.14	0.16	119.2	119.3	118.3	125.2	98.4	98.5	97.7	103.4
1989	0.19	0.19	0.16	0.17	109.6	109.4	110.9	106.6	93.0	92.8	94.1	90.5
1990	0.21	0.22	0.17	0.20	113.3	113.6	109.9	118.6	111.5	111.8	108.2	116.8
1991	0.23	0.24	0.19	0.24	109.3	109.0	112.0	117.5	105.3	105.0	107.9	113.2
1992	0.27	0.28	0.22	0.30	115.4	115.7	113.8	125.1	104.5	104.8	103.1	113.3
1993	0.32	0.33	0.27	0.39	118.0	117.2	123.2	130.2	99.3	98.7	103.7	109.6
1994	0.45	0.47	0.35	0.52	142.4	143.7	130.8	133.4	121.4	122.5	111.5	113.7
1995	0.51	0.53	0.42	0.58	114.1	113.1	120.4	111.6	94.8	94.0	100.1	92.7
1996	0.62	0.64	0.49	0.69	121.0	121.4	116.3	118.3	111.3	111.7	107.0	108.8
1997	0.70	0.72	0.55	0.79	112.9	112.7	111.1	114.4	107.9	107.7	106.2	109.4
1998	0.77	0.79	0.60	0.76	109.0	108.9	110.2	96.3	106.4	106.4	107.6	94.1
1999	0.83	0.84	0.65	0.86	107.9	107.2	107.9	113.2	109.2	108.5	109.2	96.5
2000	0.92	0.94	0.70	0.96	111.5	111.5	108.1	111.7	114.3	114.3	110.8	95.2
2001	1.05	1.09	0.72	1.04	114.1	115.5	102.4	108.8	116.4	117.7	104.4	92.7
2002	1.20	1.24	0.79	1.14	113.8	114.2	110.3	110.0	114.7	115.2	111.2	93.7
2003	1.29	1.35	0.85	1.19	107.4	108.4	107.2	103.9	106.0	107.0	105.8	88.5
2004	1.46	1.53	0.95	1.33	113.3	113.7	111.7	112.0	106.8	107.2	105.3	95.4
2005	1.61	1.69	1.05	1.49	110.7	110.3	110.5	111.9	108.8	108.5	108.6	110.1
2006	1.87	2.00	1.22	1.64	115.9	118.4	115.9	110.4	113.8	116.2	113.8	108.4
2007	2.05	2.29	1.41	1.67	109.5	114.3	115.3	101.5	103.4	108.0	108.8	95.9
2008	2.40	2.68	1.82	1.97	117.3	117.0	129.5	117.9	111.3	111.0	122.8	111.8
2009	2.70	3.03	2.14	2.16	112.3	113.3	117.7	109.9	111.8	112.8	117.1	109.4
2010	3.02	3.43	2.51	2.38	111.8	113.2	117.4	109.9	107.7	109.0	113.1	105.8
2011	3.54	4.04	3.40	2.87	117.3	117.6	135.3	120.7	111.9	112.2	129.1	115.2
2012	3.89	4.51	3.86	3.22	109.9	111.6	113.3	112.1	106.7	108.4	110.0	108.8
2013	4.40	4.90	4.50	4.00	113.6	108.7	117.8	124.3	110.2	105.5	114.3	120.7
2014	4.78	5.44	5.00	4.18	108.6	111.0	111.1	104.5	106.1	108.4	108.5	102.1
2015	5.50	6.45	5.62	4.65	115.1	118.5	112.5	111.4	113.0	116.3	110.4	109.3
2016	6.36	7.89	6.46	4.97	115.5	122.4	114.8	106.8	113.8	120.6	113.1	105.2
2017	7.35	9.57	7.30	5.45	115.7	121.3	113.0	109.5	114.7	120.3	112.1	108.7
2018	8.05	10.41	8.30	6.17	109.5	108.8	113.7	113.3	107.8	107.1	112.0	111.5
2019	9.18	10.65	7.92	7.78	114.0	102.3	95.4	126.1	111.3	99.9	93.2	123.2
2020	9.83	11.36	9.02	8.20	107.1	106.7	113.9	105.4	103.5	103.2	110.2	101.9

15−19 各州市全部职工工资总额和平均工资（2020年）

Total Wages and Annual Average Wages of Staff and Workers by Region (2020)

单位：亿元、万元/人

(100 million yuan,10 000 yuan/person)

州　市	Region	职工工资总额 Total Wages	职工平均工资 Wages Average
全　省	**Yunnan**	**3 050.83**	**9.83**
昆　明	Kunming	1 050.26	10.23
曲　靖	Qujing	265.20	8.91
玉　溪	Yuxi	158.90	9.81
保　山	Baoshan	120.26	8.37
昭　通	Zhaotong	207.31	9.49
丽　江	Lijiang	71.31	10.06
普　洱	Pu'er	119.38	9.56
临　沧	Lincang	113.30	9.83
楚　雄	Chuxiong	131.79	8.95
红　河	Honghe	213.42	8.42
文　山	Wenshan	145.89	9.79
西双版纳	Xishuangbanna	67.58	9.20
大　理	Dali	179.88	9.86
德　宏	Dehong	68.11	8.94
怒　江	Nujiang	40.60	10.02
迪　庆	Diqing	46.71	13.37

注：全省数含铁路部门数据。

Note: The data of the whole province include the data of railway.

15-20 各州市城镇单位分行业年末就业人员劳动报酬（2020年）
Earnings of Employed Persons in Urban Units by Sector and Region at Year-end (2020)

单位：亿元 (100 million yuan)

州 市	Region	劳动报酬 Earnings of Employed Persons	农、林、牧、渔业 Farming,Forestry,Animal Husbandry and Fishery	采矿业 Mining	制造业 Manufacturing	电力、热力、燃气及水生产和供应业 Production and Supply of Electric Power, Heat, Gas and Water
全 省	**Yunnan**	**3 283.58**	**12.02**	**45.87**	**320.56**	**126.11**
昆 明	Kunming	1 154.59	2.81	6.37	149.03	88.46
曲 靖	Qujing	280.88	1.15	10.86	39.65	6.55
玉 溪	Yuxi	170.15	0.44	4.31	15.52	1.40
保 山	Baoshan	125.98	0.43	0.76	13.82	3.80
昭 通	Zhaotong	215.79	0.42	4.58	6.93	4.10
丽 江	Lijiang	76.20	0.32		2.46	1.33
普 洱	Pu'er	124.79	1.22	1.44	5.63	1.42
临 沧	Lincang	121.39	0.49	0.43	5.68	0.84
楚 雄	Chuxiong	143.02	0.42	2.11	10.16	1.49
红 河	Honghe	229.54	0.96	7.95	34.56	4.32
文 山	Wenshan	155.47	0.87	4.12	10.78	5.49
西双版纳	Xishuangbanna	71.89	1.69	0.11	5.18	0.85
大 理	Dali	193.17	0.60	0.30	10.96	2.54
德 宏	Dehong	72.43	0.05	0.05	4.81	1.75
怒 江	Nujiang	42.65	0.08	0.02	4.47	0.83
迪 庆	Diqing	52.36	0.06	2.48	0.93	0.93

注：全省数含铁路部门数据。
Note: The data of the whole province include the data of railway.

15-20 续表1 continued

单位：亿元 (100 million yuan)

州 市	Region	建筑业 Construction	批发和零售业 Wholesale and Retail Trade	交通运输、仓储和邮政业 Transportation, Storage and Post	住宿和餐饮业 Hotel and Catering Service	信息传输、软件和信息技术服务业 Information Transmission, Software and Information Technology Service
全 省	**Yunnan**	**209.06**	**119.45**	**160.92**	**21.09**	**56.11**
昆 明	Kunming	114.32	50.95	70.58	10.98	25.59
曲 靖	Qujing	22.56	12.60	4.85	0.78	2.84
玉 溪	Yuxi	5.81	7.04	3.88	0.63	2.28
保 山	Baoshan	4.28	4.16	2.50	0.86	1.60
昭 通	Zhaotong	5.81	6.59	3.28	0.58	3.03
丽 江	Lijiang	1.59	2.35	1.72	1.81	1.18
普 洱	Pu'er	5.75	2.99	2.49	0.17	2.86
临 沧	Lincang	5.04	3.68	2.34	0.39	2.37
楚 雄	Chuxiong	11.38	5.18	2.67	0.47	2.07
红 河	Honghe	17.16	7.68	3.10	1.00	3.49
文 山	Wenshan	3.55	3.31	2.88	0.41	2.55
西双版纳	Xishuangbanna	1.28	2.06	1.09	0.99	1.29
大 理	Dali	6.49	7.31	3.33	1.10	2.32
德 宏	Dehong	1.92	1.56	1.07	0.28	1.24
怒 江	Nujiang	1.00	0.57	0.93	0.14	0.54
迪 庆	Diqing	1.13	1.42	0.92	0.50	0.85

15-20 续表2 continued

单位：亿元 (100 million yuan)

州 市	Region	金融业 Finance	房地产业 Real Estate	租赁和商务服务业 Leasing Trade and Business Service	科学研究和技术服务业 Scientific Research, Technology Service and Geological Prospecting	水利、环境和公共设施管理业 Water Conservancy, Admistration of Environment and Public Facilities
全 省	**Yunnan**	**162.87**	**70.91**	**65.08**	**107.82**	**38.46**
昆 明	Kunming	73.51	36.61	33.71	60.28	11.84
曲 靖	Qujing	11.94	4.97	3.08	4.26	2.98
玉 溪	Yuxi	7.52	3.74	3.26	4.88	2.48
保 山	Baoshan	4.44	2.72	1.56	2.33	1.39
昭 通	Zhaotong	6.50	1.61	2.98	3.66	0.92
丽 江	Lijiang	3.45	1.30	1.52	1.51	1.79
普 洱	Pu'er	7.51	1.29	2.39	6.18	1.55
临 沧	Lincang	3.01	2.27	1.33	2.24	0.92
楚 雄	Chuxiong	6.91	3.04	2.54	3.05	1.69
红 河	Honghe	12.29	3.47	2.99	4.41	2.65
文 山	Wenshan	5.79	1.31	1.29	2.52	1.26
西双版纳	Xishuangbanna	3.41	2.84	1.13	4.25	2.25
大 理	Dali	9.94	4.21	4.32	5.54	4.15
德 宏	Dehong	3.54	1.10	1.66	2.42	0.30
怒 江	Nujiang	1.72	0.30	0.36	0.00	0.22
迪 庆	Diqing	1.40	0.13	0.96	0.29	2.06

15-20 续表3 continued

单位：亿元 (100 million yuan)

州 市	Region	居民服务、修理和其他服务业 Services to Households,Repair and Other Services	教 育 Education	卫生和社会工作 Health Care, Social Security and Social Welfare	文化、体育和娱乐业 Culture, Sports and Entertainment	公共管理、社会保障和社会组织 Common Administration, Social security and Social Organization
全 省	**Yunnan**	**6.47**	**697.03**	**331.99**	**34.62**	**697.14**
昆 明	Kunming	3.16	158.26	94.66	15.42	148.06
曲 靖	Qujing	0.77	68.57	26.42	1.58	54.48
玉 溪	Yuxi	0.22	39.84	19.48	1.71	45.67
保 山	Baoshan	0.10	31.17	17.79	0.68	31.60
昭 通	Zhaotong	0.27	81.17	28.25	1.46	53.63
丽 江	Lijiang	0.02	20.51	9.61	0.98	22.75
普 洱	Pu'er	0.14	31.31	15.98	1.26	33.22
临 沧	Lincang	0.35	32.60	16.55	1.15	39.71
楚 雄	Chuxiong	0.17	31.10	18.01	1.72	38.84
红 河	Honghe	0.34	50.13	20.39	2.09	50.55
文 山	Wenshan	0.27	50.02	19.32	1.41	38.31
西双版纳	Xishuangbanna	0.17	10.85	10.54	1.57	20.33
大 理	Dali	0.19	58.09	20.68	1.70	49.39
德 宏	Dehong	0.08	15.34	10.52	0.58	24.16
怒 江	Nujiang	0.18	9.41	1.33	0.55	20.01
迪 庆	Diqing	0.02	8.64	2.46	0.75	26.44

15-21 各州市城镇单位分行业职工平均工资（2020年）

Average Wages of Staff and Workers in Urban Entities by Sector and Region (2020)

单位：万元/人 (10 000 yuan/person)

州市	Region	全部职工 Staff and Workers	农、林、牧、渔业 Farming,Forestry,Animal Husbandry and Fishery	采矿业 Mining	制造业 Manufacturing	电力、热力、燃气及水生产和供应业 Production and Supply of Electric Power,Heat,Gas and Water
全省	**Yunnan**	**9.83**	**5.38**	**8.08**	**8.31**	**11.31**
昆明	Kunming	10.23	6.02	7.93	9.81	11.79
曲靖	Qujing	8.91	6.45	6.26	7.69	11.31
玉溪	Yuxi	9.81	6.73	11.00	9.91	7.48
保山	Baoshan	8.37	5.74	6.69	5.86	10.58
昭通	Zhaotong	9.49	5.36	8.00	10.57	14.92
丽江	Lijiang	10.06	7.52		7.09	11.93
普洱	Pu'er	9.56	3.61	7.27	6.20	10.36
临沧	Lincang	9.83	6.22	6.69	4.66	6.35
楚雄	Chuxiong	8.95	4.16	7.85	7.18	9.98
红河	Honghe	8.42	6.29	10.40	8.03	8.65
文山	Wenshan	9.79	6.74	8.21	7.20	11.29
西双版纳	Xishuangbanna	9.20	4.28	12.70	5.86	8.27
大理	Dali	9.86	6.71	4.15	9.13	10.35
德宏	Dehong	8.94	2.99	6.22	5.90	10.66
怒江	Nujiang	10.02	3.38	6.73	7.19	7.13
迪庆	Diqing	13.37	4.49	13.33	7.52	8.77

15-21 续表1 continued

单位：万元/人 (10 000 yuan/person)

州 市	Region	建 筑 业 Construction	批发和零售业 Wholesale and Retail Trade	交通运输、仓储和邮政业 Transportation, Storage and Post	住宿和餐饮业 Hotel and Catering Service	信息传输、软件和信息技术服务业 Information Transmission, Software and Information Technology Service
全 省	**Yunnan**	**6.91**	**8.59**	**10.11**	**4.34**	**10.70**
昆 明	Kunming	9.31	8.24	10.25	4.37	9.93
曲 靖	Qujing	5.03	11.84	7.54	3.87	11.94
玉 溪	Yuxi	5.67	5.82	7.49	4.03	11.87
保 山	Baoshan	5.26	9.93	6.61	4.34	12.77
昭 通	Zhaotong	6.45	12.38	7.91	3.57	10.64
丽 江	Lijiang	3.86	8.23	6.82	4.99	11.67
普 洱	Pu'er	5.72	11.42	6.52	3.96	11.91
临 沧	Lincang	6.16	8.22	6.53	3.90	11.45
楚 雄	Chuxiong	5.21	10.05	6.33	3.65	11.53
红 河	Honghe	4.72	6.73	6.15	4.32	8.97
文 山	Wenshan	5.43	7.17	7.59	4.58	12.45
西双版纳	Xishuangbanna	5.22	7.37	7.35	5.61	11.79
大 理	Dali	4.35	9.35	7.72	3.93	12.06
德 宏	Dehong	5.58	7.56	9.21	3.73	13.18
怒 江	Nujiang	4.81	8.45	6.95	3.58	11.12
迪 庆	Diqing	5.19	9.54	9.97	4.76	15.38

15-21 续表2 continued

单位：万元/人 (10 000 yuan/person)

州　市	Region	金融业 Finance	房地产业 Real Estate	租赁和商务服务业 Leasing Trade and Business Service	科学研究和技术服务业 Scientific Research, Technology Service and Geological Prospecting	水利、环境和公共设施管理业 Water Conservancy, Admistration of Environment and Public Facilities
全　省	**Yunnan**	**16.19**	**7.13**	**5.74**	**11.51**	**6.99**
昆　明	Kunming	18.87	8.62	6.87	13.37	6.49
曲　靖	Qujing	14.96	5.83	4.86	8.57	6.87
玉　溪	Yuxi	12.99	5.19	4.94	9.92	8.83
保　山	Baoshan	13.82	6.44	4.77	9.11	5.62
昭　通	Zhaotong	14.68	7.57	6.64	10.15	9.10
丽　江	Lijiang	14.49	7.17	6.60	8.84	7.03
普　洱	Pu'er	14.90	5.83	3.69	9.84	6.91
临　沧	Lincang	13.37	5.35	4.22	9.42	8.23
楚　雄	Chuxiong	16.19	5.09	4.25	9.21	5.89
红　河	Honghe	13.51	5.02	5.50	8.63	6.62
文　山	Wenshan	15.27	6.07	5.81	9.40	8.31
西双版纳	Xishuangbanna	15.63	9.37	6.69	12.16	6.25
大　理	Dali	14.71	6.51	4.60	11.37	7.77
德　宏	Dehong	13.18	6.80	3.21	11.19	6.95
怒　江	Nujiang	13.84	6.92	5.15	5.24	10.41
迪　庆	Diqing	15.92	5.05	4.90	12.10	9.37

15−21 续表3 continued

单位：万元/人 (10 000 yuan/person)

州 市	Region	居民服务、修理和其他服务业 Services to Households, Repairand Other Services	教 育 Education	卫生和社会工作 Health Care, Social Works	文化、体育和娱乐业 Culture, Sports and Entertainment	公共管理、社会保障和社会组织 Common Administration, Social Security and Social Organization
全 省	**Yunnan**	**4.38**	**10.96**	**10.80**	**9.48**	**11.27**
昆 明	Kunming	4.21	11.67	12.59	10.63	12.15
曲 靖	Qujing	7.57	10.35	9.88	7.78	11.41
玉 溪	Yuxi	3.60	12.15	12.11	10.75	12.22
保 山	Baoshan	4.92	9.57	9.53	8.56	9.14
昭 通	Zhaotong	4.05	10.44	10.40	6.84	8.10
丽 江	Lijiang	4.57	12.18	13.83	6.26	12.29
普 洱	Pu'er	5.30	10.57	11.36	9.13	11.57
临 沧	Lincang	3.52	12.11	10.97	9.18	12.20
楚 雄	Chuxiong	2.50	10.29	10.03	8.75	11.25
红 河	Honghe	4.07	9.71	8.29	9.15	10.53
文 山	Wenshan	4.74	10.23	9.60	9.84	11.95
西双版纳	Xishuangbanna	5.71	11.53	10.14	7.26	10.55
大 理	Dali	5.46	12.60	9.54	9.27	11.62
德 宏	Dehong	4.88	9.31	10.19	9.21	10.09
怒 江	Nujiang	3.72	10.86	11.18	11.85	13.09
迪 庆	Diqing	4.19	14.34	15.07	16.55	16.77

主要统计指标解释

人口数 指一定时点、一定地区范围内有生命的个人总和。年度统计的年末人口数指每年 12 月 31 日 24 时的人口数。年度统计的全国人口总数内未包括香港、澳门特别行政区和台湾省以及海外华侨人数。

城镇人口和乡村人口 城镇人口是指居住在城镇范围内的全部常住人口；乡村人口是除上述人口以外的全部人口。

人口密度 指一定时点一定地区的人口数与该地区的面积数之比，即一定时点的单位土地面积上的人口数通常以每平方公里的居民人数来表示。计算公式：

人口密度（人/平方公里）= 该地区的人口数/该地区的土地面积

出生率 出生率(又称粗出生率)指一定时期内(通常为一年内)平均每千人所出生的人数的比例，一般用千分率表示。计算公式：出生率（‰）= 年出生人数/年平均人数 ×1000‰

出生人数 是指活产婴儿，即胎儿脱离母体时(不管怀孕月数)有过呼吸或其他生命现象。年平均人数是年初、年末人口数的平均数，也可用年中人口数代替。

死亡率 指在一定时期内(通常为一年内)一定地区的死亡人数与同期平均人数(或期中人数)之比，一般用千分率表示。计算公式：

死亡率（‰）= 年死亡人数/年平均人数 ×1000‰

人口自然增长率 在一定时期内(通常为一年内)人口自然增加数(出生人数减死亡人数)与平均人数(或期中人数)之比，一般用千分率表示。计算公式：

人口自然增长率 =（本年出生人口数 - 本年死亡人口数）/年平均人口数 ×1000%

人口自然增长率（‰）= 人口出生率 - 人口死亡率

性别比 反映男性与女性人口比例的指标，指在总人口中或各年龄组人口中，男性人数与女性人数之比。

通常以每 100 个女性人口相对应的男性人口数。计算公式：

性别比 = 男性人口/女性人口 ×100

就业人员 指年龄在 16 周岁及以上，从事一定社会劳动并取得劳动报酬或经营收入的人员。这一指标反映了一定时期内全部劳动力资源的实际利用情况，是研究我国基本国情国力的重要指标。

单位就业人员 指在各级国家机关、政党机关、社会团体及企业、事业单位中工作，取得工资或其他形式的劳动报酬的全部人员。包括在岗职工、再就业的离退休人员、民办教师以及在各单位中工作的外方人员和港澳台方人员、兼职人员、借用的外单位人员和第二职业者。不包括离开本单位仍保留劳动关系的职工。各单位的就业人员反映了各单位实际参加生产或工作的全部劳动力。

职工 指在国有、城镇集体、联营、股份制、外商和港、澳、台投资、其他单位及其附属机构工作，并由其支付工资的各类人员。不包括下列人员：(1) 乡镇企业就业人员；(2) 私营企业就业人员；(3) 城镇个体劳动者；(4) 离休、退休、退职人员；(5) 再就业的离、退休人员；(6) 民办教师；(7) 在城镇单位中工作的外方及港、澳、台人员；(8) 其他按有关规定不列入职工统计范围的人员。(1998 年及以后的数据均为在岗职工数据，其他相关指标如职工工资总额，职工平均工资等指标也从 1998 年按此口径进行了相应调整)。

国有单位 指资产归国家所有的经济组织。包括按《中华人民共和国企业法人登记管理条例》规定登记注册的非公司制的经济组织，以及中央、地方各级国家机关、事业单位和社会团体。

集体单位 指生产资料归集体所有，并按《中华人民共和国企业法人登记管理条例》规定登记注册的经济组织。

其他单位包括股份合作单位、联营单位、有限责任公司、股份有限公司、港澳台商投资单位以及外商投资单位等其他登记注册类型单位。

在岗职工 指在本单位工作并由单位支付工资的人员，以及有工作岗位，但由于学习、病伤产假等原因暂未工作，仍由单位支付工资的人员。

工资总额 指各单位在一定时期内直接支付给本单位全部职工的劳动报酬总额。工资总额的计算原则应以直接支付给职工的全部劳动报酬为根据。各单位支付给职工的劳动报酬以及其他根据有关规定支付的工资，不论是计入成本的还是不计入成本的，不论是按国家规定列入计征奖金税项目的，还是未列入计征奖金税项目的，不论是以货币形式支付的还是以实物形式支付的，均包括在工资总额内。

平均工资 指企业、事业、机关单位的职工在一定时期内平均每人所得的货币工资额。它表明一定时期职工工资收入的高低程度，是反映职工工资水平的主要指标。计算公式为：

$$平均工资=\frac{报告期实际支付的全部职工工资总额}{报告期全部职工平均人数}\times 100\%$$

平均工资指数 指报告期职工平均工资与基期职工平均工资的比率，是反映不同时期职工货币工资水平变动情况的相对数。计算公式为：

$$平均工资指数=\frac{报告期职工平均工资}{基期职工平均工资}\times 100\%$$

平均实际工资指数 职工平均实际工资指扣除物价变动因素后的职工平均工资。职工平均实际工资指数是反映实际工资变动情况的相对数，表明职工实际工资水平提高或降低的程度。计算公式为：

$$平均实际工资指数=\frac{报告期职工平均工资指数}{报告期城镇居民消费价格指数}\times 100\%$$

城镇单位就业人员劳动报酬 指各单位在一定时期内直接支付给本单位全部就业人员的劳动报酬总额。包括职工工资总额和其他就业人员劳动报酬总额。

平均劳动报酬 指企业、事业、机关等单位的全部就业人员在一定时期内平均每人所得的货币工资额。

计算公式为：

$$平均劳动报酬=\frac{\begin{array}{c}报告期实际支付的全部\\就业人员劳动报酬\end{array}}{报告期全部就业人员平均人数}\times 100\%$$

城镇登记失业人员 指有非农业户口，在一定的劳动年龄内（16周岁至退休年龄），有劳动能力，无业而要求就业，并在当地就业服务机构进行求职登记的人员。

城镇登记失业率 城镇登记失业人员与城镇单位就业人员（扣除使用的农村劳动力、聘用的离退休人员、港澳台及外方人员）、城镇单位中的不在岗职工、城镇私营业主、个体户主、城镇私营企业和个体就业人员、城镇登记失业人员之和的比。计算公式为：

$$\text{城镇登记失业率} = \frac{\text{城镇登记失业人数}}{\begin{array}{c}\text{(城镇单位就业人员 - 使用的农村劳动力 -}\\ \text{聘用的离退休人员 - 聘用的港澳台及外方人员)+}\\ \text{不在岗职工 + 城镇私营业主 + 城镇个体户主 +}\\ \text{城镇私营企业及个体就业人员 + 城镇登记失业人数}\end{array}} \times 100\%$$

Explanatory Notes on Main Statistical Indicators

Total Population refers to the total number of people alive at a certain point of time within a given area. The annual statistics on total population is taken at midnight, the 3lst of December, not including residents in Taiwan province, Hong Kong SAR and Macao SAR and Chinese national residing abroad.

Urban Population and Rural Population Urban population refers to all people residing in cities and towns,while rural population refers to population other than urban population.

Population Density refers to the ratio of population to the area at a certain point of time within a given area,i.e., the population of unit land area at a certain point of time, which is often expressed as number of inhabitants per square kilometer:

Population density = number of population in the region/land area in the region

Birth Rate or (crude Birth Rate) refers to the ratio of the number of births to the average population during a certain period of time (usually a year) which is often expressed in ‰. The formula is as follows:

Birth Rate = Number of Births/Annual Average Number of Population×1000‰.

Number of births refers to live births, i.e., the births when babies had showed any vital phenomena regardless of the length of pregnancy.

Annual Average Number of Population is the average of the number of population at the beginning of the year and that at the end of the year. Sometimes it is substituted for with the mid year population.

Death Rate (or Crude Death Rate) refers to the ratio of the number of deaths to the average population (or mid-period population) during a certain period of time (usually a year) which is often expressed in ‰. The formula is as follows:

Death Rate = Number of Deaths/Annual Average Number of Population×1000‰.

Natural Growth Rate of Population refers to the ratio of natural increase in population (number of births minus number of deaths) in a certain period of time (usually a year) to the average population (or mid-period population)of the same period which is often expressed in ‰. The formulas are as follows:

Natural Growth of Population = (Number of Birth − Number of Deaths)/Average Number of Population×1000‰.

Natural Growth Rate of Population = Birth Rate − Death Rate

Sex Ratio reflects the indicator of male population and female population, which refers to the ratio of male population to female population in total population or population by age group. It usually means relevant male population per 100 female populations. The formula is as follows:

Sex ratio = male population/female population ×100.

Employed Persons refer to persons aged 16 and over who are engaged in gainful employment and thus receive remuneration payment or earn business income. This indicator reflects the actual utilization of total labour force during a certain period of time and is often used for the research on China's economic situation and national power.

Persons Employed in Various Units refer to all the persons working in government agencies of various levels, political and party organizations, social organizations, enterprises and institutions, and receiving wages or other forms of payment. They include fully-employed staff and workers, re-employed retirees, teachers in the schools run by the local people, foreigners and Chinese compatriots from Hong Kong, Macao, and Taiwan working in various units, part-time employees, employees of other units working temporarily at current posts, and employees holding the second job, but do not include persons who have left their working units while keeping their labour contract (employment relation) unchanged. This indicator reflects the total number of laborers actually engaged in production or other operations in various units.

Staff and Workers refer to persons working in, and receive payment from units of state ownership, collective ownership, joint ownership, share holding ownership, foreign ownership, and ownership by entrepreneurs from Hong Kong, Macao, and Taiwan, and other types of ownership and their affiliated units. They do not include 1)persons employed in township enterprises, 2) persons employed in private enterprises, 3) urban self-employed persons, 4) retirees, 5) re-employed retirees, 6) teachers in the schools run by the local people, 7) foreigners and persons from Hong Kong, Macao and Taiwan who work in urban units, and 8) other persons not to be included byrelevant regulations. (Data since 1998 refer to fully employed staff and workers. Other related statistics indicators,such as total wage bill and average wage are adjusted since 1998 accordingly).

State-owned Units refer to economic units whose assets are owned by the state, including non-corporation units registered according to Regulation of the People's Republic of China on the Registration of Enterprises and Corporations, state organs, institutions and social organizations at the central-level and local levels.

Collective-owned Units refer to economic units registered according to Regulation of the People's Republic of China on the Registration of Enterprises and Corporations where the means of production are collectively owned.

Units of Other Types of Ownership refer to units registered with other types of ownership, including cooperative units, joint ownership units, limited liability corporations, share holding corporations, units funded by entrepreneurs from Hong Kong, Macao, and Taiwan, and foreign- funded units.

Employed Staff and Workers refer to persons who work in, and receive wages from their working units,including persons who have their work posts but are temporarily absent from work for reasons of study or on sick,injury or maternal leave and still receive wages from their working units.

Total Wage Bill refers to the total remuneration payment to staff and workers in various units during a certain period of time. The calculation of total wage bill is based on the total remuneration payment to the staff and workers. Therefore, all the wages and salaries and other payments to staff and workers are included in the total wage bill regardless of sources, reckoning the cost of production or not, category, listing as items of premium taxation or not, and forms, paying in cash or in kind.Average Wage refers to the average wage in money terms per person during a certain period of time for staffand workers in enterprises, institutions, and government agencies, which reflects the general level of wage incomeduring a certain period of time and is calculated as follows:

$$\text{Average Wage} = \frac{\text{Total Wage Bill of Staff and Workers at Reference Time}}{\text{Average Number of Staff and Workers at Reference Time}} \times 100\%$$

Average Wage Indices refers to the ratio of average wage of staff and workers at the reference period to that at the base period, which reflects the change of wage of staff and workers at the different period. It is calculated as follows:

$$\text{Average Wage Indices} = \frac{\text{Average Wage of Staff and Workers at Reference Time}}{\text{Average Wage of Staff and Workers at Base Period}} \times 100\%$$

Average Real Wage Indices average real wage of staff and workers refers to the average wage of staff and workers after removing the effects of the price changes and average real wage indices of staff and workers refers to the change of real wage, which reflects the relative increasing or decreasing level of real wage of staff and workers,which is calculated as follows:

$$\text{Average Real Wage Indices} = \frac{\text{Average Wage Indices of Staff and Workers at the Reference Time}}{\text{Urban Consumer Price Indices at Reference Time}} \times 100\%$$

Earning refer to total remuneration payment to all employees in various units in urban areas (did not include urban private units and self-employed individuals) during a certain period of time, including staff and workers and other employees (i.e., reemployed retirees or those who are from Hong Kong, Macao, Taiwan province or other countries).

Average Earning refer to average earning level in money terms per employee in the enterprise, institution and government organ during a certain period of time, it is calculated as follows:

$$\text{Average Earning Of Employees} = \frac{\text{Total Earnings of Employees at Reference Period}}{\text{Average Number of Employees at Reference Period}} \times 100\%$$

Registered Unemployed Persons in Urban Areas refer to the persons with non-agricultural household registration at certain working ages (16 years old to retirement age), who are capable of working, unemployed and willing to work, and have been registered at the local employment service agencies to apply for a job.

Registered Unemployment Rate in Urban Areas refers to the ratio of the number of the registered unemployed persons to the sum of the number of persons employed in various units (minus the employed rural labour force, re-employed retirees, and Hong Kong, Macao, Taiwan or foreign employees), laid-off staff and workers in urban units, owners of private enterprises in urban areas, owners of self-employed individuals in urban areas, employees of private enterprises in urban areas, employee of self-employed individuals in urban areas, and the registered unemployed persons in urban areas. The formula is as follows:

$$\text{Registered unemployment rate in urban areas} = \frac{\text{number of registered urban unemployed persons}}{\text{number of persons employed in urban units-}} \times 100\%$$

employed rural labour force unemployed persons
in urban areas urban self - employed individuals
registered of urban private enterprises employees
of urban self - employed individuals employees
urban private enterprises owners of laid - off staff
and workers owners of Macao, Taiwan or foreign
employees re - employed retirees - Hong Kong

Chapter 16

十六、资源与环境

Resources and Environment

16−1 土地利用情况（2018年）

Land Utilization (2018)

项　　目	Item	面积（万公顷） Area(10 000 hectares)	占总面积(%) Proportion to Total Area (%)
土地调查面积	**Land Survey Area**	**3 831.89**	**100.0**
农用地	Agricultural Land	3 291.67	85.9
耕地	Cultivated Land	620.91	16.2
园地	Garden Plot	162.58	4.2
林地	Forest Land	2 300.16	60.0
牧草地	Grassland	14.69	0.4
其他农用地	Others	193.33	5.1
建设用地	Construction Land	112.24	2.9
居民点及工矿用地	Residential and Industrial Land	88.14	2.3
交通运输用地	Land for Transport	12.24	0.3
水利设施用地	Water Conservancy Facilities Land	11.86	0.3
未利用地	Unused Land	427.98	11.2

注：由于全国第三次国土调查数据尚未公布，本表中数据仍然使用2018年数据。
Note: Since the data of the Third National Land Survey have not been released, data in this table are from 2018.

16-2 主要山峰高程
Height of Major Mountain Peaks

名称	Mountain Range	标高（米） Height of Mountain Peak (m)	所处州、市	Region
梅里雪山（卡瓦格博峰）	Meili Snow Mountains (Kawagebo Peak)	6 740	迪庆	Diqing
玉龙雪山（扇子陡峰）	Yulong Snow Mountains (Shanzi Peak)	5 596	丽江	Lijiang
碧罗雪山	Biluo Snow Mountains	4 141	怒江	Nujiang
点苍山（马龙峰）	Diancang Mountains (Malong Peak)	4 122	大理	Dali
拱王山	Gongwang Mountains	3 677	昆明	Kunming
大雪山	Daxue Mountains	3 504	临沧	Lincang
高黎贡山	Gaoligong Mountains	3 374	保山	Baoshan
无量山	Wuliang Mountains	3 291	大理、普洱	Dali, Pu'er
哀牢山	Ailao Mountains	2 940	普洱、玉溪、红河	Pu'er,Yuxi, Honghe
梁王山	Liangwang Mountains	2 833	曲靖	Qujing
五莲峰	Wulian Mountains	2 561	昭通	Zhaotong

注：全省最低点为河口县境内的南溪河与红河汇合处，海拔76.4米。
Note: The minimum height is that of 76.4 meters of the confluence of the Nanxi River and the Honghe River in Hekou county.

16-3 主要河流情况
Major Rivers

名称	River	境内河长(千米) Internal Length (km)	集水面积(万平方千米) Catchments Area (10 000 sq.km)
金沙江	Jinsha River	1 560	10.56
澜沧江	Lancang River	1 227	8.86
元江	Yuan River	680	3.75
南盘江	Nanpan River	677	4.33
怒江	Nu River	618	3.34
瑞丽江	Ruili River	370	0.97
大盈江	Daying River	196	0.59

16-4 主要湖泊情况

Major Lakes

名称	Lake	所属水系 River System	湖面面积 (平方千米) Lake Area (sq · km)	最大水深 (米) Maximum Depth(m)	平均水深 (米) Average Depth(m)	平均水位 (米) Average Water Level (m)	总容水量 (亿立方米) Water Volume (100 million cu.m)
滇池	Dianchi Lake	金沙江 Jinsha River	306.3	8	5	1 885	15.70
洱海	Erhai Lake	澜沧江 Lancang River	250.0	23	10.5	1 974	30.00
抚仙湖	Fuxian Lake	南盘江 Nanpan River	212.0	151.5	87	1 720	185.00
程海	Chenghai Lake	金沙江 Jinsha River	78.8	36.9	15	1 503	27.00
泸沽湖	Lugu Lake	金沙江 Jinsha River	51.8	73.2	40	2 685	20.72
星云湖	Xingyun Lake	南盘江 Nanpan River	39.0	12	9	1 723	2.30
杞麓湖	Qilu Lake	南盘江 Nanpan River	37.3	6.8	4	1 792	1.68
阳宗海	Yangzonghai Lake	南盘江 Nanpan River	31.0	30	20	1 770	6.02
异龙湖	Yilong Lake	泸江 Lu River	31.0	6.6	2.8	1 413	1.27

16-5 各州市土地利用情况（2018年）

Land Use by Region (2018)

单位：万公顷　　(10 000 hectares)

州　市	Region	土地调查面积 Area under Land Survey	农用地 Land for Agriculture Use	园　地 Garden Land	牧草地 Land Grazing and Pasture	建设用地 Land for Construction	居民点及工矿用地 Land for Inhabitation, Mining and Manufacturing	交通运输用地 Land for Transport	水利设施用地 Land for Water Conservancy Facilities
全　省	**Yunnan**	**3 831.89**	**3 291.67**	**162.58**	**14.69**	**112.23**	**88.14**	**12.23**	**11.86**
昆　明	Kunming	210.13	160.99	5.02	0.29	16.87	13.85	1.95	1.07
曲　靖	Qujing	289.35	235.76	3.12	0.88	13.54	10.77	1.29	1.48
玉　溪	Yuxi	149.42	127.63	2.65	0.02	5.71	4.56	0.68	0.47
保　山	Baoshan	190.62	169.32	5.98	0.15	6.52	5.50	0.64	0.38
昭　通	Zhaotong	224.40	187.95	3.65	1.66	7.14	6.13	0.63	0.38
丽　江	Lijiang	205.54	172.48	1.69	1.80	3.82	2.91	0.45	0.46
普　洱	Pu'er	442.66	416.81	26.66	0.08	9.42	5.33	0.77	3.32
临　沧	Lincang	236.20	214.95	16.62	0.20	5.37	4.09	0.75	0.53
楚　雄	Chuxiong	284.38	242.33	3.73		7.87	5.96	0.86	1.05
红　河	Honghe	321.73	272.41	17.07	0.09	10.35	8.18	1.18	0.99
文　山	Wenshan	314.08	257.12	6.64	0.14	7.50	5.96	0.86	0.68
西双版纳	Xishuangbanna	190.96	179.95	56.12	0.01	3.34	2.79	0.35	0.20
大　理	Dali	282.99	248.73	9.28	0.22	8.49	6.90	1.00	0.59
德　宏	Dehong	111.72	102.94	3.93	0.04	3.87	3.31	0.37	0.19
怒　江	Nujiang	145.85	119.06	0.17	0.41	0.92	0.80	0.10	0.02
迪　庆	Diqing	231.86	183.24	0.25	8.68	1.50	1.10	0.35	0.05

注：由于全国第三次国土调查数据尚未公布，本表中数据仍然使用2018年数据。
Note: Since the data of the Third National Land Survey have not been released, data in this table are from 2018.

16-6 各州市自然湿地面积（2020年）

Area of Natural Wetlands by Region (2020)

州市	Region	自然湿地面积（万公顷）Area of Natural Wetlands (1 0 000 hectares)	河流 Rivers	湖泊 Lakes	沼泽 Marshland	占土地调查面积比重(%) Proportion to Investigation Area (%)
全省	**Yunnan**	**40.69**	**24.51**	**12.12**	**4.06**	**1.06**
昆明	Kunming	4.82	1.22	3.43	0.18	0.13
曲靖	Qujing	1.72	1.49	0.18	0.05	0.04
玉溪	Yuxi	3.93	0.90	3.02	0.01	0.10
保山	Baoshan	1.80	1.68	0.06	0.07	0.05
昭通	Zhaotong	2.29	1.77	0.01	0.51	0.06
丽江	Lijiang	3.02	1.33	1.15	0.54	0.08
普洱	Pu'er	3.28	3.26	0.01	0.01	0.09
临沧	Lincang	1.35	1.34		0.01	0.04
楚雄	Chuxiong	2.09	2.04	0.01	0.04	0.05
红河	Honghe	2.23	1.48	0.70	0.05	0.06
文山	Wenshan	1.60	1.10	0.44	0.06	0.04
西双版纳	Xishuangbanna	1.29	1.29			0.03
大理	Dali	5.06	1.93	2.81	0.33	0.13
德宏	Dehong	1.41	1.28	0.09	0.04	0.04
怒江	Nujiang	1.36	1.24	0.03	0.10	0.04
迪庆	Diqing	3.41	1.16	0.17	2.08	0.09

16−7 造林面积情况（2020年）
Area of Afforestation (2020)

单位：公顷 （hectare）

州 市	Region	造林总面积 Total Area of Afforestation	#人工造林 Manual Planting	飞播造林 Airplane Planting	新封山育林 New Closing Hillsides for Afforestation	退化林修复 Restoration of Degraded Forest	人工更新造林 Artificial Regeneration
全 省	**Yunnan**	**267 497**	**254 181**		**53 854**	**25 844**	**205**
昆 明	Kunming	7 160	7 160		3 367	1 200	
曲 靖	Qujing	21 327	17 374		9 954	1 733	
玉 溪	Yuxi	12 023	12 023			4 667	
保 山	Baoshan	11 741	11 500		2 000	2 000	
昭 通	Zhaotong	83 999	80 090		6 381	2 266	
丽 江	Lijiang	12 226	11 959		13 107	4 600	
普 洱	Pu'er	18 625	18 625				72
临 沧	Lincang	15 102	15 102		1 000		133
楚 雄	Chuxiong	10 195	9 128		1 067	1 399	
红 河	Honghe	14 312	14 045		1 737	6 912	
文 山	Wenshan	36 617	33 842		8 775		
西双版纳	Xishuangbanna	5 838	5 838		867		
大 理	Dali	6 751	6 447		1 533	1 067	
德 宏	Dehong	2 169	2 169				
怒 江	Nujiang	5 588	5 588		333		
迪 庆	Diqing	3 824	3 291		3 733		

16-8 水资源状况
Water Resources

单位：亿立方米 (100 million cu.m)

年份 Year / 州市 Region		水资源总量 Total Amount of Water Resources	地表水资源量 Surface Water Resources	地表水与地下水重复计算量 Duplicated Measurement Between Surface Water and Groundwater
2001		2 561.94	2 561.94	808.50
2002		2 308.87	2 308.87	763.60
2003		1 699.36	1 699.36	592.20
2004		2 106.30	2 106.30	719.80
2005		1 846.43	1 846.43	660.30
2006		1 712.00	1 712.00	615.00
2007		2 256.00	2 256.00	794.60
2008		2 314.49	2 314.49	801.60
2009		1 577.00	1 577.00	582.60
2010		1 941.00	1 941.00	686.00
2011		1 480.19	1 480.19	548.05
2012		1 689.77	1 689.77	583.20
2013		1 706.69	1 706.69	573.29
2014		1 726.63	1 726.63	557.39
2015		1 872.00	1 872.00	615.16
2016		2 089.00	2 089.00	699.70
2017		2 202.63	2 202.63	762.00
2018		2 206.48	2 206.48	772.82
2019		1 533.81	1 533.81	554.61
2020		1 799.19	1 799.19	619.85
昆　明	Kunming	43.37	43.37	14.17
曲　靖	Qujing	95.58	95.58	24.32
玉　溪	Yuxi	24.82	24.82	10.55
保　山	Baoshan	126.30	126.30	46.25
昭　通	Zhaotong	129.19	129.19	49.00
丽　江	Lijiang	64.45	64.45	24.82
普　洱	Pu'er	237.20	237.20	79.41
临　沧	Lincang	134.93	134.93	46.05
楚　雄	Chuxiong	42.30	42.30	11.03
红　河	Honghe	165.15	165.15	65.31
文　山	Wenshan	114.51	114.51	38.84
西双版纳	Xishuangbanna	68.19	68.19	26.49
大　理	Dali	77.53	77.53	30.42
德　宏	Dehong	141.91	141.91	51.30
怒　江	Nujiang	222.28	222.28	60.66
迪　庆	Diqing	111.48	111.48	41.23

16-9 各州市水资源及供、用水情况（2020年）

Water Resource and Tap Water Supply and Use by Region (2020)

单位：亿立方米 (100 million cu.m)

州 市	Region	水资源总量 Total Amount of Water Resources	供水总量 Total Volume of Water Supply	用水总量 Total Volume of Water Use	农 业 For Agriculture Use	工 业 For Industry Use	生 活 For Residential Use	生 态 For Environmental Use
全 省	**Yunnan**	**1 799.19**	**155.99**	**156.03**	**109.98**	**16.55**	**25.06**	**4.44**
昆 明	Kunming	43.37	18.35	18.35	8.17	3.26	6.02	0.90
曲 靖	Qujing	95.58	15.16	15.17	10.24	2.35	2.38	0.20
玉 溪	Yuxi	24.82	8.11	8.12	5.36	0.87	1.33	0.56
保 山	Baoshan	126.30	11.23	11.24	8.74	1.05	1.18	0.27
昭 通	Zhaotong	129.19	9.78	9.78	5.65	0.93	2.88	0.32
丽 江	Lijiang	64.45	5.97	5.98	4.90		0.48	0.23
普 洱	Pu'er	237.20	11.99	11.99	10.02	0.54	1.29	0.14
临 沧	Lincang	134.93	8.59	8.59	7.03	0.51	0.92	0.13
楚 雄	Chuxiong	42.30	10.41	10.41	8.27	0.84	1.15	0.15
红 河	Honghe	165.15	16.40	16.41	11.40	2.38	2.29	0.34
文 山	Wenshan	114.51	10.81	10.81	7.71	1.11	1.78	0.21
西双版纳	Xishuangbanna	68.19	5.78	5.77	4.72	0.26	0.72	0.07
大 理	Dali	77.53	12.83	12.84	9.12	1.37	1.57	0.78
德 宏	Dehong	141.91	7.33	7.32	6.39	0.29	0.58	0.06
怒 江	Nujiang	222.28	1.87	1.88	1.33	0.22	0.26	0.07
迪 庆	Diqing	111.48	1.38	1.37	0.93	0.20	0.23	0.01

16-10 各州市城市人口和建设用地情况（2020年）

Basic Statistics on Urban Population and Land Use for Construction by Region (2020)

州 市	Rejion	城区人口（万人）Number of Urban Population (10 000 persons)	城区面积（平方公里）City Area (sq.km)	建成区面积 Of Which Developed Area	绿化覆盖面积（平方公里）Coverage Area of Greenery and Plants (sq.km)	建成区面积 Of Which Developed Area	人均公园绿地面积（平方米）Per Capita Public Park Area (sq.km)	建成区绿化覆盖率(%) Percentage of Coverage by Greenery and Plants in Developed Area (%)
全 省	**Yunnan**	**1 467.50**	**5 117.66**	**1 991.59**	**890.30**	**794.30**	**11.70**	**39.88**
昆 明	Kunming	474.58	2495.39	586.97	250.77	245.29	12.09	41.79
曲 靖	Qujing	170.31	279.55	230.00	93.69	88.48	12.06	38.47
玉 溪	Yuxi	65.09	238.21	74.60	44.29	30.52	12.75	40.91
保 山	Baoshan	70.94	179.23	94.27	44.13	40.02	12.26	42.45
昭 通	Zhaotong	105.25	188.29	131.88	52.27	50.47	10.13	38.27
丽 江	Lijiang	33.75	58.89	51.30	20.17	19.18	13.35	37.40
普 洱	Pu'er	53.78	141.26	77.86	35.48	31.41	11.10	40.34
临 沧	Lincang	59.37	161.31	75.61	30.86	30.36	10.54	40.15
楚 雄	Chuxiong	71.56	187.64	107.97	51.08	41.80	12.73	38.71
红 河	Honghe	130.79	297.76	170.66	77.18	68.66	12.35	40.23
文 山	Wenshan	64.15	180.63	104.91	42.88	39.00	8.44	37.18
西双版纳	Xishuangbanna	22.35	251.63	50.92	37.60	21.26	12.61	41.75
大 理	Dali	82.12	215.09	122.11	49.07	47.06	11.38	38.54
德 宏	Dehong	37.20	136.00	69.98	29.76	25.22	10.75	36.04
怒 江	Nujiang	15.23	32.21	17.76	7.95	6.83	10.42	38.44
迪 庆	Diqing	11.03	74.57	24.79	23.11	8.73	11.75	35.21

16-11 废水、废气排放情况

Waste Water, Waste Gas Discharged

单位：万吨 (10 000 tons)

年份 州市	Year Region	废水排放总量 Total Volume of Waste Water Discharged	生活污水排放量 Consumption Waste Water Discharged	化学需氧量(COD)排放量 COD Discharge	生活污水中COD排放量 COD Discharge from Consumption Waste Water	二氧化硫(SO_2)排放量 Volume of Sulphur Dioxide Emission	工业SO_2排放量 Volume of Industry Sulphur Dioxide Emission
2001		64 152.34	31 439.00	30.89	16.64	35.75	29.44
2002		66 271.02	32 575.00	30.10	18.07	36.41	29.31
2003		68 180.80	33 526.00	28.52	19.24	45.26	38.07
2004		78 302.56	39 901.00	29.02	19.26	47.75	39.99
2005		75 202.45	42 274.00	28.47	17.78	52.19	42.89
2006		80 478.36	46 192.41	29.37	18.80	55.10	45.62
2007		83 758.94	48 406.66	29.00	19.21	53.37	44.54
2008		83 864.57	50 869.04	28.05	18.86	50.17	41.99
2009		87 590.64	55 215.43	27.31	18.78	49.93	41.78
2010		91 992.68	61 066.20	26.83	17.90	50.07	43.96
2011		147 523.10	100 208.27	55.47	29.35	69.12	64.25
2012		154 008.29	111 088.18	54.86	29.17	67.22	62.26
2013		156 583.28	114 635.37	54.72	29.44	66.31	61.30
2014		157 544.15	116 905.20	53.38	28.69	63.67	58.26
2015		173 333.44	127 082.04	51.03	28.15	58.37	52.38
2016		181 089.33	131 931.52	37.38	28.03	52.62	46.13
2017		185 111.86	164 498.43	33.07	29.82	38.44	30.54
2018		194 168.64	174 353.81	33.00	30.30	36.47	29.03
2019		197 190.20	174 331.38	34.64	31.93	29.25	22.37
2020		114 641.47	73 576.50	68.75	11.37	23.94	14.62
昆明	Kunming	2 322.39	- 1 405.80	2.61	1.34	2.67	2.36
曲靖	Qujing	15 846.05	10 632.86	3.09	1.09	7.23	3.10
玉溪	Yuxi	8 954.55	6 298.09	1.42	0.63	1.52	1.16
保山	Baoshan	6 688.91	4 683.95	1.76	0.63	0.86	0.52
昭通	Zhaotong	12 628.72	5 897.93	2.38	0.25	1.14	0.81
丽江	Lijiang	3 642.01	2 814.73	1.11	0.66	0.87	0.15
普洱	Pu'er	7 388.43	4 281.76	1.60	0.50	1.10	0.29
临沧	Lincang	6 027.59	3 746.48	1.75	0.70	0.13	0.09
楚雄	Chuxiong	8 240.32	6 463.91	1.16	0.19	0.54	0.43
红河	Honghe	14 727.06	11 557.03	3.80	2.34	3.04	2.98
文山	Wenshan	7 997.88	5 381.08	2.74	1.13	2.65	0.81
西双版纳	Xishuangbanna	3 724.58	2 501.60	1.05	0.33	0.12	0.11
大理	Dali	9 254.76	6 988.61	2.38	1.08	0.82	0.60
德宏	Dehong	3 551.02	1 971.14	0.77	0.16	0.71	0.70
怒江	Nujiang	1 686.78	1 016.12	0.41	0.22	0.46	0.46
迪庆	Diqing	1 960.41	747.03	0.36	0.13	0.09	0.04

16-12 各州市工业废水排放及处理情况（2020年）

Discharge and Disposal of Industrial Waste Water by Region (2020)

州　市	Region	工业废水治理设施数（套） Number of Facilities for Industrial Waste Water Treated (set)	工业废水治理设施处理能力（万吨/日） Capacity of Facilities for Industrial Waste Water Treated (10 000 tons/d)	工业废水处理量（亿吨） Volume of Industrial Waste Water Treated (100 million tons)	工业废水排放量（亿吨） Total Volume of Industrial Waste Water Discharged (100 million tons)
全　省	**Yunnan**	**2 457**	**579.88**	**9.71**	**1.85**
昆　明	Kunming	466	111.73	2.03	0.18
曲　靖	Qujing	374	126.86	1.32	0.26
玉　溪	Yuxi	278	94.72	2.58	0.15
保　山	Baoshan	80	11.74	0.05	0.06
昭　通	Zhaotong	118	25.63	0.52	0.40
丽　江	Lijiang	40	2.34	0.06	0.02
普　洱	Pu'er	119	19.38	0.20	0.18
临　沧	Lincang	86	13.40	0.18	0.10
楚　雄	Chuxiong	165	27.42	0.68	0.06
红　河	Honghe	229	80.98	1.35	0.10
文　山	Wenshan	137	12.37	0.08	0.06
西双版纳	Xishuangbanna	104	12.87	0.12	0.03
大　理	Dali	123	8.91	0.17	0.04
德　宏	Dehong	98	8.25	0.22	0.09
怒　江	Nujiang	21	10.21	0.04	0.04
迪　庆	Diqing	19	13.06	0.09	0.10

16-13 各州市工业废气排放及处理能力情况（2020年）

Emission and Disposal Capacity of Industrial Waste Gas by Region (2020)

州 市	Region	工业废气治理设施数（套）Number of Facilities for Disposal of Industrial Waste Gas (set)	工业废气治理设施处理能力（万立方米/时）Capacity of Facilities for Disposal of Industrial Waste Gas (10 000 cu.m/h)	工业废气排放量（亿立方米）Total Volume of Industrial Waste Gas Emitted (100 million cu.m)
全 省	**Yunnan**	**6 353**	**85 731.01**	**19 689.00**
昆 明	Kunming	1 171	11 569.38	3 796.79
曲 靖	Qujing	1 173	23 214.68	4 684.09
玉 溪	Yuxi	674	11 879.86	3 132.62
保 山	Baoshan	193	2 264.05	637.30
昭 通	Zhaotong	211	2 835.08	851.63
丽 江	Lijiang	81	864.62	166.71
普 洱	Pu'er	271	2 538.06	545.85
临 沧	Lincang	286	1 331.23	280.09
楚 雄	Chuxiong	366	6 063.94	678.45
红 河	Honghe	607	6 837.50	2 205.88
文 山	Wenshan	322	8 593.29	932.87
西双版纳	Xishuangbanna	248	517.25	74.29
大 理	Dali	399	3 274.57	917.54
德 宏	Dehong	220	2 661.45	562.33
怒 江	Nujiang	113	1 175.41	145.34
迪 庆	Diqing	18	110.64	77.22

16-14 各州市工业固体废物排放及处理利用情况（2020年）

Discharge, Disposal and Recycling of Industrial Solid Wastes by Region (2020)

单位：万吨 (10 000 tons)

州 市	Region	一般工业固体废物产生量 Common Industrial Solid Wastes Produced	一般工业固体废物综合利用量 Common Industrial Solid Wastes Utilized	一般工业固体废物综合利用率(%) Rate of Common Industrial Solid Wastes Utilized (%)	一般工业固体废物贮存量 Common Industrial Solid Wastes Stored	一般工业固体废物处置量 Common Industrial Solid Wastes Disposal	处置往年贮存量 Volume of Previously Stored Industrial Solid Wastes Disposal	一般工业固体废物倾倒丢弃量 Common Industrial Solid Wastes Discharged
全 省	**Yunnan**	**17 472.63**	**9 060.15**	**50.81**	**4 609.35**	**4 621.39**	**459.38**	**0.03**
昆 明	Kunming	3 265.80	948.76	28.71	781.91	1 573.84	0.17	0.00
曲 靖	Qujing	1 764.81	1 270.13	68.63	431.45	151.05	1.90	0.00
玉 溪	Yuxi	2 551.61	1 924.19	74.97	543.93	99.27	0.74	0.00
保 山	Baoshan	247.75	214.32	86.41	6.24	27.94	0.50	0.00
昭 通	Zhaotong	333.25	238.83	71.66	86.62	7.83	0.00	0.00
丽 江	Lijiang	23.13	117.64	93.87	2.50	5.18	0.00	0.00
普 洱	Pu'er	357.22	196.26	54.90	23.72	138.05	0.52	0.00
临 沧	Lincang	312.48	266.99	85.36	42.82	2.98	0.00	0.00
楚 雄	Chuxiong	635.45	477.52	64.80	232.20	28.05	0.84	0.00
红 河	Honghe	3 297.06	2 181.20	66.09	817.66	308.36	6.83	0.00
文 山	Wenshan	1 099.03	196.51	17.70	577.12	355.30	18.83	0.00
西双版纳	Xishuangbanna	202.87	89.77	44.25	95.68	17.42	0.00	0.00
大 理	Dali	450.40	166.08	36.85	0.42	284.25	0.00	0.00
德 宏	Dehong	578.35	511.70	88.46	65.63	1.12	0.00	0.00
怒 江	Nujiang	1 154.23	5.23	0.45	0.00	1 553.16	404.16	0.00
迪 庆	Diqing	1 199.19	255.02	21.27	901.46	67.59	24.89	0.02

16-15 各州市城市（县城）污水排放和处理情况（2020年）
Discharge and Disposal of City Sewage by Region (2020)

州 市	Region	城市(县城)污水排放量(万立方米) Total Volume of City (County) Sewage Discharged (10 000 cu.m)	污水处理总量(万立方米) Total Volume of Sewage Disposal (10 000 cu.m)	污水厂污水处理量 Volume of Sewage Disposal by Sewage Disposal Plants	城市(县城)污水处理率(%) Ratio of City (County)Sewage Disposal (%)	污水处理厂集中处理率(%) Ratio of Centralized Disposal by Sewage Disposal Plants (%)
全 省	**Yunnan**	143 373.97	139 043.42	137 960.06	96.98	96.22
昆 明	Kunming	66 149.40	65 020.21	64 054.75	98.29	96.83
曲 靖	Qujing	10 982.48	10 705.39	10 705.39	97.48	97.48
玉 溪	Yuxi	6 247.72	5 955.53	5 954.72	95.32	95.31
保 山	Baoshan	4 322.29	4 071.71	4 071.71	94.20	94.20
昭 通	Zhaotong	6 992.40	6 814.29	6 814.29	97.45	97.45
丽 江	Lijiang	3 441.80	3 302.10	3 302.10	95.94	95.94
普 洱	Pu'er	4 056.34	3 913.15	3 913.15	96.47	96.47
临 沧	Lincang	3 218.67	3 191.87	3 191.87	99.17	99.17
楚 雄	Chuxiong	7 522.45	7 258.15	7 258.15	96.49	96.49
红 河	Honghe	9 411.39	8 978.86	8 978.86	95.40	95.40
文 山	Wenshan	4 364.09	4 115.89	4 115.89	94.31	94.31
西双版纳	Xishuangbanna	2 440.84	2 248.94	2 248.94	92.14	92.14
大 理	Dali	8 026.74	7 722.72	7 717.61	96.21	96.15
德 宏	Dehong	4 021.18	3 691.24	3 691.24	91.79	91.79
怒 江	Nujiang	986.49	923.94	811.96	93.66	82.31
迪 庆	Diqing	1 189.69	1 129.43	1 129.43	94.93	94.93

16−16 主要城市空气质量指标（2020年）

The Indicators of Air Quality By Main Cities and Towns (2020)

单位：微克/立方米 (μg/m³)

城 市	City	可吸入颗粒物 (PM10) Particulate Matters	细颗粒物 (PM2.5) Fine Particulate	二氧化硫 (SO_2) Sulphur Dioxide	二氧化氮 (NO_2) Nitrogen Dioxide	空气质量达到及好于二级的天数(天) Days of Air Quality Equal to and Above Grade Ⅱ	空气质量综合指数 Comprehensive Index of Air Quality
昆明市	Kunming	42	24	9	26	366	3.10
曲靖市	Qujing	35	20	11	16	365	2.75
玉溪市	Yuxi	36	20	8	18	362	2.77
保山市	Baoshan	24	19	5	11	363	2.2
昭通市	Zhaotong	39	20	8	15	365	2.61
丽江市	Lijiang	22	12	8	9	365	1.91
普洱市	Pu'er	34	22	5	15	351	2.63
临沧市	Lincang	34	26	8	14	362	2.68
楚雄市	Chuxiong	28	18	10	17	366	2.47
蒙自市	Mengzi	34	26	12	9	357	2.59
文山市	Wenshan	34	23	5	11	362	2.4
景洪市	Jinghong	47	29	6	18	329	3.23
大理市	Dali	22	16	6	11	363	2.06
芒 市	Mangshi	42	22	9	19	356	2.83
泸水市	Lushui	46	22	7	17	357	2.7
香格里拉市	Shangri-La	15	13	7	7	363	1.74

注：统计范围是州、市所在地监测城市

Note: Statistical coverage is the monitored cities of prefectures and cities.

16-17 主要城市区域环境噪声源构成情况（2020年）

Composition of Environmental Noise Source By Major Cities and Towns (2020)

单位：分贝　　dB(A)

城　市	City	等效声级 Average Equivalent Sound Level of Environmental Noise	交通噪声平均声级 Average Equivalent Sound Level of Traffic Noise	工业噪声平均声级 Average Equivalent Sound Level of Industrial Noise	施工噪声平均声级 Average Equivalent Sound Level of Construction Noise	生活噪声平均声级 Average Equivalent Sound Level of Residental Noise
全　省	**Total**	**52.2**	**51.9**	**52.8**	**51.1**	**53.5**
昆明市	Kunming	53.9	50.9	54.6	52.6	56.1
曲靖市	Qujing	51.0	51.0	53.4	50.9	50.7
玉溪市	Yuxi	51.9	54.0	53.2	51.1	53.6
保山市	Baoshan	49.2	50.0	52.5	47.1	50.6
昭通市	Zhaotong	50.8	51.0	55.0	50.0	49.6
丽江市	Lijiang	52.6			50.3	57.7
普洱市	Pu'er	52.2			52.1	57.9
临沧市	Lincang	51.6	57.2	54.2	50.6	54.3
楚雄市	Chuxiong	48.4		54.5	47.1	51.4
蒙自市	Mengzi	50.5	56.0	53.9	48.4	52.5
文山市	Wenshan	57.0		57.8	54.4	59.8
景洪市	Jinghong	51.2		51.3	51.1	51.2
大理市	Dali	50.4	57.0	51.8	49.1	50.2
芒　市	Mangshi	50.7		51.5	50.6	52.5
泸水市	Liuku	48.6		47.7	48.3	50.9
香格里拉	Shangri-La	50.3			50.5	49.3

注：统计范围是州、市所在地监测城市的昼间噪声情况。
Note: Statistical coverage is the daytime noise of monitored cities of prefectures and cities.

主要统计指标解释

土地调查面积 指行政区域内的土地调查总面积，包括农用地、建设用地和未利用地。

农用地 指直接用于农业生产的土地，包括耕地、园地、林地、牧草地及其他农用地。

耕地 指种植农作物的土地，包括熟地，新开发、复垦、整理地，休闲地（含轮歇地、轮作地）；以种植农作物（含蔬菜）为主，间有零星果树、桑树或其他树木的土地；平均每年能保证收获一季的已垦滩地和海涂。耕地中包括南方宽度 <1.0 米，北方宽度 <2.0 米固定的沟、渠、路和地坎（埂）；临时种植药材、草皮、花卉、苗木等的耕地，以及其他临时改变用途的耕地。

园地 指种植以采集果、叶、根、茎、汁等为主的集约经营的多年生木本和草本作物，覆盖度大于 50% 和每亩株数大于合理株数 70% 的土地。包括用于育苗的土地。

林地 指生长乔木、竹类、灌木的土地，及沿海生长红树林的土地。包括迹地，不包括居民点内部的绿化林木用地，铁路、公路征地范围内的林木，以及河流、沟渠的护堤林。

牧草地 指生长草本植物为主的土地。

居民点及工矿用地 指城乡居民点、独立居民点以及居民点以外的工矿、国防、名胜古迹等企事业单位用地，包括其内部交通、绿化用地。

交通运输用地 指用于运输通行的地面线路、场站等的土地。包括民用机场、港口、码头、地面运输管道和各种道路用地。

水利设施用地 指陆地水域，海涂，沟渠、水工建筑物等用地。不包括滞洪区和已垦滩涂中的耕地、园地、林地、居民点、道路等用地。

湿地 指天然或人工、长久或暂时性的沼泽地、泥炭地或水域地带，包括静止或流动、淡水、半咸水、咸水体，低潮时水深不超过 6 米的水域以及海岸地带地区的珊瑚滩和海草床、滩涂、红树林、河口、河流、淡水沼泽、沼泽森林、湖泊、盐沼及盐湖。

造林总面积 指在荒山、荒地、沙丘、退耕地等一切可以造林的土地上，采用人工播种、飞机播种、植苗造林、分植造林等方法新植成片乔木林和灌木林，经过检查验收符合《造林技术规程》要求的单位面积株数，并按《中华人民共和国森林法实施条例》规定，成活率达 85% 以上（含 85%，年降雨量在 400 毫米以下且无浇灌条件的地区造林成活率达 70% 以上）的总面积。“四旁”植树如一侧在四行以上，连片面积 0.066 公顷（一亩）以上，应统计在造林面积内。

人工造林 指在宜林荒山荒地、宜林沙荒地、无立木林地、疏林地和退耕地等其他宜林地上通过播种、植苗和分植来提高森林植被覆被率的技术措施。

飞机播种 通过飞机播种并辅以适当的人工措施，为宜林荒山荒地、宜林沙荒地、其他宜林地、疏林地补充适量的种源，在自然力的作用下使其形成森林或灌草植被，提高森林植被覆被率或提高森林植被质量的技术措施。包括荒山飞播造林和飞播营林。

新封山育林 对宜林地、无立木林地、疏林地或低质低效有林地、灌木林地实施封禁并辅以人工促进手段，使其形成森林或灌草植被或提高林分质量的一项技术措施。包括无林地和疏林地封育以及有林地和灌木林地封育。

退化林修复 为改善林分的活力和结构，有效遏制防护林退化，提高林分质量和恢复森林功能，对结构失调和稳定性降低、功能退化甚至丧失且自然更新能力弱的林分采取的结构调整、树种替换、补植补播、嫁接复壮等森林经营措施。

人工更新造林 指在采伐迹地、火烧迹地、林中空地上通过人工造林重新形成森林的过程。包括通过松土除草、平茬或断根复壮、补植补播、除蘖间苗等措施促进目的树种幼苗幼树生长发育的人工促进天然更新。

水资源总量 指当地降水形成的地表和地下产水总量，即地表径流量与降水入渗补给地下水量之和。

地表水资源量 指河流、湖泊、冰川等地表水体中可以逐年更新的动态水量，即当地天然河川径流量。

地表水与地下水重复计算量 指地表水和地下水相互转化的部分，即天然河川径流量中的地下水排泄量和地下水补给量中来源于地表水的入渗补给量。

供水总量 指各种水源工程为用户提供的包括输水损失在内的毛供水量。

用水总量 指各类用水户取用的包括输水损失在内的毛用水量。

农业用水 指农田灌溉用水、林果地灌溉用水、草地灌溉用水和鱼塘补水和畜禽用水。

工业用水 指工矿企业在生产过程中用于制造、加工、冷却、空调、净化、洗涤等方面的用水，按新水取用量计，不包括企业内部的重复利用水量。

生活用水 包括城镇生活用水和农村生活用水。城镇生活用水由居民用水和公共用水（含第三产业及建筑业等用水）组成；农村生活用水指居民生活用水。

生态环境补水 仅包括人为措施供给的城镇环境用水和部分河湖、湿地补水，而不包括降水、径流自然满足的水量。

城区（县城）人口 指划定的城区（县城）范围的户籍人口数。按公安部门的户籍统计为准填报。

城区（县城）面积 指城市和县城的面积。设市城市城区包括：市本级（1）街道办事处所辖地域；（2）城市公共设施、居住设施和市政公用设施等连接到的其他镇（乡）地域；（3）常住人口在3000人以上独立的工矿区、开发区、科研单位、大专院校等特殊区域。县城包括：（1）县政府驻地的镇（城关镇）或街道办事处地域；（2）县城公共设施、居住设施和市政设施等连接到的其他镇（乡）地域；（3）县域内常住人口在3000人以上独立的工矿区、开发区、科研单位、大专院校等特殊区域。

建成区面积 城市行政区内实际已成片开发建设、市政公用设施和公共设施基本具备的区域。对核心城市，它包括集中连片的部分以及分散的若干个已经成片建设起来，市政公用设施和公共设施基本具备的地区；对一城多镇来说，它包括由几个连片开发建设起来的，市政公用设施和公共设施基本具备的地区组成。因此建成区范围，一般是指建成区外轮廓线所能包括的地区，也就是这个城市实际建设用地所达到的范围。

绿化覆盖面积 指城市中的乔木、灌木、草坪等所有植被的垂直投影面积。包括公园绿地、防护绿地、生产绿地、附属绿地、其他绿地的绿化种植覆盖面积、屋顶绿化覆盖面积以及零散树木的覆盖面积，不含各类绿地中的水域面积以及没有被植被覆盖的面积（硬化道路、无屋顶绿化的建筑物等）。乔木树冠下重叠的灌木和草本植物不能重复计算。

人均公园绿地面积 指报告期末区域内城区人口平均每人拥有的公园绿地面积。人口数采用年底人口数。计算公式为：

$$人均公园绿地面积=\frac{公园绿地面积}{城区人口+城区暂住人口}\times 100\%$$

建成区绿化覆盖率 指报告期末建成区内绿化覆盖面积与建成区面积的比率。计算公式为：

$$建成区绿化覆盖率 = \frac{建成区绿化覆盖面积}{建成区面积} \times 100\%$$

废水排放总量 指工业废水排放量、城镇生活污水排放量和集中式治理设施污水排放量之和。

生活污水排放量 用人均系数法测算。计算公式是：

如果辖区内的城镇污水处理厂未安装再生水回用系统，无再生水利用量，则

$$城镇生活污水排放量 = 城镇生活污水排放系数 \times 城镇人口数 \times 365$$

反之，辖区内的城镇污水处理厂配备再生水回用系统，其再生水利用量已经污染减排核查确认，则

$$城镇生活污水排放量 = 城镇生活污水排放系数 \times 城镇人口数 \times 365 - 城镇污水处理厂再生水利用量$$

化学需氧量(COD) 指用化学氧化剂氧化水中有机污染物时所需的氧量。COD值越高，表示水中有机污染物污染越重。

生活污水中化学需氧量(COD)排放量 指城镇居民每年排放的生活污水中的COD的量。用人均系数法测算。测算公式为：

$$\begin{matrix}城镇生活污水中\\化学需氧量（COD）排放量\end{matrix} = \begin{matrix}城镇生活污水中\\COD产生系数\end{matrix} \times \begin{matrix}市镇非\\农业人口\end{matrix} \times 365$$

二氧化硫排放量 指报告期内工业SO2排放量与生活SO2排放量之和。

工业SO2排放量 指报告期内企业在燃料燃烧和生产工艺过程中排入大气的SO2总质量。工业中SO2主要来源于化石燃料（煤、石油等）的燃烧，还包括含硫矿石的冶炼或含硫酸、磷肥等生产的工业废气排放。计算公式为：

$$\begin{matrix}工业SO_2\\排放量\end{matrix} = \begin{matrix}燃料燃烧过程\\中废气排放量\end{matrix} + \begin{matrix}生产工艺过程\\中废气排放量\end{matrix}$$

工业废水治理设施数 指报告期内企业用于防治水污染和经处理后综合利用水资源的实有设施（包括构筑物）数，以一个废水治理系统为单位统计。附属于设施内的水治理设备和配套设备不单独计算。已经报废的设施不统计在内。

工业废水治理设施处理能力 指报告期内企业内部的所有废水治理设施实际具有的废水处理能力。

工业废水处理量 指经各种水治理设施（含城镇污水处理厂、工业废水处理厂）实际处理的工业废水量，包括处理后外排的和处理后回用的工业废水量。虽经处理但未达到国家或地方排放标准的废水量也应计算在内。计算时，如遇有车间和厂排放口均有治理设施，并对同一废水分级处理时，不应重复计算工业废水处理量。

工业废水排放量 指报告期内经过企业厂区所有排放口排到企业外部的工业废水量。包括生产废水、外排的直接冷却水、废气治理设施废水、超标排放的矿井地下水和与工业废水混排的厂区生活污水，不包括独立外排的间接冷却水（清污不分流的间接冷却水应计算在内）。

工业废气治理设施数 指报告期末企业用于减少在燃料燃烧过程与生产工艺过程中排向大气的污染物或对污染物加以回收利用的废气治理设施总数，以一个废气治理系统为单位统计。包括除尘、脱硫、脱硝及其它的污染物的烟气治理设施。已报废的设施不统计在内。锅炉中的除尘装置属于“三同时”设备，应统计在内。

工业废气治理设施处理能力 指报告期末企业实有的废气治理设施的实际废气处理能力。

工业废气排放量 指报告期内企业厂区内燃料燃烧和生产工艺过程中产生的各种排入大气的含有污染物的气体的总量，以标准状态 (273K，101325Pa) 计算。

一般工业固体废物产生量 指未被列入《国家危险废物名录》或者根据国家规定的危险废物鉴别标准（GB5085）、固体废物浸出毒性浸出方法（GB5086）及固体废物浸出毒性测定方法（GB/T 15555）鉴别方法判定不具有危险特性的工业固体废物。计算公式是：

一般工业固体废物产生量 =（一般工业固体废物综合利用量—其中：综合利用往年贮存量）+ 一般工业固体废物贮存量 +（一般工业固体废物处置量—其中：处置往年贮存量）+ 一般工业固体废物倾倒丢弃量

一般工业固体废物综合利用量 指报告期内企业通过回收、加工、循环、交换等方式，从固体废物中提取或者使其转化为可以利用的资源、能源和其他原材料的固体废物量（包括当年利用的往年工业固体废物累计贮存量）。如用作农业肥料、生产建筑材料、筑路等。综合利用量由原产生固体废物的单位统计。

一般工业固体废物综合利用率 指一般工业固体废物综合利用量占一般固体废物产生量与综合利用往年贮存量之和的百分率。计算公式为：

$$\text{一般工业固体废物处置率} = \frac{\text{一般工业固体废物处置量}}{\text{一般工业固体废物产生量} + \text{处置往年贮存量}} \times 100\%$$

一般工业固体废物贮存量 指报告期内企业以综合利用或处置为目的，将固体废物暂时贮存或堆存在专设的贮存设施或专设的集中堆存场所内的数量。专设的固体废物贮存场所或贮存设施必须有防扩散、防流失、防渗漏、防止污染大气、水体的措施。

一般工业固体废物处置量 指报告期内企业将工业固体废物焚烧和用其他改变工业固体废物的物理、化学、生物特性的方法，达到减少或者消除其危险成分的活动，或者将工业固体废物最终置于符合环境保护规定要求的填埋场的活动中，所消纳固体废物的量。

一般工业固体废物处置往年贮存量 指报告期内企业按照《关于固体废物处置、综合利用的作业方式的规定》的要求，处置的上一报告期末企业累计贮存的工业固体废物的量。

一般工业固体废物倾倒丢弃量 指报告期内企业将所产生的固体废物倾倒或者丢弃到固体废物污染防治设施、场所以外的量。

城市污水排放量 指城市生活污水、工业废水的排放总量，包括从排水管道和排水沟（渠）排出的污水量。

城市污水处理量 指城市污水处理厂和处理装置实际处理的污水量。包括物理处理量、生物处理量和化学处理量。

污水处理厂集中处理率 指城市污水处理厂处理的污水量与城市污水排放总量的比率。计算公式：

$$\text{污水处理厂集中处理率} = \frac{\text{城市污水处理厂污水处理量}}{\text{城市污水排放总量}} \times 100\%$$

Explanatory Notes on Main Statistical Indicators

Land survey area refers to the total land survey area within the administrative region, including agricultural land, construction land and unused land.

Land for Agriculture Use refers to land directly used for agriculture production, including land for cultivation, gardening, forests, herbage and other agriculture activities.

Cultivated Land refers to land mainly for the regular cultivation of farm crops (including vegetables), with some fruit trees, mulberry trees and others, covers cultivated land, newly-developed land, reclaimed land, consolidated land, fallow, beach land that can guarantee one harvest per year on average. It also covers fixed ditch, canal, road and sill (ridge) with width less than 1 meter in the South and 2 meters in the North, lands planted temporarily with herbs, grass, flowers and nursery stocks, and other cultivated land with temporary change of use.

Garden Land refers to land for intensive cultivation of perennial woody plants and herbs to collect fruits, leaves, roots, stems and juice, with a covering rate over 50% and plant number per mu over 70% of rational plant number. Land for nursery is included.

Forestland refers to land for planting arbor, bamboo, bush shrub and land in coastal zones for planting mangrove. It includes slash, but not the green belts in residential area, forests requested for railway and highway, and the dike protection forest around rivers and ditches.

Pastureland refers to land mainly for the growth of herbs.

Land for residential areas and mining refers to the urban and rural residential areas, independent residential areas and residential areas outside of the mining, national defense, scenic spots and historical sites, such as land for enterprises and institutions, including the internal transportation, landscaping.

Land used for transportation refers to the land used for transportation, such as ground lines and stations. Including civil airports, ports, docks, ground transport pipelines and various road land.

Land used for water conservancy facilities refers to land used for water area, mudflats, ditches and hydraulic structures. It's not included in flood detention areas and reclaimed beaches, such as arable land, garden land, woodland, residential areas and roads.

Wetlands refer to marshland and peat bog, whether natural or man-made, permanent or temporary; water covered areas, whether stagnant or flowing, with fresh or semi-fresh or salty water that is less than 6 meters deep at low tide; as well as coral beach, weed beach, mud beach, mangrove, river outlet, rivers, fresh-water marshland, marshland forests, lakes, salty bog and salt lakes along the coastal areas.

Total Area of A forestation refers to the total area of land suitable for a forestation, including barren hills, idle land, sand dunes, "grain for green" land, on which acres of arbores or bushes are planted through manual planting, airplane planting, plant seedlings, etc. in accordance with the required density standards of the Technical Procedures of A forestation, and with a survival rate of over 85% in line with the Implementing Rules of the Forest Law of the People's Republic of China (or a survival rate of 75% in areas with less that 400 mm of annual rainfall and without irrigation facilities). Included in this category are trees planted alone the roadsides, riversides, or next to houses that occupy an area over 0.066 hectares, or where more than 4 lines of trees are planted.

Area of Man-made Forests refer to the area of stable growing forests, planted manually or by airplanes, with a survival rate of 80% or higher of the designed number of trees per hectare, or with a canopy density of 0.20 - or above after 3-5 years of manual planting or 5-7 years of airplane planting.

Airplane sowing refers to technical measures of airplane planting with of appropriate artificial help taken under the influence of natural power to restore certain amount of seedlings on land suitable for afforestation, with an aim of increasing vegetation coverage rate of forests or improving forest quality. It includes barren afforestation and aerial seeding forest afforestation.

New Closing Hillsides to Facilitate Afforestation is a technical measure by banning and aritificial means to form forest or shrub and grass or improve forest quality land, to suitable for forest, forest land without stumpage, sparse forest land, or low quality forest, shrub forest.

Restoration of Degraded Forest In order to improve the vitality and structure of forest, effectively curb forest degradation, improve forest quality and restore forest function, management measures are taken to the forest of structural imbalance and stability reduction, function reduction or even loss and natural regeneration ability is weak, which include structural adjustment, species replacement, replanting sowing, grafting rejuvenation, etc.

Artificial Regeneration refers to forest reforming process in logging slash, Slash Burning, the glade through afforestation. Including artificially promoting natural regeneration of promoting the growth and development of target tree species seedlings by weeding, root pruning or stubble rejuvenation, sowing and replanting, removing tillering and thinning, etc.

Total Water Resources refers to total volume of surface water and groundwater and is measured as run-off for surface water and replenishment of groundwater with rainfall in local area.

Surface Water Resources refers to total volume of year by year renewable dynamic resources which exist in rivers, lakes, glaciers and other surface water and are the natural run-off of rivers.

Duplicated Measurement between Surface Water and Groundwater refers to mutual exchange between surface water and groundwater, i.e. run-off of rivers includes some depletion into groundwater while groundwater includes some replenishment from surface water.

Water Supply refers to gross water of various sources supplied to consumers, including losses during distribution.

Water Use refers to gross water used by various water users, including losses during distribution.

Water Use by Agriculture includes uses of water by irrigation of farming fields, forestry and orchards, irrigation of grassland, replenishment of fishing farms and water used by animal husbandry.

Water Use by Industry refers to new withdrawals of water, excluding reuse of water within enterprises.

Water Use by Living Consumption includes use of water for living consumption in both urban and rural areas. Urban water use by living consumption is composed of household use and public use (including tertiary industry and construction). Rural water use by living consumption includes water used by households.

Water Use by Ecological and Environmental Protection includes replenishment of rivers and lakes and use for urban environment.

Urban(County) population refers to the number of registered population within the designated urban(county) area. The household registration statistics of the public security department shall be reported.

Urban(County) area refers to the urban and county area of a city. The urban areas include: (1) the district under the sub-district office of the city; (2) other town (township) areas connected to urban public facilities, residential facilities and municipal public facilities; (3) special areas such as industrial and mining areas, development zones, scientific research units and colleges and universities with a permanent population of more than 3,000 people.

Built-up area refers to an area within an urban administrative region that has been developed and constructed on a large scale, and that has basic municipal public facilities and public facilities. For the core cities, it includes concentrated continuous parts as well as several scattered areas that have been built in pieces and have basic municipal utilities and public facilities. For more than one town, it consists of several areas developed and constructed in succession, with municipal utilities and basic public facilities. Therefore, the scope of built-up area generally refers to the area covered by the outer contour line of the built-up area, that is, the actual construction land of this city reaches.

Green cover area refers to the vertical projection area of all vegetation such as trees, shrubs and lawns in the city. It includes the green area of park, protective green space, production green space, attached green space and other green space, the green area of roof and the covered area of scattered trees, excluding the water area of all kinds of green space and the area not covered by vegetation (hardening roads, buildings without roof greening, etc.). Overlapping shrubs and herbs under the canopy of trees cannot be counted repeatedly.

Park green area per capita refers to the park green area per urban population in the area at the end of the report period. The population is to be counted at the end of the year. The calculation formula is:

park green area per capita = Green area of the park / (urban population + temporary urban residents) ×100%

Greening coverage rate of built-up areas refers to the ratio of greening coverage area and built-up area at the end of the report. The calculation formula is:

Green coverage of built-up area=Green coverage area of built-up area / Built-up area ×100%

Total amount of waste water discharge refers to the total amount of industrial waste water discharge, urban sewage discharge and sewage discharge from centralized treatment facilities.

Urban Non-industrial Waste Water Discharge refers to annual discharge of non-industrial waste water by urban households.It is estimated by per capita coefficient using the formula:

If the urban sewage treatment plant is not installed within the jurisdiction of reclaimed water reuse system, no renewable water dosage, then

$$\frac{\text{Urban non-industrial}}{\text{Waste water discharge}} = \frac{\text{Urban non-industrial waste}}{\text{Water discharge coefficient}} \times \frac{\text{Urban non-industrial}}{\text{Population}} \times 365 - \frac{\text{Urban sewage treatment plant}}{\text{Regeneration water consumption}}$$

Chemical Oxygen Demand (COD) refers to the amount of oxygen required to oxidize organic pollutants in water with chemical oxidants. The higher the COD value, the heavier the pollution of organic pollutants in the water.

Volume of Chemical Oxygen Demand (COD) Generated by Urban Non-industrial Waster Water refers to chemical oxygen demand generated through the annual discharge of non-industrial waste water by urban

$$\begin{matrix}\text{Volume of chemical oxygen}\\ \text{demand (cod) generated}\\ \text{by urban non - industrial}\\ \text{waster water}\end{matrix} = \begin{matrix}\text{Coefficient of COD}\\ \text{generated through urban}\\ \text{non -industrial waste water}\end{matrix} \times \begin{matrix}\text{urban}\\ \text{non - agricultural}\\ \text{population}\end{matrix} \times 365$$

SO2 Emission is calculated on the basis of consumption of coal by households and industrial activities.

SO2 Emission through Industrial Activities refers to volume of sulphur dioxide emission from fuel burning and production process by enterprises during a given period of time. In industry, SO2 mainly comes from the combustion of fossil fuels (coal, oil, etc.), as well as the industrial exhaust emissions from the smelting of sulphur-bearing ores or the production of sulphuric acid and phosphate fertilizers. It is calculated as :

$$\text{SO}_2 \text{ emission through industrial activities} = \text{SO}_2 \text{ emission from fuel burning} + \text{SO}_2 \text{ emission from production process}$$

Number of industrial waste water treatment facilities refers to the number of actual facilities (including structures) used by enterprises to prevent and control water pollution and comprehensively utilize water resources after treatment during the reporting period, which is counted by a waste water treatment system. Water treatment equipment and supporting equipment attached to the facilities are not calculated separately. Facilities that have been scrapped are not counted.

The capacity of industrial waste water treatment facilities refers to the actual capacity of waste water treatment facilities of the enterprises during the reporting period.

Industrial waste water treatment capacity refers to the actual amount of industrial waste water treated by various water treatment facilities (including urban sewage treatment plants and industrial waste water treatment plants), including the amount of industrial waste water discharged after treatment and reused after treatment. The amount of waste water treated but not up to national or local discharge standards should also be taken into account. When calculating, it should not double calculation of industrial waste water treatment volume if the workshop and the factory discharge outlet have treatment facilities, and the same waste water classification treatment.

Waste Water Discharged by Industry refers to the volume of waste water discharged by industrial enterprises through all their outlets, including waste water from production process, directly cooled water, waste water from waste gas treatment facilities, groundwater from mining wells which does not meet discharge standards and sewage from households mixed with waste water produced by industrial activities, but excluding indirectly cooled water discharged (It should be included if the discharge is not separated from waste water).

Number of industrial waste gas treatment facilities refers to the total amount of waste gas treatment facilities used by enterprises at the end of the reporting period to reduce the pollutants discharged into the atmosphere or to recycle and utilize the pollutants in the process of fuel combustion and production process. Including dust removal, desulphurization, denitration and other pollutant smoke treatment facilities. Abandoned facilities are not counted. The dust removal device in the boiler belongs to the "three simultaneous" equipment, which should be included in the statistics.

The capacity of industrial waste gas treatment facilities refers to the actual capacity of waste gas treatment facilities of the enterprises at the end of the reporting period.

Industrial Waste Air Emission refers to the discharge into atmosphere of waste air containing pollutants generated from fuel burning and production processes in enterprises within a given period of time. It is calculated at standard status (273K, 101325Pa) as.

Common Industrial Solid Wastes Produced refers to the industrial solid wastes that are not listed in the 《National Catalogue of Hazardous Waste》, or not regarded as hazardous according to the national hazardous waste identification standards (GB5085), solid waste-Extraction procedure for leaching toxicity (GB5086) and solid waste-Extraction procedure for leaching toxicity (GB/T 15555). The calculation formula is as followed:

Common Industrial Solid Wastes Produced = (common industrial solid wastes utilized – the proportion of utilized stock of previous years) + common industrial solid waste stock + (common industrial solid wastes disposed – the proportion of disposed stock of previous years) + common industrial solid wastes discharged.

Common Industrial Solid Wastes Comprehensively Utilized refers to volume of solid wastes from which useful materials can be extracted or which can be converted into usable resources, energy or other materials by means of reclamation, processing, recycling and exchange (including utilizing in the year the stocks of industrial solid wastes of the previous year). Examples of such utilizations include fertilizers, building materials and road materials. The information shall be collected by the producing units of the wastes.

Ratio of Utilization of Common Industrial Solid Wastes refers to the percentage of industrial solid wastes utilized over industrial solid wastes produced (including stocks of the previous years). It is calculated as:

$$\frac{\text{Rate of utilization of}}{\text{common industrial solid wastes}} = \frac{\text{volume of common industrialsolid wastes utilized}}{\text{industrial solid wastes produced + stock of previous years}} \times 100\%$$

Stock of Common Industrial Solid Wastes refers to the volume of solid wastes placed in special facilities or special sites for purposes of utilization or disposal. The sites or facilities should take measures against dispersion, loss, seepage, and air and water contamination.

Common Industrial Solid Wastes Disposed refers to the quantity of industrial solid wastes which are burnt or placed ultimately in the sites meeting the requirements for environmental protection and not salvaged or recycled (including disposition in the year of those wastes of previous years). The disposition includes landfill (Safe landfills should be conducted for hazardous wastes), incineration, containment spaces, deep underground disposal, backfill in mining pits and disposal at sea.

Stock of Common Industrial Solid Wastes refers to the volume of solid wastes placed in special facilities or special sites by enterprises for purposes of utilization or disposal during the report period. The sites or facilities should take measures against dispersion, loss, seepage, and air and water contamination.

Common Industrial Solid Wastes Discharged refers to the volume of industrial solid wastes dumped or discharged by producing enterprises to disposal facilities or to other sites.

Urban Sewage Discharge refers to volume of the domestic sewage and industrial sewage, which includes the sewage discharged from the drainage pipe and drainage channel(ditch).

Capacity of urban sewage treatment refers to the amount of sewage actually treated by urban sewage treatment plants and treatment plants. Including physical capacity, biological capacity and chemical capacity.

Centralized Treatment Rate of sewage treatment plant refers to the percentage of sewage volume disposed by the sewage treatment plants over the urban sewage discharge volume. It is calculated as:

Centralized Treatment Rate of sewage treatment plant= sewage volume disposed by the sewage treatment plants ÷ urban sewage discharge volume×100%

Chapter 17

十七、民族自治地方经济概况
Survey of National Autonomous Area

17-1 云南民族自治地方行政区划（2020年）

Administrative Division of Ethnic Minority Autonomous Regions (2020)

单位：个 (unit)

民族自治地方	National Autonomous Area	县级市 Number of Cities at County Level	非民族自治县 Number of Non-minority Autonomous Counties	民族自治县 Number of Minority Autonomous Counties
民族自治地方	**National Autonomous Area**	**12**	**37**	**29**
8个自治州	**8 Autonomous Prefectures**	**12**	**37**	**9**
楚雄彝族自治州	Chuxiong Yi Autonomous Prefecture	1	9	
红河哈尼族彝族自治州	Honghe Hani & Yi Autonomous Prefecture	4	6	3
文山壮族苗族自治州	Wenshan Zhuang & Miao Autonomous Prefecture	1	7	
西双版纳傣族自治州	Xishuangbanna Dai Autonomous Prefecture	1	2	
大理白族自治州	Dali Bai Autonomous Prefecture	1	8	3
德宏傣族景颇族自治州	Dehong Dai & Jingpo Autonomous Prefecture	2	3	
怒江傈僳族自治州	Nujiang Lisu Autonomous Prefecture	1	1	2
迪庆藏族自治州	Diqing Tibetan Autonomous Prefecture	1	1	1
自治州以外的20个自治县	**20 Autonomous Counties Except above Prefectures**			**20**
石林彝族自治县	Shilin Yi Autonomous County			1
禄劝彝族苗族自治县	Luquan Yi & Miao Autonomous County			1
寻甸回族彝族自治县	Xundian Hui & Yi Autonomous County			1
峨山彝族自治县	Eshan Yi Autonomous County			1
新平彝族傣族自治县	Xinping Yi & Dai Autonomous County			1
元江哈尼族彝族傣族自治县	Yuanjiang Hani & Yi & Dai Autonomous County			1
玉龙纳西族自治县	Yulong Naxi Autonomous County			1
宁蒗彝族自治县	Ninglang Yi Autonomous County			1
宁洱哈尼族彝族自治县	Ning'er Hani & Yi Autonomous County			1
墨江哈尼族自治县	Mojiang Hani Autonomous County			1
景东彝族自治县	Jingdong Yi Autonomous County			1
景谷傣族彝族自治县	Jinggu Dai & Yi Autonomous County			1
镇沅彝族哈尼族拉祜族自治县	Zhenyuan Yi & Hani & Lahu Autonomous County			1
江城哈尼族彝族自治县	Jiangcheng Hani & Yi Autonomous County			1
孟连傣族拉祜族佤族自治县	Menglian Dai & Lahu & Wa Autonomous County			1
澜沧拉祜族自治县	Lancang Lahu Autonomous County			1
西盟佤族自治县	Ximeng Wa Autonomous County			1
双江拉祜族佤族布朗族傣族自治县	Shuangjiang Lahu & Wa & Bulang & Dai Autonomous County			1
耿马傣族佤族自治县	Gengma Dai & Wa Autonomous County			1
沧源佤族自治县	Cangyuan Wa Autonomous County			1

17−2 全省民族自治县分布情况（2020年）
Geographical Distribution of Ethnic Minority Autonomous Counties (2020)

州 市	Region	民族自治县数（个）Number of Minority Autonomous Counties (unit)	民族自治县名称 Schedule of Minority Autonomous Counties
全 省	**Yunnan**	**29**	
昆 明	Kunming	3	石林彝族自治县、禄劝彝族苗族自治县、寻甸回族彝族自治县 Shilin Yi Autonomous County, Luquan Yi & Miao Autonomous County, Xundian Hui & Yi Autonomous County
玉 溪	Yuxi	3	峨山彝族自治县、新平彝族傣族自治县、元江哈尼族彝族傣族自治县 Eshan Yi Autonomous County，Xinping Yi & Dai Autonomous County, Yuanjiang Hani & Yi & Dai Autonomous County
丽 江	Lijiang	2	玉龙纳西族自治县、宁蒗彝族自治县 Yulong Naxi Autonomous County, Ninglang Yi Autonomous County
普 洱	Pu'er	9	宁洱哈尼族彝族自治县、墨江哈尼族自治县、景东彝族自治县、景谷傣族彝族自治县、镇沅彝族哈尼族拉祜族自治县、江城哈尼族彝族自治县、孟连傣族拉祜族佤族自治县、澜沧拉祜族自治县、西盟佤族自治县 Ning'er Hani & Yi Autonomous County, Mojiang Hani Autonomous County, Jingdong Yi Autonomous County, Jinggu Dai & Yi Autonomous County, Zhenyuan Yi & Hani & Lahu Autonomous County, Jiangcheng Hani & Yi Autonomous County, Menglian Dai & Lahu & Wa Autonomous County, Lancang lahu Autonomous County, Ximeng Wa Autonomous County
临 沧	Lincang	3	双江拉祜族佤族布朗族傣族自治县、耿马傣族佤族自治县、沧源佤族自治县 Shuangjiang Lahu & Wa & Bulang & Dai Autonomous County, Gengma Dai & Wa Autonomous County, Cangyuan Wa Autonomous County
红 河	Honghe	3	屏边苗族自治县、金平苗族瑶族傣族自治县、河口瑶族自治县 Pingbian Miao Autonomous County, Jinping Miao & Yao & Dai Autonomous County, Hekou Yao Autonomous County
大 理	Dali	3	漾濞彝族自治县、南涧彝族自治县、巍山彝族回族自治县 Yangbi Yi Autonomous County, Nanjian Yi Autonomous County, Weishan Yi & Hui Autonomous County
怒 江	Nujiang	2	贡山独龙族怒族自治县、兰坪白族普米族自治县 Gongshan Dulong & Nu Autonomous County , Lanping Bai & Pumi Autonomous County
迪 庆	Diqing	1	维西傈僳族自治县 Weixi Lisu Autonomous County

17-3 云南少数民族分布的主要地方
Geographic Distribution of Ethnic Minorities

民族	Ethnic Minority	分布的主要地方(州、市)	Main Geographic Distribution
彝族	Yi	楚雄州、红河州、玉溪市、大理州、普洱市、昆明市	Chuxiong, Honghe,Yuxi, Dali, Pu'er, Kunming
白族	Bai	大理州	Dali
哈尼族	Hani	红河州、西双版纳州、普洱市、玉溪市	Honghe, Xishuangbanna, Pu'er, Yuxi
壮族	Zhuang	文山州、红河州、曲靖市	Wenshan, Honghe, Qujing
傣族	Dai	西双版纳州、德宏州、普洱市、临沧市	Xishuangbanna, Dehong , Pu'er , Lincang
苗族	Miao	文山州、红河州、昭通市	Wenshan , Honghe , Zhaotong
傈僳族	Lisu	怒江州、迪庆州、丽江市、大理州	Nujiang , Diqing , Lijiang , Dali
回族	Hui	昆明市、大理州、曲靖市、楚雄州、红河州、玉溪市	Kunming , Dali , Qujing , Chuxiong , Honghe , Yuxi
拉祜族	Lahu	普洱市、临沧市、西双版纳州	Pu'er, Lincang , Xishuangbanna
佤族	Wa	临沧市、普洱市	Lincang , Pu'er
纳西族	Naxi	丽江市、迪庆州	Lijiang , Diqing
瑶族	Yao	文山州、红河州	Wenshan , Honghe
藏族	Tibetan	迪庆州	Diqing
景颇族	Jingpo	德宏州	Dehong
布朗族	Bulang	西双版纳州、普洱市、临沧市	Xishuangbanna , Pu'er , Lincang
普米族	Pumi	丽江市、怒江州、迪庆州	Lijiang , Nujiang , Diqing
怒族	Nu	怒江州	Nujiang
阿昌族	Achang	德宏州、保山市	Dehong , Baoshan
基诺族	Jino	西双版纳州	Xishuangbanna
德昂族	De'ang	德宏州、临沧市	Dehong , Lincang
蒙古族	Mongolian	玉溪市	Yuxi
布依族	Buyi	曲靖市	Qujing
独龙族	Dulong	怒江州	Nujiang
水族	Shui	曲靖市	Qujing

17-4 民族自治地方基本情况（2020年）

民族自治地方	National Autonomous Area	建立时间
民族自治地方	**Minority Autonomous Area**	
自治州合计	**Autonomous Prefectures**	
西双版纳傣族自治州	Xishuangbanna Dai Autonomous Prefecture	1953年1月24日
德宏傣族景颇族自治州	Dehong Dai & Jingpo Autonomous Prefecture	1953年7月24日
怒江傈僳族自治州	Nujiang Lisu Autonomous Prefecture	1954年8月23日
大理白族自治州	Dali Bai Autonomous Prefecture	1956年11月22日
迪庆藏族自治州	Diqing Tibetan Autonomous Prefecture	1957年9月13日
红河哈尼族彝族自治州	Honghe Hani & Yi Autonomous Prefecture	1957年11月18日
文山壮族苗族自治州	Wenshan Zhuang & Miao Autonomous Prefecture	1958年4月1日
楚雄彝族自治州	Chuxiong Yi Autonomous Prefecture	1958年4月15日
自治州以外的自治县合计	**Autonomous Counties Except above Prefectures**	
峨山彝族自治县	Eshan Yi Autonomous County	1951年5月12日
澜沧拉祜族自治县	Lancang Lahu Autonomous County	1953年4月7日
江城哈尼族彝族自治县	Jiangcheng Hani & Yi Autonomous County	1954年5月18日
孟连傣族拉祜族佤族自治县	Menglian Dai & Lahu & Wa Autonomous County	1954年6月16日
耿马傣族佤族自治县	Gengma Dai & Wa Autonomous County	1955年10月16日
宁蒗彝族自治县	Ninglang Yi Autonomous County	1956年9月20日
石林彝族自治县	Shilin Yi Autonomous County	1956年12月13日
沧源佤族自治县	Cangyuan Wa Autonomous County	1964年2月28日
西盟佤族自治县	Ximeng Wa Autonomous County	1965年3月5日
墨江哈尼族自治县	Mojiang Hani Autonomous County	1979年11月28日
寻甸回族彝族自治县	Xundian Hui & Yi Autonomous County	1979年12月20日
元江哈尼族彝族傣族自治县	Yuanjiang Hani & Yi & Dai Autonomous County	1980年11月22日
新平彝族傣族自治县	Xinping Yi & Dai Autonomous County	1980年11月25日
禄劝彝族苗族自治县	Luquan Yi & Miao Autonomous County	1985年11月25日
宁洱哈尼族彝族自治县	Ning'er Hani & Yi Autonomous County	1985年12月15日
景东彝族自治县	Jingdong Yi Autonomous County	1985年12月20日
景谷傣族彝族自治县	Jinggu Dai & Yi Autonomous County	1985年12月25日
双江拉祜族佤族布朗族傣族自治县	Shuangjiang Lahu & Wa & Bulang & Dai Autonomous County	1985年12月30日
镇沅彝族哈尼族拉祜族自治县	Zhenyuan Yi & Hani & Lahu Autonomous County	1990年5月15日
玉龙纳西族自治县	Yulong Naxi Autonomous County	2002年12月26日

注：2003年4月8日，普洱哈尼族彝族自治县更名为宁洱哈尼族彝族自治县。

Basic Conditions of Minority Autonomous Regions (2020)

Foundation Date	乡、镇、街道办事处合 计（个） Total(unit)	街道办事处 Community Offices	乡 Townships	镇 Towns	民族乡数(个) Number of Minority Townships and Towns (unit)
	818	**33**	**369**	**416**	**67**
	596	**18**	**274**	**304**	**53**
Jan.24,1953	33	2	12	19	7
July.24,1953	51	1	27	23	5
Aug.23,1954	29		16	13	2
Nov.22,1956	112	3	40	69	11
Sept.13,1957	29		20	9	3
Nov.18,1957	135	9	62	64	5
Apr.1,1958	104	3	59	42	16
Apr. 15,1958	103		38	65	4
	222	**15**	**95**	**112**	**14**
May.12,1951	8	2	3	3	
Apr.7,1953	20		15	5	6
May.18,1954	7		2	5	
June.16,1954	6		2	4	
Oct.16,1955	9		5	4	1
Sept.20,1956	15		11	4	1
Dec.13,1956	7	3	1	3	
Feb.28,1964	10		6	4	1
Mar.5,1965	7		2	5	1
Nov.28,1979	15		3	12	1
Dec.20,1979	16	3	4	9	
Nov.22,1980	10	3	5	2	
Nov.25,1980	12	2	6	4	
Nov.25,1985	17	2	6	9	
Dec.15,1985	9		3	6	
Dec.20,1985	13		3	10	
Dec.25,1985	10		4	6	
Dec.30,1985	6		4	2	
May.15,1990	9		1	8	
Dec.26,2002	16		9	7	3

Note: Pu'er Hani and Yi autonomous county changed its name into Ning'er Hani and Yi autonomous county in 8th April, 2003.

17-4 续表

民族自治地方	National Autonomous Area	土地面积（万平方千米）Land Area (10 000 sq.km)	占全省土地面积(%) Proportion to Provincial Total (%)
民族自治地方	**National Autonomous Area**	**27.67**	**70.2**
自治州合计	**Autonomous Prefectures**	**19.37**	**49.1**
楚雄彝族自治州	Chuxiong Yi Autonomous Prefecture	2.93	7.4
红河哈尼族彝族自治州	Honghe Hani and Yi Autonomous Prefecture	3.29	8.4
文山壮族苗族自治州	Wenshan Zhuang and Miao Autonomous Prefecture	3.22	8.2
西双版纳傣族自治州	Xishuangbanna Dai Autonomous Prefecture	1.97	5.0
大理白族自治州	Dali Bai Autonomous Prefecture	2.95	7.5
德宏傣族景颇族自治州	Dehong Dai and Jingpo Autonomous Prefecture	1.15	2.9
怒江傈僳族自治州	Nujiang Lisu Autonomous Prefecture	1.47	3.7
迪庆藏族自治州	Diqing Tibetan Autonomous Prefecture	2.39	6.1
自治州以外的自治县合计	**Autonomous Counties Except the Above Prefectures**	**8.30**	**21.1**
石林彝族自治县	Shilin Yi Autonomous County	0.18	0.5
禄劝彝族苗族自治县	Luquan Yi and Miao Autonomous County	0.44	1.1
寻甸回族彝族自治县	Xundian Hui and Yi Autonomous County	0.40	1.0
峨山彝族自治县	Eshan Yi Autonomous County	0.20	0.5
新平彝族傣族自治县	Xinping Yi and Dai Autonomous County	0.42	1.1
元江哈尼族彝族傣族自治县	Yuanjiang Hani and Yi and Dai Autonomous County	0.29	0.7
玉龙纳西族自治县	Yulong Naxi Autonomous County	0.76	1.9
宁蒗彝族自治县	Ninglang Yi Autonomous County	0.62	1.6
宁洱哈尼族彝族自治县	Ning'er Hani and Yi Autonomous County	0.37	0.9
墨江哈尼族自治县	Mojiang Hani Autonomous County	0.55	1.4
景东彝族自治县	Jingdong Yi Autonomous County	0.45	1.1
景谷傣族彝族自治县	Jinggu Dai and Yi Autonomous County	0.78	2.0
镇沅彝族哈尼族拉祜族自治县	Zhenyuan Yi and Hani and Lahu Autonomous County	0.42	1.1
江城哈尼族彝族自治县	Jiangcheng Hani and Yi Autonomous County	0.35	0.9
孟连傣族拉祜族佤族自治县	Menglian Dai and Lahu and Wa Autonomous County	0.20	0.5
澜沧拉祜族自治县	Lancang Lahu Autonomous County	0.88	2.2
西盟佤族自治县	Ximeng Wa Autonomous County	0.14	0.4
双江拉祜族佤族布朗族傣族自治县	Shuangjiang Lahu and Wa and Bulang and Dai Autonomous County	0.23	0.6
耿马傣族佤族自治县	Gengma Dai and Wa Autonomous County	0.38	1.1
沧源佤族自治县	Cangyuan Wa Autonomous County	0.25	0.6

continued

年末总人口 (万人) Total Population at Year-end (10 000 persons)	占全省人口比重 (%) Proportion to Provincial Total (%)	少数民族人口 (万人) Population of Minority Nationalities (10 000 persons)	占民族地方总人口比重(%) Proportion to Local Total Population (%)
2 205.00	**46.7**	**1 208.91**	**54.8**
1 729.90	**36.6**	**933.76**	**54.0**
241.70	5.1	81.55	33.7
447.80	9.5	255.20	57.0
350.30	7.4	201.51	57.5
130.40	2.8	86.41	66.3
333.80	7.1	167.08	50.1
131.80	2.8	60.32	45.8
55.30	1.2	49.39	89.3
38.80	0.8	32.31	83.3
475.10	**10.1**	**275.15**	**57.9**
24.08	0.5	8.07	33.5
37.89	0.8	11.35	30.0
46.07	1.0	10.35	22.5
14.39	0.3	9.04	62.8
26.28	0.6	18.33	69.8
19.56	0.4	15.26	78.0
22.41	0.5	17.42	77.7
24.45	0.5	19.63	80.3
16.30	0.3	8.79	53.9
28.20	0.6	21.47	76.1
30.30	0.6	15.06	49.7
27.70	0.6	13.26	47.9
18.00	0.4	10.03	55.7
11.10	0.2	8.40	75.7
14.50	0.3	11.23	77.5
44.10	0.9	34.14	77.4
8.70	0.2	7.90	90.8
16.47	0.3	7.16	43.5
28.57	0.6	14.31	50.1
16.02	0.3	13.95	87.1

17-5 全省民族自治地方主要指标（2015-2020年）

指　　标	Item	2015
年末总人口数(万人)	**Total Population at year-end (10 000 persons)**	**2 235.95**
农业生产	**Agriculture Production**	
农业总产值	Gross Output Value of Farming, Forestry, Animal Husbandry and Fishery	2 105.81
主要农业产品产量(万吨)	Yields of Major Agricultural Products (10 000 tons)	
粮　食	Grain	1 062.20
甘　蔗	Sugarcane	1 470.78
烤　烟	Flue-cured Tobacco	47.80
工业生产	**Industry Production**	
主要工业产品产量(万吨)	Output of Major Industrial Products(10 000 tons)	
粗　钢	Steel	363.73
生　铁	Pig Iron	235.83
原　煤	Coal	1 174.07
发电量（亿万千瓦小时）	Electricity (100 million kWh)	378.30
成品糖	Sugar of Finished Product	186.35
地方一般公共预算收支(亿元)	**Public Budgetary Revenue and Expenditure of Local Government(100 million yuan)**	
地方一般公共预算收入	Public Budgetary Revenue of Local Government	492.16
地方一般公共预算支出	Public Budgetary Expenditure of Local Government	1 916.10

注：1.2016年起地方一般公共预算收入数据为新口径。
2.2016-2017年粮食和甘蔗产量为根据第三次全国农业普查结果核定和修订数据。

Principal Indicators of Minority Autonomous Regions (2015-2020)

2016	2017	2018	2019	2020
2 231.48	**2 225.69**	**2 219.73**	**2 213.50**	**2 205.00**
2 207.40	2 318.40	2 351.16	2 811.27	3 364.27
990.91	1 009.49	1 023.17	1 034.57	1 048.08
1 188.73	1 199.86	1 289.86	1 261.27	1 315.56
47.24	45.11	44.43	42.60	44.43
411.80	402.92	486.18	532.08	514.44
268.34	238.71	280.07	301.08	317.42
1 489.31	1 516.50	1 908.10	1 809.02	1 791.16
528.78	613.42	684.61	638.54	760.35
160.20	170.18	171.10	169.70	198.56
520.58	537.69	567.10	593.55	613.12
2 070.54	2 242.61	2 540.57	2 756.03	2 805.08

Note: a. Sine 2016, The public budgetary revenue of local government in this table is new caliber.

b. From 2016 to 2017, data of grain and sugarcane are verified and revised by the Third National Agricultural Census.

17-6 民族自治地方主要社会经济指标占全省的比重（2020年）

Proportion of Principal Socio-economic Indicators in Minority Autonomous Areas to the Whole Province (2020)

指　　标	Item	全　省 Yunnan	民族自治地　方 Minority Autonomous Areas	民族自治地方占全省比重(%) Proportion of Minority Autonomous Areas to the Whole Province(%)
市县数（个）	**Number of Cities and Counties (unit)**	**129**	**78**	**60.5**
年末总人口（万人）	**Total Population at Year-end (10 000 persons)**	**4 722.0**	**2 205.0**	**46.7**
土地面积（万平方千米）	**Land Area (10 000 sq.km)**	**39.41**	**27.67**	**70.2**
生产总值（当年价）（亿元）	**Gross Domestic Product (at Current prices) (100 million yuan)**	**24 521.90**	**10 090.82**	**41.2**
农业总产值	Gross Output Value of Agriculture,Forestry,Animal Husbandry,Fishery	5 920.52	3 364.27	**56.8**
主要农产品产量（万吨）	**Output of Major Agricultural Products(10 000 tons)**			
粮　食	Grain	1 895.86	1 048.08	**55.3**
甘　蔗	Sugarcane	1 597.17	1 315.56	**82.4**
烤　烟	Flue-cured Tobacco	81.60	44.43	**54.4**
社会消费品零售总额（亿元）	**Retail Sales of Consumer Goods (100 million yuan)**	**9 792.87**	**3 973.99**	**40.6**
地方一般公共预算收支（亿元）	**Public Budgetary Revenue and Expenditure of Local Government(100 million yuan)**			
地方一般公共预算收入	Public Budgetary Revenue of Local Government	2 116.69	613.12	**29.0**
地方一般公共预算支出	Public Budgetary Expenditure of Local Government	6 974.02	2 805.08	**40.2**

17-7 民族自治地方一般公共预算收入和支出（2019-2020年）
Public Budgetary Revenue and Expenditure of Local Government in Minority Autonomous Regions (2019-2020)

单位：亿元 (100 million yuan)

民族自治地方	National Autonomous Area	地方一般公共预算收入 Government Revenue		地方一般公共预算支出 Government Expenditure	
		2019	2020	2019	2020
民族自治地方总计	**Minority Autonomous Area Total**	**593.55**	**613.12**	**2 756.03**	**2 805.08**
自治州合计	**Autonomous Prefectures**	**504.68**	**523.88**	**2 201.58**	**2 240.48**
楚雄彝族自治州	Chuxiong Yi Autonomous Prefecture	87.61	90.28	279.56	293.61
红河哈尼族彝族自治州	Honghe Hani and Yi Autonomous Prefecture	148.06	151.25	505.60	532.03
文山壮族苗族自治州	Wenshan Zhuang and Miao Autonomous Prefecture	63.72	65.66	373.09	384.38
西双版纳傣族自治州	Xishuangbanna Dai Autonomous Prefecture	34.74	35.81	139.93	133.87
大理白族自治州	Dali Bai Autonomous Prefecture	103.27	108.48	390.90	391.19
德宏傣族景颇族自治州	Dehong Dai and Jingpo Autonomous Prefecture	40.10	42.31	165.46	182.75
怒江傈僳族自治州	Nujiang Lisu Autonomous Prefecture	13.08	15.08	175.73	163.18
迪庆藏族自治州	Diqing Tibetan Autonomous Prefecture	14.10	15.01	171.31	159.47
自治州以外的自治县合计	**Autonomous Counties Except the Above Prefectures**	**88.87**	**89.24**	**554.45**	**564.60**
石林彝族自治县	Shilin Yi Autonomous County	6.89	6.22	20.65	23.93
禄劝彝族苗族自治县	Luquan Yi and Miao Autonomous County	5.31	5.01	39.54	38.27
寻甸回族彝族自治县	Xundian Hui and Yi Autonomous County	6.54	7.03	41.69	38.94
峨山彝族自治县	Eshan Yi Autonomous County	3.82	3.95	17.47	18.57
新平彝族傣族自治县	Xinping Yi and Dai Autonomous County	13.02	12.88	36.51	35.36
元江哈尼族彝族傣族自治县	Yuanjiang Hani and Yi and Dai Autonomous County	4.52	3.86	20.53	19.81
玉龙纳西族自治县	Yulong Naxi Autonomous County	7.16	7.38	27.74	28.87
宁蒗彝族自治县	Ninglang Yi Autonomous County	3.08	2.87	37.11	38.60
宁洱哈尼族彝族自治县	Ning'er Hani and Yi Autonomous County	2.96	3.11	16.94	16.94
墨江哈尼族自治县	Mojiang Hani Autonomous County	3.49	3.79	30.82	30.82
景东彝族自治县	Jingdong Yi Autonomous County	3.64	3.90	27.45	28.51
景谷傣族彝族自治县	Jinggu Dai and Yi Autonomous County	5.01	5.22	24.66	27.16
镇沅彝族哈尼族拉祜族自治县	Zhenyuan Yi and Hani and Lahu Autonomous County	4.21	4.02	21.22	21.04
江城哈尼族彝族自治县	Jiangcheng Hani and Yi Autonomous County	1.64	1.15	21.92	18.92
孟连傣族拉祜族佤族自治县	Menglian Dai and Lahu and Wa Autonomous County	1.41	1.70	16.77	19.35
澜沧拉祜族自治县	Lancang Lahu Autonomous County	4.81	5.33	56.64	58.01
西盟佤族自治县	Ximeng Wa Autonomous County	0.61	0.63	16.90	17.42
双江拉祜族佤族布朗族傣族自治县	Shuangjiang Lahu and Wa and Bulang and Dai Autonomous County	2.97	3.09	23.85	24.81
耿马傣族佤族自治县	Gengma Dai and Wa Autonomous County	4.54	4.74	30.97	32.64
沧源佤族自治县	Cangyuan Wa Autonomous County	3.24	3.36	25.07	26.63

17–8 民族自治地方生产总值及指数（2020年）

单位：亿元、%

民族自治地方	Minority Autonomous Area	生产总值 Gross Domestic Product
民族自治地方总计	**Minority Autonomous Area Total**	**10 090.82**
自治州合计	**Autonomous Prefectures**	**8 116.19**
楚雄彝族自治州	Chuxiong Yi Autonomous Prefecture	1 372.16
红河哈尼族彝族自治州	Honghe Hani and Yi Autonomous Prefecture	2 417.48
文山壮族苗族自治州	Wenshan Zhuang and Miao Autonomous Prefecture	1 185.12
西双版纳傣族自治州	Xishuangbanna Dai Autonomous Prefecture	604.18
大理白族自治州	Dali Bai Autonomous Prefecture	1 484.04
德宏傣族景颇族自治州	Dehong Dai and Jingpo Autonomous Prefecture	575.54
怒江傈僳族自治州	Nujiang Lisu Autonomous Prefecture	210.73
迪庆藏族自治州	Diqing Tibetan Autonomous Prefecture	266.94
自治州以外的自治县合计	**Autonomous Counties Except the Above Prefectures**	**1 974.63**
石林彝族自治县	Shilin Yi Autonomous County	117.07
禄劝彝族苗族自治县	Luquan Yi and Miao Autonomous County	146.50
寻甸回族彝族自治县	Xundian Hui and Yi Autonomous County	143.77
峨山彝族自治县	Eshan Yi Autonomous County	117.62
新平彝族傣族自治县	Xinping Yi and Dai Autonomous County	213.86
元江哈尼族彝族傣族自治县	Yuanjiang Hani and Yi and Dai Autonomous County	124.26
玉龙纳西族自治县	Yulong Naxi Autonomous County	90.15
宁蒗彝族自治县	Ninglang Yi Autonomous County	67.30
宁洱哈尼族彝族自治县	Ning'er Hani and Yi Autonomous County	67.24
墨江哈尼族自治县	Mojiang Hani Autonomous County	85.45
景东彝族自治县	Jingdong Yi Autonomous County	109.99
景谷傣族彝族自治县	Jinggu Dai and Yi Autonomous County	121.87
镇沅彝族哈尼族拉祜族自治县	Zhenyuan Yi and Hani and Lahu Autonomous County	88.61
江城哈尼族彝族自治县	Jiangcheng Hani and Yi Autonomous County	50.38
孟连傣族拉祜族佤族自治县	Menglian Dai and Lahu and Wa Autonomous County	51.68
澜沧拉祜族自治县	Lancang Lahu Autonomous County	120.07
西盟佤族自治县	Ximeng Wa Autonomous County	26.03
双江拉祜族佤族布朗族傣族自治县	Shuangjiang Lahu and Wa and Bulang and Dai Autonomous County	59.74
耿马傣族佤族自治县	Gengma Dai and Wa Autonomous County	121.47
沧源佤族自治县	Cangyuan Wa Autonomous County	51.57

注：本表数据为快报数，生产总值按当年价格计算，指数按可比价格计算。

Gross Domestic Product and Their Indices in Minority Autonomous Regions (2020)

(100 million yuan,%)

第一产业 Primary Industry	第二产业 Secondary Industry	第三产业 Tertiary Industry	生产总值指数 (上年=100) Indices of GDP (preceding year=100)	第一产业 Primary Industry	第二产业 Secondary Industry	第三产业 Tertiary Industry
2 005.97	**3 227.38**	**4 857.47**	**104.6**	**105.8**	**105.0**	**103.8**
1 494.72	**2 738.81**	**3 882.66**	**104.8**	**105.7**	**105.6**	**103.9**
261.93	545.89	564.34	106.0	105.7	108.8	103.0
344.78	940.44	1 132.26	105.2	105.9	105.8	104.4
241.28	396.78	547.06	105.4	105.4	106.3	104.5
138.26	151.56	314.36	103.6	106.0	110.0	99.5
338.96	405.94	739.14	102.0	105.7	96.8	104.1
120.41	121.52	333.61	107.9	105.8	112.3	106.9
30.63	74.01	106.09	107.1	105.2	108.0	107.0
18.47	102.67	145.80	105.1	105.7	108.2	102.6
511.25	**488.57**	**974.81**	**103.5**	**105.9**	**101.8**	**103.3**
30.73	16.17	70.17	97.8	105.3	79.7	101.3
41.64	22.04	82.82	106.9	105.6	139.5	99.7
38.35	24.32	81.10	104.0	106.9	121.5	97.7
17.59	31.97	68.06	101.6	105.9	98.5	102.3
29.53	87.93	96.40	104.9	105.9	103.8	105.7
31.30	33.60	59.36	101.7	105.9	96.1	103.8
18.49	32.27	39.39	104.1	105.5	112.5	96.8
12.20	20.05	35.05	110.1	104.4	116.9	108.0
17.41	17.79	32.04	103.9	106.1	101.1	104.6
24.42	17.37	43.66	102.5	105.2	94.1	105.4
36.46	18.06	55.47	103.9	106.1	97.1	105.2
40.35	29.09	52.43	100.1	106.2	90.6	102.2
29.07	22.75	36.79	105.2	105.9	102.0	107.1
13.61	11.11	25.66	104.3	106.2	95.6	108.4
17.26	6.35	28.07	105.7	106.6	100.2	106.7
30.52	34.30	55.25	102.6	105.9	95.7	106.5
5.12	4.72	16.19	106.1	106.1	110.4	104.8
16.80	14.09	28.85	102.5	105.7	93.6	106.5
45.19	31.35	44.93	104.4	105.8	103.5	104.0
15.21	13.24	23.12	103.0	105.6	99.0	104.2

Note: Data in this table are express numbers.Gross domestic value are calculated at current prices,while indices are calculated by comparable prices.

17–9 民族自治地方农、林、牧、渔业总产值（2020年）

单位：亿元

民族自治地方	Minority Autonomous Area	农、林、牧、渔业总产值 Gross Output Value of Farming, Forestry, Animal Husbandry and Fishery
民族自治地方总计	**Minority Autonomous Area Total**	**3 364.27**
自治州合计	**Autonomous Prefectures**	**2 520.04**
楚雄彝族自治州	Chuxiong Yi Autonomous Prefecture	441.12
红河哈尼族彝族自治州	Honghe Hani and Yi Autonomous Prefecture	564.39
文山壮族苗族自治州	Wenshan Zhuang and Miao Autonomous Prefecture	396.05
西双版纳傣族自治州	Xishuangbanna Dai Autonomous Prefecture	230.10
大理白族自治州	Dali Bai Autonomous Prefecture	618.35
德宏傣族景颇族自治州	Dehong Dai and Jingpo Autonomous Prefecture	192.48
怒江傈僳族自治州	Nujiang Lisu Autonomous Prefecture	47.08
迪庆藏族自治州	Diqing Tibetan Autonomous Prefecture	30.46
自治州以外的自治县合计	**Autonomous Counties Except the Above Prefectures**	**844.23**
石林彝族自治县	Shilin Yi Autonomous County	55.32
禄劝彝族苗族自治县	Luquan Yi and Miao Autonomous County	65.74
寻甸回族彝族自治县	Xundian Hui and Yi Autonomous County	65.70
峨山彝族自治县	Eshan Yi Autonomous County	26.62
新平彝族傣族自治县	Xinping Yi and Dai Autonomous County	55.24
元江哈尼族彝族傣族自治县	Yuanjiang Hani and Yi and Dai Autonomous County	52.26
玉龙纳西族自治县	Yulong Naxi Autonomous County	33.96
宁蒗彝族自治县	Ninglang Yi Autonomous County	21.43
宁洱哈尼族彝族自治县	Ning'er Hani and Yi Autonomous County	28.55
墨江哈尼族自治县	Mojiang Hani Autonomous County	40.11
景东彝族自治县	Jingdong Yi Autonomous County	59.76
景谷傣族彝族自治县	Jinggu Dai and Yi Autonomous County	65.84
镇沅彝族哈尼族拉祜族自治县	Zhenyuan Yi and Hani and Lahu Autonomous County	47.53
江城哈尼族彝族自治县	Jiangcheng Hani and Yi Autonomous County	22.45
孟连傣族拉祜族佤族自治县	Menglian Dai and Lahu and Wa Autonomous County	28.94
澜沧拉祜族自治县	Lancang Lahu Autonomous County	49.95
西盟佤族自治县	Ximeng Wa Autonomous County	8.52
双江拉祜族佤族布朗族傣族自治县	Shuangjiang Lahu and Wa and Bulang and Dai Autonomous County	25.67
耿马傣族佤族自治县	Gengma Dai and Wa Autonomous County	65.03
沧源佤族自治县	Cangyuan Wa Autonomous County	25.62

注：本表按现行价格计算。

Gross Output Value of Farming, Forestry, Animal Husbandry and Fishery in Minority Autonomous Regions (2020)

(100 million yuan)

农　业 Farming	林　业 Forestry	牧 业 Animal Husbandry	渔　业 Fishery	农、林、牧、渔服务业 Services in Support of Agriculture, Forestry, Animal Husbandry and Fishery
1 692.23	**321.92**	**1 190.42**	**63.38**	**96.32**
1 245.93	**219.24**	**936.90**	**42.03**	**75.93**
233.49	38.13	148.83	4.47	16.20
259.42	35.44	247.25	7.63	14.64
189.47	23.70	164.72	6.53	11.63
124.91	67.76	20.18	10.95	6.30
284.40	21.53	285.13	7.55	19.73
125.83	18.54	38.60	4.41	5.10
16.62	8.53	20.68	0.08	1.17
11.78	5.62	11.51	0.40	1.16
446.30	**102.68**	**253.51**	**21.35**	**20.38**
29.91	3.89	18.90	0.56	2.06
31.21	5.06	28.72	0.16	0.58
30.76	1.09	31.45	1.72	0.69
16.48	1.59	7.53	0.13	0.89
35.51	4.01	13.74	0.28	1.70
44.23	1.26	5.69	0.30	0.78
14.33	1.88	15.91	0.62	1.22
10.38	1.50	8.57	0.39	0.58
10.93	4.47	10.99	1.40	0.76
17.47	5.20	13.18	3.43	0.83
22.48	12.82	21.79	1.56	1.12
27.39	22.15	11.46	3.58	1.26
20.52	8.76	16.66	0.65	0.94
14.35	3.22	3.46	0.86	0.55
16.47	6.66	4.35	0.43	1.02
25.25	5.55	15.99	2.22	0.93
3.69	2.70	1.64	0.15	0.34
15.00	1.26	7.75	0.86	0.81
44.59	6.58	10.21	1.18	2.46
15.36	3.01	5.52	0.85	0.87

Note: Data in this table are calculated at current prices.

17−10 民族自治地方主要农作物产量（2020年）

单位：万吨

民族自治地方	Minority Autonomous Area	粮 食 Grain	稻谷 Rice
民族自治地方	**Minority Autonomous Area**	**1 048.08**	**306.15**
自治州合计	**Autonomous Prefectures**	**793.53**	**249.43**
楚雄彝族自治州	Chuxiong Yi Autonomous Prefecture	126.67	44.67
红河哈尼族彝族自治州	Honghe Hani and Yi Autonomous Prefecture	183.49	60.00
文山壮族苗族自治州	Wenshan Zhuang and Miao Autonomous Prefecture	169.76	47.58
西双版纳傣族自治州	Xishuangbanna Dai Autonomous Prefecture	47.64	18.32
大理白族自治州	Dali Bai Autonomous Prefecture	165.31	38.50
德宏傣族景颇族自治州	Dehong Dai and Jingpo Autonomous Prefecture	68.69	36.79
怒江傈僳族自治州	Nujiang Lisu Autonomous Prefecture	16.00	2.22
迪庆藏族自治州	Diqing Tibetan Autonomous Prefecture	15.97	1.35
自治州以外的自治县合计	**Autonomous Counties Except the Above Prefectures**	**254.55**	**56.74**
石林彝族自治县	Shilin Yi Autonomous County	14.23	1.73
禄劝彝族苗族自治县	Luquan Yi and Miao Autonomous County	22.91	1.89
寻甸回族彝族自治县	Xundian Hui and Yi Autonomous County	23.54	1.94
峨山彝族自治县	Eshan Yi Autonomous County	7.38	2.27
新平彝族傣族自治县	Xinping Yi and Dai Autonomous County	17.98	3.85
元江哈尼族彝族傣族自治县	Yuanjiang Hani and Yi and Dai Autonomous County	9.47	2.72
玉龙纳西族自治县	Yulong Naxi Autonomous County	10.96	0.51
宁蒗彝族自治县	Ninglang Yi Autonomous County	7.58	0.77
宁洱哈尼族彝族自治县	Ning'er Hani and Yi Autonomous County	8.56	2.33
墨江哈尼族自治县	Mojiang Hani Autonomous County	15.56	2.59
景东彝族自治县	Jingdong Yi Autonomous County	19.18	4.96
景谷傣族彝族自治县	Jinggu Dai and Yi Autonomous County	15.81	3.59
镇沅彝族哈尼族拉祜族自治县	Zhenyuan Yi and Hani and Lahu Autonomous County	12.00	2.32
江城哈尼族彝族自治县	Jiangcheng Hani and Yi Autonomous County	5.26	0.93
孟连傣族拉祜族佤族自治县	Menglian Dai and Lahu and Wa Autonomous County	7.59	4.68
澜沧拉祜族自治县	Lancang Lahu Autonomous County	25.44	10.14
西盟佤族自治县	Ximeng Wa Autonomous County	4.16	1.51
双江拉祜族佤族布朗族傣族自治县	Shuangjiang Lahu and Wa and Bulang and Dai Autonomous County	7.32	1.74
耿马傣族佤族自治县	Gengma Dai and Wa Autonomous County	11.71	4.47
沧源佤族自治县	Cangyuan Wa Autonomous County	7.91	1.80

Yields of Major Farm Crops in Minority Autonomous Areas (2020)

(10 000 tons)

小麦 Wheat	玉米 Maize	豆类 Beans and Peas	薯类（折粮） Tubers	油料 Oil-bearing Crops	甘蔗 Sugarcane	烤烟 Flue-cured Tobacco
41.90	**502.51**	**70.29**	**78.23**	**26.37**	**1 315.56**	**44.43**
30.72	**365.68**	**56.86**	**52.87**	**21.11**	**684.82**	**29.56**
11.09	48.71	13.29	3.59	6.41	5.88	8.50
5.73	77.24	11.06	17.93	3.32	84.76	7.14
5.75	92.79	10.75	8.75	6.95	122.01	4.93
	28.54	0.20	0.21	0.14	105.58	
4.75	82.73	17.51	8.36	3.09	0.65	7.03
0.75	19.51	1.23	10.28	0.64	364.60	1.81
0.84	8.09	1.63	2.47	0.11	1.35	
1.81	8.07	1.19	1.28	0.45		0.15
11.17	**136.82**	**13.44**	**25.34**	**5.26**	**630.74**	**14.87**
1.15	9.05	0.95	0.86	0.08		1.43
1.56	11.54	1.64	4.42	0.41	0.07	1.17
0.56	7.14	1.57	9.25	0.32		2.00
0.15	4.40	0.42	0.07	0.83	0.41	1.10
0.31	11.29	0.61	0.78	0.16	43.69	1.07
0.34	5.51	0.33	0.20	0.33	15.18	0.76
1.75	4.07	1.19	1.85	0.54		1.20
0.20	2.06	0.86	2.68	0.01		0.42
0.73	4.81	0.28	0.37	0.19	0.05	0.50
0.57	11.29	0.68	0.20	0.34	1.34	0.86
1.47	9.11	1.72	1.79	0.44	22.67	1.15
0.53	10.22	0.59	0.78	0.37	61.61	1.02
0.94	8.23	0.39	0.09	0.28	2.71	1.30
0.03	4.21	0.02	0.06	0.05	0.77	
	2.70	0.10	0.03	0.07	42.18	
0.24	13.22	0.63	0.69	0.31	113.11	
0.05	2.51	0.02	0.01	0.03	20.77	
0.36	4.16	0.43	0.55	0.22	40.60	0.35
0.16	5.80	0.73	0.52	0.20	208.45	0.28
0.07	5.50	0.28	0.14	0.07	57.13	0.29

17-11 民族自治地方规模以上工业主要产品产量（2020年）

单位：万吨

民族自治地方	Minority Autonomous Area	粗 钢 Steel	生 铁 Pig Iron
民族自治地方总计	**Minority Autonomous Area**	**514.44**	**317.42**
自治州合计	**Autonomous Prefectures**	**290.91**	**317.42**
楚雄彝族自治州	Chuxiong Yi Autonomous Prefecture	137.42	145.62
红河哈尼族彝族自治州	Honghe Hani and Yi Autonomous Prefecture	153.49	146.77
文山壮族苗族自治州	Wenshan Zhuang and Miao Autonomous Prefecture		
西双版纳傣族自治州	Xishuangbanna Dai Autonomous Prefecture		
大理白族自治州	Dali Bai Autonomous Prefecture		25.03
德宏傣族景颇族自治州	Dehong Dai and Jingpo Autonomous Prefecture		
怒江傈僳族自治州	Nujiang Lisu Autonomous Prefecture		
迪庆藏族自治州	Diqing Tibetan Autonomous Prefecture		
自治州以外的自治县合计	**Autonomous Counties Except the Above Prefectures**	**223.53**	
石林彝族自治县	Shilin Yi Autonomous County		
禄劝彝族苗族自治县	Luquan Yi and Miao Autonomous County		
寻甸回族彝族自治县	Xundian Hui and Yi Autonomous County		
峨山彝族自治县	Eshan Yi Autonomous County		
新平彝族傣族自治县	Xinping Yi and Dai Autonomous County	223.53	
元江哈尼族彝族傣族自治县	Yuanjiang Hani and Yi and Dai Autonomous County		
玉龙纳西族自治县	Yulong Naxi Autonomous County		
宁蒗彝族自治县	Ninglang Yi Autonomous County		
宁洱哈尼族彝族自治县	Ning'er Hani and Yi Autonomous County		
墨江哈尼族自治县	Mojiang Hani Autonomous County		
景东彝族自治县	Jingdong Yi Autonomous County		
景谷傣族彝族自治县	Jinggu Dai and Yi Autonomous County		
镇沅彝族哈尼族拉祜族自治县	Zhenyuan Yi and Hani and Lahu Autonomous County		
江城哈尼族彝族自治县	Jiangcheng Hani and Yi Autonomous County		
孟连傣族拉祜族佤族自治县	Menglian Dai and Lahu and Wa Autonomous County		
澜沧拉祜族自治县	Lancang Lahu Autonomous County		
西盟佤族自治县	Ximeng Wa Autonomous County		
双江拉祜族佤族布朗族傣族自治县	Shuangjiang Lahu and Wa and Bulang and Dai Autonomous County		
耿马傣族佤族自治县	Gengma Dai and Wa Autonomous County		
沧源佤族自治县	Cangyuan Wa Autonomous County		

注：统计范围为年主营业务收入2000万元及以上工业企业。

Output of Major Industrial Products above Designated size in Minority Autonomous Areas (2020)

(10 000 tons)

原 煤 Coal	发电量(亿千瓦小时) Electricity (100 million kWh)	成品糖 Sugar of Finished Product	农用化肥 Agricultural Chemical Fertilizer	白 酒(万升) Liquor (10 kiloliters)	啤 酒(万升) Beer (10 kiloliters)	水 泥 Cement
1 791.16	**760.33**	**198.56**	**90.46**	**5 451.60**	**26 282.75**	**6 052.73**
1 583.28	**662.15**	**116.04**	**82.30**	**4 797.54**	**23 780.25**	**4 353.84**
50.88	65.98		0.95	865.14		149.81
1 438.59	182.76	5.34	81.35	74.70		913.40
82.91	56.28	15.66		3 733.20		911.88
	6.83	26.37			2 173.95	185.82
10.90	167.86			120.30	21 606.30	1 467.45
	128.88	68.67				418.87
	25.28					97.58
	28.28			4.20		209.03
207.88	**98.18**	**82.52**	**8.16**	**654.06**	**2 502.50**	**1 698.89**
0.20	6.24					106.47
	26.45					131.46
199.94	16.16		8.16			172.57
0.04	0.92				2 502.50	103.80
	9.11	3.21				93.05
	6.86	1.02				250.82
	1.01					
	1.24			297.22		
0.53	0.37					173.19
	16.19					
3.79	1.72	1.12				5.08
	2.70	5.36		209.91		42.63
	0.44					190.33
	3.28					
	0.23	9.14				
3.38	1.58	11.85				144.67
	0.07	2.77				
	0.83	5.22		146.93		
	1.45	33.80				151.11
	1.33	9.03				133.71

Note: Statistical coverage are industrial enterprises with annual revenue over 20 million yuan from principal business.

Chapter 18

十八、县域经济概况
Survey of Intra-county Economies

18-1 各州市县生产总值及其指数（2020年）

Gross Domestic Product and Its Indices by Region (2020)

单位：亿元、% (100 million,%)

州市县	Region	生产总值 Gross Domestic Product	第一产业 Primary Industry	第二产业 Secondary Industry	第三产业 Tertiary Industry	生产总值指数（上年=100） Indices of GDP (preceding year=100)	第一产业 Primary Industry	第二产业 Secondary Industry	第三产业 Tertiary Industry
全省	**Yunnan**	**24 521.90**	**3 598.91**	**8 287.54**	**12 635.45**	**104.0**	**105.7**	**103.6**	**103.8**
昆明市	**Kunming**	**6 733.79**	**312.35**	**2 102.93**	**4 318.51**	**102.3**	**105.6**	**101.4**	**102.5**
五华区	Wuhua	1 242.35	2.59	491.86	747.90	102.6	95.0	102.4	102.8
盘龙区	Panlong	928.16	5.95	188.74	733.47	102.6	102.2	94.0	105.5
官渡区	Guandu	1 383.47	8.95	465.81	908.71	101.8	98.2	106.4	99.4
西山区	Xishan	903.98	4.81	152.23	746.94	103.6	103.0	108.5	102.6
东川区	Dongchuan	123.11	11.39	31.28	80.44	105.5	106.5	111.1	103.0
呈贡区	Chenggong	508.59	5.97	202.32	300.30	105.1	102.7	103.9	106.1
晋宁区	Jinning	194.77	31.73	39.88	123.16	102.4	106.5	95.1	104.7
富民县	Fumin	105.73	16.10	40.55	49.08	102.5	106.1	98.3	106.0
宜良县	Yiliang	211.26	70.34	39.66	101.26	99.5	106.7	88.3	101.0
石林县	Shilin	117.07	30.73	16.17	70.17	97.8	105.3	79.7	101.3
嵩明县	Songming	152.67	22.86	43.46	86.35	101.4	105.8	102.2	99.8
禄劝县	Luquan	146.50	41.64	22.04	82.82	106.9	105.6	139.5	99.7
寻甸县	Xundian	143.77	38.35	24.32	81.10	104.0	106.9	121.5	97.7
安宁市	Anning	572.36	20.96	344.61	206.79	97.9	102.4	95.5	103.3
曲靖市	**Qujing**	**2 959.35**	**553.53**	**1 094.92**	**1 310.90**	**106.6**	**105.9**	**107.0**	**106.5**
麒麟区	Qilin	905.88	38.40	434.42	433.06	107.7	105.9	109.9	105.5
沾益区	Zhanyi	305.53	59.85	116.02	129.66	105.4	105.7	102.4	108.8
马龙区	Malong	91.58	16.62	39.96	35.00	110.0	106.0	112.9	107.7
陆良县	Luliang	269.69	84.77	78.80	106.12	108.5	105.9	113.1	106.8
师宗县	Shizong	172.03	47.76	53.06	71.21	107.3	105.9	109.6	106.1
罗平县	Luoping	273.91	71.09	78.83	123.99	105.3	106.2	101.1	108.3
富源县	Fuyuan	246.96	58.54	93.58	94.84	106.0	105.7	105.7	106.7
会泽县	Huize	287.65	79.37	83.36	124.92	105.5	106.1	102.7	107.9
宣威市	Xuanwei	406.12	97.13	116.87	192.12	104.5	106.0	103.3	104.7
玉溪市	**Yuxi**	**2 058.14**	**207.26**	**864.29**	**986.59**	**102.1**	**105.8**	**99.4**	**104.4**
红塔区	Hongta	890.16	20.12	525.91	344.13	102.3	105.5	101.3	104.2
江川区	Jiangchuan	146.74	27.36	44.95	74.43	104.3	105.8	104.4	103.8
通海县	Tonghai	172.26	26.15	42.71	103.40	105.4	105.8	105.4	105.3
华宁县	Huaning	119.48	26.41	22.01	71.06	102.3	105.8	96.1	103.9
易门县	Yimen	132.52	15.53	47.51	69.48	94.0	105.8	79.4	108.3
峨山县	Eshan	117.62	17.59	31.97	68.06	101.6	105.9	98.5	102.3
新平县	Xinping	213.86	29.53	87.93	96.40	104.9	105.9	103.8	105.7
元江县	Yuanjiang	124.26	31.30	33.60	59.36	101.7	105.9	96.1	103.8
澄江市	Chengjiang	140.64	13.27	27.26	100.11	98.9	105.4	85.8	103.1

18-1 续表1 continued

单位：亿元、% (100 million,%)

州 市 县	Region	生产总值 Gross Domestic Product	第一产业 Primary Industry	第二产业 Secondary Industry	第三产业 Tertiary Industry	生产总值指数（上年=100）Indices of GDP (preceding year=100)	第一产业 Primary Industry	第二产业 Secondary Industry	第三产业 Tertiary Industry
保 山 市	**Baoshan**	**1 052.58**	**243.30**	**392.61**	**416.67**	**104.8**	**105.6**	**104.5**	**104.6**
隆阳区	Longyang	393.96	76.37	144.20	173.39	105.2	105.6	104.2	106.0
施甸县	Shidian	90.08	24.58	24.00	41.50	95.1	105.7	79.3	103.5
龙陵县	Longling	123.00	34.33	50.25	38.42	105.7	105.7	106.6	104.2
昌宁县	Changning	163.19	52.97	60.49	49.73	104.8	105.7	105.3	103.2
腾冲市	Tengchong	282.35	55.04	113.67	113.64	107.2	105.6	111.2	103.6
昭 通 市	**Zhaotong**	**1 288.74**	**226.12**	**482.78**	**579.84**	**104.2**	**105.7**	**102.9**	**105.0**
昭阳区	Zhaoyang	365.84	37.61	158.89	169.34	106.6	105.2	105.2	108.5
鲁甸县	Ludian	82.44	17.13	29.16	36.15	102.7	105.5	94.0	109.9
巧家县	Qiaojia	103.03	35.35	26.88	40.80	106.4	105.8	110.4	104.2
盐津县	Yanjin	55.61	14.65	10.85	30.11	100.8	105.8	96.5	100.4
大关县	Daguan	41.90	10.53	8.30	23.07	104.9	105.9	107.9	103.2
永善县	Yongshan	139.62	20.89	83.56	35.17	102.5	105.5	103.4	98.7
绥江县	Suijiang	37.02	6.54	10.21	20.27	100.4	106.1	93.4	103.4
镇雄县	Zhenxiong	217.82	39.27	57.64	120.91	105.2	106.2	109.3	102.6
彝良县	Yiliang	101.11	28.65	28.77	43.69	103.1	105.5	95.4	108.3
威信县	Weixin	66.83	12.11	16.03	38.69	100.8	106.2	95.8	101.9
水富市	Shuifu	77.50	3.37	52.48	21.65	100.6	105.5	99.4	103.6
丽 江 市	**Lijiang**	**512.75**	**77.53**	**165.50**	**269.72**	**104.6**	**105.5**	**109.7**	**101.0**
古城区	Gucheng	176.99	8.20	40.99	127.80	100.1	107.0	108.3	97.1
玉龙县	Yulong	90.15	18.49	32.27	39.39	104.1	105.5	112.5	96.8
永胜县	Yongsheng	104.10	28.54	35.95	39.61	101.7	106.1	98.3	102.9
华坪县	Huaping	74.21	10.09	36.24	27.88	116.5	104.0	118.5	118.0
宁蒗县	Ninglang	67.30	12.20	20.05	35.05	110.1	104.4	116.9	108.0
普 洱 市	**Pu'er**	**945.42**	**235.13**	**228.62**	**481.67**	**102.5**	**105.8**	**95.8**	**105.0**
思茅区	Simao	224.11	20.92	67.09	136.10	100.6	103.9	94.1	104.1
宁洱县	Ning'er	67.24	17.41	17.79	32.04	103.9	106.1	101.1	104.6
墨江县	Mojiang	85.45	24.42	17.37	43.66	102.5	105.2	94.1	105.4
景东县	Jingdong	109.99	36.46	18.06	55.47	103.9	106.1	97.1	105.2
景谷县	Jinggu	121.87	40.35	29.09	52.43	100.1	106.2	90.6	102.2
镇沅县	Zhenyuan	88.61	29.07	22.75	36.79	105.2	105.9	102.0	107.1
江城县	Jiangcheng	50.38	13.61	11.11	25.66	104.3	106.2	95.6	108.4
孟连县	Menglian	51.68	17.26	6.35	28.07	105.7	106.6	100.2	106.7
澜沧县	Lancang	120.07	30.52	34.30	55.25	102.6	105.9	95.7	106.5
西盟县	Ximeng	26.03	5.12	4.72	16.19	106.1	106.1	110.4	104.8
临 沧 市	**Lincang**	**821.32**	**242.34**	**203.84**	**375.14**	**103.7**	**105.7**	**101.4**	**103.9**
临翔区	Linxiang	170.20	24.49	37.50	108.21	103.0	105.6	102.2	102.8
凤庆县	Fengqing	147.27	55.48	36.64	55.15	104.5	105.8	102.4	105.0
云 县	Yunxian	130.90	45.34	35.32	50.24	103.4	105.7	102.2	102.5
永德县	Yongde	83.25	25.11	19.92	38.22	103.8	105.6	103.4	103.0
镇康县	Zhenkang	56.93	14.72	15.78	26.43	104.2	105.6	98.5	107.6
双江县	Shuangjiang	59.74	16.80	14.09	28.85	102.5	105.7	93.6	106.5
耿马县	Gengma	121.47	45.19	31.35	44.93	104.4	105.8	103.5	104.0
沧源县	Cangyuan	51.57	15.21	13.24	23.12	103.0	105.6	99.0	104.2

18-1 续表2 continued

单位：亿元、% (100 million,%)

州 市 县	Region	生产总值 Gross Domestic Product	第一产业 Primary Industry	第二产业 Secondary Industry	第三产业 Tertiary Industry	生产总值指数 (上年=100) Indices of GDP (preceding year=100)	第一产业 Primary Industry	第二产业 Secondary Industry	第三产业 Tertiary Industry
楚 雄 州	**Chuxiong**	**1 372.16**	**261.93**	**545.89**	**564.34**	**106.0**	**105.7**	**108.8**	**103.0**
楚雄市	Chuxiong	485.14	40.26	243.64	201.24	104.5	105.7	105.0	103.6
双柏县	Shuangbai	60.97	16.24	20.03	24.70	108.9	105.7	114.5	105.8
牟定县	Mouding	77.64	18.22	31.79	27.63	106.9	105.6	110.1	103.6
南华县	Nanhua	97.00	23.53	32.78	40.69	106.5	105.7	111.3	102.2
姚安县	Yao'an	74.29	23.47	20.44	30.38	106.4	105.7	109.8	104.3
大姚县	Dayao	109.47	29.89	40.10	39.48	106.3	105.8	108.2	104.3
永仁县	Yongren	55.01	13.65	16.74	24.62	106.3	105.6	109.6	104.1
元谋县	Yuanmou	96.11	24.91	29.80	41.40	109.4	105.8	116.2	106.0
武定县	Wuding	108.37	26.32	34.80	47.25	106.7	105.9	112.8	102.0
禄丰县	Lufeng	208.16	45.45	75.77	86.94	106.0	105.7	113.9	98.8
红 河 州	**Honghe**	**2 417.48**	**344.78**	**940.44**	**1 132.26**	**105.2**	**105.9**	**105.8**	**104.4**
个旧市	Gejiu	339.10	22.21	172.90	143.99	106.6	105.8	109.8	102.5
开远市	Kaiyuan	269.24	28.02	105.74	135.48	106.2	105.9	107.8	104.8
蒙自市	Mengzi	390.85	37.10	163.71	190.04	106.6	105.9	106.9	106.3
弥勒市	Mile	442.00	44.65	224.30	173.05	103.6	106.0	102.4	105.0
屏边县	Pingbian	61.04	10.70	22.90	27.44	104.3	105.9	104.2	103.8
建水县	Jianshui	224.01	46.79	51.90	125.32	103.3	105.9	99.2	104.6
石屏县	Shiping	133.02	36.51	47.59	48.92	105.9	105.8	107.1	104.6
泸西县	Luxi	152.29	31.86	37.34	83.09	102.0	106.0	98.4	102.6
元阳县	Yuanyang	83.63	20.78	18.27	44.58	106.3	105.8	112.2	104.1
红河县	Honghe	70.48	18.84	15.43	36.21	104.3	105.9	99.6	105.9
金平县	Jinping	89.01	18.45	31.76	38.80	107.0	105.8	112.7	102.5
绿春县	Luchun	52.61	13.50	14.89	24.22	104.5	105.8	103.0	104.9
河口县	Hekou	110.22	15.38	33.72	61.12	106.4	105.8	113.4	102.9
文 山 州	**Wenshan**	**1 185.12**	**241.28**	**396.78**	**547.06**	**105.4**	**105.4**	**106.3**	**104.5**
文山市	Wenshan	324.45	27.14	137.14	160.17	103.0	105.2	103.6	101.9
砚山县	Yanshan	178.39	38.31	51.50	88.58	106.2	105.4	101.0	110.2
西畴县	Xichou	56.35	15.69	13.98	26.68	106.3	105.5	108.0	105.6
麻栗坡县	Malipo	86.68	17.31	31.41	37.96	106.2	105.2	108.2	104.7
马关县	Maguan	122.21	27.60	42.56	52.05	105.0	105.1	107.5	102.3
丘北县	Qiubei	122.60	34.92	32.06	55.62	107.3	105.8	111.9	105.3
广南县	Guangnan	166.96	49.07	46.87	71.02	107.2	105.7	112.9	104.3
富宁县	Funing	127.48	31.24	41.25	54.99	106.3	105.1	109.3	104.3
西双版纳州	**Xishuangbanna**	**604.18**	**138.26**	**151.56**	**314.36**	**103.6**	**106.0**	**110.0**	**99.5**
景洪市	Jinghong	316.64	51.00	87.69	177.95	103.5	105.8	111.8	98.9
勐海县	Menghai	160.73	39.88	45.56	75.29	105.1	106.0	109.2	101.6

18-1 续表3 continued

单位：亿元、% (100 million,%)

州市县	Region	生产总值 Gross Domestic Product	第一产业 Primary Industry	第二产业 Secondary Industry	第三产业 Tertiary Industry	生产总值指数（上年=100） Indices of GDP (preceding year=100)	第一产业 Primary Industry	第二产业 Secondary Industry	第三产业 Tertiary Industry
勐腊县	Mengla	126.81	47.38	18.30	61.13	102.2	106.2	104.1	98.9
大理州	**Dali**	**1 484.04**	**338.96**	**405.94**	**739.14**	**102.0**	**105.7**	**96.8**	**104.1**
大理市	Dali	472.85	25.77	142.43	304.65	98.2	105.6	88.7	103.5
漾濞县	Yangbi	35.17	11.46	7.98	15.73	107.2	105.6	112.9	105.0
祥云县	Xiangyun	193.10	48.05	56.06	88.99	106.0	104.8	108.0	105.0
宾川县	Binchuan	143.26	63.94	23.91	55.41	103.7	106.1	100.3	102.9
弥渡县	Midu	85.99	30.64	15.79	39.56	105.1	105.8	105.7	104.3
南涧县	Nanjian	79.38	20.82	21.30	37.26	102.8	105.5	93.8	108.1
巍山县	Weishan	91.05	31.53	19.03	40.49	102.4	105.9	91.3	107.3
永平县	Yongping	64.35	24.32	12.97	27.06	103.2	106.1	97.3	104.7
云龙县	Yunlong	70.43	16.44	27.92	26.07	97.2	105.7	93.6	98.4
洱源县	Eryuan	78.09	30.64	13.24	34.21	97.5	105.4	81.4	100.9
剑川县	Jianchuan	58.97	12.24	17.87	28.86	105.4	105.9	102.5	107.5
鹤庆县	Heqing	111.40	23.12	47.43	40.85	110.1	106.2	115.5	104.5
德宏州	**Dehong**	**575.54**	**120.41**	**121.52**	**333.61**	**107.9**	**105.8**	**112.3**	**106.9**
瑞丽市	Ruili	167.02	14.83	26.02	126.17	108.1	105.6	99.9	110.3
芒　市	Mangshi	177.22	34.53	34.79	107.90	110.0	105.9	121.6	107.6
梁河县	Lianghe	40.44	10.37	9.44	20.63	109.9	105.8	141.7	100.3
盈江县	Yingjiang	118.03	36.94	36.55	44.54	102.2	105.7	104.8	97.3
陇川县	Longchuan	72.83	23.73	14.72	34.38	111.3	105.7	124.5	109.3
怒江州	**Nujiang**	**210.73**	**30.63**	**74.01**	**106.09**	**107.1**	**105.2**	**108.0**	**107.0**
泸水市	Lushui	79.16	11.05	25.78	42.33	109.0	105.2	112.8	107.5
福贡县	Fugong	24.16	4.40	6.46	13.30	109.2	105.1	121.1	105.2
贡山县	Gongshan	18.81	3.49	5.22	10.10	106.2	104.7	106.4	106.7
兰坪县	Lanping	88.60	11.69	36.55	40.36	104.4	105.3	103.2	105.4
迪庆州	**Diqing**	**266.94**	**18.47**	**102.67**	**145.80**	**105.1**	**105.7**	**108.2**	**102.6**
香格里拉市	Shangri-La	161.54	7.19	66.96	87.39	105.1	105.7	109.8	101.1
德钦县	Deqin	41.89	2.50	16.39	23.00	105.1	105.6	106.6	103.8
维西县	Weixi	63.51	8.77	19.32	35.42	105.4	105.7	104.4	105.9

18-2 各州市县人均生产总值（2019-2020年）

Per Capita Gross Domestic Product by Region (2019-2020)

单位：元 (yuan)

州市县	Region	2019	2020
全　省	**Yunnan**	**49 323**	**51 975**
昆明市	**Kunming**	**79 759**	**80 586**
五华区	Wuhua	107 358	109 473
盘龙区	Panlong	92 503	94 532
官渡区	Guandu	90 891	88 426
西山区	Xishan	92 450	95 508
东川区	Dongchuan	43 780	47 077
呈贡区	Chenggong	81 963	81 160
晋宁区	Jinning	55 658	56 751
富民县	Fumin	67 620	70 816
宜良县	Yiliang	52 977	54 814
石林县	Shilin	47 709	48 538
嵩明县	Songming	38 778	37 874
禄劝县	Luquan	35 174	38 644
寻甸县	Xundian	29 027	31 223
安宁市	Anning	124 019	119 603
曲靖市	**Qujing**	**46 281**	**51 244**
麒麟区	Qilin	86 056	91 549
沾益区	Zhanyi	68 688	75 236
马龙区	Malong	41 740	47 462
陆良县	Luliang	39 552	44 925
师宗县	Shizong	40 682	45 558
罗平县	Luoping	46 306	51 083
富源县	Fuyuan	32 554	36 449
会泽县	Huize	31 315	35 990
宣威市	Xuanwei	30 402	33 973
玉溪市	**Yuxi**	**87 770**	**91 290**
红塔区	Hongta	149 520	152 217
江川区	Jiangchuan	52 163	57 589
通海县	Tonghai	54 080	59 245
华宁县	Huaning	59 961	62 312
易门县	Yimen	89 229	86 640
峨山县	Eshan	77 469	81 120
新平县	Xinping	76 291	81 008
元江县	Yuanjiang	59 278	63 123
澄江市	Chengjiang	81 357	81 107
保山市	**Baoshan**	**39 856**	**43 200**
隆阳区	Longyang	40 321	43 536
施甸县	Shidian	31 094	30 656
龙陵县	Longling	40 054	44 906
昌宁县	Changning	46 307	50 807
腾冲市	Tengchong	39 897	43 931
昭通市	**Zhaotong**	**23 692**	**25 255**
昭阳区	Zhaoyang	38 287	40 431
鲁甸县	Ludian	19 573	20 703
巧家县	Qiaojia	19 574	22 142
盐津县	Yanjin	16 232	17 302
大关县	Daguan	17 601	19 696
永善县	Yongshan	37 590	39 675
绥江县	Suijiang	25 623	27 043
镇雄县	Zhenxiong	15 067	16 145
彝良县	Yiliang	19 025	20 040
威信县	Weixin	17 860	18 861
水富市	Shuifu	74 071	74 951
丽江市	**Lijiang**	**38 065**	**40 841**
古城区	Gucheng	62 660	62 004
玉龙县	Yulong	37 249	40 220
永胜县	Yongsheng	28 483	30 654
华坪县	Huaping	38 922	46 220
宁蒗县	Ninglang	23 866	27 376
普洱市	**Pu'er**	**36 658**	**39 172**
思茅区	Simao	54 726	54 621
宁洱县	Ning'er	37 217	40 923
墨江县	Mojiang	27 475	29 877
景东县	Jingdong	32 506	35 928
景谷县	Jinggu	42 023	43 900
镇沅县	Zhenyuan	43 783	48 821
江城县	Jiangcheng	41 074	45 100
孟连县	Menglian	32 403	35 676
澜沧县	Lancang	25 022	27 058
西盟县	Ximeng	26 969	29 794
临沧市	**Lincang**	**33 496**	**36 213**
临翔区	Lincang	44 887	46 188
凤庆县	Fengqing	34 268	37 960
云　县	Yunxian	30 711	33 410
永德县	Yongde	22 963	25 143
镇康县	Zhenkang	29 901	32 707
双江县	Shuangjiang	33 589	36 029
耿马县	Gengma	38 519	42 236
沧源县	Cangyuan	29 532	31 982

18-2 续表 continued

单位：元 (yuan)

州市县	Region	2019	2020	州市县	Region	2019	2020
楚雄州	**Chuxiong**	**51 491**	**56 433**	富宁县	Funing	29 378	32 014
楚雄市	Chuxiong	74 452	77 025	**西双版纳州**	**Xishuangbanna**	**44 784**	**46 619**
双柏县	Shuangbai	39 080	45 147	景洪市	Jinghong	47 806	49 553
牟定县	Mouding	43 864	50 997	勐海县	Menghai	41 990	45 507
南华县	Nanhua	41 240	47 201	勐腊县	Mengla	41 750	41 741
姚安县	Yao'an	39 116	44 725	**大理州**	**Dali**	**41 396**	**44 346**
大姚县	Dayao	41 875	47 340	大理市	Dali	62 530	61 649
永仁县	Yongren	50 612	55 792	漾濞县	Yangbi	32 008	35 927
元谋县	Yuanmou	41 949	47 518	祥云县	Xiangyun	43 021	47 189
武定县	Wuding	40 172	44 956	宾川县	Binchuan	38 184	41 889
禄丰县	Lufeng	51 076	56 320	弥渡县	Midu	27 798	32 628
红河州	**Honghe**	**50 081**	**53 925**	南涧县	Nanjian	37 018	40 899
个旧市	Gejiu	71 887	79 778	巍山县	Weishan	29 438	33 823
开远市	Kaiyuan	75 301	82 818	永平县	Yongping	34 103	38 942
蒙自市	Mengzi	68 671	68 720	云龙县	Yunlong	37 289	38 308
弥勒市	Mile	77 293	82 012	洱源县	Eryuan	29 317	31 322
屏边县	Pingbian	42 439	46 668	剑川县	Jianchuan	32 941	36 615
建水县	Jianshui	39 004	41 828	鹤庆县	Heqing	39 487	45 702
石屏县	Shiping	43 589	48 549	**德宏州**	**Dehong**	**39 739**	**43 817**
泸西县	Luxi	37 069	39 184	瑞丽市	Ruili	59 015	63 529
元阳县	Yuanyang	20 518	23 114	芒 市	Mangshi	36 259	40 492
红河县	Honghe	21 889	24 565	梁河县	Lianghe	25 855	29 473
金平县	Jinping	23 310	26 581	盈江县	Yingjiang	37 793	40 195
绿春县	Luchun	22 837	24 968	陇川县	Longchuan	34 557	39 997
河口县	Hekou	98 259	107 895	**怒江州**	**Nujiang**	**35 039**	**38 141**
文山州	**Wenshan**	**31 244**	**33 798**	泸水市	Lushui	35 060	38 870
文山市	Wenshan	52 777	52 899	福贡县	Fugong	19 648	21 275
砚山县	Yanshan	34 053	37 433	贡山县	Gongshan	45 202	48 924
西畴县	Xichou	23 971	27 256	兰坪县	Lanping	41 731	45 009
麻栗坡县	Malipo	31 580	35 250	**迪庆州**	**Diqing**	**64 410**	**68 711**
马关县	Maguan	34 748	37 958	香格里拉市	Shangri-La	83 987	87 459
丘北县	Qiubei	23 072	26 105	德钦县	Deqin	70 537	76 101
广南县	Guangnan	19 331	21 565	维西县	Weixi	38 800	42 754

18-3　各州市县年末总人口（2013-2020年）

Total Population at Year-end by Region（2013-2020）

单位：万人　　(10 000 persons)

州市县	Region	2013	2014	2015	2016	2017	2018	2019	2020
全　省	**Yunnan**	**4 641.0**	**4 653.0**	**4 663.0**	**4 677.0**	**4 693.0**	**4 703.0**	**4 714.0**	**4 722.0**
昆明市	**Kunming**	**700.5**	**719.9**	**739.7**	**760.4**	**782.1**	**803.1**	**824.9**	**846.3**
五华区	Wuhua	94.61	97.84	101.21	104.33	107.72	110.27	112.57	114.40
盘龙区	Panlong	86.61	88.57	90.50	92.46	94.53	96.28	97.57	98.80
官渡区	Guandu	105.85	112.88	120.50	127.72	136.13	144.10	152.65	160.26
西山区	Xishan	82.06	84.07	86.22	88.40	90.67	92.64	93.20	96.10
东川区	Dongchuan	26.80	26.72	26.52	26.43	26.37	26.25	26.20	26.10
呈贡区	Chenggong	40.39	43.27	46.12	49.44	52.64	56.70	60.27	65.06
晋宁区	Jinning	30.33	30.88	31.42	32.12	32.71	33.10	34.01	34.63
富民县	Fumin	14.62	14.71	14.73	14.75	14.77	14.82	14.91	14.95
宜良县	Yiliang	40.85	40.42	39.88	39.45	38.94	38.61	38.59	38.49
石林县	Shilin	24.43	24.40	24.36	24.31	24.28	24.20	24.16	24.08
嵩明县	Songming	30.58	31.55	32.65	33.91	35.06	36.78	39.53	41.09
禄劝县	Luquan	39.12	38.93	38.41	38.29	38.05	37.95	37.93	37.89
寻甸县	Xundian	45.83	45.85	45.89	45.91	45.94	45.98	46.02	46.07
安宁市	Anning	38.43	39.82	41.31	42.88	44.29	45.42	47.33	48.38
曲靖市	**Qujing**	**584.5**	**583.7**	**582.5**	**581.8**	**581.2**	**579.8**	**578.4**	**576.6**
麒麟区	Qilin	82.55	85.24	87.67	90.83	93.94	95.76	98.27	99.63
沾益区	Zhanyi	42.27	42.04	41.71	41.42	41.11	40.87	40.69	40.53
马龙区	Malong	18.81	18.92	19.03	19.11	19.19	19.24	19.28	19.31
陆良县	Luliang	61.51	61.27	61.02	60.84	60.61	60.35	60.13	59.93
师宗县	Shizong	38.75	38.58	38.41	38.22	38.08	37.94	37.83	37.69
罗平县	Luoping	54.55	54.40	54.24	54.11	53.96	53.81	53.68	53.56
富源县	Fuyuan	70.88	70.42	69.99	69.56	69.10	68.53	67.99	67.52
会泽县	Huize	87.35	86.09	85.15	83.77	82.56	81.78	80.42	79.43
宣威市	Xuanwei	127.83	126.74	125.28	123.94	122.65	121.52	120.11	118.98
玉溪市	**Yuxi**	**229.4**	**228.9**	**228.2**	**227.8**	**227.3**	**226.6**	**225.9**	**225.0**
红塔区	Hongta	52.34	53.25	54.19	55.20	56.21	57.14	58.09	58.87
江川区	Jiangchuan	27.32	27.06	26.75	26.49	26.22	25.93	25.63	25.33
通海县	Tonghai	30.22	30.02	29.71	29.58	29.50	29.37	29.16	28.99
华宁县	Huaning	20.81	20.57	20.29	20.06	19.83	19.57	19.31	19.04
易门县	Yimen	16.94	16.68	16.38	16.16	15.91	15.66	15.42	15.17
峨山县	Ershan	15.64	15.53	15.44	15.25	15.03	14.80	14.61	14.39
新平县	Xinping	27.99	27.76	27.47	27.27	27.03	26.78	26.52	26.28
元江县	Yuanjiang	21.20	20.99	20.75	20.54	20.30	20.05	19.81	19.56
澄江市	Chengjiang	16.94	17.05	17.22	17.24	17.28	17.30	17.36	17.32

18-3 续表1 continued

单位：万人 (10 000 persons)

州市县	Region	2013	2014	2015	2016	2017	2018	2019	2020
保山市	**Baoshan**	**249.1**	**248.3**	**247.5**	**246.8**	**246.2**	**245.2**	**244.2**	**243.1**
隆阳区	Longyang	92.59	92.20	91.83	91.59	91.40	91.25	90.68	90.30
施甸县	Shidian	30.27	30.14	30.02	29.94	29.86	29.61	29.47	29.30
龙陵县	Longling	27.74	27.71	27.68	27.67	27.65	27.52	27.50	27.28
昌宁县	Changning	33.94	33.73	33.48	33.16	32.87	32.45	32.25	31.99
腾冲市	Tengchong	64.57	64.52	64.49	64.45	64.42	64.36	64.30	64.24
昭通市	**Zhaotong**	**519.2**	**518.1**	**516.6**	**515.5**	**514.6**	**512.9**	**511.3**	**509.3**
昭阳区	Zhaoyang	82.24	83.33	84.43	85.51	87.32	88.52	89.79	91.18
鲁甸县	Ludian	39.41	39.50	39.50	39.52	39.72	39.76	39.80	39.84
巧家县	Qiaojia	50.13	49.66	49.32	48.67	47.94	47.39	46.84	46.22
盐津县	Yanjin	35.79	35.31	34.73	34.36	33.62	33.07	32.53	31.75
大关县	Daguan	24.95	24.43	23.89	23.39	22.87	22.26	21.64	20.91
永善县	Yongshan	38.32	37.88	37.41	36.99	36.48	35.97	35.46	34.92
绥江县	Suijiang	14.93	14.76	14.60	14.46	14.20	14.01	13.83	13.55
镇雄县	Zhenxiong	133.71	134.02	134.18	134.36	134.63	134.73	134.85	134.98
彝良县	Yiliang	51.73	51.52	51.24	51.18	51.14	50.86	50.57	50.34
威信县	Weixin	37.74	37.42	37.02	36.77	36.37	36.01	35.64	35.23
水富市	Shuifu	10.26	10.27	10.28	10.29	10.31	10.32	10.33	10.35
丽江市	**Lijiang**	**125.1**	**125.3**	**125.3**	**125.4**	**125.6**	**125.6**	**125.6**	**125.5**
古城区	Gucheng	23.64	24.42	25.23	25.99	26.71	27.42	28.21	28.88
玉龙县	Yulong	22.00	22.13	22.23	22.37	22.50	22.65	22.42	22.41
永胜县	Yongsheng	37.30	36.32	35.71	35.18	34.93	34.52	34.13	33.79
华坪县	Huaping	16.58	16.94	16.85	16.73	16.53	16.23	16.14	15.97
宁蒗县	Ninglang	25.60	25.49	25.31	25.15	24.95	24.81	24.72	24.45
普洱市	**Pu'er**	**250.8**	**249.4**	**247.9**	**246.6**	**245.4**	**243.8**	**242.2**	**240.5**
思茅区	Simao	33.65	34.80	35.94	37.00	39.63	39.89	40.46	41.60
宁洱县	Ning'er	18.10	17.91	17.69	17.47	17.04	16.90	16.56	16.30
墨江县	Mojiang	33.71	32.94	32.14	31.33	30.03	29.57	29.00	28.20
景东县	Jingdong	34.25	33.70	33.15	32.54	31.99	31.41	30.93	30.30
景谷县	Jinggu	28.65	28.49	28.32	28.18	28.05	27.85	27.82	27.70
镇沅县	Zhenyuan	19.98	19.70	19.41	19.16	18.91	18.58	18.30	18.00
江城县	Jiangcheng	11.98	11.88	11.77	11.65	11.58	11.44	11.24	11.10
孟连县	Menglian	13.92	14.02	14.11	14.23	14.38	14.44	14.47	14.50
澜沧县	Lancang	47.56	46.99	46.43	46.19	44.96	44.90	44.65	44.10
西盟县	Ximeng	8.99	8.97	8.94	8.86	8.83	8.82	8.77	8.70
临沧市	**Lincang**	**238.4**	**236.7**	**234.8**	**233.2**	**231.6**	**229.7**	**227.8**	**225.8**
临翔区	Linxiang	33.75	34.21	34.68	35.15	35.63	36.11	36.60	37.10
凤庆县	Fengqing	43.64	42.31	41.72	41.05	40.40	39.75	39.05	38.54

18-3 续表2 continued

单位：万人

(10 000 persons)

州市县	Region	2013	2014	2015	2016	2017	2018	2019	2020
云　县	Yunxian	42.91	42.66	41.61	41.03	40.62	40.07	39.44	38.92
永德县	Yongde	35.67	35.29	34.88	34.52	34.16	33.74	33.33	32.89
镇康县	Zhenkang	18.03	18.16	18.28	18.15	17.96	17.74	17.52	17.29
双江县	Shuangjiang	17.35	17.28	17.19	17.10	16.90	16.75	16.69	16.47
耿马县	Gengma	29.68	29.60	29.45	29.39	29.30	29.10	28.95	28.57
沧源县	Cangyuan	17.37	17.19	16.99	16.81	16.64	16.44	16.23	16.02
楚雄州	**Chuxiong**	**260.9**	**258.2**	**255.3**	**252.7**	**250.2**	**247.4**	**244.6**	**241.7**
楚雄市	Chuxiong	60.53	60.90	61.30	61.68	62.04	62.38	62.82	63.15
双柏县	Shuangbai	15.08	14.84	14.58	14.32	14.11	13.88	13.62	13.39
牟定县	Mouding	18.98	18.41	17.79	17.23	16.70	16.13	15.51	14.94
南华县	Nanhua	22.70	22.36	22.00	21.70	21.41	21.08	20.73	20.37
姚安县	Yao'an	18.80	18.47	18.12	17.81	17.52	17.18	16.80	16.42
大姚县	Dayao	26.03	25.58	25.11	24.65	24.24	23.80	23.35	22.90
永仁县	Yongren	10.61	10.49	10.36	10.25	10.14	10.03	9.92	9.80
元谋县	Yuanmou	21.14	21.01	20.87	20.75	20.64	20.46	20.30	20.15
武定县	Wuding	26.34	26.03	25.69	25.37	25.03	24.68	24.30	23.91
禄丰县	Lufeng	40.70	40.12	39.49	38.94	38.38	37.81	37.27	36.65
红河州	**Honghe**	**450.7**	**450.5**	**450.1**	**450.0**	**450.0**	**449.4**	**448.8**	**447.8**
个旧市	Gejiu	45.97	45.91	45.87	45.75	45.41	45.07	43.08	41.93
开远市	Kaiyuan	32.98	33.13	33.23	33.35	33.55	33.71	32.72	32.30
蒙自市	Mengzi	44.03	44.83	45.61	47.83	48.77	49.90	55.15	58.60
弥勒市	Mile	54.10	54.09	54.21	54.09	54.15	54.12	53.98	53.81
屏边县	Pingbian	14.77	14.57	14.32	13.77	13.67	13.48	13.22	12.94
建水县	Jianshui	53.66	53.79	53.87	53.89	54.03	54.02	53.69	53.42
石屏县	Shiping	29.28	29.01	28.78	28.45	28.32	27.99	27.60	27.20
泸西县	Luxi	39.42	39.18	38.92	38.57	38.33	38.11	38.82	38.91
元阳县	Yuanyang	38.85	38.52	38.14	37.64	37.28	36.86	36.44	35.92
红河县	Honghe	29.79	29.84	29.83	29.76	29.84	29.86	28.92	28.46
金平县	Jinping	35.69	35.59	35.48	35.27	35.19	35.04	33.83	33.14
绿春县	Luchun	21.81	21.68	21.52	21.34	21.18	20.97	21.12	21.02
河口县	Hekou	10.36	10.36	10.33	10.29	10.28	10.27	10.23	10.20
文山州	**Wenshan**	**352.4**	**352.3**	**352.0**	**351.9**	**351.9**	**351.5**	**351.0**	**350.3**
文山市	Wenshan	52.13	53.56	54.85	56.34	57.74	58.97	60.29	62.38
砚山县	Yanshan	46.96	47.10	47.24	47.38	47.55	47.65	47.65	47.66
西畴县	Xichou	24.04	23.51	23.00	22.47	21.95	21.47	20.99	20.36
麻栗坡县	Malipo	26.89	26.55	26.19	25.84	25.50	25.17	24.82	24.36
马关县	Maguan	35.46	34.97	34.47	33.98	33.49	33.02	32.52	31.87

18-3 续表3 continued

单位：万人 (10 000 persons)

州市县	Region	2013	2014	2015	2016	2017	2018	2019	2020
丘北县	Qiubei	47.70	47.61	47.50	47.41	47.34	47.25	47.11	46.82
广南县	Guangnan	78.53	78.40	78.26	78.13	78.05	77.84	77.65	77.19
富宁县	Funing	40.70	40.59	40.48	40.37	40.28	40.13	39.96	39.68
西双版纳州	**Xishuangbanna**	**118.6**	**120.2**	**121.9**	**123.6**	**125.4**	**127.1**	**128.8**	**130.4**
景洪市	Jinghong	55.60	56.70	58.00	59.30	60.70	62.00	63.40	64.40
勐海县	Menghai	33.90	34.20	34.40	34.60	34.80	35.00	35.20	35.44
勐腊县	Mengla	29.10	29.30	29.50	29.70	29.90	30.10	30.20	30.56
大理州	**Dali**	**343.0**	**341.9**	**340.5**	**339.4**	**338.4**	**336.9**	**335.5**	**333.8**
大理市	Dali	68.85	69.92	71.09	72.40	73.61	74.98	76.29	77.11
漾濞县	Yangbi	10.07	10.00	9.93	9.87	9.85	9.83	9.82	9.76
祥云县	Xiangyun	44.23	43.78	43.26	42.94	42.55	41.75	41.18	40.66
宾川县	Binchuan	34.74	34.70	34.63	34.45	34.38	34.32	34.27	34.13
弥渡县	Midu	29.71	29.16	28.55	27.96	27.41	27.09	26.59	26.12
南涧县	Nanjian	20.86	20.76	20.62	20.47	20.36	19.86	19.53	19.29
巍山县	Weishan	29.25	28.85	28.40	27.97	27.51	27.40	27.09	26.75
永平县	Yongping	17.39	17.34	17.24	17.16	17.09	16.81	16.59	16.46
云龙县	Yunlong	19.53	19.37	19.19	19.01	18.84	18.67	18.47	18.30
洱源县	Eryuan	26.40	26.25	26.05	25.87	25.69	25.32	25.05	24.81
剑川县	Jianchuan	16.76	16.68	16.56	16.44	16.33	16.28	16.16	16.05
鹤庆县	Heqing	25.22	25.11	24.98	24.86	24.79	24.59	24.45	24.30
德宏州	**Dehong**	**124.6**	**125.7**	**126.7**	**127.8**	**128.9**	**129.9**	**130.9**	**131.8**
瑞丽市	Ruili	20.81	21.92	22.81	23.55	24.39	25.12	26.15	26.43
芒市	Mangshi	40.53	40.88	41.20	41.80	42.44	43.18	43.44	44.09
梁河县	Lianghe	14.97	14.67	14.49	14.34	14.14	13.90	13.71	13.73
盈江县	Yingjiang	30.12	30.01	29.92	29.82	29.64	29.45	29.38	29.35
陇川县	Longchuan	18.18	18.22	18.27	18.29	18.29	18.25	18.22	18.20
怒江州	**Nujiang**	**54.1**	**54.3**	**54.5**	**54.7**	**54.9**	**55.0**	**55.2**	**55.3**
泸水市	Lushui	19.08	19.33	19.55	19.78	19.98	20.11	20.32	20.41
福贡县	Fugong	10.37	10.53	10.69	10.82	10.99	11.12	11.27	11.44
贡山县	Gongshan	3.81	3.82	3.82	3.83	3.83	3.84	3.84	3.85
兰坪县	Lanping	20.84	20.62	20.44	20.27	20.10	19.93	19.77	19.60
迪庆州	**Diqing**	**39.7**	**39.6**	**39.5**	**39.4**	**39.3**	**39.1**	**38.9**	**38.8**
香格里拉市	Shangri-La	17.58	17.60	17.66	17.80	17.94	18.04	18.30	18.64
德钦县	Deqing	6.25	5.98	5.87	5.80	5.71	5.65	5.54	5.47
维西县	Weixi	15.87	16.02	15.97	15.80	15.65	15.41	15.07	14.64

18－4　各州市县人口数及构成（2020年）

Population and Its Composition by Region (2020)

单位：万户、万人　　(10 000 households，10 000 persons)

州市县	Region	总户数 Total Number of Households	总人口 Total Population	按性别分 By Sex 男 Male	女 Female
全　省	**Yunnan**	**1644.50**	**4 722.0**	**2 442.6**	**2 279.4**
昆明市	**Kunming**	**351.48**	**846.3**	**432.9**	**413.4**
五华区	Wuhua	49.75	114.40	56.08	58.32
盘龙区	Panlong	43.43	98.80	49.94	48.86
官渡区	Guandu	72.70	160.26	85.42	74.84
西山区	Xishan	42.99	96.10	48.46	47.64
东川区	Dongchuan	10.00	26.10	13.44	12.66
呈贡区	Chenggong	26.34	65.06	33.16	31.90
晋宁区	Jinning	13.30	34.63	17.55	17.07
富民县	Fumin	5.29	14.95	7.82	7.13
宜良县	Yiliang	14.88	38.49	19.50	18.99
石林县	Shilin	8.22	24.08	12.28	11.81
嵩明县	Songming	14.62	41.09	20.87	20.22
禄劝县	Luquan	14.58	37.89	19.21	18.68
寻甸县	Xundian	15.35	46.07	23.48	22.59
安宁市	Anning	20.04	48.38	25.73	22.65
曲靖市	**Qujing**	**207.13**	**576.6**	**298.9**	**277.7**
麒麟区	Qilin	37.75	99.63	49.98	49.65
沾益区	Zhanyi	13.68	40.53	21.02	19.51
马龙区	Malong	6.43	19.31	10.09	9.22
陆良县	Luliang	21.94	59.93	30.99	28.94
师宗县	Shizong	11.11	37.69	19.60	18.09
罗平县	Luoping	18.20	53.56	27.96	25.60
富源县	Fuyuan	20.81	67.52	35.42	32.10
会泽县	Huize	30.42	79.43	41.67	37.76
宣威市	Xuanwei	46.78	118.98	62.13	56.85
玉溪市	**Yuxi**	**78.84**	**225.0**	**115.5**	**109.4**
红塔区	Hongta	21.29	58.87	29.41	29.46
江川区	Jiangchuan	8.64	25.33	12.96	12.37

18-4 续表1 continued

单位：万户、万人 (10 000 households、10 000 persons)

州市县	Region	总户数 Total Number of Households	总人口 Total Population	按性别分 By Sex 男 Male	女 Female
通海县	Tonghai	9.39	28.99	14.76	14.23
华宁县	Huaning	6.62	19.04	9.85	9.19
易门县	Yimen	5.68	15.17	7.93	7.24
峨山县	Ershan	5.00	14.39	7.51	6.88
新平县	Xinping	9.00	26.28	13.75	12.52
元江县	Yuanjiang	6.80	19.56	10.29	9.27
澄江市	Chengjiang	6.42	17.32	9.06	8.26
保山市	**Baoshan**	**73.81**	**243.1**	**124.8**	**118.3**
隆阳区	Longyang	28.25	90.30	45.68	44.62
施甸县	Shidian	8.77	29.30	15.02	14.28
龙陵县	Longling	7.95	27.28	14.38	12.90
昌宁县	Changning	9.68	31.99	16.39	15.60
腾冲市	Tengchong	19.16	64.24	33.31	30.93
昭通市	**Zhaotong**	**165.46**	**509.3**	**267.2**	**242.1**
昭阳区	Zhaoyang	30.86	91.18	46.61	44.57
鲁甸县	Ludian	13.30	39.84	20.90	18.94
巧家县	Qiaojia	16.18	46.22	24.96	21.26
盐津县	Yanjin	9.46	31.75	16.76	14.99
大关县	Daguan	6.82	20.91	11.12	9.79
永善县	Yongshan	12.11	34.92	18.43	16.49
绥江县	Suijiang	4.64	13.55	7.01	6.54
镇雄县	Zhenxiong	41.45	134.98	71.17	63.81
彝良县	Yiliang	15.33	50.34	26.60	23.74
威信县	Weixin	11.46	35.23	18.35	16.88
水富市	Shuifu	3.85	10.35	5.27	5.08
丽江市	**Lijiang**	**42.17**	**125.5**	**64.7**	**60.8**
古城区	Gucheng	11.77	28.88	14.65	14.23
玉龙县	Yulong	7.26	22.41	11.64	10.77
永胜县	Yongsheng	10.39	33.79	17.25	16.54
华坪县	Huaping	5.24	15.97	8.39	7.58

18-4 续表2 continued

单位：万户、万人 (10 000 households、10 000 persons)

州市县	Region	总户数 Total Number of Households	总人口 Total Population	按性别分 By Sex 男 Male	女 Female
宁蒗县	Ninglang	7.51	24.45	12.76	11.69
普洱市	**Pu'er**	**82.66**	**240.5**	**126.5**	**114.0**
思茅区	Simao	16.13	41.60	21.29	20.31
宁洱县	Ning'er	5.71	16.30	8.48	7.82
墨江县	Mojiang	9.47	28.20	15.23	12.97
景东县	Jingdong	10.03	30.30	15.84	14.46
景谷县	Jinggu	9.32	27.70	14.61	13.09
镇沅县	Zhenyuan	6.29	18.00	9.65	8.35
江城县	Jiangcheng	3.81	11.10	5.87	5.23
孟连县	Menglian	4.72	14.50	7.57	6.93
澜沧县	Lancang	14.20	44.10	23.35	20.75
西盟县	Ximeng	2.99	8.70	4.58	4.12
临沧市	**Lincang**	**70.98**	**225.8**	**118.1**	**107.7**
临翔区	Linxiang	12.15	37.10	18.96	18.14
凤庆县	Fengqing	11.84	38.54	19.77	18.77
云　县	Yunxian	12.42	38.92	20.49	18.43
永德县	Yongde	9.80	32.89	17.54	15.35
镇康县	Zhenkang	5.25	17.29	9.27	8.02
双江县	Shuangjiang	5.28	16.47	8.66	7.81
耿马县	Gengma	8.82	28.57	15.01	13.56
沧源县	Cangyuan	5.41	16.02	8.43	7.59
楚雄州	**Chuxiong**	**88.14**	**241.7**	**123.5**	**118.2**
楚雄市	Chuxiong	23.82	63.15	31.64	31.52
双柏县	Shuangbai	5.30	13.39	7.09	6.30
牟定县	Mouding	5.74	14.94	7.71	7.24
南华县	Nanhua	7.43	20.37	10.28	10.09
姚安县	Yao'an	5.86	16.42	8.48	7.94
大姚县	Dayao	8.10	22.90	11.68	11.21
永仁县	Yongren	3.51	9.80	5.12	4.68

18-4 续表3 continued

单位：万户、万人 (10 000 households, 10 000 persons)

州市县	Region	总户数 Total Number of Households	总人口 Total Population	按性别分 By Sex 男 Male	女 Female
元谋县	Yuanmou	6.88	20.15	10.38	9.77
武定县	Wuding	8.23	23.91	12.13	11.77
禄丰县	Lufeng	13.25	36.65	18.99	17.67
红河州	**Honghe**	**149.04**	**447.8**	**232.0**	**215.8**
个旧市	Gejiu	16.05	41.93	21.57	20.36
开远市	Kaiyuan	12.05	32.30	16.58	15.72
蒙自市	Mengzi	20.91	58.60	29.75	28.85
弥勒市	Mile	19.40	53.81	27.91	25.90
屏边县	Pingbian	4.61	12.94	6.84	6.10
建水县	Jianshui	17.14	53.42	27.47	25.95
石屏县	Shiping	9.44	27.20	13.78	13.42
泸西县	Luxi	12.01	38.91	20.45	18.46
元阳县	Yuanyang	10.40	35.92	18.86	17.06
红河县	Honghe	7.80	28.46	14.68	13.78
金平县	Jinping	9.63	33.14	17.67	15.47
绿春县	Luchun	5.71	21.02	11.02	10.00
河口县	Hekou	3.91	10.20	5.44	4.76
文山州	**Wenshan**	**104.38**	**350.3**	**182.5**	**167.8**
文山市	Wenshan	20.10	62.38	31.74	30.64
砚山县	Yanshan	13.80	47.66	24.82	22.84
西畴县	Xichou	6.45	20.36	10.79	9.57
麻栗坡县	Malipo	7.78	24.36	12.99	11.37
马关县	Maguan	10.17	31.87	16.78	15.09
丘北县	Qiubei	13.24	46.82	24.54	22.28
广南县	Guangnan	21.05	77.19	40.40	36.79
富宁县	Funing	11.79	39.68	20.44	19.24
西双版纳州	**Xishuangbanna**	**44.91**	**130.4**	**68.6**	**61.8**
景洪市	Jinghong	24.39	64.40	34.03	30.37
勐海县	Menghai	10.39	35.44	18.42	17.02

18-4 续表4 continued

单位：万户、万人 (10 000 households, 10 000 persons)

州市县	Region	总户数 Total Number of Households	总人口 Total Population	按性别分 By Sex 男 Male	女 Female
勐腊县	Mengla	10.14	30.56	16.16	14.40
大 理 州	**Dali**	**110.94**	**333.8**	**169.3**	**164.4**
大理市	Dali	28.85	77.11	38.76	38.35
漾濞县	Yangbi	3.17	9.76	5.06	4.70
祥云县	Xiangyun	13.34	40.66	20.60	20.06
宾川县	Binchuan	10.40	34.13	17.54	16.59
弥渡县	Midu	8.85	26.12	13.20	12.92
南涧县	Nanjian	6.25	19.29	9.80	9.50
巍山县	Weishan	8.74	26.75	13.53	13.21
永平县	Yongping	5.17	16.46	8.41	8.05
云龙县	Yunlong	5.90	18.30	9.48	8.81
洱源县	Eryuan	7.81	24.81	12.50	12.31
剑川县	Jianchuan	4.69	16.05	8.14	7.91
鹤庆县	Heqing	7.76	24.30	12.32	11.99
德 宏 州	**Dehong**	**44.05**	**131.8**	**68.7**	**63.1**
瑞丽市	Ruili	10.35	26.43	14.47	11.96
芒　市	Mangshi	14.20	44.09	22.56	21.53
梁河县	Lianghe	4.53	13.73	7.10	6.63
盈江县	Yingjiang	9.10	29.35	15.15	14.20
陇川县	Longchuan	5.87	18.20	9.46	8.75
怒 江 州	**Nujiang**	**17.80**	**55.3**	**29.0**	**26.3**
泸水市	Lushui	6.77	20.41	10.76	9.65
福贡县	Fugong	3.28	11.44	5.92	5.52
贡山县	Gongshan	1.35	3.85	2.06	1.79
兰坪县	Lanping	6.39	19.60	10.22	9.38
迪 庆 州	**Diqing**	**12.71**	**38.8**	**20.3**	**18.4**
香格里拉市	Shangri-La	6.24	18.64	9.78	8.86
德钦县	Deqing	1.60	5.47	2.83	2.64
维西县	Weixi	4.87	14.64	7.70	6.94

18-5 各州市县土地、气温、降水量（2020年）

Land Characteristics, Temperature and Precipitation By Region (2020)

州 市	Region	土地调查面积（万平方千米） Area under Land Survey (10 000 sq.km)	牧草地面积（万公顷） Area of Grazing Land (10 000 hectares)	年平均气温（℃） Annual Average Temperature(℃)	年降水量（毫米） Annual Precipitation(mm)
全 省	**Yunnan**	**38.32**	**14.69**	**17.6**	**1 001.1**
昆 明 市	**Kunming**	**2.10**	**0.29**	**17.0**	**850.1**
五华区	Wuhua	0.04	0.06	16.5	1 062.2
盘龙区	Panlong	0.03			
官渡区	Guandu	0.06			
西山区	Xishan	0.09			
东川区	Dongchuan	0.19		21.2	560.9
呈贡区	Chenggong	0.05		16.4	927.6
晋宁区	Jinning	0.13	0.01	16.0	885.7
富民县	Fumin	0.10		17.2	882.7
宜良县	Yiliang	0.19	0.01	17.7	836.5
石林县	Shilin	0.17		17.3	849.2
嵩明县	Songming	0.13		15.6	868.8
禄劝县	Luquan	0.42		16.7	904.0
寻甸县	Xundian	0.36	0.21	15.7	729.7
安宁市	Anning	0.13		16.6	844.3
曲 靖 市	**Qujing**	**2.89**	**0.88**	**15.1**	**922.6**
麒麟区	Qilin	0.15	0.05	16.3	695.5
沾益区	Zhanyi	0.28		16.0	664.5
马龙区	Malong	0.16	0.01	14.5	611.5
陆良县	Luliang	0.20		15.9	796.5
师宗县	Shizong	0.28		14.4	1 145.7
罗平县	Luoping	0.30		16.3	1 658.1
富源县	Fuyuan	0.33		14.4	866.2
会泽县	Huize	0.59	0.80	13.5	765.1
宣威市	Xuanwei	0.61	0.02	14.7	1 100.1
玉 溪 市	**Yuxi**	**1.49**	**0.02**	**18.3**	**720.5**
红塔区	Hongta	0.09		17.4	777.1
江川区	Jiangchuan	0.08		17.6	712.6
通海县	Tonghai	0.07		16.9	789.6
华宁县	Huaning	0.12		17.1	618.4
易门县	Yimen	0.15		17.5	542.4
峨山县	Eshan	0.19		17.2	659.0
新平县	Xinping	0.43		18.5	880.3
元江县	Yuanjiang	0.27		25.1	543.9
澄江市	Chengjiang	0.08	0.02	17.2	961.3

注：由于全国第三次国土调查数据尚未公布，本表土地调查面积和牧草地面积数据使用的是2018年数据。

Note: Since the data of the Third National Land Survey have not been released, data of Area under Land Survey and Area of Grazing Land in this table are from 2018.

18−5 续表1 continued

州 市	Region	土地调查面积（万平方千米）Area under Land Survey (10 000 sq.km)	牧草地面积（万公顷）Area of Grazing Land (10 000 hectares)	年平均气温（℃）Annual Average Temperature (℃)	年降水量（毫米）Annual Precipitation (mm)
保 山 市	**Baoshan**	**1.91**	**0.15**	**16.8**	**1 251.7**
隆阳区	Longyang	0.49		17.9	821.5
施甸县	Shidian	0.20		18.6	866.8
龙陵县	Longling	0.28	0.07	16.3	2 033.0
昌宁县	Changning	0.38		15.4	1 099.9
腾冲市	Tengchong	0.57	0.08	15.6	1 437.5
昭 通 市	**Zhaotong**	**2.24**	**1.66**	**15.9**	**906.7**
昭阳区	Zhaoyang	0.22		12.9	704.7
鲁甸县	Ludian	0.15		12.9	791.9
巧家县	Qiaojia	0.32	0.65	22.1	960.4
盐津县	Yanjin	0.20		18.2	1 011.4
大关县	Daguan	0.17		15.0	945.9
永善县	Yongshan	0.28	0.91	16.6	668.1
绥江县	Suijiang	0.07		18.2	1 123.9
镇雄县	Zhenxiong	0.37	0.02	12.7	839.3
彝良县	Yiliang	0.28	0.08	16.6	792.4
威信县	Weixin	0.14		13.4	1 228.6
水富市	Shuifu	0.04			
丽 江 市	**Lijiang**	**2.06**	**1.80**	**15.6**	**1 009.2**
古城区	Gucheng	0.13	0.01		
玉龙县	Yulong	0.62	1.45	14.0	892.3
永胜县	Yongsheng	0.49	0.09	14.8	960.6
华坪县	Huaping	0.21		20.4	1 209.9
宁蒗县	Ninglang	0.60	0.25	13.2	974.0
普 洱 市	**Pu'er**	**4.43**	**0.08**	**19.9**	**1 378.8**
思茅区	Simao	0.39	0.01	20.2	1 243.2
宁洱县	Ning'er	0.37		18.8	1 130.0
墨江县	Mojiang	0.53		18.4	1 341.2
景东县	Jingdong	0.45	0.01	20.1	974.9
景谷县	Jinggu	0.75		21.1	1 155.4
镇沅县	Zhenyuan	0.41		20.3	1 198.6
江城县	Jiangcheng	0.34		19.0	2 304.7
孟连县	Menglian	0.19		20.6	1 328.9
澜沧县	Lancang	0.87	0.05	20.8	1 543.8
西盟县	Ximeng	0.13		20.1	1 567.2
临 沧 市	**Lincang**	**2.36**	**0.20**	**19.3**	**1 183.1**
临翔区	Linxiang	0.26	0.01	17.7	1 237.0
凤庆县	Fengqing	0.33		17.8	1 242.9
云 县	Yunxian	0.37		21.2	712.1
永德县	Yongde	0.32		18.3	1 144.3

18-5 续表2 Continued

州 市	Region	土地调查面积（万平方千米） Area under Land Survey (10 000 sq.km)	牧草地面积（万公顷） Area of Grazing Land (10 000 hectares)	年平均气温（℃） Annual Average Temperature (℃)	年降水量（毫米） Annual Precipitation (mm)
镇康县	Zhenkang	0.25	0.18	20.2	1 585.8
双江县	Shuangjiang	0.22		20.9	824.3
耿马县	Gengma	0.37		19.7	1 197.1
沧源县	Cangyuan	0.24		18.7	1 521.3
楚 雄 州	**Chuxiong**	**2.84**		**17.6**	**701.5**
楚雄市	Chuxiong	0.44		17.6	709.7
双柏县	Shuangbai	0.39		16.3	804.2
牟定县	Mouding	0.14		16.8	782.1
南华县	Nanhua	0.23		15.4	799.5
姚安县	Yao'an	0.17		16.8	715.9
大姚县	Dayao	0.40		17.2	595.9
永仁县	Yongren	0.22		18.8	609.3
元谋县	Yuanmou	0.20		22.6	445.5
武定县	Wuding	0.29		17.0	806.5
禄丰县	Lufeng	0.36		17.0	746.8
红 河 州	**Honghe**	**3.22**	**0.09**	**19.6**	**1 140.5**
个旧市	Gejiu	0.16	0.02	16.0	757.8
开远市	Kaiyuan	0.19		20.9	602.0
蒙自市	Mengzi	0.22		19.8	438.7
弥勒市	Mile	0.39		18.5	836.5
屏边县	Pingbian	0.18		17.4	1 755.7
建水县	Jianshui	0.38		20.0	681.2
石屏县	Shiping	0.30		18.7	871.5
泸西县	Luxi	0.16		16.4	784.6
元阳县	Yuanyang	0.22		25.0	718.8
红河县	Honghe	0.20		21.6	726.8
金平县	Jinping	0.36	0.06	18.9	2 378.8
绿春县	Luchun	0.31		17.9	2 155.1
河口县	Hekou	0.13		24.2	2 118.8
文 山 州	**Wenshan**	**3.14**	**0.14**	**18.3**	**1 082.0**
文山市	Wenshan	0.30		18.8	1 006.8
砚山县	Yanshan	0.39	0.01	17.0	941.9
西畴县	Xichou	0.15		16.7	1 054.8
麻栗坡县	Malipo	0.24		18.7	885.2
马关县	Maguang	0.27		18.2	1 714.5
丘北县	Qiubei	0.50	0.10	17.6	830.0
广南县	Guangnan	0.77	0.03	18.1	1 007.8
富宁县	Funing	0.53		20.9	1 215.2

18−5 续表3 continued

州 市	Region	土地调查面积（万平方千米） Area under Land Survey (10 000 sq.km)	牧草地面积（万公顷） Area of Grazing Land (10 000 hectares)	年平均气温（℃） Annual Average Temperature (℃)	年降水量（毫米） Annual Precipitation (mm)
西双版纳州	**Xishuangbanna**	**1.91**	**0.01**	**21.9**	**1 064.9**
景洪市	Jinghong	0.69	0.01	23.9	877.7
勐海县	Menghai	0.54		19.3	1 070.9
勐腊县	Mengla	0.69		22.5	1 246.1
大 理 州	**Dali**	**2.83**	**0.22**	**16.8**	**790.6**
大理市	Dali	0.17	0.10	16.0	1 280.2
漾濞县	yangbi	0.19		17.0	880.6
祥云县	Xiangyun	0.24		16.7	758.8
宾川县	Binchuan	0.25		20.2	547.5
弥渡县	Midu	0.15		17.7	790.0
南涧县	Nanjian	0.17		19.8	679.0
巍山县	Weishan	0.22	0.01	16.9	629.1
永平县	Yongping	0.28		16.7	718.5
云龙县	Yunlong	0.44	0.11	16.4	659.3
洱源县	Eryuan	0.25		15.0	825.4
剑川县	Jianchuan	0.22		13.9	779.5
鹤庆县	Heqing	0.24		14.7	939.6
德 宏 州	**Dehong**	**1.12**	**0.04**	**20.3**	**1 470.9**
瑞丽市	Ruili	0.09		21.5	1 321.5
芒 市	Mangshi	0.29		21.0	1 511.7
梁河县	Lianghe	0.11		18.6	1 277.6
盈江县	Yingjiang	0.43	0.04	20.8	1 745.6
陇川县	Longchuan	0.19		19.6	1 497.9
怒 江 州	**Nujiang**	**1.46**	**0.41**	**16.3**	**1 225.6**
泸水市	Lushui	0.31		20.6	793.7
福贡县	Fugong	0.27		17.3	1 311.6
贡山县	Gongshan	0.44	0.06	15.1	1 829.6
兰坪县	Lanping	0.44	0.35	12.1	967.4
迪 庆 州	**Diqing**	**2.32**	**8.68**	**8.6**	**651.6**
香格里拉市	Shangri-La	1.14	6.46	6.6	599.6
德钦县	Deqing	0.73	0.11	6.8	552.5
维西县	Weixi	0.45	2.11	12.4	802.6

18-6 各州市县职工平均工资（2020年）
Average Wages of Staff and Workers by Region (2020)

单位：万元 (10 000 yuan)

州市县	Region	职工平均工资 Average Wage of Staff and Workers
全　省	**Yunnan**	**9.83**
昆明市	**Kunming**	**10.23**
五华区	Wuhua	11.07
盘龙区	Panlong	11.07
官渡区	Guandu	10.74
西山区	Xishan	11.38
东川区	Dongchuan	7.89
呈贡区	Chenggong	11.31
晋宁区	Jinning	9.16
富民县	Fuming	8.18
宜良县	Yiliang	7.72
石林县	Shilin	8.52
嵩明县	Songming	9.12
禄劝县	Luquan	9.22
寻甸县	Xundian	9.34
安宁市	Anning	9.70
曲靖市	**Qujing**	**8.91**
麒麟区	Qilin	9.32
沾益区	Zhanyi	9.57
马龙区	Malong	8.43
陆良县	Luliang	7.36
师宗县	Shizong	9.05
罗平县	Luoping	9.06
富源县	Fuyuan	8.13
会泽县	Huize	11.67
宣威市	Xuanwei	7.70
玉溪市	**Yuxi**	**9.81**
红塔区	Hongta	10.41
江川区	Jiangchuan	10.40
通海县	Tonghai	7.47
华宁县	Huaning	10.77
易门县	Yimen	10.09
峨山县	Eshan	9.33
新平县	Xinping	9.48
元江县	Yuanjiang	9.57
澄江市	Chengjiang	11.13

18-6 续表1 continued

单位：万元 (10 000 yuan)

州市县	Region	职工平均工资 Average Wage of Staff and Workers
保山市	**Baoshan**	**8.37**
隆阳区	Longyang	9.47
施甸县	Shidian	6.79
龙陵县	Longling	7.79
昌宁县	Changning	7.03
腾冲市	Tengchong	8.73
昭通市	**Zhaotong**	**9.49**
昭阳区	Zhaoyang	10.61
鲁甸县	Ludian	9.79
巧家县	Qiaojia	9.57
盐津县	Yanjin	9.29
大关县	Daguan	9.53
永善县	Yongshan	10.16
绥江县	Suijiang	7.87
镇雄县	Zhenxiong	8.33
彝良县	Yiliang	8.37
威信县	Weixin	8.49
水富市	Shuifu	8.31
丽江市	**Lijiang**	**10.06**
古城区	Gucheng	9.84
玉龙县	Yulong	10.32
永胜县	Yongsheng	10.73
华坪县	Huaping	9.11
宁蒗县	Ninglang	11.45
普洱市	**Pu'er**	**9.56**
思茅区	Simao	9.65
宁洱县	Ning'er	9.64
墨江县	Mojiang	11.25
景东县	Jingdong	9.08
景谷县	Jinggu	8.30
镇沅县	Zhenyuan	9.88
江城县	Jiangcheng	8.61
孟连县	Menglian	8.59
澜沧县	Lancang	9.64
西盟县	Ximeng	11.81
临沧市	**Lincang**	**9.83**
临翔区	Linxiang	9.74

18-6 续表2 continued

单位：万元 (10 000 yuan)

州市县	Region	职工平均工资 Average Wage of Staff and Workers
凤庆县	Fengqing	9.81
云　县	Yunxian	9.81
永德县	Yongde	9.95
镇康县	Zhenkang	9.64
双江县	Shuangjiang	9.83
耿马县	Gengma	9.81
沧源县	Cangyuan	9.86
楚 雄 州	**Chuxiong**	**8.95**
楚雄市	Chuxiong	9.19
双柏县	Shuangbai	8.24
牟定县	Mouding	8.69
南华县	Nanhua	9.06
姚安县	Yao'an	9.08
大姚县	Dayao	9.39
永仁县	Yongren	10.23
元谋县	Yuanmou	9.38
武定县	Wuding	8.61
禄丰县	Lufeng	8.18
红 河 州	**Honghe**	**8.42**
个旧市	Gejiu	7.53
开远市	Kaiyuan	7.06
蒙自市	Mengzi	9.08
弥勒市	Mile	9.98
屏边县	Pingbian	7.23
建水县	Jianshui	10.03
石屏县	Shiping	9.45
泸西县	Luxi	7.39
元阳县	Yuanyang	9.10
红河县	Honghe	7.28
金平县	Jinping	7.81
绿春县	Luchun	7.33
河口县	Hekou	7.40
文 山 州	**Wenshan**	**9.79**
文山市	Wenshan	10.24
砚山县	Yanshan	10.03

18-6 续表3 continued

单位：万元 (10 000 yuan)

州市县	Region	职工平均工资 Average Wage of Staff and Workers
西畴县	Xichou	9.07
麻栗坡县	Malipo	10.04
马关县	Maguan	10.95
丘北县	Qiubei	9.99
广南县	Guangnan	8.82
富宁县	Funing	9.67
西双版纳州	**Xishuangbanna**	**9.20**
景洪市	Jinghong	9.28
勐海县	Menghai	9.14
勐腊县	Mengla	9.04
大 理 州	**Dali**	**9.86**
大理市	Dali	9.27
漾濞县	Yangbi	10.71
祥云县	Xiangyun	10.15
宾川县	Binchuan	9.87
弥渡县	Midu	10.19
南涧县	Nanjian	9.96
巍山县	Weishan	10.89
永平县	Yongping	10.94
云龙县	Yunlong	10.58
洱源县	Eryuan	9.79
剑川县	Jianchuan	10.69
鹤庆县	Heqing	11.32
德 宏 州	**Dehong**	**8.94**
瑞丽市	Ruili	9.14
芒 市	Mangshi	9.49
梁河县	Lianghe	9.15
盈江县	Yingjiang	8.51
陇川县	Longchuan	8.26
怒 江 州	**Nujiang**	**10.02**
泸水市	Lushui	11.06
福贡县	Fugong	9.11
贡山县	Gongshan	9.83
兰坪县	Lanping	9.65
迪 庆 州	**Diqing**	**13.37**
香格里拉市	Shangri-La	12.85
德钦县	Deqin	16.96
维西县	Weixi	15.04

18-7 各州市县固定资产投资（不含农户）增长速度（2019-2020年）

Growth Rate of Total Investment in Fixed Assets (Exclude Rural Households) by Region (2019-2020)

单位：% (%)

州市县	Region	2019	2020	州市县	Region	2019	2020
全　省	**Yunnan**	**8.5**	**7.7**	**保山市**	**Baoshan**	**18.0**	**6.4**
昆明市	**Kunming**	**2.8**	**8.1**	隆阳区	Longyang	18.6	5.9
五华区	Wuhua	0.3	-2.3	施甸县	Shidian	2.2	-30.5
盘龙区	Panlong	-13.3	22.3	龙陵县	Longling	10.6	-8.7
官渡区	Guandu	0.6	14.6	昌宁县	Changning	8.0	0.7
西山区	Xishan	-1.6	10.4	腾冲市	Tengchong	35.1	31.0
东川区	Dongchuan	-32.2	27.0	**昭通市**	**Zhaotong**	**20.7**	**3.1**
呈贡区	Chenggong	13.8	5.9	昭阳区	Zhaoyang	18.1	-4.7
晋宁区	Jinning	-6.9	8.5	鲁甸县	Ludian	19.6	12.2
富民县	Fumin	29.0	6.7	巧家县	Qiaojia	-44.8	54.5
宜良县	Yiliang	-5.0	36.5	盐津县	Yanjin	-39.6	-37.1
石林县	Shilin	6.9	-30.2	大关县	Daguan	2.0	21.6
嵩明县	Songming	10.1	7.8	永善县	Yongshan	17.7	10.9
禄劝县	Luquan	27.0	-6.1	绥江县	Suijiang	28.3	18.2
寻甸县	Xundian	-4.1	-15.1	镇雄县	Zhenxiong	21.9	13.4
安宁市	Anning	19.1	22.5	彝良县	Yiliang	32.1	-26.1
曲靖市	**Qujing**	**13.5**	**10.6**	威信县	Weixin	-14.2	27.3
麒麟区	Qilin	20.9	20.3	水富市	Shuifu	-30.4	71.4
沾益区	Zhanyi	10.0	-19.4	**丽江市**	**Lijiang**	**20.2**	**12.3**
马龙区	Malong	11.4	32.5	古城区	Gucheng	21.7	20.2
陆良县	Luliang	23.1	14.5	玉龙县	Yulong	12.2	16.9
师宗县	Shizong	14.2	24.5	永胜县	Yongsheng	26.5	-9.2
罗平县	Luoping	27.3	24.8	华坪县	Huaping	-13.2	-24.4
富源县	Fuyuan	7.6	17.2	宁蒗县	Ninglang	93.4	50.0
会泽县	Huize	15.0	5.0	**普洱市**	**Pu'er**	**26.6**	**19.7**
宣威市	Xuanwei	2.5	8.4	思茅区	Simao	9.4	-26.6
玉溪市	**Yuxi**	**-8.8**	**-1.5**	宁洱县	Ning'er	32.0	39.3
红塔区	Hongta	-17.7	-8.1	墨江县	Mojiang	86.8	-26.1
江川区	Jiangchuan	6.7	-22.4	景东县	Jingdong	5.7	47.5
通海县	Tonghai	-5.5	5.0	景谷县	Jinggu	-26.2	30.9
华宁县	Huaning	3.9	2.2	镇沅县	Zhenyuan	91.5	64.8
易门县	Yimen	-19.1	-13.3	江城县	Jiangcheng	27.7	97.7
峨山县	Eshan	2.3	3.4	孟连县	Menglian	37.6	32.8
新平县	Xinping	-34.8	21.8	澜沧县	Lancang	39.0	50.0
元江县	Yuanjiang	5.8	-16.6	西盟县	Ximeng	12.1	19.9
澄江市	Chengjiang	0.7	19.4				

18-7 续表 continued

单位：% (%)

州市县	Region	2019	2020
临沧市	**Lincang**	**25.7**	**19.7**
临翔区	Linxiang	40.2	19.2
凤庆县	Fengqing	35.1	-4.8
云 县	Yunxian	26.2	9.1
永德县	Yongde	28.5	76.7
镇康县	Zhenkang	23.7	23.5
双江县	Shuangjiang	40.0	10.2
耿马县	Gengma	6.3	21.3
沧源县	Cangyuan	6.2	15.6
楚雄州	**Chuxiong**	**3.8**	**13.6**
楚雄市	Chuxiong	23.1	13.4
双柏县	Shuangbai	18.5	24.6
牟定县	Mouding	15.0	1.5
南华县	Nanhua	-33.5	23.0
姚安县	Yao'an	22.3	16.9
大姚县	Dayao	-28.1	20.7
永仁县	Yongren	23.0	2.1
元谋县	Yuanmou	22.0	16.6
武定县	Wuding	12.0	5.2
禄丰县	Lufeng	-16.9	14.1
红河州	**Honghe**	**1.4**	**6.0**
个旧市	Gejiu	10.5	6.3
开远市	Kaiyuan	12.7	5.0
蒙自市	Mengzi	15.2	2.7
弥勒市	Mile	-4.0	11.4
屏边县	Pingbian	-4.2	5.1
建水县	Jianshui	-35.4	8.5
石屏县	Shiping	15.1	17.6
泸西县	Luxi	3.1	-17.7
元阳县	Yuanyang	8.8	10.1
红河县	Honghe	-12.3	9.1
金平县	Jinping	6.8	14.0
绿春县	Luchun	-40.6	15.7
河口县	Hekou	14.1	12.3
文山州	**Wenshan**	**15.8**	**-3.6**
文山市	Wenshan	13.0	-51.0
砚山县	Yanshan	15.4	44.3
西畴县	Xichou	16.1	37.5
麻栗坡县	Malipo	18.5	17.9
马关县	Maguan	14.5	7.8
丘北县	Qiubei	20.2	18.2
广南县	Guangnan	20.2	21.7
富宁县	Funing	14.0	-2.8
西双版纳州	**Xishuangbanna**	**25.0**	**12.9**
景洪市	Jinghong	24.8	15.6
勐海县	Menghai	32.6	30.1
勐腊县	Mengla	21.8	-2.9
大理州	**Dali**	**11.5**	**9.0**
大理市	Dali	5.4	8.5
漾濞县	yangbi	32.9	20.0
祥云县	Xiangyun	20.7	12.3
宾川县	Binchuang	25.0	18.3
弥渡县	Midu	-29.7	4.9
南涧县	Nanjian	34.0	24.9
巍山县	Weishan	10.2	11.3
永平县	Yongping	14.9	7.9
云龙县	Yunlong	21.8	-10.6
洱源县	Eryuan	-9.0	0.3
剑川县	Jianchuan	33.6	22.9
鹤庆县	Heqing	21.5	-8.0
德宏州	**Dehong**	**10.4**	**15.5**
瑞丽市	Ruili	5.0	2.1
芒 市	Mangshi	7.8	38.7
梁河县	Lianghe	30.8	30.2
盈江县	Yingjiang	8.1	1.3
陇川县	Longchuan	23.5	16.5
怒江州	**Nujiang**	**17.2**	**11.0**
泸水市	Lushui	21.7	13.7
福贡县	Fugong	32.7	24.1
贡山县	Gongshan	19.6	6.5
兰坪县	Lanping	8.6	5.0
迪庆州	**Diqing**	**11.8**	**6.4**
香格里拉县	Shangri-La	13.8	6.4
德钦县	Deqin	10.8	6.3
维西县	Weixi	8.2	6.3
不分地区	**Trans-Regional**	**3.4**	**-13.4**

18-8 各州市县地方一般公共预算收入（2012-2020年）

Public Budgetary Revenue of Local Government by Region（2012-2020）

单位：亿元 (100 million yuan)

州市县	Region	2012	2013	2014	2015	2016	2017	2018	2019	2020
全　省	**Yunnan**	**1 338.15**	**1 611.30**	**1 698.06**	**1 808.15**	**1 812.29**	**1 886.17**	**1 994.35**	**2 073.56**	**2 116.69**
昆明市	**Kunming**	**378.40**	**450.75**	**477.97**	**502.22**	**530.00**	**560.86**	**595.63**	**630.03**	**650.47**
五华区	Wuhua	30.49	36.31	32.47	33.91	36.83	38.47	41.33	44.68	45.82
盘龙区	Panlong	27.20	33.25	33.40	35.19	38.03	39.34	41.40	43.81	44.99
官渡区	Guandu	37.78	45.00	41.54	41.78	38.84	39.94	43.29	48.41	49.65
西山区	Xishan	26.64	32.51	34.59	35.63	38.43	39.79	42.87	45.51	46.72
东川区	Dongchuan	6.79	6.93	7.10	5.53	6.13	6.67	7.29	5.88	6.23
呈贡区	Chenggong	9.07	11.07	14.29	17.49	20.49	21.06	23.94	25.34	27.37
晋宁区	Jinning	11.01	13.43	14.50	15.82	16.93	14.57	12.50	15.35	15.76
富民县	Fumin	3.43	4.27	4.73	4.80	5.18	5.29	5.47	5.80	6.02
宜良县	Yiliang	5.60	6.84	7.21	6.83	7.43	7.84	8.51	8.59	8.81
石林县	Shilin	6.15	7.45	5.13	5.60	6.13	6.17	6.49	6.89	6.22
嵩明县	Songming	7.39	9.03	9.70	10.48	11.53	10.80	12.02	12.12	13.11
禄劝县	Luquan	4.87	5.98	6.06	5.87	6.37	6.12	5.60	5.31	5.01
寻甸县	Xundian	5.93	7.24	7.62	6.18	6.77	6.80	6.19	6.54	7.03
安宁市	Anning	24.03	26.99	22.74	26.45	29.13	28.88	37.02	47.14	50.10
市本级	City-level	172.01	204.44	236.90	250.66	261.79	289.12	301.71	308.66	317.63
曲靖市	**Qujing**	**103.83**	**121.53**	**115.67**	**118.09**	**126.31**	**136.22**	**141.90**	**149.07**	**155.05**
麒麟区	Qilin	16.81	20.34	18.71	19.52	19.72	21.40	20.38	21.82	22.92
沾益区	Zhanyi	6.97	8.23	6.83	6.31	6.47	7.38	7.13	7.91	8.38
马龙区	Malong	3.52	4.13	4.31	4.51	4.55	5.19	5.62	6.09	6.52
陆良县	Luliang	5.42	6.37	6.38	6.61	7.07	7.78	8.41	9.26	9.87
师宗县	Shizong	4.40	5.16	5.22	5.39	5.44	5.90	6.39	6.88	7.23
罗平县	Luoping	5.08	6.11	6.70	7.03	7.20	7.80	8.43	8.93	9.03
富源县	Fuyuan	12.45	13.84	8.31	8.58	9.21	10.51	12.34	13.14	13.95
会泽县	Huize	8.00	9.40	10.10	10.78	11.05	11.94	13.13	14.06	14.13
宣威市	Xuanwei	12.50	14.70	15.00	11.28	12.07	13.06	14.19	15.12	15.59
市本级	City-level	28.68	33.25	34.12	38.10	43.52	45.26	45.89	45.86	47.43
玉溪市	**Yuxi**	**90.22**	**105.97**	**113.59**	**124.82**	**131.06**	**137.22**	**142.49**	**133.20**	**134.53**
红塔区	Hongta	13.21	18.46	19.63	20.01	21.59	16.59	17.90	18.08	18.69
江川区	Jiangchuan	3.54	4.61	5.02	5.40	5.82	7.10	7.84	5.37	5.67
通海县	Tonghai	3.54	4.14	4.41	4.79	5.19	5.58	5.15	3.95	4.12
华宁县	Huaning	2.51	3.13	3.46	3.73	3.95	4.21	4.39	3.15	3.27
易门县	Yimen	3.34	3.91	4.57	5.30	5.82	6.08	6.45	6.83	7.25
峨山县	Eshan	3.56	4.31	4.60	4.42	4.18	4.33	4.47	3.82	3.95
新平县	Xinping	8.32	10.00	10.95	11.22	12.06	12.67	13.44	13.02	12.88
元江县	Yuanjiang	2.55	3.15	3.40	3.68	4.24	4.88	4.36	4.52	3.86
澄江市	Chengjiang	3.88	4.66	5.41	5.87	7.33	8.76	9.51	9.22	7.96
市本级	City-level	45.77	49.59	52.16	60.40	60.88	67.03	68.97	65.24	66.87

注：本表中2016年起数据为新口径。

Note:Data in this table are new caliber since 2016.

18-8 续表1 continued

单位：亿元

(100 million yuan)

州市县	Region	2012	2013	2014	2015	2016	2017	2018	2019	2020
保山市	**Baoshan**	**35.55**	**42.84**	**47.18**	**52.24**	**57.51**	**62.32**	**66.16**	**67.22**	**65.54**
隆阳区	Longyang	8.78	10.07	12.91	15.35	16.79	17.89	19.25	19.79	19.80
施甸县	Shidian	2.29	3.06	3.74	4.45	5.21	5.64	5.71	6.13	6.13
龙陵县	Longling	2.67	3.47	4.21	4.86	5.37	5.85	6.44	6.53	5.93
昌宁县	Changning	5.21	5.97	4.43	4.70	5.26	5.70	5.94	6.42	5.93
腾冲市	Tengchong	12.10	14.92	15.30	15.94	16.57	16.99	17.56	18.96	16.60
市本级	City-level	4.50	5.34	6.58	6.95	8.30	10.25	11.25	9.39	11.14
昭通市	**Zhaotong**	**39.47**	**47.47**	**51.02**	**55.27**	**59.80**	**67.53**	**78.21**	**81.81**	**85.01**
昭阳区	Zhaoyang	7.71	9.01	10.61	11.46	11.60	11.38	13.09	14.04	15.06
鲁甸县	Ludian	2.26	2.49	2.07	2.63	3.06	4.01	4.78	4.79	4.10
巧家县	Qiaojia	1.72	2.15	2.67	3.08	3.45	3.80	4.41	5.00	5.32
盐津县	Yanjin	1.38	1.66	1.36	1.52	1.40	1.45	1.62	1.72	1.73
大关县	Daguan	0.87	1.06	1.18	1.24	1.14	1.19	1.23	1.26	1.14
永善县	Yongshan	2.24	2.88	3.78	4.44	6.57	7.74	7.91	7.57	7.59
绥江县	Suijiang	2.20	2.68	3.12	2.49	2.94	3.02	3.24	3.01	3.18
镇雄县	Zhenxiong	5.10	5.88	5.07	5.51	5.77	6.35	7.52	7.91	8.82
彝良县	Yiliang	2.20	2.32	2.41	2.84	2.94	3.32	4.21	5.07	5.19
威信县	Weixin	1.95	2.36	1.69	1.78	1.51	1.67	2.49	2.51	2.51
水富市	Shuifu	2.16	2.28	2.06	2.60	2.37	2.63	3.41	3.68	3.79
市本级	City-level	9.67	12.70	14.98	15.68	17.06	20.96	24.31	25.26	26.57
丽江市	**Lijiang**	**38.01**	**45.78**	**46.07**	**47.77**	**48.25**	**40.06**	**42.86**	**45.41**	**43.15**
古城区	Gucheng	9.19	10.79	12.42	13.33	13.76	10.06	10.27	10.78	10.11
玉龙县	Yulong	4.51	5.71	6.80	7.27	7.66	5.58	6.20	7.16	7.38
永胜县	Yongsheng	2.87	3.75	4.16	3.81	4.00	3.31	4.40	4.78	4.57
华坪县	Huaping	5.25	5.78	4.60	3.63	3.70	3.84	3.94	2.52	2.68
宁蒗县	Ninglang	1.87	2.34	2.39	1.79	2.10	2.42	2.86	3.08	2.87
市本级	City-level	14.32	17.41	15.71	17.95	17.02	14.85	15.19	17.09	15.53
普洱市	**Pu'er**	**47.90**	**53.72**	**44.99**	**47.49**	**50.06**	**53.22**	**54.34**	**49.84**	**51.31**
思茅区	Simao	7.10	8.38	7.17	7.53	8.00	8.03	8.91	9.08	9.20
宁洱县	Ning'er	2.36	2.71	3.01	3.20	3.39	3.60	3.79	2.96	3.11
墨江县	Mojiang	2.72	3.27	3.66	3.85	3.38	3.59	3.86	3.49	3.79
景东县	Jingdong	3.05	3.42	4.01	4.21	4.46	4.73	3.48	3.64	3.90
景谷县	Jinggu	4.28	4.80	4.76	5.01	5.41	5.84	6.31	5.01	5.22
镇沅县	Zhenyuan	2.26	2.84	3.14	3.36	3.63	3.86	4.06	4.21	4.02
江城县	Jiangcheng	1.09	1.35	1.50	1.60	1.70	1.81	1.89	1.64	1.15
孟连县	Menglian	0.92	1.14	1.33	1.43	1.52	1.67	1.62	1.41	1.70
澜沧县	Lancang	3.64	4.36	4.63	4.87	5.16	5.47	5.24	4.81	5.33
西盟县	Ximeng	0.45	0.54	0.63	0.67	0.72	0.78	0.81	0.61	0.63
市本级	City-level	20.04	20.93	11.16	11.76	12.69	13.85	14.37	12.97	13.26
临沧市	**Lincang**	**30.22**	**36.85**	**37.26**	**38.06**	**38.27**	**40.04**	**44.17**	**46.47**	**47.92**
临翔区	Linxiang	4.49	5.60	6.41	6.63	6.77	7.08	7.95	8.59	8.88
凤庆县	Fengqing	4.46	3.72	4.36	4.45	4.72	4.92	5.53	5.93	6.17
云县	Yunxian	4.06	5.05	4.02	4.18	4.45	4.63	5.10	5.43	5.63
永德县	Yongde	2.44	3.15	3.31	3.39	2.89	3.10	3.48	2.93	3.27
镇康县	Zhenkang	2.67	3.55	3.00	3.01	3.19	2.92	3.22	3.25	3.39
双江县	Shuangjiang	1.62	2.25	3.14	3.23	3.25	3.05	3.07	2.97	3.09
耿马县	Gengma	2.80	3.65	3.54	3.61	3.62	3.79	4.24	4.54	4.74
沧源县	Cangyuan	1.72	2.21	2.18	2.23	2.37	2.77	3.03	3.24	3.36
市本级	City-level	5.95	7.66	7.29	7.34	7.02	7.76	8.56	9.58	9.38

注：本表中2016年起数据为新口径。

Note:Data in this table are new caliber since 2016.

18–8 续表2 continued

单位：亿元 (100 million yuan)

州市县	Region	2012	2013	2014	2015	2016	2017	2018	2019	2020
楚 雄 州	**Chuxiong**	**46.32**	**56.37**	**63.72**	**68.19**	**73.64**	**80.26**	**86.69**	**87.61**	**90.28**
楚雄市	Chuxiong	13.93	16.30	18.43	20.00	21.61	23.19	25.04	25.41	26.17
双柏县	Shuangbai	1.42	1.97	2.28	2.51	2.74	3.01	3.19	3.35	2.76
牟定县	Mouding	1.83	2.30	2.67	2.88	3.12	3.37	3.64	3.86	3.97
南华县	Nanhua	2.49	3.21	3.86	4.10	4.43	4.78	5.16	5.42	5.59
姚安县	Yao'an	1.42	1.81	2.23	2.41	2.62	2.88	3.14	3.39	3.57
大姚县	Dayao	2.80	3.48	3.94	4.22	4.56	4.98	5.53	5.86	6.04
永仁县	Yongren	1.63	2.04	2.42	2.62	2.83	3.07	3.32	3.53	3.64
元谋县	Yuanmou	1.62	1.91	2.27	2.52	2.83	3.17	3.46	3.58	3.69
武定县	Wuding	3.68	4.31	5.00	5.00	5.40	5.81	6.25	6.41	4.56
禄丰县	Lufeng	5.61	7.46	7.66	8.05	8.69	9.61	10.49	9.78	9.30
州本级	Prefecture-level	9.89	11.58	12.98	13.89	14.82	16.40	17.45	17.02	21.00
红 河 州	**Honghe**	**84.48**	**97.25**	**111.02**	**123.24**	**133.10**	**141.28**	**142.27**	**148.06**	**151.25**
个旧市	Gejiu	8.89	9.33	10.73	11.11	11.35	12.05	12.82	13.21	13.40
开远市	Kaiyuan	8.42	9.77	11.23	12.45	13.20	13.99	14.84	15.45	16.07
蒙自市	Mengzi	10.64	12.56	15.03	16.82	17.55	18.71	15.28	15.98	16.07
弥勒市	Mile	9.50	11.13	13.09	15.01	16.22	17.22	18.26	19.03	19.45
屏边县	Pingbian	0.74	0.93	1.14	1.33	1.47	1.57	1.68	1.72	1.76
建水县	Jianshui	7.35	8.60	10.05	11.20	12.10	12.83	13.60	14.03	14.35
石屏县	Shiping	2.71	3.19	3.83	4.41	4.77	5.11	5.56	5.87	6.05
泸西县	Luxi	5.07	6.19	7.24	8.18	8.83	9.45	10.02	10.34	10.55
元阳县	Yuanyang	1.61	1.85	2.23	2.41	2.61	2.80	2.12	2.20	2.27
红河县	Honghe	0.83	1.08	1.31	1.50	1.66	1.79	1.42	1.60	1.68
金平县	Jinping	2.20	2.33	2.44	2.50	2.24	2.41	1.95	1.99	2.03
绿春县	Luchun	1.17	1.35	1.63	1.86	2.01	2.15	1.50	1.55	1.59
河口县	Hekou	1.44	1.83	2.23	2.55	2.76	3.00	3.27	3.49	3.49
州本级	Prefecture-level	23.93	27.12	28.84	31.89	36.33	38.19	39.92	41.61	42.50
文 山 州	**Wenshan**	**36.13**	**42.72**	**50.70**	**52.04**	**54.69**	**56.88**	**60.33**	**63.72**	**65.66**
文山市	Wenshan	10.70	13.30	15.60	17.20	18.24	20.07	21.32	22.40	23.18
砚山县	Yanshan	4.02	5.04	6.20	6.61	7.02	7.52	8.01	8.42	8.67
西畴县	Xichou	0.78	1.00	1.40	1.61	1.82	2.00	2.21	2.40	2.48
麻栗坡县	Malipo	2.70	3.16	3.28	2.80	2.90	3.08	3.31	3.51	3.60
马关县	Maguan	4.31	5.17	5.25	5.00	5.40	6.05	7.01	7.58	7.81
丘北县	Qiubei	2.91	3.64	4.15	4.00	4.20	4.41	4.70	4.75	4.88
广南县	Guangnan	2.40	3.00	3.78	4.00	4.15	4.32	4.74	5.32	5.51
富宁县	Funing	2.87	3.60	4.10	3.80	2.80	3.00	3.34	3.54	3.67
州本级	Prefecture-level	5.44	4.82	6.93	7.02	8.17	6.43	5.69	5.80	5.86
西双版纳州	**Xishuangbanna**	**22.26**	**26.81**	**28.79**	**30.80**	**30.48**	**28.46**	**31.29**	**34.74**	**35.81**
景洪市	Jinghong	10.18	11.98	11.73	12.10	11.59	11.03	12.21	13.96	15.01
勐海县	Menghai	2.51	3.51	4.21	4.64	4.75	4.95	5.33	5.66	5.53

注：本表中2016年起数据为新口径。

Note:Data in this table are new caliber since 2016.

18−8 续表3 continued

单位：亿元 (100 million yuan)

州市县	Region	2012	2013	2014	2015	2016	2017	2018	2019	2020
勐腊县	Mengla	2.91	3.15	3.48	3.71	3.64	3.86	4.20	4.30	3.36
州本级	Prefecture-level	6.67	8.17	9.37	10.35	10.50	8.62	9.55	10.83	11.91
大理州	**Dali**	**59.28**	**71.97**	**75.28**	**78.10**	**82.01**	**87.01**	**96.16**	**103.27**	**108.48**
大理市	Dali	21.52	25.60	27.53	29.19	30.07	31.67	36.42	37.52	37.53
漾濞县	Yangbi	1.19	1.47	0.77	0.86	1.19	1.48	1.78	2.00	2.24
祥云县	Xiangyun	5.41	6.75	7.18	7.63	8.01	8.82	10.00	10.81	11.36
宾川县	Binchuan	2.82	3.44	3.66	3.77	3.93	4.25	4.83	5.32	5.64
弥渡县	Midu	2.27	2.76	3.15	3.38	3.50	3.72	4.12	4.53	4.80
南涧县	Nanjian	2.65	2.91	2.57	2.65	2.91	3.00	3.30	3.50	3.72
巍山县	Weishan	2.58	3.23	3.39	3.07	3.20	3.42	3.77	3.96	4.16
永平县	Yongping	2.00	2.26	2.03	2.14	2.05	2.26	2.50	2.70	2.86
云龙县	Yunlong	2.07	2.66	2.87	3.12	3.29	3.39	2.40	2.69	3.02
洱源县	Eryuan	1.95	2.47	2.87	3.09	3.22	3.42	3.80	3.89	4.01
剑川县	Jianchuan	1.77	2.38	2.41	2.49	2.57	2.73	3.02	3.17	3.37
鹤庆县	Heqing	3.22	4.29	4.99	5.09	5.22	5.56	6.12	6.62	7.00
州本级	Prefecture-level	9.84	11.76	11.85	11.62	12.84	13.29	14.11	16.56	18.78
德宏州	**Dehong**	**24.32**	**27.96**	**31.00**	**31.96**	**32.61**	**33.77**	**37.04**	**40.10**	**42.31**
瑞丽市	Ruili	6.95	8.75	9.13	7.30	7.41	7.72	10.04	10.95	9.08
芒　市	Mangshi	5.66	7.02	7.11	5.80	5.81	6.00	6.24	7.02	8.00
梁河县	Lianghe	1.25	1.35	1.50	1.22	1.27	1.39	1.46	1.58	1.85
盈江县	Yingjiang	4.95	5.53	5.59	4.39	4.48	4.85	5.02	5.25	5.76
陇川县	Longchuan	1.70	1.81	2.13	1.73	1.88	2.17	2.29	3.06	3.52
州本级	Prefecture-level	3.81	3.49	5.54	11.52	11.75	11.63	11.98	12.25	14.11
怒江州	**Nujiang**	**7.51**	**8.41**	**9.33**	**9.00**	**9.46**	**9.93**	**10.86**	**13.08**	**15.08**
泸水市	Lushui	1.72	2.00	2.38	2.46	2.55	2.58	2.78	4.07	4.34
福贡县	Fugong	0.47	0.55	0.67	0.76	0.84	0.75	0.93	1.16	1.21
贡山县	Gongshan	0.38	0.48	0.60	0.68	0.79	0.75	0.80	1.07	1.14
兰坪县	Lanping	3.36	3.73	4.25	3.24	3.50	4.00	4.62	5.07	5.48
州本级	Prefecture-level	1.58	1.65	1.43	1.87	1.78	1.85	1.72	1.71	2.92
迪庆州	**Diqing**	**10.75**	**13.05**	**14.49**	**15.53**	**16.47**	**10.17**	**11.45**	**14.10**	**15.01**
香格里拉市	Shangri-La	3.50	4.37	5.05	5.50	5.84	4.86	5.56	6.63	7.62
德钦县	Deqin	1.28	1.60	1.80	1.59	1.69	0.92	1.09	1.09	1.15
维西县	Weixi	1.86	2.38	2.71	2.93	3.10	1.02	1.64	1.82	1.93
州本级	Prefecture-level	4.12	4.69	4.94	5.51	5.83	3.38	3.17	4.56	4.30
省本级	**Province-level**	**283.49**	**361.85**	**379.97**	**413.34**	**338.56**	**340.93**	**352.51**	**365.84**	**359.84**

注：本表中2016年起数据为新口径。
Note:Data in this table are new caliber since 2016.

18-9 各州市县人均地方一般公共预算收入（2016-2020年）

Per Capita Public Budgetary Revenue of Local Government by Region (2016-2020)

单位：元 (yuan)

州市县	Region	2016	2017	2018	2019	2020
全　省	**Yunnan**	**3 881**	**4 026**	**4 245**	**4 404**	**4 486**
昆明市	**Kunming**	**7 066**	**7 272**	**7 515**	**7 740**	**7 784**
五华区	Wuhua	3 584	3 628	3 792	4 010	4 037
盘龙区	Panlong	4 157	4 207	4 339	4 520	4 582
官渡区	Guandu	3 129	3 027	3 089	3 263	3 173
西山区	Xishan	4 402	4 444	4 677	4 898	4 936
东川区	Dongchuan	2 315	2 527	2 771	2 242	2 382
呈贡区	Chenggong	4 288	4 126	4 379	4 332	4 367
晋宁区	Jinning	5 329	4 494	3 798	4 574	4 592
富民县	Fumin	3 514	3 584	3 696	3 900	4 032
宜良县	Yiliang	1 873	2 001	2 194	2 225	2 286
石林县	Shilin	2 518	2 539	2 677	2 849	2 579
嵩明县	Songming	3 465	3 131	3 346	3 176	3 252
禄劝县	Luquan	1 661	1 603	1 474	1 400	1 322
寻甸县	Xundian	1 475	1 481	1 347	1 422	1 527
安宁市	Anning	6 919	6 625	8 252	10 164	10 470
曲靖市	**Qujing**	**2 170**	**2 343**	**2 444**	**2 574**	**2 685**
麒麟区	Qilin	2 210	2 316	2 149	2 249	2 316
沾益区	Zhanyi	1 556	1 788	1 739	1 940	2 064
马龙区	Malong	2 386	2 710	2 924	3 162	3 378
陆良县	Luliang	1 160	1 281	1 391	1 537	1 644
师宗县	Shizong	1 420	1 547	1 681	1 816	1 915
罗平县	Luoping	1 329	1 443	1 564	1 661	1 684
富源县	Fuyuan	1 320	1 516	1 793	1 925	2 059
会泽县	Huize	1 308	1 436	1 598	1 734	1 768
宣威市	Xuanwei	969	1 059	1 162	1 251	1 304
玉溪市	**Yuxi**	**5 748**	**6 030**	**6 278**	**5 887**	**5 967**
红塔区	Hongta	3 947	2 978	3 158	3 138	3 196
江川区	Jiangchuan	2 186	2 695	3 007	2 083	2 225
通海县	Tonghai	1 750	1 889	1 750	1 350	1 417
华宁县	Huaning	1 957	2 110	2 228	1 620	1 705
易门县	Yimen	3 577	3 791	4 085	4 395	4 742
峨山县	Eshan	2 725	2 860	2 998	2 597	2 724
新平县	Xinping	4 406	4 667	4 994	4 886	4 879
元江县	Yuanjiang	2 053	2 390	2 161	2 268	1 960
澄江市	Chengjiang	4 254	5 075	5 500	5 320	4 591
保山市	**Baoshan**	**2 327**	**2 528**	**2 693**	**2 747**	**2 690**
隆阳区	Longyang	1 831	1 955	2 108	2 175	2 188
施甸县	Shidian	1 738	1 886	1 920	2 075	2 086
龙陵县	Longling	1 940	2 115	2 334	2 374	2 165
昌宁县	Changning	1 579	1 726	1 819	1 985	1 846
腾冲市	Tengchong	2 570	2 637	2 727	2 947	2 583
昭通市	**Zhaotong**	**1 159**	**1 311**	**1 522**	**1 598**	**1 666**
昭阳区	Zhaoyang	1 365	1 317	1 489	1 575	1 664
鲁甸县	Ludian	774	1 012	1 203	1 204	1 030
巧家县	Qiaojia	704	787	925	1 061	1 143
盐津县	Yanjin	405	427	486	524	538
大关县	Daguan	482	514	545	574	536
永善县	Yongshan	1 766	2 107	2 183	2 119	2 157
绥江县	Suijiang	2 023	2 107	2 296	2 162	2 323
镇雄县	Zhenxiong	430	472	558	587	654
彝良县	Yiliang	574	649	825	1 000	1 029
威信县	Weixin	409	457	688	701	708
水富市	Shuifu	2 303	2 553	3 304	3 562	3 665
丽江市	**Lijiang**	**3 849**	**3 192**	**3 412**	**3 615**	**3 437**
古城区	Gucheng	5 373	3 818	3 795	3 876	3 541
玉龙县	Yulong	3 435	2 488	2 746	3 178	3 293
永胜县	Yongsheng	1 128	944	1 267	1 393	1 346
华坪县	Huaping	2 204	2 309	2 405	1 557	1 670
宁蒗县	Ninglang	832	966	1 150	1 243	1 167
普洱市	**Pu'er**	**2 025**	**2 163**	**2 222**	**2 051**	**2 126**
思茅区	Simao	2 194	2 096	2 241	2 260	2 242
宁洱县	Ning'er	1 928	2 087	2 233	1 769	1 893
墨江县	Mojiang	1 065	1 170	1 295	1 192	1 325
景东县	Jingdong	1 358	1 466	1 098	1 168	1 274
景谷县	Jinggu	1 915	2 077	2 258	1 800	1 880
镇沅县	Zhenyuan	1 883	2 028	2 166	2 283	2 215
江城县	Jiangcheng	1 452	1 558	1 642	1 446	1 030
孟连县	Menglian	1 073	1 168	1 124	975	1 173
澜沧县	Lancang	1 114	1 200	1 166	1 074	1 201
西盟县	Ximeng	809	882	918	694	722
临沧市	**Lincang**	**1 635**	**1 723**	**1 915**	**2 031**	**2 113**
临翔区	Linxiang	1 939	2 001	2 216	2 362	2 410
凤庆县	Fengqing	1 140	1 208	1 380	1 505	1 590
云　县	Yunxian	1 077	1 134	1 264	1 366	1 437
永德县	Yongde	833	903	1 025	874	988
镇康县	Zhenkang	1 752	1 618	1 804	1 843	1 948
双江县	Shuangjiang	1 895	1 794	1 824	1 776	1 864
耿马县	Gengma	1 230	1 291	1 452	1 564	1 648
沧源县	Cangyuan	1 402	1 656	1 832	1 984	2 083

18-9 续表 continued

单位：元 (yuan)

州市县	Region	2016	2017	2018	2019	2020
楚雄州	**Chuxiong**	**2 899**	**3 192**	**3 484**	**3 561**	**3 713**
楚雄市	Chuxiong	3 514	3 749	4 025	4 059	4 155
双柏县	Shuangbai	1 896	2 117	2 279	2 436	2 044
牟定县	Mouding	1 782	1 986	2 217	2 440	2 607
南华县	Nanhua	2 027	2 217	2 428	2 592	2 720
姚安县	Yao'an	1 458	1 630	1 810	1 995	2 149
大姚县	Dayao	1 833	2 037	2 302	2 485	2 612
永仁县	Yongren	2 745	3 010	3 290	3 537	3 692
元谋县	Yuanmou	1 360	1 531	1 684	1 757	1 824
武定县	Wuding	2 115	2 306	2 514	2 617	1 892
禄丰县	Lufeng	2 216	2 486	2 753	2 605	2 516
红河州	**Honghe**	**2 957**	**3 140**	**3 164**	**3 297**	**3 374**
个旧市	Gejiu	2 478	2 644	2 834	2 997	3 152
开远市	Kaiyuan	3 965	4 182	4 413	4 651	4 943
蒙自市	Mengzi	3 756	3 874	3 097	3 042	2 825
弥勒市	Mile	2 995	3 182	3 373	3 521	3 609
屏边县	Pingbian	1 046	1 144	1 237	1 288	1 346
建水县	Jianshui	2 246	2 378	2 517	2 605	2 679
石屏县	Shiping	1 667	1 800	1 974	2 112	2 208
泸西县	Luxi	2 279	2 458	2 622	2 688	2 714
元阳县	Yuanyang	689	747	572	600	627
红河县	Honghe	557	601	476	544	586
金平县	Jinping	633	684	555	578	606
绿春县	Luchun	938	1 011	712	736	755
河口县	Hekou	2 677	2 915	3 181	3 405	3 415
文山州	**Wenshan**	**1 554**	**1 616**	**1 715**	**1 814**	**1 873**
文山市	Wenshan	3 281	3 519	3 653	3 757	3 779
砚山县	Yanshan	1 484	1 584	1 683	1 767	1 819
西畴县	Xichou	800	901	1 018	1 130	1 199
麻栗坡县	Malipo	1 115	1 200	1 306	1 404	1 464
马关县	Maguan	1 578	1 793	2 108	2 313	2 425
丘北县	Qiubei	885	931	994	1 007	1 039
广南县	Guangnan	531	553	608	684	712
富宁县	Funing	693	744	831	884	922
西双版纳州	**Xishuangbanna**	**2 483**	**2 286**	**2 478**	**2 715**	**2 763**
景洪市	Jinghong	1 976	1 838	1 990	2 226	2 349
勐海县	Menghai	1 377	1 427	1 527	1 613	1 566
勐腊县	Mengla	1 230	1 295	1 400	1 426	1 106
大理州	**Dali**	**2 412**	**2 567**	**2 848**	**3 072**	**3 242**
大理市	Dali	4 191	4 338	4 902	4 960	4 893
漾濞县	Yangbi	1 202	1 501	1 809	2 037	2 288
祥云县	Xiangyun	1 858	2 063	2 372	2 607	2 776
宾川县	Binchuan	1 138	1 235	1 406	1 551	1 649
弥渡县	Midu	1 239	1 344	1 512	1 688	1 821
南涧县	Nanjian	1 416	1 469	1 641	1 777	1 917
巍山县	Weishan	1 135	1 233	1 373	1 454	1 545
永平县	Yongping	1 192	1 320	1 475	1 617	1 730
云龙县	Yunlong	1 723	1 791	1 280	1 449	1 642
洱源县	Eryuan	1 240	1 327	1 490	1 544	1 609
剑川县	Jianchuan	1 558	1 666	1 853	1 954	2 093
鹤庆县	Heqing	2 095	2 239	2 479	2 700	2 872
德宏州	**Dehong**	**2 563**	**2 631**	**2 862**	**3 075**	**3 221**
瑞丽市	Ruili	3 197	3 221	4 057	4 272	3 454
芒市	Mangshi	1 400	1 425	1 458	1 621	1 828
梁河县	Lianghe	881	976	1 041	1 144	1 348
盈江县	Yingjiang	1 500	1 631	1 699	1 785	1 961
陇川县	Longchuan	1 028	1 186	1 253	1 679	1 933
怒江州	**Nujiang**	**1 733**	**1 812**	**1 976**	**2 374**	**2 729**
泸水市	Lushui	1 296	1 298	1 387	2 013	2 131
福贡县	Fugong	781	687	841	1 036	1 065
贡山县	Gongshan	2 063	1 958	2 083	2 786	2 961
兰坪县	Lanping	1 719	1 981	2 308	2 554	2 783
迪庆州	**Diqing**	**4 175**	**2 585**	**2 921**	**3 615**	**3 864**
香格里拉市	Shangri-La	3 294	2 720	3 091	3 649	4 126
德钦县	Deqin	2 894	1 597	1 919	1 946	2 087
维西县	Weixi	1 951	648	1 056	1 194	1 299

18–10 各州市县地方一般公共预算支出（2012–2020年）

Public Budgetary Expenditure of Local Government by Region (2012-2020)

单位：亿元 (100 million yuan)

州市县	Region	2012	2013	2014	2015	2016	2017	2018	2019	2020
全　省	**Yunnan**	**3 572.66**	**4 096.51**	**4 437.98**	**4 712.83**	**5 018.86**	**5 712.97**	**6 075.03**	**6 770.09**	**6 974.02**
昆明市	**Kunming**	**525.50**	**585.76**	**593.66**	**615.49**	**688.40**	**775.90**	**756.80**	**820.86**	**875.05**
五华区	Wuhua	29.60	32.77	31.12	32.10	35.14	39.01	44.82	52.85	51.75
盘龙区	Panlong	31.14	37.11	36.43	39.14	43.07	48.92	50.09	51.24	52.37
官渡区	Guandu	40.41	47.05	41.46	43.00	40.71	45.37	52.34	57.85	62.98
西山区	Xishan	29.10	36.94	35.53	38.07	42.19	44.31	46.79	51.32	52.50
东川区	Dongchuan	23.23	22.21	22.31	24.85	25.27	27.67	39.31	36.65	37.56
呈贡区	Chenggong	12.27	14.75	17.22	24.92	23.35	32.68	33.54	37.46	38.36
晋宁区	Jinning	20.34	24.45	24.81	23.27	25.14	25.02	23.69	29.36	31.47
富民县	Fumin	8.40	9.83	9.97	10.49	11.25	11.40	12.50	14.43	14.61
宜良县	Yiliang	17.36	17.68	15.92	17.26	18.82	20.08	21.41	22.66	28.18
石林县	Shilin	13.52	14.30	14.09	15.30	16.26	20.35	20.10	20.65	23.93
嵩明县	Songming	17.50	17.01	18.99	21.21	22.07	25.56	23.53	23.01	24.45
禄劝县	Luquan	18.51	22.75	21.95	24.35	27.30	33.59	36.75	39.54	38.27
寻甸县	Xundian	19.57	22.90	23.05	26.26	26.55	36.42	34.82	41.69	38.94
安宁市	Anning	27.88	31.03	27.01	29.19	30.71	36.22	46.23	50.49	61.65
市本级	City-level	216.68	234.97	253.81	246.07	300.57	329.30	270.90	291.66	318.05
曲靖市	**Qujing**	**281.93**	**297.26**	**334.17**	**363.05**	**400.15**	**442.55**	**477.24**	**541.58**	**532.24**
麒麟区	Qilin	28.42	30.57	31.27	40.99	41.91	50.15	49.40	55.63	55.64
沾益区	Zhanyi	16.93	19.16	21.56	20.61	25.13	25.96	26.48	27.38	26.77
马龙区	Malong	11.50	13.25	16.78	16.60	17.75	19.01	20.07	19.74	21.46
陆良县	Luliang	21.38	22.77	25.03	29.07	30.09	34.48	34.33	38.96	41.71
师宗县	Shizong	17.96	18.88	20.15	21.54	25.51	29.30	34.63	31.20	30.40
罗平县	Luoping	22.48	23.31	26.41	30.06	32.75	35.56	35.80	34.94	37.48
富源县	Fuyuan	32.23	30.28	29.93	30.56	37.93	42.67	47.22	47.88	50.19
会泽县	Huize	35.61	38.14	50.19	58.67	52.09	55.96	73.62	107.92	102.63
宣威市	Xuanwei	49.31	52.18	59.77	61.91	69.45	77.29	83.21	106.24	93.73
市本级	City-level	46.12	48.72	53.09	53.03	67.55	72.16	72.48	71.70	72.22
玉溪市	**Yuxi**	**161.82**	**186.28**	**207.31**	**223.30**	**233.35**	**262.12**	**277.81**	**292.69**	**301.57**
红塔区	Hongta	20.16	24.74	27.48	31.06	32.31	31.42	34.64	34.49	40.37
江川区	Jiangchuan	11.53	14.08	15.56	15.98	17.42	18.40	20.53	20.72	21.05
通海县	Tonghai	11.83	14.31	13.31	15.84	16.65	18.00	18.05	18.50	18.90
华宁县	Huaning	9.69	11.72	12.17	13.83	15.47	16.07	17.59	17.41	18.50
易门县	Yimen	10.96	13.32	14.48	15.89	16.67	17.22	18.64	20.32	20.88
峨山县	Eshan	9.47	11.99	11.67	12.92	14.86	15.52	16.83	17.47	18.57
新平县	Xinping	19.45	23.56	21.92	23.60	27.06	27.88	34.02	36.51	35.36
元江县	Yuanjiang	10.75	13.18	14.63	16.00	17.62	18.89	20.09	20.53	19.81
澄江市	Chengjiang	9.17	11.16	11.56	12.69	14.26	21.85	27.25	36.10	36.32
市本级	City-level	48.82	48.24	64.54	65.47	61.02	76.88	70.16	70.64	71.81

18-10 续表1 continued

单位：亿元 (100 million yuan)

州 市 县	Region	2012	2013	2014	2015	2016	2017	2018	2019	2020
保 山 市	**Baoshan**	**141.57**	**150.32**	**164.24**	**192.13**	**212.65**	**238.03**	**261.31**	**270.92**	**270.94**
隆阳区	Longyang	37.56	36.11	39.05	48.18	50.97	62.54	66.15	60.85	60.85
施甸县	Shidian	16.97	17.92	19.66	23.93	26.36	29.14	30.41	32.89	28.71
龙陵县	Longling	15.60	18.47	21.71	22.63	25.52	29.17	32.75	32.50	30.64
昌宁县	Changning	21.52	21.38	21.18	26.92	28.32	31.45	34.95	32.50	30.00
腾冲市	Tengchong	35.94	38.71	41.86	45.37	53.32	55.14	62.63	76.36	77.80
市本级	City-level	13.98	17.72	20.79	25.10	28.16	30.59	34.41	34.93	42.94
昭 通 市	**Zhaotong**	**248.09**	**261.26**	**330.89**	**405.29**	**410.06**	**416.42**	**460.02**	**640.64**	**625.92**
昭阳区	Zhaoyang	34.03	38.07	43.48	51.12	52.52	57.55	62.35	85.36	72.36
鲁甸县	Ludian	20.27	20.39	46.66	60.11	46.78	34.93	31.57	42.63	37.86
巧家县	Qiaojia	20.67	21.50	35.60	61.17	40.10	34.15	39.08	51.32	46.98
盐津县	Yanjin	14.40	16.33	19.26	19.30	21.35	23.68	29.17	37.78	32.73
大关县	Daguan	13.09	14.41	16.89	15.52	16.43	21.67	21.82	36.84	27.43
永善县	Yongshan	16.71	19.82	25.13	36.57	30.12	34.20	38.04	62.60	44.62
绥江县	Suijiang	9.73	11.60	11.64	12.10	13.00	15.49	16.72	20.61	19.22
镇雄县	Zhenxiong	46.22	47.27	50.34	59.07	72.39	81.37	94.35	132.29	131.83
彝良县	Yiliang	32.25	27.41	26.93	27.00	32.78	36.89	40.31	73.17	53.76
威信县	Weixin	14.93	15.01	17.10	22.37	27.30	26.06	28.34	31.81	32.07
水富市	Shuifu	6.79	7.12	7.69	8.76	9.51	9.64	10.42	15.11	16.62
市本级	City-level	18.98	22.31	30.17	32.20	47.79	40.79	47.85	51.13	110.44
丽 江 市	**Lijiang**	**106.73**	**113.20**	**128.03**	**144.04**	**150.07**	**160.80**	**167.30**	**172.98**	**175.60**
古城区	Gucheng	16.31	17.05	19.82	24.44	26.82	26.12	22.29	24.93	24.37
玉龙县	Yulong	16.80	20.02	20.04	23.57	25.67	27.87	29.41	27.74	28.87
永胜县	Yongsheng	18.25	20.11	23.02	27.36	27.02	32.63	30.96	35.35	33.91
华坪县	Huaping	13.67	12.81	13.50	16.09	17.93	19.16	19.34	15.27	18.26
宁蒗县	Ninglang	21.76	19.92	21.81	22.40	24.59	28.64	34.76	37.11	38.60
市本级	City-level	19.96	23.29	29.84	30.19	28.04	26.37	30.55	32.59	31.59
普 洱 市	**Pu'er**	**170.09**	**201.61**	**224.36**	**219.10**	**245.72**	**271.78**	**293.23**	**301.43**	**323.55**
思茅区	Simao	15.72	21.40	17.46	18.21	21.18	21.93	24.83	24.59	27.18
宁洱县	Ning'er	10.72	13.39	14.64	13.89	17.86	19.65	17.34	16.94	16.94
墨江县	Mojiang	14.50	17.93	21.30	22.82	24.75	26.74	30.05	30.82	30.82
景东县	Jingdong	16.07	22.21	23.18	22.36	26.02	26.48	27.53	27.45	28.51
景谷县	Jinggu	14.91	17.88	31.65	22.91	25.45	26.98	29.10	24.66	27.16
镇沅县	Zhenyuan	12.43	15.98	18.42	19.81	19.82	22.72	22.32	21.22	21.04
江城县	Jiangcheng	8.94	10.84	12.80	12.87	14.03	15.46	18.16	21.92	18.92
孟连县	Menglian	9.50	10.04	11.04	13.16	15.13	17.56	17.13	16.77	19.35
澜沧县	Lancang	25.33	29.68	29.42	33.99	36.00	45.10	50.07	56.64	58.01
西盟县	Ximeng	7.50	8.34	9.31	12.07	13.18	13.62	15.03	16.90	17.42
市本级	City-level	34.47	33.91	35.12	26.99	32.30	35.54	41.66	43.52	58.20
临 沧 市	**Lincang**	**160.62**	**181.33**	**194.45**	**202.50**	**213.39**	**242.95**	**267.30**	**274.11**	**276.88**
临翔区	Linxiang	19.60	22.36	25.79	26.65	28.01	29.54	32.87	34.85	36.24
凤庆县	Fengqing	20.51	21.52	24.37	27.86	29.81	31.08	34.52	36.60	37.20
云 县	Yunxian	19.63	21.72	22.15	24.28	29.40	29.72	32.72	34.36	30.01
永德县	Yongde	19.07	21.76	23.40	23.43	21.08	22.57	24.85	28.26	27.33
镇康县	Zhenkang	14.35	16.80	18.96	18.98	17.82	18.80	20.71	21.42	22.30
双江县	Shuangjiang	14.01	16.07	18.12	17.53	18.69	19.97	21.97	23.85	24.81
耿马县	Gengma	19.91	22.97	20.05	23.82	25.20	26.46	29.22	30.97	32.64
沧源县	Cangyuan	14.49	17.10	19.25	18.42	19.87	21.07	23.64	25.07	26.63

18-10 续表2 continued

单位：亿元 (100 million yuan)

州市县	Region	2012	2013	2014	2015	2016	2017	2018	2019	2020
市本级	City-level	19.07	21.04	22.37	21.53	23.50	43.75	46.80	38.74	39.72
楚雄州	**Chuxiong**	**158.02**	**172.65**	**205.12**	**216.23**	**235.21**	**248.69**	**275.91**	**279.56**	**293.61**
楚雄市	Chuxiong	28.63	30.18	35.30	36.22	39.84	43.93	51.56	54.14	57.77
双柏县	Shuangbai	9.80	11.00	16.54	16.03	15.30	18.10	18.10	17.23	18.11
牟定县	Mouding	10.38	12.46	13.27	13.90	17.83	17.91	16.99	17.84	18.73
南华县	Nanhua	12.73	13.72	17.55	17.10	17.79	19.57	21.52	21.96	22.39
姚安县	Yao'an	10.60	11.20	12.88	14.59	15.25	17.27	18.67	19.60	19.61
大姚县	Dayao	14.22	16.55	18.39	19.19	21.46	23.17	24.35	24.47	25.70
永仁县	Yongren	8.19	9.47	10.75	12.05	12.84	13.95	14.84	15.59	16.06
元谋县	Yuanmou	11.35	11.79	14.92	16.03	17.65	18.06	19.57	19.97	20.36
武定县	Wuding	15.49	15.63	18.50	20.52	21.31	23.66	29.80	33.30	30.64
禄丰县	Lufeng	18.43	19.96	21.75	24.17	28.41	27.23	32.61	29.60	32.13
州本级	Prefecture-level	18.18	20.71	25.28	26.44	27.55	25.83	27.90	25.86	32.11
红河州	**Honghe**	**248.08**	**310.71**	**344.79**	**369.15**	**378.79**	**402.79**	**448.45**	**505.60**	**532.03**
个旧市	Gejiu	25.82	30.35	35.12	33.07	31.87	37.47	39.06	42.89	34.85
开远市	Kaiyuan	17.69	23.00	23.29	25.50	27.80	29.54	34.31	37.77	36.23
蒙自市	Mengzi	22.37	28.66	30.52	31.69	33.59	34.98	34.63	36.70	39.85
弥勒市	Mile	20.71	26.54	31.19	35.76	39.60	39.21	45.44	47.26	40.94
屏边县	Pingbian	9.33	12.26	13.26	14.15	14.17	14.66	17.07	19.85	18.43
建水县	Jianshui	20.49	26.21	27.53	31.53	34.15	34.98	41.51	45.66	45.14
石屏县	Shiping	13.50	17.78	18.43	23.94	24.18	25.88	27.48	28.37	29.28
泸西县	Luxi	17.62	22.97	26.79	26.17	29.24	31.00	31.77	32.09	29.10
元阳县	Yuanyang	14.44	17.81	20.51	24.07	24.62	25.60	33.86	39.01	35.91
红河县	Honghe	14.39	18.71	18.84	21.58	21.30	21.36	25.04	34.46	30.15
金平县	Jinping	15.52	18.20	20.17	24.49	23.23	26.65	30.31	41.05	38.14
绿春县	Luchun	13.68	17.35	17.30	19.06	20.71	20.77	24.56	28.05	25.93
河口县	Hekou	8.45	11.40	13.50	14.57	15.57	16.39	21.44	21.47	25.88
州本级	Prefecture-level	34.05	39.48	48.32	43.57	38.75	44.29	41.97	50.98	102.20
文山州	**Wenshan**	**167.80**	**195.46**	**217.23**	**242.76**	**272.23**	**321.57**	**343.30**	**373.09**	**384.38**
文山市	Wenshan	22.09	28.89	32.72	38.08	42.10	54.04	55.21	56.04	58.25
砚山县	Yanshan	19.59	23.11	25.78	29.44	32.22	35.43	37.79	39.74	41.44
西畴县	Xichou	11.10	12.53	14.46	18.79	23.79	25.54	27.52	26.10	26.49
麻栗坡县	Malipo	14.82	16.98	19.49	20.37	23.28	26.48	31.89	39.04	34.99
马关县	Maguan	16.77	19.66	23.30	23.83	25.86	32.19	35.61	41.67	42.16
丘北县	Qiubei	18.93	24.68	24.72	25.95	31.97	36.31	38.67	38.92	43.49
广南县	Guangnan	25.96	27.95	31.70	35.88	38.74	48.54	53.51	61.57	68.11
富宁县	Funing	20.06	22.31	25.23	27.96	29.58	34.06	38.94	34.74	38.68
州本级	Prefecture-level	18.49	19.35	19.83	22.47	24.70	28.99	24.16	35.28	30.78
西双版纳州	**Xishuangbanna**	**80.63**	**81.26**	**90.07**	**105.67**	**117.31**	**117.77**	**129.31**	**139.93**	**133.87**
景洪市	Jinghong	32.84	29.40	31.27	33.94	39.09	38.23	41.14	45.15	43.13
勐海县	Menghai	16.46	17.52	20.76	25.48	27.11	29.93	32.16	34.49	32.13

18-10 续表3 continued

单位：亿元 (100 million yuan)

州市县	Region	2012	2013	2014	2015	2016	2017	2018	2019	2020
勐腊县	Mengla	16.00	16.62	18.46	24.34	26.86	28.08	31.12	35.10	31.61
州本级	Prefecture-level	15.32	17.72	19.57	21.91	24.25	21.54	24.89	25.19	27.00
大理州	**Dali**	**200.50**	**222.93**	**243.57**	**277.43**	**294.82**	**338.18**	**366.22**	**390.90**	**391.19**
大理市	Dali	35.00	40.23	41.92	46.59	46.80	53.79	63.57	80.35	70.53
漾濞县	Yangbi	7.40	9.11	9.38	11.10	12.43	13.85	14.69	12.55	13.73
祥云县	Xiangyun	21.51	20.69	23.47	27.66	30.35	32.95	33.02	33.35	36.89
宾川县	Binchuan	15.32	16.77	19.08	20.45	22.44	24.24	25.51	24.03	26.24
弥渡县	Midu	14.71	15.81	18.77	18.74	19.82	22.89	24.71	27.05	27.81
南涧县	Nanjian	11.11	12.47	13.08	15.51	18.00	20.36	21.61	20.25	20.68
巍山县	Weishan	13.81	15.02	17.33	20.74	21.23	21.50	26.28	26.57	26.96
永平县	Yongping	10.07	10.50	11.69	14.32	15.20	17.33	21.51	22.81	23.47
云龙县	Yunlong	12.31	13.51	15.50	16.20	16.77	20.53	20.67	26.99	22.08
洱源县	Eryuan	12.70	17.77	17.30	20.39	22.63	24.51	28.28	23.60	25.01
剑川县	Jianchuan	10.21	12.29	12.90	15.01	17.75	18.73	22.91	23.89	25.63
鹤庆县	Heqing	13.50	14.31	16.37	23.95	22.26	22.93	23.72	26.04	29.36
州本级	Prefecture-level	22.85	24.45	26.76	26.78	29.12	44.56	39.76	43.41	42.78
德宏州	**Dehong**	**102.16**	**99.60**	**121.72**	**124.53**	**134.26**	**150.92**	**150.04**	**165.46**	**182.75**
瑞丽市	Ruili	15.86	16.68	20.83	17.95	21.57	26.44	27.33	29.90	38.75
芒　市	Mangshi	28.24	19.75	23.41	25.96	28.05	28.43	30.33	32.64	37.50
梁河县	Lianghe	8.89	9.28	12.02	12.51	12.76	14.21	15.55	17.80	18.13
盈江县	Yingjiang	18.07	18.15	30.60	29.81	27.45	29.40	26.75	27.11	31.95
陇川县	Longchuan	11.01	11.65	13.70	16.17	17.75	19.02	18.70	25.85	23.44
州本级	Prefecture-level	20.09	24.08	21.16	22.15	26.68	33.41	31.38	32.17	32.98
怒江州	**Nujiang**	**50.39**	**55.29**	**63.36**	**71.81**	**83.35**	**89.67**	**138.92**	**175.73**	**163.18**
泸水市	Lushui	12.71	13.22	15.86	18.29	23.80	23.57	37.00	47.57	49.48
福贡县	Fugong	8.25	9.66	12.47	14.34	14.96	15.25	24.08	35.41	34.88
贡山县	Gongshan	6.49	8.41	8.51	9.29	11.15	11.96	14.87	20.04	18.19
兰坪县	Lanping	13.87	14.71	18.98	20.83	22.76	25.47	36.28	58.71	44.80
州本级	Prefecture-level	9.06	9.29	7.55	9.06	10.69	13.42	26.68	13.99	15.82
迪庆州	**Diqing**	**73.14**	**108.85**	**101.13**	**110.47**	**118.66**	**139.94**	**160.08**	**171.31**	**159.47**
香格里拉市	Shangri-La	26.89	32.58	33.12	38.97	38.14	42.37	45.98	48.89	48.19
德钦县	Deqin	12.38	20.42	18.32	19.42	24.89	25.64	30.55	36.47	30.14
维西县	Weixi	16.50	28.06	23.43	26.42	30.66	28.69	37.10	42.97	41.56
州本级	Prefecture-level	17.37	27.80	26.27	25.66	24.97	43.24	46.44	42.98	39.59
省本级	**Provincial-level**	**695.59**	**872.75**	**873.89**	**829.88**	**830.44**	**1 092.90**	**1 101.78**	**1 253.30**	**1 351.79**

18-11 全省各州市县人均地方一般公共预算支出（2016-2020年）
Per Capita Public Budgetary Government Expenditure of Local Government by Region (2016-2020)

单位：元 (yuan)

州市县	Region	2016	2017	2018	2019	2020
全　省	**Yunnan**	**10 747**	**12 194**	**12 931**	**14 378**	**14 782**
昆明市	**Kunming**	**9 178**	**10 060**	**9 548**	**10 084**	**10 472**
五华区	Wuhua	3 419	3 679	4 112	4 743	4 560
盘龙区	Panlong	4 708	5 232	5 250	5 286	5 334
官渡区	Guandu	3 280	3 439	3 735	3 899	4 025
西山区	Xishan	4 832	4 949	5 105	5 523	5 547
东川区	Dongchuan	9 543	10 481	14 941	13 973	14 363
呈贡区	Chenggong	4 887	6 403	6 135	6 405	6 121
晋宁区	Jinning	7 913	7 717	7 198	8 749	9 170
富民县	Fumin	7 632	7 724	8 446	9 704	9 786
宜良县	Yiliang	4 745	5 124	5 521	5 870	7 312
石林县	Shilin	6 680	8 374	8 292	8 540	9 921
嵩明县	Songming	6 632	7 411	6 551	6 030	6 065
禄劝县	Luquan	7 119	8 800	9 671	10 422	10 095
寻甸县	Xundian	5 784	7 929	7 576	9 063	8 456
安宁市	Anning	7 295	8 309	10 305	10 886	12 884
曲靖市	**Qujing**	**6 874**	**7 610**	**8 221**	**9 352**	**9 216**
麒麟区	Qilin	4 696	5 428	5 208	5 734	5 623
沾益区	Zhanyi	6 045	6 290	6 460	6 714	6 592
马龙区	Malong	9 308	9 927	10 442	10 249	11 119
陆良县	Luliang	4 938	5 678	5 676	6 467	6 948
师宗县	Shizong	6 657	7 680	9 111	8 234	8 051
罗平县	Luoping	6 045	6 580	6 643	6 500	6 990
富源县	Fuyuan	5 436	6 155	6 861	7 014	7 407
会泽县	Huize	6 167	6 728	8 959	13 307	12 840
宣威市	Xuanwei	5 573	6 268	6 815	8 793	7 840
玉溪市	**Yuxi**	**10 235**	**11 519**	**12 241**	**12 937**	**13 376**
红塔区	Hongta	5 907	5 640	6 112	5 987	6 903
江川区	Jiangchuan	6 544	6 983	7 875	8 037	8 261
通海县	Tonghai	5 616	6 093	6 133	6 323	6 502
华宁县	Huaning	7 666	8 055	8 929	8 956	9 645
易门县	Yimen	10 246	10 736	11 805	13 076	13 656
峨山县	Eshan	9 687	10 251	11 288	11 876	12 807
新平县	Xinping	9 887	10 269	12 642	13 700	13 394
元江县	Yuanjiang	8 533	9 251	9 955	10 301	10 061
澄江市	Chengjiang	8 276	12 659	15 761	20 831	20 946
保山市	**Baoshan**	**8 604**	**9 656**	**10 635**	**11 072**	**11 120**
隆阳区	Longyang	5 558	6 835	7 243	6 689	6 725
施甸县	Shidian	8 793	9 746	10 225	11 134	9 769
龙陵县	Longling	9 220	10 546	11 870	11 814	11 187
昌宁县	Changning	8 499	9 525	10 701	10 328	9 340
腾冲市	Tengchong	8 271	8 557	9 727	11 870	12 105
昭通市	**Zhaotong**	**7 946**	**8 085**	**8 954**	**12 510**	**12 266**
昭阳区	Zhaoyang	6 181	6 659	7 092	9 574	7 996
鲁甸县	Ludian	11 840	8 816	7 944	10 716	9 508
巧家县	Qiaojia	8 185	7 070	8 200	10 894	10 097
盐津县	Yanjin	6 181	6 967	8 749	11 518	10 184
大关县	Daguan	6 950	9 369	9 672	16 784	12 890
永善县	Yongshan	8 097	9 309	10 500	17 525	12 680
绥江县	Suijiang	8 947	10 809	11 850	14 806	14 039
镇雄县	Zhenxiong	5 391	6 050	7 005	9 815	9 771
彝良县	Yiliang	6 401	7 211	7 904	14 426	10 654
威信县	Weixin	7 400	7 126	7 831	8 878	9 049
水富市	Shuifu	9 242	9 359	10 097	14 627	16 074
丽江市	**Lijiang**	**11 972**	**12 813**	**13 320**	**13 772**	**13 986**
古城区	Gucheng	10 472	9 913	8 237	8 964	8 536
玉龙县	Yulong	11 511	12 425	13 025	12 312	12 883
永胜县	Yongsheng	7 622	9 307	8 917	10 300	9 985
华坪县	Huaping	10 679	11 521	11 807	9 438	11 377
宁蒗县	Ninglang	9 746	11 433	13 971	14 982	15 697
普洱市	**Pu'er**	**9 938**	**11 048**	**11 988**	**12 405**	**13 406**
思茅区	Simao	5 808	5 723	6 245	6 120	6 624
宁洱县	Ning'er	10 159	11 391	10 218	10 126	10 310
墨江县	Mojiang	7 800	8 716	10 084	10 522	10 776
景东县	Jingdong	7 923	8 206	8 685	8 807	9 314
景谷县	Jinggu	9 009	9 595	10 411	8 858	9 784
镇沅县	Zhenyuan	10 280	11 939	11 910	11 508	11 592
江城县	Jiangcheng	11 981	13 305	15 778	19 330	16 938
孟连县	Menglian	10 677	12 280	11 888	11 598	13 354
澜沧县	Lancang	7 774	9 895	11 144	12 651	13 074
西盟县	Ximeng	14 809	15 407	17 041	19 226	19 954
临沧市	**Lincang**	**9 119**	**10 454**	**11 589**	**11 983**	**12 208**
临翔区	Linxiang	8 023	8 347	9 164	9 585	9 834
凤庆县	Fengqing	7 202	7 631	8 613	9 289	9 588
云　县	Yunxian	7 115	7 279	8 109	8 644	7 660
永德县	Yongde	6 075	6 573	7 320	8 428	8 254
镇康县	Zhenkang	9 786	10 416	11 602	12 150	12 816
双江县	Shuangjiang	10 898	11 747	13 054	14 264	14 964
耿马县	Gengma	8 566	9 015	10 007	10 672	11 349
沧源县	Cangyuan	11 757	12 594	14 293	15 352	16 510

18-11 续表 continued

单位：元 (yuan)

州市县	Region	2016	2017	2018	2019	2020
楚 雄 州	**Chuxiong**	**9 260**	**9 890**	**11 090**	**11 364**	**12 075**
楚雄市	Chuxiong	6 479	7 102	8 288	8 649	9 171
双柏县	Shuangbai	10 588	12 729	12 929	12 531	13 415
牟定县	Mouding	10 183	10 554	10 347	11 277	12 298
南华县	Nanhua	8 142	9 077	10 127	10 502	10 895
姚安县	Yao'an	8 486	9 774	10 761	11 536	11 806
大姚县	Dayao	8 625	9 476	10 137	10 377	11 116
永仁县	Yongren	12 454	13 676	14 708	15 621	16 288
元谋县	Yuanmou	8 482	8 725	9 523	9 799	10 064
武定县	Wuding	8 347	9 389	11 987	13 597	12 714
禄丰县	Lufeng	7 244	7 043	8 559	7 885	8 693
红 河 州	**Honghe**	**8 417**	**8 951**	**9 972**	**11 258**	**11 868**
个旧市	Gejiu	6 957	8 221	8 634	9 730	8 198
开远市	Kaiyuan	8 351	8 831	10 202	11 370	11 144
蒙自市	Mengzi	7 190	7 242	7 019	6 986	7 006
弥勒市	Mile	7 313	7 245	8 393	8 744	7 596
屏边县	Pingbian	10 085	10 685	12 570	14 869	14 090
建水县	Jianshui	6 338	6 483	7 683	8 478	8 428
石屏县	Shiping	8 449	9 116	9 759	10 205	10 686
泸西县	Luxi	7 546	8 062	8 312	8 342	7 486
元阳县	Yuanyang	6 498	6 834	9 134	10 644	9 925
红河县	Honghe	7 148	7 168	8 389	11 725	10 509
金平县	Jinping	6 566	7 565	8 630	11 919	11 388
绿春县	Luchun	9 664	9 770	11 651	13 325	12 307
河口县	Hekou	15 102	15 928	20 856	20 946	25 323
文 山 州	**Wenshan**	**7 735**	**9 138**	**9 761**	**10 622**	**10 962**
文山市	Wenshan	7 572	9 474	9 460	9 398	9 496
砚山县	Yanshan	6 810	7 464	7 939	8 340	8 695
西畴县	Xichou	10 462	11 499	12 676	12 294	12 809
麻栗坡县	Malipo	8 947	10 316	12 585	15 616	14 229
马关县	Maguan	7 555	9 541	10 707	12 716	13 093
丘北县	Qiubei	6 736	7 664	8 175	8 249	9 259
广南县	Guangnan	4 954	6 216	6 865	7 919	8 797

州市县	Region	2016	2017	2018	2019	2020
富宁县	Funing	7 316	8 445	9 684	8 674	9 714
西双版纳州	**Xishuangbanna**	**9 557**	**9 459**	**10 242**	**10 936**	**10 329**
景洪市	Jinghong	6 665	6 372	6 706	7 201	6 750
勐海县	Menghai	7 858	8 625	9 215	9 826	9 097
勐腊县	Mengla	9 074	9 423	10 373	11 642	10 405
大 理 州	**Dali**	**8 672**	**9 979**	**10 846**	**11 627**	**11 690**
大理市	Dali	6 523	7 368	8 557	10 623	9 196
漾濞县	Yangbi	12 556	14 047	14 929	12 780	14 025
祥云县	Xiangyun	7 042	7 708	7 834	8 042	9 015
宾川县	Binchuan	6 497	7 044	7 426	7 008	7 673
弥渡县	Midu	7 016	8 270	9 068	10 078	10 550
南涧县	Nanjian	8 759	9 971	10 746	10 279	10 654
巍山县	Weishan	7 531	7 751	9 574	9 754	10 015
永平县	Yongping	8 837	10 123	12 690	13 659	14 198
云龙县	Yunlong	8 780	10 845	11 024	14 534	12 007
洱源县	Eryuan	8 717	9 507	11 086	9 369	10 032
剑川县	Jianchuan	10 758	11 428	14 055	14 729	15 919
鹤庆县	Heqing	8 933	9 235	9 607	10 620	12 048
德 宏 州	**Dehong**	**10 551**	**11 758**	**11 595**	**12 689**	**13 913**
瑞丽市	Ruili	9 305	11 030	11 042	11 666	14 739
芒 市	Mangshi	6 759	6 750	7 085	7 536	8 568
梁河县	Lianghe	8 855	9 979	11 091	12 889	13 214
盈江县	Yingjiang	9 190	9 889	9 052	9 215	10 878
陇川县	Longchuan	9 710	10 399	10 235	14 180	12 872
怒 江 州	**Nujiang**	**15 266**	**16 363**	**25 281**	**31 893**	**29 535**
泸水市	Lushui	12 100	11 856	18 454	23 526	24 291
福贡县	Fugong	13 903	13 978	21 772	31 616	30 704
贡山县	Gongshan	29 112	31 227	38 724	52 188	47 247
兰坪县	Lanping	11 179	12 615	18 122	29 577	22 753
迪 庆 州	**Diqing**	**30 079**	**35 563**	**40 837**	**43 926**	**41 048**
香格里拉市	Shangri-La	21 512	23 710	25 559	26 907	26 091
德钦县	Deqin	42 620	44 514	53 785	65 125	54 701
维西县	Weixi	19 295	18 239	23 889	28 196	27 968

18-12 各州市县社会消费品零售总额（2019-2020年）
Total Retail Sales of Consumer Goods by Region (2019-2020)

单位：亿元 (100 million yuan)

州市县	Region	2019	2020	州市县	Region	2019	2020
全　省	**Yunnan**	**10 158.23**	**9 792.87**	澄江市	Chengjiang	95.22	92.64
昆明市	**Kunming**	**3 186.74**	**3 070.44**	**保山市**	**Baoshan**	**420.30**	**427.84**
五华区	Wuhua	624.26	596.12	隆阳区	Longyang	210.79	214.10
盘龙区	Panlong	604.62	625.84	施甸县	Shidian	37.10	37.68
官渡区	Guandu	683.16	601.90	龙陵县	Longling	36.59	37.23
西山区	Xishan	476.95	456.92	昌宁县	Changning	43.28	44.30
东川区	Dongchuan	44.78	45.97	腾冲市	Tengchong	92.54	94.53
呈贡区	Chenggong	147.77	160.17	**昭通市**	**Zhaotong**	**478.56**	**435.56**
晋宁区	Jinning	76.79	66.18	昭阳区	Zhaoyang	169.76	151.77
富民县	Fumin	39.50	40.09	鲁甸县	Ludian	39.39	35.13
宜良县	Yiliang	84.42	76.71	巧家县	Qiaojia	21.72	19.94
石林县	Shilin	46.22	44.98	盐津县	Yanjin	15.79	14.97
嵩明县	Songming	81.05	83.83	大关县	Daguan	16.46	14.98
禄劝县	Luquan	60.84	57.33	永善县	Yongshan	18.48	16.39
寻甸县	Xundian	65.73	62.86	绥江县	Suijiang	15.30	13.98
安宁市	Anning	150.64	151.54	镇雄县	Zhenxiong	107.47	99.80
曲靖市	**Qujing**	**915.16**	**934.86**	彝良县	Yiliang	25.44	23.07
麒麟区	Qilin	292.14	298.26	威信县	Weixin	34.40	31.95
沾益区	Zhanyi	87.20	88.85	水富市	Shuifu	14.34	13.58
马龙区	Malong	17.38	18.02	**丽江市**	**Lijiang**	**251.74**	**233.57**
陆良县	Luliang	76.86	78.40	古城区	Gucheng	132.46	114.78
师宗县	Shizong	34.63	35.87	玉龙县	Yulong	40.79	36.94
罗平县	Luoping	98.39	101.05	永胜县	Yongsheng	22.13	23.53
富源县	Fuyuan	52.90	54.06	华坪县	Huaping	27.82	28.26
会泽县	Huize	84.51	86.29	宁蒗县	Ninglang	28.52	30.06
宣威市	Xuanwei	171.15	174.06	**普洱市**	**Pu'er**	**316.13**	**292.29**
玉溪市	**Yuxi**	**814.21**	**790.29**	思茅区	Simao	104.75	95.39
红塔区	Hongta	283.18	274.42	宁洱县	Ning'er	20.40	19.37
江川区	Jiangchuan	66.51	64.60	墨江县	Mojiang	22.35	20.93
通海县	Tonghai	73.02	70.75	景东县	Jingdong	33.56	31.39
华宁县	Huaning	49.14	47.66	景谷县	Jinggu	35.16	31.84
易门县	Yimen	62.36	60.34	镇沅县	Zhenyuan	21.17	19.88
峨山县	Eshan	51.75	50.45	江城县	Jiangcheng	14.74	13.41
新平县	Xinping	80.68	78.60	孟连县	Menglian	20.37	18.92
元江县	Yuanjiang	52.34	50.83	澜沧县	Lancang	36.80	34.63

18-12 续表 continued

单位：亿元 (100 million yuan)

州市县	Region	2019	2020
西盟县	Ximeng	6.82	6.52
临沧市	**Lincang**	**338.38**	**317.02**
临翔区	Linxiang	103.70	94.06
凤庆县	Fengqing	47.86	45.40
云　县	Yunxian	54.90	52.55
永德县	Yongde	33.77	32.96
镇康县	Zhenkang	18.97	18.03
双江县	Shuangjiang	16.95	16.05
耿马县	Gengma	41.22	38.51
沧源县	Cangyuan	21.01	19.46
楚雄州	**Chuxiong**	**538.72**	**518.66**
楚雄市	Chuxiong	198.17	182.51
双柏县	Shuangbai	18.28	18.92
牟定县	Mouding	28.25	29.16
南华县	Nanhua	44.14	45.55
姚安县	Yao'an	29.97	30.84
大姚县	Dayao	33.64	32.06
永仁县	Yongren	11.64	12.01
元谋县	Yuanmou	40.14	38.13
武定县	Wuding	40.45	40.54
禄丰县	Lufeng	94.04	88.96
红河州	**Honghe**	**885.10**	**883.01**
蒙自市	Mengzi	165.00	161.30
个旧市	Gejiu	112.46	113.37
开远市	Kaiyuan	108.17	109.79
弥勒市	Mile	103.68	104.07
屏边县	Pingbian	30.75	30.87
建水县	Jianshui	89.91	89.40
石屏县	Shiping	45.72	45.88
泸西县	Luxi	63.49	64.01
元阳县	Yuanyang	38.13	38.27
红河县	Honghe	35.89	35.60
金平县	Jinping	35.72	34.71
绿春县	Luchun	32.15	32.27
河口县	Hekou	24.05	23.49
文山州	**Wenshan**	**636.44**	**578.16**
文山市	Wenshan	224.60	199.95
砚山县	Yanshan	62.02	55.94
西畴县	Xichou	33.72	30.31
麻栗坡县	Malipo	52.38	47.20
马关县	Maguan	53.05	52.49
丘北县	Qiubei	54.45	48.99
广南县	Guangnan	89.17	81.81
富宁县	Funing	67.05	61.48
西双版纳州	**Xishuangbanna**	**312.98**	**272.52**
景洪市	Jinghong	197.57	171.55
勐海县	Menghai	59.89	51.33
勐腊县	Mengla	55.52	49.64
大理州	**Dali**	**632.07**	**607.63**
大理市	Dali	285.50	275.36
漾濞县	Yangbi	10.57	10.01
祥云县	Xiangyun	74.96	72.60
宾川县	Binchuan	41.53	39.80
弥渡县	Midu	35.42	33.83
南涧县	Nanjian	28.38	27.43
巍山县	Weishan	33.85	32.65
永平县	Yongping	21.98	20.80
云龙县	Yunlong	22.05	21.05
洱源县	Eryuan	27.83	26.48
剑川县	Jianchuan	21.30	20.47
鹤庆县	Heqing	28.69	27.16
德宏州	**Dehong**	**317.41**	**328.18**
瑞丽市	Ruili	120.03	127.20
芒　市	Mangshi	113.92	116.09
梁河县	Lianghe	15.10	15.28
盈江县	Yingjiang	44.06	44.54
陇川县	Longchuan	24.29	25.07
怒江州	**Nujiang**	**42.79**	**36.62**
泸水市	Lushui	17.97	15.78
福贡县	Fugong	5.13	4.49
贡山县	Gongshan	3.85	3.46
兰坪县	Lanping	15.83	12.90
迪庆州	**Diqing**	**71.52**	**66.22**
香格里拉市	Shangri-La	49.50	42.01
德钦县	Deqin	9.38	10.32
维西县	Weixi	12.64	13.90

18–13 各州市县住户存款年末余额（2016–2020年）

Balance of Savings Deposits of Household at Year-end by Region (2016-2020)

单位：亿元 (100 million yuan)

州市县	Region	2016	2017	2018	2019	2020
全　省	**Yunnan**	**11 935.78**	**13 164.69**	**14 459.15**	**15 888.28**	**17 675.38**
昆明市	**Kunming**	**4 124.21**	**4 431.40**	**4 882.29**	**5 355.25**	**5 962.63**
五华区 盘龙区	Wuhua Panlong	1 947.17	2 014.20	2 244.90	2 493.23	2 739.35
官渡区	Guandu	700.22	790.09	839.79	876.58	1 014.01
西山区	Xishan	468.34	496.71	526.20	584.21	641.88
东川区	Dongchuan	74.81	83.45	96.49	101.07	109.86
呈贡区	Chenggong	189.58	214.47	242.64	275.08	311.29
晋宁区	Jinning	107.44	117.14	127.40	141.93	161.14
富民县	Fumin	43.45	49.02	55.87	63.97	71.55
宜良县	Yiliang	124.58	140.51	160.03	175.70	194.11
石林县	Shilin	59.41	63.17	71.77	80.37	90.67
嵩明县	Songming	97.05	109.04	121.87	130.73	145.76
禄劝县	Luquan	61.05	68.02	75.49	81.88	89.91
寻甸县	Xundian	76.57	93.58	102.22	111.41	124.62
安宁市	Anning	174.54	192.00	217.62	239.09	268.49
曲靖市	**Qujing**	**1 070.12**	**1 193.81**	**1 337.09**	**1 505.22**	**1 721.99**
麒麟区	Qilin	344.64	381.43	429.92	488.60	590.88
沾益区	Zhanyi	71.39	79.99	89.44	97.90	107.62
马龙区	Malong	34.80	38.85	44.70	51.35	55.62
陆良县	Luliang	102.52	115.03	127.94	148.50	173.34
师宗县	Shizong	57.95	62.25	69.54	75.89	84.74
罗平县	Luoping	75.61	82.61	90.69	102.67	116.54
富源县	Fuyuan	92.66	103.12	113.49	127.36	140.83
会泽县	Huize	95.72	106.73	119.16	131.80	146.94
宣威市	Xuanwei	194.84	223.80	252.20	281.15	305.48
玉溪市	**Yuxi**	**752.34**	**825.21**	**876.02**	**966.04**	**1 053.89**
红塔区	Hongta	291.76	317.82	338.21	372.76	407.76
江川区	Jiangchuan	73.98	81.57	90.71	101.82	109.76
通海县	Tonghai	102.86	109.02	116.57	123.77	136.65
华宁县	Huaning	46.53	50.07	52.46	60.89	66.29
易门县	Yimen	50.98	53.59	55.32	59.61	66.01
峨山县	Eshan	44.40	48.22	48.68	51.04	54.60
新平县	Xinping	52.84	65.45	65.33	69.14	74.48
元江县	Yuanjiang	39.02	42.30	43.45	44.95	48.75
澄江市	Chengjiang	49.98	57.17	65.29	82.06	89.59

18-13 续表1 continued

单位：亿元 (100 million yuan)

州市县	Region	2016	2017	2018	2019	2020
保山市	**Baoshan**	**518.14**	**594.07**	**643.93**	**711.69**	**781.73**
隆阳区	Longyang	203.44	239.97	261.09	284.99	312.49
施甸县	Shidian	50.12	58.85	64.18	69.67	79.05
龙陵县	Longling	55.97	59.91	63.86	73.04	78.91
昌宁县	Changning	49.26	54.18	56.03	63.84	71.13
腾冲市	Tengchong	159.35	181.17	198.76	220.15	240.14
昭通市	**Zhaotong**	**647.39**	**752.78**	**860.21**	**952.10**	**1047.37**
昭阳区	Zhaoyang	181.67	210.50	234.76	250.18	268.90
鲁甸县	Ludian	31.74	37.43	42.46	46.25	50.20
巧家县	Qiaojia	48.20	56.08	66.83	79.61	95.62
盐津县	Yanjin	36.97	42.25	49.42	54.16	59.21
大关县	Daguan	28.33	31.78	36.99	43.03	47.37
永善县	Yongshan	58.82	65.54	74.28	83.27	90.05
绥江县	Suijiang	35.03	40.09	43.53	47.82	51.42
镇雄县	Zhenxiong	106.00	127.22	150.51	167.59	187.98
彝良县	Yiliang	41.54	50.29	59.54	69.61	76.30
威信县	Weixin	46.69	57.28	65.28	71.64	77.32
水富市	Shuifu	32.42	34.30	36.60	38.92	42.99
丽江市	**Lijiang**	**330.98**	**373.43**	**419.25**	**460.02**	**494.16**
古城区	Gucheng	138.17	152.32	170.13	187.61	200.05
玉龙县	Yulong	33.28	38.47	43.60	47.69	51.91
永胜县	Yongsheng	72.61	84.78	94.66	105.61	114.68
华坪县	Huaping	56.46	61.78	67.73	71.08	76.64
宁蒗县	Ninglang	30.46	36.08	43.13	48.03	50.87
普洱市	**Pu'er**	**442.78**	**498.54**	**527.16**	**568.96**	**637.96**
思茅区	Simao	122.96	138.04	146.42	157.02	179.99
宁洱县	Ning'er	37.40	42.37	43.15	46.57	52.06
墨江县	Mojiang	39.58	44.73	48.70	52.87	56.43
景东县	Jingdong	49.71	55.85	59.82	66.18	72.67
景谷县	Jinggu	46.28	51.87	54.11	56.20	62.19
镇沅县	Zhenyuan	34.39	36.89	39.74	43.79	49.69
江城县	Jiangcheng	16.36	19.02	19.33	21.56	23.58
孟连县	Menglian	41.50	49.27	50.78	52.65	59.16
澜沧县	Lancang	45.81	50.74	54.70	61.39	69.81
西盟县	Ximeng	8.80	9.77	10.40	10.72	12.38
临沧市	**Lincang**	**305.60**	**340.39**	**368.08**	**416.56**	**482.35**
临翔区	Linxiang	74.41	85.49	92.51	101.61	116.32
凤庆县	Fengqing	42.05	46.26	51.53	59.31	69.04
云　县	Yunxian	51.33	56.38	62.06	70.65	79.49
永德县	Yongde	31.27	34.81	38.37	44.31	54.58
镇康县	Zhenkang	28.51	29.95	32.33	37.75	44.41
双江县	Shuangjiang	20.99	23.28	23.98	25.66	29.72
耿马县	Gengma	39.14	44.53	46.69	54.03	62.32
沧源县	Cangyuan	17.89	19.69	20.60	23.24	26.47

18-13　续表2　continued

单位：亿元　(100 million yuan)

州 市 县	Region	2016	2017	2018	2019	2020
楚 雄 州	**Chuxiong**	**563.39**	**629.20**	**685.33**	**748.92**	**829.65**
楚雄市	Chuxiong	181.05	199.66	220.87	244.98	273.08
双柏县	Shuangbai	26.44	30.24	33.30	34.98	38.75
牟定县	Mouding	34.48	38.41	42.48	45.77	49.73
南华县	Nanhua	38.25	44.89	47.47	50.33	55.15
姚安县	Yao'an	34.82	40.12	44.14	48.14	54.12
大姚县	Dayao	45.24	49.96	54.80	60.27	66.94
永仁县	Yongren	21.04	23.97	25.83	26.82	30.06
元谋县	Yuanmou	45.95	50.89	51.55	58.59	63.61
武定县	Wuding	45.25	51.03	56.95	63.94	70.34
禄丰县	Lufeng	90.88	100.03	107.93	115.12	127.89
红 河 州	**Honghe**	**989.68**	**1093.23**	**1210.89**	**1345.16**	**1485.71**
个旧市	Gejiu	160.34	172.02	187.43	203.59	221.64
开远市	Kaiyuan	108.02	115.86	125.22	138.20	154.35
蒙自市	Mengzi	150.87	163.51	182.26	209.32	236.57
弥勒市	Mile	111.00	123.90	137.26	151.75	169.09
屏边县	Pingbian	21.21	23.01	25.55	28.17	31.11
建水县	Jianshui	143.28	157.62	176.09	199.45	221.08
石屏县	Shiping	75.82	86.18	97.63	108.07	118.35
泸西县	Luxi	80.34	91.70	101.69	110.85	121.04
元阳县	Yuanyang	31.12	36.32	41.27	46.15	50.09
红河县	Honghe	24.82	28.79	32.53	36.13	40.43
金平县	Jinping	31.83	37.80	42.23	47.09	52.14
绿春县	Luchun	16.82	18.52	21.60	24.26	25.94
河口县	Hekou	34.21	38.01	40.13	42.13	43.90
文 山 州	**Wenshan**	**517.12**	**595.34**	**645.16**	**680.88**	**752.86**
文山市	Wenshan	167.68	192.86	197.97	205.09	225.19
砚山县	Yanshan	61.68	69.62	72.15	79.71	89.20
西畴县	Xichou	28.66	33.63	38.2	37.52	41.67
麻栗坡县	Malipo	38.39	43.34	48.11	50.79	55.52
马关县	Maguan	54.05	61.49	70.98	76.48	83.21
丘北县	Qiubei	43.24	51.21	58.01	62.08	70.66
广南县	Guangnan	76.5	89.36	99.88	105.81	116.59
富宁县	Funing	46.93	53.83	59.86	63.40	70.83
西双版纳州	**Xishuangbanna**	**339.65**	**371.15**	**398.91**	**428.81**	**465.41**
景洪市	Jinghong	203.32	220.05	239.86	259.52	279.07
勐海县	Menghai	58.63	63.28	69.37	76.29	86.90

18－13 续表3 continued

单位：亿元 (100 million yuan)

州 市 县	Region	2016	2017	2018	2019	2020
勐腊县	Mengla	77.70	87.82	89.68	93.01	99.45
大 理 州	**Dali**	**795.96**	**873.83**	**971.41**	**1 075.03**	**1 208.65**
大理市	Dali	321.90	348.73	395.69	435.42	480.37
漾濞县	Yangbi	16.83	19.19	21.34	23.15	26.19
祥云县	Xiangyun	89.06	98.29	105.36	121.00	138.52
宾川县	Binchuan	60.44	67.84	74.69	81.91	94.54
弥渡县	Midu	53.50	56.54	60.84	69.04	78.58
南涧县	Nanjian	27.06	30.55	33.74	36.50	42.27
巍山县	Weishan	41.63	44.49	49.92	55.67	63.50
永平县	Yongping	26.04	29.26	32.31	35.37	39.44
云龙县	Yunlong	27.43	30.66	32.70	36.64	39.55
洱源县	Eryuan	44.89	52.10	55.73	60.29	67.33
剑川县	Jianchuan	29.91	33.05	36.34	40.59	46.47
鹤庆县	Heqing	57.25	63.14	72.77	79.47	91.88
德 宏 州	**Dehong**	**359.35**	**387.02**	**402.24**	**431.17**	**483.79**
瑞丽市	Ruili	142.43	146.86	146.48	157.50	171.72
芒 市	Mangshi	104.86	112.90	122.92	133.88	152.81
梁河县	Lianghe	27.43	32.34	35.28	37.69	42.26
盈江县	Yingjiang	50.06	58.30	60.36	62.55	72.43
陇川县	Longchuan	34.56	36.62	37.21	39.56	44.55
怒 江 州	**Nujiang**	**79.51**	**92.29**	**104.68**	**108.63**	**119.08**
泸水市	Lushui	32.77	38.07	41.58	45.31	50.25
福贡县	Fugong	8.83	11.10	15.04	14.69	15.68
贡山县	Gongshan	6.34	7.95	9.46	9.69	10.57
兰坪县	Lanping	31.58	35.18	38.60	38.95	42.58
迪 庆 州	**Diqing**	**99.56**	**112.98**	**126.30**	**133.33**	**147.81**
香格里拉市	Shangri-La	64.32	73.34	80.58	83.56	91.59
德钦县	Deqin	11.42	12.38	14.58	15.25	16.92
维西县	Weixi	23.82	27.26	31.14	34.53	39.31

18-14 2020年各州市县城乡常住居民人均可支配收入

Per Capita Income of Urban and Rural Households by Region 2020

单位：元 (yuan)

州市县	Region	城镇 Urban	农村 Rural	州市县	Region	城镇 Urban	农村 Rural
全　省	**Yunnan**	**37 500**	**12 842**	隆阳区	Longyang	41 241	14 854
昆 明 市	**Kunming**	**48 018**	**17 719**	施甸县	Shidian	31 048	12 255
五华区	Wuhua	48 942	22 790	龙陵县	Longling	31 455	12 626
盘龙区	Panlong	49 177	22 954	昌宁县	Changning	33 853	12 992
官渡区	Guandu	48 997	24 073	腾冲市	Tengchong	35 667	13 463
西山区	Xishan	49 015	23 595	**昭 通 市**	**Zhaotong**	**31 007**	**11 283**
东川市	Dongchuan	36 610	10 243	昭阳区	Zhaoyang	35 962	12 657
呈贡区	Chenggong	48 427	23 298	鲁甸县	Ludian	29 392	11 335
晋宁区	Jinning	44 423	18 679	巧家县	Qiaojia	28 748	11 195
富民县	Fumin	43 930	17 374	盐津县	Yanjin	29 582	11 357
宜良县	Yiliang	45 015	17 701	大关县	Daguan	28 086	10 738
石林县	Shilin	45 213	17 440	永善县	Yongshan	28 573	11 148
嵩明县	Songming	44 583	17 239	绥江县	Suijiang	29 358	11 305
禄劝县	Luquan	36 807	10 553	镇雄县	Zhenxiong	28 901	11 490
寻甸县	Xundian	38 634	10 847	彝良县	Yiliang	28 192	10 467
安宁市	Anning	48 021	21 410	威信县	Weixin	28 186	11 041
曲 靖 市	**Qujing**	**38 657**	**14 793**	水富市	Shuifu	37 112	13 022
麒麟区	Qilin	42 652	19 728	**丽 江 市**	**Lijiang**	**37 022**	**12 370**
沾益区	Zhanyi	38 941	16 673	古城区	Gucheng	42 910	20 632
马龙区	Malong	37 220	13 512	玉龙县	Yulong	31 159	13 413
陆良县	Luliang	35 058	17 518	永胜县	Yongsheng	30 860	13 174
师宗县	Shizong	35 143	14 066	华坪县	Huaping	38 630	14 345
罗平县	Luoping	36 831	17 502	宁蒗县	Ninglang	26 042	8 972
富源县	Fuyuan	38 892	14 804	**普 洱 市**	**Pu'er**	**32 658**	**12 366**
会泽县	Huize	34 970	12 298	思茅区	Simao	35 477	13 236
宣威市	Xuanwei	39 637	14 442	宁洱县	Ning'er	34 503	12 949
玉 溪 市	**Yuxi**	**42 125**	**16 835**	墨江县	Mojiang	31 989	12 142
红塔区	Hongta	43 672	19 988	景东县	Jingdong	32 049	12 835
江川区	Jiangchuan	41 158	15 701	景谷县	Jinggu	34 160	13 143
通海县	Tonghai	42 267	19 397	镇沅县	Zhenyuan	32 233	13 141
华宁县	Huaning	41 371	16 535	江城县	Jiangcheng	31 953	11 879
易门县	Yimen	41 881	16 220	孟连县	Menglian	28 343	11 934
峨山县	Eshan	42 441	15 441	澜沧县	Lancang	30 651	11 779
新平县	Xinping	41 952	15 858	西盟县	Ximeng	27 865	11 736
元江县	Yuanjiang	41 120	15 128	**临 沧 市**	**Lincang**	**30 794**	**12 824**
澄江市	Chengjiang	42 741	17 966	临翔区	Linxiang	31 709	12 869
保 山 市	**Baoshan**	**36 433**	**13 426**	凤庆县	Fengqing	31 121	13 034

18-14 续表 continued

单位：元 (yuan)

州 市 县	Region	城镇 Urban	农村 Rural
云　县	Yunxian	31 208	13 561
永德县	Yongde	31 067	12 918
镇康县	Zhenkang	30 338	12 571
双江县	Shuangjiang	30 569	12 863
耿马县	Gengma	31 492	13 484
沧源县	Cangyuan	30 091	12 401
楚 雄 州	**Chuxiong**	**38 285**	**12 861**
楚雄市	Chuxiong	40 313	13 751
双柏县	Shuangbai	39 229	12 095
牟定县	Mouding	38 720	12 243
南华县	Nanhua	38 759	12 564
姚安县	Yao'an	38 259	12 890
大姚县	Dayao	38 500	12 484
永仁县	Yongren	38 275	11 922
元谋县	Yuanmou	39 651	14 671
武定县	Wuding	39 180	11 916
禄丰县	Lufeng	39 849	14 035
红 河 州	**Honghe**	**37 500**	**13 580**
个旧市	Gejiu	39 307	18 382
开远市	Kaiyuan	39 110	18 229
蒙自市	Mengzi	39 790	16 559
弥勒市	Mile	39 669	16 061
屏边县	Pingbian	34 551	10 474
建水县	Jianshui	37 241	16 560
石屏县	Shiping	35 863	15 137
泸西县	Luxi	35 906	14 825
元阳县	Yuanyang	34 217	10 251
红河县	Honghe	34 736	10 430
金平县	Jinping	34 908	10 311
绿春县	Luchun	34 290	10 266
河口县	Hekou	37 315	14 973
文 山 州	**Wenshan**	**33 709**	**12 001**
文山市	Wenshan	37 324	13 321
砚山县	Yanshan	36 213	12 705
西畴县	Xichou	30 758	11 495
麻栗坡县	Malipo	30 603	11 984
马关县	Maguan	33 824	12 054
丘北县	Qiubei	31 205	12 318
广南县	Guangnan	30 416	11 435
富宁县	Funing	33 255	12 453
西双版纳州	**Xishuangbanna**	**33 147**	**15 463**
景洪市	Jinghong	36 652	17 615
勐海县	Menghai	32 525	13 951
勐腊县	Mengla	28 077	12 777
大 理 州	**Dali**	**38 435**	**13 645**
大理市	Dali	41 147	18 968
漾濞县	yangbi	34 490	12 855
祥云县	Xiangyun	39 385	14 121
宾川县	Binchuan	38 326	18 181
弥渡县	Midu	36 285	11 981
南涧县	Nanjian	36 653	10 969
巍山县	Weishan	36 369	12 092
永平县	Yongping	36 263	12 203
云龙县	Yunlong	34 450	11 751
洱源县	Eryuan	36 408	12 733
剑川县	Jianchuan	34 368	10 728
鹤庆县	Heqing	37 845	12 457
德 宏 州	**Dehong**	**32 770**	**12 356**
瑞丽市	Ruili	39 051	13 955
芒　市	Mangshi	32 070	13 618
梁河县	Lianghe	28 780	10 375
盈江县	Yingjiang	31 269	12 679
陇川县	Longchuan	29 989	11 434
怒 江 州	**Nujiang**	**27 506**	**7 810**
泸水市	Lushui	28 455	7 973
福贡县	Fugong	26 209	7 557
贡山县	Gongshan	26 132	7 681
兰坪县	Lanping	28 249	7 920
迪 庆 州	**Diqing**	**38 547**	**10 088**
香格里拉市	Shangri-La	38 995	10 139
德钦县	Deqin	40 488	10 045
维西县	Weixi	34 940	10 076

18-15 各州市县农、林、牧、渔业总产值（2017-2020年）
Gross Output Value of Farming, Forestry, Animal Husbandry and Fishery by Region (2017-2020)

(按现行价格计算) (Calculated at current prices)
单位：亿元 (100 million yuan)

州市县	Region	2017	2018	2019	2020
全　省	**Yunnan**	**3 872.93**	**4 108.88**	**4 935.74**	**5 920.52**
昆明市	**Kunming**	**366.38**	**374.84**	**447.49**	**519.50**
五华区	Wuhua	3.43	3.40	3.95	4.06
盘龙区	Panlong	8.40	8.22	9.09	9.51
官渡区	Guandu	13.96	13.42	13.10	14.74
西山区	Xishan	6.20	6.10	7.05	7.72
东川区	Dongchuan	14.45	14.88	17.88	21.19
呈贡区	Chenggong	8.21	8.20	9.56	9.83
晋宁区	Jinning	37.98	39.07	46.97	51.17
富民县	Fumin	17.75	18.22	21.83	25.50
宜良县	Yiliang	77.98	80.22	97.58	115.24
石林县	Shilin	38.57	39.71	47.74	55.32
嵩明县	Songming	27.91	28.64	34.16	37.76
禄劝县	Luquan	43.98	45.28	54.43	65.74
寻甸县	Xundian	42.37	43.62	53.22	65.70
安宁市	Anning	25.19	25.84	30.94	36.04
曲靖市	**Qujing**	**603.74**	**596.28**	**713.19**	**911.13**
麒麟区	Qilin	45.18	45.00	51.89	63.36
沾益区	Zhanyi	60.12	60.80	72.58	88.08
马龙区	Malong	18.38	18.62	22.52	32.53
陆良县	Luliang	97.01	95.09	113.88	136.03
师宗县	Shizong	58.80	53.31	58.82	72.41
罗平县	Luoping	82.96	82.44	99.48	126.41
富源县	Fuyuan	59.48	59.58	72.03	93.57
会泽县	Huize	80.54	81.26	101.50	143.28
宣威市	Xuanwei	101.28	100.19	120.50	155.47
玉溪市	**Yuxi**	**245.58**	**250.04**	**298.79**	**343.53**
红塔区	Hongta	29.02	29.55	34.88	36.10
江川区	Jiangchuan	27.79	28.29	34.01	43.22
通海县	Tonghai	28.78	29.30	35.50	41.79
华宁县	Huaning	29.88	30.37	36.79	40.81
易门县	Yimen	20.40	20.40	24.49	24.90
峨山县	Eshan	18.61	18.95	22.75	26.62
新平县	Xinping	38.63	39.86	48.63	55.24
元江县	Yuanjiang	33.34	33.94	41.23	52.26
澄江市	Chengjiang	19.12	19.37	20.51	22.59
保山市	**Baoshan**	**262.09**	**268.93**	**321.36**	**385.41**
隆阳区	Longyang	85.84	89.10	103.48	119.23
施甸县	Shidian	32.92	32.86	39.72	47.89
龙陵县	Longling	30.56	31.81	38.43	51.28
昌宁县	Changning	55.12	54.51	67.23	80.41
腾冲市	Tengchong	57.66	60.64	72.50	86.58
昭通市	**Zhaotong**	**247.02**	**249.09**	**296.80**	**342.34**
昭阳区	Zhaoyang	44.07	44.00	52.42	59.95
鲁甸县	Ludian	18.74	19.13	22.90	26.30
巧家县	Qiaojia	37.87	38.11	45.32	55.16
盐津县	Yanjin	14.81	15.07	17.92	21.28
大关县	Daguan	10.63	10.83	12.91	14.20
永善县	Yongshan	21.48	21.99	26.07	31.49
绥江县	Suijiang	7.03	7.05	8.39	10.43
镇雄县	Zhenxiong	44.08	44.23	52.80	56.80
彝良县	Yiliang	31.76	31.71	37.81	43.07
威信县	Weixin	12.79	13.03	15.55	18.22
水富市	Shuifu	3.76	3.93	4.70	5.44
丽江市	**Lijiang**	**91.03**	**93.43**	**111.65**	**135.62**
古城区	Lijiang	10.05	10.20	11.80	13.58
玉龙县	Yulong	23.18	23.90	28.06	33.96
永胜县	Yongsheng	30.47	31.44	38.52	48.14
华坪县	Huaping	13.24	13.50	15.60	18.51
宁蒗县	Ninglang	14.09	14.39	17.67	21.43
普洱市	**Pu'er**	**273.35**	**271.95**	**324.65**	**385.88**
思茅区	Simao	25.00	25.41	30.37	34.23
宁洱县	Ning'er	19.53	19.48	23.97	28.55
墨江县	Mojiang	28.38	28.44	33.99	40.11
景东县	Jingdong	42.32	42.11	50.15	59.76
景谷县	Jinggu	49.56	48.00	55.20	65.84
镇沅县	Zhenyuan	33.53	32.81	39.87	47.53
江城县	Jiangcheng	15.71	15.61	18.70	22.45
孟连县	Menglian	19.71	20.21	24.22	28.94
澜沧县	Lancang	34.20	34.20	41.21	49.95
西盟县	Ximeng	5.41	5.67	6.97	8.52

注：因分级核算，各州(市)加总数不等于全省数，分县(市、区)加总数不等于州(市)数。
Note: Number of the whole province is not equal to the aggregate number of 16 cities and prefectures and the number of the city and prefecture is not equal to the aggregate number of its counties because of the different accounting at different levels.

18-15 续表 continued

(按现行价格计算)
单位：亿元

(Calculated at current prices)
(100 million yuan)

州市县	Region	2017	2018	2019	2020
临沧市	**Lincang**	**263.38**	**270.60**	**323.04**	**377.09**
临翔区	Linxiang	27.38	28.50	30.51	35.36
凤庆县	Fengqing	55.89	59.41	69.54	81.18
云　县	Yunxian	47.36	49.00	58.58	68.48
永德县	Yongde	28.06	28.97	43.24	50.98
镇康县	Zhenkang	18.64	17.72	21.28	24.77
双江县	Shuangjiang	18.52	18.70	22.03	25.67
耿马县	Gengma	48.78	49.92	55.85	65.03
沧源县	Cangyuan	18.74	18.38	22.00	25.62
楚雄州	**Chuxiong**	**305.62**	**311.91**	**373.06**	**441.12**
楚雄市	Chuxiong	46.44	47.29	56.22	65.88
双柏县	Shuangbai	19.85	20.22	24.12	28.65
牟定县	Mouding	20.43	20.90	24.95	29.54
南华县	Nanhua	28.48	29.13	34.45	40.95
姚安县	Yao'an	27.09	27.66	32.86	39.03
大姚县	Dayao	36.59	37.46	44.41	52.70
永仁县	Yongren	16.00	16.37	19.58	23.26
元谋县	Yuanmou	27.67	28.27	35.53	41.98
武定县	Wuding	31.74	32.38	38.47	45.38
禄丰县	Lufeng	51.33	52.24	62.47	73.77
红河州	**Honghe**	**382.73**	**385.43**	**460.57**	**564.39**
个旧市	Gejiu	25.54	25.78	31.09	38.24
开远市	Kaiyuan	29.58	29.81	35.71	42.85
蒙自市	Mengzi	38.16	38.42	45.73	56.23
弥勒市	Mile	51.47	51.70	61.26	75.33
屏边县	Pingbian	11.67	11.85	14.22	17.06
建水县	Jianshui	52.03	52.20	61.65	75.45
石屏县	Shiping	46.73	46.98	55.91	67.24
泸西县	Luxi	35.04	35.27	43.07	54.26
元阳县	Yuanyang	21.55	21.71	26.01	31.77
红河县	Honghe	19.19	19.38	23.25	28.83
金平县	Jinping	19.96	20.13	24.18	29.74
绿春县	Luchun	16.67	16.88	20.26	24.82
河口县	Hekou	15.14	15.32	18.23	22.56
文山州	**Wenshan**	**278.05**	**281.19**	**335.68**	**396.05**
文山市	Wenshan	31.70	31.96	38.72	43.75
砚山县	Yanshan	42.88	43.45	53.29	60.72
西畴县	Xichou	16.91	17.15	21.10	25.76
麻栗坡县	Malipo	19.34	19.53	23.18	27.85
马关县	Maguan	31.49	31.88	38.73	45.35
丘北县	Qiubei	40.38	40.79	48.69	60.46
广南县	Guangnan	59.34	59.95	68.39	82.05
富宁县	Funing	36.01	36.47	43.57	50.12
西双版纳州	**Xishuangbanna**	**169.59**	**173.90**	**207.60**	**230.10**
景洪市	Jinghong	68.76	70.54	83.94	92.16
勐海县	Menghai	39.02	40.10	49.72	57.28
勐腊县	Mengla	61.81	63.26	73.94	80.66
大理州	**Dali**	**407.92**	**416.01**	**495.70**	**618.35**
大理市	Dali	47.03	30.53	34.76	38.36
漾濞县	Yangbi	11.03	13.27	16.26	20.74
祥云县	Xiangyun	53.90	57.61	68.85	80.01
宾川县	Binchuan	81.73	85.21	100.42	119.54
弥渡县	Midu	32.87	35.17	43.59	59.65
南涧县	Nanjian	24.28	25.98	31.58	40.33
巍山县	Weishan	31.00	33.13	39.70	52.75
永平县	Yongping	23.25	24.88	29.49	37.90
云龙县	Yunlong	24.10	25.57	30.93	35.16
洱源县	Eryuan	39.40	41.46	47.82	63.28
剑川县	Jianchuan	13.39	15.48	18.78	24.19
鹤庆县	Heqing	25.94	27.72	33.51	46.44
德宏州	**Dehong**	**132.38**	**133.32**	**159.46**	**192.48**
瑞丽市	Ruili	15.14	14.65	17.50	21.03
芒　市	Mangshi	35.29	35.49	42.39	51.43
梁河县	Lianghe	13.11	13.79	16.49	19.91
盈江县	Yingjiang	41.50	41.83	50.06	60.20
陇川县	Longchuan	27.34	27.56	33.01	39.91
怒江州	**Nujiang**	**33.70**	**34.59**	**41.22**	**47.08**
泸水市	Lushui	11.55	12.29	14.79	17.09
福贡县	Fugong	5.24	5.40	6.46	6.86
贡山县	Gongshan	3.91	3.92	4.36	5.03
兰坪县	Lanping	13.01	12.99	15.61	18.10
迪庆州	**Diqing**	**21.26**	**21.61**	**25.80**	**30.46**
香格里拉市	Shangri-La	8.01	8.07	9.76	11.47
德钦县	Deqin	2.91	2.92	3.39	4.07
维西县	Weixi	10.34	10.62	12.65	14.92

18–16 各州市县粮食作物种植面积（2020年）

Planting Area of Major Food Crops by Region (2020)

单位:万公顷 (10 000 hectares)

州市县	Region	粮食 Grain	稻谷 Rice	小麦 Wheat	玉米 Corn	豆类 Beans	薯类 Tubers
全　省	**Yunnan**	**416.74**	**81.89**	**32.00**	**180.25**	**48.46**	**54.39**
昆明市	**Kunming**	**23.34**	**1.46**	**2.37**	**8.58**	**3.93**	**3.75**
五华区	Wuhua	0.18	0.00	0.02	0.10	0.04	0.01
盘龙区	Panlong	0.75		0.08	0.31	0.12	0.08
官渡区	Guandu	0.41		0.06	0.23	0.06	0.02
西山区	Xishan	0.23	0.00	0.03	0.14	0.04	0.01
东川区	Dongchuan	1.36	0.11	0.09	0.55	0.10	0.40
呈贡区	Chenggong	0.03			0.03	0.00	
晋宁区	Jinning	0.52	0.02	0.04	0.30	0.11	0.05
富民县	Fumin	1.33	0.10	0.19	0.50	0.42	0.07
宜良县	Yiliang	3.02	0.30	0.39	1.33	0.75	0.11
石林县	Shilin	3.06	0.26	0.36	1.29	0.54	0.23
嵩明县	Songming	1.24	0.06	0.21	0.47	0.33	0.08
禄劝县	Luquan	4.99	0.25	0.65	1.83	0.65	0.75
寻甸县	Xundian	5.75	0.32	0.23	1.18	0.72	1.93
安宁市	Anning	0.46	0.02	0.02	0.33	0.06	0.01
曲靖市	**Qujing**	**63.04**	**5.96**	**3.64**	**23.15**	**6.41**	**18.94**
麒麟区	Qilin	3.61	0.69	0.14	0.92	0.85	0.35
沾益区	Zhanyi	6.98	1.20	0.31	2.53	1.05	1.28
马龙区	Malong	3.03	0.70	0.21	0.87	0.19	0.72
陆良县	Luliang	5.51	0.63	0.10	1.55	0.54	2.37
师宗县	Shizong	4.06	0.52	0.52	1.37	0.42	0.73
罗平县	Luoping	5.54	0.67	0.34	2.67	0.64	0.90
富源县	Fuyuan	6.20	0.31	0.76	2.84	0.80	1.33
会泽县	Huize	10.86	0.56	0.43	2.99	1.12	5.41
宣威市	Xuanwei	17.24	0.69	0.84	7.41	0.80	5.86
玉溪市	**Yuxi**	**11.08**	**1.63**	**1.17**	**5.78**	**1.30**	**0.50**
红塔区	Hongta	0.53	0.01	0.03	0.33	0.14	0.02
江川区	Jiangchuan	0.63	0.18	0.07	0.11	0.17	0.08
通海县	Tonghai	0.44	0.01	0.08	0.28	0.04	0.02
华宁县	Huaning	1.21	0.10	0.23	0.66	0.14	0.07
易门县	Yimen	1.31	0.07	0.34	0.72	0.10	0.04
峨山县	Eshan	1.19	0.28	0.06	0.61	0.17	0.02
新平县	Xinping	3.43	0.56	0.15	1.94	0.26	0.18
元江县	Yuanjiang	1.88	0.41	0.17	1.00	0.16	0.06
澄江市	Chengjiang	0.45	0.01	0.04	0.12	0.11	0.01

注：全省粮食面积数据为抽样调查数，分州（市）及分县（市、区）数据为全面统计数。
Note: Data of grain area of the whole province are sampling survey data, and the data by region are comprehensive survey data.

18-16 续表1 continued

单位:万公顷

(10 000 hectares)

州市县	Region	粮食 Grain	稻谷 Rice	小麦 Wheat	玉米 Corn	豆类 Beans	薯类 Tubers
保山市	**Baoshan**	**26.34**	**5.39**	**0.88**	**10.79**	**3.63**	**2.13**
隆阳区	Longyang	6.82	0.78	0.26	3.61	1.24	0.34
施甸县	Shidian	3.46	0.13	0.22	1.81	0.72	0.16
龙陵县	Longling	3.36	0.80	0.13	1.12	0.34	0.42
昌宁县	Changning	4.41	0.75	0.27	1.72	0.78	0.39
腾冲市	Tengchong	8.30	2.93		2.54	0.54	0.81
昭通市	**Zhaotong**	**50.41**	**2.53**	**2.34**	**22.53**	**4.44**	**17.85**
昭阳区	Zhaoyang	5.12	0.32	0.01	1.85	0.39	2.35
鲁甸县	Ludian	3.69	0.13	0.19	1.62	0.41	1.25
巧家县	Qiaojia	4.70	0.09	0.36	1.59	0.50	2.01
盐津县	Yanjin	4.31	0.50	0.10	2.07	0.38	1.27
大关县	Daguan	3.28	0.16	0.23	1.47	0.27	1.15
永善县	Yongshan	4.52	0.32	0.19	1.64	0.51	1.79
绥江县	Suijiang	0.91	0.14	0.01	0.52	0.13	0.10
镇雄县	Zhenxiong	13.57	0.08	0.72	6.56	0.95	5.11
彝良县	Yiliang	4.57	0.17	0.51	2.33	0.33	1.20
威信县	Weixin	4.92	0.28	0.04	2.51	0.49	1.57
水富市	Shuifu	0.81	0.34		0.37	0.07	0.04
丽江市	**Lijiang**	**12.78**	**1.21**	**0.98**	**4.62**	**2.38**	**2.09**
古城区	Gucheng	0.92	0.05	0.10	0.38	0.17	0.11
玉龙县	Yulong	3.28	0.13	0.52	1.11	0.57	0.53
永胜县	Yongsheng	4.17	0.68	0.16	1.77	0.88	0.31
华坪县	Huaping	1.40	0.15	0.11	0.66	0.34	0.12
宁蒗县	Ninglang	3.02	0.19	0.09	0.69	0.41	1.03
普洱市	**Pu'er**	**34.22**	**7.15**	**2.57**	**18.85**	**3.31**	**1.50**
思茅区	Simao	1.72	0.26	0.14	1.14	0.14	0.03
宁洱县	Ning'er	2.78	0.56	0.38	1.44	0.20	0.15
墨江县	Mojiang	4.36	0.58	0.35	2.67	0.51	0.11
景东县	Jingdong	4.64	0.66	0.73	1.84	1.00	0.34
景谷县	Jinggu	4.63	0.76	0.23	2.61	0.49	0.47
镇沅县	Zhenyuan	3.34	0.41	0.53	2.07	0.26	0.05
江城县	Jiangcheng	1.57	0.21	0.02	1.30	0.02	0.02
孟连县	Menglian	1.93	0.99	0.00	0.80	0.07	0.01
澜沧县	Lancang	7.82	2.28	0.16	4.13	0.59	0.29
西盟县	Ximeng	1.43	0.45	0.04	0.84	0.02	0.01
临沧市	**Lincang**	**28.81**	**4.32**	**3.21**	**15.32**	**3.55**	**1.94**
临翔区	Linxiang	2.43	0.33	0.19	1.20	0.39	0.29
凤庆县	Fengqing	4.88	0.62	1.22	2.17	0.54	0.20

18–16 续表2 continued

单位：万公顷 (10 000 hectares)

州 市 县	Region	粮 食 Grain	稻 谷 Rice	小 麦 Wheat	玉 米 Corn	豆 类 Beans	薯 类 Tubers
云 县	Yunxian	5.50	0.86	0.88	2.64	0.64	0.39
永德县	Yongde	5.65	0.36	0.42	3.55	0.84	0.43
镇康县	Zhenkang	3.04	0.56	0.23	1.72	0.33	0.18
双江县	Shuangjiang	2.19	0.26	0.15	1.19	0.30	0.24
耿马县	Gengma	2.83	0.90	0.07	1.39	0.31	0.15
沧源县	Cangyuan	2.28	0.43	0.04	1.46	0.21	0.07
楚 雄 州	**Chuxiong**	**24.55**	5.85	3.86	8.08	4.21	0.83
楚雄市	Chuxiong	3.78	0.98	0.66	1.18	0.51	0.09
双柏县	Shuangbai	1.98	0.27	0.35	0.76	0.49	0.05
牟定县	Mouding	2.18	0.65	0.28	0.55	0.54	0.05
南华县	Nanhua	2.28	0.45	0.51	0.70	0.25	0.17
姚安县	Yao'an	1.63	0.33	0.16	0.60	0.42	0.03
大姚县	Dayao	2.78	0.48	0.36	0.95	0.64	0.26
永仁县	Yongren	1.34	0.29	0.15	0.47	0.24	0.09
元谋县	Yuanmou	1.72	0.52	0.18	0.80	0.12	0.05
武定县	Wuding	2.68	0.63	0.54	0.90	0.34	0.04
禄丰县	Lufeng	4.18	1.24	0.66	1.17	0.65	0.01
红 河 州	**Honghe**	**38.52**	8.81	2.68	14.30	5.03	4.21
个旧市	Gejiu	1.50	0.20	0.09	0.74	0.20	0.20
开远市	Kaiyuan	2.81	0.44	0.19	1.24	0.33	0.36
蒙自市	Mengzi	3.79	0.75	0.10	1.23	1.11	0.26
弥勒市	Mile	5.51	0.79	1.00	2.18	0.33	0.39
屏边县	Pingbian	1.83	0.49	0.06	0.58	0.33	0.28
建水县	Jianshui	4.51	0.87	0.26	1.65	0.59	1.00
石屏县	Shiping	2.60	0.67	0.43	0.60	0.30	0.50
泸西县	Luxi	3.44	0.31	0.32	1.05	0.23	0.56
元阳县	Yuanyang	3.51	1.27	0.01	1.18	0.65	0.25
红河县	Honghe	2.83	0.87	0.22	0.78	0.30	0.20
金平县	Jinping	3.04	1.17		1.36	0.37	0.07
绿春县	Luchun	2.70	0.86	0.00	1.37	0.24	0.15
河口县	Hekou	0.45	0.09		0.33	0.03	
文 山 州	**Wenshan**	**44.48**	7.52	3.66	20.22	7.22	3.90
文山市	Wenshan	5.42	1.14	0.85	2.77	0.23	0.23
砚山县	Yanshan	7.20	0.99	1.00	3.97	0.61	0.58
西畴县	Xichou	3.38	0.35	0.03	1.04	0.84	0.73
麻栗坡县	Malipo	3.23	0.38	0.06	1.31	0.59	0.38
马关县	Maguan	4.81	0.82	0.03	1.81	1.44	0.53

18−16 续表3 continued

单位：万公顷

(10 000 hectares)

州市县	Region	粮食 Grain	稻谷 Rice	小麦 Wheat	玉米 Corn	豆类 Beans	薯类 Tubers
丘北县	Qiubei	6.83	0.80	1.14	4.15	0.57	0.18
广南县	Guangnan	10.24	2.33	0.53	3.88	2.00	0.89
富宁县	Funing	3.36	0.72	0.02	1.29	0.95	0.38
西双版纳州	**Xishuangbanna**	**8.54**	2.53		5.65	0.13	0.09
景洪市	Jinghong	1.98	0.27		1.69	0.01	0.01
勐海县	Menghai	4.67	1.95		2.43	0.10	0.08
勐腊县	Mengla	1.89	0.31		1.53	0.02	
大理州	**Dali**	**29.68**	5.06	1.50	13.17	4.57	1.81
大理市	Dali	1.40	0.29	0.06	0.54	0.31	0.11
漾濞县	Yangbi	1.49	0.16	0.17	0.86	0.18	0.09
祥云县	Xiangyun	3.34	0.49	0.23	1.45	0.50	0.24
宾川县	Binchuan	2.41	0.27	0.03	1.73	0.23	0.05
弥渡县	Midu	2.47	0.59	0.17	1.06	0.15	0.13
南涧县	Nanjian	2.45	0.14	0.27	1.06	0.41	0.13
巍山县	Weishan	2.97	0.57	0.16	1.23	0.61	0.08
永平县	Yongping	2.46	0.32	0.12	1.13	0.32	0.09
云龙县	Yunlong	3.21	0.43	0.14	1.56	0.44	0.20
洱源县	Eryuan	2.75	0.51	0.03	0.76	0.93	0.24
剑川县	Jianchuan	2.09	0.48	0.08	0.70	0.31	0.34
鹤庆县	Heqing	2.63	0.80	0.04	1.06	0.18	0.12
德宏州	**Dehong**	**12.91**	5.69	0.15	4.37	0.59	2.08
瑞丽市	Ruili	0.88	0.47		0.37	0.02	0.02
芒　市	Mangshi	3.67	1.64	0.02	1.47	0.17	0.37
梁河县	Lianghe	1.47	0.72	0.00	0.44	0.08	0.23
盈江县	Yingjiang	4.70	1.90	0.00	1.23	0.22	1.32
陇川县	Longchuan	2.20	0.96	0.12	0.86	0.10	0.15
怒江州	**Nujiang**	**5.81**	0.36	0.51	2.14	1.42	0.87
泸水市	Lushui	2.05	0.15	0.08	0.91	0.51	0.31
福贡县	Fugong	0.55	0.03	0.00	0.22	0.11	0.16
贡山县	Gongshan	0.15	0.01	0.00	0.07	0.03	0.03
兰坪县	Lanping	3.06	0.18	0.43	0.94	0.77	0.37
迪庆州	**Diqing**	**4.28**	0.22	0.59	1.80	0.43	0.46
香格里拉市	Shangri-La	1.58	0.07	0.21	0.52	0.12	0.20
德钦县	Deqin	0.55	0.01	0.14	0.21	0.04	0.03
维西县	Weixi	2.15	0.15	0.24	1.07	0.27	0.23

18-17 各州市县主要农作物产量（一）（2020年）
Output of Major Farm Crops by Region (I) (2020)

单位：万吨 (10 000 tons)

州市县	Region	粮食 Grain	稻谷 Rice	小麦 Wheat	玉米 Corn	豆类 Beans	薯类（折粮） Tubers
全　省	**Yunnan**	**1895.86**	**524.91**	**69.70**	**938.00**	**123.33**	**185.03**
昆明市	**Kunming**	**103.65**	**10.51**	**6.12**	**53.57**	**8.75**	**17.86**
五华区	Wuhua	0.88	0.01	0.07	0.58	0.16	0.02
盘龙区	Panlong	3.10		0.12	1.94	0.30	0.45
官渡区	Guandu	1.66		0.10	1.32	0.13	0.05
西山区	Xishan	1.17	0.02	0.13	0.81	0.14	0.03
东川区	Dongchuan	4.90	0.73	0.10	2.26	0.11	1.53
呈贡区	Chenggong	0.15			0.15	0.00	
晋宁区	Jinning	2.17	0.12	0.12	1.37	0.29	0.26
富民县	Fuming	6.09	0.85	0.67	3.15	0.96	0.30
宜良县	Yiliang	14.62	2.63	1.14	8.66	1.49	0.36
石林县	Shilin	14.23	1.73	1.15	9.05	0.95	0.86
嵩明县	Songming	5.17	0.46	0.35	3.02	0.87	0.25
禄劝县	Luquan	22.91	1.89	1.56	11.54	1.64	4.42
寻甸县	Xundian	23.54	1.94	0.56	7.14	1.57	9.25
安宁市	Anning	3.07	0.14	0.06	2.57	0.15	0.07
曲靖市	**Qujing**	**324.08**	**42.45**	**8.61**	**164.30**	**18.40**	**78.24**
麒麟区	Qilin	23.55	6.62	0.44	8.52	3.04	2.40
沾益区	Zhanyi	36.34	7.58	1.01	19.27	2.60	4.31
马龙区	Malong	10.18	3.15	0.39	3.90	0.45	1.73
陆良县	Luliang	32.20	5.53	0.29	11.60	1.41	12.60
师宗县	Shizong	22.75	3.95	1.29	11.99	1.49	2.76
罗平县	Luoping	37.89	5.65	1.25	22.32	2.86	4.65
富源县	Fuyuan	35.92	1.93	1.72	23.02	2.44	6.55
会泽县	Huize	46.23	4.08	0.68	17.47	2.10	21.16
宣威市	Xuanwei	79.01	3.95	1.56	46.21	2.00	22.09
玉溪市	**Yuxi**	**61.20**	**12.06**	**2.81**	**38.71**	**3.20**	**2.32**
红塔区	Hongta	3.79	0.05	0.11	3.03	0.48	0.10
江川区	Jiangchuan	4.59	1.69	0.26	1.80	0.30	0.49
通海县	Tonghai	2.61	0.05	0.18	2.12	0.11	0.13
华宁县	Huaning	6.62	0.89	0.55	4.39	0.40	0.36
易门县	Yimen	6.13	0.44	0.77	4.39	0.26	0.18
峨山县	Eshan	7.38	2.27	0.15	4.40	0.42	0.07
新平县	Xinping	17.98	3.85	0.31	11.29	0.61	0.78
元江县	Yuanjiang	9.47	2.72	0.34	5.51	0.33	0.20
澄江市	Chengjiang	2.63	0.10	0.12	1.79	0.30	0.03

注：全省粮食数据为抽样调查数，分州（市）及分县（市、区）数据为全面统计数。
Note: Data of grain output of the whole province are sampling survey data, and the data by region are comprehensive survey data.

18-17 续表1 continued

单位:万吨 (10 000 tons)

州市县	Region	粮食 Grain	稻谷 Rice	小麦 Wheat	玉米 Corn	豆类 Beans	薯类（折粮） Tubers
保山市	**Baoshan**	**146.12**	**40.67**	**3.02**	**70.52**	**9.66**	**9.38**
隆阳区	Longyang	49.11	8.19	1.14	29.58	4.94	2.72
施甸县	Shidian	16.36	1.15	0.81	10.46	1.59	0.65
龙陵县	Longling	15.41	5.20	0.33	5.99	0.67	1.57
昌宁县	Changning	22.13	6.63	0.74	10.13	1.51	1.61
腾冲市	Tengchong	43.11	19.50		14.36	0.95	2.84
昭通市	**Zhaotong**	**208.02**	**15.83**	**4.14**	**120.27**	**9.46**	**56.91**
昭阳区	Zhaoyang	30.84	2.89	0.01	15.26	1.18	11.00
鲁甸县	Ludian	14.68	0.91	0.19	8.57	0.75	4.08
巧家县	Qiaojia	21.44	0.74	0.77	8.84	1.21	9.53
盐津县	Yanjin	14.47	2.75	0.14	9.33	0.66	1.59
大关县	Daguan	8.96	1.01	0.29	5.40	0.44	1.81
永善县	Yongshan	21.24	2.68	0.36	8.65	1.27	8.13
绥江县	Suijiang	3.28	0.66	0.02	2.24	0.21	0.16
镇雄县	Zhenxiong	47.80	0.30	1.66	31.90	1.82	11.93
彝良县	Yiliang	22.11	0.98	0.63	13.94	1.12	5.40
威信县	Weixin	20.38	1.59	0.08	14.81	0.71	3.18
水富市	Shuifu	2.83	1.31		1.33	0.10	0.09
丽江市	**Lijiang**	**50.40**	**8.47**	**3.22**	**21.07**	**6.41**	**6.97**
古城区	Gucheng	3.86	0.28	0.32	2.10	0.39	0.43
玉龙县	Yulong	10.96	0.51	1.75	4.07	1.19	1.85
永胜县	Yongsheng	22.04	5.88	0.52	10.07	2.79	1.47
华坪县	Huaping	5.96	1.03	0.43	2.78	1.18	0.54
宁蒗县	Ninglang	7.58	0.77	0.20	2.06	0.86	2.68
普洱市	**Pu'er**	**120.00**	**34.62**	**4.81**	**70.58**	**4.69**	**4.07**
思茅区	Simao	6.44	1.58	0.26	4.27	0.27	0.05
宁洱县	Ning'er	8.56	2.33	0.73	4.81	0.28	0.37
墨江县	Mojiang	15.56	2.59	0.57	11.29	0.68	0.20
景东县	Jingdong	19.18	4.96	1.47	9.11	1.72	1.79
景谷县	Jinggu	15.81	3.59	0.53	10.22	0.59	0.78
镇沅县	Zhenyuan	12.00	2.32	0.94	8.23	0.39	0.09
江城县	Jiangcheng	5.26	0.93	0.03	4.21	0.02	0.06
孟连县	Menglian	7.59	4.68	0.00	2.70	0.10	0.03
澜沧县	Lancang	25.44	10.14	0.24	13.22	0.63	0.69
西盟县	Ximeng	4.16	1.51	0.05	2.51	0.02	0.01
临沧市	**Lincang**	**104.00**	**21.96**	**5.15**	**64.96**	**6.20**	**4.86**
临翔区	Linxiang	9.52	1.66	0.38	6.19	0.67	0.56
凤庆县	Fengqing	16.88	3.26	1.96	9.74	1.17	0.51

18-17 续表2 continued

单位:万吨 (10 000 tons)

州市县	Region	粮食 Grain Crops	稻谷 Rice	小麦 Wheat	玉米 Maize	豆类 Beans and Peas	薯类（折粮） Tubers
云 县	Yunxian	21.59	4.51	1.25	13.75	0.97	0.93
永德县	Yongde	20.42	2.15	0.57	14.77	1.44	1.35
镇康县	Zhenkang	8.65	2.37	0.40	5.05	0.51	0.30
双江县	Shuangjiang	7.32	1.74	0.36	4.16	0.43	0.55
耿马县	Gengma	11.71	4.47	0.16	5.80	0.73	0.52
沧源县	Cangyuan	7.91	1.80	0.07	5.50	0.28	0.14
楚雄州	**Chuxiong**	**126.67**	**44.67**	**11.09**	**48.71**	**13.29**	**3.59**
楚雄市	Chuxiong	21.41	8.35	2.24	7.38	1.77	0.37
双柏县	Shuangbai	8.25	1.75	0.68	4.39	1.15	0.15
牟定县	Mouding	10.78	4.88	0.73	3.03	1.59	0.21
南华县	Nanhua	11.53	3.33	1.42	4.70	0.80	0.70
姚安县	Yao'an	9.84	2.71	0.73	4.31	1.55	0.16
大姚县	Dayao	13.55	3.20	1.14	5.31	2.38	1.32
永仁县	Yongren	6.47	2.38	0.26	2.60	0.59	0.37
元谋县	Yuanmou	9.17	3.85	0.41	4.37	0.37	0.08
武定县	Wuding	12.51	4.31	1.20	5.31	0.95	0.18
禄丰县	Lufeng	23.17	9.92	2.27	7.31	2.15	0.04
红河州	**Honghe**	**183.49**	**60.00**	**5.73**	**77.24**	**11.06**	**17.93**
个旧市	Gejiu	7.32	1.22	0.26	3.95	0.47	0.97
开远市	Kaiyuan	15.51	3.57	0.27	8.15	0.88	1.93
蒙自市	Mengzi	15.63	4.73	0.17	6.71	2.35	0.92
弥勒市	Mile	28.06	6.22	2.09	15.74	0.51	1.26
屏边县	Pingbian	6.28	2.46	0.10	2.40	0.55	0.53
建水县	Jianshui	22.54	7.24	0.49	9.58	0.89	3.98
石屏县	Shiping	11.63	4.50	0.64	2.85	0.72	2.68
泸西县	Luxi	18.72	2.82	1.09	6.93	0.58	3.04
元阳县	Yuanyang	16.55	7.71	0.02	5.87	1.80	0.90
红河县	Honghe	14.27	6.45	0.59	3.60	0.87	1.01
金平县	Jinping	13.57	7.81		4.54	0.88	0.23
绿春县	Luchun	11.18	4.73	0.00	5.31	0.47	0.49
河口县	Hekou	2.25	0.55		1.62	0.08	
文山州	**Wenshan**	**169.76**	**47.58**	**5.75**	**92.79**	**10.75**	**8.75**
文山市	Wenshan	23.24	6.81	1.35	13.55	0.52	0.67
砚山县	Yanshan	30.25	6.44	1.51	19.57	0.99	1.50
西畴县	Xichou	11.36	2.79	0.06	5.23	0.96	1.51
麻栗坡县	Malipo	10.64	2.65	0.08	5.90	0.70	0.59
马关县	Maguan	16.05	4.91	0.06	8.03	1.95	0.83

18-17 续表3 continued

单位:万吨

(10 000 tons)

州市县	Region	粮食 Grain	稻谷 Rice	小麦 Wheat	玉米 Corn	豆类 Beans	薯类（折粮） Tubers
丘北县	Qiubei	26.82	4.97	1.71	18.85	0.81	0.49
广南县	Guangnan	38.35	13.98	0.96	16.07	3.15	2.40
富宁县	Funing	13.05	5.03	0.02	5.58	1.66	0.76
西双版纳州	**Xishuangbanna**	**47.64**	**18.32**		**28.54**	**0.20**	**0.21**
景洪市	Jinghong	9.34	1.20		8.12	0.02	0.01
勐海县	Menghai	29.02	15.38		13.01	0.15	0.20
勐腊县	Mengla	9.28	1.74		7.41	0.04	
大理州	**Dali**	**165.31**	**38.50**	**4.75**	**82.73**	**17.51**	**8.36**
大理市	Dali	10.33	2.83	0.30	4.49	1.47	0.69
漾濞县	Yangbi	7.20	1.19	0.53	4.41	0.55	0.41
祥云县	Xiangyun	21.13	3.63	0.61	11.01	2.39	1.51
宾川县	Binchuan	15.42	2.43	0.11	11.35	0.89	0.21
弥渡县	Midu	18.18	5.16	0.78	8.29	1.37	0.66
南涧县	Nanjian	11.04	0.95	0.73	6.47	1.34	0.43
巍山县	Weishan	16.07	4.64	0.49	7.33	2.20	0.23
永平县	Yongping	11.07	2.47	0.44	5.60	0.94	0.30
云龙县	Yunlong	14.39	2.68	0.32	9.22	0.88	0.54
洱源县	Eryuan	17.55	4.36	0.09	5.93	3.92	1.68
剑川县	Jianchuan	8.82	2.44	0.24	3.25	0.91	1.29
鹤庆县	Heqing	14.13	5.73	0.11	5.37	0.66	0.41
德宏州	**Dehong**	**68.69**	**36.79**	**0.75**	**19.51**	**1.23**	**10.28**
瑞丽市	Ruili	4.53	2.91		1.54	0.03	0.05
芒　市	Mangshi	22.30	11.94	0.06	7.48	0.45	2.35
梁河县	Lianghe	7.36	4.47	0.01	1.71	0.14	1.03
盈江县	Yingjiang	22.69	11.44	0.01	4.73	0.36	6.05
陇川县	Longchuan	11.80	6.02	0.68	4.06	0.24	0.80
怒江州	**Nujiang**	**16.00**	**2.22**	**0.84**	**8.09**	**1.63**	**2.47**
泸水市	Lushui	5.87	1.04	0.09	3.14	0.47	0.96
福贡县	Fugong	1.65	0.17	0.00	1.19	0.07	0.18
贡山县	Gongshan	0.43	0.03	0.00	0.26	0.02	0.09
兰坪县	Lanping	8.05	0.98	0.75	3.50	1.06	1.24
迪庆州	**Diqing**	**15.97**	**1.35**	**1.81**	**8.07**	**1.19**	**1.28**
香格里拉市	Shangri-La	6.44	0.45	0.90	2.41	0.37	0.70
德钦县	Deqin	2.22	0.03	0.47	1.19	0.12	0.06
维西县	Weixi	7.32	0.87	0.44	4.47	0.70	0.52

18–18 各州市县主要农作物产量（二）（2020年）

Output of Major Farm Crops by Region (II) (2020)

单位:万吨 (10 000 tons)

州市县	Region	油料 Oil-bearing Crops	花生 Peanuts	油菜籽 Rapeseeds	甘蔗 Sugarcane	烤烟 Flue-cured Tobacco	茶叶 Tea	园林水果 Fruits
全　省	**Yunnan**	**63.09**	**7.61**	**54.23**	**1 597.17**	**81.60**	**46.32**	**880.42**
昆明市	**Kunming**	**1.47**	**0.13**	**1.26**	**0.10**	**6.80**	**0.01**	**19.44**
五华区	Wuhua	0.01				0.02		0.28
盘龙区	Panlong					0.30		0.24
官渡区	Guandu							0.40
西山区	Xishan	0.02		0.01				0.99
东川区	Dongchuan	0.11	0.06	0.05	0.03			1.88
呈贡区	Chenggong							0.41
晋宁区	Jinning	0.11	0.01	0.09		0.20		0.53
富民县	Fumin	0.10		0.08		0.23		3.13
宜良县	Yiliang	0.06	0.02	0.02		1.00	0.01	1.13
石林县	Shilin	0.08		0.06		1.43		4.82
嵩明县	Songming					0.35		0.70
禄劝县	Luquan	0.41	0.04	0.37	0.07	1.17		1.33
寻甸县	Xundian	0.32		0.32		2.00		0.52
安宁市	Anning	0.25		0.25		0.10		3.09
曲靖市	**Qujing**	**20.95**	**0.08**	**20.75**	**0.02**	**15.91**		**27.50**
麒麟区	Qilin	0.08		0.08		1.44		5.22
沾益区	Zhanyi	0.08		0.08		1.59		1.53
马龙区	Malong	0.17		0.14		1.69		4.06
陆良县	Luliang	0.13		0.13		1.34		5.23
师宗县	Shizong	3.45		3.45		2.17		1.05
罗平县	Luoping	15.16		15.16		2.73		1.90
富源县	Fuyuan	1.62		1.58		1.24		0.99
会泽县	Huize	0.21	0.08	0.13	0.02	0.68		5.68
宣威市	Xuanwei	0.04		0.01		3.03		1.84
玉溪市	**Yuxi**	**3.27**	**0.19**	**2.97**	**59.39**	**8.25**	**0.44**	**104.98**
红塔区	Hongta	0.50		0.50		0.48		1.47
江川区	Jiangchuan	0.75		0.75		1.28		1.16
通海县	Tonghai	0.14		0.14		0.68		0.83
华宁县	Huaning	0.30	0.02	0.26		1.16		31.09
易门县	Yimen	0.24	0.02	0.20	0.11	0.81		0.95
峨山县	Eshan	0.83	0.02	0.79	0.41	1.10	0.01	0.58
新平县	Xinping	0.16	0.09	0.04	43.69	1.07	0.22	27.92
元江县	Yuanjiang	0.33	0.04	0.29	15.18	0.76	0.21	40.10
澄江市	Chengjiang	0.02		0.02		0.92		0.89

18-18 续表1 continued

单位:万吨 (10 000 tons)

州市县	Region	油料 Oil-bearing Crops	花生 Peanuts	油菜籽 Rapeseeds	甘蔗 Sugarcane	烤烟 Flue-cured Tobacco	茶叶 Tea	园林水果 Fruits
保山市	**Baoshan**	**7.00**	**0.21**	**6.72**	**107.38**	**5.85**	**5.90**	**28.51**
隆阳区	Longyang	1.11	0.12	0.95	22.77	1.17	0.24	14.81
施甸县	Shidian	0.19	0.04	0.14	13.78	1.28	0.14	1.76
龙陵县	Longling	0.09	0.03	0.06	42.74	0.67	0.75	2.09
昌宁县	Changning	0.58	0.03	0.54	28.09	1.06	2.91	9.57
腾冲市	Tengchong	5.03		5.02		1.68	1.86	0.28
昭通市	**Zhaotong**	**3.44**	**0.71**	**2.70**	**2.37**	**3.42**	**0.26**	**51.24**
昭阳区	Zhaoyang	0.01			0.50	1.04		38.87
鲁甸县	Ludian	0.11	0.02	0.07	0.06	0.81		2.47
巧家县	Qiaojia	0.09	0.08	0.01	1.05	0.29		0.69
盐津县	Yanjin	0.78	0.16	0.61	0.18		0.20	0.28
大关县	Daguan	0.06	0.05	0.01	0.07	0.08	0.02	1.15
永善县	Yongshan	0.65	0.08	0.57	0.36	0.05	0.01	1.30
绥江县	Suijiang	0.12	0.01	0.12	0.06		0.02	5.05
镇雄县	Zhenxiong	0.50	0.11	0.39		0.50	0.01	0.48
彝良县	Yiliang	0.56	0.07	0.49	0.07	0.59	0.01	0.37
威信县	Weixin	0.49	0.11	0.37	0.02	0.06		0.08
水富市	Shuifu	0.08	0.02	0.06				0.50
丽江市	**Lijiang**	**1.12**	**0.17**	**0.78**	**1.15**	**3.01**	**0.10**	**44.99**
古城区	Gucheng	0.12		0.09		0.24		0.76
玉龙县	Yulong	0.54		0.53		1.20		2.34
永胜县	Yongsheng	0.36	0.11	0.11	1.04	0.92		6.54
华坪县	Huaping	0.10	0.05	0.04	0.11	0.23	0.10	34.20
宁蒗县	Ninglang	0.01		0.01		0.42		1.14
普洱市	**Pu'er**	**2.15**	**1.13**	**1.01**	**265.23**	**4.99**	**11.92**	**32.14**
思茅区	Simao	0.07	0.06	0.01	0.04	0.17	1.66	1.59
宁洱县	Ning'er	0.19	0.13	0.06	0.05	0.50	1.24	0.60
墨江县	Mojiang	0.34	0.32	0.02	1.34	0.86	1.51	1.01
景东县	Jingdong	0.44	0.08	0.36	22.67	1.15	1.34	1.07
景谷县	Jinggu	0.37	0.19	0.18	61.61	1.02	1.33	4.18
镇沅县	Zhenyuan	0.28	0.06	0.22	2.71	1.30	0.49	1.22
江城县	Jiangcheng	0.05	0.02	0.02	0.77		1.33	16.02
孟连县	Menglian	0.07	0.07		42.18		0.50	3.30
澜沧县	Lancang	0.31	0.18	0.12	113.11		2.19	2.46
西盟县	Ximeng	0.03	0.02		20.77		0.33	0.68
临沧市	**Lincang**	**2.58**	**0.26**	**2.26**	**476.70**	**3.80**	**14.65**	**17.90**
临翔区	Linxiang	1.45	0.03	1.42	11.33	0.75	1.82	0.63
凤庆县	Fengqing	0.24		0.24	28.07	0.95	3.81	0.78

18-18 续表2 continued

单位:万吨 (10 000 tons)

州市县	Region	油料 Oil-bearing Crops	花生 Peanuts	油菜籽 Rapeseeds	甘蔗 Sugarcane	烤烟 Flue-cured Tobacco	茶叶 Tea	园林水果 Fruits
云县	Yunxian	0.25	0.03	0.21	47.57	0.43	2.46	1.42
永德县	Yongde	0.12	0.07	0.01	30.58	0.55	1.81	4.96
镇康县	Zhenkang	0.02	0.02	0.01	52.97	0.21	0.78	0.35
双江县	Shuangjiang	0.22	0.02	0.20	40.60	0.35	1.60	1.42
耿马县	Gengma	0.20	0.08	0.12	208.45	0.28	1.40	7.42
沧源县	Cangyuan	0.07	0.01	0.04	57.13	0.29	0.97	0.92
楚雄州	**Chuxiong**	**6.41**	**0.31**	**6.00**	**5.88**	**8.50**	**0.15**	**39.82**
楚雄市	Chuxiong	1.12		1.11		1.40	0.02	2.09
双柏县	Shuangbai	0.27	0.04	0.23	5.46	0.70	0.06	1.64
牟定县	Mouding	0.95		0.91		0.56	0.02	1.19
南华县	Nanhua	0.52		0.51		0.99	0.05	1.26
姚安县	Yao'an	0.71		0.71		0.94		1.16
大姚县	Dayao	0.33		0.32	0.13	0.71		1.68
永仁县	Yongren	0.28	0.03	0.24	0.01	0.46		6.03
元谋县	Yuanmou	0.20	0.16	0.03	0.07	0.25		17.92
武定县	Wuding	0.48	0.03	0.44	0.10	0.99		2.28
禄丰县	Lufeng	1.55	0.04	1.50	0.09	1.50		4.57
红河州	**Honghe**	**3.32**	**1.46**	**1.81**	**84.76**	**7.14**	**2.97**	**288.50**
个旧市	Gejiu	0.16	0.13	0.03	10.20	0.13		7.58
开远市	Kaiyuan	0.15	0.12	0.02	0.05	0.41		8.35
蒙自市	Mengzi	0.27	0.13	0.12	2.40	0.54	0.01	40.11
弥勒市	Mile	0.22	0.02	0.20	18.18	2.10		27.63
屏边县	Pingbian	0.11	0.07	0.04	1.87	0.02	0.15	17.03
建水县	Jianshui	0.24	0.20	0.03	0.46	0.84		27.76
石屏县	Shiping	0.24	0.09	0.15	7.58	1.06		20.42
泸西县	Luxi	1.21	0.01	1.21		2.04		28.33
元阳县	Yuanyang	0.17	0.17		17.22		0.09	10.19
红河县	Honghe	0.22	0.22		10.61		0.43	9.45
金平县	Jinping	0.14	0.14		15.40		0.06	43.83
绿春县	Luchun	0.16	0.16		0.20		2.23	3.19
河口县	Hekou	0.02	0.02		0.60		0.01	44.63
文山州	**Wenshan**	**6.95**	**2.59**	**4.08**	**122.01**	**4.93**	**1.12**	**38.92**
文山市	Wenshan	1.25	0.61	0.53	3.40	0.43		3.60
砚山县	Yanshan	0.76	0.62	0.07	0.31	1.78		4.23
西畴县	Xichou	0.20	0.12	0.08	8.18	0.22	0.03	0.45
麻栗坡县	Malipo	0.27	0.14	0.13	17.90	0.17	0.08	3.22
马关县	Maguan	0.83	0.26	0.57	11.76	0.31	0.01	22.46

18-18 续表3 continued

单位:万吨 (10 000 tons)

州市县	Region	油料 Oil-bearing Crops	花生 Peanuts	油菜籽 Rapeseeds	甘蔗 Sugarcane	烤烟 Flue-cured Tobacco	茶叶 Tea	园林水果 Fruits
丘北县	Qiubei	0.63	0.25	0.32		1.39		1.13
广南县	Guangnan	2.58	0.45	2.10	7.52	0.63	0.97	2.34
富宁县	Funing	0.43	0.15	0.28	72.93	0.01	0.03	1.51
西双版纳州	**Xishuangbanna**	**0.14**	**0.14**		**105.58**		**5.57**	**65.55**
景洪市	Jinghong	0.04	0.04		1.59		1.77	30.06
勐海县	Menghai	0.07	0.07		102.44		3.17	12.62
勐腊县	Mengla	0.03	0.02		1.55		0.63	22.87
大理州	**Dali**	**3.09**	**0.12**	**2.87**	**0.65**	**7.03**	**1.10**	**92.22**
大理市	Dali	0.15		0.14		0.27	0.01	1.68
漾濞县	Yangbi	0.16		0.15		0.24		0.51
祥云县	Xiangyun	0.45		0.44		1.52		1.70
宾川县	Binchuan	0.53	0.05	0.47	0.12	0.59		69.38
弥渡县	Midu	0.53	0.04	0.44		0.63	0.02	1.38
南涧县	Nanjian	0.14		0.14	0.04	0.64	0.75	1.06
巍山县	Weishan	0.47		0.47		0.72	0.05	3.55
永平县	Yongping	0.18		0.18		0.50	0.23	0.37
云龙县	Yunlong	0.21		0.21	0.04	0.51	0.05	1.66
洱源县	Eryuan	0.14		0.14		0.59		1.98
剑川县	Jianchuan	0.04		0.04		0.46		0.84
鹤庆县	Heqing	0.09	0.02	0.05	0.44	0.35		8.12
德宏州	**Dehong**	**0.64**	**0.08**	**0.57**	**364.60**	**1.81**	**2.11**	**26.45**
瑞丽市	Ruili	0.01		0.01	15.76		0.03	10.48
芒市	Mangshi	0.07	0.04	0.02	58.99	0.59	1.03	10.88
梁河县	Lianghe	0.04	0.02	0.02	23.68	0.59	0.33	0.24
盈江县	Yingjiang	0.16	0.01	0.15	85.55	0.12	0.43	2.14
陇川县	Longchuan	0.37	0.01	0.36	180.63	0.51	0.29	2.71
怒江州	**Nujiang**	**0.11**	**0.03**	**0.04**	**1.35**		**0.01**	**0.97**
泸水市	Lushui	0.01		0.01	1.35		0.01	0.24
福贡县	Fugong	0.03	0.02	0.02			0.01	0.02
贡山县	Gongshan	0.02	0.01	0.01				0.04
兰坪县	Lanping	0.04		0.01				0.68
迪庆州	**Diqing**	**0.45**		**0.42**		**0.15**		**1.28**
香格里拉市	Shangri-La	0.26		0.24		0.15		0.31
德钦县	Deqin							0.57
维西县	Weixi	0.20		0.18				0.40

18-19 各州市县畜牧业、水产品生产情况（2020年）

单位:万头、万只、万吨

州市县	Region	猪 Hogs			牛 Cattle and Buffaloes			
		存栏 Stocked	出栏 Slaughtered	肉产量 Output of Meat	存栏 Stocked	出栏 Slaughtered	肉产量 Output of Meat	存栏 Stocked
全省	**Yunnan**	**3 120.43**	**3 453.23**	**291.57**	**858.78**	**335.90**	**40.94**	**1 350.66**
昆明市	**Kunming**	**145.20**	**178.26**	**14.66**	**42.89**	**21.51**	**2.34**	**121.89**
五华区	Wuhua	0.84	1.09	0.12	0.18	0.07	0.01	0.77
盘龙区	Panlong	1.03	1.36	0.11	0.38	0.19	0.02	1.25
官渡区	Guandu	0.32	0.51	0.04	0.12	0.06	0.01	0.90
西山区	Xishan	2.10	2.39	0.20	0.26	0.11	0.01	2.47
东川区	Dongchuan	6.58	7.15	0.52	2.26	1.14	0.09	20.02
呈贡区	Chenggong							
晋宁区	Jinning	4.21	6.19	0.51	0.72	0.28	0.03	2.85
富民县	Fuming	5.96	10.61	0.87	1.58	0.74	0.08	5.25
宜良县	Yiliang	27.66	41.96	3.64	3.52	1.34	0.14	10.03
石林县	Shilin	8.97	11.97	0.88	3.09	1.49	0.16	14.75
嵩明县	Songming	4.87	5.75	0.47	1.56	0.68	0.11	2.56
禄劝县	Luquan	27.37	30.57	2.32	9.48	4.25	0.54	33.45
寻甸县	Xundian	43.60	43.09	3.70	19.06	10.72	1.09	24.05
安宁市	Anning	11.69	15.62	1.28	0.68	0.44	0.06	3.54
曲靖市	**Qujing**	**755.11**	**877.25**	**75.17**	**121.62**	**61.78**	**8.55**	**286.30**
麒麟区	Qilin	52.00	72.34	6.13	3.86	3.38	0.36	9.23
沾益区	Zhanyi	80.00	104.71	8.79	9.60	6.60	0.99	32.36
马龙区	Malong	15.40	16.93	1.45	5.96	2.83	0.43	29.02
陆良县	Luliang	97.58	130.79	11.32	6.03	5.14	0.65	20.57
师宗县	Shizong	52.42	57.20	4.71	9.01	4.92	0.66	21.99
罗平县	Luoping	68.26	70.57	6.00	13.21	7.14	0.88	40.68
富源县	Fuyuan	76.10	90.72	7.66	13.03	6.79	0.95	35.79
会泽县	Huize	109.85	118.62	10.04	45.57	18.62	2.65	61.21
宣威市	Xuanwei	203.50	215.38	19.07	15.35	6.36	0.98	35.46
玉溪市	**Yuxi**	**95.10**	**106.47**	**8.91**	**19.38**	**11.25**	**1.60**	**39.45**
红塔区	Hongta	11.26	18.34	1.62	0.41	1.00	0.20	1.76
江川区	Jiangchuan	10.89	11.75	0.94	0.29	0.18	0.03	1.66
通海县	Tonghai	7.79	10.74	0.80	1.14	1.31	0.23	2.62
华宁县	Huaning	9.98	10.51	0.94	2.50	1.89	0.29	6.97
易门县	Yimen	14.32	15.09	1.31	2.13	0.89	0.13	6.04
峨山县	Eshan	11.69	12.68	0.99	1.93	1.51	0.17	4.52
新平县	Xinping	19.43	18.02	1.52	7.13	2.66	0.32	10.91
元江县	Yuanjiang	9.17	8.58	0.73	3.56	1.72	0.22	3.99
澄江市	Chengjiang	0.57	0.76	0.06	0.29	0.09	0.01	0.98

Output of Animal Husbandry Products and Aquaticts Products by Region (2020)

(10 000 heads, 10 000 units, 10 000 tons)

羊 Sheep and Goats		家禽 Poultry			禽蛋产量 Poultry Eggs Output	牛奶产量 Cow Milk Output	水产品产量 Total Output of Aquatic Products
出栏 Slaughtered	肉产量 Output of Meat	存栏 Stocked	出栏 Slaughtered	肉产量 Output of Meat			
1 177.48	**20.77**	**18 975.68**	**34 226.76**	**62.76**	**41.75**	**67.29**	**64.40**
100.37	**1.69**	**2 686.31**	**7 079.38**	**11.77**	**5.75**	**14.11**	**3.60**
0.44	0.01	26.00	17.32	0.03	0.19	0.01	0.01
0.54	0.01	31.95	41.34	0.12	0.28		0.02
0.59	0.01	59.47	85.23	0.13	0.25		0.00
1.33	0.02	20.35	50.73	0.11	0.01	0.01	0.03
12.66	0.19	103.96	227.87	0.41	0.17		0.17
							0.03
1.69	0.03	199.80	362.88	0.66	1.28	0.55	0.04
1.96	0.04	114.32	159.18	0.29	0.44		0.05
7.23	0.14	534.50	2321.13	3.69	0.48	5.26	1.63
11.21	0.21	692.62	2067.47	3.33	0.29	1.37	0.20
2.68	0.05	96.56	144.51	0.28	0.29	2.67	0.10
31.80	0.52	112.09	222.81	0.36	0.17		0.08
24.11	0.39	228.06	257.34	0.42	0.53	4.16	1.05
4.13	0.08	466.63	1121.57	1.94	1.37	0.07	0.20
277.94	**5.41**	**1 488.63**	**3 168.31**	**7.67**	**3.79**	**4.46**	**9.95**
9.23	0.25	175.84	434.71	1.25	1.27		1.09
30.96	1.01	137.64	391.86	1.24	0.30	0.12	0.92
21.58	0.38	132.04	159.50	0.36	0.24	0.14	0.32
25.61	0.43	266.55	615.37	1.28	0.30	4.20	1.97
28.48	0.57	81.59	212.73	0.52	0.17		1.07
30.29	0.48	62.77	245.14	0.47	0.15		0.94
30.90	0.54	182.68	263.64	0.57	0.30		1.28
71.52	1.12	233.10	435.19	0.88	0.51		1.78
29.38	0.64	216.40	410.16	1.10	0.56		0.58
32.43	**0.74**	**1 843.37**	**3 346.79**	**7.25**	**7.61**	**0.92**	**1.43**
1.93	0.06	384.47	591.24	1.57	2.23	0.00	0.11
1.70	0.04	149.00	325.62	0.76	1.06		0.24
2.78	0.06	634.48	729.59	1.26	3.49	0.63	0.27
4.53	0.11	84.85	205.52	0.42	0.10	0.15	0.14
4.01	0.10	302.07	791.20	1.94	0.19		0.08
4.95	0.11	68.49	185.76	0.37	0.16		0.11
8.57	0.17	150.35	406.30	0.74	0.26		0.16
3.20	0.07	61.56	99.93	0.17	0.10		0.20
0.76	0.02	8.10	11.63	0.02	0.01	0.14	0.12

18-19 续表1

单位:万头、万只、万吨

州市县	Region	猪 Hogs 存栏 Stocked	猪 Hogs 出栏 Slaughtered	猪 Hogs 肉产量 Output of Meat	牛 Cattle and Buffaloes 存栏 Stocked	牛 Cattle and Buffaloes 出栏 Slaughtered	牛 Cattle and Buffaloes 肉产量 Output of Meat	存栏 Stocked
保山市	**Baoshan**	**288.08**	**317.38**	**26.73**	**64.72**	**21.18**	**2.61**	**65.80**
隆阳区	Longyang	79.63	87.88	7.35	16.60	5.10	0.63	19.30
施甸县	Shidian	61.30	63.98	5.34	8.75	3.04	0.37	5.08
龙陵县	Longling	21.29	23.99	2.03	13.65	3.90	0.48	17.73
昌宁县	Changning	63.21	70.19	5.94	13.99	4.20	0.52	16.14
腾冲市	Tengchong	62.65	71.35	6.07	11.72	4.93	0.61	7.55
昭通市	**Zhaotong**	**288.49**	**290.73**	**24.98**	**48.13**	**16.04**	**2.03**	**68.02**
昭阳区	Zhaoyang	28.22	30.14	2.18	5.12	1.92	0.26	8.60
鲁甸县	Ludian	18.49	15.03	1.47	7.10	1.85	0.24	7.25
巧家县	Qiaojia	36.92	40.12	3.73	5.89	1.45	0.18	13.92
盐津县	Yanjin	28.38	27.43	2.22	2.52	0.74	0.11	0.78
大关县	Daguan	16.33	17.70	1.68	3.14	0.66	0.10	5.91
永善县	Yongshan	23.15	25.39	2.11	3.45	0.92	0.10	12.61
绥江县	Suijiang	7.53	7.15	0.64	0.42	0.22	0.04	1.18
镇雄县	Zhenxiong	79.38	82.05	6.68	10.80	5.60	0.64	4.51
彝良县	Yiliang	25.90	23.95	2.26	8.20	1.88	0.26	12.23
威信县	Weixin	22.04	17.80	1.60	1.44	0.76	0.09	0.39
水富市	Shuifu	2.14	3.97	0.40	0.07	0.04	0.01	0.64
丽江市	**Lijiang**	**94.03**	**89.73**	**7.07**	**36.18**	**8.38**	**0.83**	**106.26**
古城区	Gucheng	8.10	8.10	0.66	1.24	0.66	0.06	3.99
玉龙县	Yulong	34.82	35.71	2.78	11.69	2.48	0.32	22.70
永胜县	Yongsheng	27.57	28.68	2.19	12.28	3.72	0.31	39.95
华坪县	Huaping	5.53	5.45	0.46	2.24	0.65	0.06	9.18
宁蒗县	Ninglang	18.01	11.79	0.98	8.73	0.87	0.08	30.44
普洱市	**Pu'er**	**194.19**	**190.45**	**15.27**	**53.33**	**13.02**	**1.34**	**45.59**
思茅区	Simao	11.01	14.07	1.18	1.84	0.46	0.05	2.90
宁洱县	Ning'er	19.10	21.16	1.77	3.23	1.07	0.11	3.64
墨江县	Mojiang	20.22	26.52	2.13	5.80	1.66	0.16	3.91
景东县	Jingdong	39.86	30.89	2.35	10.42	2.55	0.25	14.76
景谷县	Jinggu	18.71	17.96	1.33	6.15	1.36	0.15	6.25
镇沅县	Zhenyuan	27.30	29.00	2.35	5.25	1.19	0.13	9.22
江城县	Jiangcheng	4.66	5.51	0.45	2.69	0.84	0.08	1.74
孟连县	Menglian	5.48	6.16	0.50	1.53	0.76	0.08	0.34
澜沧县	Lancang	43.85	34.80	2.86	14.86	2.68	0.30	2.42
西盟县	Ximeng	4.00	4.38	0.35	1.56	0.46	0.05	0.41
临沧市	**Lincang**	**225.03**	**252.03**	**20.74**	**55.16**	**15.43**	**1.75**	**72.11**
临翔区	Linxiang	18.13	18.05	1.41	4.25	0.98	0.11	8.33
凤庆县	Fengqing	48.82	60.50	5.20	9.61	3.41	0.36	15.82

continued

(10 000 heads, 10 000 units, 10 000 tons)

羊 Sheep and Goats		家禽 Poultry			禽蛋产量 Poultry Eggs Output	牛奶产量 Cow Milk Output	水产品产量 Total Output of Aquatic Products
出栏 Slaughtered	肉产量 Output of Meat	存栏 Stocked	出栏 Slaughtered	肉产量 Output of Meat			
65.98	**1.19**	**781.72**	**1 426.64**	**3.31**	**1.12**	**1.21**	**4.27**
17.64	0.32	211.08	439.26	1.08	0.47	0.11	1.22
5.44	0.10	141.42	255.55	0.56	0.21		0.64
18.44	0.33	99.14	110.41	0.22	0.12		0.68
15.08	0.27	126.53	222.37	0.46	0.12	0.01	0.66
9.37	0.17	203.55	399.05	1.00	0.19	1.10	1.07
55.24	**0.96**	**801.92**	**1 160.15**	**2.41**	**1.59**		**4.00**
6.70	0.11	66.84	95.30	0.17	0.11		0.59
4.91	0.08	57.66	51.32	0.10	0.06		0.26
14.83	0.25	63.84	127.19	0.22	0.18		0.33
0.77	0.02	122.92	253.56	0.56	0.12		0.51
3.81	0.08	31.44	42.66	0.08	0.04		0.23
10.97	0.15	42.25	65.26	0.12	0.04		0.30
1.13	0.02	24.95	38.03	0.06	0.08		0.53
5.10	0.10	230.54	291.71	0.69	0.46		0.40
6.01	0.13	78.88	96.74	0.21	0.34		0.33
0.45	0.01	43.99	63.72	0.13	0.09		0.30
0.56	0.01	38.63	34.66	0.07	0.07		0.23
68.38	**1.02**	**339.85**	**386.54**	**0.59**	**0.29**	**0.41**	**1.85**
4.46	0.07	21.61	21.70	0.04	0.02		0.18
16.02	0.20	60.84	60.34	0.09	0.11	0.36	0.31
29.78	0.49	120.93	126.44	0.20	0.13	0.04	0.70
4.43	0.06	88.72	128.76	0.18	0.01		0.53
13.69	0.20	47.75	49.30	0.08	0.02	0.01	0.14
29.51	**0.53**	**1 455.28**	**1 855.24**	**2.62**	**1.11**	**0.02**	**16.06**
2.06	0.04	166.63	208.54	0.30	0.27	0.02	2.36
2.31	0.05	90.18	118.68	0.17	0.12		1.35
2.93	0.06	166.89	227.09	0.32	0.12		3.30
9.82	0.17	244.91	340.35	0.51	0.10		1.50
3.80	0.07	201.72	269.45	0.39	0.14		3.45
5.20	0.09	154.31	189.20	0.27	0.13		0.57
0.82	0.02	42.17	56.31	0.09	0.07		0.83
0.35	0.01	75.18	82.49	0.13	0.07		0.42
1.91	0.03	287.63	322.45	0.39	0.06		2.14
0.31	0.01	25.68	40.69	0.05	0.04		0.14
48.89	**0.79**	**1 150.40**	**1 902.47**	**2.73**	**0.69**	**0.07**	**12.77**
5.39	0.10	116.09	214.38	0.31	0.02	0.02	0.95
10.16	0.16	135.70	249.06	0.37	0.07		2.14

18-19 续表2

单位:万头、万只、万吨

州市县	Region	猪 Hogs			牛 Cattle and Buffaloes			
		存栏 Stocked	出栏 Slaughtered	肉产量 Output of Meat	存栏 Stocked	出栏 Slaughtered	肉产量 Output of Meat	存栏 Stocked
云县	Yunxian	54.09	63.02	5.37	13.22	2.70	0.28	22.89
永德县	Yongde	49.01	59.24	4.95	9.69	3.16	0.46	10.12
镇康县	Zhenkang	13.19	12.50	0.95	4.67	1.01	0.12	6.21
双江县	Shuangjiang	13.73	12.43	0.94	3.44	1.00	0.10	2.62
耿马县	Gengma	17.27	16.26	1.25	6.94	2.14	0.21	5.39
沧源县	Cangyuan	10.79	10.02	0.67	3.34	1.03	0.12	0.72
楚雄州	**Chuxiong**	**215.43**	**217.61**	**18.71**	**67.68**	**22.66**	**3.31**	**166.72**
楚雄市	Chuxiong	25.75	32.87	2.84	7.55	4.10	0.60	17.22
双柏县	Shuangbai	23.56	18.00	1.54	7.31	1.94	0.28	21.32
牟定县	Mouding	20.66	16.01	1.43	3.59	1.33	0.20	7.10
南华县	Nanhua	17.46	17.79	1.53	6.22	2.35	0.34	10.11
姚安县	Yao'an	15.81	16.90	1.45	9.09	2.18	0.32	10.58
大姚县	Dayao	25.88	17.08	1.48	6.92	1.93	0.28	28.82
永仁县	Yongren	12.71	12.86	1.10	3.77	1.56	0.23	14.20
元谋县	Yuanmou	13.77	12.82	1.10	5.14	1.51	0.22	15.58
武定县	Wuding	23.64	26.33	2.27	6.49	2.86	0.42	20.94
禄丰县	Lufeng	36.19	46.95	3.97	11.60	2.90	0.42	20.85
红河州	**Honghe**	**290.00**	**331.40**	**29.19**	**102.35**	**36.77**	**4.62**	**115.59**
蒙自市	Mengzi	29.24	35.97	2.98	7.15	1.93	0.29	5.47
个旧市	Gejiu	17.46	15.48	1.53	11.51	4.32	0.52	12.92
开远市	Kaiyuan	11.46	13.69	1.35	5.07	1.61	0.19	10.69
弥勒市	Mile	49.12	63.16	5.32	15.38	7.04	0.78	26.71
屏边县	Pingbian	9.17	8.68	0.86	3.66	0.27	0.04	1.73
建水县	Jianshui	54.21	66.75	5.58	7.89	3.84	0.53	12.76
石屏县	Shiping	36.89	42.74	3.58	12.58	4.02	0.52	14.01
泸西县	Luxi	28.43	35.00	3.14	13.56	3.94	0.55	20.67
元阳县	Yuanyang	13.78	14.22	1.43	8.68	3.70	0.45	3.30
红河县	Honghe	17.73	14.71	1.38	7.96	3.54	0.47	5.66
金平县	Jinping	10.45	10.23	1.02	2.38	1.44	0.16	0.87
绿春县	Luchun	9.15	8.08	0.79	5.94	0.93	0.10	0.79
河口县	Hekou	2.92	2.67	0.23	0.60	0.20	0.02	
文山州	**Wenshan**	**170.69**	**189.39**	**16.65**	**112.33**	**47.92**	**4.79**	**38.75**
文山市	Wenshan	14.68	15.75	1.42	13.79	5.44	0.53	2.55
砚山县	Yanshan	16.18	16.97	1.49	15.60	7.06	0.75	7.79
西畴县	Xichou	12.10	13.16	1.21	8.37	3.79	0.36	0.58
麻栗坡县	Malipo	12.89	15.28	1.35	7.45	3.82	0.38	1.16
马关县	Maguan	17.13	18.35	1.65	11.50	4.63	0.49	0.40

continued

(10 000 heads, 10 000 units, 10 000 tons)

羊 Sheep and Goats		家禽 Poultry			禽蛋产量 Poultry Eggs Output	牛奶产量 Cow Milk Output	水产品产量 Total Output of Aquatic Products
出栏 Slaughtered	肉产量 Output of Meat	存栏 Stocked	出栏 Slaughtered	肉产量 Output of Meat			
18.19	0.27	402.34	800.84	1.15	0.09	0.05	1.99
4.75	0.08	164.53	189.66	0.26	0.20		1.15
3.73	0.07	65.49	114.87	0.17	0.02		0.86
2.61	0.05	75.67	92.28	0.12	0.15		3.09
3.51	0.05	119.35	170.54	0.24	0.10		1.49
0.55	0.01	71.22	70.83	0.11	0.04		1.10
123.44	**2.09**	**1 182.70**	**1 880.79**	**3.23**	**1.01**	**0.05**	**4.16**
13.63	0.23	187.45	375.15	0.63	0.17		0.98
12.09	0.20	79.76	80.91	0.14	0.03		0.14
6.24	0.11	52.40	72.21	0.12	0.07		0.33
8.74	0.15	133.56	246.08	0.42	0.06		0.23
8.30	0.14	80.87	152.90	0.27	0.06		0.79
19.54	0.33	90.52	114.45	0.21	0.06		0.27
14.22	0.24	47.25	69.78	0.12	0.03		0.12
13.09	0.22	51.68	80.69	0.14	0.02		0.39
18.84	0.32	159.77	428.42	0.74	0.23	0.05	0.19
8.75	0.15	299.44	260.20	0.44	0.28		0.73
95.12	**1.64**	**3 083.68**	**5 811.65**	**9.84**	**9.21**	**7.65**	**4.70**
5.07	0.09	217.41	357.66	0.67	0.75	0.07	0.35
7.30	0.14	169.09	353.42	0.55	0.65	3.52	0.53
7.62	0.10	337.69	791.93	1.45	1.30	0.01	0.34
24.09	0.44	490.02	1 416.66	2.51	0.76	1.90	0.56
0.76	0.01	113.68	141.28	0.20	0.05		0.16
13.71	0.28	626.52	851.13	1.35	2.63	0.09	0.42
9.74	0.15	197.28	251.54	0.41	0.28		0.40
15.56	0.27	336.26	556.74	0.99	2.06	2.07	0.39
2.91	0.04	105.57	205.87	0.31	0.29		0.41
6.87	0.10	177.80	330.86	0.49	0.26		0.47
0.76	0.01	137.63	285.18	0.46	0.07		0.21
0.73	0.01	149.76	243.51	0.40	0.06		0.35
		24.97	25.88	0.04	0.06		0.12
52.81	**1.01**	**1 099.14**	**1 842.33**	**3.32**	**1.69**	**0.21**	**6.03**
3.72	0.06	99.24	205.58	0.39	0.39	0.21	0.46
9.52	0.19	220.92	298.54	0.51	0.51		0.82
0.76	0.02	90.19	165.74	0.28	0.08		0.26
1.86	0.03	91.06	177.25	0.34	0.07		0.68
0.76	0.01	135.59	224.22	0.39	0.27		0.48

18-19 续表3

单位:万头、万只、万吨

州市县	Region	猪 Hogs			牛 Cattle and Buffaloes			
		存栏 Stocked	出栏 Slaughtered	肉产量 Output of Meat	存栏 Stocked	出栏 Slaughtered	肉产量 Output of Meat	存栏 Stocked
丘北县	Qiubei	47.50	54.24	4.50	23.94	10.15	1.05	17.14
广南县	Guangnan	40.35	45.04	3.89	27.03	11.00	1.02	6.93
富宁县	Funing	9.86	10.60	1.14	4.65	2.03	0.21	2.20
西双版纳州	**Xishuangbanna**	**24.72**	**32.00**	**2.34**	**5.33**	**3.29**	**0.35**	**2.85**
景洪市	Jinghong	9.43	15.08	1.06	1.56	1.12	0.11	1.15
勐海县	Menghai	5.17	3.92	0.27	1.94	0.96	0.10	0.86
勐腊县	Mengla	10.12	13.00	1.01	1.83	1.21	0.14	0.84
大理州	**Dali**	**231.10**	**264.22**	**22.31**	**85.47**	**39.67**	**4.88**	**156.92**
大理市	Dali	7.49	15.79	1.35	1.45	1.00	0.13	1.45
漾濞县	Yangbi	9.94	6.56	0.57	6.25	1.99	0.24	12.81
祥云县	Xiangyun	31.98	41.65	3.46	5.39	1.94	0.26	10.10
宾川县	Binchuan	20.03	23.56	2.06	5.15	1.76	0.21	14.79
弥渡县	Midu	39.44	43.04	3.53	10.03	3.23	0.37	6.39
南涧县	Nanjian	13.66	11.74	1.01	8.44	5.14	0.63	6.24
巍山县	Weishan	14.17	11.80	1.03	9.90	5.94	0.75	16.03
永平县	Yongping	19.83	20.32	1.72	7.44	3.60	0.41	13.45
云龙县	Yunlong	21.40	16.89	1.46	10.72	3.45	0.45	26.81
洱源县	Eryuan	9.18	22.07	1.93	6.21	5.09	0.64	19.27
剑川县	Jianchuan	11.85	9.88	0.83	8.47	3.71	0.43	15.29
鹤庆县	Heqing	32.12	40.94	3.36	6.01	2.82	0.35	14.30
德宏州	**Dehong**	**39.42**	**42.64**	**3.44**	**15.46**	**11.64**	**1.30**	**9.37**
瑞丽市	Ruili	5.60	6.05	0.47	1.34	3.47	0.38	0.35
芒市	Mangshi	10.03	10.71	0.87	4.84	3.85	0.43	3.01
梁河县	Lianghe	6.84	6.55	0.53	1.35	0.80	0.09	1.14
盈江县	Yingjiang	10.21	11.96	0.97	4.03	1.96	0.22	3.03
陇川县	Longchuan	6.74	7.37	0.60	3.89	1.56	0.18	1.84
怒江州	**Nujiang**	**36.85**	**41.24**	**2.98**	**10.37**	**2.28**	**0.27**	**36.67**
泸水市	Lushui	14.78	18.41	1.47	3.46	1.09	0.12	12.59
福贡县	Fugong	5.81	4.56	0.27	0.81	0.23	0.03	2.61
贡山县	Gongshan	2.35	1.64	0.09	0.71	0.13	0.01	1.15
兰坪县	Lanping	13.91	16.62	1.15	5.39	0.83	0.11	20.32
迪庆州	**Diqing**	**26.99**	**32.43**	**2.42**	**18.38**	**3.08**	**0.37**	**18.37**
香格里拉市	Shangri-La	11.37	13.69	1.06	9.48	1.60	0.23	6.04
德钦县	Deqin	3.65	2.85	0.20	4.19	0.55	0.05	3.11
维西县	Weixi	11.97	15.89	1.16	4.71	0.94	0.09	9.22

continued

(10 000 heads, 10 000 units, 10 000 tons)

羊 Sheep and Goats		家禽 Poultry			禽蛋产量 Poultry Eggs Output	牛奶产量 Cow Milk Output	水产品产量 Total Output of Aquatic Products
出栏 Slaughtered	肉产量 Output of Meat	存栏 Stocked	出栏 Slaughtered	肉产量 Output of Meat			
24.13	0.46	114.88	215.49	0.39	0.08		0.49
9.58	0.20	212.07	373.37	0.72	0.26		0.74
2.48	0.04	135.19	182.14	0.30	0.03		2.10
1.94	**0.03**	**498.60**	**652.15**	**0.88**	**0.41**		**8.96**
0.42	0.01	211.95	312.00	0.45	0.11		5.08
0.57	0.01	163.20	187.14	0.22	0.20		2.69
0.95	0.01	123.45	153.01	0.21	0.10		1.18
175.61	**2.91**	**1 844.01**	**2 642.34**	**5.40**	**6.87**	**35.69**	**5.93**
1.21	0.02	187.78	326.00	0.67	1.06	3.99	0.45
11.89	0.20	47.26	72.21	0.15	0.05	0.06	0.06
4.08	0.07	851.64	978.89	2.07	4.32	0.60	0.17
15.54	0.25	73.25	108.22	0.22	0.13	0.89	1.00
9.60	0.17	64.16	134.63	0.28	0.12	8.67	1.19
13.18	0.21	185.60	349.69	0.66	0.15	0.02	0.52
27.99	0.45	110.08	229.83	0.46	0.18	0.76	1.01
13.43	0.21	97.20	101.11	0.18	0.08		0.12
26.13	0.46	50.00	105.97	0.23	0.26		0.13
19.14	0.32	55.91	81.28	0.16	0.25	14.14	0.47
15.35	0.25	47.97	63.55	0.13	0.10	3.23	0.32
18.07	0.31	73.16	90.95	0.19	0.18	3.33	0.49
9.63	**0.17**	**401.91**	**769.11**	**1.24**	**0.40**	**0.24**	**4.41**
0.75	0.01	112.39	231.54	0.37	0.11		0.76
3.11	0.05	144.73	251.02	0.41	0.12	0.09	1.30
1.44	0.03	28.75	70.11	0.11	0.03	0.01	0.33
2.42	0.04	70.61	123.36	0.20	0.08	0.07	0.94
1.92	0.03	45.43	93.09	0.15	0.05	0.07	1.08
29.78	**0.44**	**201.82**	**197.35**	**0.31**	**0.15**	**0.01**	**0.07**
10.16	0.14	82.61	89.68	0.15	0.10		0.05
3.01	0.05	52.68	37.95	0.06	0.02		0.00
0.67	0.01	20.04	16.83	0.02	0.01	0.01	0.01
15.94	0.24	46.50	52.88	0.09	0.03	0.00	0.02
10.41	**0.15**	**116.34**	**105.52**	**0.19**	**0.07**	**2.21**	**0.29**
3.51	0.06	51.55	49.36	0.09	0.03	1.30	0.12
0.74	0.01	15.01	14.86	0.03	0.02	0.86	0.01
6.16	0.09	49.78	41.30	0.07	0.02	0.05	0.16

18-20 各州市县工业主要产品产量（2020年）

Output of Major Industrial Products by Region (2020)

州市县	Region	原煤（万吨）Coal (10 000 tons)	发电量（亿千瓦小时）Electricity (100 million kWh)	农用化肥（万吨）Agricultural Chemical Fertilizer (10 000 tons)	白酒（万升）Liquor (10 kiloliters)	啤酒（万升）Beer (10 kiloliters)	糖（万吨）Sugar (10 000 tons)	水泥（万吨）Cement (10 000 tons)
全省	**Yunnan**	**5 265.63**	**3 451.17**	**213.77**	**9 106.19**	**69 648.63**	**261.22**	**12 984.71**
昆明市	**Kunming**	**260.96**	**1 517.93**	**58.99**		**34 166.00**	**0.01**	**1 988.35**
五华区	Wuhua		214.99	0.21				
盘龙区	Panlong		134.29					
官渡区	Guandu		829.21					210.83
西山区	Xishan		216.88	13.29				
东川区	Dongchuan		4.21	5.53				103.67
呈贡区	Chenggong		0.96				0.01	
晋宁区	Jinning		0.61	10.41		9 202.81		
富民县	Fumin		9.41					183.74
宜良县	Yiliang	60.82	22.09	2.34				706.93
石林县	Shilin	0.20	6.24					106.47
嵩明县	Songming		0.51			24 963.19		
禄劝县	Luquan		26.45					131.46
寻甸县	Xundian	199.94	16.16	8.16				172.57
安宁市	Anning		35.92	19.05				372.68
曲靖市	**Qujing**	**2 370.32**	**233.30**	**28.20**	**1 451.70**	**2 533.58**		**1 576.91**
麒麟区	Qilin	687.08	14.19	0.64				178.24
沾益区	Zhanyi	2.43	31.56	22.60		2 533.58		
马龙区	Malong		2.57					77.87
陆良县	Luliang	351.45	15.01					451.99
师宗县	Shizong	86.02	5.78					140.48
罗平县	Luoping	46.07	26.08		676.80			75.86
富源县	Fuyuan	937.57	79.11					123.24
会泽县	Huize		19.83	0.30				180.30
宣威市	Xuanwei	259.72	39.17	4.66	774.90			348.93
玉溪市	**Yuxi**	**0.04**	**30.79**	**2.05**		**2 502.50**	**4.22**	**1 609.31**
红塔区	Hongta		2.71	2.05				333.58
江川区	Jiangchuan							17.43
通海县	Tonghai		2.89					34.94
华宁县	Huaning		5.41					333.46
易门县	Yimen		0.68					276.90
峨山县	Eshan	0.04	0.92			2 502.50		103.80
新平县	Xinping		9.11				3.21	93.05
元江县	Yuanjiang		6.86				1.02	250.82
澄江市	Chengjiang		2.23					165.34

注：本表统计范围为规模以上工业法人单位。

Note: The coverage of statistics are industrial enterprises above designated size in this table.

18-20 续表1 continued

州市县	Region	原煤(万吨) Coal (10 000 tons)	发电量(亿千瓦小时) Electricity (100 million kWh)	农用化肥(万吨) Agricultural Chemical Fertilizer (10 000 tons)	白酒(万升) Liquor (10 kiloliters)	啤酒(万升) Beer (10 kiloliters)	糖(万吨) Sugar (10 000 tons)	水泥(万吨) Cement (10 000 tons)
保山市	**Baoshan**	**2.69**	**74.22**	**0.48**	**245.47**		**11.70**	**764.33**
隆阳区	Longyang		52.40				2.44	217.57
施甸县	Shidian		3.48				1.74	378.45
龙陵县	Longling		7.76				4.13	81.12
昌宁县	Changning	2.69	3.18		245.47		3.39	8.85
腾冲市	Tengchong		7.39	0.48				78.34
昭通市	**Zhaotong**	**1 037.41**	**607.04**	**41.76**				**814.80**
昭阳区	Zhaoyang		13.77	0.97				321.99
鲁甸县	Ludian		6.12					73.31
巧家县	Qiaojia		12.59					111.06
盐津县	Yanjin	3.55	9.04					
大关县	Daguan		2.48					100.72
永善县	Yongshan		484.80					
绥江县	Suijiang	23.89	0.18					110.69
镇雄县	Zhenxiong	882.77	36.74					90.10
彝良县	Yiliang	25.07	4.51					
威信县	Weixin	102.12	33.63					
水富市	Shuifu		3.17	40.79				6.93
丽江市	**Lijiang**	**3.22**	**235.28**		**297.22**			**389.71**
古城区	Gucheng		128.13					
玉龙县	Yulong		1.01					
永胜县	Yongsheng		103.48					185.33
华坪县	Huaping	3.22	1.42					204.38
宁蒗县	Ninglang		1.24		297.22			
普洱市	**Pu'er**	**7.71**	**72.51**		**209.91**		**30.24**	**842.14**
思茅区	Simao		45.93					286.23
宁洱县	Ning'er	0.53	0.37					173.19
墨江县	Mojiang		16.19					
景东县	Jingdong	3.79	1.72				1.12	5.08
景谷县	Jinggu		2.70		209.91		5.36	42.63
镇沅县	Zhenyuan		0.44					190.33
江城县	Jiangcheng		3.28					
孟连县	Menglian		0.23				9.14	
澜沧县	Lancang	3.38	1.58				11.85	144.67
西盟县	Ximeng		0.07				2.77	
临沧市	**Lincang**		**17.94**		**2 104.35**	**6 666.30**	**99.01**	**645.32**
临翔区	Linxiang		0.07				2.97	
凤庆县	Fengqing		1.07		39.83		6.81	174.51
云　县	Yunxian		6.13		1 917.60	6 666.30	19.26	46.49
永德县	Yongde		2.82				6.43	48.91
镇康县	Zhenkang		4.22				15.48	90.59
双江县	Shuangjiang		0.83		146.93		5.22	
耿马县	Gengma		1.45				33.80	151.11
沧源县	Cangyuan		1.33				9.03	133.71

18–20 续表2 continued

州市县	Region	原 煤 (万吨) Coal (10 000 tons)	发电量 (亿千瓦小时) Electricity (100 million kWh)	农用化肥 (万吨) Agricultural Chemical Fertilizer (10 000 tons)	白 酒 (万升) Liquor (10 kiloliters)	啤 酒 (万升) Beer (10 kiloliters)	糖 (万吨) Sugar (10 000 tons)	水 泥 (万吨) Cement (10 000 tons)
楚 雄 州	**Chuxiong**	**50.88**	**65.98**	**0.95**	**865.14**			**149.81**
楚雄市	Chuxiong	0.45	1.66					82.33
双柏县	Shuangbai		3.46					
牟定县	Mouding		8.74		504.80			
南华县	Nanhua	50.43	9.17					
姚安县	Yao'an		10.63					
大姚县	Dayao		6.81					
永仁县	Yongren		2.56					
元谋县	Yuanmou		6.15		162.34			37.66
武定县	Wuding		1.65					18.50
禄丰县	Lufeng		15.16	0.95	198.00			11.32
红 河 州	**Honghe**	**1 438.59**	**182.76**	**81.35**	**74.70**		**5.34**	**913.40**
个旧市	Gejiu		5.90	7.44				26.44
开远市	Kaiyuan	968.56	70.66	73.91				333.01
蒙自市	Mengzi		11.46					144.26
弥勒市	Mile	439.59	31.45					162.49
屏边县	Pingbian		4.61					17.34
建水县	Jianshui		11.82					91.58
石屏县	Shiping	3.07	4.23				0.67	9.10
泸西县	Luxi	27.36	16.72		74.70			63.36
元阳县	Yuanyang		2.25				1.40	
红河县	Honghe		1.02				1.21	
金平县	Jinping		18.22				2.06	
绿春县	Luchun		1.08					62.29
河口县	Hekou		3.34					3.53
文 山 州	**Wenshan**	**82.91**	**56.28**		**3 733.20**		**15.66**	**911.88**
文山市	Wenshan		8.05					175.96
砚山县	Yanshan		2.43					618.42
西畴县	Xichou		0.13				5.30	
麻栗坡县	Malipo		15.07					8.12
马关县	Maguan		8.48					8.37
丘北县	Qiubei		10.00		3 733.20			
广南县	Guangnan		5.51				0.81	101.00
富宁县	Funing	82.91	6.61				9.54	
西双版纳州	**Xishuangbanna**		**6.83**			**2 173.95**	**26.37**	**185.82**
景洪市	Jinghong		2.05			2 173.95	0.93	166.75
勐海县	Menghai		4.54				14.95	
勐腊县	Mengla		0.25				10.49	19.07

18−20 续表3 continued

州市县	Region	原煤 (万吨) Coal (10 000 tons)	发电量 (亿千瓦小时) Electricity (100 million kwh)	农用化肥 (万吨) Agricultural Chemical Fertilizer (10 000 tons)	白酒 (万升) Liquor (10 kiloliters)	啤酒 (万升) Beer (10 kiloliters)	糖 (万吨) Sugar (10 000 tons)	水泥 (万吨) Cement (10 000 tons)
大理州	**Dali**	**10.90**	**167.86**		**120.30**	**21 606.30**		**1 467.45**
大理市	Dali		13.29			21 606.30		
漾濞县	Yangbi		4.23					
祥云县	Xiangyun		4.55					131.53
宾川县	Binchuan		4.42					276.28
弥渡县	Midu		1.78					354.15
南涧县	Nanjian							27.75
巍山县	Weishan		33.33					12.29
永平县	Yongping	10.90	0.31					174.42
云龙县	Yunlong							125.38
洱源县	Eryuan		6.16					
剑川县	Jianchuan		7.96					138.62
鹤庆县	Heqing		91.84		120.30			227.03
德宏州	**Dehong**		**128.88**				**68.67**	**418.87**
瑞丽市	Ruili							
芒　市	Mangshi		15.38				52.74	110.15
梁河县	Lianghe		7.28				4.86	
盈江县	Yingjiang		105.96				2.30	308.72
陇川县	Longchuan		0.26				8.77	
怒江州	**Nujiang**		**25.28**					**97.58**
泸水市	Lushui		11.72					97.58
福贡县	Fugong		4.78					
贡山县	Gongshan		8.78					
兰坪县	Lanping							
迪庆州	**Diqing**		**28.28**		**4.20**			**209.03**
香格里拉市	Shangri-La		22.24		4.20			209.03
德钦县	Deqin							
维西县	Weixi		6.04					

中国统计出版社有限公司最新图书简目

（仅供参考，以实际出版为准）

统计资料

中国统计年鉴	中国统计摘要	中国第三产业统计年鉴
中国第三次全国农业普查综合资料	国际统计年鉴	金砖国家联合统计手册
中国-东盟国家统计年鉴	中国农村统计年鉴	中国县域统计年鉴
中国农产品价格调查年鉴	中国城市统计年鉴	中国价格统计年鉴
中国贸易外经统计年鉴	中国零售和餐饮连锁企业统计年鉴	中国商品交易市场统计年鉴
大中型批发零售和住宿餐饮企业统计年鉴	中国住户调查年鉴	中国工业统计年鉴
中国环境统计年鉴	中国能源统计年鉴	中国建筑业统计年鉴
中国房地产统计年鉴	中国投资领域统计年鉴	长江经济带发展统计年鉴
中国人口和就业统计年鉴	中国劳动统计年鉴	中国社会统计年鉴
中国科技统计年鉴	中国高技术产业统计年鉴	全国企业创新调查年鉴
中国文化及相关产业统计年鉴	中国妇女儿童状况统计资料	中国青年发展统计年鉴
中国基本单位统计年鉴	中国教育统计年鉴	中国教育经费统计年鉴
中国民族统计年鉴	中国残疾人事业统计年鉴	中国电力统计年鉴
中国证券期货统计年鉴	中国医疗保障统计年鉴	国家医疗保障年鉴
中国城市建设统计年鉴	中国城乡建设统计年鉴	中国县城建设统计年鉴

省级综合统计年鉴系列

北京 天津 河北 山西 内蒙古 辽宁 吉林 黑龙江 上海 江苏 浙江 安徽 福建 江西 山东 河南 湖北 湖南 广东 广西 海南 重庆 四川 贵州 云南 西藏 陕西 甘肃 青海 宁夏 新疆 新疆生产建设兵团

市(县)级综合统计年鉴系列

滨海新区 石家庄 唐山 邯郸 邢台 保定 承德 沧州 衡水 太原 大同 晋城 晋中 长治 忻州 朔州 临汾 运城 阳泉 吕梁 呼和浩特 包头 鄂尔多斯 赤峰 大连 长春 四平 延吉 延边 哈尔滨 齐齐哈尔 黑龙江垦区 浦东新区 南京 无锡 徐州 常州 苏州 南通 淮安 盐城 扬州 镇江 宿迁 江阴 丹阳 海门 张家港 通州 如东 杭州 宁波 绍兴 台州 温州 金华 嘉兴 湖州 丽水 舟山 合肥 安庆 福州 厦门 漳州 宁德 龙岩 莆田 泉州 三明 南平 思明 南昌 上饶 抚州 赣州 九江 景德镇 宁都 济南 青岛 枣庄 潍坊 聊城 郑州 洛阳 三门峡 南阳 商丘 平顶山 信阳 济源 武汉 宜昌 十堰 荆州 荆门 咸宁 黄冈 长沙 广州 东莞 惠州 深圳 汕尾 珠海 南宁 桂林 柳州 防城港 贵港 梧州 玉林 钦州 海口 三亚 儋州 成都 贵阳 毕节 黔南 昆明 文山 德宏 西安 安康 延安 汉中 渭南 商洛 榆林 银川 兰州 庆阳 乌鲁木齐

调查年鉴系列

天津 内蒙古 上海 浙江 安徽 福建 江西 河南 湖北 湖南 广西 重庆 四川 云南 甘肃 宁夏

统计方法应用/实用手册

Python数据分析基础（第二版） 国民经济核算教程（第五版） 现代金融投资统计分析（第四版）
全国统计专业技术资格考试系列考试用书：统计业务知识（2021版） 统计业务知识学习指导与习题（2021版）
全国统计专业技术资格考试系列考试用书：统计相关知识（2021版） 统计相关知识学习指导与习题（2021版）

统计通俗读物/统计科普图书

领导干部统计知识问答（第二版） 统计公文写作及会议办理实用手册 2020中国宏观经济
中国国民经济核算知识读本 地区生产总值核算国际比较研究 中国投入产出理论与实践

重点图书

中国2020年人口普查资料 2020年第七次全国人口普查主要数据 全面建成小康社会成就报告
迈向高质量发展——“十三五”经济社会发展成就报告 人间奇迹——中国脱贫攻坚统计监测报告
中华生物医学统计大词典 挑大学选专业2021—高考志愿填报指南